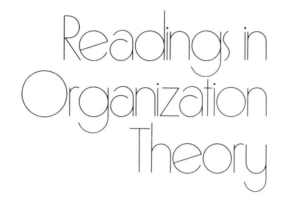

Readings in
Organization
Theory

Consulting Editor   BARRY RICHMAN   University of California

Readings in Organization Theory: ‡b

Open-System Approaches

edited by

John G. Maurer

RANDOM HOUSE NEW YORK

Foreword

The concept of the firm or the organization as an open or closed system is subject to serious ambiguity. For instance, it might be argued that every organization is necessarily an open system, depending upon inputs from some environment for its continued existence. The totality of life upon earth, the entire biosphere, depends in this way upon the sun's delivering daily a certain number of kilowatts of energy per square yard. No organization can exist, except momentarily, without energy inputs of some kind from the outside; to call an organization a closed system is technically to deny the second law of thermodynamics.

What then do we mean when we call an organization open or closed? We usually mean one of two things. First, we are often hortatory. This is the case when we point out that an organization is behaving as if it were a closed system when in fact it is open. This is sometimes necessary. Organizations need to be reminded of the external world. The difficulty is that this use of the concept throws the question of whether an organization is open or closed into the realm of psychological perception. An organization is an open system when it takes the external environment into account; it is closed when it does not. The one organization embraces the world; the other pretends that it does not exist.

Second, whether an organization is called open or closed can depend upon the purposes of the person studying it, the kinds of phenomena he is investigating, and the nature of the model he is building. Some of the things that go on in organizations can be explained by endogenous variables and a closed-system model—being more economical—is the one to use. Other things going on require the consideration of exogenous variables. Whether an organization is open or closed—either in its own eyes or the eyes of an investigator—depends upon the relative weights given to endogenous and exogenous variables.

I am not sure that Professor Maurer would agree with the foregoing, but it is certain that this collection of essays and research reports throws light upon these and similar questions. It is addressed to organizations, to organization theorists, and to students of organization. The constant theme is the need for broader and more inclusive models of organizational behavior. Doctor Maurer has documented in this book the contribution of the open-system concept to a better understanding of how organizations work and how they can be made to work more effectively.

William H. Reynolds, Dean
School of Business Administration
Wayne State University, Detroit, Michigan

Acknowledgments

I would like to thank William H. Reynolds, Dean, School of Business Administration, Wayne State University, for providing resources that made this book possible.

I would also like to thank the authors of the papers and the copyright holders thereof for their permissions to reprint.

I am greatly indebted to Gudrun Lindert, Linda Patterson, Lori Patterson, and Mary Jo Krisak for their excellent secretarial assistance.

John G. Maurer

Detroit, Michigan
March 1971

Contents

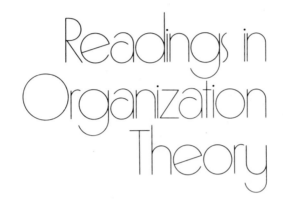

Readings in
Organization
Theory

Introduction

The objective of this book is to present the student of organizations
with a different view of the causes of organizational structure and
functioning, as well as participants' attitudes and behaviors. Although relationships between and among variables internal to the
organization have been widely and closely examined, there has been
serious neglect of the relationship between environmental variables
and internal organizational variables. For example, while economists
have studied the interaction between the firm and its environment,
their emphasis, in general, has been on the resource allocation
process, market organization, and market equilibrium (Cleland 1960,
p. 202; Krupp 1961, p. 13; Katz and Kahn 1966, p. 454). The theme of
the book is the relationship between external environmental phenomena and phenomena internal to the organization. The central
questions under consideration are: What are open systems; to what
are they open; and what is the meaning of openness for the
organization?

Hall and Fagen (1968, p. 81) define a system as "a set of objects
together with relationships between the objects and between their
attributes." An open-system approach to organizations is one in
which: (1) The organization is conceptualized as an importing-
transforming-exporting system. (2) The organization is viewed as
transacting with environmental elements with respect to the importing and exporting of people, material, energy, or information.

Environmental elements refer to "the set of all objects, a change in whose attributes affect the system and also those objects whose attributes are changed by the behavior of the system" (Hall and Fagen, p. 83). (3) The processes of importation and exportation are characterized to some degree by uncertainty (Thompson, 1967, pp. 4–6. (4) Reception of exports by elements in the external environment provides the organization with additional imports for transformation. (5) The organization is viewed as a subsystem of a supersystem. Katz and Kahn (1966, p. 58) encourage this view for research purposes: "The first step should always be to go to the next higher level of system organization, to study the dependence of the system in question upon the supersystem of which it is a part, for the supersystem sets the limits of variance of behavior of the dependent system." (6) Some phenomena internal to the organization are viewed as partially determined by phenomena external to the organization.

Buckley (1967, p. 50) states the meaning of system openness succinctly:

> That a system is *open* means, not simply that it engages in interchanges with the environment, but that this interchange is *an essential factor* underlying the system's viability, its reproductive ability or continuity, and its ability to change.

Obviously, all organizations are open to environmental influence. But some are more open than others. A monastery or prison is less open than a business or political organization. However, some business organizations are more open than others, and openness within a given business organization may vary with hierarchical level. This differential extent of openness is an important variable to isolate and study. On the other hand, some degree of closedness is necessary to prevent system disintegration and collapse. Katz and Kahn (1966, pp. 59–62) point out that not all inputs can be ingested. Loomis (1960, pp. 31–32) discusses boundary maintenance as the "process whereby the identity of the social system is preserved and the characteristic interaction pattern maintained." He notes that boundary-maintenance mechanisms may be physical, social, or consist of commitment to the system's traditions or values (p. 202 and p. 285). Monane (1967, pp. 78–100) notes that system gatekeepers "are a major bulwark of system stability." He views gatekeepers as "agents of a system's power structure" who are "customarily designed to encourage the entry of items which the power structure perceives as providing positive feedback to itself and to the system (friends) and to discourage the entry of items which the power structure regards as negative feedback for itself and for the system (enemies)."

In general, early students of business organizations employed a closed-system model of the organization. Obviously the organizations they studied were open systems. These organizations had to transact with elements in their environment. However, theorists could view a given organization *as if* it were a closed system because of the nature of the business firm's environment. At that time the paramount problem was the transformation of inputs into outputs. Inputs and outputs could be viewed *as if* they were given, constant, and certain. Consider, for example, two environmental elements. Not many years ago, a customer purchased a black car or no car; he worked under economic-man conditions or someone took his place. In the economist's terminology, the business organization enjoyed a buyer's market as regards human inputs and a seller's market as regards product outputs.

Today, the nature of the environment has changed for many organizations. The major independent variable of the Lawrence-Lorsch (1967) contingency theory of organization is environmental uncertainty. The central theme of Chamberlain's book (1968, p. 3) is "How the business firm uses the discretion available to it to attempt to establish some measure of control over its operations in an environment filled with uncertainty due to change, and to relate itself to a society which is seeking to do the same thing." Thompson (1967, p. 13) notes that "technologies and environment are basic sources of uncertainty for organizations." Modern man is more educated and appears to be climbing the Maslow need-hierarchy ladder. Rising income allows consumer choice. Product models proliferate. Organizations export not only products or services, but also information about their internal operations, their behavior on their boundaries, and functional as well as dysfunctional by-products. Increased participation in decision making in some societal institutions is imported into other institutions. In summary, many input and output relationships are becoming increasingly problematic for organizations.

An important issue is how an administrator conceptualizes the relationship of his organization to its environment. Under what conditions can he assume a closed system and act *as if* environmental elements are not critical factors for organizational survival and growth? As Hagen points out (1961, pp. 145–146), for purposes of analysis, the theorist must assume a closed system, that is, he must assume "that the operation of the system is affected only by given conditions previously established by the environment and not changing at the time of analysis, plus the relationships among the elements of the system." However, the effective administrator must not only identify and measure the impact of given conditions but also be sensitive to changes in these conditions and be able to appropriately respond to them. Monane (1967, p. 85) points out that organizational "gatekeepers tend to ignore, disregard, distort, or denigrate environmental data not providing positive feedback, and to be especially alert to that which does." Thompson (1967, pp.

151–152) distinguishes opportunistic surveillance, a monitoring of the environment for opportunities, and problemistic search which is "stimulated by a problem and directed toward finding a solution to that problem."

An open-system theorist does not conceptualize the organization as simply reacting to elements in its external environment. The model he uses is interactional. An organization shapes as well as is shaped by its environment. The environment presents the organization with opportunities for exploitation and controllable external factors as well as confronts it with uncontrollable constraints and contingencies. As Buckley (1967, p. 58) indicates, the interaction may be complex:

> . . . the behavior of complex, open systems is not a simple and direct function of impinging external forces, as is the case with colliding billiard balls or gravitational systems. Rather, as open systems become more complex there develop within them more and more complex mediating processes that intervene between external forces and behavior.

Many theorists consider business organizations in the United States as the dominant societal institution. However, each business organization must cope with a multitude of environmental constraints, uncertainties, and changes. Thompson (1967, p. 32, and Ch. 4) discusses how an organization tries to avoid becoming subservient to its environment, and how it removes or reduces environmental contingencies through organizational design.

No implication is intended that in studying organizational structure and process, external variables are more important than variables internal to the organization. The open-system model simply adds another dimension to the analysis of organizational cause-effect relationships. Thompson (1967, pp. 11–12), following Talcott Parsons, has applied both closed-system and open-system models to a single organization by distinguishing the location of organizational problems. At the technical level of the organization, it is necessary to reduce or eliminate uncertainty, and hence the closed-system model is appropriate. At the institutional level or the organization-environment interface, uncertainty is great, and hence the open-system model is appropriate. A temporal dimension also exists. In the long run, the organization is more open; in the short run, it is more closed.

Perhaps the influence of the external environment is most noticeable when external changes produce subsequent changes within the organization. However, there are relatively enduring features of the various environmental elements with which the organization must transact if it is to persist and maintain its viability and stability. Thus, an open-system model encompasses both synchronic and diachronic analysis.

INTRODUCTION

The modern organization theorist insists that there is no one best way to organize. In a field research study of Scottish firms, Burns and Stalker (1961, pp. 4–5; p. 122) delineated eleven characteristics of two polar systems of organization—the mechanistic and the organic. The former they found to be appropriate for stable environmental conditions in technology and market demands; the latter to be appropriate for changing or unstable conditions. Lawrence and Lorsch (1967, Ch. 7) in another field research study have developed a contingency theory of organization that includes both classical and human-relations organization theory. Which theory to use depends, in part, upon the nature of the environment that a given sector of the organization faces. Thompson (1967, Ch. 6) has developed an organizational typology model that is based on whether the organization faces either a homogeneous-heterogeneous or a stable-shifting environment.

This book is interdisciplinary in approach and reports on many types of organizations: businesses, hospitals, universities, research, health and welfare, voluntary associations, stock exchanges, libraries, banks, etc. The objective in article selection was to include more theoretical-conceptual articles than empirical ones. The hope is that this will increase the student's return on time invested. The assumption is that if the student is to understand organizational phenomena, he needs concepts, models, and theories, as well as concrete examples. He requires these to see "old" relationships in new ways as well as to perceive and understand "new" relationships. The articles were selected for their value in adding conceptual rather than factual material to the student's toolkit. Today, facts depreciate rapidly. By making use of the bibliographies after each chapter, as well as the footnotes contained within articles, the student can read case studies as well as obtain additional theoretical material.

Because of space constraints, two important areas were eliminated: (1) cross-cultural studies, that is, how different societal environments affect organizational structure, process, management practices, and employee behavior; and (2) the relationship between union organizations and other organizations.[1]

The basic premise in developing this book is that if the environments in which organizations are embedded become more complex, then an increasing percentage of future administrators will have to perceive and analyze their organizations *as if* they were open systems. Only in this way will their organizations escape Brillouin's "death by confinement."

NOTE

1. With regard to (1), Nath reviews 115 references. See Raghu Nath. 1968. "A Methodological Review of Cross-Cultural Management Research." *International Social Sciences Journal*, 20, 35–62. R. B. Peterson lists 278

references. Consult: *Bibliography on Comparative (International) Management,* Occasional Paper 21 (Seattle, Washington: Office of Faculty Publications, Graduate School of Business Administration, University of Washington, August 1969).

See also:

Berger, Morroe. 1956. "Bureaucracy East and West," *Administrative Science Quarterly,* 1, 518–529.

Boddewyn, J. 1969. *Comparative Management and Marketing.* Glenview, Ill.: Scott, Foresman & Co.

Crozier, Michel. 1964. *The Bureaucratic Phenomenon.* Chicago: The University of Chicago Press.

Farmer, Richard N. 1968. *International Management.* Belmont, Calif.: Dickenson.

Farmer, Richard, and Barry Richman. 1964. "A Model for Research in Comparative Management," *California Management Review,* 7 (Winter), 55–68.

Fouraker, Lawrence E., and John M. Stopford. 1968. "Organizational Structure and the Multinational Strategy," *Administrative Science Quarterly,* 13 (June), 47–64.

Mann, Charles K. 1965. "Sears, Roebuck de Mexico: A Cross-Cultural Analysis," *Social Science,* 40 (Winter), 149–157.

Megginson, Leon C. 1967. "The Interrelationship and Interaction Between the Cultural Environment and Managerial Effectiveness," *Management International Review,* 7, 56–70.

Presthus, Robert V. 1959. "Behavior and Bureaucracy in Many Cultures," *Public Administration Review,* 19 (Winter), 25–35.

Presthus, Robert V. 1959. "The Social Bases of Bureaucratic Organization," *Social Forces,* 38, 103–109.

Useem, John, Ruth Useem, and John Donoghue. 1962. "Men in the Middle of the Third Culture: The Roles of American and Non-Western People in Cross-Cultural Administration," *Human Organization,* 21 (Summer), 169–179.

Webber, Ross A. 1969. *Culture and Management.* Homewood, Ill.: Richard D. Irwin.

Zurcher, Louis A. 1968. "Particularism and Organizational Position: A Cross-Cultural Analysis," *Journal of Applied Psychology,* 52, 139–154.

Zurcher, L. A., et al. 1965. "Value Orientation, Role Conflict, Alienation From Work: A Cross Cultural Study," *American Sociological Review,* 30 (August), 539–547.

For (2), consult:

Chamberlain, Neil W. 1948. *Union Challenge to Management Control.* New York: Harper & Row.

Derber, Milton, W. E. Chalmers, and Milton T. Edelman. 1961. "Union Participation in Plant Decision-Making," *Industrial and Labor Relations Review,* 15 (October), 83–101.

Derber, M., W. E. Chalmers, and R. Stagner. 1958. "Collective Bargaining and Managerial Functions: An Empirical Study," *Journal of Business,* 13, 107–119.

Derber, Milton, W. Ellison Chalmers, and Ross Stagner. 1960. *The Local Union-Management Relationship.* Urbana, Ill.: Institute of Labor and Industrial Relations, University of Illinois.

Kuhn, James W. 1962. "Encroachments on the Right to Manage," *California Management Review,* 5, 18–24.

Slichter, Sumner H., James J. Healy, and E. Robert Livernash. 1960. *The*

Impact of Collective Bargaining on Management. Washington, D.C.: The Brookings Institution.

Strauss, George. 1962. "The Shifting Power Balance in the Plant," *Industrial Relations,* 1 (May), 65–96.

REFERENCES

Brillouin, L. 1949. "Life, Thermodynamics, and Cybernetics," *American Scientist,* 37 (October), 554–568.

Buckley, Walter. 1967. *Sociology and Modern Systems Theory.* Englewood Cliffs, N.J.: Prentice-Hall.

Burns, Tom, and G. M. Stalker. 1961. *The Management of Innovation.* London: Tavistock.

Chamberlain, Neil W. 1968. *Enterprise and Environment.* New York: McGraw-Hill.

Cleland, Sherrill. 1960. "A Short Essay on a Managerial Theory of the Firm." *Linear Programming and the Theory of the Firm,* K. E. Boulding and W. A. Spivey, eds. New York: Macmillan.

Hagen, Everett E. 1961. "Analytical Models in the Study of Social Systems," *The American Journal of Sociology,* 67 (September), 144–151.

Hall, A. D., and R. E. Fagen. 1968. "Definition of System." In *Modern Systems Research for the Behavioral Scientist,* Walter Buckley, ed. Chicago: Aldine.

Katz, Daniel, and Robert L. Kahn. 1966. *The Social Psychology of Organizations.* New York: Wiley.

Krupp, Sherman. 1961. *Pattern in Organization Analysis.* New York: Holt, Rinehart & Winston.

Lawrence, Paul R., and Jay W. Lorsch. 1967. *Organization and Environment.* Boston: Harvard University.

Loomis, Charles P. 1960. *Social Systems.* Princeton, N.J.: D. Van Nostrand.

Monane, Joseph H. 1967. *A Sociology of Human Systems.* New York: Appleton-Century-Crofts.

Thompson, James D. 1967. *Organizations in Action.* New York: McGraw-Hill.

INTRODUCTION

In excerpts from an excellent book, Katz and Kahn elaborate on the nature of open-system theory. They identify nine characteristics common to all open systems, and call attention to some of the practical and theoretical misconceptions that occur when organizations are viewed as closed rather than as open systems.

In an article noted in the additional reading section, Johnson, Kast, and Rosenzweig propose that administrators will find the systems concept a useful frame of reference to perceive, understand, and resolve complexity, and that it will also aid them in decision-making and integration. They explore the hierarchy-of-levels approach to general systems theory, identify six key subsystems, and provide an illustrative model of the system concept that integrates the "traditional" activities of management.

OPEN-SYSTEM THEORY

Daniel Katz and Robert Kahn

Organizations and Open-System Theory: A Summary

THE NATURE OF OPEN-SYSTEM THEORY

In some respects open-system theory is not a theory at all; it does not pretend to the specific sequences of cause and effect, the specific hypotheses and tests of hypotheses which are the basic elements of theory. Open-system theory is rather a framework, a meta-theory, a model in the broadest sense of that overused term. Open-system theory is an approach and a conceptual language for understanding and describing many kinds and levels of phenomena. It is used to describe and explain the behavior of living organisms and combinations of organisms, but it is applicable to any dynamic, recurring process, any patterned sequence of events.

It is such a recurrent pattern of events, differentiated from but dependent on the larger stream of life in which it occurs and recurs, that constitutes an open system. All such systems involve the flow of energy from the environment through the system itself and back into the environment. They involve not only a flow of energy but a transformation of it, an alteration in energic form the precise nature of which is one definition of the system itself.

The functioning of any open system thus consists of recurrent cycles of input, transformation, and output. Of these three basic systemic processes, input and output are transactions involving the system and some sectors of its immediate environment; transformation or through-put is a process contained within the system itself. The transactions by which agencies in the environment accept the systemic product typically are linked to the transactions by which new inputs are made available to the system. To locate a system, to specify its functions, and to understand its functions, therefore, requires that this cyclical energic process be identified and traced. An open system is defined by its boundaries for the selective reception of inputs (a coding process) and for its typical transmission of outputs. It is further characterized by such properties as negentropy to counteract the tendency of all systems to run down; by feedback or responsiveness to information provided by its own functioning; homeostasis, the tendency to maintain a steady state; by equifinality or the use of different patterns to produce the same effect; and by differentiation, i.e., the tendency toward elaboration of structure.

AN OPEN-SYSTEM APPROACH TO ORGANIZATIONAL THEORY

Some advocates of the open-system approach believe that a theory can be devised that will comprehend all levels of life. For the general-system theorists

The Social Psychology of Organizations, New York: John Wiley & Sons, Inc. (1966), 452–455, 17–28, 32–33, 59–62, 81–82, 123–124. Reprinted with the permission of the publisher, John Wiley & Sons, Inc.

this is an article of faith. Our view is that theoretical progress can best be made by attempting instead to adapt the open-system model to each genotypic category of phenomena to which it is to be applied, adding specification to the meta-theoretical framework in order to maximize its explanatory power for the population category under study. This we have attempted for human organizations.

For human organizations, as for other open systems, the basic systemic processes are energic and involve the flow, transformation, and exchange of energy. Human organizations have unique properties, however, which distinguish them from other categories of open systems. Perhaps the most basic of these unique properties is the absence of structure in the usual sense of the term—an identifiable, enduring, physical anatomy which is observable at rest as in motion and which in motion generates and performs those activities which comprise the systemic function. The human organization lacks structure in this anatomical sense; its land and buildings are trappings; its members come and go. Yet it has structure; it is not a formless aggregate of interacting individuals engaged in the creation of some random combination of events.

We have argued that the resolution of this paradox lies in the patterns of the events of organizational life themselves. The events are structured, and the forms they assume have dynamic properties. Social organizations as contrived systems are sets of such patterned behavioral events. They consist of such events and have no anatomical structure analogous to that of physical and biological systems. In the most generic sense the structure of a social organization is contained in its various functions. In small subsystems the

functions may be directly observable in the human activities involved; in dealing with larger sectors of organizational activity the patterns and functions are inferred from observable events.

This primary structural-functional quality of human organizations is closely linked to others that can be derived from it. The fact that organizational structure is created and maintained only as the members of the organization interact in an ordered way suggests a high degree of openness, a persistent and inherent vulnerability to forces in the organizational environment. It suggests also a continuing necessity to maintain the organizational structure against such forces or to adapt it to them. Much of the theorizing and empirical work about organizations has assumed explicitly or implicitly a closed system, in which the inputs into the system are regarded as constants. The open-system approach reminds us that organizational inputs are neither constant nor guaranteed. In particular, the organization lives only so long as people are induced to be members and to perform as such.

PRODUCTION AND
MAINTENANCE INPUTS

One way of giving theoretical recognition to this organizational characteristic is to distinguish between that energic flow which goes into procuring, transforming, and exporting the organizational product, and, on the other hand, that energic flow which goes into overcoming the centrifugal and permeable qualities inherent in the unique' function-structure of the human organization. We have done so by proposing an essential dichotomy between production inputs and maintenance inputs. Production inputs are the materials and energies directly related to the through-put or the work that comprises the activity of the organization in turning out a product. Maintenance inputs are the energic and informational contributions necessary to hold the people in the system and persuade them to carry out their activities as members of the system. No social organization can exist without habitual acceptance by its members of their expected activities, understanding and skill needed for the performance of those activities, and motivation to engage in that performance.

· · ·

It follows from an analysis of the nature of social systems that special attention must be given to their maintenance inputs. All open systems, of course, require *maintenance* as well as *production* inputs. *Maintenance inputs* are the energic imports which sustain the system; *production inputs* are the energic imports which are processed to yield a productive outcome. In social systems, however, the maintenance problem is more complex than in biological systems in that the maintenance requirements are much less clearly specified in the former than the latter. Certain minimum nutritive and caloric input is necessary to keep the biological organism functioning. Science can specify these inputs with precision, and most organisms show a good deal of primitive wisdom about staying alive even without such specifications. By contrast, the motivations which will attract people to a social system and keep them functioning in it are varied, the relationship between organizational inducements and the required role behavior is indirect and mediated by many factors, and too little is known either at the practical or at the scientific level about maximizing productive output in relation to main-

tenance input. Moreover, physical and physiological systems with a given physical structure can lie dormant and still maintain their basic character when revived; the social system, once it ceases to function, disappears. This difference means that the social system is more open than physical systems; it must constantly import both production and maintenance materials.

Biological systems also require nourishment and maintenance. Food, water, air, and certain conditions of pressure and temperature are essential to life. But the preservation of the physical structure is not a problem from the point of view of the parts leaving the whole. Cells do not wander away from the organs in which they are imbedded, organs do not leave the body any more than the spark plug goes AWOL. Human beings do drift away from social systems, do go on strike, and do stay at home. Hence the social sciences must go further than natural sciences in order to take into account two types of system openness: openness with respect to production inputs and openness with respect to maintenance inputs. The trend in the social sciences, however, has been to focus as does the physical scientist upon one type of openness, namely the openness to production inputs. The natural scientist can concentrate solely upon the learning function of rats in a maze with the walls of the maze as a constant. In the social system the walls of the maze are not constant because they are made up of human behavior. Classic organization theory with its machine concepts has been concerned almost exclusively with the single type of openness and has attempted to develop principles of organizational functioning as if the production input and the methods of processing it were the only variables. Holding the human

OPEN-SYSTEM THEORY

parts in the system and mobilizing their energies in prescribed patterns do not represent constant factors in the equation and cannot be ignored.

.   .   .

System Openness, System Boundaries, and System Coding

These three concepts are interrelated and have to do with the relative autonomy of system functioning and with system differentiation from the surrounding environment. *System openness* is the most general of these concepts and refers to the degree to which the system is receptive to all types of inputs. Systems vary with respect to the general range of inputs that can be absorbed and with respect to openness to particular types of inputs.

Either of the major American political parties would be an example of a system open to a fairly wide range of influences. Many types of individuals can move into the organization, bringing with them different ideas and interests. The party accepts contributions and help from many sources. As a result, American political parties tend not to present distinctive action or ideological programs or distinctive candidates. They are not highly differentiated from one another or from the surrounding environment of community activities concerned with the exertion of influence. Eisenhower was sought as a presidential candidate by both parties. It has been proposed, and from an improbable source (Luce, 1964), that the history of American political parties can be understood as a cyclical process in which the tendency of the parties to become increasingly open and undifferentiated from each other is occasionally and dramatically interrupted by some historical issue that either polarizes them or creates a re-alignment of forces and a new pair of parties. On the other hand, the Communist Party in the United States is closed to a wide range of inputs but very open with respect to input from the international communist organization.

.   .   .

The continuing and inevitable process of organizational recruitment is one of the most important sources of influence from the external environment. An organization which is completely resolute in its resistance to externally proposed suggestions and ideas may be open to the same substantive inputs when they are imported by new members. As people move into an organization, they bring with them a variety of values and interests from the external environment. It follows that any organization with easy permeability of boundaries is subject to continuing influence from the external environment. Such influence is likely to be varied in content and to affect many aspects of the organization. Indeed, the open organization is subject to transformation by its members and may have difficulty in the single-minded pursuit of given objectives.

An organization which seeks to avoid such influence must make itself less permeable to self-nominating new members. It must screen potential members more carefully and define more broadly the individual characteristics which are relevant in the screening. By so doing the organization will perhaps sharpen its sense of mission and minimize the possibilities of internal disruption. It may pay the price, however, of tending to replicate its current membership characteristics and thus coming to resemble itself more and more closely as time passes. Such organizations can turn into caricatures of themselves. Their thrift becomes miserliness, and their conservatism becomes fearfulness.

There is no prescription for such dilemmas of permeability. That organizational leadership which understands the nature of its exchange with the external environment can choose, however, the forms and degrees of permeability which best meet the contemporary requirements of the organization.

. . .

System coding is the major procedure for insuring specifications for the intake of information and energy, and it thus describes the actual functioning of barriers separating the system from its environment. One of the significant characteristics of any system is the selective intake of energy and information and the transformation of that input according to the nature of the system. Social systems develop their own mechanisms for blocking out certain types of alien influence and for transforming what is received according to a series of code categories. Though the coding concept can apply to the selective absorption and transformation of all types of input into a system, it is characteristically employed for the processing of information.

The procedure for excluding information may be deliberately and rationally developed. The judicial system, for example, has codified rules which define the nature of the evidence admissible. Hearsay evidence is excluded; so too are confessions obtained under duress; and in some states the results of lie detection tests are ruled out. Most organizations have not developed their rules for the exclusion of information in as systematic a manner, but they do possess *formal criteria* for rejecting some types of input. These criteria may specify that only information relevant to the questions posed by organizational leaders will be accepted, or that only members of a certain status or functional position will be heard on certain questions. More generally the practice is to have specialized structures for the reception of information so that any message will have to traverse and survive the "proper channels" in order to get a hearing.

System boundaries refer to the types of barrier conditions between the system and its environment which make for degrees of system openness. Boundaries are the demarcation lines or regions for the definition of appropriate system activity, for admission of members into the system, and for other imports into the system. The boundary constitutes a barrier for many types of interaction between people on the inside and people on the outside, but it includes some facilitating device for the particular types of transactions necessary for organizational functioning. The barrier condition is exemplified by national states with their border guards and customs offices which restrict the flow of people and goods across their boundaries. Within a national state, organizations are similarly characterized by boundaries, both physical and psychological, to maintain the integrity of the system.

Psychological separation is maintained by visible symbols, such as uniforms, dress, and insignia (e.g., fraternity pins), and even more subtly by speech patterns and other distinctive forms of behavior. Without such special provisions, organizational members at the boundaries would become susceptible to outside influence. The incursion of environmental influence would be uncontrolled and would vitiate the intrasystem influences. Where physical space can be employed to create separation, there is protection against such external forces. But since the organization must have interchange with its supporting environment, some of its members must occupy boundary positions to help in the export of the services, ideas, and other products of the system and in the import of materials and people into the system. Since these members face out upon the world and deal with the public, they are subject to the conflicting pressures of their own organization and the social environment. Because of their greater acquaintance with opportunities outside the organization as well as the conflicting demands of their roles, one would expect greater personnel turnover in these boundary positions than in the central production structure. Many other evidences of the stressfulness of boundary positions have already been produced (Kahn et al., 1964).

The boundary condition applies also to the process by which outsiders enter and become members of the organization. They may be physically within the organization for some time before they cross the psychological boundary and become part of the organization. Before foreigners are admitted to citizenship in the United States, they must have resided within its physical boundaries for five years, have passed required tests, and taken an oath of allegiance. Many organizations have formal induction and socialization procedures for instilling the behavior, attitudes, and values which differentiate the system from the outside environment. (Dornbusch, 1955)

We have been speaking mainly about the boundary condition with respect to maintenance inputs. Environmental transactions on the production side are also controlled by organizational boundaries. In system theory it is common to define the boundary as the area where a lower interchange of energy or information occurs than in the system proper. In social systems it is also a matter of qualitative breaks between the activity within the system and the activity on the outside.

Organizations and the System Concept

All social systems, including organizations, consist of the patterned activities of a number of individuals. Moreover, these patterned activities are complementary or interdependent with respect to some common output or outcome; they are repeated, relatively enduring, and bounded in space and time. If the activity pattern occurs only once or at unpredictable intervals, we could not speak of an organization. The stability or recurrence of activities can be examined in relation to the *energic input* into the system, the *transformation of energies within the system,* and the *resulting product or energic output.* In a factory the raw materials and the human labor are the energic input, the patterned activities of production the transformation of energy, and the finished product the output. To maintain this patterned activity requires a continued renewal of the inflow of energy. This is guaranteed in social systems by the energic return from the product or outcome. Thus the outcome of the cycle of activities furnishes new energy for the initiation of a renewed cycle. The company which produces automobiles sells them and by doing so obtains the means of securing new raw materials, compensating its labor force, and continuing the activity pattern.

In many organizations outcomes are converted into money and new energy is furnished through this mechanism. Money is a convenient way of handling energy units both on the output and input sides, and buying and selling represent one set of social rules for regulating the exchange of money. Indeed, these rules are so effective and so widespread that there is some danger of mistaking the business of buying and selling for the defining cycles of organization. It is a commonplace executive observation that businesses exist to make money, and the observation is usually allowed to go unchallenged. It is, however, a very limited statement about the purposes of business.

Some human organizations do not depend on the cycle of selling and buying to maintain themselves. Universities and public agencies depend rather on bequests and legislative appropriations, and in so-called voluntary organizations the output reenergizes the activity of organization members in a more direct fashion. Member activities and accomplishments are rewarding in themselves and tend therefore to be continued, without the mediation of the outside environment. A society of bird watchers can wander into the hills and engage in the rewarding activities of identifying birds for their mutual edification and enjoyment. Organizations thus differ on this important dimension of the source of energy renewal, with the great majority utilizing both intrinsic and extrinsic resources in varying degree. Most large-scale organizations are not as self-contained as small voluntary groups and are very dependent upon the social effects of their output for energy renewal.

Our two basic criteria for identifying social systems and determining their functions are (1) tracing the pattern of energy exchange or activity of people as it results in some output and (2) ascertaining how the output is translated into energy which reactivates the pattern. We shall refer to organizational functions or objectives not as the conscious purposes of group leaders or group members but as the outcomes which are

the energic source for a maintenance of the same type of output.

This model of an energic input-output system is taken from the open system theory as promulgated by von Bertalanffy (1956). Theorists have pointed out the applicability of the system concepts of the natural sciences to the problems of social science. It is important, therefore, to examine in more detail the constructs of system theory and the characteristics of open systems.

System theory is basically concerned with problems of relationships, of structure, and of interdependence rather than with the constant attributes of objects. In general approach it resembles field theory except that its dynamics deal with temporal as well as spatial patterns. Older formulations of system constructs dealt with the closed systems of the physical sciences, in which relatively self-contained structures could be treated successfully as if they were independent of external forces. But living systems, whether biological organisms or social organizations, are acutely dependent upon their external environment and so must be conceived of as open systems.

Before the advent of open-system thinking, social scientists tended to take one of two approaches in dealing with social structures; they tended either (1) to regard them as closed systems to which the laws of physics applied or (2) to endow them with some vitalistic concept like entelechy. In the former case they ignored the environmental forces affecting the organization and in the latter case they fell back upon some magical purposiveness to account for organizational functioning. Biological theorists, however, have rescued us from this trap by pointing out that the concept of the open system means that we neither have to follow the laws of

OPEN-SYSTEM THEORY

traditional physics, nor in deserting them do we have to abandon science. The laws of Newtonian physics are correct generalizations but they are limited to closed systems. They do not apply in the same fashion to open systems which maintain themselves through constant commerce with their environment, i.e., a continuous inflow and outflow of energy through permeable boundaries.

One example of the operation of closed versus open systems can be seen in the concept of entropy and the second law of thermodynamics. According to the second law of thermodynamics, a system moves toward equilibrium; it tends to run down, that is, its differentiated structures tend to move toward dissolution as the elements composing them become arranged in random disorder. For example, suppose that a bar of iron has been heated by the application of a blowtorch on one side. The arrangement of all the fast (heated) molecules on one side and all the slow molecules on the other is an unstable state, and over time the distribution of molecules becomes in effect random, with the resultant cooling of one side and heating of the other, so that all surfaces of the iron approach the same temperature. A similar process of heat exchange will also be going on between the iron bar and its environment, so that the bar will gradually approach the temperature of the room in which it is located, and in so doing will elevate somewhat the previous temperature of the room. More technically, entropy increases toward a maximum and equilibrium occurs as the physical system attains the state of the most probable distribution of its elements. In social systems, however, structures tend to become more elaborated rather than less differentiated. The rich may grow richer and the poor may grow poorer. The open system does not run down, because it can import energy from the world around it. Thus the operation of entropy is counteracted by the importation of energy and the living system is characterized by negative rather than positive entropy.

Common Characteristics of Open Systems

Though the various types of open systems have common characteristics by virtue of being open systems, they differ in other characteristics. If this were not the case, we would be able to obtain all our basic knowledge about social organizations through studying the biological organisms or even through the study of a single cell.

The following nine characteristics seem to define all open systems.

1. IMPORTATION OF ENERGY

Open systems import some form of energy from the external environment. The cell receives oxygen from the blood stream; the body similarly takes in oxygen from the air and food from the external world. The personality is dependent upon the external world for stimulation. Studies of sensory deprivation show that when a person is placed in a darkened soundproof room, where he has a minimal amount of visual and auditory stimulation, he develops hallucinations and other signs of mental stress (Solomon et al., 1961). Deprivation of social stimulation also can lead to mental disorganization (Spitz, 1945). Köhler's (1944, 1947) studies of the figural after-effects of continued stimulation show the dependence of perception upon its energic support from the external world. Animals deprived of visual experience from birth for a prolonged period never fully recover their visual capacities (Melzack and Thompson, 1956). In other words, the functioning personality is heavily dependent upon the continuous inflow of stimulation from the external environment. Similarly, social organizations must also draw renewed supplies of energy from other institutions, or people, or the material environment. No social structure is self-sufficient or self-contained.

2. THE THROUGH-PUT

Open systems transform the energy available to them. The body converts starch and sugar into heat and action. The personality converts chemical and electrical forms of stimulation into sensory qualities, and information into thought patterns. The organization creates a new product, or processes materials, or trains people, or provides a service. These activities entail some reorganization of input. Some work gets done in the system.

3. THE OUTPUT

Open systems export some product into the environment, whether it be the invention of an inquiring mind or a bridge constructed by an engineering firm. Even the biological organism exports physiological products such as carbon dioxide from the lungs which helps to maintain plants in the immediate environment.

4. SYSTEMS AS CYCLES OF EVENTS

The pattern of activities of the energy exchange has a cyclic character. The product exported into the environment furnishes the sources of energy for the repetition of the cycle of activities. The energy reinforcing the cycle of activities

can derive from some exchange of the product in the external world or from the activity itself. In the former instance, the industrial concern utilizes raw materials and human labor to turn out a product which is marketed, and the monetary return is used to obtain more raw materials and labor to perpetuate the cycle of activities. In the latter instance, the voluntary organization can provide expressive satisfactions to its members so that the energy renewal comes directly from the organizational activity itself.

The problem of structure, or the relatedness of parts, can be observed directly in some physical arrangement of things where the larger unit is physically bounded and its subparts are also bounded within the larger structure. But how do we deal with social structures, where physical boundaries in this sense do not exist? It was the genius of F. H. Allport (1962) which contributed the answer, namely that the structure is to be found in an interrelated set of events which return upon themselves to complete and renew a cycle of activities. It is events rather than things which are structured, so that social structure is a dynamic rather than a static concept. Activities are structured so that they comprise a unity in their completion or closure. A simple linear stimulus-response exchange between two people would not constitute social structure. To create structure, the responses of A would have to elicit B's reactions in such a manner that the responses of the latter would stimulate A to further responses. Of course the chain of events may involve many people, but their behavior can be characterized as showing structure only when there is some closure to the chain by a return to its point of origin with the probability that the chain of events will then be repeated. The repetition of the cycle does not have to involve the same set of phenotypical happenings. It may expand to include more sub-events of exactly the same kind or it may involve similar activities directed toward the same outcomes. In the individual organism the eye may move in such a way as to have the point of light fall upon the center of the retina. As the point of light moves, the movements of the eye may also change but to complete the same cycle of activity, i.e., to focus upon the point of light.

A single cycle of events of a self-closing character gives us a simple form of structure. But such single cycles can also combine to give a larger structure of events or an event system. An event system may consist of a circle of smaller cycles or hoops, each one of which makes contact with several others. Cycles may also be tangential to one another from other types of subsystems. The basic method for the identification of social structures is to follow the energic chain of events from the input of energy through its transformation to the point of closure of the cycle.

5. NEGATIVE ENTROPY

To survive, open systems must move to arrest the entropic process; they must acquire negative entropy. The entropic process is a universal law of nature in which all forms of organization move toward disorganization or death. Complex physical systems move toward simple random distribution of their elements and biological organisms also run down and perish. The open system, however, by importing more energy from its environment than it expends, can store energy and can acquire negative entropy. There is then a general trend in an open system to maximize its ratio of imported to expended energy, to survive and even during periods of crisis to live on borrowed time. Prisoners in concentration camps on a starvation diet will carefully conserve any form of energy expenditure to make the limited food intake go as far as possible (Cohen, 1954). Social organizations will seek to improve their survival position and to acquire in their reserves a comfortable margin of operation.

The entropic process asserts itself in all biological systems as well as in closed physical systems. The energy replenishment of the biological organism is not of a qualitative character which can maintain indefinitely the complex organizational structure of living tissue. Social systems, however, are not anchored in the same physical constancies as biological organisms and so are capable of almost indefinite arresting of the entropic process. Nevertheless the number of organizations which go out of existence every year is large.

6. INFORMATION INPUT, NEGATIVE FEEDBACK, AND THE CODING PROCESS

The inputs into living systems consist not only of energic materials which become transformed or altered in the work that gets done. Inputs are also informative in character and furnish signals to the structure about the environment and about its own functioning in relation to the environment. Just as we recognize the distinction between cues and drives in individual psychology, so must we take account of information and energic inputs for all living systems.

The simplest type of information input found in all systems is negative feedback. Information feedback of a negative kind enables the system to correct its deviations from course. The working parts of the machine feed back information about the effects of their operation to some central mechanism or subsystem which acts on such information to keep the system on target. The thermostat which controls the temperature of the room is a simple example of a regulatory device which operates on the basis of negative feedback. The automated power plant would furnish more complex examples. Miller (1955) emphasizes the critical nature of negative feedback in his proposition: *"When a system's negative feedback discontinues, its steady state vanishes, and at the same time its boundary disappears and the system terminates"* (p. 529). If there is no corrective device to get the system back on its course, it will expend too much energy or it will ingest too much energic input and no longer continue as a system.

The reception of inputs into a system is selective. Not all energic inputs are capable of being absorbed into every system. The digestive system of living creatures assimilates only those inputs to which it is adapted. Similarly, systems can react only to those information signals to which they are attuned. The general term for the selective mechanisms of a system by which incoming materials are rejected or accepted and translated for the structure is coding. Through the coding process the "blooming, buzzing confusion" of the world is simplified into a few meaningful and simplified categories for a given system. The nature of the functions performed by the system determines its coding mechanisms, which in turn perpetuate this type of functioning.

7. THE STEADY STATE AND DYNAMIC HOMEOSTASIS

The importation of energy to arrest entropy operates to maintain some constancy in energy exchange, so that open systems which survive are characterized by a steady state. A steady state is not motionless or a true equilibrium. There is a continuous inflow of energy from the external environment and a continuous export of the products of the system, but the character of the system, the ratio of the energy exchanges and the relations between parts, remains the same. The catabolic and anabolic processes of tissue breakdown and restoration within the body preserve a steady state so that the organism from time to time is not the identical organism it was but a highly similar organism. The steady state is seen in clear form in the homeostatic processes for the regulation of body temperature; external conditions of humidity and temperature may vary, but the temperature of the body remains the same. The endocrine glands are a regulatory mechanism for preserving an evenness of physiological functioning. The general principle here is that of Le Châtelier (see Bradley and Calvin, 1956) who maintains that any internal or external factor making for disruption of the system is countered by forces which restore the system as closely as possible to its previous state. Krech and Crutchfield (1948) similarly hold, with respect to psychological organization, that cognitive structures will react to influences in such a way as to absorb them with minimal change to existing cognitive integration.

The homeostatic principle does not apply literally to the functioning of all complex living systems, in that in counteracting entropy they move toward growth and expansion. This apparent contradiction can be resolved, however, if we recognize the complexity of the subsystems and their interaction in anticipating changes necessary for the maintenance of an overall steady state.

Stagner (1951) has pointed out that the initial disturbance of a given tissue constancy within the biological organism will result in mobilization of energy to restore the balance, but that recurrent upsets will lead to actions to anticipate the disturbance:

> We eat before we experience intense hunger pangs. . . . energy mobilization for forestalling tactics must be explained in terms of a *cortical tension* which reflects the visceral-propriceptive pattern of the original biological disequilibration . . . . *Dynamic homeostasis* involves the maintenance of tissue constancies by establishing a constant physical environment—by reducing the variability and disturbing effects of external stimulation. Thus the organism does not simply restore the prior equilibrium. A new, more complex and more comprehensive equilibrium is established. (p. 5)

Though the tendency toward a steady state in its simplest form is homeostatic, as in the preservation of a constant body temperature, the basic principle is *the preservation of the character of the system.* The equilibrium which complex systems approach is often that of a quasi-stationary equilibrium, to use Lewin's concept (1947). An adjustment in one direction is countered by a movement in the opposite direction and both movements are approximate rather than precise in their compensatory nature. Thus a temporal chart of activity will show a series of ups and downs rather than a smooth curve.

In preserving the character of the system, moreover, the structure will tend to import more energy than is required for its output, as we have already noted in discussing negative entropy. To insure survival, systems will operate to acquire some margin of safety beyond the immediate level of existence. The body will store fat, the social organization will build up reserves, the society will increase its technological and cultural base. Miller (1955) has formulated the proposition that the rate of growth of a system—within certain ranges—is exponential if it exists in a medium which makes available unrestricted amounts of energy for input.

In adapting to their environment, systems will attempt to cope with external forces by ingesting them or acquiring control over them. The physical boundedness of the single organism means that such attempts at control over the environment affect the behavioral system rather than the biological system of the individual. Social systems will move, however, towards incorporating within their boundaries the external resources essential to survival. Again the result is an expansion of the original system.

Thus, the steady state which at the simple level is one of homeostasis over time, at more complex levels becomes one of preserving the character of the system through growth and expansion. The basic type of system does not change directly as a consequence of expansion. The most common type of growth is a multiplication of the same type of cycles or subsystems—a change in quantity rather than in quality. Animal and plant species grow by multiplication. A social system adds more units of the same essential type as it already has. Haire (1959) has studied the ratio between the sizes of different subsystems in growing business organizations. He found that though the number of people increased in both the production subsystem and the subsystem concerned with the external world, the ratio of the two groups remained constant. Qualitative change does occur, however, in two ways. In the first place, quantitative growth calls for supportive subsystems of a specialized character not necessary when the system was smaller. In the second place, there is a point where quantitative changes produce a qualitative difference in the functioning of a system. A small college which triples its size is no longer the same institution in terms of the relation between its administration and faculty, relations among the various academic departments, or the nature of its instruction.

In fine, living systems exhibit a growth or expansion dynamic in which they maximize their basic character. They react to change or they anticipate change through growth which assimilates the new energic inputs to the nature of their structure. In terms of Lewin's quasi-stationary equilibrium the ups and downs of the adjustive process do not always result in a return to the old level. Under certain circumstances a solidification or freezing occurs during one of the adjustive cycles. A new base line level is thus established and successive movements fluctuate around this plateau which may be either above or below the previous plateau of operation.

8. DIFFERENTIATION

Open systems move in the direction of differentiation and elaboration. Diffuse global patterns are replaced by more specialized functions. The sense organs and the nervous system evolved as highly differentiated structures from the primitive nervous tissues. The growth of the personality proceeds from primitive, crude organizations of mental functions to hierarchically structured and well-differentiated systems of beliefs and feelings. Social organizations move toward the multiplication and elaboration of roles with greater specialization of function. In the United States today medical specialists now outnumber the general practitioners.

One type of differentiated growth in systems is what von Bertalanffy (1956) terms progressive mechanization. It finds expression in the way in which a system achieves a steady state. The early method is a process which involves an interaction of various dynamic forces, whereas the later development entails the use of a regulatory feedback mechanism. He writes:

It can be shown that the *primary* regulations in organic systems, that is, those which are most fundamental and primitive in embryonic development as well as in evolution, are of such nature of dynamic interaction. . . . Superimposed are those regulations which we may call *secondary,* and which are controlled by fixed arrangements, especially of the feedback type. This state of affairs is a consequence of a general principle of organization which may be called progressive mechanization. At first, systems —biological, neurological, psychological or social—are governed by dynamic interaction of their components; later on, fixed arrangements and conditions of constraint are established which render the system and its parts more efficient, but also gradually diminish and eventually abolish its equipotentiality. (p. 6)

9. EQUIFINALITY

Open systems are further characterized by the principle of equifinality, a principle suggested by von Bertalanffy in 1940. According to this principle, a system can reach the same final state from differing initial conditions and by a variety of paths. The well-known biological experiments on the sea urchin show that a normal creature of that species can develop from a complete ovum, from each half of a divided ovum, or from the fusion product of two whole ova. As open systems move toward regulatory mechanisms to control their operations, the amount of equifinality may be reduced.

Some Consequences of Viewing Organizations as Open Systems

At this point we should call attention to some of the misconceptions which arise both in theory and practice when social organizations are regarded as closed rather than open systems.

The major misconception is the failure to recognize fully that the organization is continually dependent upon inputs from the environment and that the inflow of materials and human energy is not a constant. The fact that organizations have built-in protective devices to maintain stability and that they are notoriously difficult to change in the direction of some reformer's desires should not obscure the realities of the dynamic interrelationships of any social structure with its social and natural environment. The very efforts of the organization to maintain a constant external environment produce changes in organizational structure. The reaction to changed inputs to mute their possible revolutionary implications also results in changes.

The typical models in organizational theorizing concentrate upon principles of internal functioning as if these problems were independent of changes in the environment and as if they did not affect the maintenance inputs of motivation and morale. Moves toward tighter integration and coordination are made to insure stability, when flexibility may be the more important requirement. Moreover, coordination and control become ends in themselves rather than means to an end. They are not seen in full perspective as adjusting the system to its environment but as desirable goals within a closed system. In fact, however, every attempt at coordination which is not functionally required may produce a host of new organizational problems.

One error which stems from this kind of misconception is the failure to recognize the equifinality of the open system, namely that there are more ways than one of producing a given outcome. In a closed physical system the same initial conditions must lead to the same final result. In open systems this is not true even at the biological level. It is much less true at the social level. Yet in practice we insist that there is one best way of assembling a gun for all recruits, one best way for the baseball player to hurl the ball in from the outfield, and that we standardize and teach these best methods. Now it is true under certain conditions that there is one best way, but these conditions must first be established. The general principle, which characterizes all open systems, is that there does not have to be a single method for achieving an objective.

A second error lies in the notion that irregularities in the functioning of a system due to environmental influences are error variances and should be treated accordingly. According to this conception, they should be controlled out of studies of organizations. From the organization's own operations they should be excluded as irrelevant and should be guarded against. The decisions of officers to omit a consideration of external factors or to guard against such influences in a defensive fashion, as if they would go away if ignored, is an instance of this type of thinking. So is the now outmoded "public be damned" attitude of businessmen toward the clientele upon whose support they depend. Open system theory, on the other hand, would maintain that environmental influences are not sources of error variance but are integrally related to the functioning of a social system, and that we cannot understand a system without a constant study of the forces that impinge upon it.

Thinking of the organization as a closed system, moreover, results in a failure to develop the intelligence or feedback function of obtaining adequate information about the changes in environmental forces. It is remarkable how weak many industrial companies are in their market research departments when they are so dependent upon the market. The prediction can be hazarded that organizations in our society will increasingly move toward the improvement of the facilities for research in assessing environmental forces. The reason is that we are in the process of correcting our misconception of the organization as a closed system.

Emery and Trist (1960) have pointed out how current theorizing on organizations still reflects the older closed system conceptions. They write:

In the realm of social theory, however, there has been something of a tendency to continue thinking in terms of a "closed" system, that is, to regard the enterprise as sufficiently independent to allow most of its problems to be analyzed with reference to its internal structure and without reference to its external environment. . . . In practice the system theorists in social science . . . did "tend to focus on the statics of social structure and to neglect the study of structural change." In an attempt to overcome this bias, Merton suggested that "the concept of dysfunction, which implied the concept of strain, stress and tension on the structural level, provides an analytical approach to the study of dynamics and change." This concept has been widely accepted by system theorists but while it draws attention to sources of imbalance within an organization it does not conceptually reflect the mutual permeation of an organization and its environment that is the cause of such imbalance. It still retains the limiting perspectives of "closed system" theorizing. In the administrative field the same limitations may be seen in the otherwise invaluable contributions of Barnard and related writers. (p. 84)

. . .

The fact that the organization is an open system means that it is constantly interacting with its environment to dispose of its product, to obtain materials, to recruit personnel, and to obtain the general support of outside structures to facilitate these functions. There is a constant need for environmental support. Hence subsystems develop within the organization to institutionalize environmental relationships and guarantee such support. An organization will often have separate departments for merchandising, advertising, and selling; for recruiting and selecting personnel; for procuring raw materials; and for public relations and contact with the larger society.

Though different organizations will assign different functions and names to these departments, three types of boundary systems can generally be identified.

The procurement operation is divided into the function of obtaining the input of materials to be converted and the input of personnel to get the job done. These two functions are characteristically found in separate bureaus or divisions of the organization. Theoretically part of the boundary subsystems, in practice the procurement of materials usually is tied into the production structure and the recruiting of personnel into the maintenance system. The basic condition for this allocation is a fairly abundant supply of materials and people in the external environment. When materials and personnel are difficult to obtain, the structures responsible for their procurement must face more completely toward the outside world and divorce themselves in part from the production and maintenance functions. Thus the securing of personnel for given periods of time in industrial organizations through contracts with unions is not handled through the personnel officer but through a vice president in charge of industrial relations.

The disposal function of marketing the product is found in its most exaggerated form in profit-making organizations with elaborate merchandising and sales systems. The primary emphasis is upon inducing the public to purchase the product of the organization, but feedback on the success of this effort will lead to changes in the product itself. Many nonbusiness organizations expend little energy in direct product disposal. They are not in the position of having their source of input support tied directly to the disposal of their output. For example, educational institutions have as their product the imparting of knowledge and the increase of knowledge, and they do little to market their graduates.

All organizations have as their essential boundary system what Parsons (1960) calls the *institutional system* or relations with the larger community or society. The operation of any organization depends not only upon the specific reception of its product but upon the support and legitimation of its activities by the larger social structure. Corporations deal with the federal government with respect to policy and practice on mergers and monopolies and tax laws, among other things. Corporations also relate to the general public regarding support for private enterprise and types of restrictions on private power. Awareness of this problem has led to concern with the image of the company in the public mind. In similar fashion, the public school interacts with the community it serves through its Board of Education. An educator named as president of a large university soon finds that little of his time is available for educational administration within the university. He is primarily its external representative, dealing with alumni groups, foundations, potential donors, governmental officers, civic and other public groups. The term *public relations* tends to be restricted to institutional advertising, and is not an adequate concept to cover this important function of relating the organization to the total social system of which it is a part.

CHANGING ENVIRONMENTAL PRESSURES AND ADAPTIVE SUBSYSTEMS

Organizations do not exist in a static world. The surrounding environment is in a constant state of flux and a rigid technical system, though preserved by an excellent structure, does not survive. The pressures for change are communicated most sharply to the organization when there is no market for its output. This is often too late for organizational survival and so many organizations develop *adaptive structures* whose function it is to gather advance information about trends in the environment, carry out research on internal productive processes, and plan for future developments.

NOTES

1. Allport, F. H. 1962. A structuronomic conception of behavior: individual and collective. I. Structural theory and the master problem of social psychology, *Journal of Abnormal and Social Psychology*, 64, 3–30.
2. Bradley, D. F., and M. Calvin. 1956. Behavior: imbalance in a network of chemical

transformations. *General Systems*. Yearbook of the Society for the Advancement of
General System Theory, 1, 56–65.

3. Cohen, E. 1954. *Human behavior in the concentration camp*. London: Jonathan Cape.

4. Dornbusch, S. 1955. The military academy as an assimilating institution. *Social Forces, 33,* 316–321.

5. Emery, F. E., and E. L. Trist. 1960. Socio-technical systems. In *Management sciences models and techniques*. Vol. 2. London: Pergamon Press.

6. Haire, M. 1959. Biological models and empirical histories of the growth of organizations. In M. Haire (Ed.) *Modern organization theory,* New York: Wiley, 272–306.

7. Kahn, R. L., D. M. Wolfe, R. P. Quinn, J. D. Snoek, and R. A. Rosenthal. 1964. *Organizational stress: studies in role conflict and ambiguity*. New York: Wiley.

8. Köhler, W., and D. Emery. 1947. Figural after-effects in the third dimension of visual space. *American Journal of Psychology, 60,* 159–201.

9. Köhler, W., and H. Wallach. 1944. Figural after-effects: an investigation of visual processes. *Proceedings of the American Philosophical Society, 88,* 269–357.

10. Krech, D., and R. Crutchfield. 1948. *Theory and problems of social psychology*. New York: McGraw-Hill.

11. Lewin, K. 1947. Frontiers in group dynamics. *Human Relations, 1,* 5–41.

12. Luce, Clare B. 1964. Address to the Detroit Economic Club.

13. Melzack, R., and W. Thompson. 1956. Effects of early experience on social behavior, *Canadian Journal of Psychology, 10,* 82–90.

14. Miller, J. G. 1955. Toward a general theory for the behavioral sciences, *American Psychologist, 10,* 513–531.

15. Parsons, T. 1960. *Structure and process in modern societies*. New York: Free Press.

16. Solomon, P., et al. (eds.) 1961. *Sensory deprivation*. Cambridge, Mass.: Harvard University Press.

17. Spitz, R. A. 1945. Hospitalism: an inquiry into the genesis of psychiatric conditions in early childhood, *Psychoanalytic Study of the Child, 1,* 53–74.

18. Stagner, R. 1951. Homeostasis as a unifying concept in personality theory, *Psychological Review, 58,* 5–17.

19. von Bertalanffy, L. 1940. Der organismus als physikalisches system betrachtet, *Naturwissenschaften, 28,* 521 ff.

20. von Bertalanffy, L. 1956. General system theory, *General systems,* Yearbook of the Society for the Advancement of General System Theory, 1, 1–10.

ADDITIONAL READINGS

Allport, Gordon W. 1960. "The Open System in Personality Theory," *Journal of Abnormal and Social Psychology,* 61, 301–311.

Andrew, Gwen. 1965. "An Analytic System Model for Organization Theory," *Academy of Management Journal,* 8 (September), 190–198.

Ashby, W. R. 1958. "General Systems Theory as a New Discipline." *General Systems Yearbook,* 3 (October), 1–17.

Boulding, Kenneth E. 1956. "General Systems Theory—The Skeleton of Science," *Management Science,* 2 (April), 197–208.

Buckley, Walter. 1967. *Sociology and Modern Systems Theory.* Englewood Cliffs, N.J.: Prentice-Hall.

Buckley, Walter, ed. 1968. *Modern Systems Research for the Behavioral Scientist.* Chicago: Aldine.

Ellis, David O., and Fred J. Ludwig. 1962. *Systems Philosophy.* Englewood Cliffs, N.J.: Prentice-Hall.

Griffiths, Daniel E. 1964. "Administrative theory and change in organizations." In *Innovation in Education,* Matthew B. Miles, ed. New York: Columbia University.

Gross, Bertram M. 1967. "The Coming General Systems Models of Social Systems," *Human Relations,* 20 (November), 357–374.

Hare, Van Court, Jr. 1967. *Systems Analysis: A Diagnostic Approach.* New York: Harcourt Brace Jovanovich.

Hopeman, Richard J. 1969. *Systems Analysis and Operations Management.* Columbus, Ohio: Merrill.

Johnson, Richard, et al. 1963. *The Theory and Management of Systems.* New York: McGraw-Hill.

Johnson, Richard A., Fremont E. Kast, and James E. Rosenzweig. 1964. "Systems Theory and Management," *Management Science,* 10 (January), 367–384.

Kaplan, Morton A. 1968. "Systems Theory and Political Science," *Social Research,* 35 (Spring), 30–47.

Kast, Fremont E., and James E. Rosenzweig. 1967. "System Concept: Pervasiveness and Potential," *Management International,* 7, 87–96.

Mesarovic, M. D., ed. 1964. *Views on General Systems Theory.* New York: Wiley.

Miller, James G. 1965. "Living Systems: Basic Concepts," *Behavioral Science,* 10 (July), 193–237.

Miller, James G. 1965. "Living Systems: Cross-Level Hypotheses," *Behavioral Science,* 10 (October), 380–411.

Miller, James G. 1965. "Living Systems: Structure and Process," *Behavioral Science,* 10 (October), 337–379.

Rice, A. K. 1963. *The Enterprise and Its Environment.* London: Tavistock Publications.

Tilles, Seymour. 1963. "The Manager's Job: A Systems Approach," *Harvard Business Review,* 41 (January–February), 73–81.

von Bertalanffy, Ludwig. 1950. "The Theory of Open Systems in Physics and Biology," *Science,* 111 (January), 23–29.

von Bertalanffy, Ludwig. 1968. *General System Theory.* New York: George Braziller.

Young, Stanley. 1968. "Organization as a Total System," *California Management Review,* 10 (Spring), 21–32.

CHAPTER TWO

Interorganizational Relationships Within an Organization's Environment

Before studying the relationships of a given organization to other organizations in its environment, it is important to consider that these other organizations are related to each other, and that the nature of their interconnectedness affects the exchanges between a given organization and any one organization with respect to both inputs and outputs. This is what Emery and Trist mean by the phrase "causal texture of organizational environments."[1]

In the first article, Evan examines the interaction between an organization and the network of organizations in its environment. He delineates seven strategic dimensions of this network or organization-set. He proposes five hypotheses concerning the effects of these dimensions on the decision-making autonomy of the focal organization, and seven hypotheses with other interorganizational processes as dependent variables.

Emery and Trist, using a case study of a British food-canning firm, discuss how a change in the degree of connectedness between organizations and events in the firm's environment, as well as increases in the rate of change and extent of interactional complexity, led to organizational change in terms of product mix and company identity. They isolate four ideal types of causal textures, and point out that in type four, a turbulent field, the firm experiences serious difficulties in prediction and control because of the degree of causal texturing. This turbulent field is not of the organization's making; that is, it is a quasi-independent domain. Evan's hypothesis of an inverse relationship between concentration in the organization-set of input-organizational resources and decision-making autonomy is supported by Emery and Trist's National Farmers Union case. In addition, this case supports the hypothesis with respect to output organization-sets. Other hypotheses of Evan are also supported by Emery and Trist, and additional ones are suggested.

Terreberry's paper elaborates the concepts of Emery and Trist, and presents evidence that strongly suggests that the environments of many organizations are evolving toward turbulent field conditions. She maintains that this turbulence is associated with an increasing proportion of externally induced organizational changes as well as increasingly unpredictable changes in an organization's transactional interdependencies. She examines four conceptual frameworks (other than oligopoly theory) for the analysis of interorganizational relationships, and outlines the beginning of an integrative framework.

NOTE

1. Boulding's "ecosystem" is a similar concept (Kenneth E. Boulding. 1953. *The Organizational Revolution.* New York: Harper & Brothers, pp. xx–xxi]. He defines this as a "self-contained and self-perpetuating system of interacting populations of various kinds." According to Boulding, "If we are to understand the laws which govern the growth and survival of any class of organization, we must understand where it fits into the social ecosystem . . . ."

THE ORGANIZATION-SET
Toward a Theory of Interorganizational Relations*

William M. Evan

Social science research on organizations has been concerned principally with *intraorganizational* phenomena. Psychologists have studied the individual in an organization; social psychologists, the relations among the members of a group in an organization and the impact of a group on the attitudes and behavior of group members; and sociologists, informal groups, formal subunits, and structural attributes of an organization.[1] With relatively few exceptions, social scientists engaged in organizational research have not taken the organization in its environment as a unit of observation and analysis. Selznick's (1949) work on the TVA is a notable exception, as are Ridgeway's (1957) study of the manufacturer-dealer relationships, Dill's (1958) comparative study of two Norwegian firms, Levine and White's (1961) research on health and welfare agencies, Elling and Halebsky's (1961) study of hospitals, and Litwak and Hylton's (1962) study of community chests and social service exchanges.

The relative neglect of *interorganizational* relations is all the more surprising in view of the fact that all formal organizations are embedded in an environment of other organizations as well as in a complex of norms, values, and collectivities of the society at large. Inherent in the relationship between any formal organization and its environment is the fact that it is to some degree dependent upon its environment; in other words, it is a subsystem of the more inclusive social system of society. As distinct from a society, which in some respects is relatively self-sufficient in that it runs the gamut of all human institutions, a formal organization is a partial social system inasmuch as it defines only a specific set of goals and statuses as relevant to its functioning.

The phenomena and problems of interorganizational relations are part of the general class of boundary-relations problems confronting all types of social systems, including formal organizations. All such boundary relations tend to be enormously complex. Apart from sheer complexity, problems of interorganizational relations have been neglected by organizational analysts in part because of the concepts and propositions of various theories of organization. For

Reprinted from *Approaches to Organizational Design*, edited by James D. Thompson, by permission of the University of Pittsburgh Press. © 1966 by the University of Pittsburgh Press.

* This is a revised version of a paper prepared for the Seminar on the Social Science of Organizations, University of Pittsburgh, June 1963. It is printed with the permission of *Management Science,* where it first appeared. The author developed the concept of organization-set in a proposal entitled, "Law, Formal Organization, and Social Change," which was submitted to the Russell Sage Foundation in the Spring of 1959. He wishes to express his gratitude to the members of his conference group at the University of Pittsburgh for their many valuable comments. He is especially indebted to John MacDougall, Robert Melson, and Sheldon Stryker for their critical reading of the manuscript.

example, the Weberian theory of bureaucracy is concerned largely with internal structural attributes and processes such as specialization of functions, allocation of authority, and formalization of rules. Taylorism and other kindred theories are also oriented toward internal relations among personnel. And the inducement-contribution theory of Barnard (1938) and Simon (1945) also has an intraorganizational focus. (cf. March and Simon, 1958, pp. 83–111.) A notable exception to the intraorganizational focus is the theoretical work of Parsons (1959, pp. 10–16; 1960, pp. 60–65) on formal organizations. As a social system theorist, Parsons is concerned with how organizations differing in their primacy of functions solve four system problems: adaptation, goal attainment, pattern maintenance, and integration. Any attempt to investigate how a particular organization solves these problems immediately involves considerations of interorganizational relations.

Notwithstanding the general neglect of interorganizational phenomena by organization theorists, managers are greatly preoccupied with interorganizational relations. Some well-known examples of interorganizational practices are allocation of resources to public relations, co-optation of personnel of environing organizations into leadership positions in order to reduce the threat they might otherwise pose, acquisition of and merging with competitors, use of espionage against competitors, and recourse to litigation, arbitration, and mediation to resolve interorganizational disputes. These and many other interorganizational phenomena and processes await systematic inquiry by organization theorists. Millett's (1962, p. 3) general observation about organization theory is particularly relevant to this problem area: "... our practice has far outrun our theory. . . . The art of organization has much more to its credit . . . than has the science of organization." Impeding progress are problems of conceptualizing and measuring interactions among organizations. Prevailing organizational concepts and theories concerned with intraorganizational phenomena are probably not adequate for a study of interorganizational phenomena.

The purpose of this paper is to explore in a preliminary manner some conceptual and methodological problems of interorganizational relations. In the process we hope to extend the scope of organization theory and to draw attention to the potentialities of comparative research on interorganizational relations.

The Role-Set

One point of departure in the study of interorganizational relations is to examine the utility of the concept of the "role-set," developed by Merton (1957, pp. 368–380), for analyzing role relationships (see also Gross et al., 1958, pp. 48–74). A role-set consists of the complex of roles and role relationships that the occupant of a given status has by virtue of occupying that status. A professor, for example, interacts not only with students but also with other professors, with the head of his department, with the dean of his school, and occasionally with the president or with the members of the board of trustees.

In all organizations the occupants of some statuses perform a liaison function with other organizations. Top executives in industrial organizations frequently confer with government officials, with executives of other firms within and without the industry, with members of trade associations, with officials in the local community. As guardians of the "public image" of the organization (cf. Riley and Levy, 1963), they are probably wary of delegating to subordinates contacts with representatives of other organizations that might have critical significance for the welfare of their own organizations.

The difference in orientation and behavior between liaison and nonliaison personnel is clearly brought out in a study by Macaulay (1963). In a study of the use of contract law among business firms, Macaulay found a high incidence of noncontractual relations. Among his other findings was a difference in orientation among the various departments in business firms toward the use of contracts, with the sales department being more negatively disposed to contracts and the comptroller departments being more positively disposed. When interdepartmental conflicts arise about the use of contracts, the house counsel, Macaulay observes, occasionally performs the function of an arbitrator.

A role-set analysis of the sales personnel as compared with the personnel of the comptroller departments suggests a possible explanation for the observed difference in attitudes toward the use of contracts (see Evan, 1963a). As the "foreign affairs" personnel of an organization, sales department employees come into recurrent contact with their "role partners" in other organizations, i.e., purchasing agents, with the result that nonorganizational norms develop, making for less recourse to contracts. In contrast, the role-sets of comptroller personnel involve a higher degree of interaction with others within the organization, thus reinforcing organizational norms—including the use of contracts. We may infer from Macaulay's study that systematic inquiry into the role-sets of boundary personnel will shed light on interorganizational relations as it bears on organizational decisions, whether pertaining to the use of contracts or other matters.

The Organization-Set

Analogous to the role-set concept is what I propose to call the "organization-set." Instead of taking a particular status as the unit of analysis, as Merton does in his role-set analysis, I shall take as the unit of analysis an organization, or a class of organizations, and trace its interactions with the network of organizations in its environment, i.e., with elements of its organization-set. In analyzing a particular organization-set I shall refer to the organization that is the point of reference as the "focal organization" (cf. Gross et al., 1958, pp. 50–56). In order to avoid the danger of reifying interorganizational relations, the relations between the focal organization and its organization-set are conceived as mediated by (a) the role-sets of its boundary personnel, (b) the flow of information, (c) the flow of products or services, and (d) the flow of personnel. As in the case of the role-set, conflicting demands by members of the organization-set may be handled by the focal organization with the help of mechanisms analogous to those described by Merton (1957), e.g., by preventing observation of behavior and by concerted action to counter the demands of other organizations.

An analysis of the organization-set of a focal organization (or of a class of focal organizations) could help explain: (a) the internal structure of the focal organization; (b) its degree of autonomy in decision-making; (c) its degree of effectiveness or "goal attainment"; (d) its identity, i.e., its public image and self-image; (e) the flow of information from the focal organization to the elements of its organization-set and vice versa; (f) the flow of personnel from the focal organization to the elements of its organization-set and vice versa; and (g) the forces impelling the focal organization to cooperate or compete with elements of its organization-set, to coordinate its activities, to merge with other organizations, or to dissolve. As an example of the possible explanatory utility of the organization-set concept we shall presently consider the effects of structural variations in the organization-set on the decision-making autonomy of the focal organization.

Some Dimensions of Organization-Sets

If we are to make any progress in analyzing interorganizational relations, we shall have to identify strategic attributes or dimensions of organization-sets. With the aid of such attributes we can formulate empirically testable propositions about interactions among organizations.

A provisional listing of dimensions of organization-sets follows; its principal value may lie in illustrating a possibly useful direction of conceptual analysis. Whether these dimensions are more heuristic than others that might be abstracted can be determined only by means of empirical research.

1. *Input vs. output organization-sets.* The focal organization's environment consists of an input and an output organization-set. As a partial social system, a focal organization depends on input organizations for various types of resources: personnel, matériel, capital, legality, and legitimacy (Evan and Schwartz, 1964). The focal organization in turn produces a product or a service for a market, an audience, a client sys-

tem, etc. For example, a private hospital may have in its input organization-set the community chest from which it obtains financial support, an association of hospitals from which it receives accreditation, and the department of public health of the local or state government from which it receives one or more licenses granting it the right to function. Its output organization-set may include other hospitals with which it cooperates or competes, medical research organizations, government agencies to which it sends data, etc.

2. *Comparative vs. normative reference organizations.* As in the case of an individual, the focal organization may evaluate its performance by using one or more organizations in its set—input or output, more likely the latter—as a standard for comparison, i.e., as a "comparative reference organization." On the other hand, if a focal organization incorporates the values and goals of one or more of the elements of its organization-sets, we would refer to it as a "normative reference organization" (Merton, 1957, pp. 283–284). For example, a firm manufacturing a particular kind of bomber might compare the quality of its product with other firms manufacturing bombers. Such outside firms would then be deemed "comparative reference organizations." Suppose, however, the Department of Defense indicates that the rapid production of a newly developed unmanned decoy bomber is urgently required by the United States. If the firm decided to convert its current bomber production into the production of an unmanned decoy bomber, it will have in effect incorporated as its goal the goal of the government and would be using a representative of the government, the Department of Defense, as a "normative reference organization."

3. *Size of the organization-set.* A focal organization may have a relatively large or a relatively small number of elements in its set. Whether it interacts with few or with many organizations presumably has significant consequences for its internal structure and decision-making. The size of the organization-set is to be distinguished, of course, from the size of the focal organization, although the two are presumably correlated.

4. *Concentration of input organizational resources.* The focal organization may depend on few or many elements in its input organization-set for its resources. Whether the concentration of input organizational resources is high or low would probably affect the structure and functioning of the focal organization.

5. *Overlap in membership.* Not infrequently there is an overlap in membership of the focal organization with one of the organizations in its set. This is manifestly the case with (a) employees of an industrial organization who belong to a trade union with which the focal organization has a collective bargaining agreement, (b) scientists or engineers who are affiliated with a professional society from or through which an employing organization recruits its employees, and (c) members of the board of directors of the focal organization who are also directors of organizations in its set.

6. *Overlap in goals and values.* The goals and values of the focal organization may overlap with those of the elements in its set. To the extent that this occurs it probably affects the nature of the interorganizational relations that develop. For example, hostility might be engendered between an American military base overseas and a political party in the country in which the base was situated if the party did not share the assessment that the base was performing a "protective and deterrent" function rather than an "offensive and provocative" function.

7. *Boundary personnel.* Classifying the personnel of an organization into those concerned principally with domestic matters and those preoccupied with "foreign affairs" is difficult, though not impossible (cf. Thompson, 1962). In a study of four manufacturing organizations, Haire (1959, pp. 272–306) analyzes the growth of external personnel in relation to internal personnel. Parsons (1959, pp. 10–16; 1960, pp. 59–96) distinguishes among three levels of personnel and functions in a formal organization: institutional, managerial, and technical. The first and third category probably involve a higher proportion of boundary personnel than the second category. In other words, top executives and some staff specialists such as sales, public relations, and house counsel are more likely to be engaged in boundary-maintenance functions than are junior and middle executives.

Some Hypotheses About Organization-Sets

Whether or not our preliminary consideration of some conceptual problems of interorganizational relations will prove useful only empirical research can establish. In the interest of stimulating inquiry in this relatively neglected area, several hypotheses on organization-sets, each assuming a *ceteris paribus* condition, will be formulated with the aid of the attributes enumerated in the foregoing section.

1. *The higher the concentration of input organizational resources, the lower the degree of autonomy in decision making of the focal organization.* A case in

38 point is the difference in degree of independence between a public and private university. A public university probably has fewer sources of revenue than a private university, and one member in its organization-set, the state legislature, probably accounts for the greatest part of its revenue. Consequently, public universities with a high concentration of input organizational resources probably exercise a lower degree of decision-making autonomy than private universities with a low concentration of input organizational resources.

2. *The greater the size of the organization-set, the lower the decision-making autonomy of the focal organization, provided that some elements in the set form an uncooperative coalition that controls resources essential to the functioning of the focal organization, or provided that an uncooperative single member of the set controls such resources.* Where there is a high degree of conflict among the elements of the organization-set, such conflict may tend to cancel out their effect on the focal organization, thus affording it more autonomy than would otherwise be the case. On the other hand, to the extent that there are coalition formations and to the extent that these coalition formations provide essential resources for or services to the focal organization, this does impose significant constraints on the degree of independence of the focal organization.

A striking example of a coalition formation against a focal organization is the boycott by druggists—organized by their trade association—of the Pepsodent Company when the latter withdrew its California fair-trade contracts (Palamountain, 1955, pp. 235–239). Also impressive is the action of the National Automobile Dealers Association, in the courts and in legislatures, to curb the power of the three large automobile manufacturers to dictate the terms of contracts and to cancel contracts (Palamountain, 1955, pp. 107–158; Evan, 1962, p. 179). By means of concerted action this trade association has become a countervailing power in the automobile industry. But size of organization-set, through an alternative sequence of variations, may produce an increase in the decision-making autonomy of the focal organization as well as the decrease hypothesized above. Quite likely there is a positive association between size of the organization-set and size of the focal organization. The larger the organization, the greater the specialization in liaison functions, the greater the number of boundary personnel, and so the greater the decision-making autonomy of the focal organization. However, some qualifications are necessary. To the extent that the proportion of boundary personnel is indicative of the *actual* rather than the *attempted* impact on the elements of its set, the greater the proportion of such personnel in the focal organization—relative to the proportion of such personnel in the set—the greater is its decision-making autonomy. Thus it may be seen that different mediators of the effects of size of organization-set yield opposite consequences for decision-making autonomy of the focal organization.

3. *The greater the degree of similarity of goals and functions between the organization-set and the focal organization, the greater the amount of competition between them, and hence the lower the degree of decision-making autonomy of the focal organization.* In their study of health and welfare agencies, Levine and White (1961, p. 598) observe that:

... intense competition may occur occasionally between two agencies offering the same services, especially when other agencies have no specific criteria for referring patients to one rather than the other. If both services are operating near capacity, competition between the two tends to be less keen, the choice being governed by the availability of service. If the services are being operated at less than capacity, competition and conflict often occur. Personnel of referring agencies in this case frequently deplore the "duplication of services" in the community.

Another illustration of this hypothesis is the enactment of a law by Congress in 1959 requiring legislative authorization of major weapons programs of the armed forces. The enactment, Section 412 of the Military Construction Authorization Act of Fiscal 1960, substantially affects the process of policy-making in military affairs. Previously, major weapons procurement was authorized on a continual basis. Section 412, however, required that procurement of aircraft, missiles, and ships by all the services would require renewed authorization on an annual basis. Section 412 was authorized by the Senate Armed Services Committee, which was seeking to expand Congress' participation in defense policy-making. Here it may be seen that the common goal of the Defense Department and of the Armed Services Committee was the adequate defense of the nation, and that efforts to achieve that goal brought them into conflict, lowering the decision-making autonomy of the Department of Defense (Dawson, 1962, pp. 42–57).

4. *The greater the overlap in membership between the focal organization and the elements of its set, the lower its degree of decision-making autonomy.* A case in point is the overlapping membership of industrial organizations and trade unions. Overlapping membership, if accompanied by overlapping goals and values, may engender a conflict of loyalties that in turn probably diminishes the autonomy of the focal organization.

In Africa trade unions have become closely associated with nationalist parties, which have almost invariably provided governments of newly independent states with important personnel. Overlapping membership then occurs between a ministry of the central government and a trade union. These union leaders then face a dilemma in the concurrent needs to meet their members' demands for higher living standards and to cooperate with the government in promoting economic expansion. Their decision-making autonomy is thus reduced relative to the autonomy present when they were only union officials.

5. *Normative reference organizations have a greater constraining effect on the decisions of the focal organization than do comparative reference organizations.* The relations between trade unions of federal civil servants and the government illustrates this hypothesis. In the American public service it has been traditional not to strike; instead public servants have been satisfied to have working conditions determined by legislation or unilateral administrative action. This is probably due in large measure to the fact that the government department for which the civil servant works constitutes a very strong normative reference organization. Civil servants have apparently incorporated the goals of government, one of which is to maintain the continuity of the government in all circumstances. A trade union of office workers outside the government that threatens to strike will be seen only as a comparative reference organization whose members perform parallel duties with government workers. In the case of the civil servant, a normative reference organization clearly

40 determines behavior to a greater extent than a comparative reference organization (Spero, 1962, pp. 1–4).

The foregoing hypotheses are but illustrations of the kinds of hypotheses that might be formulated with the help of the properties of organization-sets. These hypotheses revolve around the dependent variable of autonomy in decision making of the focal organization. Clearly, similar hypotheses are needed for various interorganizational processes, e.g., coordination, cooperation, competition, conflict, innovation, amalgamation (Thompson and McEwen, 1958). Several examples of such hypotheses will be briefly considered:

1. *The greater the size of the organization-set, the greater the degree of centralization of authority in order to prevent the "displacement of goals" (Merton, 1957, pp. 199–201) generated by subunit loyalties and actions. In turn, an increase in centralization of authority results in an increase in the formalization of rules within the focal organization as a means of guarding against the displacement of goals.*

2. *The greater the similarity of functions between the focal organization and the members of its set, the greater the likelihood that it will compete with them. Overlapping membership, however, probably tends to mitigate competition. If overlapping membership is combined with overlapping goals and values, cooperative action that could lead to amalgamation might ensue.*

3. *The greater the complementarity of functions between the focal organization and the members of its set, the greater the likelihood of cooperative action.*

4. *The greater the capacity of the focal organization to invoke sanctions against the members of its set, the greater the likelihood of coordination and cooperation, provided that members of the set do not succeed in uniting in opposition to the focal organization.*

5. *The greater the shortage of input resources on the part of the focal organization, the greater the likelihood that it will cooperate with the input organizations in its set and the more favorable its disposition toward amalgamation with one or more of them.* The academic "common market" being formed among midwest universities to pool their resources in graduate education is a case in point.

6. *The greater the competition between the focal organization and the members of the output organizations in its set, the more favorable is its disposition toward amalgamation, provided that the goals and values of the respective organizations are compatible.*

7. *If the members of the organization-set exhibit a high rate of technological change, the focal organization, in order to remain competitive, will be highly receptive to innovations.*

Some Methodological Problems

Apart from the conceptual problems awaiting analysis in this area of research, there are measurement problems of considerable difficulty. Describing and measuring networks of interorganizational relations presents a substantial methodological challenge. Some gross behavioral indicators of interorganizational relations are number of contracts, number of clients or customers, volume of sales or services, volume of telephone calls made and received, volume of mail sent and received. Mapping interactions of organizations would require special attention to boundary personnel, as noted above, and to the patterns of interaction of organizational decision-makers. Such mapping operations of the behavior of boundary personnel and decision-makers could also yield sociometric data on which of the elements in an organization-set are perceived by different categories of members of the focal organization as "comparative reference organizations" or as "normative reference organizations." Two closely related methodological tools that may prove useful in the mapping of interorganizational relations are graph theory and input-output analysis.

GRAPH THEORY

One possible use of graph theory (Cartwright, 1959, pp. 254–271; Harary and Norman, 1953; Flament, 1963) is in the construction of an index measuring the amount of decision-making autonomy of a focal organization or of any of the elements in its set. Let us consider three highly simplified organization-set configurations approximating a "wheel," a "chain," and an "all-channel network" (cf. Bavelas, 1951; Leavitt, 1964, pp. 228–241). In the three digraphs shown in Figure 1, each point represents an organization, each line a type of interaction (a flow of information, of goods, of influence, or of personnel), and an arrow the direction of interaction.

If we take A as the focal organization in the three configurations, how do they differ in their degree of decision-making autonomy? Intuitively, we would expect that I_A ranks first in autonomy, II_A ranks second, and III_A ranks third. In the automobile industry the supplier-manufacturer-dealer sequence of organizational relationships would suggest that the supplier is in a position comparable to III_A and that the manufacturers are in a position comparable to I_A

I. Wheel

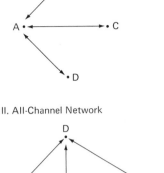

II. All-Channel Network

III. Chain

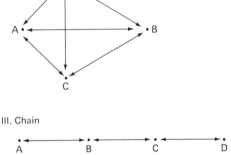

Figure 1. Three Organization-Set Configurations

(Ridgeway, 1957). Can we construct an index that would yield a "coefficient of interconnectedness" of elements in an organization-set—and hence decision-making autonomy—that would discriminate not only among the three simplified organization-sets shown in Figure 1 but also among other possible configurations?

INPUT-OUTPUT ANALYSIS

One input-output model that may prove useful in the study of interorganizational relations is that developed by Leontief (1953). In the study of the structure of the American economy, Leontief and his associates have, of course, concerned themselves with economic parameters such as prices, in-

THE ORGANIZATION-SET

vestments, and incomes. Is this mode of analysis applicable to noneconomic parameters of interorganizational relationships with which sociologists, social psychologists, and political scientists are concerned? Are the obstacles to an input-output analysis of interorganizational relations insuperable because the data most social scientists work with do not take the form of ratio scales, as is true of the data of economists? In most cases the data used by social scientists studying organizations—other than economists—frequently take the form of nominal or ordinal scales and, occasionally, interval scales, e.g., flows of information, flows of personnel, or flows of influence. Apart from the level of measurement, do noneconomic data permit the construction of "technical coefficients" of inputs to the outputs of the focal organizations?

One way of raising the question of the applicability of input-output analysis is to consider a highly simplified relationship between the members of an oligopolistic industry, such as automobile manufacturing. In Figure 2 we present a hypothetical input-output matrix consisting of the flow of influence on management decisions regarding the styling of new automobiles. It would appear from the hypothetical data in Figure 2 that G. M. is the "style leader." It receives the largest number of praiseworthy "mentions" in the minutes of management meetings of its competitors, and it in turn makes the fewest praiseworthy mentions in its meetings of its competitors' styles. Would an input-output analysis of matrices of the type shown in Figure 2—possibly in conjunction with additional data, e.g., share of the market—suggest any further operations for analyzing the data or yield any additional insights into the decision-making process concerning automobile styles?

An analogous matrix that might lend itself to an input-output analysis is shown in Figure 3. Once again it is clear from the hypothetical data that G. M. enjoys a commanding position: it has the smallest outflux of engineering personnel and the largest influx from the other automobile companies. Would an input-output analysis of this matrix, supplemented by data on other characteristics of the organizations, contribute to our understanding of the data?

The matrices shown in Figures 2 and

Flow of Engineering Personnel to

		A.M.	Ford	Chrysler	G.M.	Total
Flow of Engineering Personnel from	A.M.		15	5	40	60
	Ford	5		5	25	35
	Chrysler	7	8		35	50
	G.M.	2	12	6		20
	Total	14	35	16	100	

Figure 2. Hypothetical Matrix of Flow of Influence on Styling Decisions in the Automobile Industry (as Indexed by Frequency of Praiseworthy Mentions in the Minutes of Management Meetings)

Number of Praiseworthy Mentions Made by	A.M.	Ford	Chrysler	G.M.	Total
A.M.		10	5	15	30
Ford	2		5	15	22
Chrysler	3	8		13	24
G.M.	0	4	6		10
Total	5	22	16	43	

Figure 3. Hypothetical Flow of Engineering Personnel, 1955–1960

3 involve one point in time. Assuming that data are available for two or more time periods, can we apply a Markov chain model to analyze the processes of change in interorganizational relations?

Conclusion

The foregoing methodological discussion together with the theoretical analysis may provide guidelines for new research on interorganizational relations. Of particular promise is comparative research on the organization-sets of different classes of organizations. How different are the organization-sets of economic, political, religious, educational, and cultural organizations? And what are the consequences of variations in organization-sets for the internal structure and for the decision-making process of different types of organizations? Do "coercive" organizations have a network of interactions with other organizations different from "utilitarian" and "normative" organizations (Etzioni, 1961)? How different are the organization-sets of habit, problem solving, indoctrination, and service types of organizations (Bennis, 1959, p. 299)?

Within the confines of any one class of organizations, how different are the organization-sets of, say, industrial organizations classified by industry? Similarly, what structural variations in organization-sets are observable among therapeutic versus custodial prisons (Cloward et al., 1960; Wheeler, 1961, pp. 229–259) or among hospitals differing in the importance they attach to the goals of treatment, teaching, and research?

Another possible use of organization-set analysis is in the study of intraorganizational dynamics. If each of the major functional areas in a business organization—production, sales, engineering, personnel, etc.—is taken as a unit of inquiry, an organization-set analysis would be applicable in studying interdepartmental relations. Such an approach would probably be especially useful in investigating the problem of innovation in industrial organizations (Evan, in press).

As is generally recognized, a formal organization is a particular type of social system. The study of interorganizational relations hence involves an analysis of intersocial system relations. Systematic inquiry into the interactions among various types of organizations may not only unearth new intraorganizational phenomena and processes, but may also provide the wherewithal for bridging the gap between the microscopic *organi-*

THE ORGANIZATION-SET

zational and the macroscopic *institutional* levels of analysis. The solution of intersystem problems of the most aggregate level, viz., interrelations among societies, presupposes a knowledge of the nature of interorganizational interactions within and between the several institutions of a society.

NOTE

1. See, for example, Argyris (1957; 1964), Costello and Zalkind (1963), Haire (1964), Bennis et al. (1964), Kahn et al. (1964), Blau (1955), and Evan (1963).

REFERENCES

ABBREVIATIONS
APSR American Political Science Review
ASR American Sociological Review
ASQ Administrative Science Quarterly

Argyris, C. *Integrating the Individual and the Organization.* New York: Wiley, 1964.
———. *Personality and Organization.* New York: Harper, 1957.
Barnard, C. I. *The Functions of the Executive.* Cambridge: Harvard U. Press, 1938.
Bavalas, A. "Communication Patterns in Task-Oriented Groups." In H. Lasswell and D. Lerner, eds. *The Policy Sciences.* Stanford, Cal.: Stanford U. Press, 1951.
Bennis, W. G. "Leadership Theory and Administrative Behavior: The Problem of Authority." *ASQ,* 1959, 4, 259–301.
Bennis, W. G., Schein, E. H. Berlew, D. E., and Steele, F. I. *Interpersonal Dynamics: Essays and Readings on Human Interaction.* Homewood, Ill.: Dorsey, 1964.
Blau, P. M. *The Dynamics of Bureaucracy.* Chicago: U. of Chicago Press, 1955.
Cartwright, D. "The Potential Contribution of Graph Theory to Organization Theory." In M. Haire, ed. *Modern Organizational Theory.* New York: Wiley, 1959.
Cloward, R. A., Cressey, D. R., Grosser, G. N., McCleery, R., Ohlin, L. E., Sykes, G., and Messinger, S. L. *Theoretical Studies in Social Organization of the Prison.* New York: Social Science Research Council, 1960.
Costello, T. W. and Zalkind, S. S. *Psychology in Administration: A Research Orientation.* Englewood Cliffs: Prentice-Hall, 1963.
Dawson, R. H. "Congressional Innovation and Intervention in Defense Policy: Legislative Authorization of Weapons Systems." *APSR,* 1962, 56, 42–57.
Dill, W. R., "Environment as an Influence on Managerial Autonomy," *ASQ,* 1958, 2, 409–443.
Elling, R. H. and Halebsky, S. "Organizational Differentiation and Support: A Conceptual Framework." *ASQ,* 1961, 6, 185–209.
Etzioni, A. *A Comparative Analysis of Complex Organizations.* New York: Free Press, 1961.
Evan, W. M. "Comment on Stewart Macaulay's 'Non-Contractual Relations in Business: A Preliminary Study.'" *ASR,* 1963a, 28, 67–69.
———. "Indices of the Hierarchical Structure of Industrial Organizations." *Management Science,* 1963, 9, 468–477.
———. "Organizational Lag." *Human Organization,* 1966, 25, 51–53.
———. "Public and Private Legal Systems." In W. M. Evan, ed. *Law and Sociology.* New York: Free Press, 1962.
——— and Schwartz, M. A. "Law and the Emergence of Formal Organizations." *Sociology and Social Research,* 1964, 48, 276–279.
Flament, C. *Application of Graph Theory to Group Structure.* Englewood Cliffs: Prentice-Hall, 1963.
Gross, N., Mason, W. S., and McEachern, A. W. *Explorations in Role Analysis: Studies of the School Superintendency Role.* New York: Wiley, 1958.

Haire, M. "Biological Models and Empirical Histories of the Growth of Organizations." 45
In M. Haire, ed., *Modern Organization Theory*. New York: Wiley, 1959.

Haire, M., ed. *Modern Organization Theory*. New York: Wiley, 1959.

———. *Psychology in Management*. 2nd ed. New York: McGraw-Hill, 1964.

Harary, F. and Norman, R. Z. *Graph Theory as a Mathematical Model in Social Science*. Ann Arbor: U. of Michigan Institute for Social Research, 1953.

Leavitt, H. J. *Managerial Psychology*, rev. ed. Chicago: U. of Chicago Press, 1964.

Leontief, Wassily W. et al., *Studies in the Structure of the American Economy*. New York: Oxford U. Press, 1953.

Levine, S. and White, P. E. "Exchange as a Conceptual Framework for the Study of Interorganizational Relationships." *ASQ*, 1961, 5, 583–601.

Litwak, E. and Hylton, L. F. "Inter-organizational Analysis: A Hypothesis on Coordinating Agencies." *ASQ*, 1962. 6, 395–426.

Macaulay, S. "Non-Contractual Relations in Business: A Preliminary Study." *ASR*, 1963. 28, 55–67.

March, J. and Simon, H. A. *Organizations*. New York: Wiley, 1958.

Merton, R. K. *Social Theory and Social Structure* rev. ed. Glencoe, Ill.: Free Press, 1957.

Millett, J. D. *An Essay on Organization: The Academic Community*. New York: McGraw-Hill, 1962.

Palamountain, J. C., Jr. *The Politics of Distribution*. Cambridge: Harvard U. Press, 1955.

Parsons, T. "General Theory in Sociology." In R. K. Merton, Leonard Broom, and Leonard S. Cottrell, Jr., eds., *Sociology Today*. New York: Basic Books, 1959.

Parsons, Talcott. *Structure and Process in Modern Societies*. Glencoe, Ill.: Free Press, 1960.

Ridgeway, V. F. "Administration of Manufacturer-Dealer Systems." *ASQ*, 1957, 2, 464–483.

Riley, J. W., Jr. and Levy, M. F., eds. *The Corporation and Its Publics: Essays on the Corporate Image*. New York: Wiley, 1963.

Selznick, P. *TVA and the Grass Roots: A Study in the Sociology of Formal Organization*. Berkeley and Los Angeles: U. of California Press, 1949.

Simon, H. A. *Administrative Behavior*. New York: Macmillan, 1945.

Spero, S. D. "Collective Bargaining in Public Employment: Form and Scope." *Public Administration Rev.*, 1962, 22, 1–4.

Thompson, J. D. "Organizations and Output Transactions." *American J. Sociology*, 1962, 68, 309–324.

Thompson, J. D. and McEwen, W. J. "Organizational Goals and Environment: Goal-setting as an Interaction Process." *ASR*, 1958, 23, 23–31.

Wheeler, S. "Role Conflict in Correctional Communities." In D. Cressey, ed., *The Prison: Studies in Institutional Organization and Change*. New York: Holt, Rinehart & Winston, 1961.

THE CAUSAL TEXTURE
OF ORGANIZATIONAL
ENVIRONMENTS[1]

F. E. Emery and E. L. Trist

Identification of the Problem

A main problem in the study of organizational change is that the environmental contexts in which organizations exist are themselves changing, at an increasing rate, and towards increasing complexity. This point, in itself, scarcely needs labouring. Nevertheless, the characteristics of organizational environments demand consideration for their own sake, if there is to be an advancement of understanding in the behavioral sciences of a great deal that is taking place under the impact of technological change, especially at the present time. This paper is offered as a brief attempt to open up some of the problems, and stems from a belief that progress will be quicker if a certain extension can be made to current thinking about systems.

In a general way it may be said that to think in terms of systems seems the most appropriate conceptual response so far available when the phenomena under study—at any level and in any domain—display the character of being organized, and when understanding the nature of the interdependencies constitutes the research task. In the behavioural sciences, the first steps in building a systems theory were taken in connection with the analysis of internal processes in organisms, or organizations, when the parts had to be related to the whole. Examples include the organismic biology of Jennings, Cannon, and Henderson; early Gestalt theory and its later derivatives such as balance theory; and the classical theories of social structure. Many of these problems could be represented in closed-system models. The next steps were taken when wholes had to be related to their environments. This led to open-system models.

A great deal of the thinking here has been influenced by cybernetics and information theory, though this has been used as much to extend the scope of closed-system as to improve the sophistication of open-system formulations. It was von Bertalanffy (1950) who, in terms of the general transport equation which he introduced, first fully disclosed the importance of openness or closedness to the environment as a means of distinguishing living organisms from inanimate objects. In contradistinction to physical objects, any living entity survives by importing into itself certain types of material from its environment, transforming these in accordance with its own system characteristics, and exporting other types back

"The Causal Texture of Organizational Environments," *Human Relations*, 18, 1 (February 1965), 21–32. Reprinted with the permission of the authors and of the publisher, *Human Relations*.

into the environment. By this process the organism obtains the additional energy that renders it "negentropic"; it becomes capable of attaining stability in a time-independent steady state—a necessary condition of adaptability to environmental variance.

Such steady states are very different affairs from the equilibrium states described in classical physics, which have far too often been taken as models for representing biological and social transactions. Equilibrium states follow the second law of thermodynamics, so that no work can be done when equilibrium is reached, whereas the openness to the environment of a steady state maintains the capacity of the organism for work, without which adaptability, and hence survival, would be impossible.

Many corollaries follow as regards the properties of open systems, such as equifinality, growth through internal elaboration, self-regulation, constancy of direction with change of position, etc.—and by no means all of these have yet been worked out. But though von Bertalanffy's formulation enables exchange processes between the organism, or organization, and elements in its environment to be dealt with in a new perspective, it does not deal at all with those processes in the environment itself which are among the determining conditions of the exchanges. To analyse these an additional concept is needed— *the causal texture of the environment* —if we may re-introduce, at a social level of analysis, a term suggested by Tolman and Brunswik (1935) and drawn from S. C. Pepper (1934).

With this addition, we may now state the following general proposition: that a comprehensive understanding of organizational behaviour requires some knowledge of each member of the following set, where L indicates some po-

tentially lawful connection, and the suffix 1 refers to the organization and the suffix 2 to the environment:

$$L_{11}, L_{12}$$
$$L_{21}, L_{22}$$

L_{11} here refers to processes within the organization—the area of internal interdependencies; L_{12} and L_{21} to exchanges between the organization and its environment—the area of transactional interdependencies, from either direction; and L_{22} to processes through which parts of the environment become related to each other —i.e., its causal texture—the area of interdependencies that belong within the environment itself.

In considering environmental interdependencies, the first point to which we wish to draw attention is that the laws connecting parts of the environment to each other are often incommensurate with those connecting parts of the organization to each other, or even with those which govern the exchanges. It is not possible, for example, always to reduce organization-environment relations to the form of "being included in"; boundaries are also "break" points. As Barker and Wright (1949), following Lewin (1936), have pointed out in their analysis of this problem as it affects psychological ecology, we may lawfully connect the actions of a javelin thrower in sighting and throwing his weapon; but we cannot describe in the same concepts the course of the javelin as this is affected by variables lawfully linked by meteorological and other systems.

The Development of Environmental Connectedness (Case I)

A case history, taken from the industrial field, may serve to illustrate what is meant by the environment becoming organized at the social level. It will show how a greater degree of system-connectedness, of crucial relevance to the organization, may develop in the environment, which is yet not directly a function either of the organization's own characteristics or of its immediate relations. Both of these, of course, once again become crucial when the response of the organization to what has been happening is considered.

The company concerned was the foremost in its particular market in the food-canning industry in the U.K. and belonged to a large parent group. Its main product—a canned vegetable—had some 65 per cent of this market, a situation which had been relatively stable since before the war. Believing it would continue to hold this position, the company persuaded the group board to invest several million pounds sterling in erecting a new, automated factory, which, however, based its economies on an inbuilt rigidity—it was set up exclusively for the long runs expected from the traditional market.

The character of the environment, however, began to change while the factory was being built. A number of small canning firms appeared, not dealing with this product nor indeed with others in the company's range, but with imported fruits. These firms arose because the last of the post-war controls had been removed from steel strip and tin, and cheaper cans could now be obtained in any numbers—while at the same time a larger market was developing in imported fruits. This trade being seasonal, the firms were anxious to find a way of using their machinery and retaining their labour in winter. They became able to do so through a curious side-effect of the development of quick-frozen foods, when the company's staple was produced by others in this form. The quick-freezing process demanded great constancy at the growing end. It was not possible to control this beyond a certain point, so that quite large crops unsuitable for quick freezing but suitable for canning became available—originally from another country (the United States) where a large market for quick-frozen foods had been established. These surplus crops had been sold at a very low price for animal feed. They were now imported by the small canners—at a better but still comparatively low price, and additional cheap supplies soon began to be procurable from underdeveloped countries.

Before the introduction of the quick-freezing form, the company's own canned product—whose raw material had been specially grown at additional cost—had been the premier brand, superior to other varieties and charged at a higher price. But its position in the product spectrum now changed. With the increasing affluence of the society, more people were able to afford the quick-frozen form. Moreover, there was competition from a great many other vegetable products which could substitute for the staple, and people preferred this greater variety. The advantage of being the premier line among canned forms diminished, and demand increased both for the not-so-expensive varieties among them and for the quick-frozen forms. At the same time, major changes were taking place in retailing; supermarkets were developing, and more and more large grocery chains were coming into existence. These establishments wanted to sell certain types of goods under their own house names, and began to place bulk orders with the small canners for their own varieties of the company's staple that fell within this class. As the small canners provided an extremely cheap article (having no marketing expenses and a cheaper raw material), they could undercut the manufacturers' branded product, and within three years they captured over 50 per cent of the market. Previously, retailers' varieties had accounted for less than 1 per cent.

The new automatic factory could not be adapted to the new situation until alternative products with a big sales volume could be developed, and the scale of research and development, based on the type of market analysis required to identify these, was beyond the scope of the existing resources of the company either in people or in funds.

The changed texture of the environment was not recognized by an able but traditional management until it was too late. They failed entirely to appreciate that a number of outside events were becoming connected with each other in a way that was leading up to irreversible general change. Their first reaction was to make an herculean effort to defend the traditional product, then the board split on whether or not to make entry into the cheaper unbranded market in a supplier role. Group H.Q. now felt they had no option but to step in, and many upheavals and changes in management took place until a "redefinition of mission" was agreed, and slowly and painfully the company re-emerged with a very much altered product mix and something of a new identity.

Four Types of Causal Texture

It was this experience, and a number of others not dissimilar, by no means all of them industrial (and including studies of change problems in hospitals, in prisons, and in educational and political organizations), that gradually led us to feel a need for re-directing conceptual

attention to the causal texture of the environment, considered as a quasi-independent domain. We have now isolated four "ideal types" of causal texture, approximations to which may be thought of as existing simultaneously in the "real world" of most organizations—though, of course, their weighting will vary enormously from case to case.

The first three of these types have already, and indeed repeatedly, been described—in a large variety of terms and with the emphasis on an equally bewildering variety of special aspects —in the literature of a number of disciplines, ranging from biology to economics and including military theory as well as psychology and sociology. The fourth type, however, is new, at least to us, and is the one that for some time we have been endeavouring to identify. About the first three, therefore, we can be brief, but the fourth is scarcely understandable without reference to them. Together, the four types may be said to form a series in which the degree of causal texturing is increased, in a new and significant way, as each step is taken. We leave as an open question the need for further steps.

STEP ONE

The simplest type of environmental texture is that in which goals and noxiants ("goods" and "bads") are relatively unchanging in themselves and randomly distributed. This may be called the *placid, randomized environment*. It corresponds to Simon's idea of a surface over which an organism can locomote: most of this is bare, but at isolated, widely scattered points there are little heaps of food (1957, p. 137). It also corresponds to Ashby's limiting case of no connection between the environmental parts (1960, S15/4); and to Schutzenberger's random field (1954, p. 100). The economist's classical market also corresponds to this type.

A critical property of organizational response under random conditions has been stated by Schutzenberger: that there is no distinction between tactics and strategy, "the optimal strategy is just the simple tactic of attempting to do one's best on a purely local basis" (1954, p. 101). The best tactic, moreover, can be learnt only by trial and error and only for a particular class of local environmental variances (Ashby, 1960, p. 197). While organizations under these conditions can exist adaptively as single and indeed quite small units, this becomes progressively more difficult under the other types.

STEP TWO

More complicated, but still a placid environment, is that which can be characterized in terms of clustering: goals and noxiants are not randomly distributed but hang together in certain ways. This may be called the *placid, clustered environment,* and is the case with which Tolman and Brunswik were concerned; it corresponds to Ashby's "serial system" and to the economist's "imperfect competition." The clustering enables some parts to take on roles as signs of other parts or become means-objects with respect to approaching or avoiding. Survival, however, becomes precarious if an organization attempts to deal tactically with each environmental variance as it occurs.

The new feature of organizational response to this kind of environment is the emergence of strategy as distinct from tactics. Survival becomes critically linked with what an organization knows of its environment. To pursue a goal under its nose may lead it into parts of the field fraught with danger, while avoidance of an immediately difficult issue may lead it away from potentially rewarding areas. In the clustered environment the relevant objective is that of "optimal location," some positions being discernible as potentially richer than others.

To reach these requires concentration of resources, subordination to the main plan, and the development of a "distinctive competence," to use Selznick's (1957) term, in reaching the strategic objective. Organizations under these conditions, therefore, tend to grow in size and also to become hierarchical, with a tendency towards centralized control and coordination.

STEP THREE

The next level of causal texturing we have called the *disturbed-reactive environment.* It may be compared with Ashby's ultra-stable system or the economist's oligopolic market. It is a type 2 environment in which there is more than one organization of the same kind; indeed, the existence of a number of similar organizations now becomes the dominant characteristic of the environmental field. Each organization does not simply have to take account of the others when they meet at random, but has also to consider that what it knows can also be known by the others. The part of the environment to which it wishes to move itself in the long run is also the part to which the others seek to move. Knowing this, each will wish to improve its own chances by hindering the others, and each will know that the others must not only wish to do likewise, but also know that each knows this. The presence of similar others creates an imbrication, to use a term of

Chein's (1943), of some of the causal stands in the environment.

If strategy is a matter of selecting the "strategic objective"—where one wishes to be at a future time—and tactics a matter of selecting an immediate action from one's available repertoire, then there appears in type 3 environments to be an intermediate level of organizational response—that of the *operation* —to use the term adopted by German and Soviet military theorists, who formally distinguish tactics, operations, and strategy. One has now not only to make sequential choices, but to choose actions that will draw off the other organizations. The new element is that of deciding which of someone else's possible tactics one wishes to take place, while ensuring that others of them do not. An operation consists of a campaign involving a planned series of tactical initiatives, calculated reactions by others, and counteractions. The flexibility required encourages a certain decentralization and also puts a premium on quality and speed of decision at various peripheral points (Heyworth, 1955).

It now becomes necessary to define the organizational objective in terms not so much of location as of capacity or power to move more or less at will, i.e., to be able to make and meet competitive challenge. This gives particular relevance to strategies of absorption and parasitism. It can also give rise to situations in which stability can be obtained only by a certain coming-to-terms between competitors, whether enterprises, interest groups, or governments. One has to know when not to fight to the death.

STEP FOUR

Yet more complex are the environments we have called *turbulent fields*. In these, dynamic processes, which create significant variances for the component organizations, arise from the field itself. Like type 3 and unlike the static types 1 and 2, they are dynamic. Unlike type 3, the dynamic properties arise not simply from the interaction of the component organizations, but also from the field itself. The "ground" is in motion.

Three trends contribute to the emergence of these dynamic field forces:

(i) The growth to meet type 3 conditions of organizations, and linked sets of organizations, so large that their actions are both persistent and strong enough to induce autochthonous processes in the environment. An analogous effect would be that of a company of soldiers marching in step over a bridge.

(ii) The deepening interdependence between the economic and the other facets of the society. This means that economic organizations are increasingly enmeshed in legislation and public regulation.

(iii) The increasing reliance on research and development to achieve the capacity to meet competitive challenge. This leads to a situation in which a change gradient is continuously present in the environmental field.

For organizations, these trends mean a gross increase in their area of *relevant uncertainty*. The consequences which flow from their actions lead off in ways that become increasingly unpredictable: they do not necessarily fall off with distance, but may at any point be amplified beyond all expectation; similarly, lines of action that are strongly pursued may find themselves attenuated by emergent field forces.

CAUSAL TEXTURE OF ORGANIZATIONAL ENVIRONMENTS

The Salience of Type 4 Characteristics (Case II)

Some of these effects are apparent in what happened to the canning company of case I, whose situation represents a transition from an environment largely composed of type 2 and type 3 characteristics to one where those of type 4 began to gain in salience. The case now to be presented illustrates the combined operation of the three trends described above in an altogether larger environmental field involving a total industry and its relations with the wider society.

The organization concerned is the National Farmers Union of Great Britain to which more than 200,000 of the 250,000 farmers of England and Wales belong. The presenting problem brought to us for investigation was that of communications. Headquarters felt, and was deemed to be, out of touch with county branches, and these with local branches. The farmer had looked to the N.F.U. very largely to protect him against market fluctuations by negotiating a comprehensive deal with the government at annual reviews concerned with the level of price support. These reviews had enabled home agriculture to maintain a steady state during two decades when the threat, or existence, of war in relation to the type of military technology then in being had made it imperative to maintain a high level of home-grown food without increasing prices to the consumer. This policy, however, was becoming obsolete as the conditions of thermonuclear stalemate established themselves. A level of support could no longer be counted upon which would keep in existence small and inefficient farmers—often on marginal land and dependent on family labour—compared with efficient medium-size farms, to say nothing of large and highly mechanized undertakings.

Yet it was the former situation which had produced N.F.U. cohesion. As this situation receded, not only were farmers becoming exposed to more competition from each other, as well as from Commonwealth and European farmers, but the effects were being felt of very great changes which had been taking place on both the supply and marketing sides of the industry. On the supply side, a small number of giant firms now supplied almost all the requirements in fertilizer, machinery, seeds, veterinary products, etc. As efficient farming depended upon ever greater utilization of these resources, their controllers exerted correspondingly greater power over the farmers. Even more dramatic were the changes in the marketing of farm produce. Highly organized food processing and distributing industries had grown up dominated again by a few large firms, on contracts from which (fashioned to suit their rather than his interests) the farmer was becoming increasingly dependent. From both sides deep inroads were being made on his autonomy.

It became clear that the source of the felt difficulty about communications lay in radical environmental changes which were confronting the organization with problems it was ill-adapted to meet. Communications about these changes were being interpreted or acted upon as if they referred to the "traditional" situation. Only through a parallel analysis of the environment and the N.F.U. was progress made towards developing understanding on the basis of which attempts to devise adaptive organizational policies and forms could be made. Not least among the problems was that of creating a bureaucratic elite that could cope with the highly technical long-range planning now required and yet remain loyal to the democratic values of the N.F.U. Equally difficult was that of developing mediating institutions— agencies that would effectively mediate the relations between agriculture and other economic sectors without triggering off massive competitive processes.

These environmental changes and the organizational crisis they induced were fully apparent two or three years before the question of Britain's possible entry into the Common Market first appeared on the political agenda—which, of course, further complicated every issue.

A workable solution needed to preserve reasonable autonomy for the farmers as an occupational group, while meeting the interests of other sections of the community. Any such possibility depended on securing the consent of the large majority of farmers to placing under some degree of N.F.U. control matters that hitherto had remained within their own power of decision. These included what they produced, how and to what standard, and how most of it should be marketed. Such thoughts were anathema, for however dependent the farmer had grown on the N.F.U. he also remained intensely individualistic. He was being asked, he now felt, to redefine his identity, reverse his basic values, and refashion his organization—all at the same time. It is scarcely surprising that progress has been, and remains, both fitful and slow, and ridden with conflict.

Values and Relevant Uncertainty

What becomes precarious under type 4 conditions is how organizational stability can be achieved. In these environments individual organizations, however large, cannot expect to adapt successfully simply through their own direct actions—as is evident in the case of the N.F.U. Nevertheless, there are some indications of a solution that may have the same general significance for these environments as have strategy and operations for types 2 and 3. This is the emergence of *values that have overriding significance for all members of the field*. Social values are here regarded as coping mechanisms that make it possible to deal with persisting areas of relevant uncertainty. Unable to trace out the consequences of their actions as these are amplified and resonated through their extended social fields, men in all societies have sought rules, sometimes categorical, such as the ten commandments, to provide them with a guide and ready calculus. Values are not strategies or tactics; as Lewin (1936) has pointed out, they have the conceptual character of "power fields" and act as injunctions.

So far as effective values emerge, the character of richly joined, turbulent fields changes in a most striking fashion. The relevance of large classes of events no longer has to be sought in an intricate mesh of diverging causal strands, but is given directly in the ethical code. By this transformation a field is created which is no longer richly joined and turbulent but simplified and relatively static. Such a transformation will be regressive, or constructively adaptative, according to how far the emergent values adequately represent the new environmental requirements.

Ashby, as a biologist, has stated his view, on the one hand, that examples of environments that are both large and richly connected are not common, for our terrestrial environment is widely characterized by being highly subdivided (1960, p. 205); and, on the other, that, so far as they are encountered, they may well be beyond the limits of human adaptation, the brain being an

54 ultra-stable system. By contrast the role here attributed to social values suggests that this sort of environment may in fact be not only one to which adaptation is possible, however difficult, but one that has been increasingly characteristic of the human condition since the beginning of settled communities. Also, let us not forget that values can be rational as well as irrational and that the rationality of their rationale is likely to become more powerful as the scientific ethos takes greater hold in a society.

Matrix Organization and Institutional Success

Nevertheless, turbulent fields demand some overall form of organization that is essentially different from the hierarchically structured forms to which we are accustomed. Whereas type 3 environments require one or other form of accommodation between like, but competitive, organizations whose fates are to a degree negatively correlated, turbulent environments require some relationship between dissimilar organizations whose fates are, basically, positively correlated. This means relationships that will maximize cooperation and which recognize that no one organization can take over the role of "the other" and become paramount. We are inclined to speak of this type of relationship as an *organizational matrix*. Such a matrix acts in the first place by delimiting on value criteria the character of what may be included in the field specified—and therefore who. This selectivity then enables some definable shape to be worked out without recourse to much in the way of formal hierarchy among members. Professional associations provide one model of which there has been long experience.

We do not suggest that in other fields than the professional the requisite sanctioning can be provided only by state-controlled bodies. Indeed, the reverse is far more likely. Nor do we suggest that organizational matrices will function so as to eliminate the need for other measures to achieve stability. As with values, matrix organizations, even if successful, will only help to transform turbulent environments into the kinds of environment we have discussed as "clustered" and "disturbed-reactive." Though, with these transformations, an organization could hope to achieve a degree of stability through its strategies, operation, and tactics, the transformations would not provide environments identical with the originals. The strategic objective in the transformed cases could no longer be stated simply in terms of optimal location (as in type 2) or capabilities (as in type 3). It must now rather be formulated in terms of *institutionalization*. According to Selznick (1957) organizations become institutions through the embodiment of organizational values which relate them to the wider society.[2] As Selznick has stated in his analysis of leadership in the modern American corporation, "the default of leadership shows itself in an acute form when *organizational* achievement or survival is confounded with *institutional* success" (1957, p. 27). ". . . the executive becomes a statesman as he makes the transition from administrative management to institutional leadership" (1957, p. 154).

The processes of strategic planning now also become modified. In so far as institutionalization becomes a prerequisite for stability, the determination of policy will necessitate not only a bias towards goals that are congruent with the organization's own character, but also a selection of goal-paths that offer maximum convergence as regards the interests of other parties. This became a central issue for the N.F.U. and is becoming one now for an organization such as the National Economic Development Council, which has the task of creating a matrix in which the British economy can function at something better than the stop-go level.

Such organizations arise from the need to meet problems emanating from type 4 environments. Unless this is recognized, they will only too easily be construed in type 3 terms, and attempts will be made to secure for them a degree of monolithic power that will be resisted overtly in democratic societies and covertly in others. In the one case they may be prevented from ever undertaking their missions; in the other one may wonder how long they can succeed in maintaining them.

An organizational matrix implies what McGregor (1960) has called Theory Y. This in turn implies a new set of values. But values are psycho-social commodities that come into existence only rather slowly. Very little systematic work has yet been done on the establishment of new systems of values, or on the type of criteria that might be adduced to allow their effectiveness to be empirically tested. A pioneer attempt is that of Churchman and Ackoff (1950). Likert (1961) has suggested that, in the large corporation or government establishment, it may well take some ten to fifteen years before the new type of group values with which he is concerned could permeate the total organization. For a new set to permeate a whole modern society the time required must be much longer—at least a generation, according to the common saying—and this, indeed, must be a minimum. One may ask if this is fast enough, given the rate at which type 4 environments

Summary

1. A main problem in the study of organizational change is that the environmental contexts in which organizations exist are themselves changing—at an increasing rate, under the impact of technological change. This means that they demand consideration for their own sake. Towards this end a redefinition is offered, at a social level of analysis, of the causal texture of the environment, a concept introduced in 1935 by Tolman and Brunswik.

2. This requires an extension of systems theory. The first steps in systems theory were taken in connection with the analysis of internal processes in organisms, or organizations, which involved relating parts to the whole. Most of these problems could be dealt with through closed-system models. The next steps were taken when wholes had to be related to their environments. This led to open-system models, such as that introduced by Bertalanffy, involving a general transport equation. Though this enables exchange processes between the organism, or organization, and elements in its environment to be dealt with, it does not deal with those processes in the environment itself which are the determining conditions of the exchanges. To analyse these an additional concept —the causal texture of the environment —is needed.

3. The laws connecting parts of the environment to each other are often incommensurate with those connecting parts of the organization to each other, or even those which govern exchanges. Case history I illustrates this and shows the dangers and difficulties that arise

when there is a rapid and gross increase in the area of relevant uncertainty, a characteristic feature of many contemporary environments.

4. Organizational environments differ in their causal texture, both as regards degree of uncertainty and in many other important respects. A typology is suggested which identifies four "ideal types," approximations to which exist simultaneously in the "real world" of most organizations, though the weighting varies enormously:

a. In the simplest type, goals and noxiants are relatively unchanging in themselves and randomly distributed. This may be called the placid, randomized environment. A critical property from the organization's viewpoint is that there is no difference between tactics and strategy, and organizations can exist adaptively as single, and indeed quite small, units.

b. The next type is also static, but goals and noxiants are not randomly distributed; they hang together in certain ways. This may be called the placid, clustered environment. Now the need arises for strategy as distinct from tactics. Under these conditions organizations grow in size, becoming multiple and tending towards centralized control and coordination.

c. The third type is dynamic rather than static. We call it the disturbed-reactive environment. It consists of a clustered environment in which there is more than one system of the same kind, i.e. the objects of one organization are the same as, or relevant to, others like it. Such competitors seek to improve their own chances by hindering each other, each knowing the others are playing the same game. Between strategy and tactics there emerges an intermediate type of organizational response—what military theorists refer to as operations. Control becomes more decentralized to allow these to be conducted. On the other hand, stability may require a certain coming-to-terms between competitors.

d. The fourth type is dynamic in a second respect, the dynamic properties arising not simply from the interaction of identifiable component systems but from the field itself (the "ground"). We call these environments turbulent fields. The turbulence results from the complexity and multiple character of the causal interconnections. Individual organizations, however large, cannot adapt successfully simply through their direct interactions. An examination is made of the enhanced importance of values, regarded as a basic response to persisting areas of relevant uncertainty, as providing a control mechanism, when commonly held by all members in a field. This raises the question of organizational forms based on the characteristics of a matrix.

5. Case history II is presented to illustrate problems of the transition from type c to type d. The perspective of the four environmental types is used to clarify the role of Theory X and Theory Y as representing a trend in value change. The establishment of a new set of values is a slow social process requiring something like a generation—unless new means can be developed.

NOTES

1. A paper read at the XVII International Congress of Psychology, Washington, D.C., U.S.A., 20–26 August 1963. A French translation appeared in *Sociologie du Travail*, 4/64.

INTERORGANIZATIONAL RELATIONSHIPS

2. Since the present paper was presented, this line of thought has been further developed by Churchman and Emery (1964) in their discussion of the relation of the statistical aggregate of individuals to structured role sets:

Like other values, organizational values emerge to cope with relevant uncertainties and gain their authority from their reference to the requirements of larger systems within which people's interests are largely concordant.

REFERENCES

Ashby, W. Ross (1960). *Design for a brain.* London: Chapman & Hall.

Barker, R. G. and Wright, H. F. (1949). Psychological ecology and the problem of psychosocial development. *Child Development* **20,** 131–43.

Bertalanffy, L. von (1950). The theory of open systems in physics and biology. *Science* **111,** 23–9.

Chein, I. (1943). Personality and typology. *J. soc. Psychol.* **18,** 89–101.

Churchman, C. W. and Ackoff, R. L. (1950). *Methods of inquiry.* St. Louis: Educational Publishers.

Churchman, C. W. and Emery, F. E. (1964). On various approaches to the study of organizations. Proceedings of the International Conference on Operational Research and the Social Sciences, Cambridge, England, 14–18 September 1964. To be published in book form as *Operational research and the social sciences.* London: Tavistock Publications, 1965.

Heyworth, Lord (1955). *The organization of Unilever.* London: Unilever Limited.

Lewin, K. (1936). *Principles of topological psychology.* New York: McGraw-Hill.

Lewin, K. (1951). *Field theory in social science.* New York: Harper.

Likert, R. (1961), *New patterns of management.* New York, Toronto, London: McGraw-Hill.

McGregor, D. (1960). *The human side of enterprise.* New York, Toronto, London: McGraw-Hill.

Pepper, S. C. (1934). The conceptual framework of Tolman's purposive behaviorism. *Psychol. Rev.* **41,** 108–33.

Schutzenberger, M. P. (1954). A tentative classification of goal-seeking behaviours. *J. ment. Sci.* **100,** 97–102.

Selznick, P. (1957). *Leadership in administration.* Evanston, Ill.: Row Peterson.

Simon, H. A. (1957). *Models of man.* New York: Wiley.

Tolman, E. C. and Brunswik, E. (1935). The organism and the causal texture of the environment. *Psychol. Rev.* **42,** 43–77.

THE EVOLUTION OF ORGANIZATIONAL ENVIRONMENTS

Shirley Terreberry

Darwin published *The Origin of Species by Means of Natural Selection* in 1859. Modern genetics has vastly altered our understanding of the variance upon which natural selection operates. But there has been no conceptual breakthrough in understanding *environmental* evolution which, alone, shapes the direction of change. Even today most theorists of change still focus on *internal* interdependencies of systems—biological, psychological, or social—although the external environments of these systems are changing more rapidly than ever before.

Introduction

Von Bertalanffy was the first to reveal fully the importance of a system being open or closed to the environment in distinguishing living from inanimate systems.[1] Although von Bertalanffy's formulation makes it possible to deal with a system's exchange processes in a new perspective, it does not deal at all with those processes in the environment *itself* that are among the determining conditions of exchange.

Emery and Trist have argued the need for one additional concept, "the causal texture of the environment."[2] Writing in the context of formal organizations,

they offer the following general proposition:

> That a comprehensive understanding of organizational behaviour requires some knowledge of each member of the following set, where L indicates some potentially lawful connection, and the suffix 1 refers to the organization and the suffix 2 to the environment:
>
> $$L_{11} \quad L_{12}$$
> $$L_{21} \quad L_{22}$$
>
> L_{11} here refers to processes within the organization—the area of internal interdependencies; L_{12} and L_{21} to exchanges between the organization and its environment—the area of transactional interdependencies, from either direction; and L_{22} to processes through which parts of the environment become related to each other—i.e., its causal texture—the area of interdependencies that belong within the environment itself.[3]

We have reproduced the above paragraph in its entirety because, in the balance of this paper, we will use Emery and Trist's symbols (i.e., L_{11}, L_{21}, L_{12}, and L_{22}) to denote intra-, input, output, and extra-system interdependencies, respectively. Our purpose in doing so is to avoid the misleading connotations of conventional terminology.

PURPOSE

The theses here are: (1) that contemporary changes in organizational envi-

"The Evolution of Organizational Environments," *Administrative Science Quarterly*, 12, 4 (March 1968), 590–613. Reprinted with the permission of the author and of the publisher, the *Administrative Science Quarterly*.

ronments are such as to increase the ratio of externally induced change to internally induced change; and (2) that *other* formal organizations are, increasingly, the important components in the environment of any focal organization. Furthermore, the evolution of environments is accompanied—among viable systems—by an increase in the system's ability to learn and to perform according to changing contingencies in its environment. An integrative framework is outlined for the concurrent analysis of an organization, its transactions with environmental units, and interdependencies among those units. Lastly, two hypotheses are presented, one about organizational *change* and the other about organizational *adaptability*; and some problems in any empirical test of these hypotheses are discussed.[4]

CONCEPTS OF ORGANIZATIONAL ENVIRONMENTS

In Emery and Trist's terms, L_{22} relations (i.e., interdependencies within the environment itself) comprise the "causal texture" of the field. This causal texture of the environment is treated as a quasi-independent domain, since the environment cannot be conceptualized except with respect to some focal organization. The components of the environment are identified in terms of that system's actual and *potential* transactional interdependencies, both input (L_{21}) and output (L_{12}).

Emery and Trist postulate four "ideal types" of environment, which can be ordered according to the degree of *system connectedness* that exists among the components of the environment (L_{22}). The first of these is a "placid, randomized" environment: goods and bads are relatively unchanging in themselves and are randomly distributed

(e.g., the environments of an amoeba, a human foetus, a nomadic tribe). The second is a "placid, clustered" environment: goods and bads are relatively unchanging in themselves but clustered (e.g., the environments of plants that are subjected to the cycle of seasons, of human infants, of extractive industries). The third ideal type is "disturbed-reactive" environment and constitutes a significant qualitative change over simpler types of environments: an environment characterized by similar systems in the field. The extinction of dinosaurs can be traced to the emergence of more complex environments on the biological level. Human beings, beyond infancy, live in disturbed-reactive environments in relation to one another. The theory of oligopoly in economics is a theory of this type of environment.[5]

These three types of environment have been identified and described in the literature of biology, economics, and mathematics.[6] "The fourth type, however, is new, at least to us, and is the one that for some time we have been endeavouring to identify."[7] This fourth ideal type of environment is called a "turbulent field." Dynamic processes "arise from the *field itself*" and not merely from the interactions of components; the actions of component organizations and linked sets of them "are both persistent and strong enough to induce autochthonous processes in the environment."[8]

An alternate description of a turbulent field is that the accelerating rate and complexity of interactive effects exceeds the component systems' capacities for prediction and, hence, control of the compounding consequences of their actions.

Turbulence is characterized by complexity as well as rapidity of change in causal interconnections in the environ-

59

ment. Emery and Trist illustrate the transition from a disturbed-reactive to a turbulent-field environment for a company that had maintained a steady 65 percent of the market for its main product—a canned vegetable—over many years. At the end of World War II, the firm made an enormous investment in a new automated factory that was set up exclusively for the traditional product and technology. At the same time postwar controls on steel strip and tin were removed, so that cheaper cans were available; surplus crops were more cheaply obtained by importers; diversity increased in available products, including substitutes for the staple; the quick-freeze technology was developed; home buyers became more affluent; supermarkets emerged and placed bulk orders with small firms for retail under supermarket names. These changes in technology, international trade, and affluence of buyers gradually interacted (L_{22}) and ultimately had a pronounced effect on the company: its market dwindled rapidly. "The changed texture of the environment was not recognized by an able but traditional management until it was too late."[9]

Sociological, social psychological, and business management theorists often still treat formal organizations as closed systems. In recent years, however, this perspective seems to be changing. Etzioni asserts that interorganizational relations need intensive empirical study.[10] Blau and Scott present a rich but unconceptualized discussion of the "social context of organizational life."[11] Parsons distinguishes three distinct levels of organizational responsibility and control: technical, managerial, and institutional.[12] His categories can be construed to parallel the intraorganizational (i.e., technical or L_{11}), the interorganizational (i.e., managerial or L_{21}, and L_{12}), and the extra-organizational levels of analysis (i.e., the institutional or L_{22} areas). Perhaps in the normal developmental course of a science, intrasystem analysis necessarily precedes the intersystem focus. On the other hand, increasing attention to interorganizational relations may reflect a real change in the phenomenon being studied. The first question to consider is whether there is evidence that the environments of formal organizations are evolving toward turbulent-field conditions.

EVIDENCE FOR TURBULENCE

Ohlin argues that the sheer rapidity of social change today requires greater organizational adaptability.[13] Hood points to the increasing complexity, as well as the accelerating rate of change, in organizational environments.[14] In business circles there is growing conviction that the future is unpredictable. Drucker[15] and Gardner[16] both assert that the kind and extent of present-day change precludes prediction of the future. Increasingly, the rational strategies of planned-innovation and long-range planning are being undermined by unpredictable changes. McNulty found no association between organization adaptation and the introduction of purposeful change in a study of 30 companies in fast-growing markets.[17] He suggests that built-in flexibility may be more efficient than the explicit reorganization implicit in the quasi-rational model. Dun's Review questions the effectiveness of long-range planning in the light of frequent failures, and suggests that error may be attributable to forecasting the future by extrapolation of a noncomparable past. The conclusion is that the rapidity and complexity of change may increasingly preclude effective long-range planning.[18] These examples clearly suggest the emergence of a change in the environment that is suggestive of turbulence.

Some writers with this open-system perspective derive implications for interorganizational relations from this changing environment. Blau and Scott argue that the success of a firm increasingly depends upon its ability to establish symbiotic relations with other organizations, in which extensive advantageous exchange takes place.[19] Lee Adler proposes "symbiotic marketing."[20] Dill found that the task environments of two Norwegian firms comprised four major sectors: *customers*, including both distributors and users; *suppliers* of materials, labor, capital, equipment, and work space; *competitors* for both markets and resources; and *regulatory groups*, including governmental agencies, unions, and interfirm associations.[21] Not only does Dill's list include many more components than are accommodated by present theories, but all components are themselves evolving into formal organizations. In his recent book, Thompson discusses "task environments," which comprise the units with which an organization has input and output transactions (L_{21} and L_{12}), and postulates two dimensions of such environments: homogeneous-heterogeneous, and stable-dynamic. When the task environment is *both* heterogeneous and dynamic (i.e., probably turbulent), he expects an organization's boundary-spanning units to be functionally differentiated to correspond to segments of the task environment and each to operate on a decentralized basis to monitor and plan responses to fluctuations in its sector of the task environment.[22] He does not focus on other organizations as components of the environment, but he provides a novel perspective on structural implications (L_{11}) for organi-

zations in turbulent fields.

Selznick's work on TVA appears to be the first organizational case study to emphasize transactional interdependencies.[23] The next study was Ridgway's 1957 study of manufacturer-dealer relationships.[24] Within the following few years the study by Dill[25] and others by Levine and White,[26] Litwak and Hylton,[27] and Elling and Halebsky[28] appeared, and in recent years, the publication of such studies has accelerated.

The following are examples from two volumes of the *Administrative Science Quarterly* alone. Rubington argues that structural changes in organizations that seek to change the behavior of "prisoners, drug addicts, juvenile delinquents, parolees, alcoholics [are] . . . the result of a social movement whose own organizational history has yet to be written."[29] Rosengren reports a similar phenomenon in the mental health field whose origin he finds hard to explain: "In any event, a more symbiotic relationship has come to characterize the relations between the [mental] hospitals and other agencies, professions, and establishments in the community."[30] He ascribes changes in organizational goals and technology to this interorganizational evolution. In the field of education, Clark outlines the increasing influence of private foundations, national associations, and divisions of the federal government. He, too, is not clear as to how these changes have come about, but he traces numerous changes in the behavior of educational organizations to interorganizational influences.[31] Maniha and Perrow analyze the origins and development of a city youth commission. The agency had little reason to be formed, no goals to guide it, and was staffed by people who sought a minimal, no-action role in the community. By virtue of its existence and broad province, however, it was seized upon as a valuable weapon by other organizations for the pursuit of their own goals. "But in this very process it became an organization with a mission of its own, in spite of itself."[32]

Since uncertainty is the dominant characteristic of turbulent fields, it is not surprising that emphasis in recent literature is away from algorithmic and toward heuristic problem-solving models;[33] that optimizing models are giving way to satisficing models;[34] and that rational decision making is replaced by "disjointed incrementalism."[35] These trends reflect not the ignorance of the authors of earlier models, but a change in the causal texture of organizational environments and, therefore, of appropriate strategies for coping with the environment. Cyert and March state that "so long as the environment of the firm is unstable—and predictably unstable—the heart of the theory [of the firm] must be the process of short-run adaptive reactions."[36]

In summary, both the theoretical and case study literature on organizations suggests that these systems are increasingly finding themselves in environments where the complexity and rapidity of change in external interconnectedness (L_{22}) gives rise to increasingly unpredictable change in their transactional interdependencies (L_{21} and L_{12}). This seems to be good evidence for the emergence of turbulence in the environments of many formal organizations.

Interorganizational Environment

EVIDENCE FOR INCREASING DEPENDENCE ON ENVIRONMENT

Elsewhere the author has argued that Emery and Trist's concepts can be ex-

tended to all living systems; furthermore, that this evolutionary process gives rise to conditions—biological, psychological, and social—in which the rate of evolution of environments exceeds the rate of evolution of component systems.[37]

In the short run, the openness of a living system to its environment enables it to take in ingredients from the environment for conversion into energy or information that allows it to maintain a steady state and, hence, to violate the dismal second law of thermodynamics (i.e., of entropy). In the long run, "the characteristic of living systems which most clearly distinguishes them from the nonliving is their property of progressing by the process which is called evolution from less to more complex states of organization."[38] It then follows that to the extent that the environment of some living system X is comprised of other living systems, the environment of X is itself evolving from less to more complex states of organization. A major corollary is that the evolution of environment is characterized by an increase in the ratio of externally induced change over internally induced change in a system's transactional interdependencies (L_{21} and L_{12}).

For illustration, let us assume that at some given time, each system in some set of interdependent systems is equally likely to experience an internal (L_{11}) change that is functional for survival (i.e., improves its L_{21} or L_{12} transactions). The greater the number of other systems in that set, the greater the probability that some system other than X will experience that change. Since we posit interdependence among members of the set, X's viability over time depends upon X's capacity (L_{11}) for adaptation to environmentally induced (L_{22}) changes in its transactive position, or else upon control over these external relations.

In the case of formal organizations, disturbed-reactive or oligopolistic environments require some form of accommodation between like but competitive organizations whose fates are negatively correlated to some degree. A change in the transactional position of one system in an oligopolistic set, whether for better or worse, automatically affects the transactional position of all other members of the set, and in the opposite direction (i.e., for worse or better, as the case may be).[39] On the other hand, turbulent environments require relationships between dissimilar organizations whose fates are independent or, perhaps, positively correlated.[40] A testable hypothesis that derives from the formal argument is that the evolution of environments is accompanied, in viable systems, by an increase in ability to learn and to perform according to changing contingencies in the environment.

The evolution of organizational environments is characterized by a change in the important constituents of the environment. The earliest formal organizations to appear in the United States (e.g., in agriculture, retail trade, construction, mining)[41] operated largely under placid-clustered conditions. Important inputs, such as natural resources and labor, as well as consumers, comprised an environment in which strategies of optimal location and distinctive competence were critical organizational responses.[42] Two important attributes of placid-clustered environments are: (1) the environment is itself not formally organized; and (2) transactions are largely initiated and controlled by the organization (i.e., L_{12}).

Later developments, such as transport technology and derivative overlap in loss of strength gradients, and communication and automation technologies that increased economies of scale, gave rise to disturbed reactive (oligopolistic) conditions in which similar formal organizations become the important actors in an organization's field. They are responsive to its acts (L_{12}) and it must be responsive to theirs (L_{21}). The critical organizational response now involves complex operations, requiring sequential choices based on the calculated actions of others, and counteractions.[43]

When the environment becomes turbulent, however, its constituents are a multitude of other formal organizations. Increasingly, an organization's markets consist of other organizations; suppliers of material, labor, and capital are increasingly organized, and regulatory groups are more numerous and powerful. The critical response of organizations under these conditions will be discussed later. It should be noted that *real* environments are often mixtures of these ideal types.

The evolution from placid-clustered environments to turbulent environments[44] can be summarized as a process in which formal organizations evolve: (1) *from* the status of systems within environments not formally organized; (2) *through* intermediate phases (e.g., Weberian bureaucracy); and (3) *to* the status of subsystems of a larger social system.

Clark Kerr traces this evolution for the university in the United States.[45] In modern industrial societies, this evolutionary process has resulted in the replacement of individuals and informal groups by organizations as *actors* in the social system. Functions that were once the sole responsibility of families and communities are increasingly allocated to formal organizations; child-rearing, work, recreation, education, health, and so on. Events which were long a matter of chance are increasingly subject to organizational control, such as population growth, business cycles, and even the weather. One wonders whether Durkheim, if he could observe the current scene, might speculate that the evolution from "mechanical solidarity" to "organic solidarity" is now occurring on the *organizational level,* where the common values of organizations in oligopolies are replaced by functional interdependencies among specialized organizations.[46]

INTERORGANIZATIONAL ANALYSIS

It was noted that survival in disturbed-reactive environments depends upon the ability of the organization to anticipate and counteract the behavior of similar systems. The analysis of interorganizational behavior, therefore, becomes meaningful only in these and more complex environments. The interdependence of organizations, or any kind of living systems, at less complex environmental levels is more appropriately studied by means of ecological, competitive market, or other similar models.

The only systematic conceptual approach to interorganizational analysis has been the theory of oligopoly in economics. This theory clearly addresses only disturbed-reactive environments. Many economists admit that the theory, which assumes maximization of profit and perfect knowledge, is increasingly at odds with empirical evidence that organizational behavior is characterized by satisficing and bounded rationality. Boulding comments that "it is surprisingly hard to make a really intelligent conflict move in the economic area simply because of the complexity of the system and the enormous importance of side effects and dynamic effects."[47] A fairly comprehensive search of the literature has revealed only four conceptual frameworks for the analysis of interorganizational relations outside the field of economics. These are briefly reviewed, particular attention being given to assumptions about organization environments, and to the utility of these assumptions in the analysis of interorganizational relations in turbulent fields.

William Evan has introduced the concept of "organization-set," after Merton's "role-set."[48] Relations between a focal organization and members of its organization-set are mediated by the role-sets of boundary personnel. "Relations" are conceived as the flow of information, products or services, and personnel.[49] Presumably, monetary, and legal, and other transactions can be accommodated in the conceptual system. In general, Evan offers a conceptual tool for identifying transactions at a given time. He makes no explicit assumptions about the nature of environmental dynamics, nor does he imply that they are changing. The relative neglect of interorganizational relations, which he finds surprising, is ascribed instead to the traditional intraorganizational focus, which derives from Weber, Taylor, and Barnard.[50] His concepts, however, go considerably beyond those of conventional organization and economic theory (e.g., comparative versus reference organizations and overlap in goals and values). If a temporal dimension were added to Evan's conceptual scheme, then, it would be a very useful tool for describing the "structural" aspects of transactional interdependencies (L_{21} and L_{12} relations) in turbulent fields.

Another approach is taken by Levine and White who focus specifically on relations among community health and welfare agencies. This local set of organizations "may be seen as a system with individual organizations or system parts varying in the kinds and frequencies of their relationships with one another."[51] The authors admit that interdependence exists among these local parts only to the extent that relevant resources are not available from *outside* the local region, which lies beyond their conceptual domain. Nor do we find here any suggestion of turbulence in these local environments. If such local sets of agencies are increasingly interdependent with other components of the local community and with organizations outside the locality, as the evidence suggests, then the utility of Levine and White's approach is both limited and shrinking.

Litwak and Hylton provide a third perspective. They too are concerned with health and welfare organizations, but their major emphasis is on coordination.[52] The degree of interdependence among organizations is a major variable; low interdependence leads to *no* coordination and high interdependence leads to merger, therefore they deal only with conditions of moderate interdependence. The type of coordinating mechanism that emerges under conditions of moderate interdependence is hypothesized to result from the interaction of three trichotomized variables: the *number* of interdependent organizations; the degree of their *awareness* of their interdependence; and the extent of *standardization* in their transactions. The attractive feature of the Litwak and Hylton scheme is the possibility it offers of making different predictions for a great variety of environments. Their model also seems to have predictive power beyond the class of organizations to which they specifically address themselves. If environments are becoming turbulent, however, then increasingly fewer of the model's cells (a 3 × 3 × 3

space) are relevant. In the one-cell turbulent corner of their model, where a large number of organizations have low awareness of their complex and unstandardized interdependence, "there is little chance of coordination,"[53] according to Litwak and Hylton. If the level of awareness of interdependence increases, the model predicts that some process of arbitration will emerge. Thus the model anticipates the interorganizational implications of turbulent fields, but tells us little about the emerging processes that will enable organizations to adapt to turbulence.

The fourth conceptual framework available in the literature is by Thompson and McEwen.[54] They emphasize the interdependence of organizations with the larger society and discuss the consequences that this has for goal setting. "Because the setting of goals is essentially a problem of defining desired relationships between an organization and its environment, change in either requires review and perhaps alteration of goals."[55] They do not argue that such changes are more frequent today, but they do assert that reappraisal of goals is "a more constant problem in an unstable environment than in a stable one," and also "more difficult as the 'product' of the enterprise becomes less tangible."[56]

Thompson and McEwen outline four organizational strategies for dealing with the environment. One is competition; the other three are subtypes of a cooperative strategy: bargaining, co-optation, and coalition. These cooperative strategies all require direct interaction among organizations and this, they argue, increases the environment's potential control over the focal organization.[57] In bargaining, to the extent that the second party's support is necessary, that party is in a position to exercise a veto over the final choice of alternative goals, and thus takes part in the decision. The co-optation strategy makes still further inroads into the goal-setting process. From the standpoint of society, however, co-optation, by providing overlapping memberships, is an important social device for increasing the likelihood that organizations related to each other in complicated ways will in fact find compatible goals. Co-optation thus aids in the integration of heterogeneous parts of a complex social system. Coalition refers to a combination of two or more organizations for a common purpose and is viewed by these authors as the ultimate form of environmental conditioning of organization goals.[58]

The conceptual approaches of Levine and White and of Litwak and Hylton therefore appear to be designed for non-turbulent conditions. Indeed, it may well be that coordination *per se,* in the static sense usually implied by that term is dysfunctional for adaptation to turbulent fields. (This criticism has often been leveled at local "councils of social agencies."[59]) On the other hand, Evan's concept of organization-set seems useful for describing static aspects of interorganizational relations in either disturbed-reactive *or* turbulent-field environments. Its application in longitudinal rather than static studies might yield data on the relationship between structural aspects of transactional relations and organizational adaptability. Lastly, Thompson and McEwen make a unique contribution by distinguishing different *kinds* of interorganizational relations.

As an aside, note that Evan's extension of the role-set concept to organizations suggests still further analogies, which may be heuristically useful. A role is a set of acts prescribed for the occupant of some position. The role accrues to the position; its occupants

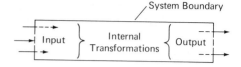

Figure 1. Structure of Living Systems such as a Formal Organization.

are interchangeable. If formal organizations are treated as social actors, then one can conceive of organizations as occupants of positions in the larger social system. Each organization has one or more roles in its behavioral repertoire (these are more commonly called functions or goals). The organization occupants of these social positions, however, are also interchangeable.

Integrative Framework

MODEL

It is assumed that the foregoing arguments are valid: (1) that organizational environments are increasingly turbulent; (2) that organizations are increasingly less autonomous; and (3) that other formal organizations are increasingly important components of organizational environments. Some conceptual perspective is now needed, which will make it possible to view any formal organization, its transactional interdependencies, and the environment itself within a common conceptual framework. The intent of this section is to outline the beginnings of such a framework.

A formal organization is a system primarily oriented to the attainment of a specific goal, which constitutes an output of the system and which is an input for some other system.[60] Needless to say, the output of any living system is dependent upon input into it. Figure 1 schematically illustrates the skeletal structure of a living system. The input and output regions are partially permeable with respect to the environment, which is the region outside the system boundary. Arrows coming into a system represent input and arrows going out of a system represent output. In Figure 2, rectangles represent formal organizations and circles represent individuals and *nonformal* social organizations. Figure 2 represents the *statics* of a system X and its turbulent environment. Three-dimensional illustration would be necessary to show the *dynamics* of a turbulent environment schematically. Assume that a third, temporal dimension is imposed on Figure 2 and that this reveals an increasing number of elements and an increasing rate and complexity of change in their interdependencies over time. To do full justice to the concept of turbulence we should add other sets of elements even in Figure 2 [below], although these are not yet linked to X's set. A notion that is integral to Emery and Trist's conception of turbulence is that changes outside of X's set, and hence difficult for X to predict and impossible for X to control, will

have impact on X's transactional interdependencies in the future. The addition of just one link at some future time may not affect the supersystem but may constitute a system break for X.

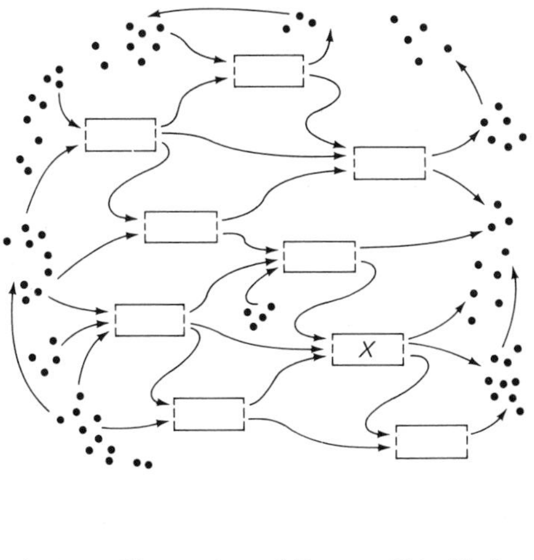

This schematization shows only one-way directionality and is meant to depict energic inputs (e.g., personnel and material) and output (e.g., product). The organization provides something in exchange for the inputs it receives, of course, and this is usually informational in nature—money, most commonly. Similarly the organization receives money for its product from those systems for whom its product is an input. Nor does our framework distinguish different kinds of inputs, although the analysis of interorganizational exchange requires this kind of taxonomic device. It seems important to distinguish energic inputs and outputs from informational ones. Energic inputs include machinery, personnel, clientele in the case of service organizations, electric power, and so on. Informational inputs are not well conceptualized although there is no doubt of their increasing importance in environments which are more complex and changeable. Special divisions of organizations and whole firms devoted to information collecting, processing, and distributing are also rapidly proliferating (e.g., research organizations, accounting firms, the Central Intelligence Agency).

An input called "legitimacy" is popular in sociological circles but highly resistant to empirical specification. The view taken here is that legitimacy is mediated by the exchange of other resources. Thus the willingness of firm A to contribute capital to X, and of agency B to refer personnel to X and firm C to buy X's product testifies to the legitimacy of X. This "willingness" on the part of organizations A, B, and C, how-

Figure 2. Illustration of System X in Turbulent Environment.

THE EVOLUTION OF ORGANIZATIONAL ENVIRONMENTS

68 ever, can best be understood in terms of informational exchange. For example, A provides X with capital on the basis of A's information about the market for X's product. Or B refuses to refer skilled workmen to X since B has information on X's discriminatory employment practices and also knows of consequences to itself from elsewhere if it is party to X's practice. Technology is also sometimes treated as an input to organizations. We use the term, however, to refer to the complex set of interactions among inputs which takes place in the internal region shown in Figure 1. It is technology which transforms the inputs of the system into the output of the system. Transportation and communication technologies, however, are of a uniquely different order; the former constitutes an energic and the latter an informational transcendence of space-time that enabled the evolution of the more complex environments (L_{22}) which concern us here. Automation and computer technologies are roughly equivalent (i.e., energic and informational, respectively) but on an intraorganizational (L_{11}) level.

Our attention to "legitimacy" and "technology" was tangential to our main theme, to which we now return. Our simplistic approach to an integrative framework for the study of organizations (L_{11}), their transactional interdependencies (L_{21} and L_{12}), and the connectedness within their environments (L_{22}), gives the following conceptual ingredients: (1) units that are mainly formal organizations, and (2) relationships between them that are the directed flow[61] of (3) energy and information. The enormous and increasing importance of informational transaction has not been matched by conceptual developments in organization theory. The importance of information is frequently cited in a general way, however, especially in the context of organizational change or innovation. Dill has made a cogent argument on the need for more attention to this dimension.[62]

The importance of communication for organizational change has been stressed by Ohlin, March and Simon, Benne, Lippitt, and others.[63] Diversity of informational input has been used to explain the creativity of individuals as well as of social systems.[64] The importance of boundary positions as primary sources of innovative inputs from the environment has been stressed by March and Simon[65] and by Kahn et al.[66] James Miller hypothesizes that up to a maximum, which no living system has yet reached, the more energy a system devotes to information processing (as opposed to productive and maintenance activity), the more likely the system is to survive.[67]

Evolution on the biological level is accompanied by improvement in the ability of systems to discover and perform according to contingencies in their environments. The random walk which suffices in a placid-randomized environment must be replaced by stochastic processes under placid-clustered conditions, and by cybernetic processes in disturbed-reactive fields. Among biological/psychological systems, only man appears to have the capacity for the purposeful behavior that may permit adaptation to or control of turbulent environments. There is some question, of course, as to whether man actually has the capacity to cope with the turbulence that he has introduced into the environment.

Analogous concepts are equally applicable to the evolution of social systems in general and to formal organizations in particular. The capacity of any system for adapting to changing contingencies in its environment is inversely related to its dependence upon instinct, habit, or tradition. Adaptability exists, by definition, to the extent that a system (L_{11}) can survive externally induced (L_{22}) change in its transactional interdependencies (L_{21} and L_{12}); therefore viability equals adaptability.

HYPOTHESES

HYPOTHESIS 1:
Organizational change is largely externally induced.

Any particular change may be adaptive or maladaptive, and it may be one of these in the short run and the other in the long run. There is *no* systematic empirical evidence on the relative influence of internal versus environmental antecedents to organizational change. The empirical task here is to identify organizational changes, and the internal or external origins of each change.

It is crucial to distinguish change on the organizational level from the multitude of changes that may occur in or among subsystems, only some of which give rise to change on the system level. Many social psychologists, for example, study change in individuals and groups *within* organizations, but with no reference to variables of organizational level. Likert's book is one noteworthy exception.[68] The important point is that change on the organizational level is analytically distinct from change on other levels.

Organizational change means any change in the kind or quantity of output. Ideally, output is treated as a function of inputs and of transfer functions (i.e., intraorganizational change is inferred from change in input-output relations). Haberstroh illustrates the use of these general system concepts in the organization context.[69] An excellent discussion

of the efficiency and effectiveness of organizations, in an open-systems framework, is given in Katz and Kahn.[70]

However, the input-output functions in diversified industries and the outputs of many service organizations are resistant to objective specification and measurement. An empirical test of this hypothesis, with presently available tools, may have to settle for some set of input and internal change that seems to be reasonably antecedent to output change.

The identification of the origin of change is also beset by difficulties. An input change may indeed have external antecedents, but external events may also be responses to some prior internal change in the focal organization. And internal change may be internally generated, but it may also be the result of an informational input from external sources. Novel informational inputs, as well as novel communication channels, often derive from change in personnel inputs. Increasingly, organizations seek personnel who bring specialized information rather than "manpower" to the organization. The presence of first, second, and higher order causation poses a problem for any empirical test of this hypothesis.

HYPOTHESIS 2:
System adaptability (e.g., organizational) is a function of ability to learn and to perform according to changing environmental contingencies.

Adaptability exists, by definition, to the extent that a system can survive externally induced change in its transactional interdependencies in the long run. Diversity in a system's input (L_{21}) and output (L_{12}) interdependencies will increase adaptability. The recent and rapid diversification in major industries illustrates this strategy. Flexible structure (L_{11}, e.g., decentralized decision making) will facilitate adaptation. Beyond this, however, adaptability would seem to be largely a function of a system's perceptual and information-processing capacities.[71] The following variables appear crucial: (1) *advance information* of impending externally induced (L_{22}) change in L_{21} or L_{12} transactions; (2) *active search* for, and activation of, more advantageous input and output transactions; and (3) *available memory store* (L_{11}) of interchangeable input and output components in the environment.

Advance information and active search might be empirically handled with Evan's concept of the role-sets of boundary personnel, along with notions of channel efficiency. For example, overlapping memberships (e.g., on boards) would constitute a particularly efficient channel. Likewise, direct communication between members of separate organizations, while less effective than overlapping memberships, would be a more efficient channel between agencies *A* and *B* than instances where their messages must be mediated by a third agency, *C*. Efficiency of interorganizational communication channels should be positively associated with access to advance information, and be facilitative of search, for example. The members of an organization's informational set may become increasingly differentiated from its energic set. Communication channels to research and marketing firms, universities, governmental agencies and other important information producing and distributing agencies would be expected to increase long-run viability. The third variable, memory store, is probably a function of the efficiency of past and present informational channels, but it involves internal (L_{11}) information processing as well.

Lastly, *any* internal change that improves an organization's transactional advantage (e.g., improved technology) will also be conducive to adaptability. Since organizational innovation is more often imitation than invention,[72] these changes are usually also the product of informational input and can be handled within the same integrative framework.

Summary

The lag between evolution in the real world and evolution in theorists' ability to comprehend it is vast, but hopefully shrinking. It was only a little over one hundred years ago that Darwin identified natural selection as the mechanism of evolutionary process. Despite Darwin's enduring insight, theorists of change, including biologists, have continued to focus largely on internal aspects of systems.

It is our thesis that the selective advantage of one intra- or interorganizational configuration over another cannot be assessed apart from an understanding of the dynamics of the environment itself. It is the environment which exerts selective pressure. "Survival of the fittest" is a function of the fitness of the environment. The dinosaurs *were* impressive creatures, in their day.

NOTES

1. Ludwig von Bertalanffy, General System Theory, *General Systems*, 1 (1956), 1–10.
2. F. E. Emery and E. L. Trist, The Causal Texture of Organizational Environments, *Human Relations*, 18 (1965), 21–31.
3. *Ibid.*, 22.

INTERORGANIZATIONAL RELATIONSHIPS

4. I am particularly grateful to Kenneth Boulding for inspiration and to Eugene Litwak, Rosemary Sarri, and Robert Vinter for helpful criticisms. A Special Research Fellowship from the National Institutes of Health has supported my doctoral studies and, therefore, has made possible the development of this paper.

5. The concepts of ideal types of environment, and one of the examples in this paragraph, are from Emery and Trist, op. cit., 24–26.

6. The following illustrations are taken from Emery and Trist, ibid.: For random-placid environment see Herbert A. Simon, Models of Man (New York: John Wiley, 1957), p. 137; W. Ross Ashby, Design for a Brain (2nd ed.; London: Chapman and Hall, 1960), Sec. 15/4; the mathematical concept of random field; and the economic concept of classical market.

   For random-clustered environment see Edward C. Tolman and Egon Brunswick, The Organism and the Causal Texture of the Environment, Psychological Review, 42 (1935), 43–72; Ashby, op. cit., sec. 15/8; and the economic concept of imperfect competition.

   For disturbed-reactive environment see Ashby, op. cit., sec. 7; the concept of "imbrication" from I. Chein, Personality and Typology, Journal of Social Psychology, 18 (1943), 89–101; and the concept of oligopoly.

7. Emery and Trist, op. cit., 24.

8. Ibid., 26.

9. Ibid., 24.

10. Amitai Etzioni, New Directions in the Study of Organizations and Society, Social Research, 27 (1960), 223–228.

11. Peter M. Blau and Richard Scott, Formal Organizations (San Francisco: Chandler, 1962), pp. 194–221.

12. Talcott Parsons, Structure and Process in Modern Societies (New York: Free Press, 1960), pp. 63–64.

13. Lloyd E. Ohlin, Conformity in American Society Today, Social Work, 3 (1958), 63.

14. Robert C. Hood, "Business Organization as a Cross Product of Its Purposes and of Its Environment," in Mason Haire (ed.), Organizational Theory in Industrial Practice (New York: John Wiley, 1962), p. 73.

15. Peter F. Drucker, The Big Power of Little Ideas, Harvard Business Review, 42 (May 1964), 6–8.

16. John W. Gardner, Self-Renewal (New York: Harper & Row, 1963), p. 107.

17. James E. McNulty, Organizational Change in Growing Enterprises, Administrative Science Quarterly, 7 (1962), 1–21.

18. Long Range Planning and Cloudy Horizons, Dun's Review, 81 (Jan. 1963), 42.

19. Blau and Scott, op. cit., p. 217.

20. Lee Adler, Symbiotic Marketing, Harvard Business Review, 44 (November 1966), 59–71.

21. W. R. Dill, Environment as an Influence on Managerial Autonomy, Administrative Science Quarterly, 2 (1958), 409–443.

22. James D. Thompson, Organizations in Action (New York: McGraw-Hill, 1967), pp. 27–28.

23. Philip Selznick, TVA and the Grass Roots (Berkeley: University of California, 1949).

24. V. F. Ridgway, Administration of Manufacturer-Dealer Systems, Administrative Science Quarterly, 2 (1957), 464–483.

25. Dill, op. cit.

26. Sol Levine and Paul E. White, Exchange as a Conceptual Framework for the Study of Interorganizational Relationships, Administrative Science Quarterly, 5 (1961), 583–601.

27. Eugene Litwak and Lydia Hylton, Interorganizational Analysis: A Hypothesis on Coordinating Agencies, Administrative Science Quarterly, 6 (1962), 395–420.

28. R. H. Elling and S. Halebsky, Organizational Differentiation and Support: A Conceptual Framework, Administrative Science Quarterly, 6 (1961), 185–209.

29. Earl Rubington, Organizational Strain and Key Roles, Administrative Science Quarterly, 9 (1965), 350–369.

THE EVOLUTION OF ORGANIZATIONAL ENVIRONMENTS

72 30. William R. Rosengren, Communication, Organization, and Conduct in the "Therapeutic Milieu," *Administrative Science Quarterly*, 9 (1964), 70–90.

31. Burton R. Clark, Interorganizational Patterns in Education, *Administrative Science Quarterly*, 10 (1965), 224–237.

32. John Maniha and Charles Perrow, The Reluctant Organization and the Aggressive Environment, *Administrative Science Quarterly*, 10 (1965), 238–257.

33. Donald W. Taylor, "Decision Making and Problem Solving," in James G. March (ed.), *Handbook of Organizations* (Chicago: Rand McNally, 1965), pp. 48–82.

34. James G. March and Herbert A. Simon, *Organizations* (New York: John Wiley, 1958), pp. 140–141.

35. David Braybrooke and C. E. Lindblom, *A Strategy of Decision* (Glencoe: The Free Press, 1963), especially ch. 3, 5.

36. Richard M. Cyert and James G. March, *A Behavioral Theory of the Firm* (Englewood Cliffs, N.J.: Prentice-Hall, 1963), p. 100.

37. Shirley Terreberry, "The Evolution of Environments" (mimeographed course paper, 1967), pp. 1–37.

38. J. W. S. Pringle, On the Parallel Between Learning and Evolution, *General Systems*, 1 (1956), 90.

39. Assuming a nonexpanding economy, in the ideal instance.

40. Emery and Trist argue that fates, here, are positively correlated. This writer agrees if an expanding economy is assumed.

41. Arthur L. Stinchcombe, "Social Structure and Organizations," in March (ed.), *op. cit.*, p. 156.

42. Emery and Trist, *op. cit.*, 29.

43. *Ibid.*, 25–26.

44. The author does not agree with Emery and Trist, that *formal* (as distinct from social) organization will emerge in placid-random environments.

45. Clark Kerr, *The Uses of the University* (New York: Harper Torchbooks, 1963).

46. Emile Durkheim, *The Division of Labor in Society*, trans. George Simpson (Glencoe: The Free Press, 1947).

47. Kenneth E. Boulding, "The Economies of Human Conflict," in Elton B. McNeil (ed.), *The Nature of Human Conflict* (Englewood Cliffs, N.J.: Prentice-Hall, 1965), p. 189.

48. William M. Evan, "The Organization-Set: Toward a Theory of Interorganizational Relations," in James D. Thompson (ed.), *Approaches to Organizational Design* (Pittsburgh, Pa.: University of Pittsburgh Press, 1966), pp. 177–180.

49. *Ibid.*, pp. 175–176.

50. *Ibid.*

51. Levine and White, *op. cit., 586.*

52. Litwak and Hylton, *op. cit.*

53. *Ibid.*, 417.

54. James D. Thompson and William J. McEwen, Organizational Goals and Environment, *American Sociological Review*, 23 (1958), 23–31.

55. *Ibid.*, 23.

56. *Ibid.*, 24.

57. *Ibid.*, 27.

58. *Ibid.*, 25–28.

59. Examples include: Robert Morris and Ollie A. Randall, Planning and Organization of Community Services for the Elderly, *Social Work*, 10 (1965), 96–103; Frank W. Harris, A Modern Council Point of View, *Social Work*, 9 (1964), 34–41; Harold L. Wilensky and Charles N. Lebeaux, *Industrial Society and Social Welfare* (New York: Russell Sage Foundation, 1958), especially pp. 263–265.

60. Talcott Parsons, "Suggestions for a Sociological Approach to the Theory of Organizations," in Amitai Etzioni (ed.), *Complex Organizations* (New York: Holt, Rinehart, and Winston, 1962), p. 33.

61. Dorwin Cartwright, "The Potential Contribution of Graph Theory to Organization

Theory," in Mason Haire (ed.), *Modern Organization Theory* (New York: John Wiley, 1959), pp. 254–271.

62. William R. Dill, "The Impact of Environment in Organizational Development," in Sidney Mailick and Edward H. Van Ness (eds.), *Concepts and Issues in Administrative Behavior* (Englewood Cliffs, N.J.: Prentice-Hall, 1962), pp. 94–109.

63. Ohlin, *op. cit.*, 63; March and Simon, *op. cit.*, pp. 173–183; Kenneth D. Benne, "Deliberate Changing as the Facilitation of Growth," in Warren G. Bennis *et al.* (eds.), *The Planning of Change* (New York: Holt, Rinehart, and Winston, 1962), p. 232; Ronald Lippitt, *The Dynamics of Planned Change* (New York: Harcourt, Brace, and World, 1958), p. 52.

64. For example: Floyd H. Allport, *Theories of Perception and the Concept of Structure* (New York: John Wiley, 1955), p. 76; Wiliam F. Ogburn and Meyer F. Nimkoff, *Sociology* (4th ed.; Boston: Houghton Mifflin, 1964), pp. 662–670.

65. March and Simon, *op. cit.*, pp. 165–166, 189.

66. Robert L. Kahn *et al.*, *Organizational Stress* (New York: John Wiley, 1964), pp. 101–126.

67. James G. Miller, Toward a General Theory for the Behavioral Sciences, *The American Psychologist*, 10 (1955), 530.

68. Rensis Likert, *New Patterns of Management* (New York: McGraw-Hill, 1961).

69. Chadwick J. Haberstroh, "Organization Design and Systems Analysis," in March (ed.), *op. cit.*, pp. 1171–1211.

70. Daniel Katz and Robert L. Kahn, *The Social Psychology of Organizations* (New York: John Wiley, 1966), especially pp. 149–170.

71. Igor Ansoff speaks of the "wide-open windows of perception" required of tomorrow's firms, and offers a perspective on the future that is fully compatible with that presented here; see The Firm of the Future, *Harvard Business Review*, 43 (September 1965), 162.

72. Theodore Levitt, Innovative Imitation, *Harvard Business Review*, 44 (September 1966), 63–70.

Bates, Frederick L. 1960. "Institutions, Organizations, And Communities: A General Theory Of Complex Structures," *Pacific Sociological Review*, 3 (Fall), 59–70.

Blau, Peter M., and W. Richard Scott. 1962. *Formal Organizations: A Comparative Approach*. San Francisco: Chandler. (Ch. 8: "The Social Context of Organizational Life").

Litwak, Eugene, and L. Hylton. 1962. "Interorganizational Analysis: A Hypothesis on Co-ordinating Agencies," *Administrative Science Quarterly*, 6 (March), 395–420.

Long, Norton E. 1958. "The Local Community As An Ecology Of Games," *The American Journal of Sociology*, 64 (November), 251–261.

Turk, Herman. 1970. "Interorganizational Networks in Urban Society: Initial Perspectives and Comparative Research," *American Sociological Review*, 35 (February); 1–19.

Warren, Roland L. 1967. "The Interorganizational Field As a Focus for Investigation," *Administrative Science Quarterly*, 12 (December), 396–419.

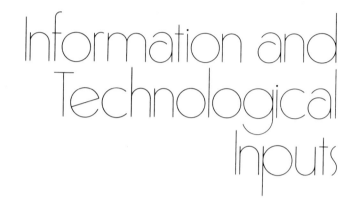

CHAPTER THREE

Information and Technological Inputs

The first article contained in this chapter is concerned with the effects of information originating in the external environment on organizational structure and process. Dill conceptualizes the environment "as information which becomes available to the organization or to which the organization, via search activity, may get access," and information "which bears potentially on goal setting and on goal attainment within the organization." He makes a critical distinction between short-run and long-run information-organization relationships, emphasizing how the effects of immediate information inputs on organizational behavior are determined by the organization's earlier interaction with its environment.

Three papers in the additional readings section that deal with information inputs are noteworthy. Meier's paper provides a description of internal changes in two organizations, a stock exchange and a library, which result from an increase in external demand for their services. He delineates fourteen policy responses that may be expected, given certain assumptions, to accompany an increasing communications load upon an organization. He points out the relationship between communication overload and stress, both organizational and personal, and discusses the structural effects that result from a mixture of policy responses and changes in strategy to deal with severe overload.

Churchill's article, elaborating on Meier's theory, presents five examples of "ignoring strategies" which indicate that some organizations can escape Meier's "salvage-of-component-units" fate. According to Churchill, whether an organization can or cannot escape this fate depends upon the time arrangement in the situation, the normalcy of social conditions, the importance of the organization's services, and the knowledge of strategy. Churchill adds an important dimension to the overload problem with his conceptualization of message load as a result of negotiations between client and organization member. Among the critical points he makes are: Demand and service are interdependent; presented demand may not be equivalent to perceived demand; and organizational participants may not accept higher error-rate behavior as legitimate. The administrator may find it valuable to use the Meier-Churchill models to analyze input-load effects for the organization and its subsystems vis-à-vis external elements.

Margolis points out the businessman's need for reliable information and how procedures and rules have been developed as a partial result of having to operate with insufficient information. Using the introduction of a new product as an example, he demonstrates how ignorance about many elements in the firm's environment is conducive to a full-cost pricing practice. This practice reflects sequential decision-making, i.e., today's actions are made under conditions of ignorance; they are partially determined by their consequences for future decisions; they alter tomorrow's information; and this alteration affects future decisions. It is interesting to note the number and type of assumptions made concerning the environment as the product price is set.

Perrow (1965, p. 915) defines technology as "a technique or complex of techniques employed to alter 'materials' (human or nonhuman, mental or physical) in an anticipated manner." According to Perrow (p. 916), "equipment is a tool of technology [and] technology rests upon knowledge of the nature of the raw material." Thus, technology does not refer only to tools and machines. For example, Perrow (p. 925) describes the large public mental hospital as "in many respects a cruel, inefficient, and irrational institution [because of] the limitations of the available technology." He discusses various treatment technologies: milieu therapy, application of learning theory, shock or drug treatment, individual psychotherapy, etc.

Although nominal definitions of technology are numerous, the concept is difficult to operationalize for purposes of research. According to Hickson, Pugh, and Pheysey (1969, pp. 380–381), the concept has three facets: (1) operations technology (the *"equipping and sequencing of activities in the workflow"*), including the subconcepts of the extent of equipment automation, the rigidity of the sequence of activities, the specificity of evaluation of operations, and the continuity of the work in process; (2) *"characteristics of the materials used in the workflow"* (i.e., characteristics of the object or raw material); (3) *"knowledge used in the workflow."*

INFORMATION AND TECHNOLOGICAL INPUTS

As was previously noted, elements in the external environment of any organization impose requirements on as well as present opportunities to the organization. Organizational administrators are continuously selecting technological elements from those extant in the external environment. The technological outputs of business research firms, governmental agencies, academic institutions, nonprofit research organizations, etc., are imported by organizations in order to efficiently transform a set of energic inputs into an exportable product or service.

The importation and utilization of specific technologies as well as changes in or replacements of given technologies may be associated with different patterns of division of labor, task design, formal organizational structure, coordination and control devices, managerial practices, informal norms and relationships, intergroup relationships, and member attitudes and behavior. In a comparative study of six firms in the container and plastics industries, Lawrence and Lorsch (1967) found distinct differences in organization structure and managerial orientations and behaviors. These differences were related to the degree of complexity, uncertainty, and rate of change in technology.

In a study of one hundred British industrial firms, Woodward (1965) concludes that organizational success is related to the degree of fit between type of production technology and formal organizational structure and certain managerial practices. Hage and Aiken (1969, p. 375) studied sixteen health and welfare agencies and report that the more routine the organization's technology, "the more centralized the decision-making about organizational policies, the more likely the presence of a rules manual and job descriptions, and the more specified the job." They also report that "In organizations with a relatively routine technology, the staff members are likely to report more emphasis on efficiency and quantity of clients than on quality of service and staff morale."

Hickson et al. (1969, p. 378 and p. 396) note the *"long-standing divergence in organization theory between statements by classical management writers of management principles irrespective of technology, and the stress by behavioral scientists on the relevance of technology (for the structure of an organization)."*

In a study of fifty-two diverse work organizations, they found in general that both groups of theorists may be right, since in larger manufacturing organizations "the basic activities of management and their structural framework are probably not much affected by the particular operations technology employed. The behavioral scientists may well be equally right (up to a point): technology makes all the difference at 'shop-floor' level, and throughout smaller organizations, where nothing is far removed from the workflow itself."

The papers in this section have been selected to explicate and stimulate thinking concerning the nature of the relationship between technological inputs and various internal organizational phenomena.

Thompson and Bates compare four different types of organizations to demonstrate how technology, defined as a set of man-machine activities, influences policy formulation, types of structures, resource management, and execution. They emphasize the adaptability of the technology and propose seventeen hypotheses that deserve the attention of administrative strategists.

Perrow elaborates on Thompson and Bates' routinization–individual judgment phenomenon. He posits two independent aspects of technology. Dichotomization of these two aspects (although Perrow stresses their continuous nature) results in a fourfold table with a routine-nonroutine diagonal. He develops an additional fourfold table derived from two aspects of the raw material. Perrow relates both tables to the task structure, social structure, and goals of the organization. The two-by-two matrix model that he develops has both sequential, interactive, and superimpositional aspects. Its value for the administrator lies in the assistance it provides in choosing from various theories of organization.

In contrast to the preceding "cross-section" papers, Burack examines a longitudinal dimension in his analysis of thirteen advanced production systems. His interest is the effects of quasiprocess and process types of manufacturing activities over time on: personnel qualities and organization, task assignment, control systems, patterns of managerial activity, administrative and technical support groups, and organization structure.

Whereas Burack's paper devotes more attention to the administrative effects of technological advances, Faunce stresses their effects on the social structure of the work place. His model relates technological development (comprised of four components) to three types of man-machine relationships that, in turn, influence the form of division of labor. He hypothesizes that the change from mechanized to automated production leads to less differentiation in the occupational structure, and cautiously suggests that this may reduce the degree of anomie and alienation.

Two articles in the additional reading section merit comment. In contrast to Faunce, who concentrates on lower-level organizational participants, Whisler and Shultz specify the impact of the computer, in combination with quantitative decision-making techniques, on: structural changes in the organization, managerial job activities, and the structure of authority and control. They provide an open-system model that traces the relationships among outside forces, technological change, employment effects, and adjustment effects.

Silverman bases his paper solely on empirical studies of the effects of automation. He delineates three types of automation and reports four effects within each type. The reader may find it challenging to fill the cells of Silverman's three-by-four matrix with emerging evidence, as well as to develop additional columnar and row headings.

INFORMATION AND TECHNOLOGICAL INPUTS

Hage, Jerald, and Michael Aiken. 1969. "Routine Technology, Social Structure and Organizational Goals," *Administrative Science Quarterly*, 14 (September), 366–376.

Hickson, David J., D. S. Pugh, and Diana C. Pheysey. 1969. "Operations Technology and Organization Structure: An Empirical Reappraisal," *Administrative Science Quarterly*, 14 (September), 378–397.

Lawrence, Paul R., and Jay W. Lorsch. 1967. *Organization and Environment.* Boston: Harvard Business School.

Perrow, Charles. 1965. "Hospitals: Technology, Structure, and Goals." In *Handbook of Organizations*, James G. March, ed. Chicago: Rand McNally.

Woodward, Joan. 1965. *Industrial Organization: Theory and Practice.* London: Oxford University Press.

THE IMPACT OF ENVIRONMENT ON ORGANIZATIONAL DEVELOPMENT

William R. Dill

In expanding our understanding of organizational behavior and in elaborating theories of organization and administration, we need to incorporate "environmental" variables more explicitly into our work. In the hopes of building simple and general theories, we have tended to assume that observations about the internal functioning of one organization would be true for others. Too often, though, when we do take the trouble to repeat a study in a new environment, we find that the old relationships disappear and new ones become prominent.

A striking example of this can be seen in the Coch and French field experiments at the Harwood Manufacturing Company on overcoming resistance to change.[1] This was an ingeniously designed and carefully conducted series of studies on different ways of getting textile workers to accept the job changes, small and large, which accompanied semiannual changes in the style and the mix of products. The results were dramatic. There was less turnover, faster relearning, and higher eventual rates of production among workers who had heard a detailed presentation of the reasons why changes were necessary[2] and who had participated in making decisions about ways in which the changes would be carried through.

This study has been widely reprinted and even more widely cited as a clear, dramatic, and generally valid example of the benefits of employee participation in company decisions. Many similar studies were done, with mixed results; but nothing approaching a direct replication was tried for about a dozen years. Then one of the original authors collaborated in an effort to replicate the study in a Norwegian textile mill.[3] The results this time were much less clear-cut. The manner of introducing change had no direct effects on turnover, learning rates, or eventual productivity. What happened seemed to depend on the meaning which workers attached to the experimental manipulations—the relevance of these manipulations to production and the legitimacy which workers assigned to opportunities for participation. The differences in results, French believes, are the results of what he calls "conditioning variables" and "cultural factors"—for the Norwegian workers, stronger group standards limiting output, stronger union traditions, and greater feelings that the proper channels for participation were through regular union representatives.

To compare these two studies of the effects of participation or to use them as a basis for interpreting other results or predicting the effects of a new experi-

William R. Dill, "The Impact of Environment on Organizational Development" in Sidney Mailick and Edward H. Van Ness, Eds., *Concepts and Issues in Administrative Behavior*, © 1962. Reprinted by permission of Prentice-Hall, Inc., Englewood Cliffs, N.J.

ment, it is clear that we need to know a lot about the environments in which the groups we are studying work. And as a first step in this process, we need some ways of talking about the environment and its interactions with an organization. Our purpose here is to outline one way of looking at the environment and its impact on organizational development.

Environment as a Flow of Information

At one level, environment is not a very mysterious concept. It means the surroundings of an organization; the "climate" in which the organization functions. The concept becomes challenging when we try to move from simple description of the environment to analysis of its properties. The complexity of what we find and the grossness of most of the data that we collect are not consistent with the standards of precision and parsimony that social scientists have come to respect. Good bases for general propositions about environmental influences or for systematic classifications and comparisons of different environments are hard to find.

The size, the diversity, and the instability of organizational environments create another handicap. In the case of simple and highly abstract laboratory experiments, we presume that we know what the environment *is* as well as how it appears to the subjects. But as we set up more complex sets of experimental conditions[4] or as we begin to look at the environments of real life groups,[5] the experimenter or the observer may not know a great deal more about the environment than the subjects whose responses he is studying. In considerable measure, his knowledge of the environment comes from the people who make up the organization.

Working under these constraints, our best strategy for analyzing the environment is probably not to try to understand it as a collection of systems and organizations external to the one we are studying. We seldom have enough data to do an adequate job of this. Instead, we can view the environment as it affects the organization which we are studying. We treat the environment as information which becomes available to the organization or to which the organization, via search activity, may get access. It is not the supplier or the customer himself that counts, but the information that he makes accessible to the organization being studied about his goals, the conditions under which he will enter into a contract, or other aspects of his behavior.

Not all of the information that an organization receives or has access to is relevant to its goals and programs. To simplify the job of description and analysis that we do, we can focus our attention on those inputs which bear potentially on goal setting and on goal attainment within the organization. These elements form, for the organization, its *task environment.*[6] The boundaries of task environment are continually changing as people within the organization do things that affect the goals to which they subscribe and toward which they want to work. The boundaries also change as action sources outside the organization persuade it to change its goals.

Short-Run Patterns of Environmental Influence

In the short-run, it is difficult to discover clear relationships between the patterns of inputs that make up the task environment and the actions which an organization takes. Because of the sheer quantity and diversity of the inputs that are accessible and relevant, no organization is likely to notice or to attend to more than a small proportion of them. The information most readily accessible from the environment is not necessarily the most relevant to the goals which the organization is trying to achieve.

As a first link between environmental inputs and action, we need to understand the process by which information "enters" the organization and is recorded or stored for its use. This involves analysis of:

1. Organizational exposure to different kinds of information. A sales group, for example, may be better situated to pick up data about customer reactions than about competitors' plans for new products. One important task for them, in fact, may be to find ways to increase their exposure to information which concerns their competitors.

2. Organizational readiness to attend to and to store various environmental inputs. Training, experience, current expectations, and a variety of other factors may heighten the sensitivity of an organization to some kinds of information or leave it totally insensitive to others. If a workman in a plant, for example, suffers a severe eye injury, his supervisors and the staff safety engineers are likely to be especially alert during the next several weeks to conditions which indicate that such an injury might happen again and to ideas which would reduce such hazards in the future.

3. Organizational strategies for searching the environment. It is necessary for organizations to go after much

of the information that they use in planning future actions. We need to know about the conditions under which they will initiate active search; the kinds of sources that they consult; and the rules which they have for terminating search or for arranging routine access to some of the new sources of information that they find.

To carry through such an analysis, we need to know a good deal about the short-run patterns of environmental inputs that are accessible to the organization. We also need to know, as Figure 1 indicates, a good deal about the *programs* which the organization and its subunits use to govern contacts with the environment. These programs may be quite informal habits or traditions, such as a morning meeting of top supervisory personnel to scan the day's mail or to review informally the previous day's production, shipment, or accident record. They may range, at the other extreme, to complex, planned patterns of search for information—formal surveys of such things as market potential, employee attitudes, the cost performance of various departments, or the return on investment in new equipment.

The programs which govern organizational action at any particular time are not often generated or created in response to short-run patterns of inputs from the environment. They are often evoked, or "triggered," by current states of the environment; but they exist as a result of earlier, longer-term interactions with the environment. The generation of programs will be discussed below.

Once information from the environment has entered the organization's communication system, the next step is usually to ascribe meaning or relevance to it. Few environmental inputs provide

84 clearly defined prescriptions for organizational action. Instead, they provide cues which members of the organization can interpret in many different ways. A major organizational function, which has so far received relatively little attention in administrative research, involves evaluation, interpreting, and combining inputs into formulations of *tasks* for the organization to perform. Tasks are the organization's own statements of the goals that it wants to achieve and of the means by which it hopes to achieve them. Task statements are more readily communicated through the organization than many forms of raw environmental inputs; and depending how and by whom they are stated, they may carry more force and lead to closer control over the behavior of the men who are to implement them.

Environmental inputs influence task formulation within organizations several ways. Inputs may serve as:

1. "Triggers" to action. News that a competitor has cut prices or that a key piece of machinery has broken down does not necessarily tell members of an organization what kind of problem they are faced with. It does tell them, though, that a problem exists and serves to switch their attention from other things that they may have been working on.

2. Sources of information about goals. Organizations are not autonomous in their selection of goals; they are subject, as many authors have shown, to a number of direct and indirect outside influences. Some inputs may directly specify goals toward which the organization should be working and may carry the force of a directive. Others are specific in content, but only sugges-

tive in force. Still others may be quite ambiguous in content and force, leaving for the organization the task of interpreting and evaluating what they mean.

3. Source of information about means to achieve goals. A major problem for any organization is to select the means (or the subgoals) which will let it achieve major objectives. A great many helpful cues are available from the environment, often from the experiences of other organizations working toward similar goals. A major focus for active search efforts in most organizations stems from a desire to find new ways to achieve predetermined objectives.

4. Sources of information about constraints. Many environmental inputs serve directly or indirectly to constrain or to channel the direction in which the organization will move, not by the specification of goals or of means to attain them, but instead by setting limits and restrictions on action. Some, like an arbitrator's decision on a grievance, can be very explicit in their consequences for the organization; others, like rumors about employees' feelings, are vague but often equally effective.

5. Source of evaluations and judgments on organizational performance. An important class of inputs, closely related to the others listed above, are those which convey to the organization assessments of how well they are doing or evidence from which they can construct their own assessments.

The different kinds of environmental inputs are not clearly separable one from another. The way in which we classify any given set of inputs depends to a large extent on our observations of how the organization uses them. Sometimes a single input may perform more than one function for the organization. For example, in some of the automated systems that exist for process control in the chemical and petroleum industries and in the highly programmed operations of the order department of a large mail-order house, we already have a situation where a single input can trigger a long, multi-stage response.

In the process of interpreting environmental inputs for itself, an organization generally formulates more tasks than it has time or resources to carry through. A full theory of environmental influence on organizational behavior, then, requires a third stage which explains why some tasks are put on the agenda for actual performance and why others never get undertaken. Evidence suggests that important tasks do not always get first priority;[7] that routine tasks tend to drive out creative planning activities,[8] that interpersonal relationships among members of an organization may facilitate or block action on various tasks; that the source and the promulgators of a task influence its chances for performance;[9] and that in the process of performance, many tasks get redefined so that final actions bear little relationship to initial formulations.

To summarize, a theory of short-run environmental impact on organizational behavior needs three elements:

1. Propositions about the transfer of environmental information into the organization, both to explain transfers in which the organization simply receives and stores inputs and to explain transfers in which the organization actively searches for information.

2. Propositions about the ways in which the organization reacts to inputs and interprets them to formulate *tasks* for organizational action.

3. Propositions about the manner in which tasks get put onto an organization's action agenda and about the differential likelihood that various tasks will be carried through.

These elements are shown diagrammatically in Figure 1.

Long-Run Environmental Influence

To unravel the effects of immediate environmental inputs on organizational action, we need to consider the longer-term patterns of inputs to which the organization has been exposed. Consider, for example, the arrival of information that a supplier is raising the price of a raw material on which a company depends. We want to know whether members of management will become aware of the price change, how quickly and how accurately they will communicate this to the men within their group who need to know about it, and what they will decide to do about it. They may miss or ignore the change. They may recognize it, but decide that compensatory action on this is less important than action on other problems that they face. They may try to persuade —or to force—the supplier to reduce his price again. They may seek an alternative source of supply, or they may raise their prices to the consumer.

What happens will depend partly on other inputs (about such things as the decisions of other suppliers or the price elasticity of consumer demand) that are available to the management group at the time they hear about the supplier's decision. But a great deal depends on the structure of the organization, on the

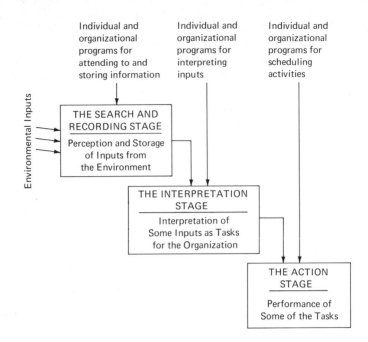

Figure 1. Short-Run Patterns of Environmental Influence

personnel that it has been able to attract and keep, on the experiences which the company has been through previously. These are products of earlier interaction with the environment, and they determine the programs which will be available to meet the new situation.

A rough model of longer-run influences on organizational development is outlined in Figure 2. Two kinds of influence need to be distinguished:

1. The concentrated influence of environmental factors at the time an organization is established or at times when it is threatened by a crisis in its relations with the environment. On such occasions, an organization is likely both to be more thorough in its analysis of the environment and to progress from an analysis of the environment to decisions and actions that will have significant long-run effects on its future programs.

2. The continuing, but less obvious, influence of environmental inputs as the main source of learning and "experience" within the organization.

As an organization begins to function, its founders and sponsors are apt to be more sensitive to environmental inputs and more anxious to seek them out than they will be at most later stages of the organization's history. At the same time, the decisions which they make take on particular significance because they determine who will staff the organization (and make future decisions), how the organization will be structured, and the basic goals and policies under which it will operate.[10]

For personnel decisions, environmental inputs provide basic information about what the organization needs and about the availability, the appropriateness, and the cost of getting certain individuals—or classes of individuals—

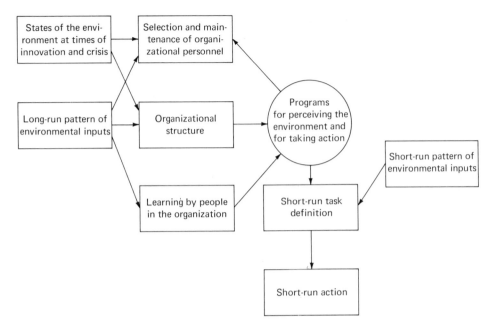

Figure 2. Long-Run Patterns of Environmental Influence

to join the organization. The key people selected have a long-range influence on others who are hired, and may in many cases have a great deal to say about the selection of their successors. They also become the arbiters in early disputes about the significance of states of the environment for the organization's policies and actions.

At the time of establishment or at times of crisis, organizations are concerned with other long-range decisions besides the selection of personnel. Environmental factors influence the choice of physical facilities—their adequacy for various kinds of technology, their location, their psychological attractiveness to the persons who must work in them. Information from the environment figures prominently in initial statements of organizational objectives and of procedures for operation —ranging from documents as lofty as the Constitution of our federal govern-

ment to the charters and by-laws of the East Jonesville Garden Club or the procedures manual of XYZ Company's sales department. Environmental conditions will affect the planners' judgments about the initial size and the projected rate of growth for the organization; the availability of capital and other resources for starting operations; and the "image" which the organization tries to create for itself with its participants, clients, and others with whom it deals.

The environment may even influence an organization's understanding of the need to build into its system ways of coping with future environmental pressures to change personnel, structure, and programs. Some organizations are set up in a way that permits them to respond effectively to new opportunities and new challenges, but many are not. Many of our states are hampered today by constitutions which, in the detail to which they specify and limit governmental action and in the hurdles that they set in the way of needed amendments, are quite inadequate to the needs of modern society. When the telephone was invented, a new company had to be established to exploit it. The telegraph industry, which had dominated communications until that time, was not interested in the new development. When radio was invented, again new companies had to be established because existing firms were unwilling to gamble on the invention. As Burns points out, the initial support for many inventions has come from the government, from dedicated individuals, and from new enterprises; not from the established organizations which have the most to gain by aiding the development (and sometimes, the most to lose by ignoring it).[11]

Little is known about the ways in which decisions made at the time an organization is established affect its later sensitivity to environmental inputs. The following propositions may merit further study:

1. An environment which gives members of a new organization the feeling that they must spell out their structure and their operating rules in detail in order to justify the appropriateness of these rules to existing conditions is likely to enhance the organization's chances for immediate survival at the expense of long-term adaptability.
2. An environment which creates pressures on members to publicize goals and policies and to differentiate them sharply from the goals and policies of other organizations will increase the costs of later changes in objectives.
3. Organizations which are estab-

lished under unstable environmental conditions will have poorer chances for short-run survival, but better chances for long-run survival than those which are established under stable conditions.
4. Organizations which are induced by technological factors and other external conditions to seek personnel who do not feel threatened by change, who have high levels of aspiration, and who are easily dissatisfied will be better able to adapt than organizations who seek other kinds of personnel.

The period of time taken to establish an organization and to get it functioning on a routine basis varies considerably. Real-life organizations often change form, personnel, and objectives several times at the beginning of their history.[12] Others stabilize early.[13] Environmental variables affect the speed with which different groups can develop a stable structure.[14] Once an organization is established, though, the importance of the environment to its long-run development does not die away. Environmental inputs provide the principal feedback to the organization about the soundness of its original decisions and about the appropriateness of short-run actions. The inputs form the basis of the organization's "experience" and lead, sometimes directly and sometimes quite subtly, to organizational learning.

Take, for example, two organizations which differ in the degree of personal autonomy which they allow to supervisory personnel. In a study which I made of two such companies, there were no differences between them in the extent to which supervisors were satisfied with the amount of autonomy they had or in the degree of change they wanted in relations with their peers and superiors. The reason was simple. One firm, and the industry in which it operated, had a reputation for offering a great deal of autonomy to supervisors; the other had a reputation in the other direction. Young men looking for supervisory careers took these differences into account as early as the time when they were planning their post-high school education. They were attentive to the differences when they chose their jobs, and if they found they had not made a satisfying choice, they were able to move to other companies. Thus, the steady-state supervisory group in one company got—and expected—a great deal of autonomy; in the other, they were expected to be—and were willing to be—dependent.

The persistent pattern of inputs from the environment over the long-run also modifies organizational objectives and programs. In responding to current inputs, an organization makes many minor changes in direction and procedure. One of the main problems of organization control is to recognize and to limit such changes, so that major objectives and programs will not be whittled away. This is not easy to manage; and it is not uncommon for a series of new environmental inputs to lead an organization, in several small stages, to reverse a stand which it had taken earlier.[15]

Finally, the environment plays an important part in remaking personalities within the organization. The degree to which the personality of individuals in their adult years can be changed is a matter both of honest conjecture and of semantics. If by personality we mean the first-level programs which govern individual choices and action, rather than more elusive traits and latent structures, there is much evidence that men do change in response to their environment.[16] We do not have much sys-tematic evidence of the impact of the environment on the men who are subjected to it—except perhaps in the study of physical and nervous breakdowns.[17] Most attention currently is placed on the effects on individuals of stress and of organizational pressures to conform.[18] These aspects of industrial experience are important, but we should not neglect more beneficial aspects of experience. Of the large number of college graduates, for example, who enter industry each year with management aspirations, only a relatively small number grow and develop to the point where these are realized. The role of the environment that these men are exposed to is an important one, but it is one that we know very little about.[19]

Multiple Environments for an Organization

So far we have proceeded as if there were one environment to analyze and understand for any organization which we wanted to study. For some gross questions, such an assumption is appropriate; but if we are trying to understand behavior within most real organizations, the assumption breaks down. Individuals and subgroups within organizations do not have the same task environments. The goals which are relevant to them include local and personal, as well as organizational, objectives. The conditions under which they have access to different kinds of information vary widely. Instead of representing a common exposure to a common environment, the actions that they take in interaction with one another represent the direct confrontation of different exposures.

Even in situations where the parties presumably have access to the same information, they may interpret it quite differently. Consider again the question of managerial autonomy. The amount of autonomy that a man has depends not only on his own actions, but on the actions of people around him. To be autonomous, he must choose independent strategies of behavior rather than seek to rely on others; but to be successfully autonomous, he must be permitted to act independently. Figure 3 shows some of the variables that influenced the amount of autonomy that men had in the organizations mentioned above and illustrates, particularly, the way in which individuals with different environments or different interpretations of their environment could have affected any one man's chances for independent action.

A Concluding Note

Most of the work of developing an adequate theory of environmental influences on organizational behavior lies ahead. Considerable work is now being done, and two directions of study seem particularly promising. One is an attempt to dimensionalize environmental variables in the same way that we have tried to dimensionalize variables of human personality and intelligence. This requires considerable faith in the adequacy of such techniques as factor analysis and the linearly independent dimensions that such techniques generate to represent significant influences on other variables that we want to study. Such faith abounds, though; and some imaginative steps have been taken to isolate the relevant dimensions of the environments in which group leaders perform,[20] in which students at various colleges and universities function,[21] and

in which college graduates take their first jobs.[22]

The second direction of investigation is more consistent with the approach that I have suggested here. This is the effort to conceptualize individuals or organizations as information processing systems and then to simulate, usually with the aid of electronic computers and related "hardware," the environment to which they are exposed. Such an approach is characteristic of the systems simulations which have been done for the armed forces;[23] the work of Newell, Shaw, and Simon[24] and others[25] on human thinking and problem-solving; and the efforts to develop "management games."[26] The trick in building a model of the environment under such circumstances is not in isolating characteristic factors or dimensions, but in writing programs and setting up systems to generate and to present information to an individual or an organization in the same manner that the "real world" would. At one level, our theory of the environment is the mechanism which we devise to simulate it; but at another level, as we gain more experience in simulation and develop more common languages in which to state our models and by which to compare them, we should be able to generalize more meaningfully than we now can about classes of environments and classes of environment-organization relationships.

We can look ahead, too, toward being able to develop new theories about organizations in interaction, where each becomes a significant element in the task environment of the others. Some of the work already being done in the simulation of large military systems is contributing to the development of such theories.

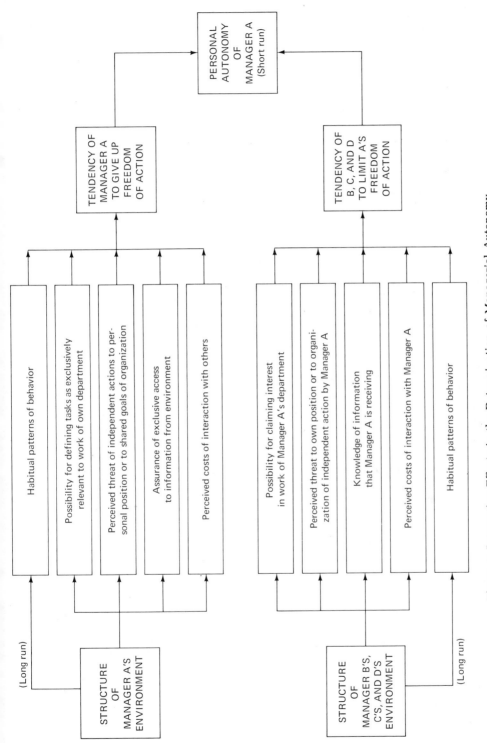

Figure 3. Interaction Effects in the Determination of Managerial Autonomy

1. See L. Coch and J. R. P. French, "Overcoming Resistance to Change," in D. Cartwright and A. Zander, *Group Dynamics* (Evanston: Row, Peterson, 1953), pp. 257–279; or in E. Maccoby, T. Newcomb, and E. Hartley, *Readings in Social Psychology* (New York: Holt, Rinehart & Winston, 1958), pp. 233–250.

2. This, to me, is a weakness in the original Coch and French report on their results. Their discussion and their theory (to say nothing of subsequent restatements by others, for which Coch and French are not responsible) stress the effects of participation in decision making. Before any decisions were made, though, management told the experimental groups (but not the control group) the reasons for change "as dramatically as possible." The possible effects of such a presentation—cognitive as well as motivational—are slighted by the authors in their discussion.

3. J. R. P. French, J. Israel, and D. Ås, "An Experiment on Participation in a Norwegian Factory," 13 *Human Relations* (1960), 3–20. A summary of these results is appended to the reprints of the original Coch and French paper cited above.

4. See, for example, R. L. Chapman and others, "The Systems Research Laboratory's Air Defense Experiments," 5 *Management Science* (1960), 250–269.

5. E. Ginzberg and others, *The Ineffective Soldier* (New York: Columbia, 1959); W. R. Dill, "Environment as an Influence Autonomy" in J. D. Thompson and others, *Comparative Studies in Administration* (Pittsburgh: University of Pittsburgh, 1960), 131–161.

6. This concept comes from the work of A. Newell and others on the air-defense simulations at the RAND Corporation. See Chapman and others, *op. cit.*

7. Dill, *op. cit.,* p. 154.

8. J. G. March and H. A. Simon, *Organizations* (New York: Wiley, 1958), p. 185.

9. H. Guetzkow and W. R. Dill, "Factors in the Organizational Development of Task-oriented Groups," 20 *Sociometry* (1957), pp. 175–204.

10. Consider, for example, a business game in which players have to decide which of 46 possible "decision questions" need attention in a given period of play. The backgrounds of the men who are selected to play and their initial assessment of the environment seem to carry a good deal of weight in the planning of their agenda throughout the game. If a decision area appears important on the first move, it is more likely to be put on the agenda for later moves. Taking the experience of two teams over 16 moves, we find:

Action on first move	No. of decision areas	Number of times considered (out of a possible 16 moves) Median	Range
Considered by both teams	10	13	4–16
Considered by one team	9	6	1–16
Considered by neither team	27	4	0–11

11. T. Burns and G. M. Stalker, *The Management of Innovation* (Edinburgh: Social Sciences Research Center, 1959), chapter II.

12. H. A. Simon, "Birth of an Organization: The Economic Cooperation Administration," 13 *Public Administration Review* (1953), 227–236.

13. H. Guetzkow and A. E. Bowes, "The Development of Organizations in a Laboratory," 3 *Management Science* (1957), 380–402.

14. H. Guetzkow and H. A. Simon, "The Impact of Certain Communication Nets upon Organization and Performance in Task-oriented Groups," 1 *Management Science* (1955), 233–250.

15. R. M. Cyert and others, "The Role of Expectations in Business Decision Making," 3 *Administrative Science Quarterly* (1958), 307–340.

INFORMATION AND TECHNOLOGICAL INPUTS

16. Writing this in the heat of the presidential campaign, it would be amusing to hear personality theorists, with their measures of basic traits to defend, debate the politicians, who are trying to persuade the voters how the candidates of both parties have grown and will continue to grow if elected.
17. See Ginzberg and others, *op. cit.*
18. C. Argyris, *Personality and Organization* (New York: Harper, 1957); W. H. Whyte, *The Organization Man* (New York: Simon and Schuster, 1956).
19. Studies are under way in at least three graduate schools of business (Carnegie, Harvard, and M.I.T.) to learn more about this. The work at Carnegie involves a study of the process by which its graduates progress toward managerial jobs and includes environmental influences as a major class of variables.
20. J. Hemphill, *Situational Factors in Leadership* (Columbus: Ohio State, 1949).
21. C. R. Pace and A. McFee, "The College Environment," 30 *Review of Educational Research* (1960), 311–320.
22. L. B. Ward has undertaken such a study for graduates of Harvard Business School.
23. Chapman and others, *op. cit.*; S. Enke, "On the Economic Management of Large Organizations: a Laboratory Study," 31 *Journal of Business* (1958), 280–292; R. M. Rauner, "Laboratory Evaluation of Supply and Procurement Procedures" (RAND Corporation report R-323, 1958).
24. A. Newell and H. A. Simon, "The Simulation of Human Thought," (RAND Corporation paper P-1734, 1959); W. R. Reitman, "Heuristic Programs, Computer Simulation and Higher Mental Processes," 3 *Behavioral Science* (1959), 330–335.
25. A. L. Samuel, "Some Studies in Machine Learning Using the Game of Checkers," 3 *IBM Journal of Research and Development* (1959), 210–229; O. C. Selfridge and V. Neisser, "Pattern Recognition," 203 *Scientific American* (August 1960), 60–68.
26. K. J. Cohen and others, "The Carnegie Tech Management Game," *Journal of Business* (October 1960).

TECHNOLOGY, ORGANIZATION, AND ADMINISTRATION

James D. Thompson and Frederick L. Bates

Large-scale organizations have evolved to achieve goals which are beyond the capacities of the individual or the small group. They make possible the application of many and diverse skills and resources to complex systems of producing goods and services. Large-scale organizations, therefore, are particularly adapted to complicated *technologies*, that is, to those sets of man-machine activities which together produce a desired good or service.[1]

"Technology, Organization, and Administration," *Administrative Science Quarterly*, 2, 3 (December 1957), 325–343. Reprinted with the permission of the authors and of the publisher, the *Administrative Science Quarterly*.

As scientific knowledge has led to increasingly complicated technologies, large-scale organizations have multiplied; they have become necessary in new fields, and they have changed their characteristics. Medical care affords a striking illustration, for in this area the technology has been revolutionized within a generation. From reliance on a few simple home remedies, passed from generation to generation, and ultimate resource to a general practitioner with standard prescriptions for standard symptoms, health-care practice in Western cultures has moved to a much more specialized, more highly divided technology. The diagnostic equipment and procedures used by the physician are no longer simply constructed and exercised, and prescriptions are no longer blended from a small list of basic powders and essences easily stocked by any local pharmacist. The "simple" treatment of a virus infection, for example, now relies on a whole series of large-scale organizations which perform research, produce pharmaceuticals, and ship, store, and prepare medications. Certain conditions which once required confinement of the patient to the home with nursing by other (amateur) members of the family now call for confinement in the hospital, where a battery of technical specialists, nurses, and dietitians can contribute specialized skills toward therapy.

The list of examples is endless, illustrating the point that the elaboration of technology usually means that activities which formerly were considered single units of effort are dissected and split into multiple units of effort, each of them specialized and highly developed. With this "elongation" of the technology comes increasing complexity of the social organization designed to operate it.

In the following paragraphs we will explore some of the ways in which technology, as a variable, may impinge on organization and on administration. We will develop the general proposition that the type of technology available and suitable to particular types of goals sets limits on the types of structures appropriate for organizations and that the functional emphases, the problems of greatest concern, and the processes of administration will vary as a result. For this exploratory effort, we will focus on four types or organizations: the mining enterprise, the manufacturing organization, the hospital, and the university. While these clearly do not exhaust the major types of organizations, they have sufficiently different goals and technologies to serve as illuminating examples.[2] The discussion necessarily will be general; we are seeking central tendencies. Each class of organization displays variations. This is particularly true in the field of manufacturing, and to make the discussion manageable we will conceive of a factory mass-producing a single line of products widely distributed to consumers. Moreover, references to technology will be based on present technology.

We will compare these types of organizations with respect to three broad functional areas of administration: the setting of objectives, or policy formulation; the management of resources (including people, authority structure, money, and materials); and execution.[3]

Determination of Objectives

Whatever the motives of its members—accumulating wealth, achieving fame, exercising power, and so on—an enterprise must in the long run produce something useful or acceptable to others in order to merit support. The determination of what the enterprise will seek to produce we will refer to as the determination of objectives or goals or, alternatively, as policy formulation.

The manufacturing enterprise may have difficulty in determining what particular demands of what potential customers it will attempt to satisfy, and this is especially true in dynamic and highly competitive markets. Unless the product is extremely costly, however, or costs vary greatly with variations in volume, the manufacturing enterprise may test its decision through pilot operations. In any event the acceptance of the product is rather quickly and accurately reflected in sales figures or ultimately in profit figures, and reappraisal of decisions regarding objectives can therefore be rapid. If reappraisal leads to a redefinition of objectives, capital goods including machinery and raw materials can often be adapted to the new purpose or be sold, so that the manufacturing enterprise may be able to convert effectively from one objective to another; the technology may be relatively flexible. Finally, policy determination in the manufacturing enterprise is largely a matter for top administrators.

The mine is less flexible. It possesses highly specialized equipment and property rights which for the most part cannot be converted to other major objectives. The objectives of the mine may be adjusted to the extent that it may offer new sizes, grades, packaging, or delivery arrangements and hence may cater to a new market, but those responsible for the mining enterprise would find it difficult to get it out of mining and into a different industry—or even to shift from the mining of coal to the mining of a different mineral. The scope of alternative objectives thus appears to be less for those enterprises with heavy, specialized capital investments.

In both the university and the hospital the general or abstract purpose of the enterprise is relatively fixed. But in both cases there is wide latitude for interpretation of the general into more specific objectives. Because knowledge is so specialized the members of the university must decide what it will teach, and as new areas of knowledge develop or split off, they must decide anew. Here the product is intangible, and reappraisal of the policy decision is difficult and drawn out. Furthermore, because of the heterogeneity of university objectives and departments, top administrative officers can reappraise decisions only in gross or general terms; professional members specialized in the particular subject can claim greater qualification to judge. The university president is also highly dependent on that professional staff to interpret and implement a new educational policy. Hence, in a real sense, power to determine or veto objectives in the university is widely diffused.

The hospital, likewise, is highly dependent in the matter of objectives on the decisions of its professional medical members, who are the obvious authorities on health matters and who in the final analysis must implement the policy they believe in. Any shift in emphasis, for example, from treatment of the ill to maintenance of health can become effective only through the persuasion and conviction of professional members.

Thus in both the university and the hospital the general goal of the organization specifies an area of activity instead of a specific activity and therefore is subject to wide differences in specific interpretations. Since the technology employed by both types of organizations is relatively flexible as compared to that of the factory or the mine, goals may be revised or adjusted more easily to the technological resources available.

It appears, therefore, that the following variables are of particular importance as conditions affecting policy formulation:

(1) *Degree of concreteness of the goal,* as expressed in the product. This is a matter of tangibility and is verbally expressed by such questions as the precision with which the product can be described, the specificity with which it can be identified, and the extent to which it can be measured and evaluated.

(2) *Adaptability of the technology* associated with the goal. Here the question is the extent to which the appropriate machines, knowledge, skills, and raw materials can be used for other products.

While these definitions have not been operationalized, they seem to be adequate for our exploratory purposes, and we can advance the following hypotheses regarding these two variables and their relationships to policy formulation:

(1) If the product is concrete, such as mined material, and the technology unadaptable, the major concerns over policy will be the possibility that the environment may reject or dispense with the product. This is happening now in the case of the tuberculosis hospital, for example.

(2) If the product is concrete or tangible and the technology adaptable, the major concerns over policy will be when to shift to new products and which of the possible alternative uses of the technology present the most favorable opportunities. For example, should the watch manufacturer shift to cosmetic jewelry, to armament mechanisms, or to still another product calling for the machinery and skills at his disposal?

(3) If the product is abstract and the technology adaptable, the organization again has great adaptability to its environment, and the major policy-formulation problem will be achieving agreement on goals and on the appropriate application of technologies in pursuit of them. The modern university, for example, seems torn between emphasis on applied and on traditional studies; the National Foundation for Infantile Paralysis is seeking new causes to support, having all but achieved its original purpose.

(4) If the product is abstract but the technology unadaptable, environmental redefinition of goals presents a serious threat to the organization, since the technology can be adapted to redefined goals only within limits. The administrative problem here is to "educate" or influence relevant parts of the environment to accept those products which are possible with existing technology. Political parties and fundamentalist churches seem to be facing this problem in modern America.

Management of Resources

Every enterprise has problems of acquiring and employing people, finances, materials, and authority. The difficulties of management are not necessarily equal in each of these four resource areas, however, and the amount of attention given to each probably varies from enterprise to enterprise as well as within one enterprise at different stages of its development. Likewise, the content of those activities which serve to manage any one resource varies, as the following paragraphs will illustrate.

MANAGEMENT OF MANPOWER

The factory and the mine, as enterprises operating on physical objectives, have relatively few problems of personnel selection below the management level, since the operational activities are either standardized or are settled by experience, and the training of operators is not overly difficult. There may be a high degree of functional differentiation in the factory, but this differentiation tends to be based on the machine rather than on the operator; operation of a complicated machine may be so simplified and repetitive that individuals are relatively interchangeable. Hierarchical distinctions tend to be shaded or gradual, with normal skill and experience qualifying the operator for advancement. Vacancies, therefore, can be filled from below. Since machinery is so important, a major personnel-management problem is to ensure safety in its operation.

Because many members of the general population are potentially qualified as members of the factory or the mine and because training to entrance-level standards is quick, expansion of activities may be undertaken on relatively short notice. Long-range forecasting of personnel needs may be an important factor in factory location, but "personnel-development" or training programs can be confined largely to preparation for future executive or supervisory positions. The large percentage of operative personnel, coupled with an open hierarchy, provides the factory enterprise with opportunity to screen members on the job and hence to locate future supervisory or executive talents. This is less likely in the mine, where the division between those working above and below ground is rather sharp, and mobility between these categories is low. In the mine, moreover, flexibility of daily operations is necessary because of the lack of control over the natural environment from which the material is taken. This front-line flexibility requires the exercise of judgment, and hence experience is a major basis for functional and hierarchical differentiation.

Both the hospital and the university must rely heavily on professionally trained people. In the case of the hospital, moreover, the situation is complicated by the fact that some of the key professionals are not employees of the hospital, in the sense of being on the pay roll. They are not, therefore, recruited as employees. This is true also for many supporting activities which are performed by a voluntary "staff." Functional differentiation is extreme in both the hospital and university, and the intensity of training required for each special area is so great that interchangeability is virtually unknown. There is sharp differentiation between student, clerical, and professional ranks in the university, as well as little opportunity within a given university for a member to move from one level to another. Similar distinctions exist between patient, nurse, and doctor levels in the hospital. The length and cost of medical training mean that for practical purposes members cannot move from one category to a higher category; experience and seniority have nothing to do with a nurse's becoming a doctor.

The long periods of training required for professional competence in universities and hospitals mean that recruitment of professionals is not easy. On-the-job training may enhance the member's value within his specialty, but it is not a major means of obtaining replacements for vacancies in upper-level jobs. Moreover, while professional recognition or licensing presumably guarantees a minimum level of competence, there are many shades of ability above that minimum which are not easily judged until the individual member has already been established in the enterprise.

TECHNOLOGY, ORGANIZATION, AND ADMINISTRATION

Thus in the modern factory and mine the technology relies largely on mechanical facilities supported by "know-how" which grows out of familiarity with the mechanical operation. But in the hospital and university, even complicated mechanical devices play second fiddle to professional expertise which is wrapped up in the human being and which grows out of long exposure to academic and abstract systems of thought. These differences are reflected in recruitment, allocation, and training of personnel.

MANAGEMENT OF AUTHORITY STRUCTURE

In the factory, authority may be highly centralized or, conversely, the discretion of individual operators may be severely circumscribed, since activities are relatively routine and engineering standards such as quality controls can be used extensively. Particularly where various subassembly products feed into a final assembly line, central direction of the speed of operations and of the size, quality, or color mix is essential. The factory also has problems in maintaining a recognized position of authority for the supervisor, since experience tends to be a major basis for supervisory selection and the "boss" was formerly "one of us."

The mine, too, is predominantly staffed by "blue-collar" members, but the lack of standardization of the environment, together with distance and communication difficulties, requires a more decentralized day-to-day operation, with greater discretion lodged in the mine team and the supervisor. Constant danger, coupled with discomfort and darkness, makes members of the mining team somewhat reluctant to ac-

cept authoritative communications from executives above ground, and the mining enterprise probably would run into severe resistance if it attempted to set up and enforce rigid, disciplinary communications. Instead, authority or the exercise of discretion tends to be based on familiarity with the problem, and hence it is lodged in the most experienced member of the work team.

In the university, traditionally dominated by professional persons, authority on educational matters must be highly decentralized, since knowledge rather than title or seniority is recognized as the basis for authority—as reflected in "academic freedom"—and knowledge is highly specialized. Discretion in academic activities is controlled less by university executives than by professional peers of the faculty member. Student members of the university are more subject to centralized authority, but this is limited by a tradition that faculty members determine academic or educational policies, and anything which affects the student can be construed as an educational matter.

The authority structure of the modern hospital is an even more complicated matter. Since treatment of patients is not easily standardized, judgment must be exercised frequently by those with greatest knowledge of the case. The professional physician has the greatest knowledge about the ailment or disease, but on the other hand the nurse who is with the patient much more often may believe she has more knowledge of the patient. The social distance between physician and nurse is great, however, and the exercise of authority by the physician tends to be resented by the nurse (or vice versa) unless a strong informal organization bridges the two ranks. The bridging of this gap may be helped by the fact that both the nurse and the doctor know that the nurse cannot really threaten the doctor's position either in the hospital or in the larger community.

Thus it appears that in the mine and the factory, which rely heavily on mechanical aspects of the technology, authority is allocated primarily as control over the mechanical operation and takes the form of authority over people to the extent that behavior must be disciplined to the requirements of the mechanical operation. In the hospital and university, however, the heavy reliance on human (professional) abilities means that authority is exercised primarily with reference to people. Lacking the mechanical referent to bolster authoritative behavior, the university and hospital must depend to a much greater extent upon agreement or consensus, backed up by professional ethics and standards.

MATERIALS MANAGEMENT

The factory is concerned with acquiring and changing things, and there is emphasis, therefore, on moving inventory and on plant and machinery. Achieving volume and quality at low cost usually requires routinization of operations, and this in turn requires standardization of raw materials. Because a steady flow of standardized raw materials is so important to the factory and often constitutes a rather high portion of costs, purchasing, inventory, and transportation procedures attract a large amount of attention in day-to-day operations. The emphasis on precision scheduling and on predictability of production means that equipment failure may seriously cripple an entire operation, and preventive maintenance receives much

time and thought. Control over use of materials can be approached in the factory through measurement of spoilage or waste. Since standardization is high, deviation can be measured readily. Hence responsibility for materials management can be widely diffused in the factory.

In the mining enterprise, rights to deposits replace plant as a major concern, and preventive maintenance and steps to control the sources of the mineral against flooding, cave-ins, and so on are particularly important. These can be standardized only in a rough way, and therefore judgment must be exercised frequently. Furthermore, maximum "winning" of the material must be balanced against risk to personnel and to the remaining deposits. Machinery is cumbersome and difficult to move, hence effective placement is important. Purchasing is not the major matter in the mine that it is in the factory, but shipping is extremely important, since storage facilities can be depleted rapidly by the bulky product, and breakdown of transportation facilities can lead to shutdown of operations. Materials management in the mine is by and large a matter for supervisory and executive personnel rather than for operators.

Both the hospital and the university have important interests in plant, since both deal with people (who are "bulky") and both must provide space and facilities for a variety of human needs, including sleeping, eating, and recreation. Management frequently involves decisions as to the allocation of activities to various parts of the physical plant as shifts occur in technological procedures or in work loads.

Since in the university symbolic materials are major aids to the student and instructor, the collection, storage, and issuance of books require constant attention. These materials, moreover, are far from standardized and are highly specialized, so that judgment regarding new materials must be exercised constantly and must be made frequently by the instructor concerned. Again, because symbolic materials are easily lost, stolen, or damaged, rigorous procedures must be established to maintain inventories.

The hospital has additional complications, since many of its expendable materials are highly specialized, easily confused, and perishable and since the hospital must be prepared for any of a variety of possible emergencies. Improper storage or errors in labeling medicines can be extremely costly, and the hospital often must rely on the health team to exercise care and discretion in these matters. Professional standards, reinforced by dread of being the cause of human suffering or loss of life, facilitate this decentralization of responsibility. Nevertheless the hospital provides a number of security routines, including the keeping of complete accounts of the disposal of certain materials and restriction on the identity of persons who can withdraw or use them.

MANAGEMENT OF MONEY

During periods of economic stability, at least, the manufacturing firm may be able to estimate its money needs rather accurately. Since its inventories and other assets are largely tangible, it can obtain needed money by frank exchange of the product for cash, by pledging assets as collateral, or by sale of an interest in the firm. Hence frequently the question of acquisition of money becomes one of seeking the most favorable terms, and large errors in such decisions can be detected relatively rapidly. During growth periods, however, investment matters may become more compli-

cated, involving broader and less easily established alternatives and considerable risk. Expenditure of available money can be allocated within the manufacturing enterprise on the basis of expected return on yield and can be controlled by budgetary and accounting procedures, since standardization and predictability are relatively great. While neither allocation nor control are foolproof, such procedures are effective in the factory, and operating members can be held responsible for costs.

The mining enterprise can estimate its needs for money less precisely, since the cost of winning coal or ore is never perfectly known in advance, and disaster or geological fault may abruptly increase costs. Acquisition of money is again more difficult; reserves are less easily pledged as collateral than are the easily accessible inventories of the manufacturing firm. Allocation of available money may be budgeted on the basis of periodic estimates, but the technological requirements for flexibility may require frequent change of these programs. Formal control over the expenditure of money remains rather centralized, since the miner tends to be more safety conscious than cost conscious; and because mining operations call for judgment by the mining team, economic use of costly resources is not easily ensured.

For the university the determination of need is not difficult on the face of it, since enrollments and other costs can be fairly well forecast. But the intangibility of the product means that whether enough money has been raised is always a moot question. Acquisition, especially for the privately financed university, is a constant problem because those who most directly benefit from university activities usually are not able to pay the total costs for their training, and it is difficult to demonstrate graphically to potential contributors the indirect benefits they receive from the university's activities. Financial support rests largely on appeal, not trade.

Allocation of money is a time-consuming activity in the university. It cannot be accomplished by a few central officers because the various departments of a university are so specialized that there are few standards for evaluating the strength of their claims to scarce money. Control of expenditures through budgeting and accounting practices is relatively easy, although it tends to be accomplished only through administrative policing, since professional members of the university tend to place knowledge values above cost values.

Monetary needs of the hospital can be determined reasonably well; although work loads may vary widely from day to day or week to week, general trends can be predicted and irregularities averaged out. Acquisition of needed funds, however, presents another and more important problem, for the hospital in our culture is expected to render service on the basis of health needs rather than on ability to pay, and recovery of expenses often has been a drawn-out procedure. As far as operating costs are concerned, hospitalization insurance is relieving this problem, but capital funds still are difficult to acquire.[4] Allocation of funds may depend partly on budget procedures, but changes in work loads or new technological developments may require frequent revision. Control over the use of funds is accomplished largely by centralized handling of purchasing, but professional norms of service sometimes conflict with cost-reduction norms, and professional personnel tend to feel that cost drives interfere with their activities. Control over expenditure of items which eventually are translated into monetary terms is therefore some-what difficult. Waste and spoilage are not easily checked.

Implications of Change for Resource Management

From the foregoing section, it appears that an important variable distinguishing various types of organizations is the extent to which the technology is lodged in human as contrasted with nonhuman resources. For the sake of simplicity we will refer to this variable as the *ratio of mechanization to professionalization*. Reflecting this variable against the *adaptability of the technology*, discussed earlier, it is possible to hypothesize the following:

(1) If the technology of an organization has a high ratio of mechanization and is readily adaptable, the major resource problem involved in a change of product is likely to center around properly standardized raw materials.

(2) If the technology of an organization has a high ratio of mechanization but is not adaptable, the problem will be to avoid technological obsolescence; major resource concerns will involve materials and money and the maintenance of fluidity by amassing financial reserves.

(3) If the technology has a low ratio of mechanization but the human abilities are easily refocused on new products, the major problems are likely to be those involved in execution, to be discussed below.

(4) If the technology has a low ratio of mechanization and at the same time is not easily adapted to other goals, personnel-management problems are likely to come to the fore, with emphasis on replacing and retraining members of the organization.

The problem of welding an enterprise into an integrated whole varies with the amount and kinds of differentiation of its parts and with the kinds of relationships which the technological process requires; that is, different kinds of heterogeneity call for different ways of homogenizing. The technology appropriate to a particular purpose not only determines in an important way the extent and type of differentiation but also determines the amount of coordination and cooperation required and the locus of responsibility for these.

The manufacturing enterprise, for example, may have major need for sequential interdependence, with each work team or section depending on others only for the timely and satisfactory completion of certain prior operations. Coordination required by this type of interdependence can be achieved largely by work scheduling and controls over the flow of materials and the quality of operations. In the factory, then, coordination between individual members of the work team may be the responsibility of an on-the-spot supervisor, but the linking together of various functional activities can be achieved largely by executives at relatively centralized points in the enterprise.

Mining involves separation or removal of minerals from their environment, and mining operations are therefore subject to unpredictable environmental changes —water seepage, geological faults, cave-ins, gas pockets, and so forth. Routinization is not easily achieved, and even with mechanized equipment environmental changes may make schedules inapplicable. The judgment of the miner is therefore indispensable, and the communication difficulties introduced by the above-ground and below-ground dichot-omy increase the importance of the miner's reliability. Because day-to-day activities are somewhat unpredictable, relationships among members of the mining team can be specified only abstractly; specific relationships must be worked out on the spot, spatial requirements present close constant supervision, and coordination therefore is highly dependent on the informal organization.

Routinization of many aspects of hospital activity is essential, both to prevent dangerous omissions or oversights and to provide some predictability as the basis for carrying on when crises occur. On the other hand, each medical case is considered unique, and hence considerable flexibility (based on professional judgment) is required. To a much greater extent than in the factory, the hospital has need for collateral coordination, with the nurse, doctor, laboratory technician, dietitian, and so on integrating their activities simultaneously around the needs of the patient. In these cases central executives may act to facilitate coordination, but in the final analysis it must come largely through the cooperative efforts of operating individuals. Moreover, while there is ordinarily a certain rhythm in the amount and type of attention required during each twenty-four-hour period, the patient is an around-the-clock charge and requires periodic attention. Hence communication between shifts is vital, and there is considerable attention given to accurate posting of elaborate records. Nevertheless the specialized and complicated nature of medical technology means that records and charts cannot convey everything of importance, and informal organization of the therapy team is essential.

In the university routinization of a superficial sort is easily achieved. Hours of class meetings, systems of examinations and grading, and so forth usually are standardized. But in teaching matters routinization is not easily achieved because the imparting of knowledge remains a matter of judgment. The ability of the instructor to inspire and motivate the student cannot be centralized, and the integration of extracurricular activities can be centralized only partially. The instructor is free to maintain that he and only he can determine what his students should know and how they should proceed to acquire that knowledge about his special area of competence. Routinization tends, therefore, to be by discipline or topic rather than university-wide, and standardization is accomplished more by professional codes and standards than by administrative directive. Traditionally there is little interdependence between faculty members; although it is recognized that each deals with only "part" of the student, the integration of these part activities has been up to the student or is accomplished through informal interaction among faculty members and students. Faculty members typically are "not interested" in administrative matters except to escape interference by administrators, but the faculty may involve itself in many matters outside the classroom under the guise of "educational policy," since the development of the "whole" student is believed to result from his total experience in the university setting.

Under the more standardized conditions of the manufacturing firm, and to a lesser extent the mine, coordination can be planned and controlled relatively effectively from the center. In the less standardized, more professional fields, this is less likely to be the case—but at the same time more types of supporting activities usually are required. In the hospital and university these include feeding, housing, providing recreation, and providing opportunities for spiritual or religious expression, and so on.

Thus while responsibility for the integration of primary operations is relatively diffuse in professional-type enterprises, central executives tend to have a greater variety of activities and departments to integrate. Generally, it would seem, the greater the differentiation of an enterprise into identifiable parts, the greater is the need for fitting those parts together. Add to this the fact that human beings set themselves apart from one another on bases other than those officially arranged by administrators—on such bases as sex, age, ethnic origin, religion, style of living, political views, professional or union affiliations, and so on, and one perceives that the heterogeneity of the modern enterprise can be amazing.

Every criterion for differentiation of functions or hierarchy presents a possible or potential basis for cleavage and conflict—for the withholding of cooperation. Hence the more functional or hierarchical distinctions there are within the enterprise, the greater the problems of integration. Since systems low in mechanization of the technology and high in professionalization tend to be more clearly differentiated in this respect, it is in this kind of system that coordination problems are greatest.

Furthermore, it is in the enterprises where human differentiation is greatest that collateral types of coordination are most required, and hence interaction between people of various categories is the more intense. This interaction among people who are different or who have been led to believe they are different means that interpersonal frictions or tensions are to be expected. And yet it is in these same enterprises that interpersonal interaction must carry much of the burden for necessary coordination. In the hospital and the university, then, leadership in the form of emphasizing objectives and of stressing such factors as common devotion to a cause loom more important than they do in the manufacturing enterprise or the mine. And while resource management is important in the hospital and the university, the problems this presents are less demanding on the administrator than are those of executing.

The following hypotheses can now be advanced, based on the variable *ratio of mechanization* as it is related to the executing function of administration:

(1) If the technology has a high ratio of mechanization, executing problems are likely to be of an engineering nature since specialization is largely in the machine, the bases for human differentiation are small, and the human "zones of indifference" are great.

(2) If the technology has a low ratio of mechanization, however, the coordination and integration of human activities will be a major administrative concern. Members of the organization differentiate among themselves as specialists, a distinction leading to problems of status and authority relationships. Any change in technology is likely to upset established relationships among members. Furthermore, if the goal is abstract, there is likely to be disagreement over the interpretation of the goal in terms of products; the human "zones of indifference" are small.[5]

Conclusions

The foregoing paragraphs have attempted to illustrate some of the differences that various goals—and appropriate technologies—can make for organization and administration. At one level of analysis, all large organizations have similar problems, but at a more detailed level of analysis, these problems become variables.

We have attempted to show that the following three variables are important enough to deserve extended research: (1) abstractness of the goal, as expressed in the product, (2) adaptability of the technology, and (3) ratio of mechanization to professionalization of the technology. We may perhaps underscore our argument that the general relationships between technology, organization, and administration provide important areas for study by advancing a final set of more general propositions:

(1) An organization overly identified with a particular technology may lose its opportunity to produce a particular product as more effective technologies are adopted by other organizations pursuing the same goal. This proposition simply applies the concept of "trained incapacity" to the organizational level rather than the personal level.[6]

(2) As a technology becomes more specialized, it appears that the organization's flexibility in shifting from one goal to another is curtailed. The corporation desiring to withdraw from a given industry, for example, no longer rearranges its resources once applied to that industry, but rather sells a division or subsidiary as a unit to another corporation.

(3) As a technology becomes more complicated, entry of a new organization into a field becomes more difficult. Entrance seems to occur usually in the case of (a) an existing organization with tremendous resources, shifting part of those into a new field, or (b) the formation of a new enterprise at a time when a new technology is appearing; by avoiding problems of relearning and reequipping itself, the new organization

may be able to exploit a new technology more advantageously than an established organization.

(4) As a technology becomes elongated, any particular organization will tend to have less control over the total technological process, to be more dependent on other organizations for prior or subsequent operations in the total process (for resources and so on). This, again, tends to reduce flexibility in deciding goals and managing resources. The increased dependence on specialists, for example, means greater reliance on pretraining of personnel by organizations specializing in that training, such as universities and institutes.

(5) The organization adapting to new technology—as most are doing constantly—will be faced with "new" resource-management problems which established procedures and strategies will not always handle satisfactorily. Hence improvisation and constant learning will be characteristic of such organizations.

(6) Technological development, by requiring more specialization of personnel and equipment, adds to the heterogeneity of an organization. Related skills and knowledge formerly lodged in one person or one group are split. While such divisive developments undoubtedly allow for greater precision within an area of activity, they also intensify the need for, and concern over, integration of the several activities.

(7) Increasing technological complication is accompanied by the proliferation of professional and technical societies and associations, each with its unique values and code of ethics. Hence there is more likelihood for organizational members to owe loyalty or allegiance to a profession as well as to the organization, greater opportunity for the demands of the organization to conflict with those of the profession, and at the same time a greater opportunity for the individual employee to enforce demands on the organization by invoking sanctions from the profession.[7] Finally, the proliferation of specialization provides additional bases for organizational members to differentiate among themselves and hence for cleavage to develop.

NOTES

1. We are thus using the term *technology* in its broad sense as a system of techniques. Similar usage is made by E. D. Chapple and C. S. Coon, who say: "Our present purpose is to show how different peoples combine their various techniques into total adjustments (to their environments), which we shall call technologies" (*Principles of Anthropology* [New York, 1942], p. 223).

2. A number of valuable studies throw light on these four kinds of organizations. While our gross examination here is highly simplified and is not necessarily an accurate reflection of any of these studies, we are indebted to the following: On mining: J. F. Scott and R. P. Linton, *Three Studies in Management* (London, 1952); A. W. Gouldner, *Patterns of Industrial Bureaucracy* (Glencoe, Ill., 1954). On the factory: E. Jaques, *The Changing Culture of a Factory* (London, 1951); H. Ronken and P. R. Lawrence, *Administering Changes* (Boston, 1954); and Scott and Linton, cited above. On the hospital: A. H. Stanton and M. S. Schwartz, *The Mental Hospital* (New York, 1954); T. Burling, E. M. Lentz, and R. N. Wilson, *The Give and Take in Hospitals* (New York, 1956). On the university: L. Wilson, *The Academic Man* (New York, 1942); F. Znaniecki, *The Social Role of the Man of Knowledge* (New York, 1940).

3. This framework is taken from E. H. Litchfield, Notes on a General Theory of Administration, *Administrative Science Quarterly,* 1 (1956), 3–29.

4. This is evidenced by the fact that fund-raising organizations have grown up to provide money-gathering services primarily for hospitals, churches, and colleges.

5. The concept "zone of indifference" was advanced by Chester I. Barnard, *The Functions of the Executive* (Cambridge, Mass., 1938), pp. 167 ff. See also Herbert A. Simon, *Administrative Behavior* (New York, 1955), pp. 11 ff. Simon prefers the term "zone of acceptance."

6. This is a restatement of Thorstein Veblen's concept. For a penetrating discussion of this and similar concepts at the personal level, see R. K. Merton, "Bureaucratic Structure and Personality," in his *Social Theory and Social Structure* (Glencoe, Ill., 1949), pp. 151–160.

7. The organization may also resort to the reverse of this procedure.

A FRAMEWORK FOR THE COMPARATIVE ANALYSIS OF ORGANIZATIONS*

Charles Perrow

This paper presents a perspective on organizations that hopefully will provide a basis for comparative organizational analysis, and also allow one to utilize selectively the existing theories of organizational behavior. There are four characteristics of this perspective.

First, technology, or the work done in organizations, is considered the defining characteristic of organizations. That is, organizations are seen primarily as systems for getting work done, for applying techniques to the problem of altering raw materials—whether the materials be people, symbols or things. This is in contrast to other perspectives which see organizations as, for example, cooperative systems, institutions, or decision-making systems.

Second, this perspective treats technology as an independent variable, and structure—the arrangements among people for getting work done—as a dependent variable. Goals are conceived of

"A Framework for the Comparative Analysis of Organizations," *American Sociological Review,* 32, 3 (April 1967), 194–208. Reprinted with the permission of the author and of the publisher, The American Sociological Association.

* Revision of a paper read at the 1966 Annual Meeting of the American Sociological Association. This paper was prepared during the course of research on industrial corporations supported by Grant No. GS-742, National Science Foundation. Numerous colleagues criticized an earlier version unstintingly, but I would like to single out Ernest Vargas, Geoffrey Guest and Anthony Kovner, who transcended their graduate student roles at the University of Pittsburgh during the formulation of these ideas in sticky field situations.

INFORMATION AND TECHNOLOGICAL INPUTS

as being in part a dependent variable. What is held to be an independent and dependent variable when one abstracts general variables from a highly interdependent and complex social system is less of an assertion about reality than a strategy of analysis. Thus, no claim is made that for all purposes technology need be an independent variable.

Third, this perspective attempts to conceptualize the organization as a whole, rather than to deal only with specific processes or subparts. Thus, while the importance of technology has often been demonstrated within work groups or for particular organizational processes, here it will be used as a basis for dealing with the organization as an organization.

Finally, and in the long run perhaps most importantly, the perspective holds that technology is a better basis for comparing organizations than the several schemes which now exist.[1]

None of these points in itself is new, and the last section of this article discusses the uses to which the concept of technology has been put by others. However, the attempt to deal with all four points simultaneously, or, to put it differently, to pay systematic attention to the role of technology in analyzing and comparing organizations as a whole, is believed to be distinctive.

Technology and Raw Materials

By technology is meant the actions that an individual performs upon an object, with or without the aid of tools or mechanical devices, in order to make some change in that object. The object, or "raw material," may be a living being, human or otherwise, a symbol or an inanimate object. People are raw materials in people-changing or people-processing organizations; symbols are materials in banks, advertising agencies and some research organizations; the interactions of people are raw materials to be manipulated by administrators in organizations; boards of directors, committees and councils are usually involved with the changing or processing of symbols and human interactions, and so on.

In the course of changing this material in an organizational setting, the individual must interact with others. The form that this interaction takes we will call the structure of the organization. It involves the arrangements or relationships that permit the coordination and control of work. Some work is actually concerned with changing or maintaining the structure of an organization. Most administrators have this as a key role, and there is a variety of technologies for it. The distinction between technology and structure has its gray areas, but basically it is the difference between an individual acting directly upon a material that is to be changed and an individual interacting with other individuals in the course of trying to change that material. In some cases the material to be changed and the "other individuals" he interacts with are the same objects, but the relationships are different in each case.

There are a number of aspects of technology which are no doubt important to consider in some contexts, such as the environment of the work (noise, dirt, etc.) or the possibilities of seductive or exploitative relationships with clients, patients or customers. For our purposes, however, we are concerned with two aspects of technology that seem to be directly relevant to organizational structure. The first is the number of exceptional cases encountered in the work,[2] that is, the degree to which stimuli are perceived as familiar or unfamiliar. This varies on a scale from low to high.

108   The second is the nature of the search process that is undertaken by the individual when exceptions occur. We distinguish two types of search process. The first type involves a search which can be conducted on a logical, analytical basis. Search processes are always exceptional actions undertaken by the individual. They are nonroutine. No programs exist for them. If a program exists, only a very trivial search is involved in switching from one program to another program when the stimuli change.[3] But though nonroutine, one type of search may be logical, systematic and analytical. This is exemplified by the mechanical engineering unit of a firm building large machinery, or by programmers writing individual programs for slow readers in a special school. The second type of search process occurs when the problem is so vague and poorly conceptualized as to make it virtually unanalyzable. In this case, no "formal" search is undertaken, but instead one draws upon the residue of unanalyzed experience or intuition, or relies upon chance and guesswork. Examples would be work with exotic metals or nuclear fuels, psychiatric casework, and some kinds of advertising. We can conceive of a scale from analyzable to unanalyzable problems.

If we dichotomize these two continua into the presence or absence of exceptional cases and into the presence or absence of analyzable problems, we have a four-fold table as in Figure 1. The upper right-hand quadrant, cell 2, where there are many exceptional cases and a few analytic techniques for analyzing them, is one extreme to which we will refer as nonroutine. In the lower left-hand quadrant, cell 4, we have the routine extreme, where there are few exceptions and there are analytic techniques for handling those that occur. A one-dimensional scheme would follow the dotted line from routine to nonroutine. But note that the other two quadrants may represent viable cases in themselves and they have been labeled with some industrial examples. Few cases would probably fall in the upper left-hand corner of cell 1, or lower right-hand corner of cell 3, but otherwise many organizations are expected to appear in these two cells.

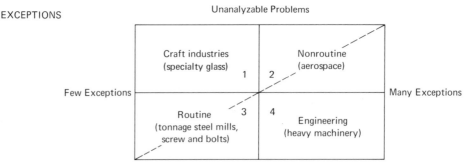

SEARCH

Figure 1. Technology Variable (Industrial Example).

INFORMATION AND TECHNOLOGICAL INPUTS

Techniques are performed upon raw materials. The state of the art of analyzing the characteristics of the raw materials is likely to determine what kind of technology will be used. (Tools are also necessary, of course, but by and large, the construction of tools is a simpler problem than the analysis of the nature of the material and generally follows the analysis.) To understand the nature of the material means to be able to control it better and achieve more predictability and efficiency in transformation. We are not referring here to the "essence" of the material, only to the way the organization itself perceives it.

The other relevant characteristic of the raw material, besides the understandability of its nature, is its stability and variability; that is, whether the material can be treated in a standardized fashion or whether continual adjustment to it is necessary. Organizations uniformly seek to standardize their raw material in order to minimize exceptional situations. This is the point of de-individualizing processes found in military academies, monasteries and prisons, or the superiority of the synthetic shoe material Corfam over leather.

These two characteristics interact, of course. On the one hand, increased knowledge of the nature of the material may lead to the perception of more varieties of possible outcomes or products, which in turn increases the need for more intimate knowledge of the nature of the material. Or the organization, with increased knowledge of one type of material, may begin to work with a variety of related materials about which more needs to be known, as when a social service agency or employment agency relaxes its admission criteria as it gains confidence, but in the process sets off more search behavior, or when a manufacturing organization starts producing new but related products. On the other hand, if increased knowledge of the material is gained but no expansion of the variety of output occurs, this permits easier analysis of the sources of problems that may arise in the transformation process. It may also allow one to prevent the rise of such problems by the design of the production process.

A recent analysis of a public defender system by Sudnow highlights the twin characteristics of the material variable.[4] On the one hand, offenders are distributed into uniform categories by means of the conception of the "normal crime," and on the other hand, control over the individual offender is insured because the public defender well understands the offender's "nature"—that is, his low status, limited understanding and intellectual resources, and his impecunious condition. The technology, then, can be routine because there are few exceptions (and these are handled by a different set of personnel) and no search behavior on the public defender's part is required. The lawyer in private practice, of course, is a contrasting case.[5]

It will readily be seen that these two characteristics of the raw material are paralleled in the four-fold table of technology (Figure 2). If the technology of an organization is going to move from cell 2 to any of the other cells, it can only do so either by reducing the variability of the material and thus the number of exceptional cases that occur, or by increasing the knowledge of the material and thus allowing more analytic techniques to be used, or both. One may move from cell 2 to cell 1 with increasing production runs, clients served, accounts handled, research projects underway, agency programs administered and so forth, since this allows more experience to be gained and thus reduces the number of stimuli seen as exceptions. If technical knowledge increases, increasing the reliability of search procedures, one may move from cell 2 to cell 3. If both things happen—and this is the aim of most organizations—one may move from cell 2 to cell 4.[6]

Task and Social Structure

For our purpose, the task structure of an organization is conceived of as consisting of two dimensions, control and coordination. Control itself can be broken up into two components. They are the degree of discretion an individual or group possesses in carrying out its tasks, and the power of an individual or group to mobilize scarce resources and to control definitions of various situations, such as the definition of the nature of the raw material. Discretion here does not mean freedom from supervision or freedom simply to vary task sequences or pace of work. Both of these are compatible with routine activities, and some nonroutine tasks must be closely supervised or have precise sequences of tasks, once a program is selected, be-

cause of their critical nature. Nor does the length of time between performance reviews[7] necessarily indicate discretion. Rather, discretion involves judgments about whether close supervision is required on one task or another, about changing programs, and about the interdependence of one's task with other tasks.[8] Discretion and power may often be correlated,[9] but there is an important distinction. Power affects outcomes directly because it involves choices regarding basic goals and strategies. Discretion relates to choices among means and judgments of the critical and interdependent nature of tasks. The consequences of decisions in the case of discretion have no direct influence on goals and strategies; these decisions are formed within the framework of accepted goals and strategies.

Coordination, on the other hand, can be achieved through planning or feedback, to use the terms proposed by March and Simon.[10] Coordination by planning refers to the programmed interaction of tasks, which interaction is clearly defined by rules or by the very tools and machinery or the logic of the

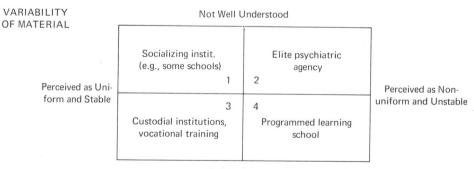

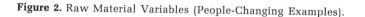

Figure 2. Raw Material Variables (People-Changing Examples).

INFORMATION AND TECHNOLOGICAL INPUTS

transformation process. Coordination by feedback, on the other hand, refers to negotiated alterations in the nature or sequence of tasks performed by two different units.

It is now necessary to distinguish three functional or task areas within management in organizations. Area One, the design and planning function, entails such major decisions as what goods or services are to be produced, who the customers will be, the technology employed, and the source of legitimacy and capital. Area Two, the technical control and support of production and marketing, includes such functions (to use industrial terms) as accounting, product and process research, quality control, scheduling, engineering, plant management, purchasing, customer service, advertising, market research, and general sales management. (Not all are important, or even existent, of course, in all industrial organizations.) This is distinguished as a function, though not necessarily in terms of actual persons or positions, from Area Three, the supervision of production and marketing. This area involves the direct supervision of those dealing with the basic raw materials and those doing direct selling.[11] In the subsequent discussion we shall ignore marketing, and, for a time, Area One.

Figure 3 shows crudely the kinds of values that might be expected to appear in the task structure, considering only Areas Two and Three—technical control and support of production, and the supervision of production. Some global organizational characterizations of structure are given at the bottom of each cell. Those familiar with Burns and Stalker's work will recognize cell 2 as closest to the organic structure and cell 4 as closest to the mechanistic structure.[12]

In cell 2, we have nonuniform raw materials in both areas which are not well understood, and thus present many occasions for exceptional handling. However, the search required cannot be logically conducted, but must involve a high degree of experimentation and "feel." In such a technological situation, the discretion of both those who super-

Task-Related Interactions

	Discretion	Power	Coord. w/in gp.	Interdependence of groups	Discretion	Power	Coord. w/in gp.	Interdependence of groups
Technical Superv.	Low	Low	Plan	Low	High	High	Feed	High
	High	High	Feed		High	High	Feed	
	Decentralized			1	2 Flexible, Polycentralized			
Technical Superv.				4	3			
	Low	High	Plan	Low	High	High	Feed	Low
	Low	Low	Plan		Low	Low	Plan	
	Formal, Centralized				Flexible, Centralized			

Figure 3

vise the transformation of the basic raw material, and those who provide technical help for this process, must be high. The supervisors will request help from technical personnel rather than receive orders from them, or there may not even be a clear line of distinction between the two in terms of persons. That is, the clinical psychologist or the quality control engineer will find himself "on the line" so to speak, dealing directly with patients or exotic metals and working side by side with the supervisors who are nominally of lower status. The power of both groups will be high, and not at the expense of each other. The coordination will be through feedback— that is, considerable mutual adjustment must be made. The interdependence of the two groups will be high. The development of product groups and product managers in industry provides an example, as does the somewhat premature attempt of one correctional institution to utilize a cottage system bringing both clinical and line personnel together with joint responsibility for running autonomous cottages.[13]

In the case of cell 4, uniform stable materials whose relevant nature is perceived as well understood can be handled with few exceptions occurring, and those that do occur can be taken care of with analytical search processes. In such a situation the discretion of both groups is likely to be low. This is a well-programmed production process and there is no need to allow much discretion. Indeed, there is danger in doing so. However, the power of the technical group over the supervisory group is high, for they direct the activities of the supervisors of production on the basis of routine reports generated by the supervisors. Those in Area Three are likely to see those in Area Two as hindrances to their work rather than aides. Coordination can be through planning in both groups, and the interdependence of the two groups is low; it is a directive rather than an interdependent relationship.

Cell 3 represents a variation from either of these extremes, for here, in contrast to cell 2, the existence of many exceptions which require search procedures increases both the power and the discretion of the technical group, which handles these exceptions, at the expense of the supervisory group. The supervisors of production respond to the results of these search processes rather than undertake search themselves. In the case of cell 1, the situation is re-

Social identity (communal)		Goal identification (mission, "character" of organization, distinctive competence, etc.)
	1	2
	3	4
Instrumental identity (job security, pay, protection from arbitrary power)		Work or task identification (technical satisfactions)

Figure 4

INFORMATION AND TECHNOLOGICAL INPUTS

versed. Because search cannot be logical and analytical, when the infrequent exceptions occur they are handled by those in closest contact with the production process such as teachers and skilled craftsmen, and there is minimal development of administrative services. Of course, in schools that attempt to do little socialization but simply offer instruction and provide custody, technical (administrative) services grow and we move to cell 2.

Having thus related technology to task structure, let us turn to another aspect of structure—the non-task-related but organizationally relevant interactions of people. We call this the social structure.

Figure 4 follows our previous fourfold classification and indicates the variety of bases for non-task-related interactions. All are present in all organizations, but the saliency varies. In cell 2, these interactions are likely to revolve more around the mission, long-range goals, and direction of development of the organizations than around the other three bases. This is because of the task structure characteristic of a flexible, polycentric organization, or at least is related to it. The category "social identity" in cell 1 is meant to convey that the non-task-related interactions of personnel that are organizationally relevant revolve around communal or personal satisfactions born of long tenure and close working relationships. This is true especially at the supervisory level, which is a large management group in this type of structure. However, it is very possible, as Blauner and others have shown, for communal relations to develop in cell 4 types of organizations if the organization is located in a rural area where kinship and rural ties are strong.[14] The basis of interaction in cell 3 is instrumental identity and in cell 4, work or task identification. These would

also be predicted upon the basis of the technology.

So far we have ignored Area One—design and planning. This area receives more inputs from the environment than the other areas, and thus its tasks and technologies are derived from both internal and external stimuli. If the product environment of the organization—a term meant to cover competitors, customers, suppliers, unions and regulatory agencies—were the same in all four cells of Figure 3, we would expect the design and planning areas in cell 4 to have routine tasks and techniques, and nonroutine ones in cell 2. This is because the occasions for design and long-range planning would be few in the one and many in the other. For example, at least until very recently, the decisions that executives in the primary metals industries, railroads and surface mining had to make were probably rather routine, while those of executives in new industries such as electronics and aerospace were probably nonroutine.[15] One would expect that cell 1 would also be routine, and cell 3 somewhat nonroutine. But the product environment can alter all this. Organizations in cell 4 can be in a rapidly changing market situation even though the technical control and the supervision of production are fairly routine. Consumer goods industries probably deal with many decisions where the search behavior confronts unanalyzable problems such as the hemline of women's clothes, fads in the toy industry, or the length of time that tail fins or the boxy look in autos will last. Generally speaking, however, though the intrinsic characteristics of the product remain the same, rapid changes in the extrinsic characteristics will introduce nonroutine tasks in the design and planning area, even though [they] hardly alters the routine character of the

114 technical control and the supervision of production.[16]

These are industrial examples, but it also seems likely that the tasks of Area One in custodial mental hospitals are quite different from those in treatment-oriented hospitals. Relations with the regulatory agencies, supplying agencies, the consumers such as courts and families, and the other agencies that compete for funds or clients, will be rather routine in the first, while they will be quite nonroutine and sensitive in the second. This would not be true, of course, if the latter have the means of isolating themselves from their environment.[17] Similarly, the market situation of vocational training institutions may change rather quickly as industrial technologies change, requiring changes in the design and planning of the institution, while the market of a public school that attempts to socialize youths will not change as often.

Goals

Finally, let us turn to the last major variable, goals. Three categories of goals can be distinguished for present purposes.[18] These are system goals, which relate to the characteristics of the system as a whole, independent of its products; product characteristic goals, which relate to the characteristics of the products the organization decides to emphasize; and derived goals, which refer to the uses to which power generated by organizational activities can be put, independent of system or product goals.

We would expect completely routinized organizations to stress those "system" goals of organizational stability, low risk, and perhaps high profits or economical operations rather than growth. (See Figure 5.) In terms of "prod-

uct characteristic" goals, they would be more likely to emphasize quantity than quality, stable lines over unstable or diversified lines, superficial transformations (e.g., instilling discipline in deviant clients) over basic transformation (such as character restructuring), and so forth. Their "derived" goals are likely to emphasize conservative attitudes towards the government, conservative political philosophies, conservative forms of corporate giving. Also, they are perhaps more likely to have individuals who exploit, for their own benefit, relations with suppliers, and who have collusive arrangements with competitors and devious and excessive forms of management compensation. Obviously, these comments upon possible goals are open to serious question. For one thing, we lack such data on goals for a large number of organizations. Furthermore, personalities and the environment may shape goals more than the other variables of technology and structure. Finally, the link between structure and goals is an intuitive one, based upon unproven assumptions regarding attitudes generated by task relations. But the comments are meant to suggest how goals may be shaped or constrained, though hardly specified, through the influence of technology and structure.

Some Cautions

This truncated perspective ignores the role of the cultural and social environment in making available definitions of raw material, providing technologies, and restricting the range of feasible structures and goals.[19] It also ignores, for the most part, the role of the product environment—customers, competitors, suppliers, unions and regulatory agencies—and the material and human

System	Product	Derived	System	Product	Derived
Stability Few risks Moderate to low profit emphasis	Quality No innovations	Conservative 1	High growth High risks Low emphasis on profit 2	High quality Innovative	Liberal
Stability Few risks High profit emphasis	Quantity No innovations	4 Conservative	3 Moderate growth Some risks Moderate profit emphasis	Reliability Moderate innova- tions	Liberal

Figure 5

resources. These will have their independent effect upon the major variables.

In addition, it is not proposed here that there are four types of organizations. The two-dimensional scheme is conceived of as consisting of two continua. Nor are the dimensions and the specifications of the variables necessarily the best. It is argued, however, that the main variables—raw materials, technology, task and social structure, goals, and some differentiation of task areas within organizations, are critical ones. As to the assignment of independent and dependent variables, occasions can be readily cited where changes in goals, for example those brought about by changes in the market place or the personalities of top executives, have brought about changes in the technology utilized. The argument is somewhat more subtle than one of temporal priorities. Rather, it says that structure and goals must adjust to technology or the organization will be subject to strong strains. For a radical change in goals to be a successful one, it may require a change in technology, and thus in structure, or else there will be a large price paid for the lack of fit between these variables.[20] Furthermore, as one proceeds, analytically, from technology through the two kinds of structure to goals, increasingly the prior variable only sets limits upon the range of possible variations in the next variable. Thus, technology may predict task structure quite well in a large number of organizations,[21] but these two predict social structure less well, and these three only set broad limits upon the range of possible goals.

Comparative Analyses

If all this is at all persuasive, it means that we have a powerful tool for comparing organizations. The first implication of this for comparative studies is that we cannot expect a particular relationship found in one organization to be found in another unless we know these organizations are in fact similar with respect to their technology. Thus, the fact that the cosmopolitan-local relationship that worked so well in Antioch College was not found in the outpatient department of a hospital should not surprise us; the work performed by the professionals in each case was markedly different.[22] That morale was associated with bureaucracy in fairly routine public schools, but not in research organizations, is understandable.[23] Less obvious, however, is the point that types of organization—in terms of their function in society—will vary as much within each type as between types. Thus, some schools, hospitals, banks and steel companies may have more in common, because of their routine character, than routine and nonroutine schools, routine and nonroutine hospitals, and so forth. To assume that you are holding constant the major variable by comparing several schools or several steel mills is unwarranted until one looks at the technologies employed by various schools or steel mills. In fact, the variations within one type of organization may be such that some schools are like prisons, some prisons like churches, some churches like factories, some factories like universities, and so on.[24] Once this is recognized, of course, analysis of the differences between churches or whatever can be a powerful tool, as witness the familiar contrast of custodial and treatment-oriented people-changing institutions.

Another implication is that there is little point in testing the effect of a parameter variable, such as size, age, auspices, geographical dispersion, or even national culture, unless we control for technology. For example, in the case of size, to compare the structure of a small R and D lab where the tasks of all three areas are likely to be quite nonroutine with the structure of a large bank where they are likely to be quite routine is fruitless. The nature of their tasks is so different that the structures must vary independently of their different sizes.[25] A meaningful study of the effect of size on structure can be made only if we control for technology, and compare, say, large and small banks all of which have similar services, or large and small R and D labs. Similarly,

though the brilliant work of Crozier on French culture is very suggestive, many of his conclusions may stem from the fact that only very routine organizations were studied, and even those lacked many critical elements of the bureaucratic model.[26] Equally routine organizations in a protected product environment in the U.S. might have displayed the same characteristics.

Finally, to call for decentralization, representative bureaucracy, collegial authority, or employee-centered, innovative or organic organizations—to mention only a few of the highly normative prescriptions that are being offered by social scientists today—is to call for a type of structure that can be realized only with a certain type of technology, unless we are willing to pay a high cost in terms of output. Given a routine technology, the much maligned Weberian bureaucracy probably constitutes the socially optimum form of organizational structure.

If all this is plausible, then existing varieties of organizational theory must be selectively applied. It is increasingly recognized that there is no "one best" theory (any more than there is "one best" organizational structure, form of leadership, or whatever) unless it be so general as to be of little utility in understanding the variety of organizations. The perspective proposed here may allow us to utilize existing theories selectively.

For example, a characteristic of thoroughly routinized organizations is the programmatic character of decisions, and perhaps the infrequency with which important decisions have to be made. A decision-making framework that attempts to simulate executive behavior would be fruitful in such cases, for decisions are programmed and routinized.

There are fairly clear guidelines for decisions, and clear routing maps, flow charts, and so forth. (See the examples in the second half of the Cyert and March volume, *The Behavioral Theory of the Firm*.[27]) However, a decision-making perspective which emphasizes uncertainty, such as Herbert Simon's, or that illustrated in the first part of the Cyert and March volume, would not be fruitful here.[28] It would be fruitful where nonroutine tasks are involved.

The study of organizations with a moderate or high component of non-routine activities, especially at the design and planning level, would benefit from the institutional analysis proposed by Selznick, whereas more routine organizations would not. Selznick, himself, would see them as technical tools. The Communist Party is engaged in nonroutine activities and Selznick chose to analyze the nonroutine rather than the routine aspects of the multi-organization, the Tennessee Valley Authority.[29] Except for its Bell Laboratories, the American Telephone and Telegraph Corporation is probably a rather routine organization in a stable product environment and Barnard's equilibrium analysis works well.[30] Equilibrium analysis also works well for the routine operatives at the production level in economic organizations that constitute most of the subjects for the discussion by March and Simon of the contribution-inducement model.[31] Where nonroutine activities are involved, however, the measurement of both inducements and contributions tends to be difficult, and little is gained by this model except the unenlightening assertion that if the person stays in the organization and produces, there must be some kind of an inducement at least to match his contribution.[32]

There are, of course, many aspects of the general perspectives or theories of organizations that apply to all organizations, and many more will be forthcoming. What is asserted here is that we know enough about organizations in general, at this point, to suggest that more of our effort should be directed toward "middle range" theories which attempt to increase their predictive power by specifying the types of organizations to which they apply. To do this we need far better classification systems than we now have. A better classification system will be based upon a basic aspect of all organizations. In this paper we have suggested that a better system would be one which conceptualizes organizations in terms of the work that they do rather than their structure or their goals.

Other Studies Utilizing Technology

If there is anything novel in the present essay it is the setting forth of an integrated and somewhat comprehensive viewpoint on technology and complex organizations. Numerous studies have dealt with specific aspects of this viewpoint and some are discussed here.

There have been a few general theoretical statements regarding technology and structure. The one closest to the perspective presented here is a seminal essay by Litwak[33] which distinguishes uniform and nonuniform tasks. His framework received some empirical support in an interesting essay by Hall.[34] One of the first attempts to specify some structural and goal concomitants of technology in general terms was by Thompson and Bates.[35] March and Simon,[36] and Simon alone,[37] proposed and discussed a distinction between programmed and nonprogrammed decisions in general terms. Bennis[38] verges

118 upon a technological conceptualization in parts of his excellent review of leadership theory and administrative behavior.

There have been numerous studies of the role of technology in work groups and small groups. One of the most widely cited is that of the long-wall coaling method by Trist and Bamforth.[39] In our terms this represents a premature attempt at rationalizing nonroutine activities. An assembly-line work layout was imposed on a craft and job-shop operation which was essentially nonroutine, and the results were predictably unfortunate, as were similar attempts to impose a bureaucratic structure on the nonroutine underground mining operations described by Gouldner.[40] Those interested in human relations in organizations have increasingly toyed with technology as an independent variable, but with mixed feelings and reluctance, since it appears to jeopardize some implicit values of this school of thought. See, for example, the curious chapter in Likert[41] where many of the central hypotheses of previous and subsequent chapters are undermined by observing that the consequences of leadership style varied with the routine and nonroutine nature of the work. More sophisticated statements of the impact of technology upon work groups can be found in Dubin[42] and in the comparative study of Turner and Lawrence.[43] The most sophisticated statement of the impact upon workers is presented by Blauner,[44] who uses a comparative framework to great effect; he also summarizes the vast literature on this topic which need not be cited here. Studies of experimental groups have provided evidence of the effect of technology upon small group structure. See the work of Bavelas,[45] Guetzkow and Simon,[46] and Leavitt.[47]

The impact of routine technologies upon both managerial and nonmanagerial personnel is apparent, though not explicit, in Argyris' study of a bank,[48] in Sudnow's study of a court system,[49] and in two studies of French organizations by Crozier.[50]

Technology plays an explicit and important role in a number of studies of single types of organizations, such as Janowitz's outstanding study of the military,[51] and Rose Coser's contrast of two units in a long-term hospital.[52] It is implicit in her contrast of a medical and a surgical ward.[53] It is also implicit in Rosengren's analysis of milieu therapy.[54] It plays the key role in the author's analysis of the literature on general and mental hospitals,[55] and in his longitudinal study of a maximum security institution for juveniles.[56] It plays an ambiguous role in the Street, et al., study of six correctional institutions where its impact is obscured by a competing emphasis upon executive goals and behavior, and an inappropriate reliance upon a simple custodial-treatment continuum which leads to many ambiguities about the middle organizations where components of treatment vary independently.[57]

Explicit contrasts of organizations have utilized technological variables. The most ambitious, of course, is Udy's analysis of simple organizations in nonindustrial societies where the emphasis upon technology is explicit.[58] Unfortunately, it is difficult to import his techniques of operationalization and his theory into the world of complex organizations in industrialized societies. As is noted in the preceding essay, technology is a relevant variable, and is sometimes made explicit, in Stinchcombe's discussion of structure and time periods.[59] It also plays a role, though not the key one, in his discussion of craft and bureaucratic organization.[60] The key role is reserved for market factors, and this is true of two other comparative studies—the study of two business concerns by Dill[61] and an ambitious study of two industrial firms by Lorsch.[62] In both these cases it would appear that technology is an important variable but is absorbed in the broader variable, environment. A study of several British firms by Burns and Stalker[63] uses technology as an important variable, though in a quite nonrigorous fashion; their one explicit comparison of a routine and a nonroutine firm is excellent.[64]

The most ambitious and stimulating comparative study using technology as an independent variable is Joan Woodward's survey of 100 industrial organizations.[65] Her independent variable is not, strictly speaking, technology, but is a mixture of type of production, size of production run, layout of work and type of customer order. These distinctions overlap and it is difficult to decide how a particular kind of organization might be classified in her scheme, or how she made her final classification. An examination of the actual types of organizations (bakery, electronic firm, etc.) utilized in her study, kindly provided by Miss Woodward, suggests that most of those in the general category "small batch and unit" are probably involved in nonroutine production; those in the "large batch and unit" are probably involved in routine production; those in the "large batch and mass production" category have a mixture of routine and nonroutine technologies, but are predominantly routine. If so, her findings would be consistent with our perspective. However, her analysis of continuous process firms unfortunately cannot easily be incorporated in the scheme advanced here. Efforts to do so after her book appeared floundered because of lack of crucial data.

Considering the strong empirical tradition of sociology, it is surprising that so few studies actually give details regarding the kind of work performed in organizations that permit technological generalizations. Two of the best are Gouldner's contrast of mining and manufacturing within a gypsum plant,[66] and Blau's implicit contrast of a routine employment agency and a nonroutine regulatory agency.[67] The works of Argyris,[68] Crozier,[69] Sudnow,[70] and Trist and Bamford[71] also are exceptions.

Finally, we should mention the problem of operationalizing the various concepts of technology—programmed and nonprogrammed decisions, uniform and nonuniform events, routine and nonroutine techniques, simple and complex technologies, and so forth. This has rarely been systematically handled. Udy's procedures do not seem to be applicable to complex organizations.[72] Neither Lorsch[73] nor Hall[74] indicate in detail how they make their distinctions. March and Simon provide some general guidelines,[75] but Litwak[76] provides none. It is impossible to determine how Woodward[77] or Burns and Stalker[78] arrived at their classifications of companies. Street, et al.,[79] provide indications of operationalization, but these are not particularly applicable to other types of organizations nor are the authors particularly sensitive to the problem. Only Turner and Lawrence[80] have approached the problem systematically and fully described in an appendix the measurement of their variables. The level of conceptualization is not general enough to apply to other types of organizations than industrial firms, and the material is limited to blue-collar workers, but it is at least encouraging that in our own study of industrial firms we arrived independently at some roughly similar measures.

Udy, in a discussion of this paper,

aptly noted the difficulty of reconciling the respondent's perception of the nature of his work with the observer's perception, which is based upon a comparative view. Few organizations will characterize themselves as routine, and most employees emphasize the variability of their jobs and the discretion required. Nevertheless, contrasts between extreme examples of a single type of organization appear to present no problem. It seems clear that the technology of custodial and therapeutic mental hospitals, or of firms producing ingot molds and those producing titanium-based metals, differ greatly. On the other hand, to say precisely wherein these differences occur, and how one might compare the two routine examples, is far more difficult. Such operationalization, however, depends first upon adequate conceptualization. That proposed in this essay—the two continua of exceptions and search procedures—hopefully can be operationalized for a variety of settings. (An attempt is made, with fair success, by Kovner in his study of nursing units.[81]) But much more research and theory will be required to determine if these concepts are relevant and adequate. Meanwhile, we are aware of a number of other studies of technology and organization currently under way or even in press; other concepts will no doubt be formulated and perhaps will be given systematic operational definition.

NOTES

1. E.g., social function (schools, business firms, hospitals, etc.), as used by Talcott Parsons in *Structure and Process in Modern Society*, Glencoe, Ill.: The Free Press, 1960, pp. 44–47; who benefits, proposed by Peter M. Blau and William R. Scott in *Formal Organizations*, San Francisco: Chandler, 1962, pp. 42–45; or compliance structure, as used by Amitai Etzioni, *A Comparative Analysis of Complex Organizations*, New York: The Free Press, 1961.
2. Cf. James March and Herbert Simon, *Organizations*, New York: Wiley, 1958, pp. 141–142, where a related distinction is made on the basis of search behavior. In our view the occurrence of an exceptional case is prior to search behavior, and various types of search behavior can be distinguished.
3. *Ibid.*, p. 142.
4. David Sudnow, "Normal Crimes: Sociological Features of the Penal Code in a Public Defender Office," *Social Problems*, 12 (Winter, 1965), pp. 255–276.
5. For a more extensive treatment of raw material somewhat along these lines, see David Street, Robert Vinter and Charles Perrow, *Organization for Treatment, A Comparative Study of Institutions for Delinquents*, New York: The Free Press, 1966, Chap. 1.
6. Some organizations, such as mental hospitals, perceive that their technology is inadequate to their goals, and try to move from cell 4 to cell 2 in the search for a new technology.
7. Eliot Jaques, *The Measurement of Responsibility*, Cambridge: Harvard University Press, 1959.
8. This raises serious operationalization problems. In my own work, first-line supervisors were said to have considerable independence in some routine production situations, and to have little in some nonroutine situations, according to a questionnaire, though it was observed that the former had little discretion and the latter a good deal. Kovner found the same kind of responses with a similar question regarding control of job and pace of work among nurses in routine and nonroutine nursing units. See Anthony Kovner, "The Nursing Unit: A Technological Perspective," unpublished Ph.D. dissertation, University of Pittsburgh, 1966. See also the discrepancy between

scores on a similar matter resulting from different interpretations of discretion in two studies: Rose L. Coser, "Authority and Decision-Making in a Hospital," *American Sociological Review*, 23 (February, 1958), pp. 56–64, and James L. Hawkins and Eugene Selmanoff, "Authority Structure, Ambiguity of the Medical Task, Absence of Doctor from the Ward, and the Behavior of Nurses," Indiana University, mimeo.

9. See, for example, a developmental scheme which holds that critical tasks requiring considerable discretion are the basis for group domination in hospitals and other organizations, in Charles Perrow, "Analysis of Goals in Complex Organizations," *American Sociological Review*, 26 (April, 1961), pp. 335–341. See also the compelling illustration presented in the discussion of maintenance personnel in a thoroughly routinized cigarette factory by Michel Crozier, *The Bureaucratic Phenomenon*, Chicago: University of Chicago Press, 1964, Chap. 4.

10. *Op. cit.*, p. 160.

11. The distinction between Areas Two and Three is based upon a more limited distinction used by Joan Woodward in her brilliant study, *Industrial Organization*, London: Oxford University Press, 1965.

12. Tom Burns and G. M. Stalker, *The Management of Innovation*, London: Tavistock Publications, 1961.

13. Street, *et al., op. cit.*, Chaps. 5, 6. The organization is called Milton.

14. Robert Blauner, *Alienation and Freedom: The Factory Worker and His Industry*, Chicago: University of Chicago Press, 1964, Chap. 4. Blauner's theory, incidentally, is entirely consistent with the perspective proposed here, even though we do not concern ourselves explicitly in this article with the morale of hourly employees.

15. On the former see Alfred D. Chandler, Jr., *Strategy and Structure*, Cambridge, Mass.: MIT Press, 1962, pp. 329–330, and Chap. 7 in general. The discussion of social structure and time periods by Stinchcombe can be interpreted in this manner also. Those exceptions that occur in his data appear to be examples of nonroutine technologies established in periods of predominantly routine technologies, or *vice versa*. See Arthur Stinchcombe, "Social Structure and Organizations" in James March (ed.) *Handbook of Organizations*, Chicago: Rand McNally, 1965, pp. 142–169, esp. p. 158.

16. On the distinction between intrinsic and extrinsic prestige, see Charles Perrow, "Organizational Prestige, Some Functions and Dysfunctions," *American Journal of Sociology*, 66 (January, 1961), pp. 335–341.

17. Cf. Street, *et al., op. cit.*, Chap. 4.

18. For a full discussion of these and three others see Charles Perrow, "Organizational Goals," *International Encyclopedia of the Social Sciences* (rev. ed.), David L. Sills (ed.), vol. 2, 1968, The Macmillan Co. and The Free Press, pp. 305–311.

19. The role of the cultural and social environment is developed in somewhat more detail in a review of studies of general and mental hospitals in Charles Perrow, "Hospitals: Technology, Structure and Goals," in James March, *op. cit.*, Chap. 22.

20. This is argued in detail in Perrow, *ibid.*, pp. 926–946. Kovner finds those nursing units with the greatest divergence between technology and structure to have the lowest scores on a dimension of goal realization. *Op. cit.*, pp. 96–97.

21. Unfortunately, verification of the predicted relationships would require a large sample of organizations since there are bound to be many examples of incompatibility between the variables. However, even in a small sample, those whose structure was appropriate to their technology should have fewer "strains" than those whose structure was inappropriate. Joan Woodward, using a similar approach with 100 industrial firms found strong relationships between production systems and certain aspects of structure, though the rudimentary information and analysis on the 100 firms leaves one in doubt as to how strong. See Joan Woodward, *op. cit.*

22. Cf. Alvin Gouldner, "Cosmopolitans and Locals: Toward an Analysis of Latent Social Roles," *Administrative Science Quarterly*; 2 (December, 1957, March, 1958), pp. 281–306, 444–480, and Warren G. Bennis, N. Berkowitz, M. Affinito, and M. Malone, "Reference Groups and Loyalties in the Out-Patient Department," *Administrative Science Quarterly*, 2 (March, 1958), pp. 481–500.

122   23. Gerald H. Moeller and W. W. Charters, "Relation of Bureaucratization to Sense of Power Among Teachers," *Administrative Science Quarterly,* 10 (December, 1966), pp. 444–465. In addition, for this reason one becomes wary of propositional inventories that fail to make sufficient distinctions among organizations, but attempt to support the propositions by illustrations that are likely to restrict the scope of the proposition to the particular type of organization used in the illustration. For the most recent example, see William A. Rushing, "Organizational Rules and Surveillance: Propositions in Comparative Organizational Analysis," *Administrative Science Quarterly,* 10 (December, 1966), pp. 423–443.

24. Many of the frameworks for comparative analysis, such as those cited in footnote 1, break down because of their broad categories. The failure of some of these schemes to meaningfully order the data from a large sample of a great variety of organizations is discussed in J. Eugene Haas, Richard H. Hall and Norman J. Johnson, "Toward an Empirically Derived Taxonomy of Organizations," in Raymond V. Bowers (ed.), *Studies on Behavior in Organizations,* Atlanta: University of Georgia Press, 1966, pp. 157–180.

25. This may be a basic error in the ambitious survey conducted by Haas and his associates, *ibid.*

26. Crozier, *op. cit.*

27. Richard M. Cyert and James G. March, *The Behavioral Theory of the Firm,* Englewood Cliffs, New Jersey: Prentice-Hall, 1963, Chaps. 7–11.

28. *Ibid., Chaps.* 1–4, 6.

29. Philip Selznick, *The Organizational Weapon,* New York: McGraw-Hill, 1952, and *TVA and the Grass Roots,* Berkeley: University of California Press, 1949. See also *Leadership in Administration,* Evanston, Ill.: Row, Peterson, 1957, Chap. 1.

30. Chester Barnard, *The Functions of the Executive,* Cambridge: Harvard University Press, 1938.

31. March and Simon, *op. cit.,* Chap. 4.

32. Woodward's remarkable book offers several implicit examples of selective utility. It seems clear, for example, that firms in her middle category (large batch, assembly and mass production) exhibit the characteristics of political science models such as Melville Dalton (*Men Who Manage,* New York: Wiley, 1959) and the first part of Cyert and March (*op. cit.*). But this view would not illuminate the other two categories in her scheme; application must be selective.

33. Eugene Litwak, "Models of Organization Which Permit Conflict," *American Journal of Sociology,* 67 (September, 1961), pp. 177–184.

34. Richard H. Hall, "Intraorganizational Structural Variation: Application of the Bureaucratic Model," *Administrative Science Quarterly,* 7 (December, 1962), pp. 295–308. However, the normative anti-bureaucratic tone of many of Hall's questionnaire items precludes an adequate test. An affirmative response to an item such as "I have to ask my boss before I do almost anything" probably indicates a very poor boss, rather than a situation where a bureaucratic structure is viable. A factor analysis of Hall's items was utilized to construct several discrete dimensions of some aspects of bureaucracy in connection with research reported by Aiken and Hage. It appears that the groupings are not on the basis of content, but on the evaluative wording of the items. Those stated negatively, as in the above example, group together, and those implying "good" leadership techniques (rather than bureaucratic or nonbureaucratic techniques) group together. It is doubtful that anything but good or bad leadership in a gross sense is being tested here. A valid item for degree of bureaucratization would permit respondents to approve of the necessity for close supervision, for example, as well as to indicate it is not appropriate. See Michael Aiken and Jerald Hage, "Organizational Alienation: A Comparative Analysis," *American Sociological Review,* 31 (August, 1966), pp. 497–507.

35. James D. Thompson and Frederick L. Bates, "Technology, Organization, and Administration," *Administrative Science Quarterly,* 2 (March, 1957), pp. 325–343.

36. James March and Herbert Simon, *Organizations,* New York: Wiley, 1958.

INFORMATION AND TECHNOLOGICAL INPUTS

37. Herbert Simon, *The New Science of Management Decisions,* New York: Harper, 1960. **123**
38. Warren G. Bennis, "Leadership Theory and Administrative Behavior: The Problem of Authority," *Administrative Science Quarterly,* 4 (April, 1959), pp. 259–301.
39. Eric L. Trist and E. K. Bamforth, "Some Social and Psychological Consequences of the Long-Wall Method of Coal-Getting," *Human Relations,* 4 (1951), pp. 3–38.
40. Alvin W. Gouldner, *Patterns of Industrial Bureaucracy,* Glencoe, Ill.: The Free Press, 1954.
41. Rensis Likert, *New Patterns of Management,* New York: McGraw-Hill, 1961, Chap. 7.
42. Robert Dubin, "Supervision and Productivity: Empirical Findings and Theoretical Considerations," in Robert Dubin, George C. Homans, Floyd C. Mann and Delbert C. Miller, *Leadership and Productivity,* San Francisco: Chandler, 1965, pp. 1–50.
43. Arthur N. Turner and Paul R. Lawrence, *Industrial Jobs and the Worker,* Cambridge: Harvard University Press, 1965.
44. Robert Blauner, *Alienation and Freedom: The Factory Worker and His Industry,* Chicago: University of Chicago Press, 1964.
45. Alex Bavelas, "Communication Patterns in Task-Oriented Groups," *Journal of the Statistical Society of America,* 22 (1950), pp. 725–730.
46. Harold Guetzkow and Herbert Simon, "The Impact of Certain Communication Nets Upon Organization and Performance in Task-Oriented Groups," in Albert H. Rubenstein and Chadwick J. Haverstroh, eds. *Some Theories of Organization,* Homewood, Ill.: The Dorsey Press, 1960, pp. 259–277.
47. Harold J. Leavitt, "Some Effects of Certain Communication Patterns on Group Performance," *Readings in Social Psychology,* Eleanor Maccoby, *et al.,* eds., New York: Holt, Rinehart & Winston Inc., 1958, pp. 546–563.
48. Chris Argyris, *Organization of a Bank,* New Haven, Conn.: Yale University Press, 1954.
49. David Sudnow, "Normal Crimes: Sociological Features of the Penal Code in a Public Defender Office," *Social Problems,* 12 (Winter, 1965), pp. 255–276.
50. Michel Crozier, *The Bureaucratic Phenomenon,* Chicago: University of Chicago Press, 1964.
51. Morris Janowitz, *The Professional Soldier,* Glencoe, Ill.: The Free Press, 1960.
52. Rose L. Coser, "Alienation and the Social Structure: A Case Analysis of a Hospital," in Eliot Freidson (ed.), *The Hospital in Modern Society,* New York: The Free Press, 1963, pp. 231–265.
53. Rose L. Coser, "Authority and Decision-Making in a Hospital," *American Sociological Review,* 23 (February, 1958), pp. 56–64.
54. William R. Rosengren, "Communication, Organization and Conduct," *Administrative Science Quarterly,* 9 (June, 1964), pp. 70–90.
55. Charles Perrow, "Hospitals: Technology Structure and Goals," in James March, ed., *Handbook of Organizations,* Chicago: Rand McNally, 1965, Chap. 22.
56. Charles Perrow, "Reality Adjustment: A Young Organization Settles for Humane Care," *Social Problems,* 14 (Summer, 1966), pp. 69–79.
57. David Street, Robert Vinter and Charles Perrow, *Organization for Treatment: A Comparative Study of Institutions for Delinquents,* New York: The Free Press, 1966.
58. Stanley Udy, *Organization of Work,* New Haven: Human Relations Area Files Press, 1959.
59. Arthur L. Stinchcombe, "Social Structure and Organization," in James March (ed.), *Handbook of Organizations,* Chicago: Rand McNally, 1965, Chap. 4.
60. Arthur L. Stinchcombe, "Bureaucratic and Craft Administration of Production: A Comparative Study," *Administrative Science Quarterly,* 4 (September, 1959), pp. 168–187.
61. William Dill, "Environment as an Influence on Managerial Autonomy," *Administrative Science Quarterly,* 2 (March, 1958), pp. 409–443.
62. Jay W. Lorsch, *Product Innovation and Organization,* New York: Macmillan, 1965.
63. Tom Burns and G. M. Stalker, *The Management of Innovation,* London: Tavistock Publications, 1961.

64. *Ibid.,* Chap. 5.
65. Joan Woodward, *Industrial Organization: Theory and Practice,* London: Oxford University Press, 1965.
66. Gouldner, *op. cit.*
67. Blau, Peter, *Dynamics of Bureaucracy,* Chicago: University of Chicago Press, 1955.
68. Argyris, *op. cit.*
69. Crozier, *op. cit.*
70. Sudnow, *op. cit.*
71. Trist and Bamford, *op. cit.*
72. Udy, *op. cit.*
73. Lorsch, *op. cit.*
74. Hall, *op. cit.*
75. March and Simon, *op. cit.,* pp. 142–143.
76. Litwak, *op. cit.*
77. Woodward, *op. cit.*
78. Burns, *op. cit.*
79. Street, *et al., op. cit.*
80. Turner, *op. cit.*
81. Anthony Kovner, "The Nursing Unit: A Technological Perspective," unpublished Ph.D. dissertation, University of Pittsburgh, 1966.

INDUSTRIAL MANAGEMENT IN ADVANCED PRODUCTION SYSTEMS
Some Theoretical Concepts
and Preliminary Findings

Elmer H. Burack

Enormous technological changes have been taking place in the industrial sector of the economy, particularly in the means by which manufacturing operations are technically organized and managed. Often, these changes have not been as dramatic or obvious as information automation (use of the computer) in which changes have been discrete and often readily visible; nevertheless, they have greatly affected managerial areas such as planning, control, and the organization of man-machine systems. Analysis of these changes frequently requires a view of developments over time as well as of a point in time.

Characteristically, the changes in process technology are a phenomenon of

"Industrial Management in Advanced Production Systems: Some Theoretical Concepts and Preliminary Findings," *Administrative Science Quarterly,* 12, 3 (December 1967), 479–500. Reprinted with the permission of the author and of the publisher, the *Administrative Science Quarterly.*

INFORMATION AND TECHNOLOGICAL INPUTS

accretion so that the impact of each modification is not always immediately apparent, although the cumulative effect of the changes often makes it seem that serious organization dislocations have suddenly developed. Typically, improvement tends to center around a machine, a given procedure, or occasionally, the total process itself. Sometimes information automation supplements changes that have taken place in manufacturing processes and procedures.

This paper focuses on industrial manufacturing systems in which organizational-management changes have been most pronounced; that is, production systems characterized by quasi-flow or flow types of processes, such as are commonly found in food processing, oil refining, electric power generation, meat processing, and high-speed automatic packaging. Some of these manufacturing procedures are mixtures of mechanically based and flow elements designated as *quasi-process* units in contrast to continuous-flow, integrated types of systems designated as *process* units. Both have been particularly amenable to advanced technical innovations. Manufacturing improvements, facilitated by product standardization and volume, often can be attributed to advancements in process instrumentation and controls (including use of the computer) as well as the joining together of related production units. The automating of sub-units of the production systems, the integration of these subsystems into a total system, and the incorporation of advanced control concepts led to some of the management changes described in this paper.

A technological approach to the organizational analysis of advanced production systems considers characteristics of the manufacturing activity that affect the organization and performance of work functions and activities. The characteristics of the technological systems influence the organization of personnel, the allocation of functions and responsibilities, design of the organizational control system, and managerial activity patterns. This approach to organizational analysis sometimes treats the same output variables of interest to the behavioral scientist (e.g., productivity and quality); however, the focus here is not primarily on behavioral factors (e.g., attitude, motivation), despite the relevancy of socio-technical approaches in the confrontation of managerial and operating problems.

Preliminary Concepts

TECHNICAL INNOVATION AND IMPROVEMENTS IN PROCESSING

Quasi-process and process types of manufacturing activities have developed away from a purely product orientation and have increasingly involved managerial and information innovations as an integral part of the production or management systems. Industrial units can be viewed along a technological continuum: at one end are production units in which manufacturing procedure is characteristically intermittent, volumes are low, general-purpose equipment tends to predominate, and there is little division or specialization of labor- and staff-support function. Intermediate level production systems are associated with "mass production" such as those operations found in final assembly lines for automotive manufacturing, the assembly of appliances, and other types of high volume assembling associated with consumer products. Such systems are characterized by product standardization, integration of supporting

126 subsystems of production, extensive commitments to mechanically based production equipment, division of labor, and elaborate organizational hierarchies for administration, planning, and control. Some features of intermediate and more advanced systems are depicted in Table 1. Quasi-process and process type systems represent those advanced units which possess flow-like characteristics, high volume, and product standardization; these are of particular interest in this paper. Here, there is often the opportunity for use of some of the most advanced process controls, management science and material handling techniques. Companies, such as those in the oil industry, reached an advanced state of process development and refinement many years ago. With the attainment of advanced stages of technological development, managerial attention is increasingly focused on *system* refinement, which includes process improvement, technical innovation, and the incorporation of these advanced production systems into a comprehensive management network.

ORGANIZATION DEVELOPMENT IN ADVANCED PRODUCTION SYSTEMS

Several large-scale studies provide a basis for anticipating the emerging organization relationships and characteristics of advanced production units.[1]

TABLE 1. Comparison of different forms of advanced operating systems.

Level of tech- nology*	Desig- nation	Example(s)†	Characteristics	
			Process	Management
Interme- diate	Advanced mass produc- tion	Semi-automatic machinery lines	Semi-continuous or continuous production. Low level of worker interspersion. Largely based on mechanical arts. Characteristically an assembly procedure. Mechanization of material handling.	Specialization and division of effort. Elaborate organizational controls.
	Quasi- process systems (low)	Automatic pack- aging. Processed meats. Galvaniz- ing lines. Com- mercial bread plant.	Semi-continuous or continuous. Low level of worker interspersion. Equipment combines concepts based on mechanical arts and sci- ence areas (e.g., chemistry).	
	Quasi- process systems (high)	Automatic fill- ing lines. Plastic extrusion.	Continuous process. Largely automatic controls. No feed- back. Intermediate to high volume. Process integration.	
Ad- vanced	Process systems	Refining. Power generation. Chemical plant.	Continuous processes. High volume. Automatic con- trols with or without com- puters, off-line or on-line.	Management sci- ence concepts‡ Advanced infor- mation support.‡

* The more advanced portion of a technology continuum which spans a range from low level, intermittent (batch) operations to advanced managerial operating systems.

† Suggestive of manufacturing applications recognizing that wide variation exists in individual cases.

‡ Managerial innovation supporting advanced operational systems.

The analyses made for this study suggest that the quasi-process type of company will be concerned with additional refinements in processing and continued development towards an integrated system, whereas the process type of company, since it has already reached an advanced stage of technological development, will be increasingly concerned with the development of significant managerial innovations[2] or approaches to the management of these manufacturing systems. In these systems, job orientation shifts to system orientation: the interdependency between operations increases and the cost of disrupting the production system becomes significant, because of lost sales opportunities represented by the product which could have been made as well as the actual loss of the product. As technical complexity increases, more complex organizational structures develop to regulate the multiplicity of variables, equipment and facilities often become more compact, counteracting the otherwise continued growth in size of production units that is associated with volume increases. These physical and technical changes in the manufacturing process require changes in the organization's control system. Because of the complexity of the evolving production systems, both the controls necessary for the regulation of process functions, and management controls such as job procedures, job descriptions, and systems analyses are extended and become a more pervasive feature of the production network. The idea of skill based on various combinations of on-the-job training or work experiences found in traditional production systems, no longer adequately describes the job requirements for these advanced manufacturing units. Output features such as productivity and quality, which depend so much on direct supervisory and worker effort in low-level systems, give way to *indirect* worker involvement in the quasi-process and process type installations. In low-level work systems, work typically tends to be non-routine and often involves exacting work requirements. These work features are in sharp contrast to the mass production where operations have tended to become standardized with repetitive line pacing or the so-called automated types of production units, where the operator is completely in a stand-by role and can only indirectly influence output characteristics such as quality and productivity.

Preliminary analyses of about 150 manufacturing units suggest a major modification of managerial features as quasi-process and process-type units are approximated. Modifications in managerial structure and activities appear to be related to (1) elements of the work environment, including both control and work characteristics of the process which affect requisite qualities of both supervisor and worker, and (2) emergence and growing importance of administrative and technical support groups, such as production control, planning, and industrial engineering. Other modifications that develop are: (1) more complex organization structures, (2) a shift in the role of supervision (and historically important functions such as direction) to patrol on a process-wide basis, and (3) a shift in the role of the workers to stand-by functions, with emphasis on mental skills. The following generalizations appear relevant to these modifications:

1. The *level* from which technological change takes place helps to determine the *extent* to which organizational dislocations take place.

2. It is of importance to know the *absolute change* in level involved in production improvements in a particular production system.

3. The rate at which technological change takes place is related to the available time for principal organization groups to adjust to the changes.

The studies undertaken in these advanced systems have been directed towards examining some of the preliminary notions advanced in the foregoing discussion more closely and identifying some of the underlying structure of these relationships.

Data Development

The data and information presented were derived from 13 companies in a 22-company study of technical innovation in product and service type companies.[3] Information was developed through questionnaires, interviews, records analysis, and observation. Company documents and supporting records were employed whenever available. Unfortunately, in these companies, as in many others, documentation was inadequate, so that some of the data depend on recall to fill in missing details or major omissions. The companies not included in this study showed less technological development. This study has built on the results of analyses undertaken in earlier years. In many cases, the complexity of the variables involved often prevented developing sharply defined or quantifiable results. Data and information from studies that have appeared in the literature were incorporated where the results of studies appeared to bear directly on the technological-management approaches out-

lined in this paper. The usual problems arise in the interpretation of data from the research and analyses of others. Some of the data were not directly comparable in form and required some redevelopment. Results must be viewed as tentative, pending the development of a considerably greater body of data.

Data derived from the 13-company study suggest some of the underlying structural changes taking place in advanced production systems. These analyses are presented at two levels: (1) an *overview* of organization and structural developments (levels of hierarchy and supervisory span of control), and (2) *detailed* analysis of information derived in several quasi-process (baking, steel, and prepared meats) and process (oil refining and electric power) type industries.

Changes in number of hierarchical levels and numbers of workers per supervisor are illustrated in Figure 1. For convenience, range figures as well as the median values (characteristic of the middle firm in the range) from the large-scale, Joan Woodward study are superimposed on these plots. The number of hierarchical levels characteristic of these companies indicate a clustering of values on the lower side of the Woodward figures which might result from cultural differences between the organization of U.S. and English industry.[4] Four of the companies studied (9, 13, 17 and 18) illustrated some of the organizational-technological dynamics of change.

BUSINESS VOLUME AND STRUCTURE: MEAT PROCESSING

Company No. 13, a processor of meat products showed an *increase* in authority levels from three to four.[5] From 1950 to 1962, it underwent a substantial change in marketing, business organiza-

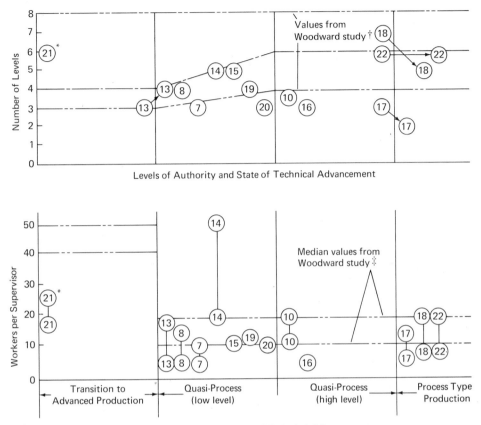

Figure 1. Comparative Analysis of Some Structural Characteristics of Supervisory Organization and the Level of Technical Advancement for 13 Companies.

† Values include range (extreme) values and median (number of levels for the middle firm in the range) from Joan Woodward, *Management and Technology,* cited in footnote 1.

‡ Median value is for the span, 11 to 20 workers.

* Company key:

No.	Type of firm	No.	Type of firm
7	Aluminum rolling mill	16	Industrial chemicals
8	Steel rolling mill I	17	Power plant
10	Plastic extrusion	18	Oil refining
13	Processed meats I	19	Commercial bread I
14	Processed meats II	20	Commercial bread II
15	High speed packaging	21	Final assembly plant—autos
		22	Steel rolling mill II

130

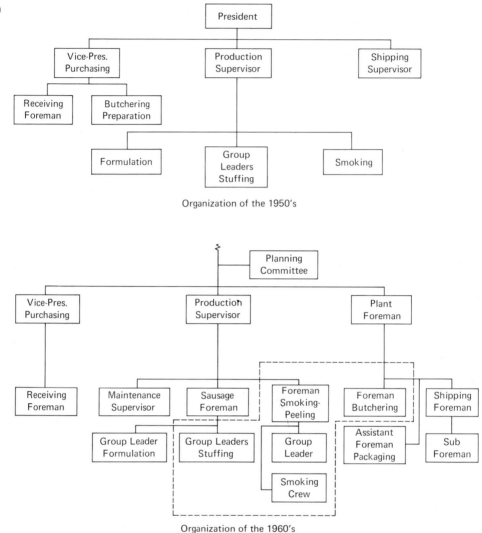

Figure 2. Organizational Structure of Meat Plant in 1950 and 1960. Dashed line indicates portion of organization affected by integrated equipment. Source for formal organization is plant records.

tion, and production technique as the company was transformed from a small volume, informal operation to a highly formalized organization with substantial business volume. Initially, the prepared meats were furnished in an unpackaged form to small retailing businesses. Substantial market expansion and the necessity for furnishing a packaged product led to a significant organization expansion to manage and contain the rapid growth in business effectively. The magnitude of these organizational changes can be readily assessed from Figure 2, which shows the 1950 and 1960 organizational structures.

Specialization and division of labor are evident in the development of new jobs, departments, several new functions, and in the formalization of responsibilities and authority. Increased organizational complexity was reflected in two additional authority levels. The system of the 1950's was of the batch type with intermittent production. From 1950 to the early 1960's, gradual modernization resulted in the mechanical and electronic bridging of many points in the process that had previously been controlled by the worker on the floor, and the corresponding displacement of personnel or modification in their work routines. The total production procedure was transformed into a semi-integrated production system. The transformations that took place show: (1) scale-of-operation effects, related to the changing nature and growth of marketing opportunities; and (2) technological change, resulting in the transformation of islands of equipment and work into a more integrated production system.

Organization structure became more complex as this unit achieved a quasi-process type of system. The potential simplification of supervisory organization through the integration of successive production units and the addition of mechanical and electronic control components was more than counterbalanced by market developments and growing organizational sophistication which resulted in (1) a vastly increased level of business volume, necessitating expansion of the production organization; (2) newly emerging marketing demand that necessitated the addition of a whole new departmental function in packaging; and (3) addition of a new staff level function-planning.

FACTORS IN ORGANIZATIONAL SIMPLIFICATION: STEEL MILL

Changes in Technology. The simplification of organization structure and relationships in several advanced production units (companies No. 9, 17 and 18) contrasted with developments in the meat processing organization.

In company No. 9, a hot rolling mill, computer control was introduced. This change resulted in a modification of departmental structure and organization; organizational levels were reduced from eight to five, with the elimination of several positions including the "assistant" type of classification. The radical change in the managerial structure of this steel processing unit was difficult to explain. It appeared that managerial ineptitude may have allowed an elaborate organization to develop over an extended time period. Consequently, the change in organizational structure in another steel production unit, company No. 22, was studied. Here, changes were substantial, but differed from the level changes in the first company. In this second company, a comparative analysis was made between the older style 76-inch hot rolling mill and an 80-inch, computer-controlled installation. The computer-controlled facility required two less operating foremen and general foremen per production day, a reduction in the overall production supervisory staff from ten to eight. In mechanical maintenance, the total number of foremen was reduced by one; but in the electrical maintenance groups, three new foremen were added to handle the more complex motor controls, motors, and other electrical equipment associated with closer regulation and computer operation. In addition, two computer analysts were added at the supervisory level to deal with the new control and operational problems of the *computer-controlled* system. The new mill was able to achieve an output some 50 percent greater than that obtainable in the old facility, as well as greatly

132 improved quality. The organization changes in the first steel mill chiefly led to a flattening of the managerial structure, whereas in this mill, there were major shifts in the qualitative composition of the whole productive organization. In the erection of the new 80-inch mill, the opportunity was provided for modernizing the technical aspects of the production facility significantly. The new mill not only had the capacity to produce a somewhat wider sheet, but also new technical features which included automatic gauge control and descaling water operating at very high pressure. These technical innovations contributed to the higher level of production and quality assurance. To some extent, the organization changes in this mill were affected by past management practices. The company had always been run with limited production supervision and staff, so that over-supervision was unlikely; if anything, the organization was under-supervised. Consequently, with the installation of the new, integrated, computer-operated facility, the organization changes led to a significant redistribution of supervisory effort, and even greater changes in the worker groups.

Changes in Worker Groups. In the analyses undertaken on worker groups, it was apparent that large quantitative and qualitative changes took place. An over-all work force reduction of 20 percent was associated with significant changes in the composition of work force. Mill operating groups were reduced by some 60 percent, whereas worker groups for the electrical control systems and the electrical-mechanical aspects of the integrated line increased by almost 85 percent. The mechanical categories showed a nominal decrease of some 10 percent. These changes in the supervisory force and workers suggested that changes might have taken place within the supervisory-managerial group, in job qualifications or capabilities related to the new computer-controlled production processes.

Experience and Educational Requirements of Supervisors. The management of this steel mill attributed several major changes in experience and educational requirements directly to computer control. The computer-controlled operation had a higher percentage of college graduates in the production, mechanical, and electrical supervisory groups. In some cases, men had advanced degrees. Furthermore, a new supervisory classification was added—"computer analyst." The job activities of the operating supervisor also changed, in a direction noted in several other studies. The number of workers controlled by a single first-line supervisor decreased from ten workers to six. This change was almost entirely due to the disproportionate reduction in ranks of each of these groups: the worker group incurred greater losses than production supervision.

Other interesting and revealing changes in the first-line supervisory span of control were encountered in analyses undertaken in the high-volume baking industry.

ORGANIZATIONAL FEATURES AND TECHNICAL INNOVATION: BAKING INDUSTRY

Companies No. 19 and No. 20, members of the high-volume baking industry, provided an example of industry development which started to approximate advanced stages of production some years ago.[6] The simplified process-type characteristics of the manufacturing procedure readily lent itself to technical innovations, such as mechanization of material transport (conveyors and bulk-

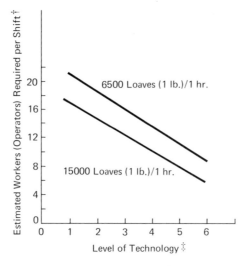

Figure 3. Relation of number of workers to level of technology in commercial baking units.*

* For details on this approach and information for graph, see Edward Van Poolen, "Automate or Abdicate," Ninth Annual General Manager's Conference, Independent Baker's Cooperative (Chicago, 1964); and Evert Kindstrand, "Planning a Plant Modernization Program," house publication Baker-Perkins, Inc. (Saginaw, Mich., 1962).

† Based on multiple shift operations exclusive of packaging.

‡ Technological changes from level one to level six include such things as the addition of automatic machines, transfer equipment, motorized conveyors and continuous processing equipment.

material handling systems) and various types of control instrumentation characteristically associated with the chemical and petroleum industries. This resulted in organizations with much more simplified management systems. The more advanced production unit (company No. 20) had a single foreman per shift who was assigned on a total process basis; company No. 19 (the technologically less advanced unit) had a somewhat more complex managerial organization because of the departmental organization of the production process.

In this industry, the high level of technical development facilitated a systematic approach to management level problems. Many standardized types of plant layouts, each associated with some advanced type of process configuration, were part of the organized approaches taken to process development. Engineering approaches to process development and organizational manning led to codification of most of the information. Figure 3 shows the worker requirements for various types of production facility, at given levels of plant capacity.

As an example in the application of these data, consider a proposed plant (15,000 loaves per hour) modernizing from level 1 to level 6. Worker requirements are lessened from sixteen to six; that is, worker requirements for a plant of the most advanced design are some ten less per shift than less advanced units, but both the level 1 and level 6 plants have the same supervisory re-

134 quirements—one person. This suggests that the first line supervisory ratio decreased from some eighteen to one in low-level plants to that of six to one in the most advanced types of production units.

Interplay of Technical and Managerial Developments. In the progression towards advanced production systems, features of both a technical and managerial nature sustained appreciable changes. These semi-continuous process units (meat processing and baking) contained both mechanical and process types of elements, required close time conformity and demanded extensive systems of both process and managerial types of controls—workers and supervisors were unable to exercise a degree of discretion possible in lower-level processes. In the more advanced plants, both worker and supervisor were removed from direct interspersion in the process and carried out a wholly monitoring type of activity. Technical innovations established the basis for an advanced type of time-interdependent production system within these quasi-process types of units. Human variability and ineptitude were bridged by mechanical and electrical elements in the process. Slowly, the basis for managerial expertise shifted from one based on experience to that of technical education. Here, concern was evidenced with overall system performance as opposed to responsibility within functional units of the process.

Although large, systematic reductions of the work force took place with the updating of *facilities,* technical support groups such as industrial engineering and quality control were often required to reinforce the process changes. However, a *clear* case was *not made* for *advanced* educational requirements in the companies contacted; the supervisor

with general industry experience and high school background had proven adequate, although there was some de-emphasis on experience and increasingly greater pressure for extending certain technical or educational capabilities. More functions were relegated to a standby basis and broader managerial functions were largely removed from the supervisory ranks and directed to more advanced levels of management or into corporate staff groups.

Studies in these two companies, as well as several other companies in this industry, indicated a widening educational gap between plant managers, supervisors, and certain technical support groups. Even in high-volume baking operations where increasingly advanced educational requirements had not yet become operational, a plant manager indicated that:

> Given a condition where comparable people were available at the available salary, those with the more advanced education would be chosen. Furthermore, in the future, our practices will more consciously reflect this move towards better educated supervision.

In several other plants, it was evident that managerial capabilities had not kept pace with the very rapid technological developments. Consequently, personnel in some of these groups found themselves seriously lacking requisite technical insights and unable to cope with disruptive breakdowns, which occasionally took place. Developments in these quasi-process companies were suggestive of changes in advanced productions systems.

THE SOCIOTECHNICAL SYSTEM: POWER PLANTS

Several power plants and oil refineries (companies No. 17 and No. 18) provided examples of some of the significant changes in the organization and technology of process companies. Both showed simplification of organizational structure. In company No. 17, an electrical power-generating unit, Mann and Hoffman noted a reduction in authority levels from three to one: the assistant foreman and shift engineers were eliminated, and a single shift foreman assumed a key operating role.[7] Where the foreman and assistant foreman (a total of six on three shifts) had supervised some 42 operators, giving a ratio of first-line supervisor to worker of one to seven; in the new plant, the ratio was approximately one to fourteen. The traditional pyramidal structure was flattened with only a single supervisory level between worker and plant engineer. Supervision incurred a *relatively* greater reduction in numbers so that the first line ratio in the new plant was greater.

Process Sensitivity and New Control Requirements. The new high-performance power plants had more critical process points. In a group of power plants studied by Emery and Marek,[8] the number of *critical* operational points increased.

In the older installation, three points existed at which at least five minutes was available for correcting the equipment or process and *only two* at which there was *less* than five minutes available. In the new plant, there were no critical points at which more than five minutes was available for corrective measures but nine points with less than five minutes. Furthermore, the *total* number of critical points was *increased* by four. The increased sensitivity to disruptive changes made the new stand-by functions and the timely, corrective response to potentially disruptive conditions extremely important.

Skill Concept in Transition. The advanced technological developments and the lessening of human operating requirements facilitated reduction of human participation in the process and affected managerial, engineering, and operating personnel alike. Operating problems involved considerably more complex technical and scientific concepts. The process imposed new requirements on supervisory and operator abilities to conceptualize the implications of instrument readings or process developments.[9] These problems posed a new challenge to the supervisory or engineering groups for appropriate, timely, remedial action. The importance of traditional man-to-man skills such as supervisory direction were de-emphasized. The personnel classified as "operator" in the new plants differed considerably from their predecessors in the old plants. The traditional concept of skill associated with worker job experiences or manipulative abilities was no longer appropriate in these stand-by functions. The necessary set of experiences and abilities employed in this work system needed to be redefined.

THE SOCIOTECHNICAL SYSTEM: PETROLEUM REFINERIES

The petroleum refining industry used advanced concepts of process development and control instrumentation many years prior to the so-called era of automation. For example, one of the executives in the petroleum firm suggested:

We had automation in our company 15 years ago. All of our major processes had extensive amounts of automatic equipment and controls for the various complex process variables. In addition, many of these units were controlled from points which were physically removed from the process equipment it-

136   self. Most of the important process and distribution steps from the oil field to the bulk station were handled largely with automatic equipment.

Despite the advanced technical position of manufacturing units in this industry, *additional advances* were made in the recent decade, including the utilization of advanced information developments associated with the computer. Characteristically, many of the leading companies in the industry reached a technological plateau in the period (1957–1962). However, advanced companies were able to obtain additional work force reductions of some 12 to 21 percent. In the refinery incorporated in this study, the reduction in the plant work force was about 33 percent, while output increased some 50 percent.

Change in Work Environment. The significance of technological changes in these industries is illustrated by the drastic physical changes in the work environment of the refinery. In the period from 1947–1962, the reduction in plant area utilization for some key units was (approximately) as follows: 11:1 for tank blending (to be interpreted as about a 90 percent reduction), 8:1 for crude units, 4:1 for catalytic cracking, 4:1 for dewaxing units, and 3:1 for reforming units.[10] These reductions in area, supported by "research," consulting and plant engineers, ranged from some 25 to 90 percent of the previously existing plant space. In some cases, the units were more compact; in other cases, there was a great increase in height. Some processes were improved to the point that previously existing equipment could be eliminated. Refinery technology had so improved as to require clean-up or maintenance much less frequently. The utilization of outside contracting services was more easily accomplished.

The magnitude of changes noted in the technical process was paralleled by the major dislocations in the plant managerial organization.

Simplification in Organization Structure. Significant changes in managerial structure accompanied the major technological developments in this refinery. The comparative organization charts in Figure 4 highlight the differences from 1950 to 1964. In a fifteen-year period, the functional plant organization corresponding to the process gave way to a compact, simplified product-line organization. The bases for these organizational changes were related to the following important technical changes: (1) the compacting of the production equipment, (2) the incorporation of process-type computers, (3) the establishment of remote control and operating booths, and (4) the integration of much of the control within the production process itself.

Both workers and supervision were increasingly on a stand-by basis, and the reduction of the supervisor's area of surveillance permitted extensive personnel reorganization. For this plant, company No. 18, the number of supervisory levels decreased from seven to four; however, the structural changes were not accompanied by any significant shift in the ratio of supervisors to operators, since similar percentage changes took place in the supervisory and work groups. In the supervisory ranks, however, all of the "assistant" supervisory classifications were eliminated. Where the assistant general foreman had shared in the direct responsibilities for the men on the production equipment, the shift foreman (a trained engineer, often chemical or petroleum), was now *directly* in charge of the operators on the production units. Much of his activity was concerned with attempting to anticipate

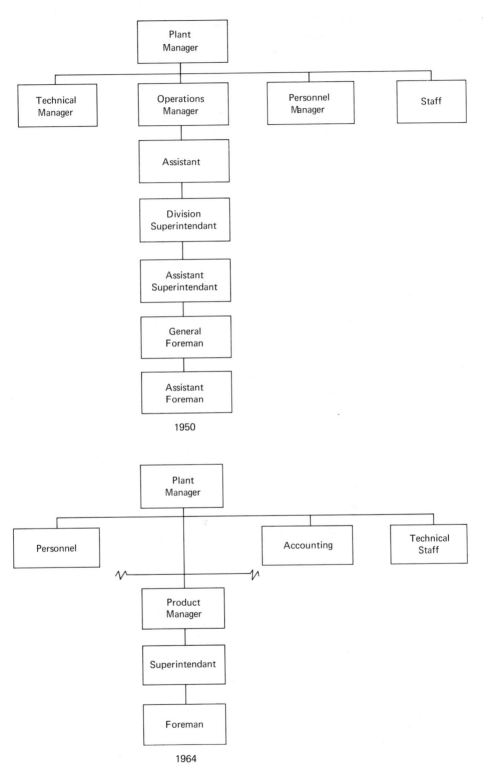

Figure 4. Organization of Refinery, 1950 and 1964.

138   disruptions and minimize down time.[11] Again, there was a redefinition of the skills or experience of supervisor, manager, and worker, as they worked within these advanced types of technological systems.

Importance for Technical Support Groups. Technical support groups, including quality control, process and plant engineering, and production planning, assumed more important responsibilities in total refinery operations. More staff activities were carried out as part of a total system at the corporate level. These groups utilized more sophisticated means for achieving high levels of performance. Many of these approaches were built around complex mathematical models and the computer. Major technological changes in this refinery were accompanied by an equally great modification of managerial organization and activities. Structure was simplified by the elimination of several supervisory levels. The new superintendent classification had no direct counterpart in the old organization and combined responsibilities from several of the previously existing jobs. In addition, with the more complex technical operations and with personnel increasingly on a stand-by basis, the role of supervisory and managerial personnel with respect to worker was closer and more supportive.

Summary

This study of the dynamics of organizational change in conjunction with technical innovation provides the basis for detecting some underlying shifts in managerial organization and functions. The producer of prepared meats provided an example of the interplay of marketing and technological forces, with increased organization complexity associated with the growth in the scale of operation and modification in response to consumer demand. In the other companies studied, there was a flattening of organizational structure and a simplification of supervisory relationships. Attributes of the job changed as experience requirements were modified by an increasing emphasis on technical education and, in advanced process units, the minimum educational need was seen as the bachelor's degree.

Additional research is required to relate more clearly the interchange of experience, technical and general education as these relate to the level of technical advancement and authority level in quasi-process and process units.

NOTES

1. These studies included: Inferences based on the some 100 companies studied by Joan Woodward, *Management and Technology* (London: Her Majesty's Stationery Office, 1958); the 46-company study of Richard A. Beaumont and Roy B. Helfgott, *Management, Automation, and People* (New York: Industrial Relations Research Counselors, 1964); and the intensive, 13-company study of James R. Bright, *Automation and Management* (Boston: Harvard Graduate School of Business, 1958).

2. Managerial innovation is used to mean such things as the incorporation and use of the computer and management science concepts in decision making, planning, and control.

3. This study has focused on technological change in both information and manufacturing procedures and is part of a long-term study in this area. Help of several research assistants was quite valuable including C. Meyer and R. A. Mann.

4. The Woodward selection of companies included some one-third with corporate affiliation while the firms reported on in the thirteen-company group included twelve
units with broader corporate affiliation. The existence of both executive and operating managements at the same physical location would thereby influence the number
of authority levels. The heavier representation of single unit, private firms in the
Woodward study, other factors being equal, would tend to increase the number of
authority levels of the English firm in comparison to the U.S. counterpart. See Joan
Woodward, *Industrial Organization: Theory and Practice* (London: Oxford University
Press, 1965), p. 9.
5. In a more advanced meat production unit, the integration of production equipment
vastly simplified the industrial management organization by complete elimination of
several production operations.
6. These two companies, their technologies, organizations and activities are examined
in considerable detail in Elmer H. Burack, Technology and Supervisory Function: A
Preliminary View, *Human Organization*, in process.
7. Floyd Mann and F. Richard Hoffman, *Automation and the Worker* (New York: Holt,
Rinehart, 1960). The shift supervisors appeared to be the principal management
representatives.
8. F. E. Emery and Julius Marek, "Some Socio-Technical Aspects of Automation,"
Human Relations, 15 (February 1962).
9. This was particularly true in those processes which did not employ process computers for on-line control.
10. Additional details are provided on this group of advanced quasi-process and process
installations in Elmer H. Burack, *Industrial Management and Technical Innovation*,
in process.
11. However, several managers noted the increasing inability of supervision to deal with
people-related problems. Woodward takes up some of these problems of change in
greater detail; see *Industrial Organization, op. cit.*, pp. 73–74; 190–205; 233–238.

AUTOMATION AND THE DIVISION OF LABOR

William A. Faunce

Specialization of function has been a cardinal principle of business organization since the beginning of the industrialization process. From Adam Smith's famous example of job specialization in the manufacture of pins to Frederick Taylor and Scientific Management, the idea that increasing job simplification meant increasing efficiency of operation has been among the principles applied

"Automation and the Division of Labor," *Social Problems*, 13, 2 (Fall 1965), 149–160. Reprinted with the permission of the author and of the publisher, The Society for the Study of Social Problems, publisher of *Social Problems*.

to the organization of production. The division of labor resulting from industrial machine technology and large scale organization has been so continuous that it appeared to be an irreversible direction of change in contemporary societies.

According to Durkheim, division of labor normally produces increased interdependence and organic solidarity, but, in an extreme and abnormal form, may result in alienation and *anomie*.[1] Georges Friedmann has recently suggested that most instances of contemporary division of labor would be "abnormal" if we use Durkheim's classification.[2] While job specialization has raised productivity, it has also been directly or indirectly responsible for a wide variety of problems in industrialized nations.

Much has been written about the effect of excessive job simplification upon motivation to work. The prototypic industrial worker is described as alienated because of the meaninglessness to him of his highly specialized tasks. Extensive occupational differentiation has also been accompanied by status ambiguities that have undoubtedly contributed to the level of status anxiety in industrial societies. The structural complexity of the labor market has increased the difficulty of balancing labor supply and labor demand. A great deal of time and effort is expended in the accommodation of conflicting interests also engendered by a highly segmentalized occupational structure. Increases in efficiency of operation in many organizations are beginning to be limited by the difficulty of coordinating and integrating complex and highly differentiated production systems.

The link between problems of this kind and the characteristic form of division of labor in industrial societies is well documented, and the only lasting solution to most of these problems would be a reversal of the long term trend toward increased job specialization. The purpose of this paper is to suggest the possibility that just such a reversal may be taking place.

Organizational forms that may be rational in the sense of their appropriateness to organizational objectives at certain stages of technological and social structural development become irrational at other levels of development. A major point in Georges Friedmann's *The Anatomy of Work* is that business managers are becoming increasingly aware of the diminishing returns from additional specialization of function. He regards recent increases in the use of job rotation and job enlargement plans as evidence of a turning point in the evolution of division of labor.[3] Other authors have also described current applications of job enlargement as a trend away from job specialization and a "revolution in job design."[4]

Possibilities for job enlargement, however, are limited so long as the form of production technology remains the same. Division of labor is linked in a fundamental way to level of technological development. Automation, because it represents a major change in production technology, may in the long run produce basic changes in occupational structure. What the consequences of widespread use of automation will be, of course, remains to be seen but the available evidence suggests that a less anomic division of labor may be the direction of change.

No attempt will be made here to add to the already extensive literature cataloguing the social problems associated with extreme functional specialization. The focus of this paper is upon technological development with an emphasis upon processes contributing to normal or to anomic forms of division of labor. Technological development is described as a sequence of changes in separate production components that form developmental stages characterized by different types of man-machine relationships. Both office and factory automation will be discussed in the context of these developmental stages. Available data regarding the effect of automation upon division of labor will be summarized and their implications for related problems discussed.

Production Components and Technological Change

A common shortcoming in discussions of the social consequences of technological change is the treatment of production technology as a unitary phenomenon. Change in certain production functions may have quite different consequences from change in others. Dividing the production process into its component functions permits analysis of these varying consequences and has the additional advantage of revealing sequences in technological development that would not otherwise be apparent.

The production process can be divided into four basic components with which more or less independent technologies are associated. The first of these is *power technology* dealing with the sources of energy used in production. A second is *processing technology* which refers to the tools and techniques used in the actual operations performed upon raw materials. A third is *materials handling technology* dealing with the transfer of materials between processing operations. The final component of production technology is *control* or the regulation of quality and quantity of

output. Any production process involving the conversion of raw materials into finished products can be separated into its power, processing, materials handling, and control components. In contemporary plants manufacturing automobile engine blocks, for example, the crude blocks are mechanically *transferred* between machines which automatically perform the various broaching, boring, milling, and other *processing* operations. Automatic inspection instruments are used, and, in some instances, feedback devices automatically *control* quality and quantity of output. Since the function of workers in these plants is limited, for the most part, to monitoring the machines, the source of *power* for each of the production components is almost exclusively electrical. Examples illustrating the fact that the production process can be divided into these four component functions could also be drawn from situations involving little or no mechanization of production operations.[5]

Technological advance in each component occurs in two phases: first, the substitution of inanimate for human performance of the function and, second, increases in the efficiency of the machinery that is introduced. While technological development may occur independently in any one of the production components, *a certain level of development of each is a necessary condition for further development of the others*. In the cotton textile industry, for example, the spinning jenny had been developed and was in widespread use prior to the introduction of either water or steam power. The use of multiple spindle jennies and spinning frames with a greater production capacity, however, was limited by the inadequacies of human power. Recourse to inanimate energy sources was thus prerequisite to further technical advance of this processing operation.

This example suggests that we may be able to see in the evolution of production technology a sequential relationship between developments in the production components described above. Examination of the history of technological change in various industries indicates that the substitution of inanimate for human power initiates a sequence of similar changes, first in processing, next in materials handling, and eventually in production control. A certain level of development of power technology is prerequisite to the use of higher speed, special purpose processing machines. In order to get maximum utilization of these new machines, it eventually becomes necessary to substitute mechanical for human handling of materials between processing operations. The development of conveyor belts and, more recently, high speed, in-line transfer equipment is an example of this change. As processing and materials handling devices become increasingly efficient and production begins to approximate a continuous flow, exercising human control of quality or quantity of output limits production capacity. Developments in processing and materials handling in themselves, of course, involve some substitution of mechanical for human control of production. A drill press and a conveyor belt, for example, involve less human control of quality and quantity of output than an auger or a wheelbarrow. High levels of development in these areas do not in themselves, however, solve problems stemming from the limitations of human control but, in fact, create such problems when their speed begins to exceed the ability of human operators to regulate quality of output. We are currently witnessing the emergence of a separate technology of production control. Computers and feedback devices are examples of developments in this area.

Stages of Technological Development

Mechanization of any one production function may have different social consequences from the others irrespective of the point at which it falls in the overall development of production technology. Our concern here, however, is with the effect upon division of labor of various phases in the developmental sequence that has been described. In most industries, three such phases can be identified. The first is the handicraft stage of production that exists prior to the sequence of technological changes with which we are primarily concerned. The second period is that in which mechanization of energy conversion and processing operations occurs. The final stage is characterized by a highly developed materials handling technology and by the introduction of automatic production control. The early developments in materials handling procedures, i.e., the initial substitution of mechanical for human transfer of materials, belong in the second rather than the third phase. The effects of the first conveyor belts were generally similar to those resulting from change in power sources and processing procedures. It is the linking together of separate operations into a continuous and automatic system which distinguishes this third period.[6]

These three phases, which will be referred to as craft production, mechanized production, and automated production, may last varying numbers of years in different industries and occur at various points in their histories. While mechanization of processing occurred very early, for example, in the production of textiles, there is still little integration of these processes around centralized, automatic controls. Oil refining, chemical processing, and the manufacture of glass are currently highly automated industries where, in some instances, basic changes in processing, materials handling, and control took place almost simultaneously. Mechanization of processing and materials handling in the automobile, steel, and rubber industries has just recently reached a point where it is becoming not only feasible but increasingly necessary to introduce automatic controls.

In spite of these variations, the form of division of labor associated with each developmental phase appears to be similar in all industries. This similarity can be accounted for, in part, by the fact that there is a unique man-machine relationship that is characteristic of each period. The worker in the craft production stage is typically an artisan whose skill lies in his ability to manipulate tools. Where the mechanization of processing has occurred, the worker becomes an operator of a special purpose machine. The development of automatic materials handling and automatic controls results in jobs in which the primary responsibility of the worker is the monitoring of an integrated production system.

The nature of the man-machine relationship is a primary link between technological development and changes in the form of division of labor. There are, of course, other ways in which these processes are linked: technologically based changes in the organizational structure of the firm that, in turn, have an effect upon division of labor will be referred to in the discussion that follows. Our major concern, however, is with the relationships among stages in the mechanization of production components, phases in the man-machine relationship, and types of division of labor. The specific relationships that have been hypothesized in the preceding pages are summarized in Table 1. The next two sections of this paper contain a more detailed discussion of these relationships, first in manufacturing and then in office operations.

From Craft Production to Industrial Automation

In the handicraft stage of production, tools are an adjunct to the skill of the craftsman, and it is primarily his ability and not his equipment that determines the quality and quantity of his output. With the mechanization of processing operations, however, skill is increasingly built into the machines. Mumford has described the difference between machines and tools as lying in the "degree of independence in the operation from the skill and motive power of the operator: the tool lends itself to manipulation, the machine to automatic action."[7] The industrial revolution of the Eighteenth Century had the frequently noted and well documented effect of replacing skilled, tool-using artisans with semi-skilled machine operators.

The significance of this change for the present analysis is two-fold. First, the development of each special purpose machine was likely to create a new job. Processing operations were not linked together and a separate operator was generally required for each piece of equipment. The Department of Labor's *Dictionary of Occupational Titles* includes thousands of jobs that are products of this process. An example from the hat manufacturing industry is the "jigger-crown-pouncing-machine opera-

TABLE 1. Relationship of production technology to division of labor.

Stage of mechanization of production components	Phase in man-machine relationship	Type of division of labor
(1) Power source: animate (2) Processing procedure: tools and simple machines (3) Materials handling procedures: not mechanized (4) Control procedures: not mechanized	Craft Production (Worker as skilled artisan)	Low degree of differentiation
(1) Power source: inanimate (2) Processing procedures: low-speed, special purpose machines (3) Materials handling procedures: early stages of mechanization (4) Control: not mechanized	Mechanized Production (Worker as machine operator)	High degree of differentiation
(1) Power source: inanimate (2) Processing procedures: high-speed, multi-purpose machines (3) Materials handling procedures: automatic (4) Control: automatic	Automated Production (Worker as machine monitor)	Low degree of differentiation

tor" whose responsibility is smoothing hat crowns. While there are some obvious similarities in the tasks performed by all semi-skilled machine operators, variations in the nature of the product and in the nature of the processing equipment result in jobs that are not simply terminologically distinct but are genuinely different occupational specialties. Secondly, the technological changes that contributed to this increased division of labor occurred almost *exclusively* in power sources and processing operations. The human operator was still, in most instances, responsible for checking quality of output and making adjustments for error in the machinery. The operator or his assistants were also responsible for handling materials between separate processing operations.

Various histories of technology lend support to the assertion that the mechanization of energy conversion and processing procedures were initial developments in most industries and that a breakdown of craft skills was associated with these changes.[8] There are also a few sociological studies that relate increased division of labor to this phase in the development of production technology. Neil Smelser's *Social Change in the Industrial Revolution* is a major work in this area.[9] The primary dependent variable in this study is structural differentiation in the British cotton textile industry and in the family economy of its working classes. Smelser found that increased structural differentiation, the generic process of which division of labor is a part, is associated with technological changes occurring primarily in power sources and processing techniques. Cottrell, in *Energy and Society*, also attributes the extensive division of labor in industrial societies to greater amounts of available energy and to the application of machines to specialized

operations.[10] The Lynds in *Middletown*, Warner and Low in *The Social System of the Modern Factory*, and Smith and Nyman in *Technology and Labor* all analyzed the social consequence of changes that were primarily developments in these two production components.[11] While their major concerns were with other matters, some of which we will have occasion to refer to later, increased division of labor may be inferred from the findings of each of these studies.

With the advent of automation there appears to be another basic change in the man-machine relationship. We have briefly described the transition from the craftsman as a skilled manipulator of tools to the industrial worker as an operator of a special purpose machine. In the automated plant the worker is increasingly a *monitor* of a *group* of special purpose machines and, in some instances, of a completely integrated production system. His responsibility may be limited to watching a panel of lights or gauges that indicate whether all production components are functioning as expected. He does not initiate processing operations nor does he have any control of quality or quantity of output. Materials handling between processing stations is automatic and the substitution of inanimate for human energy used directly in production is virtually complete.

One effect of these changes may be a reversal of the long-term trend toward increasing occupational differentiation. Automation may decrease division of labor in at least four ways. First, in a production process from which direct human involvement has been eliminated, machine monitoring and machine maintenance are almost the sole remaining functions for production workers. The task of watching or monitoring a

146   panel of lights and gauges is basically the same irrespective of the part of the production process involved or even the type of end product being produced. Automation thus reduces the variety of tasks to be performed.

Secondly, it requires a recombination of the remaining tasks. The type of worker who is best equipped to repair and maintain automated machinery, for example, is one who has a combination of mechanical, hydraulic, electrical, and other skills. The personnel manager in one automated plant described the kind of person needed to repair automated equipment as "an engineer who is willing to get his hands dirty." It is important to note, however, that automation does not result in job enlargement or increased skill requirements for all workers in automated industries. In spite of earlier enthusiastic predictions, it has not produced a general upgrading of industrial workers.[12] The integration of previously separate processing operations does have the effect, however, of recombining some tasks and is particularly likely to reduce specialization among skilled maintenance workers.

A third way in which automation may reduce division of labor is its effect upon the structure of production organizations. There is a common managerial philosophy underlying the various applications of automation. It involves a conception of the entire production process as an integrated system and not simply as a series of steps. It has been suggested that even major divisions like that between plant and office in manufacturing firms may be eliminated as a result of changes associated with the view that they are linked together in a single, interconnected system.[13] Increases in the integration of organizational structure are almost certain to produce integration of previously separate jobs into new positions involving broader responsibilities.

Finally, automation may decrease division of labor through its long run effects upon distribution of employment opportunity. Earlier studies suggest that mechanization of different production components has different effects upon the structure of demand for labor.[14] Automation appears to contribute to a general shift in the labor force from more specialized to less specialized occupations. Some degree of specialization is characteristic of almost all work in industrial societies. In expanding professional and technical fields, however, polyvalent or generalized training is required, the practitioner is likely to identify primarily with the total occupation and only secondarily with his specialty, and the public image of the professional and technician usually involves general rather than special labels. These characteristics tend to minimize the distinction between sub-specialties in these fields and have an important bearing upon the social and psychological consequences of division of labor.

It is generally conceded that we have arrived at only the early stages in the development of automation and there have been relatively few studies of the kinds of automatic materials handling and control systems currently in use. Although generalization from these studies is hazardous, the available data do support the hypothesis that one consequence of automation is decreased division of labor. Robert Blauner, after an extensive analysis of inter-industry differences in the nature of blue collar jobs, concludes that "continuous process technology . . . reverses the historic trend toward greater division of labor and specialization."[15] Various case studies have shown that the elimination and recombination of tasks in automated plants result in a decrease in the number of separate job classifications. In a large automated bakery the number of separate positions was reduced from sixteen to seven.[16] In a steel mill producing seamless pipe, automation reduced the number of job levels from seventeen to eight.[17] The following description of recombination of jobs in a highly automated power plant is a particularly dramatic example of the effect of automation upon division of labor:

... The distinctions among operators in the older (non-automated) plant according to the type of equipment they operated were eliminated in the new plant. Only one class of operators was established for the new plant: power plant operator.[18]

The combination or elimination of supervisory levels is another type of decreased job specialization which often accompanies automation. This finding is reported, for example, in both the study of the seamless pipe mill and the study of the power plant cited above. Research in a variety of other industries suggests that automation produces job enlargement in the sense of responsibility for a greater span of production.[19] While this change does not necessarily increase either the skill level or variety of tasks performed, it does tend to reduce the number of job classifications.

In a summary of studies dealing with the effects of automation in manufacturing plants, Floyd Mann has included the following statement that succinctly describes the process we are concerned with here:

The integration of what were formerly discrete units of equipment also means the integration of jobs. Old boundaries between tasks are being wiped out as jobs are combined and enlarged.[20]

We have been concerned so far in this paper primarily with technological change in manufacturing operations. Studies of the introduction of electronic data processing systems in offices suggest a somewhat different pattern of effects upon division of labor than that associated with factory automation. Analyzing work performed in offices in terms of its component functions and in terms of various developmental phases in the relationship between office workers and office machines may help in understanding this difference.

There is at least an analogy between the four production components discussed above and the elements of office work. The flow of work in the office is primarily a flow of information that must be transferred in some way between processing operations. Included in these processing operations are a wide variety of activities such as information storage or filing, changing the form of information as in typing or key punching, adding to the amount of information, sorting it in ways that make it more meaningful, etc. The major end products of this work are decisions of various sorts. Control within the total system is a matter of regulation of the "quality" of decisions in the sense of their correctness and of the "quantity" of decisions in the sense of the speed with which they can be made. Some source of energy is, of course, required for any activity.

As in the factory, each of the component functions of office work may be performed by humans or by machines and the level of mechanization of each function may vary. There also appear to be similar phases in the relationship between men and machines and these phases are apparently associated with

148 mechanization of the same components.

Until fairly recently the stage of development of most office work was comparable to that described above as the handicraft period. The equipment in use did not have skills built into it but was an adjunct to whatever ability was required of the officer worker. The typewriter is an example of equipment of this kind. In recent years the increasing use of more complex business machines has made semi-skilled machine operators of many office workers. The substitution of "key-punch operators" and "tabulating-machine operators" for "clerks" and "bookkeepers" is certainly reminiscent of the changes accompanying the mechanization of manufacturing. Specialization of office functions, of course, began prior to the development of office machines. Our concern here, however, is with *technologically* induced changes in division of labor. The initial impact of such office machinery as card sorters, key punchers, and tabulators upon man-machine relationships appears to be like that associated with factory mechanization involving the breakdown of previous functional specializations into job classifications tied to particular, special purpose machines.

Current developments like the use of computers appear to be *increasing* the number of people in job classifications of this type because they increase the need for operators of equipment peripheral to the computer, such as converters, printers, and key-punchers. Except for the people working directly with the computer, office automation may produce increased specialization of function in the sense that a narrower range of the total amount of information processed is handled by each machine operator. The similarity in the functions performed by lower level clerical workers to those performed by industrial workers in the period of mechanized production is suggested by the following quotation:

> After the conversion (to a computer), the detailed repetitive work of this function was done on machines, and the job of the clerks was either to *control* the accuracy of the work performed by the machines, or to *operate* the machines themselves.[21]

The discussion thus far suggests that what has been called office "automation" might be more appropriately seen as a major advance in the *mechanization* of information processing. Most computers in use today perform primarily a processing function. Computer technology, however, makes *possible* a system in which all information necessary for the management of an organization is stored and automatically retrieved and processed when required. Improvements in data input and output procedures will undoubtedly eliminate the peripheral processing operations. The printing out of information coming from the computer, for example, is increasingly tied directly into the computer system so that an operator of separate printing equipment is no longer necessary. This example of elimination of a functionally specialized task through the integration of production processes is a direct equivalent of the effects of factory automation described above.

Studies of office automation have produced varying and sometimes contradictory findings regarding its effect upon division of labor. Some of these contradictions are accounted for by variations in the size of the data processing systems studied and by the varying purposes for which the computers are used. Other differences in findings may be accounted for by variations in the level of mechanization of the office prior to the introduction of the computer. The organizational level studied accounts for still other differences in the results of research dealing with office automation. An illustration of some apparently contradictory findings can be seen in the two studies described below.

In a study of twenty electronic data processing installations, one of the major conclusions was that increased functional specialization is contributing substantially to the development of *anomie* among lower level clerical workers.[22] It should be noted, however, that the reported increase in job specialization occurred among workers not directly involved in the operation of the computers but in the operation of auxiliary equipment. These particular jobs most clearly illustrate the man-machine relationship characteristic of mechanization rather than automation. That an increase in division of labor is not necessarily associated with the introduction of computers is clearly indicated by a study conducted in a large electric power company. As a result of the change-over to an electronic data processing system, there was a 50 percent reduction in the number of separate jobs in the central accounting area of this company.[23]

There is both greater consensus and more information available regarding the effects of office automation upon division of labor at higher organizational levels. The installation of large scale computers generally produces more centralized decision making, decreased specialization among organizational units, and the elimination of some levels of authority.[24] There are two factors which appear to account for these changes. First, decision-making involving a limited number of alternatives, a function customarily performed by people in middle management positions, can now be taken over by large scale computers.

This change represents mechanization of certain elements of control. Secondly, the greater speed and accuracy with which information can be handled and processed with a computer make possible more centralized decision-making and permit the recombination of organizational units. The accessibility of larger amounts of more accurate information makes it possible to manage organizations of increasing size without increasing the differentiation of organizational structure.

Automation, Alienation, and Anomie

The data available regarding effects of automation suggest that a decrease in division of labor in both offices and factories is at least a reasonable hypothesis. Decreasing functional specialization can also be seen as a logical consequence of a pattern of change in production technology that begins with the development of new energy sources and culminates in a production system integrated through the use of automatic control devices. If automation contributes to a change in division of labor from, in Durkheim's terms, its anomic to its normal form, it should have important consequences for the function and meaning of work in industrial societies.

While the available data permit only very cautious generalizations, they do suggest that highly automated production systems reduce the alienation of the industrial worker. This finding is reported, for example, in both the major studies conducted thus far in automated, continuous process plants.[25] While there is apparently contradictory evidence from some other studies, it is important to note that these studies were of factories and offices in which there is not yet a high level of integration of operations through the use of centralized automatic controls.[26] In the settings where this level of integration has been achieved, increased responsibility on the job, greater control over the work process, a more meaningful in-plant status structure, and more frequent teamwork apparently contribute to feelings of social solidarity and a greater sense of involvement in the total work process.

Job enlargement in the sense of responsibility for a larger share of the production process appears to be the key element in this change. Durkheim noted but tended to de-emphasize the fact that functional interdependence does not *necessarily* produce social solidarity and meaningful work experience. Interdependence is characteristic of work on an assembly line as well as in an integrated, automatic production system. The form of division of labor associated with the latter, however, apparently tends to produce organic solidarity while the result of the assembly line is increased *anomie*.[27]

Summary and Conclusions

The development of production technology has been viewed in this paper as a sequence of innovations in particular components of the production process. Various stages in this sequence are accompanied by important differences in the relationship between men and machines. These differences tend to produce distinctive patterns of division of labor. Automation, in its most advanced form, completes the mechanization of production components and introduces basic changes in the man-machine relationship. The evidence from the few studies that have been completed suggests that automation may eventually reverse the long-term trend toward an increasingly differentiated occupational structure and may reduce the amount of alienation and *anomie* characteristic of earlier stages in the development of industrial technology.

In diversified economies like our own, there are industries that represent each of the phases in the developmental sequence that has been described. Only a small proportion of office and factory workers are now in highly automated settings. Although some industries may never go through the whole sequence, most major industries appear to be moving toward the stage of automated production. If automation becomes more widely used its effects will be more pervasive. While our attention has been focussed in this paper upon changes occurring in the social structure of the work place, the pattern of effects noted cannot help but have important consequences for the structure of other social systems as well. The effects of contemporary division of labor are so pervasive that they include most of the major characteristics of industrial societies. If the long-run consequence of automation is a basic change in this form of division of labor, its effects should be equally profound.

NOTES

1. Emile Durkheim, *The Division of Labor in Society*, Glencoe, Ill.: The Free Press, 1933, pp. 353–373.
2. Georges Friedmann, *The Anatomy of Work*, New York: The Free Press of Glencoe, 1961, pp. 68–81.
3. *Ibid.*
4. L. E. Davis, "Job Design and Productivity: A New Approach," *Personnel*, 33 (March, 1957), pp. 418–430; R. H. Guest, "Job Enlargement—A Revolution in Job Design," *Personnel Administration*, 20 (March–April, 1957), pp. 9–16.

5. There are, of course, other types of technological developments that have had major consequences for industrial societies. The invention of new products (automobiles, television, etc.) and the invention or discovery of new materials (steel, nylon, aluminum, etc.) are cases in point. Our concern in this paper, however, is not with either the materials used or the end product but only with change in the production *process*.

6. Buckingham has described the technological developments leading to automation in a somewhat similar fashion. See Walter Buckingham, *Automation: Its Impact on Business and People*, New York: Harper and Bros., 1961, pp. 5–15. Both Robert Blauner and Alain Touraine have distinguished similar phases in man-machine relationships. See Robert Blauner, *Alienation and Freedom*, Chicago: The University of Chicago Press, 1964, and Alain Touraine, *L'évolution du travail ouvrier aux usines Renault*, Paris: Centre National de la Recherche Scientifique, 1955.

7. Lewis Mumford, *Technics and Civilization*, New York: Harcourt, Brace, 1934, p. 10.

8. Mumford, *ibid.*; T. K. Derry and Trevor I. Williams, *A Short History of Technology*, London: Oxford University Press, 1961; John W. Oliver, *History of American Technology*, New York: Ronald Press, 1956.

9. Neil J. Smelser, *Social Change in the Industrial Revolution*, Chicago: The University of Chicago Press, 1959.

10. Fred Cottrell, *Energy and Society*, New York: McGraw-Hill, 1955, pp. 209–211.

11. Robert S. and Helen M. Lynd, *Middletown*, New York: Harcourt, Brace, 1929; W. Lloyd Warner and J. O. Low, *The Social System of the Modern Factory*, New Haven: Yale University Press, 1947; E. Smith and R. Nyman, *Technology and Labor*, New Haven: Yale University Press, 1939.

12. For a general discussion of the effect of automation on skill level, see J. R. Bright, *Automation and Management*, Boston: Division of Research, Graduate School of Business Administration, Harvard University, 1958.

13. John Diebold, "Automation as a Management Problem," in Howard Boone Jacobson and Joseph S. Roucek, *Automation and Society*, New York: Philosophical Library, 1959, pp. 318–320.

14. Harry Jerome, *Mechanization in Industry*, New York: National Bureau of Economic Research, 1934, pp. 391–403.

15. Robert Blauner, *op. cit.*, p. 143.

16. U.S. Department of Labor, Bureau of Labor Statistics, *A Case Study of a Large Mechanized Bakery*, Washington: U.S. Government Printing Office, 1956, p. 16.

17. Charles R. Walker, *Toward the Automatic Factory*, New Haven: Yale University Press, 1957, p. 61.

18. Floyd C. Mann and L. Richard Hoffman, *Automation and the Worker*, New York: Henry Holt, 1960, p. 72.

19. J. R. Bright, *op. cit.*; Robert Blauner, *op. cit.*; William A. Faunce, "The Automobile Industry: A Case Study in Automation," in Howard Boone Jacobson and Joseph S. Roucek, *op. cit.*, pp. 44–53.

20. Floyd C. Mann, "Psychological and Organizational Impacts," in John T. Dunlop (ed.), *Automation and Technological Change*, Englewood Cliffs, N.J.: Prentice Hall, 1962, p. 51.

21. Testimony of Howard Coughlin, U.S. Congress, 84th Congress, Joint Economic Committee, Subcommittee on Economic Stabilization, *Automation and Technological Change*, October 14–28, 1955, pp. 215–216. (The italics are mine.)

22. Ida R. Hoos, *Automation in the Office*, Washington: Public Affairs Press, 1961.

23. Floyd C. Mann and Lawrence K. Williams, "Organizational Impact of White Collar Automation," *Annual Proceedings, Industrial Relations Research Association*, 1958, p. 66.

24. Floyd C. Mann and Lawrence K. Williams, *op. cit.*; Ida Hoos, *op. cit.*; Thomas L. Whisler and George P. Shultz, "Automation and the Management Process," *The Annals*, 340 (March, 1962), pp. 81–89.

25. Robert Blauner, *op. cit.*; Floyd C. Mann and L. Richard Hoffman, *op. cit.*

26. Ida R. Hoos, *op. cit.*; Charles R. Walker, *op. cit.*; William A. Faunce, *op. cit.*

INFORMATION INPUTS

Brown, Warren B. 1966. "Systems, Boundaries, and Information Flow," *Academy of Management Journal*, 9 (December), 318–327.

Churchill, Lindsey. 1965. "Some Sociological Aspects of Message Load: 'Information Input Overload and Features of Growth in Communications-Oriented Institutions.' " In *Mathematical Explorations in Behavioral Science*, F. Massarik and P. Ratoosch, eds. Homewood, Ill.: Richard D. Irwin and The Dorsey Press.

Deutsch, Karl W. 1952. "On Communication Models in the Social Sciences," *Public Opinion Quarterly*, 16 (Fall), 356–380.

Ericson, Richard F. 1969. "The Impact of Cybernetic Information Technology on Management Value Systems," *Management Science*, 16 (October), B-40 to B-60.

Fair, William R. 1966. "The Corporate CIA—A Prediction of Things to Come," *Management Science*, 12 (June), B-489 to B-503.

Feld, M. D. 1959. "Information and Authority: The Structure of Military Organization," *American Sociological Review*, 24 (February), 15–22.

Janowitz, Morris, and William Delany. 1957. "The Bureaucrat and the Public: A Study of Informational Perspectives," *Administrative Science Quarterly*, 2 (September), 141–162.

Malmgren, H. B. 1961. "Information, Expectations and the Theory of the Firm," *Quarterly Journal of Economics*, 75 (August), 399–421.

Margolis, Julius. 1958. "The Analysis of the Firm: Rationalism, Conventionalism, and Behaviorism," *Journal of Business*, 31 (July), 187–199.

Margolis, Julius. 1960. "Sequential Decision Making in the Firm," Papers and Proceedings of the Seventy-Second Annual Meeting of the American Economic Association, *American Economic Review*, 50 (May), 526–533.

Meier, Richard L. 1963. "Information Input Overload: Features of Growth in Communications-Oriented Institutions," *Libri*, 13, 1–44.

Meier, Richard L. 1963. "Communications Overload: Proposals from the Study of a University Library," *Administrative Science Quarterly*, 7 (March), 521–544.

Milgram, Stanley. 1970. "The Experience of Living in Cities," *Science*, 167 (March 13), 1461–1468.

Richardson, G. B. 1959. "Equilibrium, Expectations, and Information," *The Economic Journal*, 69 (June), 223–237.

Shubik, Martin. 1952. "Information, Theories of Competition, and the Theory of Games," *The Journal of Political Economy*, 60 (April), 145–150.

Shubik, Martin. 1954. "Information, Risk, Ignorance and Indeterminacy," *Quarterly Journal of Economics*, 68 (November), 629–640.

TECHNOLOGICAL INPUTS

Ackoff, Russell L. 1955. "Automatic Management: A Forecast and Its Education Implications," *Management Science*, 2 (October), 55–60.

Banks, Olive. 1960. *Attitudes of Steelworkers to Technological Change*. Liverpool: Liverpool University Press.

Bowers, Raymond V., et al. 1962. "Technological Change and the Organization Man: Preliminary Conceptualization of a Research Project," *Sociological Inquiry*, 32 (Winter), 117–127.

Bright, J. R. 1958. "Does Automation Raise Skill Requirements?" *Harvard Business Review*, 36 (July–August), 85–98.

154 Brozen, Yale. 1951. "Adapting to Technological Change," *Journal of Business*, 24 (April), 114–126.

Burack, Elmer H. 1967. "Technology and Supervisory Functions: A Preliminary View," *Human Organization*, 26 (Winter), 256–264.

Burack, Elmer H., and Frank H. Cassell. 1967. "Technological Change and Manpower Developments in Advanced Production Systems," *Academy of Management Journal*, 10 (September), 293–308.

Burlingame, John F. 1961. "Information Technology and Decentralization," *Harvard Business Review*, 39 (November–December), 121–126.

Champion, Dean J. 1967. "Some Effects of Office Automation upon Status, Role Change, and Depersonalization," *The Sociological Quarterly*, 8 (Winter), 71–84.

Fadem, Joel A. 1967. "The Case of the Australian Waterfront: Organizational Design," *The Journal of Industrial Relations*, 9 (March), 26–36.

Faunce, William A. 1958. "Automation and the Automobile Worker," *Social Problems*, 6 (Summer), 68–78.

Faunce, William A. 1958. "Automation in the Automobile Industry: Some Consequences for In-Plant Social Structure," *American Sociological Review*, 23 (August), 401–407.

Faunce, William A., et al. 1962. "Automation and the Employee," *The Annals of the American Academy of Political and Social Science*, 340 (March), 60–68.

Feldman, Arnold S. 1967. "The Interpenetration of Firm and Society." In *Dynamics of Modern Society*, William J. Goode, ed. New York: Atherton Press.

Hage, Jerard, and Michael Aiken. 1969. "Routine Technology, Social Structure, and Organization Goals," *Administrative Science Quarterly*, 14 (September), 366–376.

Harvey, Edward. 1968. "Technology and the Structure of Organizations," *American Sociological Review*, 33 (April), 247–259.

Hutton, Geoffrey. 1962. "Management in a Changing Mental Hospital," *Human Relations*, 15 (November), 283–310.

Janowitz, Morris. 1959. "Changing Patterns of Organizational Authority: The Military Establishment," *Administrative Science Quarterly*, 3 (March), 473–493.

Janowitz, Morris. 1960. *The Professional Soldier*. Glencoe, Ill.: Free Press.

Janowitz, Morris, ed. 1967. *The New Military: Changing Patterns of Organization*. New York: Wiley.

Jasinski, Frank J. 1959. "Adapting Organization for New Technology," *Harvard Business Review*, 37 (January–February), 79–86.

Karsh, Bernard, and Jack Siegman. 1964. "Functions of Ignorance in Introducing Automation," *Social Problems*, 12 (Fall), 141–150.

Lipstreu, Otis. 1960. "Organizational Implications of Automation," *Academy of Management Journal*, 3 (August), 119–124.

Lipstreu, Otis, and Kenneth A. Reed. 1965. "A New Look at the Organizational Implications of Automation," *Academy of Management Journal*, 8 (March), 24–31.

Lodahl, Thomas M. 1964. "Patterns of Job Attitudes in Two Assembly Technologies," *Administrative Science Quarterly*, 8 (March), 482–519.

Mann, Floyd C., and L. Richard Hoffman. 1956. "Individual and Organizational Correlates of Automation," *The Journal of Social Issues*, 12 (April), 7–17.

Mann, Floyd C., and L. K. Williams. 1960. "Observations on the Dynamics of a Change to Electronic Data-Processing Equipment," *Administrative Science Quarterly*, 5 (September), 217–256.

Mann, Floyd C., and L. K. Williams. 1962. "Some Effects of the Changing Work Environment in the Office," *Journal of Social Issues*, 18 (July), 90–101.

Meyer, Marshall W. 1968. "Automation and Bureaucratic Structure," *The American Journal of Sociology*, 74 (November), 256–264.

Michael, Donald N. 1966. "Some Long-Range Implications of Computer Technology for Human Behavior in Organizations," *The American Behavioral Scientist*, 9 (April), 29–35.

Myers, Charles A., ed. 1967. *The Impact of Computers on Management*. Cambridge, Mass.: M.I.T. Press.

INFORMATION AND TECHNOLOGICAL INPUTS

Rubenstein, Albert H., et al. 1967. "Some Organizational Factors Related to the Effective- **155**
ness of Management Science Groups in Industry," *Management Science,* 13 (April),
B-508 to B-518.

Schoen, Donald R. 1969. "Managing Technological Innovation," *Harvard Business Review,* 47 (May–June), 156–167.

Shultz, George P., and Thomas Whisler, eds. 1960. *Management, Organization, and the
Computer.* Glencoe, Ill.: Free Press.

Siegman, Jack, and Bernard Karsh. 1962. "Some Organizational Correlates of White
Collar Automation," *Sociological Inquiry,* 32 (Winter), 108–116.

Silverman, William. 1966. "The Economic and Social Effects of Automation in an Organization," *The American Behavioral Scientist,* 9 (June), 3–8.

Smith, Michael A. 1968. "Process Technology and Powerlessness," *The British Journal
of Sociology,* 19 (March), 76–88.

Trist, E. L., et al. 1963. *Organization Choice.* London: Tavistock.

Vergin, Roger C. 1967. "Computer Induced Organization Changes," *Business Topics,* 15
(Summer), 61–68.

Walker, Charles R. 1968. *Technology, Industry, and Man: The Age of Acceleration.* New
York: McGraw-Hill.

Weber, C. E. 1959. "Change in Managerial Manpower with Mechanization of Data-
Processing," *Journal of Business,* 32 (April), 151–163.

Whisler, Thomas L., and George P. Shultz. 1962. "Automation and the Management
Process," *The Annals of the American Academy of Political and Social Science,* 340
(March), 82–89.

CHAPTER FOUR

Human Inputs

The first part of this chapter examines the effects of boundary as well as imported clients on internal organizational phenomena.

Thompson identifies four types of boundary-spanning output roles, develops a typology of transaction structures, and utilizes sequential analysis to study the contingent interaction process. He provides numerous examples of external environmental influences on internal organizational behavior: nonmember bribes evoking one of three responses; a nonmandatory exchange relationship associated with an array of programs for the boundary spanner; and the internal effects of "impurities" introduced into the transaction structure by nonmembers.

Katz and Eisenstadt also add to our knowledge of the effects of boundary clients on the organization. They find interesting evidence of debureaucratization in official-client interactions and cite various factors accounting for this phenomenon, the major one being various types of official-client dependence. The authors consider debureaucratization to be caused by a "disturbance in the relationship between an organization and its environment," characterized by the "impinging of nonbureaucratic roles, or of other bureaucratic roles, on the specific bureaucratic role in question." The concepts and observations they and Thompson offer should stimulate the administrator to examine the perimeter of his organization as well as the boundaries of the various organizational subsystems.

Bidwell and Vreeland distinguish three types of client-serving organizations and explore the effects of the professional-client relationship for each type on authority structures and control.

Lefton and Rosengren also view the client-organization relationships as critical factors influencing organizational structure and functioning. Their premise is that organizations may vary in their interest in the biographical careers of clients along a social space and a social time dimension. Utilizing the variations that this typology yields, they delineate the consequences for client compliance problems, staff consensus about means and ends, and modes of interorganizational collaboration.

The second part of the chapter focuses on the effects of a new human input, the new successor to a management position, on the organization.

Guest, in a comparative study of two "outsider" management successors, outlines seven inherited institutional pressures and traditions that shaped their disparate administrative actions. He also discusses the consequences associated with these different actions, e.g., tension and stress, hostility, group meetings, use of formal rules, character and content of interaction, and performance.

The last part of the chapter considers the effects of participant-inputs on the organization. Gamson develops a typology of organizational responses to members and explores the conditions under which each type may occur. She specifies six conditions under which the impact of members of an organization would be maximized.

Four noteworthy papers are found in the additional readings section. Grusky develops a dual orientation to the successor problem. He considers succession in terms of the successor's role-set and in terms of structural factors. Four hypotheses are proposed for the former orientation and six for the latter. The dependent variable for both is organizational instability.

Two papers scrutinize the consultant-client relationship from a theoretical and a case-study perspective. Tilles posits sixteen propositions and six corollaries that he derives from a paired-phenomena approach. This approach is used to analyze four variables affecting the outcome of the consulting relationship. In a stimulating paper, Argyris attempts to delineate issues, generate hypotheses, and develop models concerning consulting relationships designed to change interpersonal relationships within an organization. He identifies a major dilemma a consultant may experience, the basis of which is a value incongruency between client and consultant. One method in which the dilemma is resolved may be costly to the organization. Argyris believes that human-relations consultants should "practice" in their relationships to clients what they "preach" to them about clients' relationships with other organizational members. Among the insights in the article are: a dependency relationship should not be established in either direction; the consultant should emphasize

HUMAN INPUTS

the process of development; and defensiveness is a major interpersonal problem. Argyris also employs the marginal-man concept to generate five problems that the consultant may experience.

Brown discusses how the informal and the formal organization do and should reflect member characteristics. He examines six possible organizational adjustments to reflect member characteristics.

ORGANIZATIONS AND OUTPUT TRANSACTIONS[1]

James D. Thompson

Complex purposive organizations receive inputs from, and discharge outputs to, environments, and virtually all such organizations develop specialized roles for these purposes. *Output roles,* designed to arrange for distribution of the organization's ultimate product, service, or impact to other agents of the society thus are *boundary-spanning* roles linking organization and environment through interaction between member and non-member.

Organizational output roles are defined in part by reciprocal roles of non-members. Teacher, salesman, and caseworker roles can only be understood in relation to pupil, customer, and client roles. Both member and non-member roles contain the expectation of closure or completion of interaction, leading either to the severance of interaction or bringing the relationship into a new phase.[2] Each output role, together with the reciprocating non-member role, can be considered as built into a *transaction structure.*

Because output roles exist in structures that span the boundaries of the organization, they may be important sources of organization adaptation to environmental influences. Empirical studies reflect this fact more than do theories of organization.

Classic bureaucratic theory is preoccupied with behavioral relations ordered by a single, unified authority structure from which the client is excluded,[3] and only recently has an explicit correction for this one-sided approach been introduced by Eisenstadt's theory of debureaucratization.[4] Another strain of organization theory, following Chester Barnard, clouds the significance of input-output problems by lumping investors, clients, suppliers, and customers, as members of the "co-operative system."[5] The developing inducements-contributions theory of March and Simon has so far been directed primarily at the problem of recruiting and motivating members or employees.[6]

One purpose of this paper will be to focus theoretical attention on boundary-spanning behavior by way of output roles. A second will be to indicate that there are several types of transaction structures, each having peculiar significance for the comparative analysis of organizations. A third aim will be to indicate that transaction processes can be studied profitably through sequential analysis. Finally, some larger consequences of output relationships will be suggested.

Consideration will be limited to those transaction structures that call for face-to-face interpersonal interaction between member and non-member, thus ignoring the cigarette "salesman" who may periodically load a vending machine without seeing his customers or knowing who

"Organizations and Output Transactions," *The American Journal of Sociology,* 68, 3 (November 1962), 309–324. Reprinted with the permission of the author and of the publisher, The University of Chicago Press.

they are, and the soldier who may deliver destruction to an enemy he neither sees nor could identify. Consideration will also be limited to those cases in which the output role is occupied by an employed agent of the organization.

Characteristics of Transaction Structures

For any transaction structure there appear to be three possible outcomes: (1) *completion* of a transaction as defined by organizational norms, (2) *abortion,* in which interaction is terminated without completion of the transaction, or (3) *side transaction,* in which member and non-member complete an exchange not desired or approved by the organization.[7] Which of these three outcomes emerges will in part be determined by the desires, attitudes, and actions of the two parties involved. But the likely paths from initiation of interaction to termination, and the branching points which lead to one or another outcome, are largely defined by the type of transaction structure.

Elements of a Typology

The organization cannot predict in advance of any specific encounter just what desires, attitudes, or actions the non-member will bring to the transaction structure, but the organization can estimate in advance with reasonable accuracy two things: (1) the extent to which it has armed its agents with routines, and (2) the extent to which the non-member is compelled to participate in the relationship.

The first dimension will be labeled one of *specificity of control over member.* Undoubtedly this forms a continuum, but it will be discussed here only in its ex-

tremes. At one extreme the member is equipped with a single, complete program—a standard procedure which supposedly does not vary, regardless of the behavior of the non-member. At the other extreme, the member's behavior is expected to be guided primarily by the behavior of the non-member, although always in relation to some organizational target or goal.[8] The supermarket checkout clerk approximates the *programmed* role, while the social caseworker illustrates the *heuristic* variety.

The second dimension, also a continuum but here dichotomized, will be labeled *degree of non-member discretion.* At one extreme the non-member finds interaction *mandatory,* at the other it is *optional.* It may be presumed that the prisoner, for example, finds interaction with the guard mandatory. To be sure the prisoner may evade interaction by escape or by behavior which results in transfer to another cell block or prison. But short of these extremes the prisoner cannot choose whom he will interact with or whether to interact; the relationship is mandatory.

The optional state is exemplified by the salesman-customer relationship under conditions of "perfect competition," where the prospect has a wide choice of salesmen. Not only does the customer have discretion over whether to interact, but he also may terminate it at will, before completion of a transaction.

When these two dichotomized dimensions are combined, four types of output structures emerge:

Degree of non-member discretion	Specificity of organizational control	
	Member programmed	Member heuristic
Interaction mandatory	I	III
Interaction optional	II	IV

Temptation to label each cell is strong, since there are familiar categorizations readily available which appear to correspond to each. Cell I, for example, might be considered "clerical," Cell II "commercial," Cell III "semi-professional," and Cell IV "professional." The temptation has been resisted, however, because casual, traditional categorizations may in fact hide some of the distinctions which this typology attempts to bring out. Thus, transactions which might typically be lumped under the term "commercial" may, in fact, appear in any of the cells defined here.

Occurrence of Transaction Structures

Organizations which develop elaborate programs for those in output roles appear to be those that either (1) provide services for large numbers of persons and, therefore, face many non-members relative to each member at the output boundary, or (2) employ a mechanized production technology which places a premium on large runs of standardized products, attaches heavy costs to retooling, and, therefore, depend on a large volume of standardized transactions per member at the output boundary.[9] The first condition seems appropriate for clerical activities, such as the issuance of licenses or permits by a government bureau, and is especially likely when the organization holds a monopoly position, as a government often does. This seems to correspond to Cell I in the typology above, and to classic bureaucratic theory.

The second condition seems to describe commercial transactions of mass-produced products under competitive conditions and corresponds to Cell II in the typology. When competition is removed, as in the seller's market for auto-mobiles after World War II, the role of salesman can be redefined into a clerical role, with the salesman merely writing orders and adding names to the waiting list—and perhaps adding a side transaction to give the customer a priority rank in exchange for private payment.[10] Under competitive conditions, however, the sales person expresses one or more organizational programs governing size, style, color, price, terms, delivery schedules, and so on, and the customer either takes it or leaves it to search among other organizations for a more suitable program.

Neither of these transaction structures is appropriate for the organization which must "tailor" its output, for here the exigencies make it impractical if not impossible to develop standard programs in advance. Instead the organization must rely on the judgment of the member at the output boundary. Such roles tend to be assigned to professionally trained or certified persons, for it is believed that the professional type of education qualifies individuals to make judgments or exercise discretion in situations appropriate to their specialization.

When non-member participation is mandatory the transaction structure corresponds to Cell III in the typology above. Examples would include the therapy-oriented prison and the military hospital, the public school, and the *public* (as distinguished from "voluntary") welfare agency. In each case, the non-member (prisoner, patient, pupil, or applicant) is obliged to participate in the structure, and in each case the member is expected to vary his behavior to suit the particular condition of the non-member.

When interaction of the heuristic variety is optional for the non-member, the transaction structure corresponds to Cell IV in the typology. This would encompass the "voluntary" (non-governmental)

164 welfare agency and the voluntary hospital. Many of the services which fit this category are dispensed by private entrepreneurial arrangements—by private practitioners—rather than in large-scale organizational contexts. It appears that this reflects the relative complexity of the process in this kind of transaction structure, which makes it especially difficult when subjected to the additional constraints of an organizational context.

It is suggested that in the order listed above, and numbered in the typology, the four types of transaction structures are increasingly difficult to operate.

Transaction Processes

The same three types of outcomes—successful transaction, abortion, and side transaction—are available for all of the transaction structures, but significant contrasts appear in the possible courses of interaction. The final state, and the paths to it, *depend in each case on contingencies and on responses to contingencies.*

Our conceptual apparatus for analyzing contingent interaction is ill-developed, since interaction theory has been preoccupied with structure-maintaining behavior, that is, with behavior conforming to stable norms and with social control mechanisms to correct deviation. The contingencies and possible paths of interaction, therefore, will be shown in flow diagrams. These are offered as hypothetical, for literature search did not reveal sufficient data to "test" them, but illustrative citations will be made.

For illustration, the possibilities for Type I, where the member is programmed and the non-member finds interaction mandatory, are shown in Figure 1. Once contact is made, the non-member may respond in one of three ways, and each, in turn, presents several response possibilities to the member. *If,* following initial contact, the non-member responds appropriately by offering necessary information, the member may routinely complete the transaction. Instead of responding appropriately, however, the non-member may resist or offer a bribe. *If* the non-member resists, the member applies punishments, and the non-member may respond by increasing resistance, by co-operating, or by offering a bribe. The bribe attempt thus may be made immediately upon initial contact or following an exchange of activity. In either case, however, the member may elect one of three alternative responses to the bribe offer: accept it, apply additional punishments, or explore the pros and cons of the bribe possibility. And so on, as is indicated in Figure 1. In each flow diagram we have attempted to depict as the central pattern that course of interaction most desired by the organization. In each, however, there are several possibilities for the interaction to digress from the desired path, swinging either to the right or left. In the more complex transaction structures, the course of interaction may swing from one stream to the other several times before the final outcome is reached, and one of the major problems for the member is to counter each digression so that it returns to the central path and ultimately results in a successful transaction.

Why members and non-members elect one route rather than another at each switching point is a subject for microanalysis and is beyond the scope of this paper.

The number of "ifs" or contingencies —even in this simplest type of transaction—is impressive when diagrammed, but too large to make verbal reproduction possible. The following discussion will focus, therefore, on certain implica-

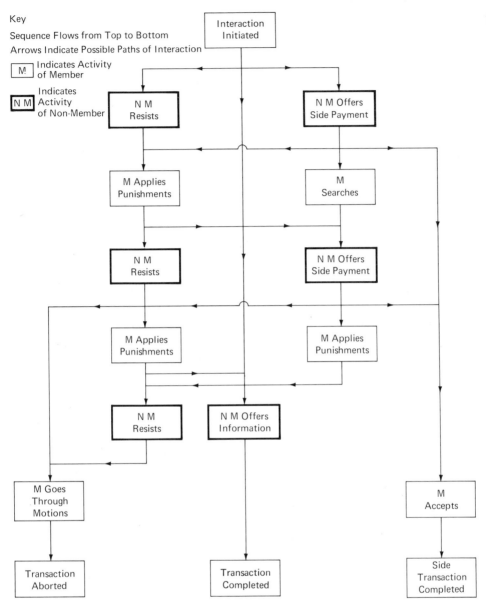

Key

Sequence Flows from Top to Bottom

Arrows Indicate Possible Paths of Interaction

M̱ Indicates Activity of Member

N M Indicates Activity of Non-Member

Interaction Initiated

N M Resists

N M Offers Side Payment

M Applies Punishments

M Searches

N M Resists

N M Offers Side Payment

M Applies Punishments

M Applies Punishments

N M Resists

N M Offers Information

M Goes Through Motions

M Accepts

Transaction Aborted

Transaction Completed

Side Transaction Completed

Figure 1

tions of contingencies for behavior within each type of transaction structure.

Interaction in Type I Structures

Here the non-member's participation is mandatory, the member is programmed, and the organization expects a large number of output transactions from the member (see Fig. 1).

The course of interaction is simplest if the non-member chooses to complete the transaction speedily, for he appears to the member to be co-operative. The member scores a completed transaction in a minimum of time, which contributes toward maximizing the number of transactions in serial and not only puts the member in line for organizational rewards but may provide the personal satisfaction of a "job well done." Blau, for example, noted that employment interviewers in a government agency avoided operations that took time without helping to improve their statistical records. Since the records served as the basis for evaluating performance, concentration on this goal made interviewers "unresponsive to requests from clients that would interfere with its attainment." [11]

If the non-member chooses to seek concession from the member, he must offer personal satisfactions sufficient to induce the member to risk penalties that the organization can apply if deviation from programs is detected. Blau found that at times the social reward of the client's appreciation led governmental employment interviewers to offer extra help,[12] and students of prisons have reported favored treatment by guards of prisoners who could exercise (or withhold) informal control over other inmates.[13]

That the opposite result—penalties for seeking too much help—can occur is suggested by the analysis of another employment office. Francis and Stone note that the client's eligibility for unemployment compensation is in effect determined by the interviewer's report, and that this report reflects the interviewer's *judgment* as to whether the claimant has given an accurate or exaggerated account of his history and present circumstances.[14] Blau also reports the use of punitive measures to vent *antagonism against aggressive clients*.[15]

The bribe attempt involves risk for both member and non-member. If the inducements offered by the non-member are insufficient, the member may regard him as unco-operative and therefore apply penalties. If, on the other hand, the non-member's offer is sufficiently inducing, the member must somehow hide his deviation from the program, and runs the risk of being caught. The bribe attempt, therefore, often calls for a rather delicate "sounding out process." [16]

If neither party is able to marshal enough power to bring a transaction or a side transaction to a conclusion, this mandatory relationship is likely to settle into a going-through-the-motions, with each party seeking to maximize his rewards or minimize his costs.[17] From the standpoint of official organizational goals, then, the transaction is aborted. If interaction must be sustained, as in the prison, it is likely to become a struggle for control. That the struggle for control can be most subtle is brought out by Gresham Sykes' study of the corruption of authority in the maximum security prison.[18]

Interaction in Type II Structures

In this case the non-member's participation is optional, the member is programmed, and the organization expects a large number of output transactions from the member (see Fig. 2).

Since the relationship is not mandatory, the organization usually develops an *array* of programs, one to appeal to each class or category of potential customer. The non-member, in interacting with this organization, is foregoing interaction with another, and hence seeks to determine rapidly whether a satisfactory program is available. The "gambit," or "opening move," is therefore a crucial issue in this interaction process. Lombard reports some of the difficulties salesgirls faced in "sizing up" prospective customers. In a children's clothing department, for example, "each customer presented . . . a different set of values that determined her taste in the clothes she bought for her children." Knowledge of style was not alone sufficient to make a sale, for the salesgirl could not express this in a way that criticized the customer's taste. With respect to price, the store suggested that "unless a customer made some other request, a salesgirl would do well to show her clothes in a middle price range."[19]

The simplest situation in this output transaction occurs when the gambit is successful, either because the non-member offers enough accurate information or the member "sizes up" the non-member correctly. On either basis the most suitable program is offered and the non-member accepts or rejects. The transaction has been completed successfully in short order, or has been aborted clearly and speedily, permitting the member to devote attention to other prospects and the non-member to seek a more satisfactory supplier.

A complication arises when the member selects from his repertoire of programs an unsuitable one because of inaccurate "size up," incorrect interpretation of the information given by the non-member, or false or misleading information offered by the non-member. The result may be (a) further exploration until a fitting program is identified, which is relatively costly to both parties, (b) withdrawal of the non-member from the output structure, in which case a potential transaction is lost to a competitor, or (c) continued interaction on the basis of false optimism, with mounting frustration for one or both parties as they find the investment mounting and the possibility of satisfaction dwindling.[20] In the latter case, the eventual abortion of the

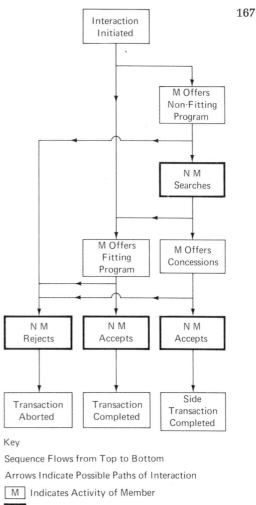

Key

Sequence Flows from Top to Bottom

Arrows Indicate Possible Paths of Interaction

M   Indicates Activity of Member

NM Indicates Activity of Non-Member

Figure 2

transaction is likely to be unpleasant, reducing the possibility of future interaction between member and non-member. It is in this frustrating situation that the member is most likely to deviate from approved programs, misrepresenting the product, offering inferior substitutes, or finding ways of offering arrangements not approved by the organization, such as special deliveries or price reductions by shaving commissions. Another possible outcome of this situation is for the non-member to reduce his standards—accepting another color, style, or settling for a different size, delivery date, and so on. When this occurs, the transaction is completed, although perhaps at the expense of future transactions.

Because prolonged search behavior is "costly," requiring investment of the time and energy where the outcome is problematic, ability to "close the deal" as early as possible becomes almost as crucial as the gambit.

Interaction in Type III Structures

Here the non-member's participation is mandatory, the member must tailor his service to the particular needs of the non-member, and the organization must therefore judge the member's performance in terms of results rather than in terms of conformity to prescribed procedures (see Fig. 3).

The straight-forward and relatively easy case occurs when the non-member elects to complete the transaction with least effort and responds appropriately. The ability of the non-member to take *active* part in the heuristic process seems frequently to be important, and especially so in comparison with the Type I output structure. Nurses were found to prefer an active patient who could make his needs and wants known, if for no other reason than to help his own treatment. In contrast, ward aides, whose duties defined the patient as "something like a necessary evil, preferred the passive patient above all others." [21]

When the non-member's responses are appropriate, both parties achieve a satisfactory outcome at minimum cost, and the member has the additional reward of evidence that his skills were instrumental—that he did a job well. But what happens when the response of the non-member is inappropriate? [22] The inappropriate response might come either from a non-member with a sincere desire to co-operate or from a non-member who is resisting. Co-operation by the non-member does not guarantee his appropriate response, for he may be incapable of articulating appropriate information, may not understand which responses are desired by the member, or may zealously offer a flood of irrelevant information. Extreme status differences between member and non-member, often found in the "helping professions," can lead to this situation. Fanshel concludes that casework help is tailored more for the verbal, communicative group than it is for "the significantly large group of clients who find difficulty in expressing their feelings and their basic ideas about the problems that bring them to the agency." [23]

When an inadequate or inappropriate response is made, therefore, the member must form a judgment (or leap to a conclusion) about the reason. If he defines the non-member as unco-operative he may apply punishments, while if he defines the non-member as sincere but inept, he may search for relevant information by seeking to educate the non-member to the appropriate role. This educational activity under such circumstances is clearly brought out by Israeli responses to large numbers of immigrants who had yet to learn client roles, [24] but there is no reason to believe that it does not occur in more "normal" or less striking situations.

Whether the member will search for information or, rather, punish the non-member for inappropriate responses, will depend largely on the member's conclusions regarding the reasons for inappropriate responses. If the non-member's search for the proper role is unsuccessful, or if he responds to punishment by

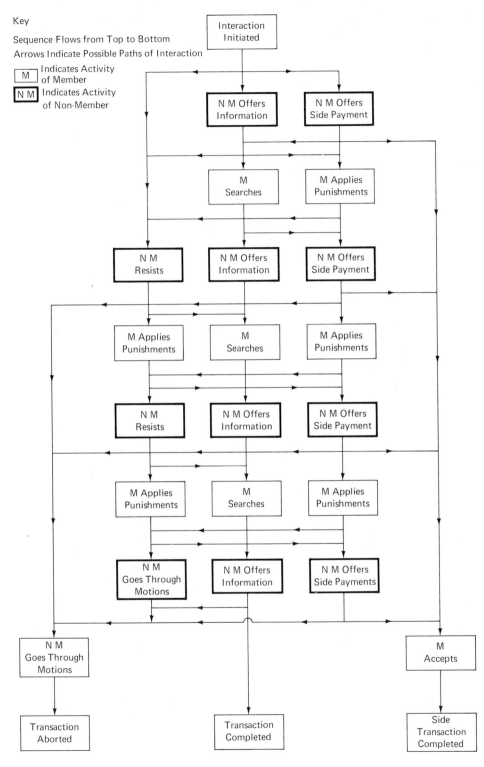

Key

Sequence Flows from Top to Bottom

Arrows Indicate Possible Paths of Interaction

M ☐ Indicates Activity of Member

N M ☐ Indicates Activity of Non-Member

Figure 3

resisting (or increasing resistance), the interaction process in this output structure is likely to degenerate into a struggle for control. This would appear, perhaps, in the relationship between high-school students and teachers, in the therapy-oriented prison, and in the therapy-oriented mental hospital.[25] Often the non-member will resist "help" but will "go through the motions," appearing to co-operate to escape punishments. Eaton has suggested that for the social caseworker the client may effectively control the relationship by "presenting a challenge," by "showing appreciation," or by promising to change his behavior at some future time—provided that the caseworker keep trying.[26]

The abortive struggle for control can also occur when the non-member offers inadequate bribes for a side transaction. A bribe offer that is rejected, however, gives the member added leverage in avoiding the stand-off, and, instead, completing a transaction successfully. Blau reports that being offered a bribe constituted a special tactical advantage for the field agent of a law enforcement agency. A non-member who had violated one law was caught in the act of compounding his guilt by violating another one. He could no longer claim ignorance or inadvertence as an excuse for his violations, and agents exploited this situation to strengthen their position in negotiations.[27]

Interaction in Type IV Structures

Now the interaction is heuristic, the relationship is optional for the non-member, and the member must attract clients and maintain interaction before he can complete a transaction (see Fig. 4).

Whether interaction is initiated by the member or by the non-member, making the initial contact is likely to be a difficult experience. Lack of knowledge of appropriate role behavior may indeed lead many individuals who need "professional help" to avoid interaction with appropriate professionals. In a sample survey seeking to determine "normal" American attitudes toward mental health, "lack of knowledge about means" of seeking professional help was a major reason given by those who felt they could have used help but did not seek it.[28] A study of "well-trained" life insurance underwriters concluded that "anxiety over intrusion on prospect privacy" was a major deterrent to making contacts,[29] and it has been reported that "a salesman of accident and health insurance is expected to make at least 36 prospect contacts by cold canvass each week. If he can sell four of these, he is regarded as performing very well. Thus he must steel himself to an average of 32 rejections 50 weeks in the year."[30]

Initial contact, at best, simply sets the stage for further exploration. Friedson concludes that the first visit by urban patients to a medical practitioner is often tentative, a tryout. Whether the physician's prescription will be followed, and whether the patient will come back, seem to rest at least partly on his retrospective assessment of the professional consultation.[31] Kadushin reports a considerable amount of shopping around by individuals undertaking psychotherapy.[32] The organizational counterpart of shopping around is exercised, for example, by the intake committee of the psychiatric clinic that, on the basis of initial exploration, may select those most likely to succeed as patients.[33]

Nevertheless, both parties enter this transaction structure with a measure of uncertainty, because the behavior of each must be keyed to information possessed by the other. The potential client

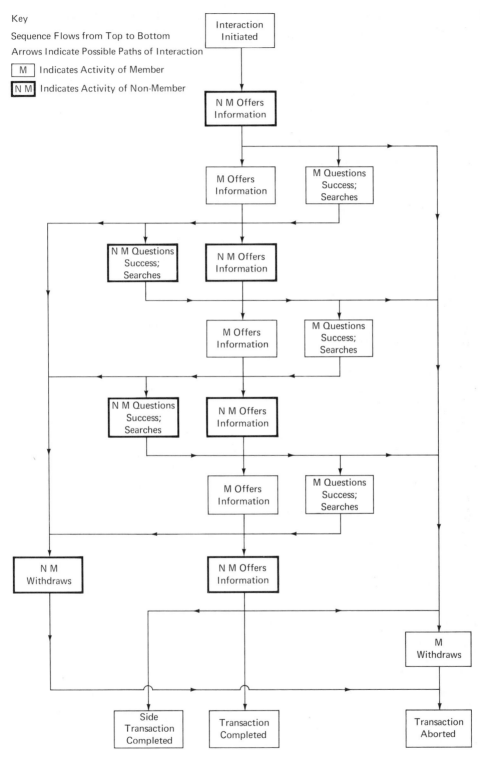

Key

Sequence Flows from Top to Bottom

Arrows Indicate Possible Paths of Interaction

M Indicates Activity of Member

N M Indicates Activity of Non-Member

Interaction Initiated

N M Offers Information

M Offers Information

M Questions Success; Searches

N M Questions Success; Searches

N M Offers Information

M Offers Information

M Questions Success; Searches

N M Questions Success; Searches

N M Offers Information

M Offers Information

M Questions Success; Searches

N M Withdraws

N M Offers Information

M Withdraws

Side Transaction Completed

Transaction Completed

Transaction Aborted

Figure 4

seeks a personalized transaction for which there may be no standard pattern, and hence, no readily available schedule of costs or of probabilities of satisfactory outcome. The member's diagnosis and prognosis depend on the unfolding of information during the interaction process; hence the member cannot at the outset guarantee success, nor can he predict the complete costs to the non-member. The member must hold out enough hope of results to maintain interaction in the face of uncertainty—but he also needs "escape clauses." The client likewise must disclose enough information and motivation to enable the member to make estimates—but without irrevocable commitment to the transaction.

If the non-member becomes fully committed to the transaction he can make few choices and exercises little control. Friedson notes that when the patient penetrates into "organizational practice" such as found in hospitals, he is well into the professional referral system, which involves maximal restriction on client choice of services, and his efforts at control are most likely to take the form of evasion.[34] In other words, when the client becomes fully committed to the transaction, the transaction structure is converted into a Type III structure.

Short of this conversion, however, there is a fully developed sounding-out process. In the early stages of interaction, a large proportion of behavior of both parties is oriented toward establishment of *rapport* and a small proportion to the substance of the transaction relationship. As the interaction process nears successful achievement the proportions are reversed, but en route the joint search may yield information that changes the prognosis of one or both parties, either making costs appear higher than anticipated or making success appear less likely. When the unfolding of the relationship in this way changes the conditions for the client, the transaction may be aborted. Each successive time the relationship is thus challenged by the unfolding of information which bears on costs and rewards, *rapport* must be re-established. Eaton notes that an evaluation of the actual results of treatment is often impossible until a good deal of time has elapsed. "Along the way, during this protracted search for happiness, both practitioner and client want to know if there is evidence of progress, and often a judgment is made with an implied presumption that the *quality of the therapeutic relationship* is predictive of its outcome."[35]

Each successive time that the relationship is questioned, additional investment has been made and thus the magnitude of the dilemma is greater. This may be true for the member as well as for the non-member, for crisis over rapport is likely to be personally dissatisfying to the practitioner as well as threatening to his organizational rewards; thus, he may be reluctant to alter early diagnosis and prognosis (in a direction more costly to the client) so long as there appears to be a possibility of success on the original terms. This would operate, then, to diminish the heuristics of the interaction process; the early prognosis becomes a program not easily disrupted.

The possibility of a side-transaction occurs when the member has exclusive access to something desired by the non-member, such as drugs that only a licensed physician can prescribe, or when the non-member seeks some form of attention rather than technical treatment. In medicine, under these circumstances, the placebo may satisfy the patient's need for attention and maintain the physician-patient relationship. Friedson notes that whether their motive be to heal the patient or to survive professionally, physicians dependent on the lay referral system will feel pressure to accept or manipulate lay expectations by administering harmless placebos or by giving up unpopular drugs.[36]

Because of the uncertainties of the heuristic transaction process and the difficulties of establishing and maintaining rapport, it would appear that the distinction between a process leading toward side transaction often is difficult to distinguish from one leading toward transaction. For this reason, Figure 4 does not distinguish a separate flow for transactions and side transactions.

The theme of the Type IV transaction structure thus appears to be rapport, and members must not only be able to establish and maintain rapport but, it would seem, to "cool out" the non-member if rapport cannot be re-established at one of the crisis points;[37] that is, when the transaction is aborted, the member needs some means of convincing the disappointed non-member that the attempt was a reasonable one.

Dynamics of Output Relations

Because disposition of its product is imperative for any complex, purposive organization, the transaction structure is crucial. It may dictate or place significant constraints on (a) the acquisition of necessary inputs by the organization, (b) the internal arrangements for allocation and co-ordination of resources and activities, and (c) the political or "institutional" requirements of the organization. The pivotal nature of the output relationship thus claims the attention not only of those in output roles but also of those at the several administrative levels.

Significance of Supervision

At the technical level of the organization is found not only the output role but, inevitably, a supervisory role—charged with direct responsibility for evaluating, facilitating, or modifying the behavior of those in output roles vis-à-vis non-members. The foregoing analysis has suggested differences in the role of the supervisor for each type of transaction structure. For the Type I structure, supervisory responsibility revolves around enforcement of conformity to program and detection of deviation. The supervisory focus on the Type II structure is on subordinates' skills in gambits and in closing transactions. For the Type III structure, the supervisory problem centers on the maintenance of heuristics—and preventing the development of *ad hoc* programs. For the supervisor of a Type IV relationship, the concern is with balancing rapport and treatment.

Though the content of the supervisory role differs from one type of structure to another, its significance is common to all; the supervisory role reinforces the organizational dimension in the definition of the output role. Since the non-member also is important in defining the role of member, the stage is set for a three-person game, with the supervisor having to make sure that the coalition always is between himself and the member in the output role, and not between member and non-member, that is, a side transaction.

Even when the coalition includes the supervisor, however, satisfactory disposal of output is not assured, for performance at the output boundary always is subject to the constraints of the transaction structure. If the structure departs from one of the "pure types" discussed above, members at the technical level can only adapt to those impurities, but administrators at other levels of the organization may have the resources necessary to reinforce or "purify" the structures. If it is to the organization's advantage to convert from one type of structure to another, that too must result from administrative decision and action. Finally, if the organization faces a changing environment for which existing transaction structures are inadequate, the necessary adaptation can come only from administrative action.

Mixed Structures and Managerial Action

Poetic license was exercised earlier to deal only with the polar extremes of two variables that in reality are continuous. The four pure types yielded by this maneuver may indeed describe the "ideal models" toward which organizations strive—but often only approximate. Impurities may stem from the situation of the non-member or of the member.

Non-members may be *more or less* under compulsion to interact with members, rather than at the mandatory or optional poles. Even where the government has a monopoly on licensing certain activities, the potential non-member may choose to risk illegal activity rather than to negotiate for a license. The member in the output role and his supervisor are powerless to combat this. If the transaction structure is to be reinforced in this case, it requires managerial policies and commitment of resources to find and punish evaders. Prisoners may be unable to effect escape, but the fact that they are *batched*[38] makes rioting possible, and the fact that they and their guards engage in a prolonged series of transactions gives prisoners a certain subtle bargaining power that can place limits on the complete arbitrariness of the prison.[39] If the transaction structure is to be reinforced

in this case, it requires managerial policies and commitment of resources to provide for segmentation of prisoners or rotation of guards.

Potential customers may, of course, "do without" or find alternative sources of supply, but there are inconveniences of time and place involved in both alternatives. Potential clients may have a choice of suffering without professional help or seeking out other professionals, which often is difficult for the layman, and there are costs attached to these alternatives also. If the transaction structure is to be purified in these cases where the non-member's discretion is limited, policies stressing service or professional norms must be adopted and emphasized by managers.

Impurities can be introduced into the transaction structure from the organization's side also. The programmed member can be furnished with such a large number of programs that he must, in fact, behave heuristically. If this situation is to be purified, it must be through managerial action to reduce the number of programs or, more likely, to departmentalize, with non-members initially screened and routed to the appropriate department. Scarcity of prospects, in the Type II structure, also leads to impurities, for this structure operates on a statistical rather than an absolute basis, that is, a percentage of interactions are expected to abort. When prospects are scarce, members in the output role may be reluctant to permit an abortion, seeking instead to complete a side transaction. If this situation is to be purified, it is likely to be through managerial action to increase the flow of prospects. Advertising, extension of credit, or emphasis on convenience are among the tactics employed.

An overload on the member in the structure calling for heuristics also introduces impurities by limiting the time available to engage in heuristics and encouraging the use of *ad hoc* programs. Here again, if impurities are to be removed, managerial action is required. In the Type IV structure managerial policies can turn away prospective clients, but in the Type III structure the most likely course is to increase the size of the output staff.

Management of Organizational Posture

Managerial or administrative influence over transaction structures rests less on authority to dictate standards or procedures than on ability to negotiate changes in *organizational posture*, that is, a relationship between the organization and its relevant environment resulting from the joint action of both.[40]

Hawkes has shown, for the psychiatric hospital case, how the contractual negotiations of the administrator can significantly influence transactions at the boundaries. Both patient input and patient output are affected by the administrator's activities outside the hospital.[41] Levine and White have indicated that administrative negotiations can affect the *domain* of a welfare agency within the larger welfare system, and hence affect what are here termed transaction structures.[42] Economic evidence clearly indicates that administrative negotiation can arrange for monopoly or cartel systems, which in turn have important implications for output relationships.

While most of the illustrations given above were of actions that rectify some imbalance caused either by (a) a positive advantage held by the prospective non-member or (b) a disadvantage imposed on the member, administrative maneuvers can sometimes result in a posture more favorable to the organization than

to the non-member. It can be hypothesized that organizations faced with Types II or IV transaction structures will attempt to reduce the freedom of prospective non-members, thus converting the structures into Types I or III. Achievement of a monopoly, of course, accomplishes this immediately.

While monopoly is illegal for certain types of American organizations, many others are not subject to such constraints. Governments usually operate monopolistic agencies, and public school systems are monopolistic or quasi-monopolistic. Hospitals, clinics, and voluntary social welfare organizations are monopolistic in many non-metropolitan settings. In larger cities they may achieve monopoly or near-monopoly by actions of the referral system, if referring agencies recognize the organization's claim to exclusive domain or jurisdiction for certain types of cases.

Even in the commercial sphere where legal codes prohibit economic monopoly, social-psychological monopoly can be achieved or approached through extension and control over credit purchasing, through brand-name advertising, or by the achievement of *extrinsic prestige* by the organization.[43]

Conclusion

It is hoped that this paper has called attention to the need for further consideration by organization theorists of the output relationship, by showing that it occurs in transaction structures built in part of elements not within the organization and hence that it cannot be authoritatively dictated.

Finally, it is hoped that a case has been made for the necessity of developing or adapting analytic tools—such as flow charts—for the investigation of contingent interaction in social roles.

1. I am indebted to my colleagues—Robert Avery, Carl Beck, Richard Carlson, Joseph Eaton, Robert Hawkes, Axel Leijonhufvud, Morris Ogul, and C. Edward Weber—for helpful reactions to earlier versions of this paper.
2. Role theory has devoted much more attention to structure-maintaining behavior than to transaction behavior, in spite of the variety and quantity of transaction in modern societies. See, however, William J. Goode, "A Theory of Role Strain," *American Sociological Review*, XXV (August, 1960), 483–96; George C. Homans, *Social Behavior: Its Elementary Form* (New York: Harcourt, Brace & Co., 1961), and John W. Thibaut and Harold H. Kelley, *The Social Psychology of Groups* (New York: John Wiley & Sons, 1959).
3. Max Weber, *The Theory of Economic and Social Organization* (Glencoe: Free Press, 1957), and Robert K. Merton, *Social Theory and Social Structure* (rev. ed.; Glencoe: Free Press, 1957), chap. vi.
4. S. N. Eisenstadt, "Bureaucracy, Bureaucratization, and Debureaucratization," *Administrative Science Quarterly*, IV (1959), 302–20.
5. *The Functions of the Executive* (Cambridge, Mass.: Harvard University Press, 1938).
6. James G. March and Herbert A. Simon, *Organizations* (New York: John Wiley & Sons, 1958).
7. This concept was suggested by that of "side payment" as developed by R. M. Cyert and J. G. March, "A Behavioral Theory of Organizational Objectives," in Mason Haire (ed.), *Modern Organization Theory* (New York: John Wiley & Sons, 1959).
8. March and Simon make a similar distinction by referring to programs specifying activities (means) and programs specifying product or outcome (ends). They observe that the latter allow discretion to the individual (*op. cit.*, p. 147).
9. I am indebted to Axel Leijonhufvud for contributing this insight from economic theory.
10. When competition returned to this field, dealers complained frequently that their "salesmen" had forgotten how to "sell."
11. Peter M. Blau, *The Dynamics of Bureaucracy* (Chicago: University of Chicago Press, 1955), pp. 43, 70.
12. *Ibid.*, p. 70.
13. See summary in Lloyd E. Ohlin, *Sociology and the Field of Corrections* (New York: Russell Sage Foundation, 1956), pp. 20–21.
14. Roy G. Francis and Robert C. Stone, *Service and Procedure in a Bureaucracy* (Minneapolis: University of Minnesota Press, 1956), pp. 83–84.
15. *Op. cit.*, pp. 24, 87.
16. For analysis in another context of the "sounding out process" see James D. Thompson and William J. McEwen, "Organizational Goals and Environment," *American Sociological Review*, XXIII (February, 1958), 23–30.
17. Thomas C. Schelling, *The Strategy of Conflict* (Cambridge, Mass.: Harvard University Press, 1960), reports an unusual case. This involved a club for motorists, and the membership card identified the holder as a person who would keep quiet if his bribe offer was accepted by a policeman. Schelling also reports, however, that if the police could identify card-carrying motorists by sight, they could concentrate arrests on card-carrying drivers, threatening a ticket unless payment were received! (See pp. 140–41.)
18. "The Corruption of Authority and Rehabilitation," in Amitai Etzioni (ed.), *Complex Organizations* (New York: Holt, Rinehart & Winston, 1960), pp. 191–97.
19. George F. Lombard, *Behavior in a Selling Group* (Boston: Harvard Business School, 1955), pp. 176–80.
20. *Ibid.*, p. 177. When "merchandise which a customer liked was not available in the desired color or size, the situation could quickly become most difficult for both salesgirl and customer."

HUMAN INPUTS

21. Reported in Leonard Reissman and John H. Rohrer (eds.), *Change and Dilemma in the Nursing Profession* (New York: G. P. Putnam's Sons, 1957), p. 143.

22. This dilemma frequently arises in treatment-oriented organizations which also have a custodial responsibility. Oscar Gursky notes that if an inmate in a traditional prison system violates the rules, the guard simply writes up a "ticket" and the inmate is punished by a central disciplinary court or a disciplinary officer; the transaction fits our Type I. However, if the same violation occurs in a treatment-oriented prison, it complicates the guard's response and creates conflict, for he must decide whether he ought to write up a ticket or whether, for treatment reasons, he ought to let the inmate "express his emotions" (see "Role Conflict in Organization," *Administrative Science Quarterly*, Vol. III [March, 1959]).

23. David Fanshel, "A Study of Caseworkers' Perceptions of Their Clients," *Social Casework*, XXXIX (December, 1958), 543–51.

24. Elihu Katz and S. N. Eisenstadt, "Some Sociological Observations on the Response of Israeli Organizations to New Immigrants," *Administrative Science Quarterly*, Vol. V (June, 1960).

25. Morris S. Schwartz and Gwen Tudor Will describe "mutual withdrawal" in a mental hospital ward, with the withdrawal of the nurse perpetuating the withdrawal of the patient and the withdrawal of the patient reinforcing the nurse's withdrawal. Withdrawal in this case was described as affective, communicative, and physical (see "Low Morale and Mutual Withdrawal on a Mental Hospital Ward," *Psychiatry*, XVI [November, 1953], 337–53).

26. Joseph W. Eaton, private conversation.

27. Blau, *op. cit.*, p. 151.

28. Gerald Gurin, Joseph Veroff, and Sheila Feld, *Americans View Their Mental Health* (New York: Basic Books, 1960), chap. xi.

29. Herbert E. Krugman, "Salesman in Conflict," *Journal of Marketing*, XXIII (July, 1958), 59–61.

30. Robert N. McMurry, "The Mystique of Super-Salesmanship," *Harvard Business Review*, XXXIX (March–April, 1961), 113–22.

31. Eliot Friedson, "Client Control and Medical Practice," *American Journal of Sociology*, LXV (January, 1960), 374–82.

32. Charles Kadushin, "Individual Decisions To Undertake Psychotherapy," *Administrative Science Quarterly*, III (December, 1958), 379–411 (see also his "Social Distance between Client and Professional," *American Journal of Sociology*, LXVII [March, 1962], 517–31).

33. Kadushin, "Individual Decisions To Undertake Psychotherapy," *op. cit.*

34. *Op. cit.*, p. 381.

35. Joseph W. Eaton, "The Client-Practitioner Relationship as a Variable in the Evaluation of Treatment Outcome," *Psychiatry*, XXII (May, 1959), 189.

36. *Op. cit.*, p. 378.

37. The "cooling out" concept appears to have been first introduced into sociological literature by Erving Goffman in his analysis of confidence games, in "On Cooling the Mark Out: Some Aspects of Adaptations to Failure," *Psychiatry*, XV (November, 1952), 451–63. The concept appears to be relevant to other types of activities where, acting in good faith, the practitioner must disappoint the client and faces the need to "let him down gently." For the application of the cooling-out concept in the junior college see Burton R. Clark, "The 'Cooling-Out' Function in Higher Education," *American Journal of Sociology*, LXV (May, 1960), 569–76.

38. See Goffman, "On the Characteristics of Total Institutions," *Proceedings of the Symposium on Preventive and Social Psychiatry* (Washington: Walter Reed Army Institute of Research, 1957).

39. For a discussion of the substitution of functional diffuseness and particularism for functional specificity and universalism under similar conditions, see Peter B. Hammond, "The Functions of Indirection in Communication," in James D. Thompson *et al.* (eds.), *Comparative Studies in Administration* (Pittsburgh: University of Pittsburgh Press, 1959), pp. 183–94.

40. For a discussion of the concept of organizational postures see James D. Thompson, "Organizational Management of Conflict," *Administrative Science Quarterly*, V, No. 4 (March, 1960), 389–409.

41. Robert W. Hawkes, "The Role of the Psychiatric Administrator," *Administrative Science Quarterly*, VI (June, 1961), 89–106.

42. See Sol Levine and Paul E. White, "Exchange as a Conceptual Framework for the Study of Interorganizational Relationships," *Administrative Science Quarterly*, V (March, 1961), 583–601.

43. For the concept of extrinsic prestige and its implications for output relationships see Charles Perrow, "Organizational Prestige: Some Functions and Dysfunctions," *American Journal of Sociology*, LXVI (January, 1961), 335–41.

SOME SOCIOLOGICAL OBSERVATIONS ON THE RESPONSE OF ISRAELI ORGANIZATIONS TO NEW IMMIGRANTS[1]

Elihu Katz and S. N. Eisenstadt

This paper has its origin in preliminary observations on the patterns of contact between Israeli organizations and recent immigrants from non-Western countries. The pilot study resulting from these observations is concerned, first with "the socialization of the client," that is, with the adaptation of newcomers from traditional familistic backgrounds to new role expectations such as those implicit in becoming a factory worker, a hospital patient, a client of a social welfare worker, or even a bus passenger. Secondly, the study is equally concerned with the changes that occur in the organizations themselves in response to the large influx of clients new to Western ways. It is to preliminary reflection on this second problem that the present paper is devoted.

Rather than consider the organization as a whole, we are restricting our focus to those officials having direct dealings with new immigrants. We are concerned, in other words, with the official-client relationship where the official is usually of European birth or parentage and where the client is a recent immigrant from a non-Western country.

According to sociological theory, there was good reason to expect that the rapid influx of large numbers of new immi-

"Some Sociological Observations on the Response of Israeli Organizations to New Immigrants," *Administrative Science Quarterly*, 5, 1 (June 1960), 113–133. Reprinted with the permission of the authors and of the publisher, the *Administrative Science Quarterly*.

grants would increase the bureaucratization of the organizations to which they came.[2] This meant that one could expect, first, an increasing impersonality of relations between bureaucrats and clients.[3] One could also expect an increase in the degree of universalism—equality before the law—in the orientation of bureaucrat toward client. Similarly, the pressure of work resulting from the large influx ought to make the official more stringent in his enforcement of the rules. And, of course, one could expect official-client relations to become more businesslike and specific, becoming more narrowly limited to officially relevant concerns. Finally, one could expect the official to rely more heavily on the ascribed authority of his office and on the symbols and the power accompanying it to get his job done.[4]

These are some of the dimensions in which we expected to find changes in the official-client relationship as a result both of the large and rapid increase of clients and of the tensions arising from the radical cultural differences between officials and clients. We found such examples, of course, but we also found many examples of change in exactly the opposite direction. Rather than a marked increase in the degree of bureaucratization in official-client relations, we found evidence of debureaucratization. We often found officials relating to clients personally, taking sympathetic account of the status "new immigrant," and not confining themselves to their officially relevant roles. And frequently we found officials trying to get their job done, not so much by means of the power and symbols of office, but on the basis of exchange of services, or persuasion, or personal charisma.

In the pages that follow, we shall try to explain how such relationships appear to arise. But it is important to bear in mind that these are, so far, only impressionistic observations. The pilot study and, ultimately, the full-scale research, we hope, will be better founded.

Theory and Research on Bureaucratization

In the broadest sense, the theoretical problem here deals with the conditions affecting the degree of bureaucratization of an organization, specifically of the bureaucrat-client relationship. We are interested in the factors that make for varying degrees of bureaucratization as well as the factors (presumably the same ones) that influence the direction of organizational change. Indeed, in the writings of Max Weber and Robert Michels the problem of organizational change is essentially identical with the theme of bureaucratization.[5] If the classical sociological writings were concerned with bureaucratization, the later writings have devoted themselves to the problems of overbureaucratization. Thus, discussions of deviations from the ideal-type bureaucracy outlined by Weber focused on overbureaucratization as a threat to the attainment of the very goals for which the organizations were established. The leading character in these discussions, the official who converts means into ends, has been frequently described both in literary and scientific publications. The same is true for the accompanying manifestations of exaggerated hierarchy and red tape.[6]

Recently, however, with the beginning of empirical research on organizational behavior, these assumptions about the unidirectional evolution of organizations have been put into broader perspective. Thus, recent empirical research seems to suggest that (1) the trend toward total bureaucratization of organizations may sometimes be averted;[7] (2) actual bureaucracies are compounded of non-bureaucratic elements also;[8] (3) bureaucracies, once established, are by no means unchanging;[9] and (4) when changes do take place, they are not always in the direction of greater bureaucratization and formalism.[10]

FACTORS AFFECTING BUREAUCRATIZATION IN THE OFFICIAL-CLIENT RELATIONSHIP

The literature provides a number of suggestions concerning the factors affecting bureaucratization in general. Weber's emphasis has already been noted.[11] Succession is another familiar example. When a new director takes over from a predecessor, he has little choice but to insist on relatively greater formal relations, to demand adherence to the appointed channels of communication, and the like.[12] Another factor is monopolization. When an organization has a monopoly on certain goods or services (as most public bureaucracies have, of course), there is little chance of effective protest on the part of the client and no possibility of recourse to a competitor; under such conditions, bureaucrats may permit themselves an attitude of detachment and ritualistic formalism vis-à-vis their clients.[13]

The reverse of each of these influences should be associated with a lesser degree of bureaucratization. Thus, a smaller organization or one which suffers a reduction in size ought to be less bureaucratic. So should an organization that is aware that its clients have a choice between it and a competitor.

Each of these factors, of course, has its impact on the official-client or the superior-subordinate relationships.[14] But there are other factors worth singling out for their specific impact on these relationships. It is well known, for example, that soldiers in combat relate to others and to their officers in a much less bureaucratic way than they do behind the front lines or in peacetime.[15] Closely related findings emerge from a study of the informal social organization that superseded the formal organization of a naval unit on a tiny, unpopulated Pacific island.[16] Similarly, workers on the night shift were treated differently by their supervisors than were day-shift employees,[17] just as, in Gouldner's study, workers in the mine successfully resisted greater bureaucratization while office workers in the same company did not.[18] The common elements in these situations would seem to be the relative danger or unusualness of the task, the relative isolation from social contacts outside the organization, and relative independence from the immediate presence of upper echelons in the hierarchy. One suspects that certain of these factors would also be appropriate to cases such as Diamond's study of the debureaucratization of a quasi-military group by early American settlers organized as the Virginia Company.[19]

As a final example of debureaucratization, Turner's study of the navy disbursing officer during wartime will serve particularly well.[20] Turner indicated several factors that influenced these officers to depart from the orientation prescribed by the rule book to establish more diffuse relations with some of their clients and to show favoritism. First, many clients of the disbursing officer were his superiors in rank and, consequently, his superiors in other role relationships. Secondly, he found it advantageous to help others who could reciprocate, such as the mess officer. This dependence, in part a function of his isolation from other social contacts, was embedded in a more general interdependence created by the war.[21] Finally, client and bureaucrat were dependent on each other because, especially during the war, the higher authorities who were to be consulted in case of doubt were both physically and psychologically distant.

This dependence of clients and officials on each other appears as a key factor in the other cases as well, and for much the same reasons.[22] The danger, the isolation, the aborted hierarchy of combat, the night shift, the mine, the Virginia Company, and the naval unit on the Pacific island made men dependent upon each other over and above the specific relations defined for them by their formal organizations. The attempt to enforce ordinary peacetime or daytime relations under such circumstances —that is, the attempt to behave in the accepted bureaucratic manner, or even more, to be overbureaucratic—is what apparently leads to desertion (where one is able to leave) or to mutiny (where one cannot).

ROLE IMPINGEMENT AS A CHARACTERIZATION OF BUREAUCRATIZATION AND DEBUREAUCRATIZATION

The notion of dependence may be viewed sociologically as a special case of the impingement of other role relationships on a given bureaucratic relationship. In Turner's study, for example, the observed debureaucratization could be considered a product of the regularized contacts in other roles that existed between the disbursing officer and his clients. Moreover, if debureaucratization may be characterized in terms of the impingement of nonbureaucratic roles on bureaucratic ones, then overbureaucratization may be characterized as either the formalistic segregation of a bureaucratic relationship from

all other role relations (even relevant ones) or, in its totalitarian form, as the imposition of the bureaucratic relationship on relations outside the scope of the bureaucracy. The bureaucratic ritualist would be an example of one who arbitrarily views all extrabureaucratic roles as irrelevant to the conduct of his office, while the totalitarian bureaucrat "takes his authority home," as, for example, the sergeant bullying his men off duty.

In effect, overbureaucratization and debureaucratization represent a disturbance in the relationship between an organization and its environment that is not envisioned by the classical model of bureaucracy. This model envisages the roles of both bureaucrat and client as segregated to some extent from their other roles; their roles are "specific" to the interaction setting and in this bureaucratic setting it is irrelevant, for example, that both bureaucrat and client belong to the same political club. However, even in the ideal-type bureaucracy a role is not completely independent of other roles; some outside roles clearly may be, or must be, considered. If an old man, obviously unable to wait his turn in a long queue, is given special attention by a clerk, this is not a case of an irrelevant role relationship being allowed incorrectly to impinge on the bureaucrat-client relationship. In general, the classic model of bureaucracy requires only that the bureaucratic organization not be directly dependent on external factors for its manpower, its resources, or its motivation for carrying out its organizational task. If an organization relies directly upon any one segment of the population for financing, or for political protection, these sources of support will clearly receive particularistic attention in the dispensation of the organization's services. It is such direct dependence that mechanisms such as boards of trustees, budget bureaus, and the like try to avert by insulating bureaucratic organizations from their sources of support. What is true for the organization as a whole is true for its members as well. If a bureaucrat receives direct rewards from outside the organization in addition to, or instead of, his rewards from within, obviously his independence of action as a bureaucrat is thereby reduced.[23]

Clearly, then, there is a very delicate balance—varying from organization to organization—between the specific roles defined as relevant to relations within the bureaucracy and those outside roles defined as irrelevant. Note the parallel to our notion of role impingement in Gouldner's concept of "latent identity."[24]

Israeli Officials and New Immigrants

Increasingly, in recent years, the contact between immigrants and the new society to which they have come are mediated by professionals and bureaucrats. The customs agent, the social worker, the policeman, the public health nurse, the housing administrator, and the like, constitute the immigrants' main connections with the community to which they come, and it is these officials who provide aid and advice, which in earlier migrations were obtained more informally or not at all. This change is characteristic not only of the reception of immigrants in present-day Israel but also of the reception of Puerto Ricans and southern Negroes in New York and Chicago, and of other immigrant groups in the areas receiving them.[25] This change is in part a consequence of the greater bureaucratization of these areas in the last generation and in part a consequence of the theory and practice of the welfare state which,

adapting itself to the immigrant, proffers many social services unknown to the immigrant of an earlier generation. In Israel, this change is also a consequence of the different pattern of motivation and different demographic composition of present-day immigrants compared with the "pioneer" immigrants of the turn of the century.[26]

The remainder of this paper is devoted to a preliminary discussion of some of the problems arising out of the contact between immigrants to Israel and the officials with whom they deal, viewed against the theoretical considerations set forth in the first part of this paper. The kind of immigrant with whom we are particularly concerned comes from non-Western countries (such as Yemen, Morocco, Iraq, and so on), where he is likely to have had little or no contact with formal organization.

The question to which we now turn is why so many of the official-client relations observed seemed to be moving in the direction of lesser bureaucratization. We do not mean to imply that Israeli organizations prior to the influx of the non-Western immigrants were close approximations of the Weberian ideal-type; for the small size of the country and the common struggle made for wide networks of interpersonal relations embracing officials and clients alike. The pioneering and egalitarian ideologies frowned on status differentiation, differential distribution of rewards, as well as on formalities of all sorts. Not least important, political parties exerted considerable influence on appointments to and conduct of the public bureaucracies.

As we have already said, the mere increase in organizational size and responsibility might have been expected to result in increased bureaucratization of relations between official and client, between supervisor and worker, and so forth. To this rapid increase in numbers add the divergence of cultural background between the majority of recent immigrants coming from non-Western countries and the European bureaucrats dealing with them, and one would certainly expect an increase in bureaucratic formalism.[27]

Yet our preliminary observations indicate that this is not the case. We have, of course, found some evidence of increasing bureaucratization as a response to the influx of new immigrants. Thus, in one co-operative organization, for example, the hierarchy became sharply elongated. Previously any member was able to reach the highest official of the organization rather directly and informally, nor was it particularly important whether he brought his problem to one or another of the top officials. Now, the same organization has developed a strict chain of command and a new immigrant with a problem must proceed strictly through the established channels and talk only to the relevant official. Yet, even in this organization, as far as the actual interaction between official and client is concerned, there is evidence of considerable debureaucratization.

Repeatedly, however, we have found in institutions as diverse as health clinics and bus companies, widespread evidence of debureaucratization in the relationship between officials and new immigrants. We have found cases where the official has assigned himself a greater number of tasks vis-à-vis his clients than those assigned him by his organization. We find considerable evidence of the growth of personal relationships between officials and new immigrants. We have even found cases where the official becomes the leader of a kind of "social movement" composed of new immigrants, thus completely reversing the expected trend which is supposed to lead from movements to bureaucracy. A major key to this unanticipated phenomenon is the notion of dependence we have developed, which takes quite a different form at this point. We shall try to describe what we think we have found and, in part, we shall do this in terms of case studies. In one case, officials assumed a teaching role vis-à-vis their clients. In another, officials departed from their prescribed role as agents of socialization in certain patterned ways. In the third case, officials became the leaders of an incipient social movement.

BUREAUCRATS AS TEACHERS:
DEPENDENCE ON THE CLIENT'S
PERFORMANCE OF HIS ROLE

The most characteristic form of debureaucratization in the relationship between bureaucrats and new immigrants in Israel is the assumption by the bureaucrat of the role of teacher along with (or at the expense of) his other functions. Consider, for example, the bus driver who gets out of the bus to teach the idea of a queue—"first come, first served"—an idea which is new to many of his new immigrant passengers. Similarly, the nurse at the well-baby clinic may be seen teaching women, informally, which of their needs are appropriate to the health services and which should be taken to other organizations. Or, the manager of the government-subsidized grocery in the new immigrant settlement may take the initiative and go into homes to teach housewives how to prepare certain foods with which they have had no previous experience.

In all these examples, the bureaucrat takes the time and effort to teach a client something about his (the bureaucrat's) expectations concerning how the client role is to be played. In other words, the bureaucrat teaches the client how to be a client so that he (the bureaucrat) can go on being a bureaucrat. This, it seems to us, is a form of dependence, but one which we have not considered so far; it is dependence on the client to act in a way which makes it possible for the bureaucrat to do his job.

In other words, it is expected by the bureaucrat and the bureaucracy that the client will bring with him to the bureaucratic context certain knowledge of expected roles from "outside," even though he may have had no previous contact with this particular bureaucracy. In Western society, for example, one is prepared for one's first encounter with a customs inspector by virtue of one's single-purpose relationships with other officials, tradesmen, and the like. When this preparation is lacking, the bureaucrat himself, in the examples cited, added a dimension—teaching—to his relationship with the client. And this change is an example of debureaucratization both because it adds another role to the specifically prescribed one and because the quality of interaction in the teacher-student relationship necessarily impinges on the more formal bureaucrat-client relationship. Yet these are the very elements which are officially alien to the ideal-type bureaucracy.[28] What is more, as we shall presently see, the teaching relationship may bring further debureaucratization, although conceivably it may simply permit the bureaucrat to perform his role as originally prescribed.

Consider the case of the bus driver. Introductory texts in sociology like to cite the driver-passenger relationship as an example of a purely instrumental, secondary relationship. Neither party matters to the other as an individual. One would not expect the bus driver to modify his behavior vis-à-vis new immigrants or anybody else, yet our preliminary observations seem to indicate that he does. Like other bureaucrats who come into contact with new immigrants, the bus driver tends to assume a teaching role, too. Besides trying to teach the idea of queuing, bus drivers were observed trying to persuade immigrant passengers that the cost of a ride on one bus was the same as the cost on the bus that had just gone by, or that the driver did not personally profit from each fare he collected, or that the decision for the bus to leave the terminal was not his. The consequences of the formal organization of a bus company that are understood by client and bureaucrat in modern society are simply not "obvious" to the non-Western immigrant.

Moreover, we have the impression—and the research now in progress will permit confirmation—that a kind of joking relationship grows up between drivers and new-immigrant passengers. This seems to be the case particularly where the passengers in the bus know one another—as in buses serving suburban settlements and city neighborhoods populated largely by new immigrants. Indeed, drivers on routes with concentrations of new immigrants have told us explicitly that they consider it desirable to get to know their passengers personally, because a new driver is likely to encounter "trouble" with non-Western immigrants, who may become unruly or begin to ask the usual questions anew: "How much is the fare?" "May I get off here?" and so on. In fact, we have had some indication that the bus companies recognize the desirability of less frequent changes of drivers on lines serving new immigrants. This "personalization" of the bureaucratic relationship represents a deviation from the impersonal, universalistic, specific relationship between driver and passenger which, in principle, ought to be unaffected by the substitution of one driver for another. It is an example of debureaucratization, which is the product of the dependence of the bureaucrat on the client's ability and motivation to perform his role as client.

It is important to note, however, that an official's dependence on the client to perform his role is probably of a different order from the kinds of dependence we discussed in the other examples reviewed in the first part of this paper. In the earlier examples, the client actually had power over the bureaucrat—he could affect his well-being both as a member of the bureaucratic organization and as an individual. Thus, the clients of the disbursing officer were his superiors in other relationships, or the men in combat or in the mine could withdraw their reciprocal protection of their superior. In the present instance, however, the passenger has power over the driver in very much the same sense that a baby has power to disrupt the family schedule, and clearly this creates dependence of quite a different order.[29]

BUREAUCRATS AS SOCIALIZING AGENTS

The process of a bureaucrat stepping outside his role to teach a new immigrant how to act his role as client is highly reminiscent of the processes of socialization and social control as analyzed by Parsons.[30] In the socialization of the child, or in the process of psychotherapy, the socializing agent steps out of his place in the larger social system and assumes a role in the "deviant" subsystem. Thus, the mother is a member of the inclusive family system consisting of father, mother, and children. To bring a new child into this more inclusive system, she must use her role in the earlier mother-child subsystem and selectively reward the child for obedience and disobedience to the new expectations of the inclusive system while at the same time providing a basis of support for the child in his effort to learn the new role. At times, however, the mother may fail as socializing agent, because she herself prefers to remain in the "deviant" subsystem and, ignoring the father and the rest of the family, acts to "keep the child for herself."

The parallel seems striking to us. The assumption of a teaching role by the bureaucrat and the "personalizing" of the bureaucrat-client relationship seems to function for the process of immigrant socialization as does the behavior of the socializing agent vis-à-vis the child. One of the objects of our empirical study will be to determine whether this kind of bureaucratic behavior (whatever its dysfunctions for the organizational routine) contributes more to the adaptation of the new immigrant than the unbending bureaucrat-client relationship.

Even more striking, perhaps, is the parallel to the kind of mother who "keeps the child for herself." Thus, a bureaucrat who has assumed a teaching role may fail to bring the new immigrant client to play the role expected of him by the bureaucracy and may, instead, remain a member of the "deviant" subsystem. This possibility is most conspicuous perhaps in the case of the village instructors who are assigned to each new settlement of immigrants. These instructors are part of a regional Settlement Authority which, in turn, is part of a nationwide Settlement Department. Sometimes, instead of mediating between the new immigrants and the authorities, the instructor becomes so much a part of his village community that his major effort is devoted to "representing" the interests of his clients vis-à-vis the authorities.

The village instructor typically lives among his clients and is potentially available all day long. His job, as compared with the bus driver's, is a highly diffuse one and includes teaching the settlers, who were semiskilled craftsmen or peddlers, to be farmers, cooperators (as this is understood in the moshav)[31] and Israelis. In this case debureaucratization is manifested not merely in the establishment of informal relations, but rather in the surrendering of part of the bureaucrat's commitment to his bureaucracy in favor of acceptance of a role in the system which he is expected to change.

Of course, this is only one of the ways that the instructor—given his highly diffuse and flexible role—can shape his relations with his clients. Some instructors, obviously, take quite the opposite position. Their control of the resources necessary for the very existence of their clients permits them to move in the direction of overbureaucratization. They may interfere in matters—religious observance, for example—which ought properly to be outside their (very broad) spheres of influence.

An even more complicating factor is that the instructor, apart from his bureaucratic role, is often eager to make his clients full-fledged members of the nationwide small-holders co-operative movement or even of his political party, and to have them identify with its ideology, participate in its activities, and so on. Among the instructors who play this double role—which is by no means always considered illegitimate by the upper echelon of the Settlement Authority —many tend to view the various aspects of their bureaucratic role of training immigrants in agriculture and administration as a means to the end of full citizenship. This goal, for the ideologically oriented Israeli, implies the assumption of political and ideological commitments. Such instructors aim at making their clients members of a solidary movement of which they themselves are a part. This subsidiary aim makes the instructor even more dependent on the settlers. They may easily threaten not to participate in the movement unless the instructor provides them with various benefits and allocations for which he is the intermediary, though these may not be their due. In response the instructor may either move in the direction of debureaucratization and succumb to these demands, or he may attempt to use his bureaucratic position to force the clients to assume the political and ideological roles he envisages for them.

BUREAUCRATS AS LEADERS

A bureaucrat serving as "representative" or as "organizer" of his clients is by no means the extreme example of the kind of debureaucratization which may result from the bureaucrat's assumption of the role of socializing agent. Sometimes bureaucrats become charismatic leaders of groups of their clients.

Consider, for example, the case of several nurses employed at a well-baby clinic in a relatively segregated immigrants' "transitional community" within one of the major cities. In this setting the nurse—like the village instructor—is expected to be a teacher and to establish the kind of relationship required for successful teaching. Thus, along with the curative and preventive medicine practiced in such clinics, she must teach the women how to care for themselves and for their children in the particular manner prescribed by the modern scientific and philosophical orientation of the well-baby clinic. The authority of the nurses observed, however, extended beyond these rather broadly defined functions. They became generalized counselors and the clinic soon took on the air of a kind of social center where women gathered to greet each other, to gossip, and to move within the orbit of the nurses.

Some of the nurses had become preoccupied with the position of women in non-Western families. Apparently, this particular problem had first attracted attention as a result of the frequently negative reactions of their clients' husbands to one or another of the practices recommended by the clinic. Having thus become sensitized to the subordinate role of their clients within their families, the nurses added the reconciliation of family conflict to their counseling efforts and, in fact, some of the nurses considered it part of their job to teach women their "rights" vis-à-vis their husbands. In several instances, we have even heard nurses recommending divorce to their clients! Step by step, then, these nurses seem to have moved out from their broad but relatively well-defined functions (which include teaching) to assume an even broader teaching and counseling role and, in some instances, to leadership of a kind of "suffragette" movement among their clients. In such cases, the leader does not appear averse to illustrating her message with reference to her own private life or that of her friends. And to the extent that they follow, the clients look to their leaders for active support and guidance, and to sharing in the consequences of their behavior.

The leadership role, as played by the bureaucrat, represents a considerable degree of debureaucratization. It represents, in part, exchange of the authority vested in the bureaucratic office for the "voluntary" loyalty of clients; that is, such leadership exists not only by

virtue of an "appointment" but by virtue of being "chosen" by followers as well. To that extent, the bureaucrat must submit himself to the authority, and to some of the norms, of his followers. Moreover, he has considerably extended the sphere of his influence from the specific tasks assigned to him to the wider, more diffuse, tasks inherent in the leadership role.

Direction of Future Research

The variety of official relations with new immigrants in Israel provides us with a unique opportunity to locate the conditions under which debureaucratization, overbureaucratization, or both these organizational changes take place. Thus, we would expect debureaucratization to occur more often in relatively isolated settlements of new immigrants than in immigrant communities within the larger cities. In the isolated settlement the bureaucrat is far more dependent on the voluntary co-operation of his clients, both for the performance of his task and for his social and emotional (i.e. non-bureaucratic) well-being. One would also expect a greater dilution of the bureaucratic role with the teaching role in situations where a community of immigrants is transplanted more or less at the same time, compared with situations where migration was stretched over a long period of time. Under the former conditions, the immigrant community will have had less opportunity to educate itself and to develop the leaders, intermediaries, and interpreters who permit the bureaucrat to play his role uninterruptedly. In both the isolated immigrant community and in the transplanted immigrant community, the "segregated" equilibrium between the organization and its environment is likely to be more upset, and hence more marked organizational change may be anticipated. In both these cases, one might argue that the direction of change might well be toward greater, rather than lesser, bureaucratization in the sense that the organization has a unique opportunity to impose itself on more aspects of its clients' lives than is usual. Our hypothesis holds otherwise, as we have tried to argue above, but the plausibility of the competing hypothesis illustrates how the two ostensibly opposite directions of organizational change stem from closely similar conditions.

Our study will enable us to make other comparisons, too. For example, we can compare bureaucrats who come into contact with clients of their own ethnic origin with bureaucrats whose clients are not of their own group. We can compare bureaucrats who are relatively isolated from contacts with their colleagues—instructors who live in the villages—with those who live among their colleagues in the newly built Rural Centers and commute daily to the nearby villages. In the same way, we can compare the pattern of official-client relations characteristic of the bus companies whose drivers have only sporadic and brief contact with their new immigrant clients to the behavior of bureaucrats in organizations which require more extended contacts.

Again, it is easier to choose the situations in which deviation from the ideal bureaucratic norm is more likely to occur than it is to predict the direction of the deviation. Thus, when the bureaucrat is confronted primarily by clients of his own group he is likely to move either in the direction of bureaucratic formalism, studiously seeking to demonstrate his rootedness in Israeli life and to resist the particularistic expectations of the relative newcomers to Israel, or he may move in the direction of debureaucratization in the sense of reaccepting portions of the pattern of traditional authority and behavior of which he was once a part. Compared to the bureaucrat dealing with members of his own ethnic group (who may, because of his better understanding of the group, be more successful in his task), the bureaucrat without an ethnic affiliation with his clients will display more affective neutrality, though this may still lead to overbureaucratization. Again, we expect to find that bureaucrats in close touch with their colleagues can maintain a more detached, objective, service-oriented attitude to their clients than bureaucrats dependent on their clients for social and emotional acceptance and interaction. And, for the same reason, we expect bureaucrats with more extended contacts with a given group of clients to depart from the norms of bureaucratic behavior to a greater extent than bureaucrats with relatively brief and less regular contact.

In this report of preliminary observations on the contact between Israeli organizations and the mass immigration from non-Western countries into Israel in recent years, we have tried to formulate an approach to the study of organizational change, particularly to change in the official-client relationship in response to this new kind of clientele.

Contrary to the expectations of classical sociological thinking, we have considerable impressionistic evidence pointing to a process of decreasing bureaucratization, at least in the relations between immigrant-clients and those parts of the bureaucracy which come into contact with them. We have tried to explain this finding by reference to the constraints operating on the bureaucrat who comes into contact with the public to train the immigrant client to perform the client role in order that he (the bureaucrat) may perform his own role adequately.

It seems to us that this process implies a certain kind of dependence on the client as far as the bureaucrat is concerned. Specifically, the bureaucrat is dependent on the client's proper performance of the client role, although in a different sense than the client is dependent on the bureaucrat's performance of his. Beyond this, the kinds of situations we are exploring include those where the bureaucrat may look to his client for sociability, or may recognize him as a member of the same ethnic group, or may seek to enlist his client in other organizations of which he is a member. All these exemplify situations of heightened dependence and, presumably, greater deviations from bureaucratic norms.

We have tried to suggest that the various forms of dependence which we found to be related to the process of debureaucratization may be subsumed under the more general heading of the articulation of role relations in modern society. The bureaucrat-client relationship is presumed to be segmented in certain ways from other kinds of social relations. Variations in the degree to which a given role relationship is insulated from other role relationships af-

fects the degree of its bureaucratization. Thus, the process of debureaucratization may be characterized as an impinging of nonbureaucratic roles, or of other bureaucratic roles, on the specific bureaucratic role in question, while over-bureaucratization may be expressed either in terms of the artificial insulation of the bureaucratic relationship from all other roles (however relevant) or, in its more totalitarian form, in the impinging of the bureaucratic relationship on relations not relevant to the bureaucratic role.

We have tried to set down some theoretical guidelines for a discussion of the problems of organizational change, with specific reference to the official-client relationship in a situation where there has been a rapid influx of immigrants having little previous contact with formal organization. We have tried to show that, in Israel, the process of decreasing bureaucratization is not an uncommon response in this situation, although we wish to emphasize that both increasing and decreasing bureaucratization may find simultaneous expression in different parts of the organization and, sometimes, in the very same relationship between official and client. It remains for the pilot study now in the field and the projected full-scale study to substantiate the general approach and the specific hypotheses we have proposed.

NOTES

1. This paper is a by-product of a collaborative effort to design research on the developing bureaucratic framework of immigrant absorption in Israel. In 1957–1958 a research seminar on this topic was conducted by the authors at the Hebrew University in Jerusalem. Participating in the seminar, and in the pilot study that emerged from it, were the following faculty members and students: Rivka Bar-Yossef, Batsheva Bonné, Esther Carmeli, Nina Toren, Arie Eliav, Uri Horowitz, Rivka Kaplansky, Yael Lissak, Pnina Morag, Dorit Pedan, Ozer Schild, Dov Weintraub, and Rina Zabelevsky. Mr. Schild and Mrs. Bar-Yossef are currently directing the pilot study, which is being supported, in part, by the Ford Foundation. We are indebted to Professors Peter M. Blau and David Riesman for a critical reading of an earlier draft.

RESPONSE OF ISRAELI ORGANIZATIONS TO NEW IMMIGRANTS

190   2. An elaboration of the well-known Simmel hypothesis on the effects of the size of a group for the specific case of migration can be found in Frank E. Jones, A Sociological Perspective on Immigrant Adjustment, *Social Forces*, 35 (1956), 39–47.

3. In general, our use of the terms official (or bureaucrat) and client is meant to refer also to superior-subordinate relationships within an organization.

4. Here and elsewhere we make use of Parsons' terminology. Although we make an effort to communicate the meaning of the several concepts we employ, for a full discussion see Talcott Parsons, *The Social System* (Glencoe, 1951), ch. ii.

5. Max Weber, "The Presuppositions and Causes of Bureaucracy," in Robert K. Merton, Ailsa P. Gray, Barbara Hockey, and Hanan Selvin, eds., *Reader in Bureaucracy* (Glencoe, 1952), 60–68. Of course, Weber was also concerned with the role of internal factors making for a greater degree of bureaucratization in the organization, a notable example being his discussion of "The Routinization of Charisma," which tends to develop when a group faces the problem of leadership succession, *ibid.*, pp. 92–100. This also gives a brief statement of Robert Michels' argument (pp. 88–92), as does his *Political Parties* (Glencoe, 1949).

6. The best known of these essays is probably Robert K. Merton, "Bureaucratic Structure and Personality," in Merton *et al., op. cit.*, pp. 361–371.

7. Seymour M. Lipset, Martin A. Trow and James S. Coleman, *Union Democracy* (Glencoe, 1956), try to specify the conditions that contribute, in at least one case, to the maintenance of trade-union democracy rather than oligarchic bureaucracy.

8. This, of course, refers to the dominant trend of present-day research, which has been concerned with the existence and the functions of informal social relations in the context of formal organization. But more important for our present purpose is the incipient concern for informal aspects of relationships between bureaucrats and the public. See, for example, Morris Janowitz, Deil Wright, and William Delany, *Public Administration and the Public* (Ann Arbor, 1958); Edwin J. Thomas, Role Conceptions and Organizational Size, *American Sociological Review*, 24 (1959), 30–37; and George F. Lombard, *Behavior in a Selling Group* (Cambridge, Mass., 1955). For a recent critique of the assumption that the several elements of Weber's ideal-type bureaucracy are necessarily intercorrelated, see Stanley H. Udy, Jr., "Bureaucracy" and "Rationality" in Weber's Organization Theory, *American Sociological Review*, 24 (1959), 792–795.

9. See Peter M. Blau, *The Dynamics of Bureaucracy* (Chicago, 1955), esp. ch. iii.

10. See Ralph H. Turner, "The Navy Disbursing Officer as a Bureaucrat," in Merton *et al., op. cit.*, pp. 372–379. Also compare Blau, *op. cit.*, for an example of the way in which variations in supervisory practice affected the extent to which employment agency officials used racial bias vis-à-vis their clients.

11. Max Weber, "The Presuppositions and Causes of Bureaucracy," in Merton *et al., op. cit.*, pp. 60–68.

12. See Alvin W. Gouldner, *Patterns of Industrial Bureaucracy* (Glencoe, 1954), pp. 59–101.

13. See Merton, *op. cit.*, p. 369.

14. For a discussion of the effect of size, see Thomas, *op. cit.*

15. Samuel A. Stouffer, *et al. The American Soldier: Combat and Its Aftermath* (Princeton, 1949), p. 100.

16. Charles H. Page, Bureaucracy's Other Face, *Social Forces*, 25 (1946), 89–91.

17. Lipset *et al., op. cit.*, p. 139.

18. Gouldner, *op. cit.*, pp. 105–154.

19. Sigmund Diamond, From Organization to Society: Virginia in the 17th Century, *American Journal of Sociology*, 63 (1958), 588–594.

20. Turner, *op. cit.*

21. For example, Turner omits the interdependence based on the common danger.

22. Note again that we are using "bureaucrat-client" in a generic sense, implying superordinate-subordinate relations (such as in combat, the mine, the Virginia Company, etc.) as well.

23. To cite a familiar example, a civil servant looking to a political party for rewards for

24. After developing this analysis of role impingement, we encountered Gouldner's concept and noted its close similarity. "It is necessary to distinguish," says Gouldner, "between those social identities of group members which are consensually regarded as relevant to them in a given setting and those which group members define as being irrelevant, inappropriate to consider, or illegitimate to take into account. The former can be called the manifest social identities, the latter, the latent social identities . . . . When group members orient themselves to the latent identities of others in their group, they are involved in a relationship with them which is not culturally prescribed by the group norms governing their manifest roles . . . . It would seem clear that latent identities and roles are important because they exert pressure upon the manifest roles, often impairing conformity with their requirements and endemically threatening the equilibrium of the manifest role system." Gouldner goes on to give an example concerning deference to elders in a universalistic setting which is very similar to the one we have presented. See Alvin W. Gouldner, Cosmopolitans and Locals: Toward an Analysis of Latent Social Roles, I and II, Administrative Science Quarterly, 2 (1957–1958), 281–306 and 444–480, esp. pp. 282–287. It should be noted also that the problem of role impingement or latent social identity differs from the problem of role conflict. Role impingement refers to the multiple role relations played by official and client vis-à-vis one another. Role conflict generally implies the multiple (and conflicting) roles of a given actor vis-à-vis several different others— e.g., the official's relationships to his wife and to his boss. Still a further distinction, recently introduced by Merton, is that of the role set, which has to do with the multiple role relations implicit in any given role—e.g., the official's relationship to his boss, his secretary, his colleagues, etc. Others who have employed analytic concepts similar to the concept of role impingement are Lloyd Fallers, Bantu Bureaucracy (Cambridge, Eng., 1957); Frank Jones, "The Infantry Recruit: A Sociological Analysis of Socialization in the Canadian Army" (unpublished doctoral dissertation, Harvard, 1956); and Thomas, op. cit.

25. A review, by Nathan Glazer, of several recent books treating Puerto Rican migration makes this point; see New York's Puerto Ricans, Commentary, 26 (1958), 469–478.

26. See S. N. Eisenstadt, The Absorption of Immigrants (Glencoe, 1955), pp. 64–68, and 172 ff., "The Framework of Bureaucratic Absorption."

27. In 1948, at the time of the establishment of the state of Israel, persons born in Africa and Asia constituted 15 per cent of the population; five years later, in 1953, they constituted 38 per cent of the population. See Moshe Sicron, Immigration to Israel: 1948–1953 (Jerusalem, 1957), pp. 43–50.

28. This would be particularly true when a bureaucrat's aim is to bring his client to want the bureaucrat's services; thus, this might be more true of a storekeeper than a nurse, and more true of a nurse than a bus driver.

29. Replying to the query whether the "dependency" of the child does not sometimes confer power equal to or superior to that of the person on whom dependency exists, Parsons distinguishes between power defined as "relative importance in carrying out the functional performance of the system" and as the "ability to cause trouble by threatening to disrupt the system." In this latter sense, "the child, and other persons or groups in dependent positions have considerable 'power.' " See Talcott Parsons and Robert F. Bales, Family, Socialization and Interaction Process (Glencoe, 1955), p. 46, n. 18. It is this second type of power which concerns us at this point.

30. Ibid., ch. ii.

31. See S. N. Eisenstadt, Sociological Aspects of the Economic Adaptation of Oriental Immigrants in Israel: A Case Study of Modernization, Economic Development and Cultural Change, 4 (1958), 269–278; and Alex Weingrod, From the Millah to the Moshav: Culture Contact and Change in a New-Immigrant Village in Israel (unpublished doctoral dissertation, University of Chicago, 1959).

RESPONSE OF ISRAELI ORGANIZATIONS TO NEW IMMIGRANTS

AUTHORITY AND CONTROL IN CLIENT-SERVING ORGANIZATIONS*

Charles E. Bidwell and Rebecca S. Vreeland

Formal organizations, as well as individual practitioners, are important agents of professional service. Yet, despite the attention which has been given to the relations between clients and free professionals, relations between clients and client-serving organizations largely remain to be explored.[1] Since the form of the professional-client relationship has significant effects on the behavior of the free professional, presumably it has an equally marked impact upon the structures and activities of client-serving organizations. Our purpose here is to suggest what some of these effects may be.

We have chosen to analyze effects upon authority structures and control within the staff, assuming that these structures have a central, strategic position vis-à-vis other attributes of organization.[2] We shall attend especially to the effects of variations in the form of the organization-client relationship. The analysis begun here could be extended profitably to a number of other organizational characteristics.

The Organization-Client Relationship

The model of the dyadic professional-client relationship is applicable with certain modifications to the organization-client relationship. This model depicts face-to-face interaction which is affectively neutral and functionally specific.[3] The professional commands specialized esoteric skills; the client needs the services these skills make possible. Between them the specific service to be rendered and the fee to be paid are agreed upon; that is, they consummate a utilitarian contract.[4]

But the client is in no position adequately to evaluate the professional's competence. His choice among available professionals usually is based upon general reputation and fragmentary information. Consequently the client must put himself in the hands of the professional, and the latter's willingness to add the former to his clientele is contingent upon this act. In other words, a normative contract also is consummated, the client, within the service relationship, subordinating himself on the basis of trust, to the professional. If for the client the normative contract is an expression of trust, for the professional it is the assumption of responsibility for the client's welfare. This responsibility is dual—to the client himself and, through the professional community, to the larger society. The normative contract, therefore, distinguishes clients

"Authority and Control in Client-Serving Organizations," *The Sociological Quarterly,* 4, 3 (Summer 1963), 231–242. Reprinted with the permission of the authors and of the publisher, the Midwest Sociological Society.

* This paper derives from some of the work being done in the Harvard Student Study, a longitudinal investigation of undergraduate life, supported by the National Institute of Mental Health, under Grant No. 3M—9151, and by a grant from the Hazen Foundation.

from customers, who must observe the principle of *caveat emptor*.

When an organization becomes the serving agent, face-to-face interaction occurs between the client and members of the professional staff, who employ both their skills and the resources owned by the organization. The utilitarian contract occurs between the client and the organization rather than the individual professionals.

But the level and form of the normative contract varies. It may occur at either the staff or the organizational level. Moreover, the organization-client relationship may be either functionally specific or diffuse. These variations in the normative contract give rise to three types of client-serving organizations.

NONINDUCTING ORGANIZATIONS

These are organizations such as the law firm or social service agency. The normative contract is located at the staff level. That is, while the client buys a service from the organization, he puts himself in the hands only of the professionals who provide it. Strictly speaking, the client is a customer of the organization, a client of certain of the staff. The client's participation in the organization is functionally specific and limited to his interaction with these professionals. He is not inducted as a member of the organization, and its authority structure does not extend to him. He is subordinate only to the moral authority of the staff members as professionals.

Professional responsibility, but not client trust, is in part diffused at the organizational level. The professional staff incur the dual responsibility for client welfare, but also are responsible to the organization. The organization in turn is responsible to the client and to the environing society for his welfare.

Inducting organizations, such as schools or hospitals, consummate the normative as well as the utilitarian contract at the organizational level. Their clients are inducted into the organization as client-members, subordinate in the authority structure to the professional cadre. The client-members put themselves in the hands of the organization rather than of its professional staff as individuals, for the client-member is in no better position to evaluate the competence of a client-serving organization than he is of a free professional. Indeed he is often less informed because the means of service are more differentiated and complex. In inducting organizations, the organization's responsibility for client welfare is reciprocated by the trust the client-member places in the organization itself.

THE ASSOCIATIONAL SUBTYPE

Among these inducting organizations, the normative contract remains functionally specific. Day schools and commuter colleges are inducting organizations of this kind. The scope of the client-member role is defined narrowly as the pattern of activity required in face-to-face interaction with the professional staff.[5] The client-member role here is a segment of the client-member's life space.

That is, in associational inducting organizations the utilitarian contract is an agreement to exchange *only* professional services for a fee. Neither his organizational participation nor the organization's authority pervades his total personality.

THE COMMUNAL SUBTYPE

These inducting organizations—for example hospitals and residential schools and colleges—approximate total environments for their client-members. Face-to-face interaction with the professional staff defines only one sector of the client-member role.

The utilitarian contracts between these organizations and their client-members are agreements to provide not only professional services for a fee but also a wide range of auxiliary services for fixed charges (or charges hidden in the fee or absorbed by subsidies from other sources). Residential colleges, for instance, provide food and lodging and typically a variety of extracurricular activities and counselling services for their students.

The normative contract in inducting organizations of this type is diffuse. Although the auxiliary services which are provided for the client-members usually do not themselves require professional skills, they are defined as ancillary to, and thus inextricably linked with, the organization's central professional activity. Hospital food services, for instance, are usually viewed as therapeutic, and college dormitories often are seen as at least potentially educational. Consequently the trust-responsibility bond between the client-member and the communal inducting organization must be diffuse. When, for instance, a student contracts for a dormitory room, he also agrees, perhaps implicitly, to abide by the rules of dormitory life and to accept the authority of the dormitory heads and residents. The hospital patient must eat what doctor and dietician prescribe.

Consequently, the client-members of communal inducting organizations participate in these organizations as total personalities and the scope of organizational authority is co-extensive with this participation.

Authority Structures and Problems of Control

Client-serving organizations must control the activities of both their staff members and clients. Although each area of control presents significant problems for the analysis of these organizations, the present discussion is limited to the control of staff behavior. We shall consider how authority over staff performance is variously allocated among staff roles in each of the three types of client-serving organizations and results in distinctive authority structures. We shall also examine some of the problems of staff control generated by these structures.

While differences among client-serving organizations arising from their characteristic relations with clients in themselves affect the distribution of authority among the staff, this distribution also is affected by the power of the professional cadres. We therefore approach authority structures as an interaction effect of variations in this power and in organizational type.

The power of the professional cadres may be viewed as an outcome of their bargaining positions in the environing society and of the normative contract. In general the bargaining positions of professionals depend upon the extent of social demand for their services and the criticalness of these services.[6] Thus doctors or lawyers are in a stronger position than teachers or social workers. Moreover, client-serving organizations seek a mandate from the society on the basis of their professional activities, and with this mandate, they attempt to legitimate their claims to resources and support apart from the competitive criteria of the economic market. The organization's mandate depends heavily upon the mandates of the professions represented in its staff, and the scope and strength of these mandates in turn are a function of the profession's bargaining position. Finally, the stronger the profession's bargaining position, the stronger and better organized the professional community tends to be, exercising close control over the supply of professionals and effective enforcement of the demands of its members.

While differences of bargaining positions thus lead to variations in the power of professional cadres within client-serving organizations, the normative contract sets a floor under this power. Relative to the organization, professional personnel therefore always are in a comparatively powerful position. As we have seen, the normative contract, whether it occurs at the staff or organization level, renders the organization responsible for client welfare. This responsibility opens the organization to supervision by professional associations and government agencies. Witness the triads of law firm-client-bar association or hospital-patient-medical society and public health department. Through their joint memberships in the organization and the professional community, the professional staff are in a key position to modify or intensify intervention by professional and governmental agencies. In this way, a client-serving organization is dependent upon its professional staff, whatever their bargaining strength.

What kinds of authority do client-serving organizations use to control the activities of their professionals? The possible alternatives are to employ financial or solidary incentives.[7] Perhaps the central problem of control in client-serving organizations is the necessary autonomy of the professionals which arises from their monopoly of *expertise* and the relative inaccessibility of their activities to direction by others. While the organization can indirectly control professional performance, for example, by the placement of the professional in the flow of work or by the allocation of resources, central decisions about the kind and quality of professional activities are made individually by the professional. This tendency to autonomy is, of course, increased by occupational ideologies which stress freedom from interference. To maintain sufficient quality to meet client welfare responsibilities and to maximize goal attainment, the professional must be brought to identify himself strongly with the organization.

Therefore solidary incentives centered upon professional values and commitments are necessarily the principal means of control in client-serving organizations.[8] The solidary incentive to which professionals will respond is colleague esteem. Consequently authority in these organizations must be in some way collegial. Moreover, the organization must identify its goals with the values and aims of the profession. Under these circumstances, adequate organizational performance is also competent professional performance, and it brings the rewards of colleague acceptance. In other words, the professional staff are controlled by the blending of occupational social controls and organizational authority.

From this analysis, it follows that the management of client-serving organizations will either be vested in the hands of the professional cadre, with administrative roles occurring as variants of professional ones, or maintain colleagueship among professionals and administrators, although their organizational roles are distinct. In the latter case administrators probably will be recruited from the professional ranks.

AUTHORITY AND CONTROL IN NONINDUCTING ORGANIZATIONS

When the client-serving organization is noninducting, the tasks of administration center upon the management of professional activities and the maintenance of relations with the external society. Under these circumstances, two kinds of authority structure are probable, according to the power of the professional cadre.

Pure Collegial Authority. This structure should occur when the professionals are relatively strong, and indeed it is most common in legal firms and medical clinics. In this structure the distinction between the administrative and professional cadres is blurred. The combined professional - administrative hierarchy may be ordered according to professional seniority or according to the principle of *primus inter pares.*

Here the professional staff operate with broad autonomy in their interactions with clients. Control is primarily informal, exercised as the situation requires. Rules of procedure are few, centered more upon organization maintenance than upon professional tasks. Management of environmental relationships is diffused throughout the professional staff, although perhaps an especial responsibility of the senior men.

These structures are subject especially to two sources of strain. Strains may arise from power plays by individuals who seek to maximize their collegial advantage. Strains may also mirror tensions and uncertainties within the professional community over the domains and status of specialties and other subgroups.[9] The extent to which these strains can be contained will rest largely upon the integration of the professional community itself and the extent to which the organization has become identified with it.

Hierarchic authority. This authority structure should occur when the professionals are relatively weak and may be observed in such noninducting organizations as social service agencies. Here there is a distinct separation between subordinate professionals and superordinate administrators, who represent the goals and demands of the organization in contrast to the personal or occupational interests of the professionals. The administrators manage the professionals' activities and handle external relations. The professional tasks are given a more narrow "technical" definition and typically are subject to specific rules of procedure.

The administrators usually are drawn from the professional cadre, but cease active practice upon assuming their new roles. Their professional identity gives them access to solidary occupational incentives, although diminished by their occupational defection. In view of the weaker position of the professionals, these incentives likely will suffice. This identity also makes it possible for the administrators to mediate effectively between the organization and professional and governmental regulators.

However, the asymmetrical normative contracts in noninducting organizations, in which client trust reposes in the professionals rather than in the organization, heightens organizational dependency upon its professionals and thus limits administrative control. If for no other reason than the risk of losing substantial numbers of clients, the administrator cannot afford to alienate his professional subordinates. The hierarchic authority structure, then, is prone to administrator-professional strains, as the latter seek to extend their own authority. At the same time there is a strong tendency for occupational social controls and organizational authority to become divorced, because of the subordination of the professional staff, so that financial incentives become predominant and the professional effectively withdraws from the organization. The professional then is likely to pursue his own and not the organization's interests. The problem of control in these structures is to maintain staff identification without undermining administrative authority.

AUTHORITY AND CONTROL IN INDUCTING ORGANIZATIONS

The existence of a client-membership introduces new service functions. The complexity of these functions obviously varies with the scope of the normative contract. But even in associational inducting organizations, record-keeping will probably become more elaborate, client-members must be processed in and out of the organization, and the possibility of interactions among client-members, as well as with the professionals, may give rise to disciplinary tasks of a nonprofessional nature. In communal inducting organizations, these auxiliary functions further expand and typically include provision of residential facilities, health services, and leisure activities. The resulting authority structures are a mixture of segmental differentiation with either collegial or hierarchical arrangements.

Let us consider first communal inducting organizations. Auxiliary services require their own staff. In communal organizations, the auxiliary cadre will be larger and more differentiated and its power relatively greater than in their associational counterparts. When the professionals also are relatively powerful, the professional and auxiliary cadres are likely to be completely separate, as in hospitals where both the medical director and the hospital administrator report directly to the board of trustees. Here one finds the collegial professional structure preserved within a larger authority structure, employing segregation as a means for controlling conflicts between the interests of professional and auxiliary personnel.[10]

When the professionals are relatively weak, the auxiliary staff more probably will be only partially separate from the professional one. Both will be subordinate to a top administrator, drawn however from the professional group. Hierarchical structure is imposed upon segmental differentiation. This is the typical authority structure of residential colleges, for example. One of the functions of the administrator in these client-serving organizations is to mediate conflicts of interest between the professional and auxiliary staffs.

Collegial authority does not seem to occur in associational inducting organizations, probably because critical—that is, dangerous and complex—services require communal participation by client-members. Thus authority in these organizations, e.g., day schools, is hierarchically structured. But in associational inducting organizations, the auxiliary cadre, because they are relatively weak, are not in a position seriously to challenge the interests of the professionals or claim a co-ordinate position. Therefore segmental differentiation tends to be minimal, with auxiliary roles attached to the office of the top administrator or subordinated to the professional staff, at least to its senior members. Both structures may be observed in school systems, where a business manager works in the superintendent's office and counsellors work under school principals.

In inducting organizations, either communal or associational, the professionals' power is lessened since the normative contract is symmetrical, i.e., occurs at the organizational level. Even when client-members initially are recruited through individual professionals, as in private hospitals, once in the organization they come under the authority of auxiliary as well as professional personnel. The professionals no longer can claim sole competence *vis-à-vis* the client-membership. Conflicts of interest between professionals and auxiliary staff now may center upon the boundaries and exercise of their respective domains of authority over client-members.

If the professional and auxiliary staffs are completely separated, these strains may seriously lower the organization's effectiveness in the absence of a competent court of appeal. The more likely criterion for resolution is the comparative social status of the competing occupational groups. This situation is evanescent and shifting, liable to recurrent, never-resolved, organizational strains. If there is a top administrator, the problem is his. Given his professional identification he is likely to resolve such conflicts in favor of his former colleagues. In so doing, he risks alienating the auxiliary staff, but this is not as serious as alienating the professionals. As a result, these conflicts probably will be resolved by compromises which preserve the essential perquisites of the professional cadre.

In both associational and communal inducting organizations, auxiliary staff are likely to become professionalized. Many auxiliary roles involve face-to-face interaction with client-members

and either require, or are defined as requiring, the skills of a professional group, e.g., social service in hospitals and counselling and guidance in schools. As an inducting organization recruits substantial numbers of professionally trained persons into these roles, it comes to contain multiple professional cadres which perform functions different in content but not in form. It follows that the power of these newer professional cadres will be considerably enhanced *vis-à-vis* the older professionals and the organization. Differences in the power of these groups in the organization will now be based upon their bargaining positions and upon their claims to status according to the centrality of their contributions to goal attainment.

In communal inducting organizations, when the professional and auxiliary staffs are completely separated, one of two adaptations is likely. If the older professionals continue to be more powerful, one would expect them to assimilate the new professional group, although at a subordinate level. The collegial element of the authority structure would then be partially destroyed with the professional ranks now differentiated into two strata. One stratum would provide the older, and purportedly more central, services and would preserve collegiality. The other stratum would provide the newly professionalized services and be subordinate to the collegial stratum. Under these circumstances we should expect the new professionals to continue to press for more equal status. But if the older professionals do not maintain a clear power advantage, multiple separate professional staffs should develop—a situation prone to conflict and instability as each group maneuvers for advantage.

If the professional and auxiliary staffs of a communal inducting organization are united in a top administrator, the professionalization of auxiliary roles generates strong pressure for the establishment of multiple professional staff groups, each perhaps with its own chief, but all still responsible to a single administrative head. The possibilities for conflicts of interest are obvious. The criteria for their resolution are the power positions of these staff groups and their claim to central functions. The top administrator, however, cannot go too far in recognizing the claims of certain of these groups without endangering the organization by alienating the others. A series of uneasy compromises is likely to result which satisfy no one and give rise to further strains. The professional origin of the top administrator now becomes a central concern for the professional cadres, as it provides an additional resource in the struggle for advantage. Accession to this role consequently is a further source of intense struggle and may well give rise to deep and enduring cleavages between the professional groups.

If we turn to associational inducting organizations, the effect of professionalization of auxiliary roles is to move these organizations toward this same pattern. The auxiliary staff first should become larger and more differentiated and press increasingly for a co-ordinate position with the older professionals. When their power becomes sufficiently great, multiple professional staffs, with separate administrative hierarchies united in the top administrator will emerge. School counselling services, for example, have displayed this process. Consequently conflicts and control problems like those just discussed will be observed. They are unlikely to be as severe, however, since the associational participation of client-members in these organizations limits the costs of auxiliary services and tends to diminish their importance.

A Concluding Note

The different authority structures which we have discussed have often been described by students of organizations. But the approach taken in this paper suggests how their variety can be accounted for systematically. It also has allowed us to predict some of the distinctive problems of organizational control which each engenders. These predications await verification. If the organization-client relationship does appear to be a fruitful starting-point for studying client-serving organizations, the analysis begun here might well be extended to other attributes of these organizations.

NOTES

1. For analyses of the relations of free professionals and clients, see especially the work of Everett Hughes and his students; Talcott Parsons, "The Professions and Social Structure," *Essays in Sociological Theory* (Glencoe, Ill.: The Free Press, 1954), pp. 34–49; and A. M. Carr-Saunders and P. A. Wilson, *The Professions* (Oxford: The Clarendon Press, 1933). The general problem with which we here are concerned has also interested Amitai Etzioni (*A Comparative Analysis of Complex Organizations* [New York: The Free Press of Glencoe, 1961]), and Peter Blau and W. R. Scott (*Formal Organizations* [San Francisco: Chandler Publishing Co., 1962] especially pp. 27–58, 81–85, 167–93). It has been most insightfully addressed by Erving Goffman in "The Medical Model and Mental Hospitalization," *Asylums* (Garden City: Doubleday Anchor Books, 1961), pp. 323–86.
2. Cf. Etzioni, *op. cit.,* pp. 3–22.

3. Cf. Parsons, *op. cit.;* Carr-Saunders and Wilson, *op. cit.*

4. For the distinction between utilitarian and normative contracts discussed in some-what different terms, see Talcott Parsons, "The Mental Hospital as a Type of Organization," in *The Patient and the Mental Hospital,* ed. by Milton Greenblatt *et al.* (Glencoe, Ill.: The Free Press, 1957), pp. 113–17.

5. This statement is subject to many exceptions which result from attempts by associational inducting organizations to capture increasing amounts of client-member participation and thus to approach the communal extreme. The extensive extracurricula of some commuter colleges or day schools are examples of this.

6. Cf. Edward Gross, "Sociological Aspects of Professional Salaries," *Educational Record,* 41:130–37 (1960).

7. Cf. Peter B. Clark and James Q. Wilson, "Incentive Systems: A Theory of Organizations," *Administrative Science Quarterly,* 6:129–66 (1961).

8. In this analysis we are ignoring, for the sake of simplicity, modifications of authority and control which will occur when, as in hospitals, the professional staff retain the status of free practitioners. This question is well worth pursuing within the frame set here.

9. Cf. Rue Bucher and Anselm Strauss, "Professions in Process," *American Journal of Sociology,* 66:325–34 (1961).

10. See Eugene Litwak, "Models of Bureaucracy which Permit Conflict," *American Journal of Sociology,* 67:177–84 (1961).

ORGANIZATIONS AND CLIENTS: LATERAL AND LONGITUDINAL DIMENSIONS*

Mark Lefton and William R. Rosengren

This paper sets forth a framework for the development of an analytic model of formal organizations which views the clients of organizations as integral factors influencing the structure and functioning of such systems. Three reasons are basic to this effort. Of first importance is the fact that our age is witness

"Organizations and Clients: Lateral and Longitudinal Dimensions," *American Sociological Review,* 31, 6 (December 1966), 802–810. Reprinted with the permission of the authors and of the publisher, The American Sociological Association. William R. Rosengren is chairman of the Department of Sociology and Anthropology at the University of Rhode Island.

* We would like to thank Irving Rosow, Charles Perrow, and Robert Habenstein for offering us a number of helpful comments and criticisms. Many of their suggestions will also be incorporated in the further elaboration of the lateral-longitudinal model in a forthcoming monograph by William R. Rosengren and Mark Lefton, *Hospitals and Patients: A Theory of Clients and Organizations.*

to a new phase in the organizational revolution, one which is marked by a phenomenal growth in the number, variety, and importance of formal organizations which serve people as persons, rather than catering exclusively to material needs and wishes. Second, this transition appears to involve a major shift in the criteria by which the operations of organizations must be evaluated.[1] That is, the substitution of what may be called "humanitarian" values for purely economic and administrative considerations will eventually demand organizational responsiveness to an ethic of service rather than to one of efficiency. The third consideration has to do with the fact that emphasis upon such issues as rational efficiency, internal structures of authority and control, and the maintenance of organizational autonomy, while of obvious importance for the sake of better understanding economic and administrative organizations, may be of less utility in the analysis of organizations concerned with the social and personal dilemmas of men. In addition, the existing conceptions of organizations may have to be broadened to cope with the interorganizational demands engendered by large-scale action programs in the fields of human welfare.

There are four distinct traditions in organizational analysis, none of which, for different reasons, has yet codified the linkages between clients and formal organizational structure. The first of these is perhaps best represented by the work which owes its principal intellectual debt to Weber's original conception of bureaucracy as a form of legitimate authority.[2] The second includes those studies dealing with the impact of the demographic and ecological characteristics of the surrounding community upon the formal structure and functioning of organizations.[3] Third, the social system perspective focuses more upon the structural linkages by which the functional requisites of formal organizations—seen as subsystems—are integrated with and accommodated to the institutional systems of the larger social order.[4] Finally, the fourth tradition in the study of organizations is represented by the symbolic interactionists.[5]

A diversity of organizational contexts have been examined from the perspective of Weber's ideal type, but the central focus has remained consistent with the bureaucratic model. The prime concern has been with the operating functionaries of organizations rather than with the clients they serve. The structural approach has yielded a large body of literature which compares and contrasts the formal properties of organizations with expectations derived from the ideal type.[6]

In contrast, the community structure approach has tended to focus either on co-optation, competition and other processes by which "publics in contact" are made congruent with organizational needs, or upon the manner in which organizations emerge as the demographic and ecological products of the host community.[7] A variant of this approach focuses specifically on the need for an organization to manipulate its incentive system in order to maintain the commitment of its members. Effort along these lines has attempted to link particular types of organizational incentive to varying "publics" and emphasize the strategic importance of examining an organization's sensitivity to changing motives as well as to environmental conditions.[8]

The social system approach, in its focus upon the systemic relations between organizations and the institutional sub-systems of which they are but a part, has tended to preclude a deliberate concern with the role of clients in organizations, precisely because of the level of analysis at which such concerns are generally expressed.

Finally, the symbolic interactionist approach leads to a conception of formal organizational structures and processes as having only secondary importance, providing only a contextual backdrop against which processes of self-identity, situational definitions, role emergence, and symbol verification are brought into bold relief.[9]

This brief discussion is designed to make one point: Insofar as they do not explicitly deal with the clients of organizations, the major traditions in organizational analysis remain conceptually divergent and substantially distinct.

ATTEMPTS TO RELATE CLIENTS TO ORGANIZATIONS

Congruent with the concerns indicated above, there has recently been an increased awareness on the part of several students of formal organizations of the need to regard clients as critical factors in organizational structure and functioning. For example, Parsons states: ". . . in the case of professional services there is another very important pattern where the recipient of the service becomes an operative member of the service-providing organization. . . . This taking of the customer *into* the organization has important implications for the nature of the organization."[10] But then the discussion is directed once again to a systematic analysis of the strategies by which organizations meet system-maintenance requisites without pursuit of the implications of the previous insight.

Blau and Scott explicitly identify some of the instances in which organizations might better be understood in the light of client characteristics. They say:

> It is perhaps a truism to say that organizations will reflect the characteristics of the publics they serve. A technical high school differs in predictable ways from a college preparatory school, and an upper-middle class church is unlike the mission church of the same denomination in the slums. While such differences seem to be important and pervasive, there has been little attempt to relate client characteristics systematically to organizational structures.[11]

It should be obvious that clients may present organizations with a wide range of characteristics. Any specific clientele characteristic may have a varying impact upon organizational functions, but only if such a characteristic is regarded as relevant. In this regard, organizations must select and define those client characteristics which are salient for their purposes. In a discussion of hospital structures, Perrow argues that hospitals belong to that class of organizations which attempt as their primary goal the alteration of the state of human material —such material being at once self-activating, subject to a multitude of orientations, "encrusted with cultural definitions," and embodying a wide range of organizational relevancies. Perrow then indicates the impacts that contrasting definitions of the client material are likely to have upon the technologies employed in hospitals and of their structural properties as well.[12]

The importance of contrasting definitions by organizations of the publics they serve, particularly for internal as well as external control processes, has been emphasized by Etzioni. From his perspective, a critical dimension in this respect derives from the confrontation between service as an ideology and service as an organizational instrument of manipulation and control.[13]

Another hint at the importance of clients is provided by Eisenstadt's discussion of debureaucratization. The client is here perceived as a scarce resource—a fact having implications for internal structure as well as for interorganizational relationships. To the extent that the client does constitute a scarce resource upon which organizational survival depends, "the more (the organization) will have to develop techniques of communication and additional services to retain the clientele for services in spheres which are not directly relevant to its main goals." [14]

Finally, the symbolic interactionist tradition has recently been represented by the work of Glaser and Strauss. Their paradigm of "contexts of awareness" is designed to explain the interpersonal contingencies of dying in a hospital. A critical aspect of this scheme is the fact that staff and patients often interact in terms of very different definitions of the situation. They conclude that, ". . . in so much writing about interaction there has been much neglect or incomplete handling of *relationships* (italics ours) between social structure and interaction that we have no fear of placing too much emphasis upon those relationships . . . the course of interaction may partly change the social structure within which interaction occurs." [15]

Suggestive as these remarks are, their essentially descriptive character has precluded a realization of their points of convergence and their analytic potential. The purpose of the remainder of this paper is to set forth a model of formal organizations with two uses: first, to provide a frame of reference which facilitates a synthesis of previous work dealing with clients and organizations; and second, to provide an analytical point of departure from which other hypotheses may be generated concerning relationships between organizations and their clients.

A Perspective Toward Clients and Organizations

Notwithstanding the apparently divergent interests in the works referred to above, a major theme is discernible, viz., organizations have contrasting interests in their clients. Furthermore, these organizational interests in the "client biography" may vary along two major dimensions. First, such interests may range from a highly truncated span of time (as in the emergency room of a general hospital) to an almost indeterminate span of time (as in a long-term psychiatric facility or a chronic illness hospital). There is, moreover, a second range of interests which considers the client not in terms of biographical time, but rather in terms of biographical space. That is to say, some organizations may have an interest in only a limited aspect of the client as a person—as in the case of a short-term general hospital—whereas other organizations may have a more extended interest in who the client is as a product of and participant in society—as in the case of a psychiatric out-patient clinic.

The analytically important fact is that lateral and longitudinal interests in the biographical careers of clients may vary independently of one another. There are four logically different kinds of arrangement—each of which is likely to have significantly different impacts upon the internal structure and interpersonal processes of organizations, as well as upon extra-organizational relationships.

The four biographical variants may be depicted as follows:

Empirical examples	Biographical interest	
	Lateral (social space)	Longitudinal (social time)
Acute general hospital	−	−
TB hospital, rehabilitation hospital, public health department, medical school	−	+
Short-term therapeutic psychiatric hospital	+	−
Long-term therapeutic hospital, liberal arts college	+	+

The logic of this typological system suggests that certain similarities ought to be found between those organizations manifesting a similar lateral interest in their clients, even though they may differ sharply in the extent of their longitudinal concern. Thus, for example, one would expect to find some structural similarities between a general hospital and a tuberculosis hospital, in spite of the fact that the latter has an extended longitudinal interest in the client, while the former does not. That is to say, the orientation of both institutions toward their clients, i.e., patients, is highly specific, focusing as each does upon relatively well-defined disease entities. Thus, though each organization may take account of such lateral life-space factors as occupation, family life, age, and sex, the relevance of these to the defined client problem is minimal. Conversely, those institutions which have a similar stake in the longitudinal careers of their clients should share some features in common despite possible marked differences along the lateral di-

mension. Thus, a long-term psychiatric hospital, for example, should logically resemble in some respects a tuberculosis hospital, even though the former has a broad lateral interest in the client, while the latter does not. And similarly, each of the four types should reflect some organizational characteristics which distinguish them.

CLIENT BIOGRAPHIES AND
ISSUES OF COMPLIANCE

One of the persisting theoretical issues in organizational analysis has to do with the strategies by which participants are made tractable to the internal needs of organization.[16] This issue is of equal importance when the client becomes the focus of attention rather than the operative functionaries. The four types of client biographical interests outlined here appear to give rise to different kinds of control problems, and, therefore, to different structural arrangements for achieving compliance.

In utilizing the client as the point of departure by which to examine organizational dynamics, an immediate issue concerns the distinction between conformity and commitment as different modes of client compliance. In the former instance, clients' adherence to conduct rules in the organization is the key problem; in the latter the investment of the client in the ideology of the institution is at issue. These modes of compliance pose different organizational problems in each of the four types. Thus, the greater the laterality of the organization's interest in the client's biography, the greater is the variety of conduct alternatives on the part of the client which are regarded as organizationally relevant. This sets the stage for the emergence of contrasting control strategies. Conversely, those institutions with a minimal lateral interest in their clients are likely to be those in which the conformity of clients to organizational rules is of less concern. In extreme examples, in fact, conformity may be regarded as given and hence unproblematic, because of the physical structure of the institution, e.g., close security cells in custody prisons, or by the physical incapacitation of the client, e.g., quadriplegics in rehabilitation hospitals.

In the longitudinal institution, however, the compliance problem is of a somewhat different order since such organizations have a long-term commitment to the client's future biography which in some cases may extend beyond the time he will actually be physically present in the institution. In these circumstances, the re-arrangement of the client's future biography cannot be accomplished merely by the exercise of coercion. It would appear that for this type of institution the client is controlled by getting him to believe either in the moral goodness or in the practical fitness of the biography the organization is attempting to shape for him. This problem is often attacked by way of an elaborate ideology which the organization attempts to transmit to the client so that self-control is exercised once he is outside the physical confines of the institution.[17]

In terms of the client biography model, the patterns of conformity and commitment take the following shape:

| Orientations toward clients | | Compliance problems | |
Lateral	Longitudinal	Conformity	Commitment
−	−	No	No
+	+	Yes	Yes
−	+	No	Yes
+	−	Yes	No

In summary to this point: These problems of client control, which derive logically from a presumed differential institutional investment in the biographies of their clients (laterally and/or longitudinally), give rise to a series of different types of organizational problems and are attended by different modes of resolution.

CLIENT BIOGRAPHIES AND PROBLEMS OF STAFF CONSENSUS

In addition to the contrasting problems of client conformity which derive from the model, the organization's concern with client biography also gives rise to contrasting problems of staff consensus. That is, organizations also may be described by the extent to which conflict between and among staff members is present with regard either to means or to ends. It is our contention that the patterns of consensus relevant to organizational means and ends are systematically related to laterality and longitudinality. Specifically, they take the following form:

| Orientations toward clients | | Difficulties over consensus | |
Lateral	Longitudinal	Means	Ends
−	−	No	Yes
+	+	Yes	Yes
−	+	No	No
+	−	Yes	No

With respect to the non-lateral and non-longitudinal institution, the specificity of the orientation toward clients results in clear priorities and consensus as to the relative efficacy of different skills in the repair job to be done. Hence there is little ground for competing orientations to be developed. Similarly, this specificity of orientation and subsequent instant removal of the client implies that there is no compulsion to devise criteria or mechanisms for evaluating long-term outcome, the allocation of organizational resources for these purposes, nor need to establish boundaries to longitudinal responsibility.

This does not mean that stress and strain do not occur in the non-lateral/non-longitudinal organization. It means simply that they seldom become subject to *formal procedures,* but occur at the informal and extra-institutional level. Thus, claims for status are made by those whose place in the hierarchy of professional priorities is somewhere other than the top.[18] Informal negotiations are engaged in for scarce organizational resources. Power alignments develop among staff, involving agreement of a *quid pro quo* kind.[19] Moreover, such an institution is continually subject to pressures from outside, generally in the direction of pressing for greater laterality and longitudinality. Internally as well, informal negotiations develop regarding the ultimate goals and purposes of the institution, again in the direction of more broadly defining the goals of the establishment.

The most contrasting situation with regard to staff competition and conflict is to be found in the lateral and longitudinal organization, in which there is a heightened organizational response to the ubiquitous pressures for formal resolution which stem from the existence of diverse postures toward means and ends. In view of the felt need for official consensus regarding means and ends, such an organization continually devises officially established devices for making such resolutions. While the initial roots of conflict regarding means and ends may well emerge from within the context of the informal system of power alignments and personal negotiations, these issues are swiftly legitimized and made subject to formal means of solution. Here is to be found a proliferation of formal systems of communication, specialized staff meetings, and increased attempts to make the organization conform to some popularized conception of bureaucracy. The not infrequent outcome is a repeated re-organization of the system of authority and decision-making, and continual addition of staff personnel with finely discriminated skills and techniques. In short, the lateral-longitudinal organization involves a continually changing formal system of authority, with a conflict culture the content of which is co-opted into the formal system.

Although there are other obvious consequences of laterality and longitudinality for the internal structure and dynamics of organizations, we turn now to a consideration of some of their consequences for one type of inter-organizational dilemma, namely, collaborative relations between organizations.

CLIENT BIOGRAPHIES AND
INTER-ORGANIZATIONAL
COLLABORATION

It is useful to make the distinction between formal and informal processes of inter-organizational collaboration. We shall define formal processes as those ways in which members of organizations engage in collaboration *in their capacities as members of the organization.* By informal we mean those ways of collaborating which involve either an *intervening* organization, e.g., a professional association, or those in which the collaborators act in some capacity other than as organizational members, e.g., a voluntary community organization. Finally, we emphasize the importance of the

Orientations toward clients		Formal		Informal	
Lateral	*Longitudinal*	*Operating*	*Admin.*	*Operating*	*Admin.*
−	−	No	No	Yes	Yes
+	+	Yes	Yes	No	No
−	+	Yes	No	No	Yes
+	−	No	Yes	Yes	No

distinction between administrative-financial concerns as compared with collaborations involving operational facilities. It seems reasonable to argue that these modes of inter-organizational collaboration are also systematically related to the character of the organization's interest in the client's biography. With respect to these distinctions we suggest specifically that the four types of organizations differ in their *propensities* for kinds of collaboration.

The non-lateral/non-longitudinal organization (the acute general hospital, for example), typically has little propensity for formal collaboration at either the administrative or operating levels. The specificity of its interest in the client and its concern with discriminating strategies of care tend to make such organizations isolated professional islands in the community.[20] Moreover, while this situation may result in the efficient operation of separate institutions, such efficiency does not necessarily extend to the community as a whole. In fact, the reverse may indeed be true—that is, the very efficiency of separate institutions may imply duplication of expensive services such as a cobalt machine, and may thus be detrimental for the needs of the community which they independently serve.[21]

In addition, because they do have a truncated longitudinal interest in their clients, such organizations need not devise strategies to follow their departed

clients. "Checking" on clients requires the development of administrative mechanisms for getting information from other organizations which may later be responsible for the welfare of the client. In addition, such organizations normally stand as splendid pillars of financial isolation in the community, with little need (or capacity) to develop "master plans" with other organizations.[22] But again, this is only at the formal level; such organizations are involved in networks of informal relationships. In the case of the general hospital, for example, such networks may extend through the local medical society and health insurance programs in the community as well as to the local community power structure. We do not mean that the non-lateral/non-longitudinal organization does not engage in collaboration, but only that control of the kind and extent of collaboration has been co-opted by extra-organizational agencies.

On the other hand, the lateral-longitudinal organization stands as the most contrasting type. The long-term therapeutically oriented psychiatric institution, for example, is customarily involved in a massive and sometimes conflicting set of administrative and operating linkages at both the formal and the informal level. The wide range of professional personnel it utilizes tends to extend their professional contacts into other similarly organized institutions. Further, the fact of a longitudinal interest in the client's future biography means that the organization must devise ways of establishing working relationships with other organizations which may ultimately be held responsible for the later career of the client. Thus one is likely to find that the non-lateral/non-longitudinal organization (hospital or not) has no established linkages with the juvenile court, nursing homes, family welfare agencies, the probation office, and so forth, while the administrative personnel in the longitudinal institution are often intimately tied in with a wide range of other interested institutions.[23]

In sum, there appear to be variable relations between an organization's structural extensions in time and space toward other organizations, and its functional commitments to the client.

For purposes of this paper, we shall not pursue the other two types. It is rather more strategic on both theoretical and practical grounds to consider what is likely to happen when two organizations of the same type or of sharply divergent type are faced with a potential collaborative relationship. We would expect that a similarity in laterality or longitudinality would be likely to enhance formal collaboration, while contrasting types would be inhibited in collaboration and even experience open conflict.

In the field of rehabilitation, for example, one may find illustrations of these divergent types. Deliberately contrived programs of collaboration involving the consolidation of different rehabilitation agencies, such as organizations for the blind, the mentally retarded, or the physically handicapped, often flounder at the operational level. This situation may be explained by the fact that rehabilitation agencies are differentially committed to the lateral careers of their clients. What appears to account for the collaborative effort in the first place is

their common interest in the longitudinal dimensions of the client biography. The logical outcome of this duality leads to harmony in terms of effective dialogue at the administrative level but to a great deal of conflict and stress at the operational level. Furthermore, this condition may become characterized over time by elaborate administrative superstructures rather than by operational effectiveness.[24]

These illustrations point to but a few of the logical outcomes for collaboration problems between organizations which stem from the client biography model herein considered. We would expect that the nature of the analysis indicated would also be relevant and useful for an understanding of the organizational dilemmas encountered by such agencies as public health facilities, custodial and punishment-centered institutions, schools, and other client-oriented organizations.

SUMMARY AND CONCLUSION

The client biography model discussed in this paper provides a framework conducive to a more systematic linkage between four major, but often divisive, orientations associated with organizational analysis; namely, the classical bureaucratic, the systemic, the communal, and the symbolic interactionist traditions. The importance of this potential is underscored by the fact that although sociologists are generally aware of the need to better integrate these orientations, attempts to do so have tended to remain implicit and have failed to specify the theoretical link between clients and organizations. This is not to say that the importance of clients in organizations has been overlooked—the point to be emphasized is that existing theories have not incorporated client characteristics in the propositions with which they deal.

The conception of relations between organizations and their clients as varying along the lateral and longitudinal dimensions may be regarded as an initial step toward just such a synthesis.

NOTES

1. Warren Bennis, "Beyond Bureaucracy," *Transaction,* 2 (July–August, 1965), pp. 31–35.
2. See, for example, T. R. Anderson and S. Warkov, "Organizational Size and Functional Complexity: A Study of Administration in Hospitals," *American Sociological Review,* 26 (February, 1961), pp. 23–28; Peter M. Blau, *The Dynamics of Bureaucracy,* Chicago: University of Chicago Press, 1955; Amitai Etzioni, *A Comparative Analysis of Complex Organizations,* New York: The Free Press of Glencoe, 1961; Alvin Gouldner, *Patterns of Industrial Bureaucracy,* Glencoe: The Free Press, 1954.
3. For example, Ivan Belknap and J. Steinle, *The Community and Its Hospitals,* Syracuse: Syracuse University Press, 1963; Ray H. Elling, "The Hospital Support Game in Urban Center," in Eliot Friedson, ed., *The Hospital in Modern Society,* Glencoe: The Free Press, 1963; Basil Georgopoulous and F. Mann, *The Community General Hospital,* New York: Macmillan Co., 1962; Delbert Miller, "Industry and Community Power Structure: A Comparative Study of an American and an English City," *American Sociological Review,* 23 (February, 1958), pp. 9–15; Harold W. Pfautz and G. Wilder, "The Ecology of a Mental Hospital," *Journal of Health and Human Behavior,* 3 (Summer, 1962), pp. 67–72; Stanley Lieberson, "Ethnic Groups and the Practice of Medicine," *American Sociological Review,* 23 (October, 1958), pp. 542–549.
4. Philip Selznick, "Foundations of the Theory of Organizations," *American Sociological Review,* 13 (February, 1948), pp. 25–35; *TVA and the Grass Roots,* Berkeley: University of California Press, 1953; Talcott Parsons, "Suggestions for Sociological Approach to the Theory of Organizations," *Administrative Science Quarterly,* 1 (June, 1956), pp. 63–85.
5. For example, J. Bensman and I. Gerver, "Crime and Punishment in the Factory," in A. Gouldner and H. Gouldner, eds., *Modern Society,* New York: Harcourt Brace and World, 1963, pp. 593–596; Barney Glaser and Anselm Strauss, *Awareness of Dying,* Chicago: Aldine Press, 1965; Erving Goffman, *The Presentation of Self in Everyday Life,* Edinburgh: University of Edinburgh Press, 1956; Julius Roth, *Timetables,* Indianapolis: Bobbs-Merrill, 1963.
6. For example, Michel Crozier, *The Bureaucratic Phenomenon,* Chicago: University of Chicago Press, 1964; Eugene Haas, R. Hall and N. Johnson, "The Size of Supportive Components in Organizations," *Social Forces,* 42 (October, 1963), pp. 9–17; Robert Merton, "Bureaucratic Structure and Personality," in *Social Theory and Social Structure,* Glencoe: The Free Press, 1949, pp. 151–160; Melvin Seeman and J. Evans, "Stratification and Hospital Care: I. The Performance of the Medical Interne," *American Sociological Review,* 26 (February, 1961), pp. 67–80; Arthur Stinchcombe, "Bureaucratic and Craft Administration of Production," *Administrative Science Quarterly,* 4 (September, 1959), pp. 168–187; Stanley Udy, Jr., "Bureaucratic Elements in Organizations: Some Research Findings," *American Sociological Review,* 23 (August, 1958), pp. 415–418.
7. For example, Blau and Scott, *op. cit.,* especially chapter 3, "The Organization and Its Publics," pp. 59–86; Burton R. Clark, *The Open Door College,* New York: McGraw-Hill, 1960; Charles Perrow, "Goals and Power Structures: A Historical Case Study," in Eliot Friedson, ed., *op. cit.,* pp. 112–146; Erwin Smigel, "The Impact of Recruitment on the Organization of the Large Law Firm," *American Sociological Review,* 25 (February, 1960), pp. 56–66; James D. Thompson and W. McEwen, "Organizational Goals and Environment: Goal Setting as an Interaction Process," *American Sociological Review,* 23 (February, 1958), pp. 23–31.

210   8. The classic discussion of this issue is found in James March and H. Simon, *Organizations*, New York: John Wiley, 1958; a specific statement of the relationship between incentives and organizational types is found in Peter B. Clark and J. Q. Wilson, "Incentive Systems: A Theory of Organizations," *Administrative Science Quarterly*, 6 (September, 1961), pp. 129–166.

9. For example, Fred Davis, "Definitions of Time and Recovery in Paralytic Polio Convalescence," *American Journal of Sociology*, 61 (May, 1956), pp. 582–587; Barney Glaser and Anselm Strauss, "Temporal Aspects of Dying as a Non-Scheduled Status Passage," *American Journal of Sociology*, 71 (July, 1965), pp. 48–59; Erving Goffman, "The Moral Career of the Mental Patient," in *Asylums*, New York: Doubleday, 1961, pp. 125–170; Erving Goffman, *The Presentation of Self in Everyday Life*, Edinburgh: University of Edinburgh Press, 1956.

10. Talcott Parsons, "Suggestions for a Sociological Approach to the Theory of Organizations," in A. Etzioni, ed., *Complex Organizations: A Sociological Reader*, New York: Holt, Rinehart and Winston, 1961, pp. 39–40.

11. Blau and Scott, *op. cit.*, p. 77.

12. Charles Perrow, "Hospitals: Technology, Structure, and Goals," in James March, ed., *Handbook of Organizations*, Chicago: Rand-McNally, 1965, pp. 650–677.

13. Amitai Etzioni, *Modern Organizations*, Englewood Cliffs: Prentice-Hall, 1964, p. 94.

14. S. N. Eisenstadt, "Bureaucracy, Bureaucratization, and Debureaucratization," in Etzioni, *Complex Organizations: A Sociological Reader*, p. 276.

15. Glaser and Strauss, *Awareness of Dying*, *op. cit.*, p. 284.

16. Amitai Etzioni, "Organizational Control Structure," in James March, ed., *Handbook of Organizations*, *op. cit.*, pp. 650–677.

17. A dimension of clients in organizations which is not pursued here has to do with the intrinsic content of the socialization process and its effects upon the individual. A major issue along these lines has to do with the consequences of conformity for behavior expectations on the one hand, and for the internalization of values on the other. See, for example, Robert Dubin, "Deviant Behavior and Social Structure," *American Sociological Review*, 24 (April, 1959), pp. 147–164; and Irving Rosow, "Forms and Functions of Adult Socialization," *Social Forces*, 44 (September, 1965), pp. 35–45.

18. One of the key organizational issues which stems from lateral interests, particularly in psychiatric institutions, has to do with the presumption of rank-equality among clinical staff. See for example, Milton Greenblatt, R. York and E. Brown, *From Custodial to Therapeutic Patient Care in Psychiatric Hospitals*, New York: Russell Sage Foundation, 1955; Mark Lefton, S. Dinitz and B. Pasamanick, "Decision-Making in a Mental Hospital: Real, Perceived, and Ideal," *American Sociological Review*, 24 (December, 1959), pp. 822–829; Robert Rapoport and Rhona Rapoport, "Democratization and Authority in a Therapeutic Community," *Behavioral Sciences*, 2 (April, 1957), pp. 128–133; William Rosengren, "Communication, Organization, and Conduct in the 'Therapeutic Milieu'," *Administrative Science Quarterly*, 9 (June, 1964), pp. 70–90.

19. For example, Richard McCleery, "Authoritarianism and the Belief System of Incorrigibles," in D. Cressey, ed., *The Prison: Studies in Institutional Organization and Change*, New York: Holt, Rinehart and Winston, 1961, pp. 260–306; William R. Rosengren and S. DeVault, "The Sociology of Time and Space in an Obstetrical Hospital," in Friedson, *op. cit.*, pp. 266–292; Anselm Strauss, *et al.*, "The Hospital and Its Negotiated Order," in E. Friedson, ed., *op. cit.*, pp. 147–169.

20. See, for example, Ray Elling, "The Hospital Support Game in Urban Center," in Friedson, *op. cit.*, pp. 73–112; Oswald Hall, "The Informal Organization of the Medical Profession," *Canadian Journal of Economics and Political Science*, 12 (February, 1946), pp. 30–44.

21. For example, J. H. Robb, "Family Structure and Agency Co-ordination: De-centralization and the Citizen," in Mayer N. Zald, *Social Welfare Institutions: A Sociological Reader*, New York: John Wiley, 1965, pp. 383–399; Oliver Williams, *et al.*, *Suburban Differences and Metropolitan Policies: A Philadelphia Story*, Philadelphia: University of Pennsylvania Press, 1965.

HUMAN INPUTS

22. See, for example, Charles V. Willie and Herbert Notkin, "Community Organization for 211 Health: A Case Study," in E. Gartley Jaco, *Physicians, Patients, and Illness,* Glencoe: The Free Press, 1958, pp. 148–159.

23. For example, Sol Levine and P. White, "Exchange as a Conceptual Framework for the Study of Interorganizational Relationships," *Administrative Science Quarterly,* 5 (March, 1961), pp. 583–601; Eugene Litwak and L. Hylton, "Interorganizational Analysis," *Administrative Science Quarterly,* 6 (March, 1962), pp. 395–420; J. V. D. Saunders, "Characteristics of Hospitals and of Hospital Administrators Associated with Hospital-Community Relations in Mississippi," *Rural Sociology,* 25 (June, 1960), pp. 229–232; James D. Thompson, "Organizations and Output Transactions," *American Journal of Sociology,* 68 (November, 1962), pp. 309–324.

24. A clear example of this process can be discerned in the recent history of the National Mental Health Association. A short time ago this existed merely as a loosely held together congeries of autonomous, local mental health societies. Some of these groups were laterally and others non-laterally committed to their clientele. However, they shared in common a longitudinal interest in the careers of locally-defined client groups. The original move toward official collaboration came through the New York office and has persisted at the administrative and fund-raising level. It has now reached the point where most of the originally autonomous local societies provide little or no service to clients. They function merely as linkages in a nationwide administrative system. It should be added, lastly, that this decline of service functions and preeminence of administrative functions had also resulted in a dramatic shift in the sources of recruitment and staffing patterns of these organizations.

MANAGERIAL SUCCESSION IN COMPLEX ORGANIZATIONS[1]

Robert H. Guest

This paper compares two studies of managerial succession in complex industrial organizations: (1) Alvin W. Gouldner's study of a gypsum plant reported in *Patterns of Industrial Bureaucracy,*[2] and (2) a study recently completed by this observer in a large American automobile plant.[3]

Both studies examine the process by which organizational tensions are exacerbated or reduced following the succession of a new leader at the top of the hierarchy. Succession in Gouldner's case resulted in a sharp increase in tension and stress and, by inference, a lowering of over-all performance. The succession of a new manager had opposite results in the present case. Plant Y, as we chose to call it, was one of six identical plants of a large corporation. At one

"Managerial Succession in Complex Organizations," *The American Journal of Sociology,* 68, 1 (July 1962), 47–54. Reprinted with the permission of the author and of the publisher, the University of Chicago Press.

period in time the plant was poorest in virtually all indexes of performance—direct and indirect labor costs, quality of output, absenteeism and turnover, ability to meet schedule changes, labor grievances and in several other measures. Interpersonal relationships were marked by sharp antagonisms within and between all levels.

Three years later, following the succession of a new manager, and with no changes in the formal organizational structure, in the product, in the personnel, or in its basic technology, not only was there a substantial reduction of interpersonal conflict, but Plant Y became the outstanding performer among all of the plants.

The difference between what happened in Gouldner's study and this observer's study is explained by the kinds of administrative actions which each manager initiated: These actions were shaped in large measure by the social system which each inherited upon succession to office.

The analytical framework used by Gouldner was derived from his modification of Weber's concept of authority based on "discipline" as distinguished from authority based on "expertise." The former mode of administration he calls "punishment-centered," the latter, "representative."[4] The Plant Y study made use of the Homans' thesis which held that effective authority as measured by performance is related to reciprocal interactions and favorable sentiments.

In spite of differences in the way the empirical material was handled the two central hypotheses in each study are quite similar.

Gouldner says: "Internal tensions are more likely to be associated with the punishment-centered bureaucracy than with representative bureaucracy" (p. 243). In the Plant Y study the hypothesis was phrased in these terms: "To the extent that interactions between people at various levels of a hierarchy are originated primarily by superiors, sentiments of hostility will increase and performance will be lowered." Gouldner's association of "close" supervision and rule enforcement with the punishment-centered mode of administration is empirically similar to the notion that sentiments of hostility to superiors can be associated with an administrative pattern in which interactions are originated primarily by superiors.

What follows is a comparison of the conditions in the two organizational systems before and after succession which in large measure influenced the way authority was exercised by the respective managers.

The successor at the gypsum plant (Peele) and the successor at Plant Y (Cooley) had similar mandates from the parent organization. Both men were told that their respective plants had been "slipping" and that production had to improve. In assigning them to their new jobs, both men were told that the primary criterion on which they would be judged would be results—increased production to meet competitive market conditions.

"Peele, therefore, came to the plant sensitized to the rational and impersonal yardsticks which his superiors would use to judge his performance" (p. 72).

Cooley came to Plant Y "sensitized" to the same yardstick. Like Peele, he knew he was "on trial" with his superiors and that to hold his job or to expect future promotion he had to "make good." The promotion of both in itself symbolized the power which higher management held over both men, and they knew it. Both were expected to take action in keeping with the rational value system of higher management.

As Gouldner observed, Peele, by the sheer fact of succession, "had heightened awareness that he could disregard top management's rational values only at his peril" (p. 72). Cooley was aware of these same risks but, according to what he said and did at the time of his succession, one can see the beginnings of a fundamental difference in his perception of his role vis-à-vis his superiors. Cooley accepted his role as top management's agent charged with achieving the goals of greater production, but he did not necessarily accept his superiors' value system when it came to the *method* of fulfilling their expectations. His superiors (at least some of those in the main office) made it quite plain what methods he was expected to use. He was expected, and they said so, to utilize to the fullest extent the power formally vested in the office of manager, the power of discipline. He was told to "clean house" and to get rid of those in supervision who were failing to perform properly. Like Peele, he was told he could make what Gouldner called "strategic replacements," and that top management would wholly support him in such action.

Although Gouldner never said it explicitly, he inferred that Peele took the same instructions of "tightening up" and of "cleaning house" as an order. Cooley on the other hand did not accept his instructions as orders. Indeed, pressures were brought to bear on his immediate divisional superior to "allow Cooley to run his own show" without close supervision from his superior.

That Peele was deeply concerned about top management's expectations is revealed in Gouldner's observation that his behavior in the early period of succession was marked by considerable anxiety. "Comments about Peele's anxiety were made by many main office

personnel as well as by people in the plant who spoke repeatedly of his 'nervousness' " (p. 72). If Cooley had deep anxieties he never displayed any signs of "nervousness" either to his superiors, to members of the plant organization, or to this observer. A point to make here is not to deny basic differences in personality traits, but to suggest that there was also some difference, at least, in the *strength* of the organizational pressures from above that were brought to bear on each man. Putting it another way, Peele was under some of the same kinds of pressures that Cooley's predecessor, Stewart, had been under.

Stewart's feelings and perceptions are revealed in one comment he made during a crisis:

> The central office keeps saying to me, "Why can't you [keep to the schedule]? So and so in another plant can." When I get this kind of pressure on me I get butterflies in my stomach. We have a labor turnover hitting close to sixty men a day (in a plant of 5,000). Just yesterday I jumped a man who was not on his job. It's impossible for me alone to keep everybody in line but I do the best I can.

Thus, Stewart, like Peele in Gouldner's study, found it expedient and even necessary to initiate punishment-centered methods of administration.

The two successors, Peele and Cooley, shared one thing in common upon succeeding to office. Both were "outsiders" to their respective plant organizations. Neither had had any previous involvement in the social system of the plant. This allowed both men, as Gouldner stated it with respect to Peele, "to view the plant situation in a comparative dispassionate light" (p. 72). They were unhampered by previous personal commitments to the ingroup. They did not have to be concerned about breaking any long-standing friendship ties. The only "commitments" were to their superiors.

Peele, however, faced two problems that Cooley did not have to face. First, it had been a tradition at the gypsum plant that the "legitimate heir" to the manager's job had always been someone promoted from within the local organization. Also, the previous manager, who had held the job for several years, was well known and highly thought of in the close-knit community surrounding the plant. Thus, the condition which allowed Peele to view the organization with impersonal detachment was the same condition which, in the eyes of his subordinates, denied from the start the legitimacy of his succession.

Peele faced a second, related problem. His predecessor had left behind a core of supervisors who had been intensely loyal to him. And because of the "indulgency pattern," which had characterized the previous administration, authority had been derived from a *personal* loyalty and not an impersonal respect for the office of manager. Peele could not count on an automatic transfer of respect for the office such as one might find in a military or other highly bureaucratized organization.

At Plant Y managers changed frequently, a new manager taking over once every three to five years.[5] New managers almost always came from other plants in the division. Being in a large metropolitan area there had developed no close association between a manager and the local community. Thus, Cooley was not, by the act of succession, breaking any precedent that otherwise might have generated resistance from the start. More important, Cooley's predecessor had not left behind a core of "lieutenants" who were personally loyal to him. Just about everyone was glad to see his predecessor, Stewart, "retired."

The fact that Peele's succession in itself generated some intense "institutional" hostilities and Cooley's did not must be given considerable weight in explaining what Gouldner would call the "type of bureaucratic method" which each man, following his succession, found legitimate and expedient.

Not long after Peele took over he became aware of the resistance that he could expect from the subordinate organization. Gouldner points out that Peele never carefully analyzed the causes of resistance or the implications of the causes to the methods he would use to institute changes. It was simply resistance and it had to be overcome.

According to Gouldner, Peele had "two major avenues of solution available to him: (a) He could act upon and through an informal system of relations, (b) He could utilize the formal system of organization in the plant. Stated differently, Peele could attempt to solve his problems and ease his tensions either by drawing upon his resources as a 'person,' or by bringing into operation the authority invested in his status as plant manager" (p. 84).

Peele chose the latter course. Given the situation he faced, he found it was difficult to do otherwise. As he perceived the situation he could not use the "personal touch" because his aim—and his mandate from above—was to uproot precisely this kind of informal "indulgent" pattern of relationships which had existed earlier at all levels from manager on down. Nor were his subordinates too concerned with cutting costs and raising productivity. This lack of interest was all part of the general indulgency pattern. Peele's aims and those of his subordinates were different from the start. As Gouldner points out: "It is difficult to maintain, and *especially to create,* informal solidarity in pursuit of ends which are so differently valued by group members" (p. 84).

In many respects Cooley had available to him the same two general alternatives of action when he became manager. He could establish informal personal ties with his subordinates as preliminary action leading ultimately to action that would cut costs and increase productivity. On the other hand, he could use the raw power of his office to force changes and bring about improvements. He could immediately issue new orders, institute new rules; he could insist on stricter enforcement of old rules. He could let it be known that any deviations would be punished. He could insist that all information flow through the formally established vertical channels and that various control, reporting, and service functions live up to the letter of the operating manual. In short, he too had the alternative of bringing about further bureaucratization of Plant Y.

Such measures had been undertaken by his predecessor—and had failed. Cooley, therefore, found it more legitimate and expedient to take the path which Peele could not, or at least did not, take. He decided to ignore the legal powers vested in the office of manager and find out through informal contacts with his subordinates what they thought was needed to raise the plant's operating efficiency.

Here again it is necessary to underscore the historical conditioning factors explaining why Peele took one course of action and Cooley another. Putting it simply, Peele's subordinates wanted no change either in interpersonal relationships or in production results. Cooley's entire group was anxious to change both. It is perhaps more accurate to say that Cooley's subordinates wanted to eliminate both the "fear-pressure complex" which had pervaded the organization

and the technical and administrative bottlenecks which prevented the assembly line from operating smoothly and which in turn, intensified interpersonal hostilities.

In the process of trying to bridge the communications gap between manager and subordinates both men took different steps. Peele, not trusting his subordinates' willingness to give him the necessary information on which to base decisions, personally went out into the plant at unexpected times and places to "check up" on supervisors and hourly workers to see to it that they were working properly and obeying the rules and regulations. Cooley also spent considerable time "out in the shop," also showing up at unexpected times and places. In Peele's case, his object, which he acknowledged and which others perceived, was to personally "straighten out the shirkers." Cooley's acknowledged intention was to observe the technical problems and to encourage subordinates to suggest improvements.

Peele's actions, part of many to follow, signaled the beginning of the punishment-centered mode of administration based on *discipline*. Cooley's actions were the manifest start of the representative mode based on Gouldner's elaboration of Weber's term "expertise." In the language of Homans, Cooley was, by his own behavior, encouraging subordinates to initiate interactions *to* superiors.

Peele, finding it difficult to maintain direct and "close supervision" over all of his subordinates simultaneously, looked for some other alternative. He decided to bring in some "trusted lieutenants" from the outside. Gouldner labels these as "strategic replacements." They enabled "the new manager to form a new informal social circle, which revolves about himself and strengthens his status. It provides him with a new two-way communication network; on the one hand, carrying up news and information that the formal channels excluded; on the other hand carrying down the meaning or 'spirit' of the successor's policies and orders" (p. 92). Gouldner goes on to make the important observation that a successor under these circumstances is relying not on the existing bureaucratic structure, but is in fact establishing an additional structure based upon "extra-formal" ties (p. 92).

Cooley brought in no trusted lieutenants to serve as the communication link between himself and the three hundred members of supervision and five thousand workers below him. For most routine communications he used normal channels. No alterations were made in the structure. He did, however, introduce one communication mechanism which his predecessor did not adopt and which Peele in the Gouldner study could not adopt—group meetings at all levels within and between departments. In his early period in office Cooley met regularly with his immediate staff. The purpose of these meetings was not to relay pressures down from the corporate organization, but rather to encourage ideas from below which had been withheld previously. In time, and without the manager's directing the action, similar meetings "sprang up" at all levels and departments. The manifest purpose of the group meetings was to solve "business" problems, yet the experience had unanticipated consequences. Each member gained a feeling of reinforcement and support not provided for in the formal "scalar" relationships. Those at higher levels were able to return to their separate departments knowing that they had the support of peers and superiors. This reinforcement process carried down through each level. There was a reverse process as well. Subordinates, having the opportunity to interact frequently and without restraint in a group situation, felt they had more "organized" support in bringing suggestions and complaints to those at higher levels. The reinforcement effect was especially important to the manager himself in his dealings with corporate officials. He had full support from below, a condition which neither his predecessor nor Peele in Gouldner's study ever enjoyed.

The sharpest contrasts between Peele's and Cooley's methods of administration can be seen with respect to the way each made use of the formal rules. One of Peele's first acts, one which generated considerable hostility within the organization, was to fire an employee for violating a rule that had rarely been enforced by his predecessor. In time, as Gouldner points out, many formal rules "that had been ignored were being revived, while new ones were established to supplement and implement the old" (p. 69). New directives and daily reports on production, accidents, and breakdowns were required. Restrictions were imposed for loitering. Rest periods were banned. A system of warning notices was installed on a series of "offenses" including smoking, absenteeism, safety, and others. Rules were set up regulating the times for punching in and out. A "cold impersonal 'atmosphere,' " Gouldner noted, "was slowly settling on the plant" (p. 69).

After he took over as manager of Plant Y Cooley showed little indication that he was concerned about rule enforcement as the primary and legitimate means for motivating his group of three hundred supervisors. This is not to say that rules were not being enforced. There were elaborate "legal" mandates and restrictions superimposed on the plant in keeping with standard requirements of the division and corporation. The actions of the manager and his staff were highly circumscribed by the labor agreements, budgetary restrictions, work standards, and a system of paperwork required by higher authorities. The point is that Cooley, unlike Peele, relegated rule enforcement to a second level of importance. Again, unlike Peele and unlike his own predecessor, Stewart, he rarely found it necessary to use the extreme penalty of discharge against his supervisory staff. This was his announced policy, and he abided by it throughout his term of office.

At this point it would be more useful to compare Peele not with Cooley but with Cooley's predecessor, Stewart. Just as Peele "was seen as bringing the plant into line with established company rules" (p. 95), so Stewart was seen turning more and more to the impersonal mechanism of rule enforcement as greater pressures were brought to bear on him from higher management. Stewart to an increasing extent was demanding rigid enforcement of the rules relating to absenteeism. Wash-up time was eliminated as supervisors were ordered to work the men from "whistle to whistle" as required by the rules. With more intense rule enforcement the union was filing more grievances, arguing not that the rules were not "in the books," but that according to past practice many rules had not been enforced previously. When disputes arose between production and non-production departments, Stewart stressed the separate responsibility of each as prescribed by the formal rules rather than subordinating the rules themselves to the practical solution of problems.

Stewart's use of punishment-centered actions and their consequent effects is revealed typically in the following comment by an inspection foreman:

I remember one time getting called on the carpet by the plant manager, and he told me, "If you're afraid of the production people, then you're not a good inspection foreman. If you don't like the way it's going, then you just stop the line. If you can't do that, then you're not an inspector. Never be afraid of the production people." The manager ordered me to have the maintenance department install a series of buttons throughout the shop, and he told me that any time I didn't like something to just go over and push the button and stop the line. Well, I had the buttons installed all right, but I never used them. I thought it would do more harm than good. After all, I have to live with those production people every day.

This comment illustrates the dilemma in which members of Plant Y often found themselves—that of carrying out orders and enforcing rules which they did not feel were legitimized by subordinates.

Just as Peele was anxious to justify his punishment-centered actions "should the main office ever examine or challenge them" (p. 94), so Stewart took steps to assure the legitimacy of his actions. On at least two occasions Stewart recorded his staff meetings and played them back to his corporate superior to demonstrate that he was issuing the proper orders and carrying out the rules as prescribed by superiors. "He did it just to put us on the spot" was the typical reaction of his staff members.

Thus, the actions of Peele, the successor at the gypsum plant, and those of Stewart, the predecessor at Plant Y, show remarkable parallels: the methods used clearly followed the punishment-centered pattern.[6]

We can now briefly sum up the "institutionally derived pressures" which, apart from possible differences in individual personalities, shaped the actions

218 of the two "successors," Peele and Cooley.

1. Peele was under constant pressure, or so he perceived it, by his superiors to institute bureaucratic routines and to use disciplinary measures to gain efficiencies.

   Cooley, after his initial instructions, was not under these pressures from superiors. They wanted results but left the methods up to him.

2. Peele had to overcome a deeply embedded tradition that only "insiders" should succeed to the office of manager. There was no such tradition at Cooley's plant.

3. Managerial authority at the gypsum plant had been based on *personal* loyalty. Authority in the much larger and more complex Plant Y organization had been based on respect for the office of manager.

4. Lack of community acceptance was a source of resistance for Peele. The plant-community relationship in the Plant Y metropolitan area was no problem for Cooley.

5. Peele faced the pressures of subordinates who wanted to hold on to the old "indulgency" pattern based upon close informal ties. The pressure from above was to destroy this pattern through the impersonal mechanism of rule enforcement.

   The pressure from Cooley's subordinate group was to do away with the former authoritarian mode of administration and to adopt not necessarily an "indulgency" pattern, but one that would allow greater participation in decision-making.

6. Peele was under pressure from above to increase productivity, but there were no complementary pressures on him from below to run the plant more efficiently. Cooley's subordinate group was anxious to eliminate the technical difficulties which had kept productivity low and which had generated interpersonal hostility.

7. Peele brought in strategic replacements as his communications link. Cooley used the personnel at hand without superimposing an extraformal link. He also encouraged the establishment of groups which served as communication and decision-making centers.

In a general qualitative sense the two studies confirm Gouldner's hypothesis that internal organizational tensions are more likely to be associated with a punishment-centered bureaucracy than with a representative bureaucracy. The need the present writer saw was not only to confirm or reject the hypothesis. In the Plant Y study an attempt was made to add a quantitative dimension to the vague terms "punishment-centered" and "representative." This was done by extrapolating from the eighty interviews conducted before and after the succession of the manager certain *interaction* data. In most interviews it was possible to determine (a) how frequently subordinates, superiors and peers interacted with one another under both administrations, and (b) who tended to originate action for whom.

It was found that total interaction frequencies had not changed quantitatively. Closer examination, however, revealed that the character and content had changed considerably. During the Stewart administration the plant operated under chronic emergency conditions. As one foreman put it, "This place is just one damned emergency after another." Members of the organization were forced to interact frequently in order to take care of immediate emergencies. Under the new administration the rate of "emergency interaction" was sharply reduced. The organization as a technical system functioned more smoothly. But new kinds of interactions could be observed. Members were engaged much more frequently in long-range planning sessions in pairs and in groups.

The more significant change was in *direction* of interaction. In Period I there were approximately five superior-originated interactions for every one subordinate-originated interaction. After three years under the new manager the ratio was approximately two to one. Standing alone such data take on meaning only when coupled with the pattern of sentiment change under the administration of the successor. Whereas formerly all forty-eight of those members of supervision interviewed expressed a high degree of hostility toward top plant management almost no one expressed any hostility toward top management in Period II.

The modest suggestion implied here is that the use of quantitative interaction data plus information on sentiments may help to give a more sophisticated operational meaning to general terms Gouldner uses, such as "punishment-centered" versus "representative" modes of administrative behavior in complex organizations.

Finally, quantification of *performance results* is crucial if any significance is to be attached to one form of administrative behavior as contrasted with another. In the present study such evidence was clear cut. By every measure of performance Plant Y improved following the succession of the new manager, and in most performance indexes it went from bottom to top position among six plants which were almost identical in size, technology, and organizational structure.[7]

As a conclusion one is tempted to go beyond the limited substantive and methodological comparisons of the present study and that of the gypsum plant. On a level of practical and theoretical interest there emerges from both studies encouraging evidence suggesting that it is possible for democratic processes to function in an otherwise authoritarian bureaucratic social system. The successful efforts of the mining group in Gouldner's gypsum plant to resist increased bureaucratization was due to what he calls a "proto-*democratic* process of legitimation" of the supervisor's authority. If one goes to the heart of what caused Plant Y to become an outstanding success it was that the leader's authority was derived in large part from the "consent of the governed." In an era when social scientists are "under the gun" from business for suggesting that greater democracy in business enterprises is not only possible but desirable, these findings, limited as they are, are encouraging.

NOTES

1. An expanded version of a paper presented at the fifty-fifth annual meeting of the American Sociological Association, New York, 1960. The study was conducted when the author was associate director of research at the Yale Technology Project, Charles R. Walker, director.
2. Alvin W. Gouldner, *Patterns of Industrial Bureaucracy* (New York: Free Press of Glencoe, Inc., 1954). Page references in the text refer to this work.
3. Robert H. Guest, *Organizational Change: The Effect of Successful Leadership* (Homewood, Ill.: Irwin-Dorsey Press, 1962).

4. Gouldner separated two broader strands of Weber's theory which Weber himself had not clearly distinguished. The first was Weber's observation that modern bureaucratic organization was effective and maintained itself because the organization was administered by "experts." Members willingly obeyed the directions of superiors, reasoning that such obedience was the best way of realizing the acknowledged goals of the organization (Gouldner, *op. cit.*, p. 32).

Weber's second emphasis, Gouldner observed, was that bureaucracy was a mode of organization in which "obedience was an end in itself. The individual obeys the order, setting aside judgments either of its rationality or morality, primarily because of the position occupied by the person commanding" (*ibid.*, p. 32).

5. This fact appears consistent with Grusky's findings with respect to large bureaucracies (see Oscar Grusky, "Corporate Size, Bureaucratization, and Managerial Succession," *American Journal of Sociology*, LXVII [1961], 262, and O. Grusky, "Administrative Succession in Formal Organization," *Social Forces*, XXXIX [December, 1960]).

6. Peter M. Blau in personal correspondence made the enlightening observation that "the person who comes in after an indulgent leader has a very difficult time trying to establish bureaucratic procedures, while the person who comes in after a disciplinarian leader can maintain bureaucratic disciplines and still not appear as a disciplinarian. He can be perceived as a 'good guy' because he can relax a few of the authoritarian measures the former administrator had instituted. This suggests that bureaucratic institutions help a manager to achieve a position of genuine leadership, help him to be perceived by subordinates as carrying out legitimate ends, simply by his not enforcing all the bureaucratic procedures available to him."

7. For quantitative information on performance results see Guest, *op. cit.*, pp. 97–107.

Comment
Alvin W. Gouldner

Guest's work is among a number of welcome indications that we are presently acquiring the kind of data that can further the development of a modestly circumscribed, "middle-range" theory of succession. It is, I believe, a most valuable documentation of the cumulative development that can be derived from theoretically sensitive and conscientious case studies; it manifests that increasingly rare quality in sociological work, a detailed and first-hand knowledge of "natural" groups, viewed systematically. The following comments should be understood within this over-all, very positive appreciation of what Guest has done. Since Guest's article appears to be a synopsis of his forthcoming book, in which his evidence is presented and

his analysis elaborated, comments about the article as such are, in a sense, not based on "best evidence," and can only be very tentative and general. I therefore confine myself to a very brief discussion of a few salient points:

1. I have the impression that the drift in some current analyses of succession, perhaps including Guest's, has been toward a more synchronic and less diachronic treatment which may be due more to the nature of the formal models that are being applied to it than to the requirements of the data itself. Continuance in this direction would, however, be unfortunate (and unnecessary), for some of the key variables are manifestly activated at different points in time. Everything does not occur at once: the successor is appointed, he is briefed by his sponsoring superiors, initial reactions are made by his subordinates,

"Comment," *The American Journal of Sociology*, 68, 1 (July 1962), 54–56. Reprinted with the permission of the author and of the publisher, the University of Chicago Press.

the successor attempts to implement his policies, etc. It is, of course, appropriate that efforts to develop more formal models of succession be made but there is no reason why these cannot systematically take account of the processual aspects. This temporal dimension can be analyzed formally in various ways already available, in terms of a Markov chain, for example, or through computer simulation.

2. I would think it also appropriate that we begin to develop models to deal with some of the larger changes in organization structure, for example, a shift from punishment-centered to representative bureaucracy, and begin to fit analyses of the microdynamics of succession into these. For it seems clear that the administrative constraints on, or opportunities available to, a successor will differ radically with the structural arrangements prevailing under his predecessor. For example, the successor who follows a situation in which punishment-centered bureaucracy was established has an opportunity to recharge subordinates' motivations by withholding or reducing the constraints previously in effect. The very possibility of the *success* of a representative bureaucracy may depend on the subordinates' experience with the prior, less gratifying organizational structure. If, however, a successor enters a situation in which representative bureaucracy had prevailed, it may be more difficult for him to improve upon the prior level of gratifications supplied subordinates. The latter may come to take the gratifications which they had previously experienced for granted, and there may be a tendency for their motivation (to conform and to produce) to run down even in a representative bureaucracy, perhaps thereby readying the organization for a swing back to more punishment-centered

forms. It is clear that only temporally oriented organizational research can clarify such problems, and organizations must be studied over much longer spans of time than most of us have usually done.

3. Structurally significant adaptations to the tensions of succession, such as punishment-centered or representative bureaucracy, are obviously not the only adaptive responses possible. Close supervision and strategic replacements, among others, are also possible adaptive mechanisms. We need to clarify further the links between these more ephemeral adaptations and the more structurally enduring forms, and the conditions under which the former will occur. For example, Guest notes that Cooley did not make any strategic replacements while Peele did. To what extent is this due to Cooley's definition of his plant situation and to what extent is this due to the constraints of the larger labor market in which he was operating? Peele was operating during a period of increasing recession and retrenchment following World War II, which made labor relatively more plentiful than it had been. (Correspondingly, it is possible that these different economic circumstances exposed both managers to different degrees of anxiety-inducing pressure from their own superiors.) Perhaps Guest will care to comment on the larger economic situation during Cooley's succession and how, if at all, this may have affected his succession in general, and his failure to make strategic replacements, in particular. Guest acknowledges that Cooley did for a while engage in forms of close supervision and, like Peele, visited the plant at unexpected times and places. While Cooley's stated intentions for doing so apparently differed from Peele's, it is not clear from Guest's report why Cooley did not feel he could rely on his supervisory force to do what he wanted,

nor is it clear whether the latter found this practice acceptable or whether some felt that it might undermine their authority. This uniformity in the behavior of the two managers is especially notable in view of their other differences and perhaps, therefore, deserves fuller discussion.

4. I am inclined to register a mild demurrer with respect to only one of Guest's comments, specifically where he characterizes punishment-centered and representative bureaucracy as "vague" concepts. The fact is, I do define both repeatedly throughout *Patterns of Industrial Bureaucracy* and, indeed, give them formal, tabular, summary definitions on two whole pages (pp. 216–17) of that study. I must confess that it is I who find unclear Guest's effort to "use . . . quantitative interaction data plus information on sentiments . . . to give a more sophisticated operational meaning to [these] general terms . . . ." I cannot understand how an operational definition can be "more sophisticated" than the connotative definitions with which I was concerned and which, it would seem, must logically precede operationalization. In any event, it seems impossible to appraise and discuss Guest's index further on the basis of the brief allusion he makes to it.

The most valuable contribution that Guest makes is to focus attention on the ways in which succession is an opportunity as well as a threat (something that Selznick has also done with great theoretical effectiveness) and may help an organization to solve problems as well as induce them. It thus provides an illuminating and much needed corrective to my own one-sided emphasis on succession tensions.

Rejoinder
Robert H. Guest

Gouldner is quite right in taking me to task for failing to note his repeated definition of terms. What I meant to say was something more on the order of his own words on paragraph (2), namely, that the terms "punishment-centered" and "representative bureaucracy" can be refined further and sharpened after deeper analyses of what Gouldner calls the "microdynamics of succession." As to the diachronic versus synchronic argument, evidently I failed to make it patently clear that my succession study was diachronic and that the *processual* aspects were central to the method of analysis. On Gouldner's questions about "conditions" of succession: the new manager—Cooley—operated in periods of both increased production *and* of retrenchment. Also, for a period of at least three years *after* the successor—Cooley—had moved out of the organization it continued to improve with no evidence of "a swing back to more punishment-centered forms."

"Rejoinder," *The American Journal of Sociology*, 68, 1 (July 1962), 56. Reprinted with the permission of the author and of the publisher, the University of Chicago Press.

ORGANIZATIONAL RESPONSES
TO MEMBERS*

Zelda F. Gamson

We usually ask how organizations affect their members when we attempt to relate social structure and personality. Instead, let us ask what effects members have on organizations. A member of an organization, as used in this paper, is a person who participates regularly in the organizational activities, has a set of rights and obligations within the organization, and has his performance rated and remunerated in some way. Members can vary in rank, power, and commitment to the organization.

Are there developments and changes in complex organizations which can be traced to the influence of members? Assuming that there are, how can we characterize these developments systematically? That is the problem of this paper: to develop a typology of organizational responses, particularly organizational responses to members.

American sociologists have been accused many times of neglecting problems of change and instability. In the study of organizations, the opposite is true. Researchers seem to have chosen organizations which optimized the conditions for change.[1] It is not too surprising, therefore, that these studies have stressed changes, modifications, adapta-tions, adjustments, and transformations in large-scale organizations. Many of these studies have focused, particularly, on modifications of organizational goals and purposes.

Less attention has been paid to new organizational features which are not reflected in goal modification, yet these new features may entail some major redistributions of resources and the introduction of new departments, procedures, and people. They often have the effect of preventing changes in organizational goals by containing or transforming possible pressures for change. These new features are particularly important when the pressures for change come from members. Are these new features really changes? I shall avoid this question by using the term "organizational response" to mean any activities, procedures, norms, or goals which come into being during an organization's history because of some internal or external pressure.

Two types of organizational response may be identified. *Controls* are a type of organizational response which attempt to alter or manipulate the *source* of pressure. Another type of response does not attempt to alter the source of pressure

"Organizational Responses to Members," The Sociological Quarterly, 9, 2 (Spring 1968), 139–149. Reprinted with the permission of the author and of the publisher, the Midwest Sociological Society.

* This paper is based on the author's doctoral dissertation, "Social Control and Modification: A Study of Responses to Students in a Small Nonresidential College," Harvard University, 1964. A predoctoral fellowship from the Social Science Research Council and Research Training Fellowship 2 F1–MII–9141–04A1 (BEII) from the National Institutes of Health supported this work.

but, rather, tries to alter the conditions in the organization which are the *targets* of influence. Responses of this type will be called "organizational modifications." The following outline summarizes the different kinds of controls and modifications to be discussed below.

ORGANIZATIONAL RESPONSES

Any new activities, procedures, norms, or goals that result from internal or external pressure on the organization

1. *Controls.* Attempts to manipulate, alter, or contain the *sources* of pressure
   a. *Social controls.* Attempts to manipulate, alter, or contain pressures from members
      (1) *Insulation.* Attempts to manipulate who has access to the organization
          (a) *Selective recruitment:* Who will enter the organization
          (b) *Selective access:* Who will have access to rewards and high status within the organization
          (c) *Selective elimination:* Who will remain in the organization
      (2) *Sanctioning.* Attempts to manipulate members' situation
      (3) *Normative controls.* Attempts to manipulate members' intentions
2. *Organizational modifications.* Attempts to manipulate the *targets* of pressure
   a. *Dissolution*
   b. *Modifications of organizational goals*
      (1) *Goal succession.* Introduction of new goals
      (2) *Goal displacement.* Abandonment of old goals
   c. *Modifications of organizational procedures and rules*
   d. *Modifications of informal norms and staff perspectives*

Before looking at the major subtypes within these two classes of organizational response, we should recognize what they have in common. First, both controls and organizational modifications attempt to reduce the pressure on the organization—the former, by modifying the source of pressure; the latter, by modifying the target. Second, both types of response may or may not involve a major redistribution of organizational resources. And third, both controls and modifications have costs for the organization. Increased use of control mechanisms involves the diversion of organizational resources into communication techniques, counseling services, public relations, recreational activities, and recruitment programs. Such a diversion may lower the effectiveness of the organization in achieving its goals. On the other hand, organizational modification may subvert some fundamental goals.

Social Control

All social systems have the problem of instilling and maintaining member motivation at the level and in the direction necessary for their continuing operation. Since complex organizations depend on the coordination of specialized roles and the performance of specialized tasks, they face more serious problems of integration than other social systems. Specialized performance "cannot be presumed to be motivated by the mere 'nature' of the participants." [2] Indeed, Parsons postulates "an inherent centrifugal tendency" in such organizations, which reflects "pulls" deriving from the personalities of the participants, from the special adaptive exigencies of their particular job situations, and possibly from other sources, such as the pressure of other roles in which they are involved."

Organizational activities which attempt to cope with these problems may be viewed as a subcategory of controls. Social controls are controls which attempt to manipulate or contain pressures deriving from members. They occur because of some actual or perceived incompatibilities between the organization and some or all members. Rather than submit to possible influence from members resulting from lack of congruence, the organization attempts to limit members' influence.[3]

There are several distinct types of social controls. Some recent writers[4] have attempted to classify types of power or influence; for our purposes, these can be viewed as classifications of social controls. Since Etzioni's classification was developed in the context of a discussion of organizations, it will receive greater attention here than the typologies introduced by the other writers. Etzioni distinguishes among three types of power: *coercive* power, which "rests on the application, or the threat of application, of physical sanctions such as infliction of pain, deformity, or death; generation of frustration through restriction of movement; or controlling through force the satisfaction of needs such as those for food, sex, comfort, and the like"; *remunerative* power, "based on control over material resources and rewards through allocation of salaries and wages, commissions and contributions, 'fringe benefits,' services and commodities"; *normative* power, which "rests on the allocation and manipulation of symbolic rewards and deprivations through employment of leaders, manipulation of mass media, allocation of esteem and prestige symbols, administration of ritual, and the influence over the distribution of 'acceptance' and 'positive response.'"

This classification is based essentially on differences in the kinds of resources used in the influence relationship—coercive power uses physical sanctions, remunerative power uses material resources, and normative power uses symbolic resources. When we think of actual examples, however, Etzioni's classification breaks down. Material resources can be used symbolically. A corporation executive's high salary, which may be more than he knows what to do with, is not only accorded to him in exchange for the services he renders but has meaning which, in Etzioni's terms, is symbolic; i.e., it indicates esteem and may be a source of prestige. Similarly, symbolic resources can be used materially. To take the same example, the corporation executive's prestige may have exchange value. He may use his esteem with the public to give or withhold support from political candidates in exchange for some concessions. The point here is that the important distinction rests not with the things being given or withheld, but in the use made of them.

A more fruitful scheme for classifying social controls is in terms of what the organization does in the process of attempting to exercise influence over members. One approach is to manipulate who will have access to the organization. This can be accomplished in several ways; I will call all of these ways of controlling access *insulation*. (a) Through *selective recruitment*, social structures can recruit their members disproportionately from certain populations. By letting in only those who have the requisite goals, motivations, etc., and by keeping out those who do not, organizations can limit possible sources of influence from members. (b) *Selective access* for certain members—which usually brings with it differential access to rewards and to elite positions—can operate after admission to the organization. (c) *Selective elimination* by the organization of those who do not have the requisite goals, motivations, etc., is another way of exercising control over who will have access to the organization.

In general, successful insulation lessens the need for other social controls. Most organizations, however, cannot rely completely on insulation. Once individuals have attained membership, two additional types of social controls can be employed. One approach manipulates members externally, by adding to or subtracting from the situation in which they are placed. For example, the recipients of high grades in colleges are in a position to compete for prizes, scholarships, fellowships, and graduate schools for which students with low grades would rarely be eligible. I will call this type of social control *sanctioning*.

Another approach is to manipulate members internally, by attempting to change their attitudes, beliefs, values, motivations. I will call this type of social control *normative control*.[5] Using grades not so much as rewards and punishments, but as means of communicating instructors' evaluations of students' progress or of their personality characteristics, transforms grades into normative controls. In other words, many of the resources Etzioni talks about in his discussion of types of power can be used in several ways; i.e., they can be used either as sanctions or as normative controls.

Type of Relationship and Effectiveness of Sanctioning vs. Normative Controls

Although the relationship between organization and members may not differ in the two types of social control, some relationships seem to facilitate sanctioning while others seem to facilitate normative controls. More interesting, the attempt to use a type of social control inappropriately—i.e., when the relationship is not optimal—tends to reduce its effectiveness in the future.

What kinds of relationships are connected with what kinds of social controls? Parsons, and Bidwell and Vreeland have suggested that persuasion and "moral socialization" require a particularistic, diffuse solidarity between organization and member.[6] On the other hand, a specific, distant, contractual relationship between organization and member is more suitable for sanctions.[7] We must not assume that there will always, or even frequently, be a perfect fit between forms of relationships and types of controls. Even when there is such harmony, new forces may upset the equilibrium. What happens in these cases? What happens to the effectiveness of normative controls when universalistic standards are introduced into a relationship which was previously particularistic and which relied on normative controls? What are the consequences for sanctions when particularistic ties are introduced into a previously universalistic relationship which relied on sanctioning? Table 1 presents these two cases.

Sociologists have been concerned with Case 1, stemming historically from their interest in the effects of urbanization and industrialization on *Gemeinschaft* solidarity. It has been assumed in such

TABLE 1. Changes in relationship and effectiveness of social controls

Case	Time 1	Time 2	Outcome
Case 1	Relationship particularistic, etc. Social controls normative	Universalism develops	Normative controls less effective
Case 2	Relationship universalistic, etc. Social controls sanctions	Particularism develops	Sanctions less effective

cases that the particularistic-normative controls combination has stronger and deeper effects than universalism-sanctioning, that it builds greater commitment, and that, ultimately, it promotes social integration. The conclusion which follows is that the introduction of a contractual relationship will tend to "neutralize" or weaken the effectiveness of normative controls.[8]

Less attention has been paid to the reverse question, the effect of particularism on sanctioning. There are, however, examples of Case 2: the "human relations" school in industrial sociology, the emphasis on rehabilitation and therapy as opposed to custodialism in prisons and mental hospitals, and the greater use of persuasion as a means of control in the military.[9] Because of the presumed greater potency of particularistic relationships and normative controls in building commitment, it has been assumed that introducing these practices will promote greater member commitment to the goals of these organizations. Yet, one consequence—usually unanticipated—is the weakening of sanctioning as a control. Gresham Sykes describes such a case in prison settings.[10] The development of friendship ties and intimate reciprocities between prison guards and prisoners corrupts the legitimate authority of the guard and of the institution over the prisoners. Sykes writes: "When guards and inmates are enmeshed in a pattern of quasi-friendship and reciprocity, punishments by prison officials easily come to be interpreted as personal, vindictive attacks . . . . Similarly, rewards tend to be redefined as a 'pay-off' and expedient product of a 'deal.'"

Organizational Modification

An organization can respond to lack of congruence with members by accepting their influence, i.e., by modifying the conditions which contribute to the incongruence. In organizations, a number of different modifications can occur.

DISSOLUTION

The organization can, of course, dissolve. Such an outcome, although a possibility when there is massive pressure, seems less likely than other responses.

MODIFICATIONS OF GOALS

The organizational goals, either manifest or latent, can become modified. This can happen in several ways. For example, the original goals can be abandoned and alternative goals adopted. Sills' analysis of the succession of goals in the March of Dimes indicates such an adaptation.[11] What seems to happen in such

228 cases is that the existing goals are broadened or redefined to include new goals, latent goals, or the goals of subunits within the organization. Goals are rarely changed overnight or through conscious choice, although the transformation of the March of Dimes comes closest to direct manipulation. Another example of a modification of organization goals is goal displacement or goal deflection, when the original goals are abandoned without the substitution of alternative goals. The organizational structure comes to exist primarily for the satisfaction of its members.

MODIFICATIONS OF ORGANIZATIONAL PRACTICES AND PROCEDURES

Most goal modifications involve changes in practices. There are some practices which can be modified, however, and not affect goals (at least, not immediately). The shift from a piece-rate system to a wage system in factories is an example of such a procedural modification.

MODIFICATIONS OF INFORMAL NORMS AND STAFF PERSPECTIVES

Changes in the informal norms and perspectives of subunits can occur, often imperceptibly. Perrow's description of "reality shock" in a treatment-oriented correctional institution involves, in part, a discussion of changes in staff definitions of clients and norms for dealing with clients.[12]

Choice of Response to Members

Having a more differentiated vocabulary for discussing organizational responses allows us to ask our original question more precisely. Given some pressure on an organization from its members, under what conditions will social controls occur and under what conditions will organizational modifications occur?

As a first step, let us assume that every organization has a repertoire of preferentially ordered responses. Every organization's repertoire will be unique, depending on its peculiar history, goals, and position in larger social structures. Despite this fact, there should be some uniformities in the types and ordering of responses across organizations.

Let us assume also that most organizations are generally resistant to organizational modification because of the development of vested interests, external commitments, and organizational character which help to build in inertia. Particularly when the pressure derives from subordinate members, over whom the organization has some power, one would expect an organization to resist change and to deploy resources so as to control the sources of influence. In general, social control mechanisms should be a preferred response.

Organizations differ in the range and number of social controls available to them. Residential colleges, for example, have a larger number and wider range of social controls over students than nonresidential colleges.[13] Organizations differ also in the effectiveness of their attempts at controlling pressures on them. When an organization has exhausted its supply of social controls, either because it has few available or because the attempted social controls were ineffective, organizational modifications should occur.

Conditions for Maximal Effects of Members

What conditions would make organizations most open to members' influence?

There are general conditions which predispose organizational responsiveness to any source of influence and special conditions for responsiveness to members. First, it seems reasonable to assume that new organizations would be most responsive to any influence. In new organizations particularly, goals and procedures have not been institutionalized enough to protect them from internal and external influences. Early experiences define what a new organization will be at later times—a kind of "institutional imprinting." In Selznick's terms, commitments are generated which determine the future development of an organization.[14] The concept of commitment "indicates the ways in which present constraints are outcomes of earlier decisions and choices on the actors' part. This implies that the earlier choices were in some sense freer and possessed a greater variety of functional alternatives than did later ones."[15]

New organizations are more vulnerable because their goals and role-demands are likely to be undefined, implicit, unclear, and diffuse. Nevertheless, even older organizations will differ in their responsiveness because they vary in the explicitness and clarity òf their goals. Burton Clark attributes the susceptibility to clientele influence of the California adult education system to the diffuseness of its goals.[16]

Competition over resources, members, or power also heightens susceptibility to influence. In his study of adult education, Clark compares public schools to business firms in a highly competitive market. "When it is threatened by competitors, a business firm will become more sensitive to its customers and their wants. The effect of competition among schools is much the same. The scramble for students and public support is intensified."[17]

Thus far, we have considered the conditions which predispose organizations to any kind of influence. There are additional conditions which increase the pressure for adaptability to members. One of the clearest is the inability of some organizations to control who will become a member. Rigid control over selection of personnel is one of the crucial ways an organization protects itself from unwanted influence. When an organization cannot control admission, it will have to use other controls if it wants to limit member influence; an example is a draft army. We expect, then, that responsiveness to members would be maximized under conditions of little or no selectivity over members. Clark's findings that nonselection in the junior college is "the ultimate variable of the determination of the character of the public two-year college"[18] and Clark and Trow's contention that "little or no selection greatly reduces the general influence of the official establishment"[19] support this expectation.

Another condition for members' influence is the type of organization in which they participate. Some organizations, such as schools, prisons, and hospitals, "produce" people. Their effectiveness is judged by the qualities and changes they have produced in this human output. These organizations will be responsive to the personal characteristics of their members to a much greater extent than purely technical organizations. They involve members as total personalities in a broad range of activities which are seen as related to the achievement of organizational tasks. These organizations have been labeled variously as socializing, cultural, normative, people-processing. As Parsons puts it, they use people as the "materials on which technical operations are performed. The conditions under which the

230 'objects' of the technical process will co-operate satisfactorily" become a matter of paramount importance.[20] Thus, it is necessary for the effectiveness of organizations of this type that a normative relationship be established between them and their "materials." A first step toward the establishment of such a normative tie is the acceptance of the human material into membership status.

All of the above are necessary, but not sufficient, conditions for organizational responsiveness. A further condition is simply that there be some pressures which require response. For responses to members, there must be some gap between the organizational goals and operations and the skills, needs, values, interests, and expectations of members. This is simply to say that incompatibilities between the organization and at least some of its members provide the impetus for organizational reactions. Whether or not responses will occur depends on the other conditions described above.

In sum, there are six conditions under which the impact of members on an organization would be maximized: (1) in new organizations, (2) when goals, procedures, and role demands are implicit, undefined, and vague, (3) when there is competition over scarce resources, (4) in organizations which exercise little control over the selection of members, (5) in organizations whose members are the major output, and (6) when there is some incongruence between members and organization.

Summary

This paper is concerned with the effects of members on organizations. We looked at the kinds of responses organizations can make to members, the connection of different responses to the type of relationship between organization and members, the choice of different organizational responses, and the conditions maximizing effects of members.

The term "organizational response" is used to cover both new developments which are customarily thought to be changes and those which are not usually viewed as changes. The basis for distinguishing two major types of responses to members is how the pressure for change is handled: Any new activities, procedures, norms, or goals introduced in order to alter or manipulate the source of pressure on the organization are called controls. Any new activities, etc., introduced in order to alter or manipulate the targets of pressure are called organizational modifications.

The most important organizational responses to members are social controls. These may involve major redistributions of resources, the creation of new departments and services, dramatic shifts in conceptions of the organization's purposes, and so on. At the same time, they represent attempts by agents of the organization to resist, control, contain, manipulate, and prevent possible influence from members on the organization. Many times, these attempts to protect the organization are more costly than modifying those aspects of the organization which are the targets of influence. The social controls can backfire and engender greater member disaffection. Nevertheless, it was assumed that social controls should be a preferred response when pressures from members occur. Should the range of controls available to an organization become depleted—either because it has few available or because previous attempts at control have failed—organizational modifications then occur.

1. For example, Burton R. Clark, "Organizational Adaptation and Precarious Values: A Case Study," *American Sociological Review*, 21:327–36 (1956); Sheldon L. Messinger, "Organizational Transformation: A Case Study of a Declining Social Movement," *American Sociological Review*, 20:3–10 (1955); Charles Perrow, "Reality Shock: A New Organization Confronts the Custody-Treatment Dilemma," *Social Problems*, 10:374–82 (1963); Philip Selznick, *TVA and the Grass Roots* (Berkeley, Calif.: Univ. of California Press, 1953); David Sills, *The Volunteers* (Glencoe, Ill.: The Free Press, 1957).

2. Talcott Parsons, "Suggestions for a Sociological Approach to the Theory of Organizations," *Administrative Science Quarterly*, 1:63–85 (1956).

3. Note that we are speaking of the actions which the organization's agents take in such a situation. We say nothing about the effects of these actions. Members may or may not conform or cooperate as a result of these efforts; they may or may not act in the ways intended by the agents. Even if the agents of the organization succeed in controlling members in the intended ways, there may be unanticipated consequences of the application of particular social controls which affect their relationships with members or the functioning of the organization.

4. Amitai Etzioni, *A Comparative Analysis of Complex Organizations* (Glencoe, Ill.: The Free Press, 1961); Herbert Kelman, "Processes of Opinion Change," *Public Opinion Quarterly*, 25:57–78 (1960); Talcott Parsons, "On the Concept of Influence," *Public Opinion Quarterly*, 27:37–62 (1963).

5. The distinction between sanctioning and normative control is similar to Parsons' types of influence. Sanctioning is similar to inducement-deterrence, which manipulates alter's situation, and normative control is similar to persuasion-activation of commitments, which manipulates alter's intentions.

6. Parsons, "On the Concept of Influence"; Charles E. Bidwell and Rebecca S. Vreeland, "College Education and Moral Orientations: An Organizational Approach," *Administrative Science Quarterly*, 8:166–91 (1963).

7. Etzioni, *op. cit.*

8. Cf., *ibid.*

9. Reinhard Bendix and Lloyd H. Fisher, "The Perspectives of Elton Mayo," in Amitai Etzioni (ed.), *Complex Organizations: A Sociological Reader* (New York: Holt, Rinehart and Winston, 1961), pp. 113–26; D. R. Cressey, "Achievement of an Unstated Organizational Goal," *ibid.*, pp. 168–76; A. H. Stanton and M. S. Schwartz, *The Mental Hospital* (New York: Basic Books, 1954); Morris Janowitz, "Hierarchy and Authority in the Military Establishment," in Etzioni, *Complex Organizations*, pp. 198–212.

10. Gresham M. Sykes, "The Corruption of Authority and Rehabilitation," *Social Forces*, 34:257–62 (1956).

11. *Op. cit.*

12. *Op. cit.*

13. Charles E. Bidwell and Rebecca S. Vreeland, "Authority and Control in Client-Serving Organizations," *The Sociological Quarterly*, 4:231–42 (1963).

14. *Op. cit.*

15. Alvin W. Gouldner, "Theoretical Requirements of the Applied Social Sciences," *American Sociological Review*, 22:92–102 (1957).

16. *Op. cit.*

17. *Ibid.*

18. Burton Clark, *The Open Door College: A Case Study* (New York: McGraw-Hill), 1960.

19. Burton Clark and Martin Trow, "The Organizational Contest," in *College Peer Groups*, ed. by T. M. Newcomb and E. K. Wilson (Chicago: Aldine Publishing Co., 1966), pp. 17–70.

20. Talcott Parsons, "Some Ingredients of a General Theory of Formal Organizations," in *Administrative Theory in Education*, ed. by A. Halpin (Chicago, Ill.: Univ. of Chicago Press, 1958).

ORGANIZATIONAL RESPONSES TO MEMBERS

Argyris, Chris. 1958. "Some Problems in Conceptualizing Organizational Climate: A Case Study of a Bank," *Administrative Science Quarterly,* 2 (March), 501–520.

Argyris, Chris. 1959. "The Individual and Organization: An Empirical Test," *Administrative Science Quarterly,* 4 (September), 145–167.

Argyris, Chris. 1961. "Explorations in Consulting-Client Relationships," *Human Organization,* 20 (Fall), 121–133.

Bar-Yosef, R., and E. O. Schild. 1966. "Pressures and Defenses in Bureaucratic Roles," *The American Journal of Sociology,* 71 (May), 665–673.

Beckhard, Richard. 1959. "Helping a Group with Planned Change: A Case Study," *Journal of Social Issues,* 15 (April), 13–19.

Benne, Kenneth D. 1959. "Some Ethical Problems in Group and Organizational Consultation," *Journal of Social Issues,* 15 (April), 60–67.

Blau, Peter M. 1960. "Orientation toward Clients in a Public Welfare Agency," *Administrative Science Quarterly,* 5 (December), 341–361.

Brown, David S. 1966. "Shaping the Organization to Fit People," *Management of Personnel Quarterly,* 5 (Summer), 12–16.

Carlson, Richard O. 1961. "Succession and Performance among School Superintendents," *Administrative Science Quarterly,* 6 (September), 210–227.

Carlson, Richard O. 1962. *Executive Succession and Organizational Change.* Chicago: Midwest Administrative Center, University of Chicago.

Chadwick-Jones, J. K. 1964. "The Acceptance and Socialization of Immigrant Workers in the Steel Industry," *The Sociological Review,* 12 (July), 169–183.

Charters. W. W., Jr. 1955. "Stresses in Consultation." *Adult Leadership,* 3 (April), 21–22.

Christensen, C. R. 1953. *Management Succession in Small and Growing Enterprises.* Boston: Division of Research, Graduate School of Business Administration, Harvard University.

Denhardt, R. B. 1968. "Bureaucratic Socialization and Organizational Accommodation," *Administrative Science Quarterly,* 13 (December), 441–450.

Eisenstadt, S. N. 1958. "Bureaucracy and Bureaucratization, a Trend Report and Bibliography," *Current Sociology,* 7, 99–164.

Etzioni, Amitai. 1958. "Administration and the Consumer," *Administrative Science Quarterly,* 3 (September), 251–264.

Glaser, Edward M. 1958. "Psychological Consultation With Executives: A Clinical Approach," *American Psychologist,* 13 (August), 486–489.

Greiner, Larry E. 1967. "Patterns of Organization Change," *Harvard Business Review,* 45 (May–June), 119–130.

Grusky, Oscar. 1960. "Administrative Succession In Formal Organizations," *Social Forces,* 39 (December), 105–115.

Grusky, Oscar. 1962. "Authoritarianism and Effective Indoctrination: A Case Study," *Administrative Science Quarterly,* 7 (June), 79–95.

Grusky, Oscar. 1963. "Managerial Succession and Organizational Effectiveness," *The American Journal of Sociology,* 69 (July), 21–31.

Jones, Maxwell, and Robert Rapoport. 1957. "The Absorption of New Doctors into a Therapeutic Community." In *The Patient and the Mental Hospital,* M. Greenblatt, D. J. Levinson, and R. H. Williams, eds. Glencoe, Ill.: Free Press.

Killian, Lewis M. 1952. "The Effects Of Southern White Workers On Race Relations In Northern Plants," *American Sociological Review,* 17 (June), 327–331.

Kotin, Joel, and Myron R. Sharaf. 1967. "Management Succession and Administrative Style," *Psychiatry,* 30 (August), 237–248.

Kriesberg, Louis. 1953. "Customer Versus Colleague Ties Among Retail Furriers," *Journal of Retailing,* 29 (Winter), 173–191.

HUMAN INPUTS

Macaulay, Stewart. 1963. "Non-Contractual Relations in Business: A Preliminary Study," 233
American Sociological Review, 28 (February), 55–67.

McEwen, Robert J. 1967. "Strange Business Reactions to Consumer Complaints," *The Journal of Consumer Affairs,* 1 (Summer), 42–51.

McMurry, Robert N. 1958. "Recruitment, Dependency, and Morale in the Banking Industry," *Administrative Science Quarterly,* 3 (June), 87–117.

Merton, R. K. 1940. "Bureaucratic Structure and Personality," *Social Forces,* 18 (May), 560–568.

Merton, R. K. 1965. "The Environment of the Innovating Organization: Some Conjectures and Proposals." In *The Creative Organization,* Gary A. Steiner, ed. Chicago: University of Chicago Press.

Miller, Stephen J. 1964. "The Social Base of Sales Behavior," *Social Problems,* 12 (Summer), 15–24.

Miner, John B. 1969. "An Input-Output Model For Personnel Strategies," *Business Horizons,* 12 (June), 71–78.

Miner, John B. 1969. *Personnel Psychology.* New York: Macmillan (Ch. 14: "The Input-Output Model for Human Resources Utilization").

Monsen, R. Joseph, Jr., and Anthony Downs. 1965. "A Theory Of Large Managerial Firms," *The Journal of Political Economy,* 73 (June), 221–236.

Moskos, Charles C., Jr. 1966. "Racial Integration in the Armed Forces," *The American Journal of Sociology,* 72 (September), 132–148.

Palmore, E. 1955. "The Introduction of Negroes into White Departments," *Human Organization,* 14 (Spring), 27–28.

Robertson, Thomas S., and Richard B. Chase. 1968. "The Sales Process: An Open Systems Approach," *MSU Business Topics,* 16 (Autumn), 45–52.

Rosengren, William R. 1968. "Organizational Age, Structure, and Orientations Toward Clients," *Social Forces,* 47 (September), 1–11.

Rubington, Earl. 1965. "Organizational Strains and Key Roles," *Administrative Science Quarterly,* 9 (March), 350–369.

Saenger, Gerhart, and Emily Gilbert. 1950. "Customer Reactions To The Integration Of Negro Sales Personnel," *International Journal of Opinion and Attitude Research,* 4 (Spring), 57–76.

Segre, Eugene J., and Nelson W. Polsby. 1961. "Dilemmas of Air Traffic Control Operators," *Administrative Science Quarterly,* 5 (March), 602–606.

Selznick, Philip. 1952. "Cooptation: A Mechanism for Organizational Stability." In *Reader in Bureaucracy,* R. K. Merton, A. P. Gray, B. Hockey, and H. C. Selvin, eds. Glencoe, Ill.: Free Press.

Sjoberg, Gideon, Brymer, Richard A., and Bufford Farris. 1966. "Bureaucracy And The Lower Class," *Sociology and Social Research,* 50 (April), 325–337.

Smith, Edmund A. 1957. "Bureaucratic Organization: Selective or Saturative," *Administrative Science Quarterly,* 2 (December), 361–375.

Tilles, Seymour. 1962. "Some Propositions Concerning the Relationship Between Business Consultants and Their Clients," *Management International,* 5, 55–64.

Trow, Donald B. 1960. "Membership Succession and Team Performance," *Human Relations,* 13 (August), 259–268.

Trow, Donald B. 1961. "Executive Succession in Small Companies," *Administrative Science Quarterly,* 6 (September), 228–239.

Ziller, Robert C. 1965. "Toward A Theory Of Open And Closed Groups," *Psychological Bulletin,* 64 (September), 164–182.

ADDITIONAL READINGS

CHAPTER FIVE

Community and Culture

This chapter considers the effects on the organization of community and culture elements in its external environment. William Form and Delbert Miller (1960, p. 19) define community as "people living in one locality or region under the same culture and having some common geographical focus for their major activities. The distinctive characteristic of the community is that a constellation of institutional organizations have grown up around a particular center of specialized function." Robert Bierstedt (1957, pp. 106–169) has defined culture as "the complex whole that consists of everything we think and do and have as members of society." According to him, it is synonymous with: learned and shared methods of believing and behaving; social heritage; the social meaning of things and acts independent of their physical and biological characteristics; and a design for living. According to Arnold Rose (1956, p. 33), "The important idea in the concept of culture is that there are common understandings as to how individuals are to behave toward one another."

Based on recent industrial field studies, Blood and Hulin formulate a continuous construct with the extremes of "integration with middle-class norms" and "alienation from middle-class norms." In a pilot study, they hypothesize that workers in communities fostering integration respond differently than alienated workers in terms of job behavior, satisfaction, and values. The hypothesis was confirmed for blue-collar workers. They conclude that the alienation construct is useful and that need-theoretic models of motivation should take cultural differences into account.

Habenstein develops five dichotomous variables that cluster to form the establishment orientation of either a mass mortuary or a local funeral home. A somewhat different interpretation of his data suggests that the definition variables (Table 1) are related to each other within each polar type of establishment. For the mass mortuary, the independent variable may be the "refractive nature of the community orientation," while for the local funeral home it may be its "reflective community orientation." The remaining four definition variables appear to depend on this refraction or reflection. If the local funeral home becomes an "institutional element of community life," one might then expect focalized service contact, the social vestment of the unit of operation, the "business-limited" nature of the occupational goal, and the traditional organization of personnel. This sequential interpretation of Habenstein's stimulating paper raises interesting questions concerning strategy for many types of professional and quasi-professional service establishments vis-à-vis their environment.

Turner and Lawrence attempt to account for an unexpected and sharp difference between town and city workers in their study of the relationship between task attributes (independent variable) and job satisfaction and work attendance (dependent variable). They consider motivational predispositions, subcultural norms, need for achievement, and exchange theory as possible explanations.

In the last paper, Becker and Geer discuss the "conditions under which the cultures men participate in elsewhere may furnish the substance of the culture of the work group." They use Gouldner's concept of latent social identities and suggest that if these identities are shared they may lead to latent structures and cultures within an organization. Sensitization to concepts such as these is necessary if an administrator is to comprehend the determinants of organizational behavior.

REFERENCES

Bierstedt, Robert. 1957. *The Social Order.* New York: McGraw-Hill.
Form, William H., and Delbert C. Miller. 1960. *Industry, Labor, And Community.* New York: Harper.
Rose, Arnold M. 1956. *Sociology.* New York: Knopf.

ALIENATION, ENVIRONMENTAL CHARACTERISTICS, AND WORKER RESPONSES

Milton R. Blood and Charles L. Hulin

Some recent industrial field studies have pointed up the importance of community variables as determiners of workers' responses. Katzell, Barrett, and Parker (1961) and Cureton and Katzell (1962) found job satisfaction and performance inversely related to the degree of urbanization of the community. They attribute this relationship to differences in needs and expectancies of the workers in the various environments. With increased urbanization, needs and expectancies rise and there is less satisfaction from any specific return. Hulin (1966), using the worker's frame of reference as an intervening variable, predicted and empirically verified that job satisfaction is higher in communities with substantial slum areas. The assumption of his discussion is that the worker assesses his present status by referring to the alternative positions which are available to him. Since attractive alternatives are not readily apparent in slum conditions, the worker's present job will be seen as relatively more satisfactory. Turner and Lawrence (1965), in a study of workers' responses to the technological aspects of the work situation, found that rural and small town workers were more satisfied when their jobs were more autonomous, required more skill, were more varied, and contained more social interaction and re-

sponsibility. In essence, the most satisfying jobs demanded greater personal involvement. This was, of course, the "expected" result. In contrast to this, city workers were more likely to be satisfied when their jobs were less personally involving. One of the possible explanations offered by Turner and Lawrence for this unexpected response from city workers is the notion of anomie, a state of societal normlessness brought about by industrialization, which has been frequently investigated in recent sociological researches.

In addition to these studies there are a growing number of studies of "job enlargement" which present conflicting results. In general, results in line with predictions are obtained if the studies are done on workers with rural backgrounds, but contrary results are obtained if the workers are from urban backgrounds (see Friedlander, 1965; Kennedy & O'Neill, 1958; Kilbridge, 1960).

From these studies and from sociological studies of anomie and alienation a construct can be formulated which can be used in structuring and predicting workers' responses. This construct might most efficiently be conceived as a continuum running from "integration with middle-class norms" to "alienation from middle-class norms." However, it

"Alienation, Environmental Characteristics, and Worker Responses," Journal of Applied Psychology, 51, 3 (June 1967), 284–290. Reprinted with the permission of the authors and of the publisher, the American Psychological Association.

should be pointed out that this is a complex phenomenon described as unidimensional only for ease of conceptualization. At the integrated end of the construct are found workers who have personal involvement with their jobs and aspirations within their occupations. Their goals are the type of upward mobility, social climbing goals generally associated with the American middle class. At the opposite pole of the construct, workers can be described as involved in their jobs only instrumentally; that is, the job is only a provider of means for pursuing extraoccupational goals. The concern of these workers is not for increased responsibility, higher status, or more autonomy. They want money, and they want it in return for a minimal amount of personal involvement. This difference between integrated and alienated workers is similar to Dalton's (1947) discrimination between overproducers who are likely to hold middle-class aspirations and underproducers who do not identify with middle-class ideals. The construct of alienation being proposed in this study stands in obvious relation to the Protestant ethic proposed and discussed by Weber (1958). It is likely that conditions fostering integration with middle-class norms will also foster adherence to the Protestant ethic since the latter is an aspect of the former.

What environmental conditions should lead to alienation from middle-class norms? Data have suggested that anomie is associated with lower-class highly industrialized situations (Bell, 1957; Dean, 1961; Killian & Grigg, 1962; Mayo, 1933; McClosky & Schaar, 1965; Ruitenbeck, 1964; Simpson & Miller, 1963; Turner & Lawrence, 1965). Though anomie is different conceptually from the construct being defined here, the measurement of anomie has been such

that it might just as easily be interpreted as alienation from the middle class. It is postulated that "alienation from middle-class norms" results from lack of socialization to middle-class norms. That is, where a segment of society exists which holds non-middle-class norms and which is large enough to sustain its own norms, the members of that subculture will become socialized to the norms of that subculture. A handful of industrial workers in a small community could not be expected to sustain a separate set of norms, but persons separated from middle-class identification by low educational attainment or low occupational status and living in ghettos, slums, and highly industrialized communities could develop and sustain a distinct norm system. Alienation from middle-class norms, then, is fostered by industrialized, socially heterogeneous, metropolitan conditions. This conceptualization of the background of the alienated worker coincides with the characterizations by Whyte (1955) of restrictors and rate busters. The social and family background of restrictors was urban, working class, whereas rate busters were from farms or lower-middle-class families. Worthy (1950) has also pointed out the possible effects of living in urban areas on the motivation and especially the morale of industrial workers.

Method

Before describing the methods of this investigation, two cautions must be invoked. First, though the data to be presented are not such that they could support the contention of causality, a causal discussion is used here. A causal theory in this sense serves only as a working hypothesis to be altered as the data demand. This does not detract, however, from the usefulness of the construct as a guide to research and application. Second, no value judgment is intended by the use of the word "alienated." It would be as logical to consider such workers integrated to their norms from which middle-class persons are alienated (and whether or not it would be better for the workers or for society for them to be integrated to middle-class norms is a social question beyond the proper boundaries of this paper). Orientation to middle-class norms has been adopted as the point of reference here because middle-class norms predominate in our culture and among social scientists.

Data for this study were provided from a study carried out at Cornell University (Smith, Kendall, & Hulin, in press). Subjects (Ss) were 1,390 male blue-collar workers and 511 male white-collar workers representing 21 different plants located throughout the eastern half of the United States. These data were gathered in 1961 and 1962 as part of a large-scale study of retirement satisfaction sponsored by the Ford Foundation.*

STIMULUS VARIABLES

To predict from the alienation construct it was necessary to have stimulus variables which indexed the environmental conditions which foster alienation and another set of variables which indicated the responses of workers to their jobs. The variates used to index community characteristics which should foster alienation among the workers were chosen from a principal component analysis of an intercorrelation matrix of per capita census variables originally provided by Kendall (1963). While the

original solution was simply a set of statistical variates which could be used to describe communities, several of these dimensions appear to be useful as indexes of alienation. These variates consisted of the weighted sum of variables where the weights were proportional to the loadings of the variables on the component. The complex variates

TABLE 1. Worker response variables and the condition under which the variable is predicted to be higher

Variable	Alien-ated	Inte-grated
1. Importance of planning for retirement		x
2. Made plans yet for retirement		x
3. Preparation for retirement index		x
4. Look for other work after retirement	x	
5. Personal satisfaction from the job		x
6. JDI work satisfaction-Skill correlation		x
7. JDI work satisfaction-Job-level correlation		x
8. JDI work satisfaction-JIG correlation		x
9. JDI pay satisfaction-JIG correlation	x	
10. JDI promotion satisfaction-JIG correlation		x
11. JDI work satisfaction-LIG correlation		x
12. JDI pay satisfaction-LIG correlation	x	
13. JDI promotion satisfaction-LIG correlation		x
14. JIG-LIG correlation		x

were used since it was felt that the variates would provide more reliable and meaningful indexes than would individual variables. See Kendall (1963) for a complete description of this solution.

* The authors would like to thank Patricia Cain Smith of Bowling Green University who very generously made these data available for this analysis.

The variates used in this research were descriptively named *Slum Conditions* indexed mainly by the weighted sum of the standard scores of percentage of native white (reversed scoring), percentage of nonwhite, and percentage of owner-occupied housing (reversed scoring); *Urbanization* indexed mainly by the sum of percentage of rural nonfarm (reversed scoring), percentage of urban population, total population, and per capita motor vehicle deaths (reversed scoring); *Urban Growth* indexed mainly by percentage of immigration, percentage of dwellings vacant (reversed scoring), and percentage of new homes; *Prosperity and Cost of Living* indexed by the sum of percentage of sound housing, medium income, percentage of workers in wholesale, per capita retail sales, and percentage with income over $10,000; and *Productive Farming* indexed by the sum of percentage of workers in wholesale (reversed scoring), average farm income, percentage of workers in agriculture, and percentage of change in farm level of living. A sixth variable *Population Density* (population per square mile) was chosen as a final index of alienating conditions.

There were no data indicating that these variates behave in the manner predicted. Thus, confirmation of the predictions of this report would serve also to enlarge existing knowledge of the community conditions fostering alienation. It was possible that one or more of the variates would prove to be a poor index for the present purpose, and it was almost certain that these six indexes would differ in the strength with which they gauge the postulated conditions. For this reason, all of them were used in the position of the independent variable. Even if some of them did not show the anticipated relationship or showed it only weakly, the considera-

tion of all six of them together provided more understanding of the construct (cf. Webb, Campbell, Schwartz, & Sechrest, 1966).

RESPONSE VARIABLES

Fourteen variables were chosen which were expected to show differences between integrated and alienated workers. Four of them concerned retirement. Workers were asked to rate the importance of planning for retirement, whether or not they had made plans yet for retirement, and whether they would look for other work after they retired. Also a Preparation for Retirement Index was established for each worker indicating the extent of preparation the worker had made for his retirement years. On the three planning-and-preparation-for-retirement variables it was predicted that the integrated workers would score higher since it was felt that the desire for a leisurely retirement has become imbued with a great deal of prestige or status significance in the middle class. For the same reason, integrated workers were expected to be less likely to say that they would look for other work after retirement.

Workers were asked to rank their job as well as their family life, hobbies, etc., as a provider of personal satisfaction. Integrated workers were expected to be more likely to rank their job first or second as a provider of personal satisfaction.

It was predicted that the correlation of the work satisfaction scale of the Job Description Index (JDI) with a rating of job level would be lower for alienated workers than for integrated workers since alienated workers are more satisfied when their jobs are *less demanding*. The same prediction was made for the correlation of the JDI work satisfaction

TABLE 2. Prediction tests using all workers: correlations (Pearson r's) between stimulus and response variables

Response variables	Predicted direction	Stimulus variables					
		Slum conditions	Urbanization	Urban growth	Cost of living	Productive farming (reversed)	Population density
Importance of planning for retirement	−	**−.05**	**−.46**	+.31	**−.42**	**−.16**	**−.51**
Made plans yet for retirement	−	**−.18**	**−.60**	+.24	**−.57**	**−.20**	**−.61**
Preparation for retirement index	−	**−.37**	**−.33**	+.15	**−.28**	**−.01**	**−.41**
Look for other work after retirement	+	**+.35**	**+.11**	**+.21**	**+.18**	−.36	**+.25**
Personal satisfaction from the job	−	+.50	+.16	+.43	+.19	**−.15**	00
Correlations between:							
Work satisfaction–Skill level	−	00	**−.03**	**−.07**	**−.05**	+.07	+.06
Work satisfaction–Job level	−	**−.25**	**−.23**	**−.14**	**−.19**	**−.24**	**−.13**
Work satisfaction–Job-in-general satisfaction	−	+.26	+.31	**−.04**	+.33	+.32	+.38
Pay satisfaction–Job-in-general satisfaction	+	−.19	−.02	−.06	**+.04**	**+.19**	**+.09**
Promotion satisfaction–Job-in-general satisfaction	−	**−.31**	**−.15**	**−.38**	**−.19**	+.18	**−.04**
Work satisfaction–Life-in-general satisfaction	−	+.39	+.32	+.08	+.30	+.27	+.34
Pay satisfaction–Life-in-general satisfaction	+	−.28	00	−.21	−.01	**+.28**	**+.28**
Promotion satisfaction–Life-in-general satisfaction	−	00	**−.05**	**−.20**	**−.13**	+.28	+.04
Job-in-general satisfaction–Life-in-general satisfaction	−	+.16	+.14	**−.11**	+.07	+.19	+.02

Note.—N=21 companies. Bold-faced numbers are in the direction of the prediction.

scale and ratings of job-skill requirements.

As the job was expected to play a more central role in the lives of the integrated workers, the correlation between satisfaction with the job in general (JIG) and satisfaction with life in general (LIG) was predicted to be higher for them. JIG and LIG were measured by General Motors Faces Scales (Kunin, 1955). Using JDI scales, satisfaction with work and satisfaction with promotional opportunities should be more highly correlated with JIG and LIG in the integrated sample. On the other hand, pay satisfaction should be more highly correlated with JIG and LIG in the alienated sample because these are the persons who view their job as primarily an activity which is instrumental to the achievement of other goals. A summary of these predictions can be seen in Table 1 where the response variables are listed and an "x" is placed under the heading of the situation in which the level of the variable was predicted to be higher.

It was possible to assign each of the 21 plant locations a score on each of the indexes of alienating conditions and on each of the indexes of workers' responses. The analysis was carried out by correlating these two sets of variables—the alienation indexes and the response variables. It should be noted that the n for each of these correlations was 21 and not 1,900. This of course means that this study, in spite of the large number of subjects, was a very small study considering the type of analysis which was being carried out. Further, 54 of the predictions are predictions about the relative size of a *correlation*. Differences were being predicted in the relationship between two response variables as determined by differences in the stimulus condition. For these two reasons a prediction will be simply regarded as being supported if the finding was in the expected direction and the results will be discussed as a whole and not as specific findings.

Results

Using all of the workers of the sample, the correlations were computed and the results can be seen in Table 2. The first column gives the predicted direction of the correlations for each row. Of the 84 predictions represented in this table, 45 are in the predicted direction. This, of course, does not support the construct.

It scarcely seemed appropriate to abandon the construct after such limited analysis, and a further step was proposed. It was assumed that middle-class ideals were much more likely to be found among white-collar workers than among blue-collar workers, regardless of community environment. If that assumption is correct, the results might have been masked by the inclusion of white-collar workers in the sample. Accordingly, the 511 white-collar workers were dropped, and the analyses were redone. Again showing the direction of predictions in the first column, the results using only blue-collar workers are shown in Table 3. Here 61 of 84 predictions are in the proper direction. Using the normal approximation to the binomial distribution, the probability of finding this many confirmations out of 84 predictions by chance is less than .001. Though extreme caution must be used in attempting to interpret the results of any specific variable, three of the response variables warrant mention. Those are the three which did *not* confirm the construct. JDI work–JIG correlation, and JDI work–LIG correlation do not present any clear pattern. The equivocal results with these two correlations

TABLE 3. Prediction tests using blue-collar workers: correlations (Pearson r's) between stimulus and response variables

Response variables	Predicted direction	Stimulus variables					
		Slum conditions	Urbanization	Urban growth	Cost of living	Productive farming (reversed)	Population density
Importance of planning for retirement	−	+.23	**−.22**	+.42	**−.18**	**−.09**	**−.35**
Made plans yet for retirement	−	**−.25**	**−.55**	+.09	**−.57**	**−.05**	**−.65**
Preparation for retirement index	+	−.46	−.19	−.11	−.20	**+.20**	−.28
Look for other work after retirement	+	**+.32**	**+.11**	**+.02**	**+.16**	−.22	**+.23**
Personal satisfaction from the job	−	+.52	+.16	+.46	+.20	**−.21**	+.01
Correlations between:							
Work satisfaction–Skill level	−	**−.03**	**−.07**	**−.10**	**−.09**	**−.02**	+.07
Work satisfaction–Job level	−	**−.65**	**−.18**	**−.47**	**−.20**	+.17	**−.14**
Work satisfaction–Job-in-general satisfaction	−	**−.12**	+.20	**−.34**	+.17	+.37	+.25
Pay satisfaction–Job-in-general satisfaction	+	**+.13**	**+.02**	**+.18**	**+.11**	**+.09**	**+.12**
Promotion satisfaction–Job-in-general satisfaction	−	**−.31**	**−.23**	**−.30**	**−.23**	**−.02**	**−.17**
Work satisfaction–Life-in-general satisfaction	−	**−.31**	+.15	**−.48**	+.05	+.47	+.13
Pay satisfaction–Life-in-general satisfaction	+	**+.05**	**+.13**	**+.09**	**+.10**	**+.37**	**+.28**
Promotion satisfaction–Life-in-general satisfaction	−	**−.48**	**−.10**	**−.47**	**−.18**	+.26	**−.06**
Job-in-general satisfaction–Life-in-general satisfaction	−	**−.30**	+.03	**−.22**	**−.01**	00	**−.21**

Note.—N = 21 companies. Bold-faced numbers are in the direction of the prediction.

are not easily explained. Perhaps the relationship between work satisfaction and global satisfaction is too strong to allow modification by the social environmental differences which are being measured here. The other nonconforming variable, "Personal satisfaction from the job," is in the direction opposite the prediction in five of the six opportunities. The present analysis is not so powerful that this response can be concluded to act in this direction in all cases. This particular response and related areas should certainly enjoy increased interest in any continuation of this line of research.

The Slum Conditions, Cost of Living, and Urban Growth variates work best as predictors of alienated responses having 12, 11, and 11 correct predictions, respectively. Urbanization and Population Density each had 10 correct predictions, while Productive Farming had only 7. Thus, empirically as well as logically, the Slum Conditions variate is the one most closely aligned with the alienation construct. The Productive Farming variate does not seem useful.

Discussion

In general it appears that the construct of alienation has been demonstrated to be useful for structuring workers' responses. It has been shown that workers living in communities which should foster alienation from middle-class norms structure their jobs and their lives predictably differently from workers in communities where adherence to middle-class norms would be expected. Further, these differences were predicted from a theoretical framework consistent with the construct of alienation. Since this study should be regarded as a pilot study, this discussion will emphasize the problems and future research direction rather than the implications of the findings.

It is true that in this study as in the previous research, "alienation from middle-class norms" is not the only tenable hypothesis. Katzell et al. (1961) invoked an explanation based on differing "needs" being generated by urban and rural environments. Hulin (1966) and Kendall (1963) used the concepts of "frame-of-reference" and the "alternatives available to the workers" in economically depressed and slum-ridden communities. Turner and Lawrence (1965) used the concept of "anomie" to explain their results. Even in the present study it is possible that an economic-frame-of-reference hypothesis would be useful in understanding the results. The cost of living variate made 11 out of 14 correct predictions suggesting that frames of reference of the workers in the community play a significant role in structuring workers' jobs. On the other hand, communities with a high cost of living would be expected to be less than optimal as places for workers to live. Alienation from the norms of the dominant social group might be a reasonable response of the economically disadvantaged workers who might well see the "middle class" as the cause of their unenviable position. Thus, both of these constructs may be similar. Also, since "productive farming" proved useful in predicting *level* of pay satisfaction consistent with a frame-of-reference explanation (Hulin, 1966; Kendall, 1963) but not alienated responses regarding job structure, the economic-frame-of-reference explanation in the present study is a bit tenuous. It also could be argued that anomie remains a tenable explanation for these findings and all that has been found is that "integrated" workers are more predictable than "alienated" workers who are truly normless (anomic). Table 1 indicates that in the majority of the cases prediction has been made for stronger relationships between response variables for the integrated sample. However, of the 18 cases where higher relationships were predicted for the alienated workers, 17 were in the expected direction. Thus, it does not appear that anomie is a tenable explanation. The alienated workers are not normless. They have norms but they are different from those of the middle classes. It would appear that "alienation from middle-class norms" is the only construct so far invoked which is capable of structuring all of the diverse findings.

The construct was not confirmed above the level of skilled blue-collar workers. The fact that it was not found in a sample of white-collar workers is in line with the definition of the construct. The possibility that different occupations may generate different susceptibility to alienation is similar to Blauner's (1964) reasoning and certainly has not been ruled out. While the upper boundary of blue-collar workers was arbitrarily set at the level of skilled workers in this study, future research may show that some other level will be optimal in applications of the construct.

The present data delineate attitude changes which accompany alienation. An area of at least equal and probably greater importance will be to see if there are related behavioral changes. Related to job-performance differences is the question of what job-design criteria will be most effective in maximizing satisfaction and performance among alienated workers. As the Turner and Lawrence (1965) findings suggest, the best job design in alienating conditions may be contrary to the models usually proposed by human-relations-oriented investigators. Although integrated workers desire greater responsibility and autonomy, alienated workers may be happiest when given a job which demands little personal involvement either in terms of task skills or identification with the goals of management.

It should be reiterated that this represents a pilot study and although predictions regarding all of the relationships were made a priori there is still only a rudimentary knowledge of the effects of the independent variable. Eventually, with increasing knowledge and sophistication one may know enough about alienation to attempt direct psychological assessment rather than indexing it by means of environmental variables. To the deplorers of "actuarial research" (such as has been conducted here) this would represent a significant step forward. However, if this direct assessment is carried out, researchers will be back in the domain of verbal response–verbal response correlations with all of the attendant problems of response sets, halo, acquiescence, and unreliability. Even with the "slippage" that occurs between an index and a construct, it seems preferable to use a stimulus-response paradigm as was employed in this study.

This study does seem to have strong implications for theorists who would like to talk about "basic human needs." Both the currently popular need hierarchy approach and the human relations theorists talk about needs for self-actualization, needs for autonomy, needs for a demanding job, etc., which are supposedly basic needs of all people. These data indicate that at the very least these systems need to be revised to take cultural differences into account.

Bell, W. Anomie, social isolation, and the class structure. *Sociometry,* 1957, **20,** 105–116.

Blauner, R. *Alienation and freedom: The factory worker and his industry.* Chicago: University of Chicago Press, 1964.

Cureton, E. E., & Katzell, R. A. A further analysis of the relations among job performance and situational variables. *Journal of Applied Psychology,* 1962, **46,** 230.

Dalton, M. Worker response and social background. *Journal of Political Economy,* 1947, **55,** 323–332.

Dean, D. G. Alienation: Its meaning and measurement. *American Sociological Review,* 1961, **26,** 753–758.

Friedlander, F. Comparative work value systems. *Personnel Psychology,* 1965, **18,** 1–20.

Hulin, C. L. Effects of community characteristics on measures of job satisfaction. *Journal of Applied Psychology,* 1966, **50,** 185–192.

Katzell, R. A., Barrett, R. S., & Parker, T. C. Job satisfaction, job performance, and situational characteristics. *Journal of Applied Psychology,* 1961, **45,** 65–72.

Kendall, L. M. Canonical analysis of job satisfaction and behavioral, personal background, and situational data. Unpublished doctoral dissertation, Cornell University, 1963.

Kennedy, J. E., & O'Neill, H. E. Job content and workers' opinions. *Journal of Applied Psychology,* 1958, **42,** 372–375.

Kilbridge, M. D. Do workers prefer larger jobs? *Personnel,* 1960, **37**(5), 45–48.

Killian, L. M., & Grigg, C. M. Urbanism, race, and anomia. *American Journal of Sociology,* 1962, **67,** 661–665.

Kunin, T. The construction of a new type of attitude measure. *Personnel Psychology,* 1955, **8,** 65–77.

Mayo, E. *The human problems of an industrial civilization.* New York: Macmillan, 1933.

McClosky, H., & Schaar, J. H. Psychological dimensions of anomy. *American Sociological Review,* 1965, **30,** 14–40.

Ruitenbeck, H. M. *The individual and the crowd.* New York: Nelson, 1964.

Simpson, R. L., & Miller, H. M. Social status and anomia. *Social Problems,* 1963, **10,** 256–264.

Smith, P. C., Kendall, L. M., & Hulin, C. L. *Measurement of satisfaction in work and retirement.* Chicago: Rand McNally, 1969.

Turner, A. N., & Lawrence, P. R. *Industrial jobs and the worker: An investigation of response to task attributes.* Boston: Harvard University Press, 1965.

Webb, B, J., Campbell, D. T., Schwartz, R. D., & Sechrest, L. *Unobtrusive measures: Nonreactive research in the social sciences.* Chicago: Rand McNally, 1966.

Weber, M. *The protestant ethic and the spirit of capitalism.* (Tr. by Talcott Parsons) New York: Scribner, 1958.

Whyte, W. F. *Money and motivation: An analysis of incentives.* New York: Harper, 1955.

Worthy, J. C. Organizational structure and employee morale. *American Sociological Review,* 1950, **15,** 169–179.

CONFLICTING ORGANIZATIONAL PATTERNS IN FUNERAL DIRECTING

Robert Habenstein

This article deals with funeral directing as it takes place within the context of a business operation performed in service establishments. As a business with professional overtones, funeral directing has before it the socially legitimate goal of profitable enterprise, and the successful pursuit of business profit carries with it in our society a fair share of social prestige. The critical problem of orientation from the standpoint of the funeral director is not whether he should make a profit, but in light of so many imponderables and variables that can affect vitally his pursuit of this goal, what scheme, what pattern of social and economic activity may he follow to ensure his success?

Establishment Orientations

The fact of the matter is that there is no single dominant occupational model toward which the work of the funeral director may be ordered. Rather, the choices are several, and, although the elements and implications of each or any may not be clear to the individuals involved, organizational analysis indicates that the structural principles of operation may be separated into at least two highly different patterns. It is convenient to term these alternative pat-

terns "establishment orientations," first, because the significant part of the service of the funeral director goes forward in a physical establishment, and, second, the imagery suggested by the term leads easily into social psychological analysis based on concepts of dramatic reference—as laid down by Goffman, and recommended by Meadows, Burke, and others.[1]

From the data of nine years of intermittent research,[2] I have built these polar establishment types, which are to be seen as rational, analytical constructs, the specific elements of which, hereinafter called "definitions," are proposed to "go together" in such fashion as to form one of two theoretically meaningful configurations. (See Table 1.) [page 257] Each of the five particular definitions is held to stand in less ambiguous relation to its configuration than does its logical opposite. Any mixture of these elements at the concrete level of action, it follows, should give rise to an organizational dilemma, or, in the vernacular, "structural strain." In short, the two establishment orientations or types are composite polar opposites, as are each of the specific sets of alternative definitions that go into their making. Preliminary leads in the development of these types came from funeral director

"Conflicting Organizational Patterns in Funeral Directing," *Human Organization*, 21, 2 (Summer 1962), 126–132. Reprinted with the permission of the author and of the publisher, The Society for Applied Anthropology.

respondents who, in answer to the question,

> What different kinds of funeral directors are there?

would reply

> . . . curb-stone operators, advertisers, old-time undertakers, operators gone commercial, real professional, promotors, chain, big operators, independent, community, family,

among other casual terms of reference. In addition to these verbal leads, it became apparent that the two major associations representing funeral directors tended to differ on so many basic points that one might suspect their divergencies to be a reflection of two differing modes of funeral service operation. Finally, the trade journals, and the one authoritative "handbook for morticians" reflected similar differing perspectives, as a clear cleavage in views often revealed itself in the "impartial" editorial comment.

From such various kinds of research data, then, the writer has been able to distinguish the five different sets of "definitional variables," basic to the operation of funeral establishments. These differ both in form and content from Parsons' "pattern variables" in that they are intended to operate analytically at a lower and more manageable level of abstraction (Table 1). Each variable is dichotomous, consisting, as indicated, of two polar opposite definitions of situations. The variables, in order of their presentation, are (1) Nature of Service Contact; (2) Community Orientation; (3) Conceived Unit of Operation; (4) Establishment Goal; and, (5) Personnel Organization. It will be the task of the remainder of this paper to elaborate the polar-opposite dichotomies of definitional variables, and to show the manner in which they cluster to form the basic establishment orientations of funeral directing.

The Mass-Mortuary

The writer has used the term "mass-mortuary" as a collective designation for one cluster of characteristic definitions. Beyond its alliterative quality in relation to "mortuary," the term "mass" has an orientational, or sensitizing nature, as derived from its use by Park, Wirth, Blumer, and among others, Arnold Rose.[3] The mass-mortuary, obviously, should have more than a passing relation to the more general mass dimension of modern society.

(1) THE DIFFUSED SERVICE CONTACT

The mass-mortuary is organized in such manner that *no one person can assume a consistently central role in the conduct of each funeral service.* The impossibility of one funeral director taking charge, and in the English sense being "in attendance," is obvious for establishments that operate upon the principle of a high volume of cases. It is simply physically impossible for any one person personally to attend five, ten, or fifteen funerals *per day*. As a consequence the operations must be so organized that there is no one person known as *the* funeral director, but there is instead a corps of trained specialists, standardized in demeanor and action, and interchangeable, as it were, at any stage of the funeralization process.

What exactly may the client expect by way of attention and service in the mass-mortuary? Inevitably he faces up to the functionary, the arranger-for-things-which-obviously-need-to-be-done. The structure of interaction between the two is characterized by a set of relationships that cannot be based in sympathetic understanding generated out of a personal relationship historically existing between funeral director and the family of the deceased. Moreover, since the mass operation demands the maximum utilization of energies and funeral paraphernalia, there is an underlying sense of urgency imparted to the situation. Time, not rapport, becomes of the essence.

Thus, the contact is segmental in the sense that there is lacking the organization and focus of a personal, symmetrical relationship grounded in understanding based on acquaintance through time. In the mass-mortuary one does not get service—he gets services.

(2) THE REFRACTIVE NATURE OF THE COMMUNITY ORIENTATION

As regards the community, the definition prevailing in the mass-mortuary is directly affected by the fact of *transcendence beyond community expectations and controls.* (This is central to the sociological use of the term "mass" generally.) There is no reflection of expression of local community by the mass-mortuary, mainly because the clientele served do not come as community members to a community institution; they come as customers from a trade area or area of mass appeal. For example, the largest funeral service operation in Chicago, organized to serve over five million inhabitants, has three large establishments, one north, one south, and one southwest. It goes without saying that these branches are each organized to serve areas constituted by something more than a community! From the wide use of billboards, streetcar and bus advertising signs, and other media of mass communication there can be no

doubting the factor of community transcendence. When the writer asked the manager of one of Chicago's largest single establishments if he had a local business, the response was a hearty laugh and the comment that

> . . . there weren't enough people passing away in the locality to keep them in business, [and that they had cases] from as far away as Evanston, Chicago Heights, Argonne, and all over Chicago.

In Los Angeles one gigantic combination mortuary and cemetery has as its market area the whole of Southern California.

From the veteran director of an association coordinating livery and handling problems of the funeral directors of Chicago come the following observations:

> Take out in Los Angeles, or any of the large scale operations anywhere else, I think they will pretty much confine themselves to the areas they are now in. A lot of people *without families and communities* will see some advertising and perhaps remember the name. These are the people that advertising can appeal to, and they make up most of the trade for the large scale establishments. In the more settled areas, in communities, you will find that advertising has a more limited appeal, with the business that you can get this way.

> The large operations have hit a norm [sic]—they have hit a peak and there they will probably stay. Right now they are staying pretty level. *Most undertakers serve family groups:* people who have had twenty-five years elapse will still go back to the one that buried grandpa, or perhaps mother. This is true all over, not just in rural areas, but in most parts of the city too. And this is the kind of family trade that doesn't get influenced by advertisement.

In the far west there are two giant mortuary "chains," one with thirteen and the other with sixteen mortuaries scattered over Southern California, centering about Los Angeles. It should be pointed out that a large profit from a funeral establishment is not *ipso facto* an index of its mass character, although high gross receipts and corporate rather than individual proprietorship organization are closely associated with such type of funeral service operations. More importantly, since the clientele do not bring with them a direct expression of community controls, the mass-mortuary has little incentive for expressing in the services performed the definitions and relationships that make up a specific community way of life.

Thus, the community folkways and mores are *refracted* by the mass-mortuary insofar as the attitudes, convictions, and definitions of the clients are at best hurdles to be cleared, or raw materials to be worked until pliable. They do not constitute a framework of action. They are, as will be shown later, the stuff from which the sales arrangements are made. In the interactive process of what amounts to a buyer-seller relationship there is an erosion of community controls, and to some extent a depersonalization of the actors involved. A mass appeal backdrops a commercial relation; in short, it is the "mass-cash-nexus."

(3) THE SOCIAL DIVESTMENT OF THE UNIT OF OPERATION

When *the dead are atomistically conceived as "cases,"* or *"units"* and stripped of their kinship and locality attachments, so that to the mortician each funeral becomes simply an item in its own right, and divested of any relationships with the survivors except the contractual obligation to pay costs of burial, there emerges another polar definition making up the mass-mortuary type of funeral operation.

In such cases just as the dead lose their social attributes, so do the clients fall into a "customer-mass" about whom the mass morticians can make only the vaguest and most general identifying characterizations.

Services to a client, when seen in the light of a personal service relation, cannot easily be rationalized into precisely determinate units. However, an ideological element in most mass-mortuary operations is exhibited in the term "service rendered." Such definition of situation is a far cry from a professional service relationship of the doctor-client, or for that matter, the service rendered to one's person by his barber. In bringing to light these two considerations, i.e., the divestment of the social characteristics of the dead and defining the relationship during the making of arrangements as a "buying" relationship, then, we find emerging the third polar definition in the characterization of the mass-mortuary type of funeral operation.

(4) THE "BUSINESS UNLIMITED" NATURE OF THE OCCUPATIONAL GOAL

The goal of any mortuary or funeral home includes the socially legitimated idea of profit. But the goal of the mass-mortuary is *unlimited business and untrammeled growth of profit.* There is no more consideration given to the limitation of profit than might be found in corporation operations generally. Profit, expansion, added "branches," higher volume of sales, lower cost per unit, better sales techniques, higher profits, renewed expansion, etc.—the cycle is unending. There is only one standard, which in no way is a limitation, against which the mass-mortuary measures its business health—other than by the profit and loss column—and that is the mortician's "share" of the total amount of retail and service trade business in a particular market area.

In sum, the goal of business operation of the mass-mortuary is, simply, "business unlimited." Extra-business norms are without relevance; what is good for business is excellent for the mass-mortician.

(5) THE BUREAUCRATIC ORGANIZATION OF PERSONNEL

A final defining element deals with the mode of personnel organization. *Employees are categorized in terms of their specialties in such way that the "occupational distance" between the levels of organization is emphasized,* and the personal characteristics of the help becomes important only to the extent that they have a bearing on the flow of work or the selling of services and merchandise. As is generally the case with service establishments the list of occupational specialties tends to elaborate with the size of the establishment. Usually the mass-mortuary will have maintenance and custodial personnel; apprentice embalmers—who often are putting in their apprenticeship as sort of low-paid labor and who will go to a different establishment for more permanent jobs—embalmers, salaried usually on a per-week basis; cosmeticians and beauticians, quite often women; assistants to the managing director; assistant managing director, and director. Above these offices may be a series of corporation executives, proprietors, or managers. Chauffeurs are likely to be organized with hackmen generally, and have become a quasi-independent group.

The role of union organization of employees is interesting. Most of the lower echelon workers in mass-mortuaries are either organized or drifting toward union organization. In their anxiety to join unions embalmers have found themselves members of gravediggers and teamsters unions! There is no single nationwide union specifically for embalmers.

On the other hand, the presence or absence of union organization in a funeral establishment is not an unambiguous criterion for defining a type of operation. Union organization admittedly is much more likely to be present in the large corporation-type operations, but the "union idea" has been creeping into smaller, non-mass types too. What is important is the attitude toward unionization. The mass-mortuary operators look upon the union as does American business management generally— as a sort of necessary evil, not without some advantages, yet not to be encouraged. Union contracts are often handled by a local funeral director's association. To the mass-mortuaries, union organization of employees is understandable; there is no *moral* injunction used to keep away the unions. Personnel managers fight union organization with plans to give better conditions of work and rewards to the employees.

The personnel in mass-mortuaries are diversified as to specialty, dealt with somewhat categorically, and are most likely to seek mobility within their specialty. An embalmer, no matter how he may have seen himself in training at a school of mortuary science, must come to see himself in the future as still an embalmer, and not as *the* funeral director of the establishment. In the first place, as noted above, there is not *the* funeral director in a mass-mortuary establishment; and in the second place the embalmer in such an establishment is likely to have been hired for his technical skill in performing a specific task;

thus the chances favor his staying in his particular *metier*. If he is taken "up front" he crosses the line between management and worker, and assumes a management role. As the number of employees increases it follows that the executives' and managers' offspring will more likely stand in a direct competitive relation to categories of persons rather than to specific individuals. Mobility, although decreased by the appearance of distinct categories of work specialties nevertheless is not blocked completely in the mass-mortuary by someone standing in a particular relation to the manager, or director. Different skills and special knowledge, not the boss's son, stand in the way.

Thus the mass-mortuary orientation to personnel is bureaucratic. It operates upon the premise of interchangeability of performers of skills, so that it is more a question of what is to be done, than of the person who does it, that is important. In a real sense the employee works *in* such an establishment, he is not *of* it.

The Local Funeral Home

This term has been chosen to represent the polar opposite conception to the mass-mortuary type of funeral service. It is conceived to have more than an ecological referent; basically the local funeral home operates on the premise that the clientele receive, or should receive personal, i.e., sympathetic understanding, in a social, or status-connected relationship to the funeral director. The full meaning of the type, "local funeral home," will emerge, it is hoped, with the redelineation of the five definitional variables—this time from the standpoint of the definitions dichotomous to those that were elaborated in defining the mass-mortuary.

(1) THE FOCALIZED SERVICE CONTACT

The local funeral home is organized so that *the clientele can always feel certain that they will have their funeral services handled by THE funeral director, whom they know personally*. Within the structure of community relationships the funeral director occupies a highly legitimated position with social status as diffuse as, but probably well below that of the family doctor. It should be noted that analytically for the operation of the local funeral home the personal relation of funeral director to client is indispensable; its presence in empirical, concrete situations is not always certain. Theoretically, however, the orientation of the local funeral home is toward clients who are known, both personally and in terms of their status in the community.

A funeral director from an incorporated establishment in an industrial satellite of Chicago remarks:

We have what you would call a community business but what I call a home type of business. The other kind is the apartment-type business. When you have mostly apartments, you have congestion. When you have congestion, everybody wants to move out of it. So with apartments you get a moving population and sometimes a floating population. With this you get a big funeral home where you do not offer a personal service, like a bank teller who lets you draw your money out . . . . This is the kind of place where the personal family type of undertaker does best. I . . . could never set up a place in this community and run it in the volume scale that he does in the apartment house area.

Your personality is one of the big things in the small businesses. Not in the big places, maybe, where they have 1500–2000 a year. You can't be a Jim Farley and remember all the people you serve in a place like that. In a place like this we have the facilities for more services and it is *personal service.* It is the comfort we give that counts and brings the people back. If you don't have the kind of personality that will permit you to give comfort and sincere sympathy to the people, you just don't stay in the game.

It is necessary to emphasize what I term the "focusing" process. It is a process precisely because in rendering his service to the client, the funeral director makes it increasingly clear that *he* is taking over the necessary details and is actually directing the organization and disposal of the dead. A young college instructor remarked to the writer,

What a relief, when my father died suddenly, to be able to call somebody to take over the whole thing. I couldn't even stop my mother from being hysterical, much less think what to do about the funeral, relatives, and all that.

In this case, the respondent was so anxious to have something done that, when the Jewish funeral director said he could not pick up the body until after sundown, he called a Polish mortician who made an immediate "first call." The aftermath came when the relatives pressured the son into having the body shifted to a Jewish funeral home on the following day. So great, apparently, is the alienation of the dead in American society that ethnic and religious customs and traditions may—temporarily at least—be dissolved in the frantic efforts of the family to have some immediate action taken toward the corpse. The "focalizing" funeral director brings as many necessary actions as possible under his immediate supervision.

(2) THE REFLECTIVE NATURE OF THE COMMUNITY ORIENTATION

I would like to suggest that not only can the community enter into the operation of the funeral home, but that *the establishment may become an institutional element of community life.* Typically, the local funeral director is passive in his client relationships. The passivity stems from the historic roots of Western funeral service where the status expression for the dead in funeral service was not defined nor delimited by the undertaker but *arranged* to be expressed, by ceremony and trappings. Today the local funeral director still does not take an active role in the application of community sanctions and controls as regards burial practices. However, at the same time he would never deny that he is part of the community nor feel that his round of life is outside it. From a small town funeral director it is put in the following fashion:

Like any funeral director in a small town I am part of it. Everybody knows everybody, and community opinion is very strong in deciding what is right and wrong. Take the case of the fellow who lost his wife and a few months after was going steady with a school teacher. The community didn't like it and she lost her job. Either you fit in, or you get out. I try to tell people that they are absolutely free to choose who shall bury their dead. But suppose a person in this community dies and relatives from another town have the funeral service there and the business goes to the funeral director there? The people in my community will explain the situation over and over again to me —why it was I didn't get the funeral.

Local funeral directors are notorious for expending time and giving money to worthwhile community projects. Philanthropic drives in particular are often sparked by them. The writer finds it difficult to recall a case where a local funeral director did not mention active participation in community affairs. For analytic purposes the important factor involved is the perspective: is the community being taken into account, or is the gesture part of being *of* the community?

From the standpoint of orientation to the community the local funeral home may be considered as integrally a part of the community round of life. We have used the term "reflective" to indicate that there is no distortion, refraction, or erosion of community folkways and mores as is the case in the mass-mortuary operation. Community and family sentiments are not considered malleable material for the fashioning of a funeral service that will bring the maximum profit to the establishment. The local funeral home provides, theoretically, an instrumentality for the expression of personal sentiment and family and community social relationships.

(3) THE SOCIAL VESTMENT OF THE UNIT OF OPERATION

Only in an incidental way can the dead in the local funeral home be conceived as units, or cases. By virtue of the fact that the general business dimension to funeral service demands some sort of bookkeeping unit, and that associations base dues, services, and other organizational items around the amount of business a funeral home enjoys, *all* funeral directors have occasion to speak of "cases," meaning number of dead bodies funeralized in some period of time. However, this is a far cry from thinking about one's operations *solely* in terms of such units. *What the local funeral director thinks is basically his unit of operation turns out to be a set of social and personal relations in which kinship attachments are usually primary.* He conceives of the dead, then, primarily in relation to social factors. Economic factors consequently are nearly always mediated by social circumstances. A funeral is both a family and community event; to the local funeral director the social reality is the *service-to-family*, and his return on the funeral service is attuned to the socioeconomic circumstances of the dead as a member of a family and holder of a community status. The wife of a local funeral director in west-side Chicago remarks:

> There may be exploitation of the families in some places, maybe the bigger ones, but it is far from the case here. We never try to pressure the customer, and we do some work where we are sure to lose money. Nearly every family has one relation that has hard luck or in some way has not done as well as the rest. Then we are asked by those who are better off to do something for poor so-and-so. My husband does a lot of this, maybe too much for his own good.

If the mass-mortician conceives of the dead as "units," and the person making the arrangements as a "customer," his sense of responsibility is inevitably geared to the economic potential of the interaction, i.e., the size of the sale. The feeling of responsibility generated by the operation of funeral organization along local funeral direction lines is qualitatively different. Its focus is on the family. Remarks another funeral director:

> I feel my closest responsibility to my families. Remember that the funeral director gets to see some of the most intimate aspects of the private lives of the families he sees. Take insurance. We often get to know the insurance situation. But sometimes I can sense when a group of survivors get together that something is not right. What I usually do is to tell them we will meet tomorrow. Sure enough within a half hour I am getting telephone calls from them individually saying that so and so had an insurance policy on the dead and he is going to have to come through with a larger share of payment. And once in a while we get a case where the survivors say there is just one little insurance policy, so can we bury the case

cheap? We do, and then we find a request for six duplicates of death certificate, meaning there are five hidden insurance policies. But despite this a funeral director can't get casual, can't get hardened.

A funeral director is in a "personal service profession" and must guard against those who would make the service big business.

one of the most prominent Milwaukee funeral directors advised the Wisconsin Funeral Directors' Association a few years ago. He went on to say:

We must *never allow clients to become just another case on the books that must show profit* . . . We should be demonstrating our value to the profession and to the community not through high pressure salesmanship but in good personal relations with those we serve.

In addition to being a well-to-do funeral director, this particular speaker has been one of the eight district governors of the largest national association of funeral directors. It is a fair judgment to say that these remarks represent an expression of the principle of the investment of unit of operation with social attributes, and in making the statements the speaker was representing, association-wise, the local funeral home form of funeral operation.

(4) THE "BUSINESS LIMITED" NATURE OF THE OCCUPATIONAL GOAL

Almost all funeral homes in America operate within the context of exchange of goods and services for profit. All funeral directors expect to make money, none, that the writer knows of, expects to perform his tasks as a purely philanthropic gesture. Yet there is a decided difference in the way the business goal of funeral service operation becomes defined, either according to the *mass*

principle, or in the organization and operation of the *local* funeral home. In the first place the status of the local funeral director in an on-going community falls somewhere between family doctor on the one hand and independent merchant on the other. Should it appear that the funeral director is "profiteering in sorrow" community sanctions in the form of withdrawal of trade and "talk" will either force his operations into an approved form, or eventually he will be out of business. In a remarkably frank response a funeral director from Texas (interviewed at the National Foundation of Funeral Service School of Management in Evanston, Illinois) elaborated the occupational goals of the two different types—as he conceives them in terms of size:

As the establishment becomes larger the attitudes change radically. The smaller establishment is based and founded on the reputation and personality of the individual owner, or owners. His contact with the public in general is on a much greater intimate basis. He is better respected in his own service area than the funeral director with the large establishment and service area. His attitude is more of a sincere service nature. *He knows that his volume is set, and could not possibly* be in the field for monetary gain alone. Similar to the small town doctor, he gets a greater personal satisfaction out of a "job well done."

Conversely, the larger operator's establishment is based and founded on the reputation of the establishment. The *contact* with the general public is more on an impersonal basis. By this I mean that they are considered by the public —especially by professional men—as less professional. *Their attitude again is one of volume. How this volume is gained is immaterial.* They have an open field—and the tactics used sometimes would alarm the public, if known.

The occupational goal intrinsic to the local funeral home type of funeral serv-

ice operation is one of profitable operation to the end that the funeral director can live a comfortable, middle-class quasi-professional existence. His sales do not have a clear-cut unity to them. They are, one might say, socially encumbered. The well-to-do of an extended family grouping in the community may easily spend fifteen hundred dollars on one funeral. But even though the profit on the "case" might be a clear five hundred dollars, the encumbering principle would be present in the fact that other, perhaps distant members of the same family may have to be buried at a loss. County cases are almost inevitably losses to local funeral directors; yet while the burial of a county case at a loss might, in strict business terms, be unwise, the wealthier clients' funeral expenses will be high enough to carry the loss-funerals. Many local funeral directors never send a bill; conversely, mass-mortuary practice sanctions the use of collection agencies which not only collect the unpaid bills but include interest on the unpaid sums as well!

(5) THE TRADITIONAL ORGANIZATION OF PERSONNEL

The last defining element for the local funeral home type of funeral service operation stresses the traditional orientation of the funeral director toward the help. The essence of this orientation is *the sense of reciprocal commitment that exists between personnel at different levels of work.* This relation is tinctured by a sense of overall unity of performance of tasks within the funeral establishment. In the traditional mode of occupational organization such factors as age, length of time served, and mastery of skill were important. More important was the incorporation of the help into a form of quasi-family relationship. For over a hundred years undertakers in America had apprentices, journeymen (called "assistants") and, as partners, sometimes brothers living and working with them. The son was likely to begin as an apprentice working with his father. When licensing was introduced the son would first have to spend six to nine months in an embalming school. Then, having formally qualified to become an embalmer and a funeral director by passing state examinations, he would begin the serious work of understudying funeral direction, knowing that someday the establishment would be his to operate and eventually to pass on to his own offspring. In cases where a funeral director had no sons to take over and the sons-in-law, if any, were not interested in learning the trade, a promising assistant would be worked into a partnership, and would eventually have the business as his own. Significantly each specialty had its meaning inside the funeral establishment operation, and all events, circumstances, and conditions relevant to the work were defined, controlled, or worked out without reference to extra-establishment considerations. For the local funeral home to operate, typically, this condition—the circumscription of work within the establishment operation—has to be maintained. The local funeral director has no categories such as "management" and "labor" to cut sharply across the organization of operations; he has instead a small group, possibly two or three members of a work family to whom he is committed with respect to security, advancement, and concern for their selves —as persons. They in turn express a unity of purpose and an unthinking association of their selves with the establishment family. As problems arise the examples and experiences of the past stand as guideposts. The idea of a labor union representing any class of worker to the local funeral director is almost self-contradictory, as the help in the local funeral home are intrinsically a part of it as much as is the director himself.

Recapitulation of Definitional Variables as Dichotomies

Based in social reality, i.e., the objective conditions of human existence in the society about us, two rationalized, analytically purified types of funeral service operations have been constructed. The empirical materials out of which these constructs have been built were gathered in the course of the research, and the

theoretical components were drawn from the general sociological field of social organization expressed at the level of abstraction known familiarly as "middle range." Briefly recapitulated, these types line up schematically in Table 1.

IMPLICATIONS

Like most sociological schemes the terms used do not speak for themselves, yet it is believed in the present case the context makes the meanings implied in the concepts relatively easy to grasp. They have been constructed crescively over a several year period of time in which methodologically the writer went back and forth from tentative concepts to the growing research materials. The value of such effort can be gauged by asking two questions: one, is understanding added to what is already casually known about funeral directors and funeral direction?, and two, can structural stresses, strains, and adaptive devices be located and explained in empirical situations through analysis by the type constructs? In the writer's judgment the answer to the first is a limited "yes," but the second question will only be adequately answered by additional investigations into the areas where these constructs are relevant. However, if, as proposed, the definitional variables in terms of their dichotomies *imply* each other, the testing of the constructs will be considerably facilitated.

TABLE 1. Funeral service establishment orientations.

Definitional variables	Mass-mortuary	Local funeral home
Nature of service contact	Diffused	Focalized
Nature of community orientation	Refractive	Reflective
Unit of operation	Socially divested	Socially vested
Occupational goal	Unlimited	Limited
Personnel organization	Bureaucratic	Traditional

NOTES

1. The most complete statement of the dramatic frame of reference is found in Erving Goffman's *The Presentation of Self in Everyday Life,* Doubleday & Co., Inc., Garden City, New York, 1959.
2. Research began in 1952 as a dissertation project and has continued with lessened emphasis until the present. C.f. "The American Funeral Director, A Study in the Sociology of Work," unpublished Ph.D. Dissertation, University of Chicago, 1954.
3. Arnold Rose, "The Problem of a Mass Society," *Antioch Review,* X (September, 1950), 378–394.

THE TOWN-CITY DIFFERENCE
Possible Explanations

Arthur N. Turner and Paul R. Lawrence

In the previous chapter we reported the major "unexpected" finding of this research, namely, that two different patterns of response to task attributes were discovered in our total sample: high job satisfaction with complex (high scoring RTA*) work in Town settings and high job satisfaction with simple (low scoring RTA) work in City settings. The purpose of this chapter is to discuss this finding, its possible significance, and how it may be explained. In doing so we will bring in some additional data not yet presented. However, as is often the case, what turned out to be perhaps the most interesting outcome was not hypothesized in the original design. From the beginning we assumed that we might discover different patterns of response to work for various subpopulations, but we did not predict the "subcultural" basis for such differences. Consequently in this chapter we can no longer limit ourselves to a straightforward presentation of findings, but must begin more speculatively to discuss their meaning. We will be raising some questions for which we have no clear answers; we will be turning more frequently to the research and theory of others in searching for explanations for what we found; and we will be implying some relevant directions for further research and ex-perimentation which will be made more explicit in Chapter 6 when we summarize implications from the total study.

To set the stage for the following discussion, it is helpful to review briefly the major difference in the response and behavior of the Town and City subpopulations. Workers in Town settings, almost without exception, behaved and responded in accordance with the prior hypotheses of the researchers. The Town workers on high RTA Index jobs had both high Attendance and high Job Satisfaction, and expressed greater satisfaction with both their company and their union. The older and more senior Town workers tended to be assigned to higher RTA jobs, and they were both better satisfied and better paid. Town workers perceived the attributes of their tasks in much the same way as the researchers, and they especially saw high opportunities to contribute on high RTA jobs. Pay in the lowest quartile was associated with dissatisfaction, but at higher levels Pay had no discernible effect on Job Satisfaction.

These "expected" findings for Town workers stand in sharp contrast to the findings for City workers. City workers found higher Job Satisfaction on low RTA jobs. For City workers there was no significant relation between Attend-

Arthur N. Turner and Paul R. Lawrence, Chapter 5, pages 91 to 108, "The Town-City Difference: Possible Explanations," in *Industrial Jobs and the Worker: An Investigation of Response to Task Attributes.* (Boston: Harvard University, Division of Research, Graduate School of Business Administration, 1965. Reprinted by permission.)

* RTA refers to a "Requisite Task Attribute Index" which measured job attributes such as the amount of variety, autonomy, responsibility, and interaction in the job.

ance and task attributes. They also expressed higher satisfaction with their company, their union, and their foreman when they were working on low RTA jobs. The older and more senior men among them were not more satisfied and were significantly lower paid than the younger, junior men. Many City workers perceived high opportunities to contribute on *low* scoring jobs. And we have not been able, as yet, to find any meaningful relation between their pay level and their level of Job Satisfaction.

How can we account for these differences? The remainder of this chapter will be concerned primarily with this question. We will not expect to find any final answers but will be seeking to fit the evidence of this study into a more general theoretical explanation.

Before proceeding with the discussion, an obvious but important point should be made about satisfaction as a response to work. Any person's level of satisfaction with a particular circumstance depends not only on the rewards available to him in that situation, but also on his needs and wants. Or, as Nancy Morse puts it, "The greater the amount the individual gets, the greater his satisfaction and, at the same time, the more the individual still desires, the less his satisfaction."[1] This formulation serves as a useful reminder that the Town-City difference in satisfaction with the same kind of job attributes implies a difference in what is wanted or expected at work. Unless we understand this difference in wants or expectations, we cannot understand the difference in response. This is why we have sometimes referred to the variation in response between Town and City settings as a difference in "motivational predispositions." Now we need to consider in more detail these two different patterns of expectation or predisposition toward the

job, where they may come from, how they may be explained, and the extent to which they may be subject to change.

Town Predispositions

The positive relationship for Town workers between task attribute scores and Job Satisfaction indicates that what they wanted out of their job experience was a relatively large amount of variety, autonomy, interaction, skill, and responsibility. Put in other terms, they were seeking a work environment in which they were expected or permitted a relatively rich and varied behavioral pattern in terms of activities, interactions, and mental states. Apparently they were predisposed to respond favorably to a relatively "challenging" or "involving" work environment, in which more of their potential ways of behaving could be constructively engaged with the task.

It can be seen that statements like those in the preceding paragraph are consistent with a widely held set of assumptions about the relationship between needs and behavior. Under this mode of theorizing about motivation, it is assumed that men will seek out and feel rewarded by situations in which there is a challenge or opportunity to engage more of their ability to enrich their experience, to explore and achieve more varied relationships with their environment.

A number of theories of motivation, differing from one another in important respects, share in common this emphasis. For example, White, in developing his theory of "effectance motivation," has described a persistent human need to attain increasing levels of competence in exploring and dealing with the environment.[2] Other writers stress the idea of the individual's need to develop and grow, to achieve the potentials in himself of which his previous experience has taught him to be aware. Thus, according to Combs and Snygg: "Man . . . is an insatiably striving organism forever seeking the maintenance and enhancement of the self. From birth to death he is continually engaged in the search for greater feelings of adequacy."[3] Perhaps the leading exponent of this point of view is Gordon Allport, with his stress on the "proactive" nature of man, his concept of "functionally autonomous" motives, and his view of personality as "a wide open system seeking progressively new levels of order and transaction."[4]

While the theories just cited differ from one another in many important ways, they, as is true of many others that could be added, have in common that they could without difficulty be used to "explain" the response to task attributes we discovered in Town settings. The greater the requirement and opportunity inherent in the job for the Town worker to exercise increasing competence, to enhance his concept of himself as an adequate person, to attain new levels of order and transaction with his environment, the more favorable his response to the job should be, according to theories of this kind.

An opportunity to explain in more specific terms our data in terms of this way of thinking about motivation is offered by the "need hierarchy" of Maslow (1954). In his theory, Maslow postulates that man is a wanting creature who will under all circumstances be seeking to achieve certain goals, but that these goals will change as he satiates some needs and turns his attention to others. Maslow has worked out a hierarchy of needs that he believes man follows in general terms, being "concerned at the outset" in physiological gratifications, and, as these are partially filled, moving his seeking attention in sequence to "safety" needs, "social" needs, "ego" needs, and "self-actualization" needs. McGregor has written of the relevance of Maslow's theory to industrial settings and has shown how management beliefs and practices can be built upon Maslow's conception of motivation.[5] Clark has carried this line of theory one step further by testing it in one industrial organization.[6] He found some evidence supporting the hypothesis that certain specified combinations of industrial conditions (job security, work group characteristics, supervisory style, company support, and task attributes) induced seeking, concerned behavior in workers that would support the need hierarchy theory.

Following Maslow, McGregor, and Clark, we would predict that a certain minimal level of pay and job security would be a preoccupation of industrial workers until their basic physiological and safety needs were met. Then we would predict a preoccupation with social needs—the need to be liked and enjoy friendly associations at work. As this need became at least partially satisfied at work, the theory would predict a growing concern with accomplishments that would bring the respect of others and self-respect to the worker. If the opportunity existed to meet these ego needs by the performance of complex tasks, the theory would predict that these task opportunities would be sought and valued as sources of need gratification.

The record of findings in regard to both Town and City workers can usefully be reviewed with this theory in mind. As reported in the previous chapter, Town workers in the lowest pay quartile were preoccupied with pay to the extent that for them low pay was associated significantly with lower Job Satisfaction. Once this minimal level of pay was achieved, however, it seemed to have no consistent or meaningful relation to variance in Job Satisfaction. This relation between Pay and Job Satisfaction did not hold for City workers. In order to test the need hierarchy against our data, two further analysis steps can be reported. First we took those workers who received pay in the upper three quartiles (on the assumption that for them safety needs would be fairly well satisfied) and examined the relation between Work Group Satisfaction (as a means of fulfilling social needs) and Job Satisfaction. We found that for both Town and City workers in the upper three pay quartiles, the majority who were satisfied with their work group also had a high Job Satisfaction score ($p < .01$ in both subpopulations). Next we took those workers who were not only in the upper three pay quartiles but also in the upper three quartiles in Work Group Satisfaction, and investigated how for them Job Satisfaction was associated with the RTA Index. For these men, who were presumably meeting both their minimal pay and work group satisfaction needs, we found the now familiar pattern: high satisfaction with high RTA for Town workers, and high satisfaction with low RTA for City workers ($p < .05$ in both cases).

The need hierarchy theory fits quite well the response of Town workers: when their pay was unusually low they tended to be dissatisfied; when satisfied with pay, they responded favorably to a congenial work group; when satisfied with their work group they responded favorably to the challenge of a relatively complex task. But this explanation, as with the other "striving" type theories we examined briefly, fails as an explanation of the City response. City workers did not necessarily express dissatisfaction with unusually low pay. Whether pay was high or low they tended to express high Job Satisfaction when satisfied with their work group. And regardless of either pay or Work Group Satisfaction, they were likely to be more satisfied with more simple, less demanding jobs. In short, the various "striving" theories of motivation are not consistent with our total findings; what is a useful explanation of the City workers' response?

City Predispositions

One plausible explanation of the response of City workers is, quite simply, that they are motivated exactly like Town workers except for a subcultural norm or ground rule against appearing "eager for responsibility." In effect, this idea holds that City workers have been taught by their parents and friends that to express openly an interest in more complex and responsible work is to expose oneself unnecessarily to disappointment and ridicule. Hence, the norm. In conformance with this norm, they express high satisfaction with low scoring jobs, but are aware, at least dimly, of inner feelings of desire for the more psychologically involving aspects of more complex work irrespective of other extrinsic rewards such as pay.

In order to test the validity of this explanation of the City workers' behavior, the researchers thought of two questions that could be put to our available research data, questions which could be stated so that the resulting findings would or would not give support to this "latency" explanation.

TEST ONE

The latency explanation assumes that the City worker has a norm against "appearing eager" that serves the function of protecting him against the disappointment and ridicule of failing to secure more complex work. To justify and sustain such a norm the City worker would be expected to feel discriminated against in terms of opportunities to secure more complex work relative to Town workers. In our questionnaire we asked a question that provides a fair test of the existence of this feeling of discrimination. The question was designed to measure the degree to which each worker saw opportunities to advance in his job situation. The hypothesis was that if City workers scored lower on this question than Town workers, the latency explanation would be supported. The data indicated that there was no association at all between perceived opportunities to advance and the two subcultures and on this test the latency explanation was not supported.

TEST TWO

The latency explanation is based on the assumption that City workers employed on low RTA jobs are experiencing more or less of some form of distress even though they tended to express high Job Satisfaction in the questionnaire. Our Psychosomatic Response Index, as a measure of the freedom from nervous strain and tension in connection with work, could be expected to indicate this latent distress on low RTA jobs. Therefore, if City workers on low content jobs scored as low or lower in Psychosomatic Response than Town workers on low scoring jobs, the latency explanation would be supported. Once again the data fail to support this explanation. On jobs in the lowest Requisite Task tertile, 71% of the City workers scored high in their Psychosomatic Response and 68% of the Town workers scored low ($\chi^2 = 5.05$, $p < .02$).

In short, our data indicated that the City response was more than an outward conformity to a subcultural norm. City workers appeared genuinely to find more simple tasks less stress producing and more satisfying than more complex work. A low score on the RTA Index, in other words, was more in line with what they were looking for in work, apparently, and their favorable response to low scoring jobs appeared to be the consequence of a fairly basic predisposition or value position inherent in the City subcultural setting.

One way of describing this kind of underlying difference in orientation is to say that relative to Town workers, City workers would presumably produce low scores in "need for achievement," as conceived and measured by McClelland and his associates.[7] According to McClelland's theory, to the extent that industrial workers have achievement needs, we could expect them to seek progressively more complex tasks as appropriate settings for demonstrating their excellence of performance and their rights to preferred social standing; whereas for workers with low achievement needs, task complexity would be a matter of relative indifference, or even have a negative value if it was seen as interfering with other, more important motivations, such as "need for affiliation."

In order to see whether McClelland's ideas about these inherently different motivational sets do in fact help to explain our Town-City difference, we would have had to obtain need for achievement and need for affiliation scores for the members of our sample. Unfortunately, we do not have these data. The only personality measure that we secured, a modified F-scale score, failed to discriminate in a useful manner, as already reported. However, a study by Rosen reports findings that are highly relevant in this respect, and reinforce the indications already given that the City response differed from the Town response because of a basically different set of predispositions toward work on the part of the City subpopulation.[8]

Rosen made use of McClelland's method of measuring the strength of an individual's achievement motivation by scoring the achievement themes in the stories he tells in response to ambiguous pictures in a Thematic Apperception Test. This and two other related methods were used by Rosen in a comparative study of the achievement beliefs of several American subcultures. Rosen's study involved 954 subjects in four northeastern states. The six American subcultures studied were Greek, Jewish, Negro, French-Canadian, Italian, and Protestant. The last three of these are uniquely relevant to this study, since of the four companies in City settings three had predominantly French-Canadian work forces and the fourth was predominantly Italian. All of the companies in Town settings employed predominantly Protestant work forces, with the exception of two companies where French-Canadians were in a large majority.

Rosen reports that the average need for achievement score for French-Canadians was 8.82; for Italians, 9.65; and for Protestants, 10.11. When the scores for French-Canadians and Italians were combined, they were found to be signifi-

cantly lower than the scores for Protestants ($p<.01$). Rosen also secured data on the age at which children were given "independence training" in the home by these subcultures, and the mean age for this was: French-Canadian, 7.99; Italian, 8.03; and Protestant, 6.87. As a third measure Rosen asked his subjects questions designed to elicit their value position as between (1) an activistic or a passivistic orientation, (2) an individualistic or a collectivistic orientation, and (3) a future or a present time orientation. Each response to seven questions that favored activistic, individualistic, and future-oriented values was taken to facilitate achievement and was given a point. The mean scores of French-Canadians on this value index was 3.68; of Italians, 4.17; and of Protestants, 5.16. The score for Protestants was significantly higher than the combined French-Canadian and Italian scores ($p<.001$).

This evidence goes a long way to support the idea that there are some important and not merely superficial differences between the particular subcultures we are concerned with in this study. Rosen, of course, points out that these differences are in the process of change as each of these subcultures is exposed to the shared American culture. Nevertheless, the fact of these cultural differences at this point of time provides additional understanding of why these subcultures respond so differently to industrial work.

We have seen that the Town response to work was more congruent than the City response to the kind of motivational theory which stresses striving as a basic human motive, and that the City response becomes more understandable in terms of McClelland's notion that "need for achievement" is subject to significant variations between one group or culture and another. An alternative way of thinking about motivation can be applied to our data, namely the body of theory that emphasizes not the striving but rather the *exchange* aspects of behavior. In this case we have an approach to the problem of explanation which at first thought seems to fit more closely the City than the Town response.

Exchange Theory as an Explanation

The underlying idea of this body of theorizing about motivation is of course fundamental to much of economics. Men are viewed as always seeking to engage in favorable exchanges with the persons and things in their environment; they are looking for transactions that will be favorable to them in the sense that their "rewards" will be greater than their "costs."

If we are thinking in exchange terms, the question of whether or not we "like or want something" is meaningless unless we add "at what cost to ourselves." City workers may be looking at the nature of their work in these exchange terms. But the question immediately arises, what will these workers treat as the costs and the rewards of their work situation?

Most labor economics is built upon the premise that workers will strive to maximize their economic rewards with the least cost to themselves, in time and mental or physical effort. In terms of the variables of this study, this economic view of motivation assumes that workers are motivated to maximize their pay while minimizing the cost of a psychologically demanding job. We would expect people so motivated to seek situations and to be satisfied with situations where pay is high and task complexity is low, and, conversely, to avoid and feel dissatisfied with situations where pay is low and task complexity is high.

To test this theory in concrete terms we chose to define favorable "economic exchange" as a job with Pay in the higher half of the range and an RTA score in the lowest third of our sample. We defined an unfavorable economic exchange as a job with Pay in the lower half of the range and an RTA score in the highest third. We stated two hypotheses in regard to these variables:

1. That City workers will seek favorable economic exchanges and avoid unfavorable economic exchanges, compared with Town workers.
2. That City workers finding favorable economic exchanges will report higher Job Satisfaction than those experiencing unfavorable economic exchanges and that this difference in Job Satisfaction would not hold for Town workers.

Exhibit 1 summarizes the findings on this test. The hypothesis is supported in both parts. A majority of the workers with high pay in the lowest Requisite Task tertile are City workers, and their mean Job Satisfaction score is 5.4 compared with 3.9 for the Town workers in the same situation. Most workers receiving an unfavorable economic exchange, on the other hand, are Town workers with a relatively high Job Satisfaction score (5.0) compared to the 4.4 of the City workers. Apparently, City workers not only have a significant tendency to seek favorable economic and avoid unfavorable economic exchanges, as opposed to Town workers, but we find here for the first time a way in which the pay of City workers has an accountable relationship to Job Satisfaction. It seems that it is not the absolute amount of pay which influences them, but its relation to the "investment" of coping with a complex task. In this sense, City

JOB SATISFACTION

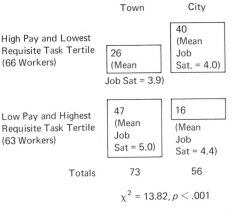

	Town	City
High Pay and Lowest Requisite Task Tertile (66 Workers)	26 (Mean Job Sat = 3.9)	40 (Mean Job Sat. = 4.0)
Low Pay and Highest Requisite Task Tertile (63 Workers)	47 (Mean Job Sat = 5.0)	16 (Mean Job Sat = 4.4)
Totals	73	56

$$\chi^2 = 13.82, p < .001$$

Exhibit 1. Test of Economic Motivation for Town and City Workers (129 Workers).

workers are responding in accordance with an economic exchange theory of motivation. Town workers are not.

The "test" we have just applied, however, is of a very narrow view of the exchange process; it sees it primarily in traditional economic terms. In recent years a number of sociologists have greatly expanded the number of commodities relevant to the exchange process beyond the traditional concern of economics with labor, time, money, and tangible goods. In exchange as a social process, other "goods" become equally relevant, such as respect, power, affection, responsibility, knowledge. The literature of this exchange theory has been contributed by writers such as Homans, Blau, Gouldner, and Zaleznik, and has introduced such concepts as "distributive justice."[9]

Under this expanded way of thinking about exchange, the response of Town workers can be explained as well as the City response, by supposing that for Town workers different commodities are relevant to the exchange process. What is a cost to the City worker (investment in a demanding task) may be for the Town worker an important reward (op-

portunity to express needs for competence and achievement). And what may be a reward for a City worker (for example, the "traction" of a low variety, low required interaction job) can be a cost for a Town worker (monotony).

Conclusion

We have examined two general ways of theorizing about human motivation to see how they were relevant to the Town-City difference in response which was the most intriguing emergent finding of this study. Some theories emphasize the purposive, *striving* aspects of personality and seem at first to point toward useful explanations of Town but not of City workers. Other theories emphasize the *exchange* aspects of behavior and seem at first to explain the City but not the Town response. However, we have also seen that in reality both Town and City behavior can be discussed under either group of theories. Whichever vocabulary for discussing the response is used, the important question is basically the same: what underlying needs motivate the striving, what kinds of commodities are seen as relevant to the exchange, and how are they valued?

The discussion, whichever type of motivation theory is used, serves the more to emphasize that the difference in response comes about because the two subpopulations in our sample represent two different systems of beliefs and values that affect how work experience is perceived and what aspects of it are felt to be rewarding. These different attitude sets came to light in our study, we must emphasize, not as individual (F-scale or surname) factors but as social system variables, in the sense that they were associated with the dominant ethnicity and size of the community within which each plant was found.

This fact tends toward an explanation of the difference in terms of culturally determined patterns of religious beliefs. Lenski's (1961) research[10] amply indicates the extent to which religion influences attitudes toward many aspects of experience. Furthermore, his finding that favorable job attitudes were more frequent among lower class Catholics than among lower class Protestants strengthens the plausibility of explaining the Town-City difference primarily in terms of religious belief. It is undoubtedly true that to a large extent the dominant religion in a particular group does strongly influence the values of individuals at a quite basic level, and thereby influences what they perceive as relevant and rewarding in their work experience. Not only Weber's (1958) theory but also McClelland's (1961) cross-cultural research indicates that task accomplishment at work *is* often (*not* invariably) perceived by the individual as more important to him (i.e., more central to his concept of himself) in predominantly Protestant than in predominantly Catholic cultures.

We should emphasize that the relationship between religious background and attitude toward work is complex. It is not simply an outcome of religious belief in the narrow sense; rather it is presumably part of a whole culturally determined way of thinking that leads to higher value being placed in a given group on certain activities than on others. Weber himself in a paper on "The Protestant Sects (in the United States) and the Spirit of Capitalism," apparently seeking to correct a mistaken interpretation of his earlier essay on the Protestant ethic, emphasized that the influence of religion on work attitudes was not through religious doctrine, as such, but through a religious tendency to place "premiums" on certain kinds of activity, leading to a characteristic "ethos" in a particular society.[11]

In other words, according to Weber's theory, the role of Protestantism in influencing work attitudes was that the religion taught a value system which created conditions favorable to the growth of capitalistic enterprise. It is important to remember, however, that basically Weber's theory is concerned with middle-class values toward thrift and investment. Although he did refer to Protestantism's influence on a ready supply of "solemn, conscientious and unusually industrious workmen,"[12] his main focus is on the role of the Protestant bourgeois businessman, as far as his thesis on the rise of capitalism is concerned.

Moreover, in our sample the difference we are considering was *not* based simply on religion. We have been talking about a Town-City, not a Protestant-Catholic, difference for a very good reason. Although it happened that none of our City settings was predominantly Protestant, we did have predominantly Catholic workers in Town settings, and *their* response was a Town, not a "City," response. Ethnic-religious background did not by itself predict the direction of the response to the task. It was important for another reason: in the groups with "mixed" ethnic-religious background, no clear-cut response in either direction was found (and in these groups, as for the total population, religion did not predict response on an individual basis). In other words, ethnic-religious homogeneity, whether "Protestant" or "Catholic," was prerequisite for any clear response to the task in terms of job satisfaction. Given such cultural homogeneity, the direction of the response was determined by whether the plant environment was rural or urban.

Why should a rural or small town environment be associated with a more favorable response to task complexity than an urban or large city environment? Again the relevant question is why in City settings there should be a different set of expectations concerning the rewards attainable from the job. One theoretical approach to this problem is by means of Durkheim's concept of the "anomie" associated with urban life.[13] Under conditions which are more likely to be found in urban than in rural settings, the division of labor, argues Durkheim, becomes associated with a sense of impersonality and alienation from others and from any larger purpose in the task.[14] If this were true, one would expect to find a greater tendency among City workers to avoid the kind of personal involvement with the job which would be necessary in order to experience satisfaction on more demanding tasks. In developing Durkheim's ideas about "Social Structure and Anomie," Merton stresses the importance of levels of aspiration relative to perceived means for reaching them.[15] Under conditions of anomie, Merton argues, people perceive no institutionalized means for achieving the goals which the culture defines as desirable. This suggests that in order to understand the City workers' response we should attempt to measure their level of aspiration, and then estimate the possibility of achieving culturally derived goals within their work experience. The theory would predict that in urban settings the job would be less frequently perceived as a relevant means for achieving the important goals.

Unfortunately our data do not provide a test for the usefulness of this theory in explaining the City workers' response. In fact we discovered no significant tendency for City workers to report less opportunity to advance at work than Town workers. However, this does not deny the general relevance of *anomie* as at least a partial explanation, since we did not attempt to measure levels of aspiration, nor did we discover whether "advancement" on the job has a different meaning for City than for Town workers. This approach should be followed in future research on this subject.

In order to pursue further the Town-City difference in response, motivational predispositions need to be measured adequately and at a more basic level than we were able to in the present study. Specifically, McClelland's methodology for investigating underlying needs for achievement (and other needs) is perhaps the most relevant in this connection. We have repeatedly been forced to the conclusion that in a somewhat crude way the Town-City dichotomy we discovered in the course of analyzing our data points to some important and relatively deep-seated differences in the perceived salience of task attributes. It seems as if these differences can best be explained by supposing that our City subcultures produce and reinforce an attitude of relative noninvolvement with the job, in which work is not perceived as a relevant means for attaining goals that are central to the individual's way of thinking about himself.

The question of the durability of these attitudes, whether and by what means they might be changed, along with some further suggestions for additional research on this topic, will be considered in the next and final chapter.

NOTES

1. Morse (1953), p. 23. See especially the discussion of this point by Homans (1961), pp. 265–282.
2. White (1959). A useful discussion of motivational theories of White and others is provided by Gellerman (1963).
3. Combs and Snygg (1959), p. 54.
4. Allport (1960), p. 51. See also Allport (1955) and (1961), pp. 212–257.
5. McGregor (1960).
6. Clark (1962). See also Clark (1960–1961).
7. McClelland and others (1953), and McClelland (1961).
8. Rosen (1959).
9. See, for example, Gouldner (1960), Homans (1961), Zaleznik, Christensen, and Roethlisberger (1958), Blau (1955), Blau and Scott (1962).
10. Lenski (1961), Table 10, p. 87.
11. Gerth and Mills (1958), pp. 302–322.
12. Weber (1958), p. 177.
13. Durkheim (1951).
14. Durkheim (1947).
15. Merton (1957), pp. 131–194.

REFERENCES

Morse, Nancy. *Satisfactions in the White-Collar Job.* Ann Arbor: University of Michigan, 1953; Homans, G. C. *Social Behavior: Its Elementary Forms.* New York: Harcourt, Brace, 1961.

White, R. W. "Motivation Reconsidered: The Concept of Competence," *Psychological Review,* Vol. 66, No. 5, September, 1959, pp. 297–333; Gellerman, S. W. *Motivation and Productivity.* New York: American Management Association, 1963.

Combs, A. W., and Donald Snygg. *Individual Behavior. A Perceptual Approach to Behavior.* New York: Harper, 1959.

Allport, G. W. *Becoming. Basic Considerations for a Psychology of Personality.* New Haven: Yale University Press, 1955; "The Open System in Personality Theory," *Personality and Social Encounter.* Boston: Beacon Press, 1960, pp. 39–54; *Pattern and Growth in Personality.* New York: Holt, Rinehart, & Winston, 1961.

McGregor, Douglas. *The Human Side of Enterprise.* New York: McGraw-Hill, 1960.

Clark, J. V. "A Healthy Organization," *California Management Review,* Vol. 4, No. 4, Summer 1962, pp. 16–30; "Motivation in Work Groups: A Tentative View," *Human Organization,* Vol. 19, No. 4, Winter 1960–1961, pp. 199–208.

McClelland, D. C., and others. *The Achievement Motive.* New York: Appleton-Century-Crofts, 1953. McClelland, D. C. *The Achieving Society.* New York: Van Nostrand, 1961.

Rosen, B. C. "Race, Ethnicity, and the Achievement Syndrome," *American Sociological Review,* Vol. 24, No. 1, February 1959, pp. 47–61.

Gouldner, A. W. "The Norm of Reciprocity: A Preliminary Statement," *American Sociological Review,* Vol. 25, No. 2, April 1960, pp. 161–178; Homans, G. C. *Social Behavior: Its Elementary Forms.* New York: Harcourt, Brace, 1961; Zaleznik, A., C. R. Christensen, and F. J. Roethlisberger. *The Motivation, Productivity, and Satisfaction of*

Workers: A Prediction Study. Boston: Division of Research, Harvard Business School, 1958; Blau, P. M. *The Dynamics of Bureaucracy*. Chicago: University of Chicago Press, 1955; Blau, P. M., and W. R. Scott. *Formal Organizations*. San Francisco: Chandler, 1962.

The identification of Protestantism with greater commitment to a work-oriented value system has been a well-known idea at least since the work of Weber (1958, originally published in 1904) and Tawney (1937). This notion implies that attitudes toward work and values in relation to it are essentially culturally determined, as Hearnshaw (1954) argued in an interesting cross-cultural survey of the problem. This area has recently become accessible to systematic research, thanks to McClelland's (1961) notable cross-cultural investigations of "achievement motivation." In a recent article Rosen (1959), making use of McClelland's methodology, has investigated similar differences identified with discrete ethnic-religious subcultures; we make use of Rosen's study in Chapter 5. Lenski's (1961) detailed study of the relationship between religious background and attitudes toward political and economic issues is equally relevant. Most interesting for our purposes is Lenski's finding (in a 1958 survey in the Detroit metropolitan area) that positive attitudes toward work are more frequent among upper-middle-class white Protestants and lower-working-class white Catholics, whereas negative attitudes toward work are more frequent among lower-working-class white Protestants and middle-class white Catholics (Lenski (1961), Table 10, p. 87). With the exception of Rosen's and Lenski's contributions, there has apparently been little systematic research on the effect of subcultural identifications on response to work, although a number of case studies have pointed in this direction. More specifically, our own attention to the difference that ethnic-religious and urban or rural background might make was suggested by several studies involving very small numbers of workers, such as the "prediction study" of our colleagues, Zaleznik, Christensen, and Roethlisberger (1958), the article by Whyte (1944) on attitudes toward unionism, and the characterization by Dalton (1948) of the nine outstanding "rate busters" in a department of 300. (See also Dalton, 1947, and Faunce, 1960.)

Weber, Max. *The Protestant Ethic and the Spirit of Capitalism*. Tr. by Talcott Parsons. New York: Scribner, 1958; Tawney, R. H. *Religion and the Rise of Capitalism*. New York: Harcourt, Brace, 1937; Hearnshaw, L. S. "Attitudes to Work," *Occupational Psychology*, Vol. 28, No. 3, July, 1954, pp. 129–139; McClelland, D. C. *The Achieving Society*. New York: Van Nostrand, 1961; Rosen, B. C. "Race, Ethnicity, and the Achievement Syndrome," *American Sociological Review*, Vol. 24, No. 1, February 1959, pp. 47–61; Lenski, Gerhard. *The Religious Factor: A Sociological Study of Religion's Impact on Politics, Economics, and Family Life*. Garden City, N.Y.: Doubleday, 1961; Zaleznik, A., C. R. Christensen, and F. J. Roethlisberger. *The Motivation, Productivity, and Satisfaction of Workers: A Prediction Study*. Boston: Division of Research, Harvard Business School, 1958; Whyte, W. F. "Who Goes Union and Why," *Personnel Journal*, Vol. 23, No. 6, December 1944, pp. 215–230, also Chapter 15 of *Men at Work*, pp. 268–279; Dalton, Melville. "The Industrial Rate Buster: A Characterization," *Applied Anthropology*, Vol. 7, No. 1, Winter 1948, pp. 5–18, also "Worker Response and Social Background," *Journal of Political Economy*, Vol. 55, No. 4, August 1947, pp. 323–332; Faunce, W. A. "Social Stratification and Attitude Toward Change in Job Content," *Social Forces*, Vol. 39, December 1960, pp. 140–148.

Gerth, H. H. and C. W. Mills (editors). *From Max Weber. Essays in Sociology*. New York: Oxford University Press, 1946. (A Galaxy Book, 1958.)

Weber, Max. *The Protestant Ethic and the Spirit of Capitalism*. Talcott Parsons, trans. New York: Scribner, 1958.

Durkheim, Emile. *Suicide: A Study in Sociology*. J. A. Spalding and G. Simpson, trans. Edited by and Introduction by G. Simpson. Glencoe, Ill.: Free Press, 1951.

Durkheim, Emile. *The Division of Labor in Society*. G. Simpson, trans. Glencoe, Illinois: Free Press, 1947.

Merton, R. K. *Social Theory and Social Structure*. Rev. ed. Glencoe, Illinois: Free Press, 1957.

THE TOWN-CITY DIFFERENCE

LATENT CULTURE
A Note on the Theory of Latent Social Roles

Howard S. Becker and Blanche Geer

Administrators have always known that workers' behavior is affected by what they are and who they are away from the job. But we have had few conceptual tools for analyzing this relation. In this paper we discuss the conditions under which the cultures men participate in elsewhere may furnish the substance of the culture of the work group.

Gouldner's paper on latent social roles[1] makes a distinction that is both long-needed and provocative. He distinguishes those social roles related to identities which the group agrees are relevant to a particular social setting from those related to identities conventionally defined as "being irrelevant, inappropriate to consider, or illegitimate to take into account" in the same context. The latter he terms *latent*, as distinguished from *manifest*, roles and identities. His research indicates that latent roles can be empirically distinguished and that they have important consequences for the behavior of people in organizations.

The importance of this conceptual advance leads us to raise the question of whether there may not be a useful distinction between characteristics of *organizations* that parallels Gouldner's distinction between roles of individuals. The role concept implies an organizational setting but does not itself describe it. Are there not distinct group characteristics which result from the operation of forces related to latent social identities on the one hand and manifest identities on the other?

Two concepts frequently used to describe organizations are *structure* and *culture*. The structure of an organization is an orderly arrangement of social relations, a continuing arrangement of kinds of people (named and defined), governed by a concept of proper behavior for them in their relations with one another. The culture of an organization consists of the conventional understandings shared by the participants in it.[2] Gouldner's analysis suggests that we might well look for manifest and latent structures and cultures that would correspond to the manifest and latent roles he has described.

The distinction between "formal" and "informal" organization closely parallels, for structures, Gouldner's distinction between kinds of roles. We would like to suggest a similar distinction for the concept of culture and examine some of its implications. Classically, culture is conceived as arising in response to some problem faced by a group.[3] The problem is one that individual members of the group see as common to all members; it is a shared problem. In some way, a way of meeting the problem is arrived at, a mode of action that is agreed to be the best or most proper solution. The solution leads to, or implies, more general views and assump-

"Latent Culture: A Note on the Theory of Latent Social Roles" (Research Notes and Comments), *Administrative Science Quarterly*, 5, 2 (September 1960). 304–313. Reprinted with the permission of the authors and of the publisher, the *Administrative Science Quarterly*.

tions—the perspectives and values underlying the culture, its "world view." The organized whole of such problem solutions is the culture of the group.

People carry culture with them; when they leave one group setting for another they do not shed the cultural premises of the first setting. This phenomenon is in part what Gouldner describes in discussing latent roles and identities. Something is true of a person by virtue of the fact that he has some other social identity, which draws its being from some other social group. Among the things true by virtue of this fact is that he holds some ideas that are part of the culture of that group. In short, the members of a group may derive their understandings from cultures other than that of the group they are at the moment participating in. To the degree that group participants share latent social identities (related to their membership in the same "outside" social groups) they will share these understandings, so that there will be a culture which can be called *latent*, i.e., the culture has its origin and social support in a group other than the one in which the members are now participating.

These latent identities are not necessarily based on prior group membership, for Gouldner's example of "cosmopolitan" and "local" identities makes clear that such identities may arise out of the internal "politics" of organizations (although his distinction seems to imply membership in outside professional groups as one of the loci of "cosmopolitanism"). It seems likely that they will usually be related to what are called "background variables" (social class, or ethnic origin, for example), but, whether they are or not, what is important is that latent identities will not affect either individual behavior within the group or the collective behavior of the group unless they are in some way mobilized and brought into play in the daily interaction of group members.

In other words, these latent identities must be taken account of; people must orient their behavior toward latent as well as manifest identities if understandings that are part of latent culture are to have any influence on behavior in the group. The fact of being an "old-timer" in the organization or of being a member of some particular ethnic group will not affect behavior unless these distinctions are made use of in daily interaction in groups that support and maintain the culture associated with these irrelevant identities. Latent culture is thus only *potential*; it needs to be developed in the new setting, in the sense that it has to be brought into play and applied to the new problems arising for group members. It does not influence group behavior simply by virtue of members having similar latent identities.

This culture stemming from latent identities can be contrasted with the culture peculiar to the group setting, the culture that has arisen in response to the problems its members share. This culture is not, in the pure case, affected by other (latent) identities of those participating in it. To the degree that group members face similar problems and contingencies, this culture is operative. It can be called the *manifest* culture. It need not be approved or formally specified by institutional rules and may even support deviation from those rules. But it is a culture that grows around the roles and identities relevant to the specific setting rather than those that are irrelevant or inappropriate.

An example from our current study of a medical school will clarify the distinction.[4] Medical students are alike in that they are all training to become physicians, but they differ in many other ways. In our study many of the students were from small towns and rural areas in Kansas, while others came from larger towns and cities in Kansas, Missouri, and elsewhere. Although these (latent) identities seldom became the basis of stable social groupings, they frequently underlay casual groupings arising in conversations about the best place to practice and the best style of practice (general practice or specialty). The student's latent culture associated with the size of his home town influenced his opinion in such conversations. (Several latent cultures of this kind operated among the students, particularly the latent culture associated with social class identities, which we discuss later.) But the students of this school shared another culture, which we have referred to as "student culture."[5] This culture grows around those problems shared by all students in the school, problems related to their manifest identities as students: the immediate necessity of mastering a vast amount of factual material, the more distant threat of failing, the difficulties of dealing with details of work in the hospital, and the peculiarities of certain teachers and departments. A set of perspectives on these problems and specific solutions for them constituted a manifest culture, dealing with different problems in different ways, quite distinct from any latent cultures we discovered.

One point needs clarification here. The use of the terms "manifest" and "latent" connotes nothing about whether the cultural items operate with or against the openly expressed aims of the organization. It might be thought that manifest culture, for instance, would not operate at cross-purposes with stated organizational aims, but it well may. In medical school, the student culture has as one of its functions the support of organized deviance from the goals of the administration and faculty.[6] Yet we refer to this as manifest culture because it is tied to the students' identities as students and grows up around problems of the students' identity. Similarly, latent culture may support stated organizational aims.

We now consider some of the concomitants of this distinction between latent and manifest culture and suggest some propositions about them.

The strength and unity of a group's latent culture will, of course, depend on the character of the recruitment to the group. If recruitment is restricted to persons coming from a similar cultural background, latent culture will be strong and consistent; there will be no variant subcultural groups within the larger group and everyone will share the premises of the culture associated with the common latent identities. To the degree that group members have different latent identities, a latent culture will not be possible. Thus, one of the conditions for the existence of latent culture is some degree of exclusiveness or restriction of recruitment. Latent cultures are not likely to develop where recruitment to the group is indiscriminate in that latent identities of recruits are diverse (in the pure case, where no two group members share any latent identity). They are likely to develop where recruitment is selective (in the pure case, where every member shared some particular latent identity).

This suggests the proposition that the independence of the manifest from the latent culture will vary with the diverseness of latent identities in the group. Manifest culture—the organized solutions to common problems of an immediate kind—may be dictated by latent culture when latent social identities are similar and the immediate problem is conceptualized by the group in terms that are restricted by their common culture associated with these identities. For instance, an occupational group drawn largely from one social class will have its occupational culture dictated by social class premises more than one which draws from all levels of the class system. One might expect the occupational culture of bankers to reflect upper-middle or upper-class culture and that of steel workers to reflect lower or lower-middle-class culture, while that of jazz musicians, who are recruited from all class levels, would not reflect the culture of any particular stratum. The latent culture would restrict solutions to immediate occupational problems within the framework of the given class culture; other solutions would not occur to members of the occupation or would be rejected as illegitimate or improper. Both bankers and musicians, let us say, may find their clients or customers difficult.[7] The musicians' solution to this problem—open hostility—might not be available to bankers because of the restrictions on such behavior in their social class culture.

But if latent culture can restrict the possibilities for the proliferation of the manifest culture, the opposite is also true. Manifest culture can restrict the operation of latent culture. The problems facing group members may be so pressing that, given the social context in which the group operates, the range of solutions that will be effective may be so limited as not to allow for influence of variations resulting from cultures associated with other identities. That is, solutions suggested by latent culture could be utilized only at the expense of breaking some very important group rule or threatening the unity and continued existence of the group.

The corollary of this proposition is that latent culture operates most in social contexts and with regard to problems that are not defined as critical for the group. The problems left to latent culture may not be of great moment, i.e., they may be considered trivial and not worthy of collective attention. Or they may be considered serious, but serious for the individual rather than the group. In either event, solutions can be derived from the culture associated with latent identities. For instance, medical students have difficulty carrying on their necessary interaction with patients; they do not at first know how to talk to them so as to make sociable intercourse easy. But this problem is not regarded as a serious one; it is not expected to lead to drastic consequences either for the individual student or for the students collectively. The student may be embarrassed by the faulty interaction, but he will not fail his course and his professional future will not be affected; nor will his failure affect the other students with whom he works. The solution is consequently left to the individual and appears to be derived from two sources: (1) from observation of practicing physicians, and (2) from past experiences in dealing with persons of various social types. Thus the upper-middle-class student, who has had more experience in dealing with persons of his own social class and with those of lower social classes, experiences less difficulty than the lower-middle-class student whose social awareness is more limited.

If problems have potential consequences for the group, however, they are not influenced by latent culture, although they might be thought equally the concern of the individual rather than the entire student group. Thus the problem of how to deal with oral quizzing by faculty members is settled by each student for himself, as he works out methods of making a good impression and avoiding censure; but these individual solutions are guided by understanding reached by the students about the kinds of solution to this problem which will not jeopardize the fate of other students. It is not solved by application of culture gained in interaction in other roles.

Problems that are serious, but affect only the individual, are more likely to be solved individually—the solutions stemming from a latent culture where this is operative. Thus a medical student has the problem of supporting himself. All students recognize this as a serious problem, but it is not one they face collectively. The problem presents a different set of contingencies and possible solutions to each student, at least theoretically. Social class subgroups among students may have some latent cultural agreements as to proper solutions to this problem, but it is not a problem that has any status in student (manifest) culture. It is left to individual solution, and thus potentially to solutions from latent culture.

We do not want to imply that behavior based on latent culture is individual behavior, as the above examples seem to suggest. It is still culturally influenced in the sense that the person is constrained in formulating his action by the premises of some subculture. But the actions we speak of as being based on latent culture will appear on the surface to be individual and not be constrained by such influences. This is so because latent culture, relating as it does to identities considered irrelevant and inappropriate in the setting, appears in the form of attitudes and cultural premises that are often unstated and undiscussed. These attitudes have not been consciously worked out in their relevance to the immediate situation through group discussion and interaction. Instead, they were formed in other settings and in this setting are taken for granted, although they may be shared and supported by other group members of similar latent identity.

So far we have considered only the case in which the participants either share a latent identity or do not. A further complication may be introduced by considering the possibility of several kinds of latent identities within a group, each person having one from among these kinds, so that there are several possible latent cultures and each person a potential participant in one of them. An example might be latent ethnic identities in a business organization; there might be people of several ethnic backgrounds in the organization, and each ethnic type would be a possible basis for the operation of a latent culture, but each person would be able to participate in only one of these.

In considering the consequences of such a situation, we need to repeat a point made earlier, namely, that latent identities and latent cultures associated with them are likely to furnish the bases for the formation of latent social structures. What are more usually known as "informal" groupings may tend to cluster around a latent culture, the members of these groupings sharing some particular latent identity. The interaction in such groups helps to maintain the person's sense of his latent identity and to maintain the latent culture by providing a group which gives social support for the use of that culture as a basis for behavior. This is important because it suggests the mechanism by which these latent identities are maintained operable in an environment in which they are regarded as irrelevant or improper, and in which they might be expected to die out.

In the situation in which several kinds of mutually exclusive latent identities are present, there may also be several latent structures (informal groups) present as well. We can now ask under what circumstances the latent culture of one of these groups might affect manifest culture by providing the solution to a problem in the immediate setting, which the whole group eventually adopts. One possibility is that groups with greater prestige or power will be more able to mold manifest culture in this way. It may be, however, that differentials in prestige or power between subgroups are not great enough for one of them to rule in this way, in which case we would expect the eventual solution to be arrived at by some process of compromise. This, of course, would only occur where the problem under consideration was not serious enough for the entire group that the solution would be dictated by the immediate setting (manifest culture) and not be subject to influence from the latent culture of any group.

In addition to the situation where there are many subgroups present, there may be only one subgroup that shares a common latent identity and culture while the remainder of the larger group is relatively diverse, not having such common identities and culture. The members of such a group will be more able to influence manifest culture than their unorganized counterparts: communication between them will proceed more easily because of culturally shared premises; they will have operating agreements almost before others are aware that there is any problem calling for solution; and so on. This suggests the more general proposition that the development of latent culture will depend on the relative strength of organization of people of differing latent identity. One subgroup may have such strength and others not.

It appears that this process operated with respect to certain problems of the medical students who had several kinds of (latent) social class identities. Some were upper middle class while the others came from lower strata. When the freshman class faced the problem of what facts and theories they should attempt to learn out of the bewildering variety they were faced with, the eventual solution—learning what the faculty wanted as evidenced by examinations and quizzes—was one which bore the mark of the (latent) social class culture of the upper-middle-class students. These students were members of medical school fraternities and thus more highly organized than the other members of the class who did not belong to fraternities. (Formal organization, as in a fraternity, should not be taken as an infallible index of the existence of latent culture, for such an organization may in fact recruit haphazardly and end with a membership with diverse latent identities, thus weakening its organization. One of the three medical fraternities in the school we studied had these characteristics. Furthermore, when people sort themselves out into groups in this way, as the students did when they joined fraternities, many "mistakes" may be made so that people gain membership in the formal organizations without sharing the latent culture.)

Such situations warn us to keep other variables in mind. For instance, two groups defined by common latent identities may be present, yet the cultural background of one is such as to make it less likely that its members will combine effectively. It may be that upper-middle-class culture provides more experience in "combining" of this sort so that where this group participates in an organization with members of a lower social class the situation would resemble that in which one group participates with a diverse aggregate. Also, even where the background culture did not provide this dividend of combining power, it might be that persons with certain kinds of latent social identities and cultures are more visible to one another than other persons sharing a different latent identity, thus making it easier for them to combine (as, for example, Jews as contrasted with Protestants, drug addicts in many settings, homosexuals, and so on).

Where there are two groups distinguished by common latent identities and a third which is an aggregate of diverse identities, the group with less power to maintain exclusiveness may find itself further weakened by the fact that it becomes, in effect, a residual group: everyone who does not belong to the more exclusive groups finds his place in the less exclusive group, which then has even less strength to achieve latent cultural consensus and so to make its contribution to the manifest culture.

In cases where one group's latent culture furnishes the material for the manifest culture, the process can be aided or hindered depending on whether this group more nearly fits the general public's cultural image of what members of the organization or group should be like.

Everett Hughes has noted that auxiliary status traits are attached in the public mind to many statuses and that status contradictions can arise when a person possesses the key or master status trait but is deficient in the auxiliary status traits.[8] Thus all one needs to be a doctor is a license, yet it is typically assumed that an M.D. will be male, white, and upper middle class. A group which most nearly fits the auxiliary status specifications attached to the manifest identity (has the proper associated latent identities) may be seen as having more authoritative information or more legitimate right to suggest solutions for the manifest culture. (This process operates among medical students, where the upper-middle-class students have more influence by virtue of this; likewise among drug addicts, where those who most nearly fit the public stereotype of the depraved "dope fiend" are commonly viewed as having the "real lowdown" by other addicts.)

Although we have clearly done no more here than suggest many questions to be explored more fully, we have used some of these propositions in our work on medical students and hope that others may find these ideas suggestive enough to merit consideration in their own research.

NOTES

1. Alvin W. Gouldner, Cosmopolitans and Locals: Toward an Analysis of Latent Social Roles—I, *Administrative Science Quarterly*, 2 (1957), 281–306.
2. Cf. Robert Redfield, *The Folk Culture of Yucatan* (Chicago, 1941), p. 132: "In speaking of 'culture' we have reference to the conventional understandings, manifest in act and artifact, that characterize societies. The 'understandings' are the meanings attached to acts and objects. The meanings are conventional, and therefore cultural, in so far as they have become typical for the members of that society by reason of intercommunication among the members. A culture is, then, an abstraction: it is the type toward which the meanings that the same act or object has for the different members tend to conform. The meanings are expressed in action and the results of action, from which we infer them; so we may as well identify culture with the extent to which the conventionalized behavior of members of the society is for all the same."

3. See W. G. Sumner, *Folkways* (Boston, 1907), §1–3.

4. This research, a sociological study of some problems of medical education, is sponsored by Community Studies, Inc., of Kansas City, Missouri, and is being carried out at the University of Kansas Medical School, to whose dean, staff, and students we are indebted for their co-operation. Professor Everett C. Hughes of the University of Chicago is director of the project. Some portions of the study are reported in Howard S. Becker and Blanche Geer, The Fate of Idealism in Medical School, *American Sociological Review,* 23 (1958), 50–56; and Student Culture in Medical School, *Harvard Educational Review,* 28 (Winter 1958), 70–80. A monograph reporting the entire study is in preparation.

5. *Ibid.*

6. *Ibid.*

7. On the jazz musician, see Howard S. Becker, The Professional Dance Musician and His Audience, *American Journal of Sociology,* 62 (1951), 136–144.

8. Everett C. Hughes, Dilemmas and Contradictions of Status, *American Journal of Sociology,* 50 (1945), 353–359.

ADDITIONAL READINGS

Baker, Frank, et al. 1969. "The Changing Mental Hospital—Its Perceived Image and Contact with the Community," *Mental Hygiene,* 53 (April), 237–244.

Behrend, H. 1953. "Absence and Labour Turnover in a Changing Economic Climate," *Occupational Psychology,* 27 (April), 67–79.

Bennis, W. G., et al. 1958. "Reference Groups and Loyalties in the Out-Patient Department," *Administrative Science Quarterly,* 2 (March), 481–500.

Clark, Burton R. 1960. *The Open Door College.* New York: McGraw-Hill.

Collins, Orvis. 1946. "Ethnic Behavior In Industry: Sponsorship And Rejection In a New England Factory," *American Journal of Sociology,* 51 (January), 293–298.

Duncan, Otis D., and Leo F. Schnore. 1959. "Cultural, Behavioral, And Ecological Perspectives in the Study Of Social Organization," *The American Journal of Sociology,* 65 (September), 132–146.

Dyer, William G. 1956. "The Interlocking Of Work And Family Social Systems Among Lower Occupational Families," *Social Forces,* 34 (March), 230–233.

Eisenstadt, S. N. 1959. "Bureaucracy, Bureaucratization, and Debureaucratization," *Administrative Science Quarterly,* 4 (December), 302–320.

Elling, Ray H., and Sandor Halebsky. 1961. "Organizational Differentiation and Support: A Conceptual Framework," *Administrative Science Quarterly,* 6 (September), 185–209.

Etzioni, Amitai. 1960. "Interpersonal and Structural Factors in the Study of Mental Hospitals," *Psychiatry,* 23 (February), 13–22.

Etzioni, Amitai, and William R. Taber. 1963. "Scope, Pervasiveness, and Tension Management in Complex Organizations," *Social Research,* 30 (Summer), 220–238.

Form, William H., and James A. Geschwender. 1962. "Social Reference Basis of Job Satisfaction: The Case of Manual Workers," *American Sociological Review,* 27 (April), 228–237.

Goldthorpe, John H. 1966. "Attitudes and Behaviour of Car Assembly Workers: A Deviant Case and a Theoretical Critique." *British Journal of Sociology,* 17, 227–244.

Golembiewski, Robert T. 1965. *Men, Management, and Morality.* New York: McGraw-Hill.

Gouldner, Alvin W. 1957. "Cosmopolitans and Locals: Toward an Analysis of Latent Social Roles—I," *Administrative Science Quarterly,* 2 (December), 281–306.

Gouldner, Alvin W. 1958. "Cosmopolitans and Locals: Toward an Analysis of Latent Social Roles—II," *Administrative Science Quarterly,* 2 (March), 444–480.

Greenblatt, M., and T. Lidz. 1957. "Some Dimensions of the Problems," in *The Patient and the Mental Hospital.* M. Greenblatt, D. J. Levinson, and R. H. Williams, eds. Glencoe, Ill.: Free Press.

Gross, Neal. 1959. "Some Contributions of Sociology to the Field of Education," *Harvard Educational Review,* 29 (Fall), 275–287.

Grosser, George H. 1960. "External Setting and Internal Relations of the Prison." In *Theoretical Studies in Social Organization of the Prison,* Richard A. Cloward et al. New York: Social Science Research Council.

Hanson, Robert C. 1962. "The Systemic Linkage Hypothesis And Role Consensus Patterns In Hospital-Community Relations." *American Sociological Review,* 27 (June), 304–313.

Hulin, Charles L. 1969. "Sources Of Variation In Job And Life Satisfactions: The Role Of Community And Job-Related Variables." *Journal of Applied Psychology,* 35 (August), 279–291.

Hulin, Charles L., and M. R. Blood. 1968. "Job Enlargement, Individual Differences, And Worker Responses," *Psychological Bulletin,* 69 (January), 41–55.

Katz, Fred E. 1965. "Explaining Informal Work Groups in Complex Organizations: The Case for Autonomy in Structure," *Administrative Science Quarterly,* 10 (September), 204–223.

COMMUNITY AND CULTURE

Kerr, Clark, and Abraham Siegel. 1954. "The Interindustry Propensity to Strike—An International Comparison," in *Industrial Conflict*, Arthur W. Kornhauser, Robert Dubin, and Arthur M. Ross, eds. New York: McGraw-Hill.

Kimmelman, Barry. 1969. "Executives' Wives—The Need for a Positive, Company Sponsored Approach," *California Management Review*, 11 (Spring), 7–10.

Lidz, T., G. Hotchkiss, and M. Greenblatt. 1957. "Patient-Family-Hospital Interrelationships: Some General Considerations." In *The Patient and the Mental Hospital*, by M. Greenblatt, D. J. Levinson, and R. H. Williams, eds. Glencoe, Ill.: Free Press.

Long, Norton E. 1962. "The Corporation and the Local Community," *The Annals of the American Academy of Political and Social Science*, 343 (September), 118–127.

Mack, Raymond W. 1954. "Ecological Patterns in an Industrial Shop," *Social Forces*, 32 (May), 351–356.

Maniha, John, and Charles Perrow. 1965. "The Reluctant Organization and the Aggressive Environment," *Administrative Science Quarterly*, 10 (September), 238–257.

Messinger, Sheldon L. 1955. "Organizational Transformation: A Case Study of a Declining Social Movement," *American Sociological Review*, 20 (February), 3–10.

Paine, Frank T., et al. 1967. "Relationship Between Family Backgrounds and Work Values," *Journal of Applied Psychology*, 51 (August), 320–323.

Peters, Lynn H. 1968. *Management and Society*. Belmont, Calif.: Dickenson.

Photiadis, John D. 1967. "Community Size And Aspects of the Authoritarian Personality Among Businessmen," *Rural Sociology*, 32 (March), 70–77.

Photiadis, John D. 1967. "Social Integration of Businessmen in Varied Size Communities," *Social Forces*, 46 (December), 229–236.

Rapoport, Robert, and Rhona Rapoport. 1965. "Work and Family in Contemporary Society," *American Sociological Review*, 30 (June), 381–394.

Schiff, Ashley L. 1966. "Innovation and Administrative Decision Making: The Conservation of Land Resources," *Administrative Science Quarterly*, 11 (June), 1–30.

Sommer, Robert. 1958. "The Mental Hospital in the Small Community," *Mental Hygiene*, 42 (October), 489–496.

Warner, W. Lloyd, and J. O. Low. 1947. *The Social System of the Modern Factory*. New Haven: Yale University Press.

Zald, Mayer N. 1967. "Urban Differentiation, Characteristics Of Boards Of Directors, and Organizational Effectiveness," *The American Journal of Sociology*, 73 (November), 261–272.

Zald, Mayer, and Patricia Denton. 1963. "From Evangelism to General Service: The Transformation of the YMCA," *Administrative Science Quarterly*, 8 (September), 214–234.

ADDITIONAL READINGS

CHAPTER SIX

Competition, Cooperation, and Crisis

What are the effects of interorganizational competition and cooperation, or a crisis facing a given organization, on internal organizational structure and functioning? This chapter attempts to develop preliminary answers to this question.

Lekachman proposes that business managers in oligopolized industries, in order to gain "peace of mind," have responded to their power and size, and the legal constraints thereon, by engaging in price leadership, advertising, and product differentiation through styling and packaging. He views the organization's role-set as sensitizing corporate managers to the limitations of their power and explains the electrical industry conspiracy as managers' carrying "an existing tendency to a logical and illegal extreme."

In a comparative study of two university research groups, Bennis' thesis is that differences in market-structure forces for the two groups caused one to be market-oriented and the other to be task-oriented. He concludes that science organizations require some degree of buffering from competitive and market pressures to avoid the lowering of professional standards. This paper should generate some practical ideas for administrators about budgeting for science organizations as well as for science departments within organizations.

Aiken and Hage are interested in the internal organizational consequences of organizational interdependence. The latter was measured by the number of joint-cooperative programs that a given organization maintained with other organizations. The authors view interdependence as the result of a trade-off between the need for organizational autonomy and the need for resources. In an empirical study of sixteen social welfare and health agencies, they found that organizations with many joint programs were more complex, more innovative, had more active internal channels of communication, and had slightly more decentralized decision-making structures than did those organizations with few joint programs. It may be well worth the time of administrators, regardless of organizational affiliation, to consider the effects on their organization of the joint-program phenomenon, as it is destined to become an increasingly common feature of an increasingly complex interorganizational environment.

In a stimulating paper, Litwak and Meyer discuss how bureaucratic organizations and external primary groups, which are characterized necessarily by antithetical atmospheres, can cooperate to solve mutual problems of social control and goal achievement. They propose eight mechanisms of cooperation, discuss the major principles of communication that govern mechanism selection, and derive specific predictions from their balance theory of coordination. They develop a typology of bureaucratic organizations that they relate to the mechanisms of coordination. Finally, they present hypotheses concerning balance achievement as a function of the relationship between type of primary group, type of bureaucratic structure, and type of coordination mechanism.

In the final paper, Hermann analyzes the dysfunctional intraorganizational processes that may result from a crisis in an organization's external environment. He develops a model that relates crisis to seven variables. Interaction among these variables results in a pattern of fourteen relationships, each of which he supports with illustrative empirical evidence.

Three papers in the additional readings section are called to the reader's attention. The Cyert and March paper provides an example of a fairly closed-system organizational model that needs to be "opened up." The authors hypothesize that six organizational characteristics, clustered around communication patterns and decision-making units, determine passive as opposed to leader price behavior vis-à-vis competitors in an oligopoly market. One can add to their excellent paper by speculating about the influence of the oligopoly's external environment on: the nature of a "given [my italics] communication chain"; "power differentials within the formal decision-making units"; "firm policy on organizational goals" [see also Thompson and McEwen's paper in Chapter 8]"; "sales-minded" members of a decision-making group; and the obtaining of information about competitors. In summary, analysis of the reaction to competitors using only those characteristics internal to the reacting organization ignores salient historical and current external factors that also influence reaction. The effective administrator must also recognize these factors and "manage" their influence.

Rose tests five hypotheses that compare voluntary associations facing competition or conflict in the same community with other associations that do not. He reports differences with regard to group goals, complexity of structure, frequency of meetings, flexibility in activities and techniques, and cohesiveness.

Gusfield's paper deals with the tactical reaction of the WCTU to a crisis in its external environment, that is, the repeal of the Eighteenth Amendment. In terms of the environment-organization relationship, tactical response was found to be polarized into "conviction-oriented" and "public-oriented" camps. Gusfield discusses, given the factionalism, the mechanisms whereby the "old guard" kept control of the organization for a generation. The value of this generation-gap analysis for any organization facing a changing environment is obvious.

BUSINESSMEN AND THEIR RIVALS

Robert Lekachman

A long time ago, Adam Smith remarked that "people of the same trade seldom meet together, even for merriment and diversion, but the conversation ends in a conspiracy against the public, or in some contrivance to raise prices." This passage in the *Wealth of Nations* is not an isolated one. Writing at the beginning of England's Industrial Revolution, Smith suspected the motives of the businessmen who were to be its agents and celebrated the virtues of the country gentlemen and farm laborers whose lives were to be disrupted.

Yet Smith did see how business activity might benefit the community. But it was a curiously indirect way, for it depended upon motives which had little or nothing to do with the pursuit of the general welfare. The "natural" harmony of interests among businessmen, farmers, and laborers could be attained if, and only if, commerce and manufacture were truly competitive. True competition compelled the inefficient either to match the methods of the efficient or suffer the salutary pain of bankruptcy. Competition was the shield of the consumer. If a seller sold him merchandise which was inferior, the customer as a reasonable man rapidly shifted to other sources of supply. Thus, the greediest merchant recognized that the facts of his market compelled him to operate at low cost, offer fair quality, and charge competitive prices. Only ruthless efficiency enabled

him to fend off his competitors and please his customers.

Thus, in Smith's commercial utopia, each businessman's hand was raised against his fellows. Indeed, so long as the businessman obeyed the laws of the land, refrained from theft or assault, and faithfully fulfilled his contracts, he served the public interest in spite of himself. It exaggerates only a trifle to say that, until near the end of the nineteenth century and the emergence of trusts in the United States and cartels in Europe, economists perceived small need to modify Smith's judgment that mutual hostility among business rivals was by all odds this most satisfactory state of affairs. Even as economists refined their analysis of markets and substituted elegant marginalism for clumsy real cost explanations of price, they retained a confidence in the benefits of competition in atomistic markets, populated by hordes of buyers and legions of sellers.

Such markets may or may not have existed in the nineteenth century. It is plain that they do not now exist. If we run down the list of leading American manufacturing industries, autos, steel, aluminum, electrical equipment and appliances, chemicals, rubber tires, and cigarettes—we must be struck time and again with the huge size and public renown of the industry leaders. In 1954, to take instances almost at random, four companies—of which the biggest was

"Businessmen and Their Rivals," *The Annals of the American Academy of Political and Social Science,* 343 (September 1962), 110–117. Reprinted with the permission of the author and of the publisher, The American Academy of Political and Social Science.

the Aluminum Company of America (Alcoa)—controlled 100 per cent of the output of primary aluminum. The largest four firms in telephone equipment, electric light bulbs, breakfast foods, and cigarettes in each instance accounted for 75 per cent or more of their industry's total employment. A complex combination of technical, financial, and marketing elements explains this phenomenon. But suffice it to say here that in 1960 the 500 largest industrial organizations in the United States sold merchandise priced at $197.4 billion, or more than half of the total sales achieved by all American manufacturing and mining firms. These same 500 corporations earned 70 per cent of all manufacturing and mining profits.

No one in his senses believes that General Motors, the employer of more than half a million men and women, can or will act in the same way and according to the same rules as a small employer of half a dozen souls in a garment-district loft in New York's Seventh Avenue. Size implies power and power confers choice. Here is the heart of the problem. The American oligopolist—the unpleasant term economists apply to large corporations—chooses policies which affect his customers, his suppliers, his government, his community, and his rivals. Although these choices are limited and fallible, he does possess the opportunity to choose a high-price, low-volume policy or a low-price, high-volume policy. He can tie his suppliers to him or deliberately diversify his orders. By moving his plant, he can ruin one community and enrich another. By investing abroad, he can make the American balance of payments tremble, as did American Ford when it bought up complete control of British Ford. These choices are his. The market does not make them. Rather, what the oligopolist does shapes the market.

Here we are particularly concerned with the relations of business firms to each other. Accordingly, we shall commence with a glance at the legal framework which is designed to curb economic power. Next we shall look at some of the ways in which the large corporation in actual practice has come to terms with its own size and power. The suggestion will be made that business practice and business ideology are increasingly disparate. Finally, we shall illustrate this proposition with several recent examples of the tension between the public expectation of business rivalry and the actual corporate practice of rivalry.

The Law

Of all major industrial nations, the United States has tried the hardest to translate the official, national ideology of free competition and individual action into binding legislation. The focus of such law as the Sherman Act (1890), the Clayton Act (1914), and the Federal Trade Commission Act (1914) is upon the avoidance of monopoly in the interest of competition and for the welfare of the consumer. Thus, Section 1 of the Sherman Act grimly warns the potential malefactor that "every contract, combination in the form of trust or otherwise, or conspiracy, in restraint of trade . . . is hereby declared to be illegal." Section 2 closes the door against any effort to monopolize: "Every person who shall monopolize, or attempt to monopolize, or combine or conspire with any other person or persons to monopolize any part of the trade or commerce among the several States, or with foreign nations, shall be deemed guilty of a misdemeanor." The language is so forbidding that it is an anticlimax to see that only a misdemeanor is in question.

Congressional concern has been persistent. The Clayton Act prohibited four monopolistic practices, among them price discrimination in favor of some customers and against others and acquisitions of competing enterprises. More recently, the Robinson-Patman Act of 1936 revised the section on price discrimination, and the Celler-Kefauver Act of 1950 amended and tightened the ban against the purchase of rival companies.

In general, these laws were written out of a sensitive awareness that inordinate private power is a menace to free consumer choice, a threat to individual initiative, and a handicap to effective democracy. Inevitably, much in these laws affects the relationships of businessmen to each other. What do we ask of our businessmen in our laws? We forbid them to indulge in a great many practices which are legal in other countries. They may not collude with their competitors in the setting of prices, the conditions of sale, and the division of markets. A seller may offer a customer discounts only if cost savings justify this reduction. Otherwise, it is an unfair practice directed as much against other sellers as against other buyers. Nor may one enterprise merge with another if the consequence of the amalgamation is a decrease in competition. No business may so act as to become a monopoly.

The federal government has enforced these prohibitions with sporadic vigor. There was a time when Thurman Arnold could argue with some plausibility in *The Folklore of Capitalism* that the major consequence of the antitrust laws was the capacity of monopolists to flourish while a complacent public soothed itself with the antitrust statutes. The joke was on Mr. Arnold when President Roosevelt appointed him head of the De-

partment of Justice's antitrust division and he set out to disprove his own analysis. Still, litigation has been copious and many points are still in dispute. It is broadly true that contemporary judicial interpretations at the least do provide a list of prohibited business acts. What is much less clear and a source of justified complaint by businessmen is precisely how we want our businessmen to act in their legal pursuits. If any ideology informs antitrust legislation, it is the outdated ideology which clings to nineteenth-century models of atomistic competition.

Business Practice

How have business managers in oligopolized industries actually responded to their size and power and its legal limitation? What they appear to have done is make serious efforts to limit the scope of effective competition and to diminish the uncertainty which has always accompanied genuine competition. Their favorite instruments have been price leadership, advertising, and enhanced emphasis upon styling and packaging. As they have perfected these tools of tolerable competition, business managers have insensibly shifted from the single-minded maximization of profit to a complex blend of economic and political objectives which ratify the recognition that the giant corporation serves many constituencies.

PRICE LEADERSHIP

Take, first, price leadership. In the atomistic market of classical competition, no seller possessed the power to set his product's price. The price which he "found" in the market was the resultant of the interplay of a great many offers of merchandise by a host of small sellers and a great many demands for merchandise on the part of myriads of buyers. Perhaps such sellers were fortunate: they needed no price policy. But the contemporary American oligopolist does badly need such a policy, for he can depend on no market to set his prices for him. This is not to say that some of the consequences of atomistic competition might not be approximated if the most efficient producer in an oligopolized industry set low prices which compelled his less efficient rivals to emulate his methods or leave him in possession of the economic battlefield.

But such a procedure is risky not alone for the inefficient but also for the efficient. Rivals might be stimulated into damaging activity. The costs of price wars might exceed the probable gains. If, by some chance, the most efficient producer drove his rivals out, his reward might be an indignant antitrust action. Sensible men take sensible actions. Hence, the institutional form of pricing in the concentrated or oligopolized industries has been price leadership. At its simplest and purest, price leadership demands no collusion, generates no trail of paper to be followed by the sleuths of the antitrust division, and requires no formal ratification. What is necessary is the existence of a single firm willing to set its prices publicly and a general willingness on the part of other firms to accept the price leader's price decisions. The mill prices which United States Steel sets are rapidly emulated by smaller steel producers. Model for model, there is little difference in price among Ford, General Motors, and Chrysler automobiles. In these and other industries, competition by price is tacitly eschewed. The consequence is considerable price stability over a wide range of American manufacturing.

In its way, this price stability is a considerable economic and political accomplishment. For it implies, in each of the concentrated industries, a pattern of prices which is mutually tolerable to small companies and large ones, to efficient producers and inefficient ones. It necessitates the persistence of markedly different levels of profit among the various producers, a condition which classical theory would have considered implausible.

There are two other implications which are less happy in their consequences. In the first place, this arrangement of pricing requires that prices be high enough to permit even the relatively inefficient to survive. And, in the second place, the capacity of the weak to continue their inefficient use of economic resources is paralleled by the excess profits which will be earned by the strong. Thus, the pressure to improve efficiency and to innovate vigorously is sensibly diminished by indulgent pricing by the price leaders in the concentrated industries.

What is gained is peace of mind. Price competition is risky even for the strong. Price leadership is a formula for peace among natural enemies. Severe economic adversity during a depression may imperil price unity. Severe public and political pressure of the variety which United States Steel encountered in April 1962 (the time this essay was written) may breach a usually united front. But, by and large, the benefits of harmony are sufficiently attractive to make price leadership both pervasive and durable.

ADVERTISING

It can be argued that advertising is another way of confining competition within limits tolerable to businessmen and another means of promoting friendly relations among the competing units of a concentrated industry. Let us, therefore, examine advertising as a natural concomitant of a general decision to get along with rivals rather than to eliminate them. Among the merits of advertising from this standpoint is its target. Advertising is only partly directed against the advertiser's direct rivals. A really successful Marlboro or Viceroy campaign is likely to expand cigarette smoking in general as well as the sales of the brand which does the advertising. The man whose yearning for a new car in the spring is magnified by Ford advertising will, in all probability, shop around before making a major investment. His final choice may well fall upon a Chevrolet. But, save for the Ford advertising campaign, he might have postponed buying a car until next year and gone on a chartered flight to Europe instead. This is a specific way of making the general point that advertising is capable of diverting consumer expenditures from one type of product to another in addition to persuading buyers to switch from one maker of a given product to another one. Within an industry, mutual good will is enhanced when advertising expands the market for all producers. Doubtless it is a recognition of this gain which induces meat packers to finance the campaigns of the American Meat Institute and Irish whiskey distillers to promote their delicacy co-operatively as well as individually.

STYLING AND PACKAGING

Closely allied to advertising is rivalry in styling and packaging. Here, competition may be as fierce as price competition used to be, but certainly this new competition is more consonant with the mutual harmony of producers. Styling and packaging variations share some of the characteristics of advertising. At their best, they enlarge the total market. Moreover, they can readily be emulated, so that the tail fins of the Cadillac sprout soon enough on the Chrysler and the Lincoln. A price reduction is a clear lure to all buyers. But styling competition is ambiguous and diffuse in its impact, attractive to some and repellent to others. Finally, advertising and competitive styling alike turn the buyer's mind away from the hard facts of price and toward the fanciful universe of style and presentation.

Industries which sell directly to consumers—auto manufacturers, distillers, meat packers, and their peers—can deploy all three of these weapons: price leadership, advertising, and product differentiation. Industries like steel and aluminum, which typically sell to other businesses, are more or less confined to price leadership. The meretricious claim and the trivial variation in product bounce off the hard-boiled purchasing agents of other business organizations. Hence, they tend to be reserved for ordinary consumers.

As businessmen have adapted themselves to the realities of their situation, what has happened to their own conception of their proper role? Adolf Berle has argued in the *20th Century Capitalist Revolution* that a corporate conscience and a body of corporate public law are in the course of evolution. Herbert Simon has advanced a model of the manager's function which emphasizes the social and political as well as the economic functions which are performed and the manager's necessity to balance satisfactorily among these functions. Some changes are evident. As the business unit has expanded, the time horizon of its managers has grown more distant, the meaning of profit maximization has become beclouded, and the existence of many corporate constituencies has become clearer.

CORPORATE CONSTITUENCIES

Of these numerous constituencies to which the manager owes if not allegiance at least tribute, stockholders are only one. The traditional rhetoric of annual statements and annual stockholders' meetings still emphasizes the wish of the corporation to increase its earnings and its dividends. But implicit in these restatements of the old faith is the reservation that suppliers, customers, rivals, trade unions, communities in which plants are located, and governmental agencies are observers, critics, and sometimes participants in corporate acts of decision. It is this reservation which inhibits the corporation from stating the single objective of making as much money as possible. Nowadays, even internal corporate targets are likely to take the shape of aspirations for market shares and minimum rates of return on specific investments.

Menacing as the power of the large corporation is to many who observe it, it is quite probable that corporate managers are more aware of the limitations of their power than of its extent. High earnings may stimulate trade union demands which dissipate the earnings. Earnings which are too low or dividends which are too scanty may spark an expensive proxy fight. Market penetration which extends too far may threaten the demise of rivals and the unwelcome attentions of the Department of Justice. A decision to close an inefficient or uncompetitive plant may set off a community clamor which damages a company's public relations, if not its very corporate image, and may even injure its sales. Major technological innovations may be installed only at the price of a major row with a union.

Under the circumstances, corporation managers cannot often feel free to make the simple choices of a more primitive and a more ruthless capitalism. One need not accept the hypothesis that these managers have acquired social consciences and ethical sensitivities to the problems of others to suspect that the sheer facts of the distribution of social, economic, and political power within American society lend considerable plausibility to J. K. Galbraith's judgment that countervailing power limits even the strongest industrial enterprise. A major consequence of this comparatively new situation is the tacit, mutual treaty among the rivals in the major industries to compete within limits, place price competition out of bounds, and hope that nobody wins a complete victory.

Law, Business Behavior, and Public Policy

However, such adaptations cannot be made without strain. Practice and precept seldom completely match. Over the broad spectrum of industrial management, corporate leaders have not reached unanimity. Of the numerous instances in which law and business practice, or public policy and business action, have come into conflict, let us glance at three.

Let us start with the projected steel merger between Bethlehem and Youngstown Sheet and Tube. In the steel industry, Bethlehem ranks second and Youngstown seventh in size. Even now, the steel industry is notable for the somber dignity with which it conducts its version of competition. Would such a merger have increased competition by making Bethlehem a worthier rival of United States Steel? Would it, as the government argued, have diminished competition by reducing by one the number of competitors? In the event, a federal court was persuaded by the government's argument and enjoined the merger. Although it cannot be said that, to an economist, the government's case was entirely convincing, both of the companies were sufficiently healthy economic organisms to continue independent existences. Vary the situation. Suppose that Ford wished, by taking over the assets of Chrysler, to increase its own size to a nearer approximation of the dimensions of General Motors. Is there more competition in an industry when two colossi dominate the market than when a single colossus (General Motors), a healthy giant (Ford), and an ailing giant (Chrysler) control the bulk of the market? Here is an area where the antitrust laws speak in an uncertain voice.

Much more sensational cases await us. In February 1961 a forthright federal judge in a Philadelphia courtroom imposed $822,500 in fines on twenty-one corporations, including General Electric, Westinghouse, and Allis Chalmers; $109,000 in fines on thirty-six officers of these companies; and thirty-day jail terms on a General Electric vice-president and six other executives. The sentences, which climaxed one of the biggest antitrust prosecutions in Sherman Act history, followed guilty pleas in December 1960 by nineteen of these companies and thirty-five individuals. What the companies and their officials confessed was systematic rigging of government bids on turbines, switchgears, controls, and other items of heavy electrical equipment. In the language of the law, their crime was among other things, conspiracy to divide markets, suppress competition, and charge artificially high prices.

In the wake of this business sensation, aggrieved stockholders brought suit; sixty major cities contemplated a single consolidated damage suit; James Carey, President of the International Union of Electrical Workers, demanded and General Electric agreed that stockholders should judge whether convicted officials should be retained in the company's employ; and, in the end, General Electric did discharge a number of its own officials. On the whole, business opinion condemned the guilty. The *Wall Street Journal* and *Fortune* could discover little in the way of extenuation. At the Harvard Business School, where corporate ethics are a precious charge, students and faculty talked of little else for several days after the news broke.

Although there can be no doubt of the legal guilt of the companies and their officers, was not the uproar in business circles somewhat exaggerated? Had the overenthusiastic vice-presidents and division managers done a great deal more than carry an existing tendency to a logical and illegal extreme? As we have examined corporate policy, it appears directed toward order and stability. Although there are occasional ominous rumbles from the government and the persistent Senator Kefauver, price leadership has thus far avoided serious legal censure. Was it not natural for corporate officials, anxious about their own security, to go a step or two farther to avert another attack of the price competition which had broken out only recently in their industry? One need not be derisive in perceiving the complicated collusive arrangements of the electrical-equipment cases as apparently sensible extensions of accustomed patterns of behavior. Indeed, there is something strange about condemning some devices which limit competition, among them collusive bidding and market division, and sanctioning others which serve the same purpose, among them price leadership and product variation.

Our last illustration is best. The conflict among law, ideology, business practice, and the realities of power has seldom been more fascinating than in the unsuccessful attempt of the major steel producers to raise their prices some 3.5 percent in April of this year. The circumstances need little recapitulation. Almost from the outset of his administration, President Kennedy has centered his attention on the steel industry as the key to the restraint of inflation. For at least a decade, steel had set the pattern of wage and price inflation. Working persistently at less than capacity, the steel industry in recent years had little market justification for a price increase. Administration pressure helped persuade the steelworkers' union to accept an agreement which contained no wage increase. Then, while the President took public credit for a noninflationary labor settlement, on the premise that steel prices would remain stable, United States Steel as the price leader announced its increase. In a cold fury, the President set in motion a grand-jury investigation of the increase, urged the unreluctant Senator Kefauver to activate his Senate Anti-Monopoly Subcommittee, announced the diversion of an important Defense Department order from United States Steel, and placed pressure on Inland, Armco, and Kaiser—three smaller companies which had not immediately followed United States Steel, to hold the price line. Under this attack, industry solidity cracked. Inland refused to go along with United States Steel, Bethlehem rescinded its own increase, and, within seventy-two hours, United States Steel bowed to these consequences of presidential power and returned to its original prices.

What are the morals of this clash of titans? The first is the sudden revelation that United States Steel's behavior was atavistic. Deluded by their own ideology, convinced by their own press releases, the officials of United States Steel really seemed to believe that to raise or lower the price of steel was entirely a private, corporate choice. Americans may owe a debt for the lesson in the realities of industrial power to the maladroit managers of Big Steel. The second moral is this: United States Steel or any other business giant retains the right to its power only on a condition. The condition is that it must use that power for purposes wider than the interests of its own stockholders or its own managers. There is a third moral. As a nation we prefer to employ the rhetoric of free enterprise. Even the President at his most excoriating carefully reaffirmed his wish to intervene as little as might be in the affairs of private enterprise. On the whole, this is a harmless indulgence, for, when it comes to a crisis, we prefer to control individual corporate power even if the price is contradiction of our usual platitudes. The President persistently reverted to the formula of his right to define the national interest and the consequent obligation of the steel industry to pay heed to his definition. We will allow our price leaders to maintain order and coherence in their industries, provided their rule is that of constitutional monarchs.

Conclusion

Is it all for the best in this best of all possible worlds? I should hesitate to leave the subject on such a note. Is this era of gentlemanly rivalry a "good thing," as the authors of the immortal *1066 And All That* might have asked the question? Until the last decade, a fair case might have been made that oli-gopoly and industrial progress had been intimately linked. Such a case, in fact, was made by the late Joseph A. Schumpeter in *Capitalism, Socialism and Democracy*. But, if we are to link the economic growth of the past to the large corporation, how can we avoid linking the comparative stagnation of the present to the same agent: the great corporation has not declined in significance. I end, then, with the possibility that oli-gopoly has become enervating, that the giant corporation has fallen prey to its bureaucracy, that soft corporate living has sapped efficiency, and that the innovating spirit which sparked economic growth in the past is in the present too weak to overcome the lures of the new "competition." The consequences are unpleasant: slow growth and lagging redistribution of income.

THE EFFECT ON ACADEMIC GOODS OF THEIR MARKET

Warren G. Bennis

Research in the physical sciences is perhaps more certain to be directed toward useful ends than research in humanistic fields, because the former is most commonly carried on in organized laboratories, where consultation is almost inevitable and a consensus of opinion as to what is worthwhile is easily formed, and has its effect on the investigator, whereas in most humanistic and social subjects the researcher can work in comparative isolation.—J. Franklin Jameson[1] (1927).

As the design engineers in an industry feel harried by the demands and expectations of product engineers who want to produce, and the sales engineers who want to sell, so the design engineers of social science are under the pressures just indicated from the production and sales staff who insist on putting on the social science assembly line what is still necessarily in the handicraft and mock-up stage. In many quarters, the promoters of social science have aroused such unfillable expectations as to risk a disillusioning bust of the whole enterprise.—David Riesman.[2]

In less than two decades we have seen the emergence in the United States of a new industry: the organized production of new social knowledge. While Slichter and other economists cite the rise of industrial, mostly physical, research as one of the main developments in the national economy, the use of teams of

"The Effect on Academic Goods of Their Market," *The American Journal of Sociology*, 62, 1 (July 1956), 28–33. Reprinted with the permission of the author and of the publisher, The University of Chicago Press.

social scientists working on practical problems has turned social research into a million-dollar business.[3] Although comprehensive and comparable statistical data on the growth of social science research are non-existent, certain clues indicate the magnitude of this development: (1) The combined expenditures for social research of the twenty largest universities in 1928 would probably support only one present-day university research organization.[4] (2) While the government disbursed practically no funds for social research twenty-five years ago, in 1952 eleven million dollars was spent on psychological research alone. (3) The National Science Foundation estimates that a hundred million dollars was spent on research in the social sciences in 1953.

Perhaps the most important circumstances in stimulating large-scale programs of research are the increased specialization of the social disciplines which has created a need for interdisciplinary and team research,[5] the magnitude of world problems, the proved usefulness of social science findings for policy-makers, the availability of large sums of money from foundations and the United States government, and the quantifiability of social data. These developments have created sweeping changes in the structure of social research. A new type of intellectual organization is emerging, replete with big budgets and the growing pains of managerial responsibility. The purpose of this paper is to examine an organization which has been under study by the author for over fifteen months and describe its chief organizational syndrome: exposure to market forces.

The organization, the "Hub," is located in a large university, is under the jurisdiction of its College of Social Studies, and is equivalent to an academic department. Its growth was spurred both to strengthen the social sciences at the university and to offer social scientists the opportunity to influence the nature of American foreign policy by tackling problems of major interest to the government. Hence its main activity centers around international affairs and economic development.

The total personnel numbers about eighty-five: twelve equivalent to full or associate professors, twenty-six research associates, twenty research assistants (chiefly graduate students), twenty-two secretaries, and four administrative assistants. These persons are connected with one or the other of two main research projects: a Development program to examine three countries with contrasting geographical and economic environments and a Communications program to study the interaction of words, impressions, and ideas which affect the attitudes and behavior of different peoples toward one another. Each program has its own director who attempts to co-ordinate the activities of the staff prescribed by the research goals.

The Hub is almost completely dependent upon outside financing by a large private foundation.[6] An indication of the anxiety concerning the granting of funds was shown in the Hub's 1953–54 Annual Report, the first sentence of which reads: "The most important event in the life of the Hub last year was the receipt at the year-end of a substantial grant from the foundation for the conduct of research. This grant removed a major uncertainty which had hovered over a major portion of the Hub's forward planning. . . ."

The program on Communications has been established with a four-year grant, while that on Development has been awarded a grant on a year-to-year basis. While even four years is short, considering the gestation period of research, the Development project was threatened by the yearly scrutiny of the foundation and by its annual uncertainties. For the preceding two years the foundation had not announced the grant until the end of May.

Market Versus Task Orientation

One chief conception of work in a research organization varies with the degree of control the organization maintains over exogenous forces—in this particular case, market forces. Where financial security provides protection from the market, the organization and the scientists within it are safe from the vagaries of the market. This situation we call "task-orientation." Where there is little protection from the market place, the organization becomes intimately concerned with financial matters. Attention, for sheer sake of survival, is diverted from the task to the sponsors of research. This we call "market-orientation."

Unless there is some degree of insulation from competitive and market pressures on the science organization, professional standards are likely to be lowered, if not entirely rejected. In industrial laboratories, firms with large research budgets and some modicum of protection from the market have an opportunity to offer their scientists more freedom and hence more opportunities for "pure" research.[7] If the market structure of a particular project is insecure and tenuous, the individual researcher faces a peculiar type of role conflict: duty as a scientist qua scientist and the demands of the market. Putting it differently, he is torn between organizational demands and his own professional demands. Hans Zinsser once

described how the competitive milieu affects scientific performance in medical work:

> It puts a premium upon quantitative productiveness, spectacular achievement and practical success, which will bring administrative applause, often because of its advertising value in institutional competition. These tendencies, to be fair, are in every university known to be resisted by the men who have the determining influence; but the psychology of the situation is too logical to be offset by individual idealism, the natural pressure too strong.[8]

The thesis presented here is that the Development program, because of its tenuous financing, is market-oriented while the Communications program is task-oriented. How was this difference in forces (market structure) reflected in the data?

The Problems

One of the questions asked of all Hub researchers in the course of an interview was "What do you consider the three main problems of research at the Hub?" The 186 responses were then categorized in five classes: organizational, external, substantive, bureaucratic, and interpersonal. We are concerned here with the "external problems" category, which deals specifically with those issues concerned exclusively with "instability and uncertainty due to precarious relations with the sponsor of research." Almost 30 per cent of the total responses fell into this category. The Communications staff made the fewest responses in this category (four times) and when they did, barely mentioned the foundation. The following representative responses were made by the Development staff:

> "I would take a job at X college in preference to the Hub based not on criteria

of teaching over research but just that the Hub's future is not as certain as X college."

"One of the major problems here has been and continues to be the uncertainty of the budget. You have to know the scale of funds before you can plan. We got only a fraction of what we had planned for. Now we're looking for other funds, etc. We cannot recruit too well because we cannot make a firm offer. If we had a budget—a firm budget—we would have no personnel problems."

"The main problem here is doing research and justifying ourself to the foundation. The thing that's annoyed me the most is that we spend so much time looking at our navel without doing anything—except justifying our existence."

"The main problem is the uncertain environment. This is an uneasy life . . . tougher than a real university life . . . this time-uncertainty and shoestring operation. If I were given dough when I first came here—say so many thousand per annum, I may have hired not *better* people but people more akin to project needs."

"I have to spend up to 25 per cent of my time working on the foundation submission."

"The tightest pressure I've felt is the annual soul-searching with the foundation. I've been through it two years now and it wears me out."

"Ever since January, tension has been awful. Everyone has been watching, waiting, and, in general, usurping valuable time because of the terrible fear of not getting the contract renewed be-cause of budget cuts. This takes a large part of group conversation."

"I've Just Received Word from the Foundation That . . ."

Few members of the Hub, according to responses to a cartoon,[9] were free of anxiety concerning relations with the foundation. In point of fact, of the eighteen cartoons used, the one dealing with foundation relations attracted the second highest responses, twenty-five completions. This particular cartoon depicted five men seated around a table, one of whom is shown saying, "I've just received word from the foundation that. . . ." Those interviewed were asked to complete the statement of the speaker by filling in the space above the speaker's head. In addition to the straight-line box extending over the speaker, there was a cloudlike "bubble" over another member's head. Subjects were also asked to supply a response in this space to the speaker's statement but to consider it an unspoken, private thought. Thus, with a device borrowed from the cartoonist, it was possible to derive public or "overt" responses as well as private or "covert" reactions. Of nineteen overt statements, seventeen dealt specifically with the question of grants. Moreover, Table 1 shows that in their covert remarks thirteen subjects revealed anxiety about financing.

Again there was a clear distinction between responses from the Communica-

TABLE 1. Attitudes toward foundation. (N = 25)

Overt response		Covert response	
Grant was awarded	8	Insecurity from uncertainty	13
Grant was cut	9	Hostile to foundation	3
Other	2	Personal insecurity stemming from fragile situation	7
Total	19	Total	23

COMPETITION, COOPERATION, AND CRISIS

tions project and those from Development. Of the seven responses showing "severe" insecurity in the covert box, six were made by Development personnel. By "severe" we mean that the individual voiced serious personal problems as a result of foundation vagaries, such as: "My job will be lost" or "Whew! Another year accounted for. . . . At last." This is not to say that the Communications staff was unconcerned about the foundation. But, judging from their responses, they tended to react more *aggressively* to the foundation. At the same time they were less worried about *personal* insecurities and more concerned with having "to revise my works" or deleting research problems of great interest. In short, while the Development staff was anxious about the possible loss of a job, the Communications group was concerned with the research goals. Examples

of cartoon responses are shown in 297 Table 2.

In addition to the data presented here the effects of the situation upon project functioning were reflected in the Communications program in the following ways: (1) more perceived freedom and scope for the staff member; (2) less time spent in writing up research proposals and progress reports; (3) greater satisfaction with the work in progress.[10] Perhaps equally important was the impression gained that more frequent offhand, somewhat parenthetical allusions to the foundation were made by the Development program. Many of these remarks were humorous. It can be argued that they were a mechanism for dealing with tension. This argument is strengthened by the fact that there seemed to be an increase in these remarks as the time drew near for the foundation decision. The following are examples:

TABLE 2. Overt and covert responses to cartoon.

Overt	Covert
Communications Program Responses	
". . . they'll give us half the money we asked for." ". . . have cut our grant in half."	"Oh God! Some jerks have no sense of the realities of life. We'll either have to get more money or revise our objectives completely." "There goes our non-economic research!" "Here we go! Another 'revision.' "
Development Program Responses	
"The Development grant will probably come up for action at the May meeting of the Board of Directors."	"How can you run a research outfit with all this uncertainty and delay? That foundation is all 'snafu'd' and unless they get straightened out they're not going to measure up to X or Y foundations—no matter how much money they have."
"We will not be given a final answer to our submission until mid-summer. By that it seems as if our request will be cut in part even if finally accepted." "They are greatly pleased with our plans and will cut our request only by 75%." "They will continue the present subsidies through the coming year."	"Planning research under foundation sponsorship is uncertain!" "We still got away with murder! (Will I keep my job?)" "I'm delighted. That means my own subsidization will continue unimpaired."

STAFF MEMBER (*pointing to foundation proposal which is nearing completion*): "There it is—about seven thousand dollars a page . . . . We have talked of matters serious—but of that— it is a matter of life and death."

(*Backing up intellectual point*): "All I'm saying is what our submission to the foundation says."

CHAIRMAN OF SEMINAR: "Well, that settles it!"

"We sent off the submission to the foundation and, after we totaled up what all the problems of development would cost, found that it would break the foundation, so we cut it down a little."

"Why are we studying X country? Well, the last time this came up we had to hunt around for a slip of paper. Unfortunately today I couldn't find that, so I have to give you my own ideas for it. Where is the submission?"

Usually one does not think of knowledge and research findings in terms of the pricing mechanism, but it does offer insight in understanding the difficulties of organized research. Because of methods of financing, the Development group was in a more "competitive" position than was the Communications group, which was protected from the market forces for at least four years. While the latter was aware of the foundation's importance, the Development personnel saw the foundation as a towering overshadowing Jehovah. (One of the Development directors once substituted the name of the foundation in the phrase, "God willing!") Each year during the last two years, with growing intensity from January to May, the question asked by the Development personnel has been, "Will the funds come through?" More indirectly, "What does the foundation want from us?" Or "How can we make our research proposals so attractive that we can get funds other institutions won't get?"

Without stretching the analogy, there was a good deal of concern with a form of market activity, "product differentiation." This was evidenced when a project group from the Hub visited a neighboring research group financed by the same foundation and working on the same country. The latent function of this trip, it can be argued, was to look over the "competitor," to insure the marketing of a unique and more appealing product. The effects of the anxiety over uncertain economic returns were reflected in various ways. At times it took the form of advanced gamesmanship, that is, how to impress the foundation and still keep the research plans fluid. As one member put it: "They [the foundation] want a research proposal now, but, after all, our hypotheses will come only after six months or so." Indeed, one of the most important functions of the Hub director was to keep a balance between the pressures of exogenous influences (demands of the country under study, foundation, users of research) and the pressures made upon him by individual researchers to keep insulated from market demands.

Another effect of the uncertain environment was the attitude toward the foundation. In reality the foundation exerted no pressure on the substantive efforts of the Hub. However, social and objective realities in this case were not consonant. Thus various individuals felt that the foundation placed unbearable constraints on research proposals; that the main problem at the Hub, as one member quoted before said, "was doing research and having to justify ourself to the foundation."

We see here a tendency, not uncommon in an organized milieu, to project blame upward and away.[11] This tendency may be exacerbated in social research, where uncertainty and the unknown are daily companions, where physical and social comparisons are ambiguous, and where authority is not definite. Hence the foundation, much as in the other cases, the civil service or "bureaucracy," may be made the scapegoat.

NOTES

1. Cited in F. A. Ogg, *Research in the Humanistic and Social Sciences* (New York and London: Century Co., 1928), p. 17.
2. "Observations on Social Science Research," from *Individualism Reconsidered* (Glencoe, Ill.: Free Press, 1954), p. 475.
3. Sumner Slichter, address at the Business Executive Conference at the University of Omaha, Omaha, Nebraska, May 15, 1953.
4. Ogg, *op. cit.,* reported that the following universities spent under $350,000 on social research in 1926–27: California, Chicago, Illinois, Indiana, Kansas, Michigan, Minnesota, Missouri, Nebraska, Harvard, Yale, Columbia, Johns Hopkins, and Cornell. The total budget of the research organization which will be described here is larger; indeed, it maintains the largest budget in the College of Social Studies.

   For accounts of the growth of expenditures in social science, see H. Alpert, "National Science Foundation," *American Sociological Review,* XIX, No. 2 (1954), 208; R. G. Axt, *Federal Government and Financing Higher Education* (New York: Columbia University Press, 1952); B. Barber, *Science and the Social Order* (Glencoe, Ill.: Free Press, 1952), p. 132; W. G. Bennis, "The Structure of Social Science: An Organizational Study" (paper read at the American Sociological Society Annual Meetings, Urbana, Ill., September 9, 1954), pp. 2–3; L. P. Lessing, "National Science Foundation Takes Stock," *Scientific American,* March, 1954; *Federal Funds for Science: National Science Foundation, 1950–52* (Washington: U.S. Government Printing Office).
5. The Russell Sage Foundation, Brookings Institution, and the Social Science Research Council stress this development as one of the most significant in the social sciences in the last two decades. See M. Graham, *Federal Utilization of Social Science* (Washington, D.C.: Brookings Institution, 1954), pp. 18–21; *Effective Use of Social Science Research in the Federal Services* (New York: Russell Sage Foundation, 1950), p. 21; *The Social Sciences in Historical Study* (Social Science Research Council Bulletin 64 [1954], pp. 31–33).
6. Since the field work for this paper was completed, i.e., during the very early days of the organization's life, important changes have been made toward a more permanent footing of research projects. The Hub director and other officers, fully aware of the problems of tenuous short-term financing, submitted a proposal urging a long-term commitment, and a five-year grant was issued by the foundation just as this study was closing.
7. W. Bennis, "Role Conflict and Market Structure" (Massachusetts Institute of Technology, 1953) (mimeographed).
8. Cited in L. Wilson, *Academic Man* (Oxford University Press, 1942), pp. 206–7.
9. These cartoons evolved out of the problem areas mentioned by Hub members in the initial interviews. The most prominent problems were reduced to simple sketches which allowed for "projections" by the subjects. The original impetus for the use of cartoons was made by H. A. Shepard, and June Moyer is responsible for the drawing.
10. These data were taken from the author's unpublished doctoral dissertation, "The Social Science Research Organization: A Study of the Institutional Practices and Values in Interdisciplinary Research" (Massachusetts Institute of Technology, Department of Economics and Social Science, 1955).
11. Paula Brown's study of a government laboratory indicates that people tend to attack and blame the far-off civil service and that there is a "reluctance to accept responsibility for making decisions easily rationalized." Thus the projection of blame upward

THE EFFECT ON ACADEMIC GOODS OF THEIR MARKET

300   ("Bureaucracy in a Government Laboratory," *Social Forces*, XXXII, No. 3 [March, 1954], 266). For a laboratory experiment showing somewhat similar social processes see L. Festinger, "A Theory of Social Comparison Processes," *Human Relations*, VII, No. 2 (May 1954), 119.

ORGANIZATIONAL INTERDEPENDENCE AND INTRA-ORGANIZATIONAL STRUCTURE*

Michael Aiken and Jerald Hage

The major purpose of this paper is to explore some of the causes and consequences of organizational interdependence among health and welfare organizations. The aspect of organizational interdependence that is examined here is the joint cooperative program with other organizations. In particular, we are interested in relating this aspect of the organization's relationships with its environment to internal organization behavior.

Thus this paper explores one aspect of the general field of interorganizational analysis. The effect of the environment on organizational behavior as well as the nature of the interorganizational relationships in an organization's environment are topics that have received increasing attention from scholars in recent years. Among studies in the latter category, there are those that have attempted to describe the nature of organizational environments in terms of the degree of turbulence (Emery and Trist, 1965; cf. Terreberry, 1968) and in terms of organizational sets (Evan, 1966). Others have emphasized transactional

"Organizational Interdependence and Intra-Organizational Structure," *American Sociological Review*, 33, 6 (December 1968), 912–930. Reprinted with the permission of the authors and of the publisher, The American Sociological Association.

* This is a revised version of a paper read at the annual meetings of the American Sociological Association, San Francisco, California, August 30, 1967. This investigation was supported in part by a research grant from the Vocational Rehabilitation Administration, Department of Health, Education, and Welfare, Washington, D.C. We are grateful to Charles Perrow for helpful comments on an earlier version of this paper. In addition, we would like to acknowledge the cooperation and support of Harry Sharp and the Wisconsin Survey Laboratory during the interviewing phase of this project.

interdependencies among organizations (Selznick, 1949; Ridgeway, 1957; Dill, 1962; Levine and White, 1961; Levine et al., 1963; Guetzkow, 1966; Litwak and Hylton, 1962; James Thompson, 1962; Elling and Halbsky, 1961; Reid, 1964.) Still others have emphasized the importance of an understanding of interorganizational relationships for such problem areas as education (Clark, 1965), medical care (Levine and White, 1963), rehabilitation and mental health (Black and Kase, 1963), delinquency prevention and control (Miller, 1958; Reid, 1964); services for the elderly (Morris and Randall, 1965); community action (Warren, 1967); and community response to disasters (Form and Nosow, 1958).

Few studies, however, have examined the impact of the environment on internal organizational processes. One such study by Thompson and McEwen (1958) showed how the organizational environment can affect goal-setting in organizations, while a study by Dill (1958) examined how environmental pressures affect the degree of managerial autonomy. Simpson and Gulley (1962) found that voluntary organizations with diffuse pressures from the environment were more likely to have decentralized structures, high internal communications, and high membership involvement, while those having more restricted pressures from the environment had the opposite characteristics. Terreberry (1968) has hypothesized that organizational change is largely induced by forces in the environment, and Yuchtman and Seashore (1967) have defined organizational effectiveness in terms of the organization's success in obtaining resources from the environment. Recently, James D. Thompson (1967) and Lawrence and Lorsch (1967) have suggested some ways in which elements in the environment can

affect organizational behavior. There are also other studies which argue that another aspect of the environment—variations in cultural values and norms—may also affect the internal structure of organizations (Richardson, 1959; Harbison et al., 1963; Crozier, 1964). Each of these studies, then, suggests ways in which the organization's environment affects the internal nature of the organization. The purpose of this study is to show how one aspect of the organization's relationship with its environment, i.e., the interdependence that arises through joint cooperative programs with other organizations, is related to several intraorganizational characteristics. We shall do this by describing a theoretical framework about organizational interdependence and then by examining some results from an empirical study of organizational interdependence.

A second objective in calling attention to this relatively neglected area of organizational analysis is to suggest that the processes of both conflict and cooperation can be incorporated into the same model of organizational interdependence. The concept of interdependence helps us to focus on the problem of interorganizational exchanges. At the same time, the exchange of resources, another aspect of the relationships between organizations, is likely to involve an element of conflict. While Simmel has made the dialectic of cooperation and conflict a truism, as yet there has been little work that explains interorganizational cooperation and conflict. Caplow (1964) has suggested a model of conflict involving the variables of subjugation, insulation, violence, and attrition, but this model focuses neither on the particular internal conditions that give rise to interorganizational relationships nor on the consequences of them for organizational structure. These are key intellectual problems in attempting to understand exchanges among organizations.

The models of pluralistic societies described by Tocqueville (1945) and more recently by Kornhauser (1959) underscore the importance of autonomous and competing organizations for viable democratic processes. Such theoretical models assume that the processes of conflict as well as cooperation inhere in social reality. Recent American social theory has been criticized for its excessive emphasis on a static view of social processes and for failing to include conflict in its conceptual models (Dahrendorf, 1958; Coser, 1956; Wrong, 1961). The study of interorganizational relationships appears to be one area which can appropriately incorporate the processes of both conflict and cooperation. Therefore the concept of organizational interdependence becomes a critical analytical tool for understanding this process.

Most studies of organizational interdependence essentially conceive of the organization as an entity that needs inputs and provides outputs, linking together a number of organizations via the mechanisms of exchanges or transactions. (Cf. Ridgeway, 1957; Elling and Halbsky, 1961; Levine and White, 1961; Dill, 1962; James D. Thompson, 1962.) Some types of organizational exchanges involve the sharing of clients, funds, and staff in order to perform activities for some common objective (Levine et al., 1963). The measure of the degree of organizational interdependence used here is the *number of joint programs* that a focal organization has with other organizations. The greater the number of joint programs, the more organizational decision-making is constrained through obligations, commitments, or contracts with other organizations, and the greater the degree of organizational interdependence. (Cf. Guetzkow, 1966.) This type of interdependence among health and welfare organizations has variously been called "functional co-operation" by Black and Kase (1963), and "program co-ordination" by Reid (1964), and is considered a more binding form of interdependence and therefore a more interesting example of interorganizational cooperation. This does not suggest that the cooperation that is involved in joint programs is easily achieved. On the contrary, there are a number of barriers to establishing such interdependencies among organizations (cf. Johns and de Marche, 1951), and the probability of conflict is quite high, as Miller (1958) and Barth (1963) point out.

The reader may wonder why the concept of the joint program is apparently such an important kind of interorganizational relationship. The answer is that, unlike exchanges of clients or funds (which may only imply the *purchase* of services) or other types of organizational cooperation, a joint program is often a relatively enduring relationship, thus indicating a high degree of organizational interdependence.

The *joint program* needs to be carefully distinguished from the *joint organization*. The latter refers to the situation in which two or more organizations create a separate organization for some common purpose. For example, the Community Chest has been created by health and welfare organizations for fund-raising purposes. Similarly, Harrison (1959) has noted that the Baptist Convention was created by the separate Baptist churches for more effective fund raising. Guetzkow (1950) has described interagency committees among federal agencies, representing a special case of the joint organization. Business firms have created joint organizations in order to provide service functions. These are clearly different from the joint program because these joint organizations have separate corporate identities and often their own staff, budget, and objectives.

Some examples of joint programs in organizations other than those in the health and welfare field are the student exchange programs in the Big Ten. Harvard, Columbia, Yale, and Cornell Universities are developing a common computerized medical library. Indeed, it is interesting to note how many universities use joint programs of one kind or another. We do not believe that this is an accident; rather, it flows from the characteristics of these organizations. In our study, which includes rehabilitation centers, we have observed the attempt by one organization to develop a number of joint programs for the mentally retarded. These efforts are being financed by the Department of Health, Education, and Welfare, and evidently reflect a governmental concern for creating more cooperative relationships among organizations. Even in the business world, where the pursuit of profit would seem to make the joint program an impossibility, there are examples of

this phenomenon. Recently, Ford and Mobil Oil started a joint research project designed to develop a superior gasoline. This pattern is developing even across national boundaries in both the business and nonbusiness sectors.

It is this apparently increasing frequency of joint programs that makes this form of interdependence not only empirically relevant but theoretically strategic. In so far as we can determine, organizational interdependence is increasingly more common (Terreberry, 1968), but the question of why remains to be answered.

Theoretical Framework

The basic assumptions that are made about organizational behavior and the hypotheses of this study are shown in Figure 1. These assumptions provide the argument, or model, to use Willer's (1967) term, for the hypotheses to be tested below.

The first three assumptions deal with the basic problem of why organizations, at least health and welfare organizations, become involved in interdependent relationships with other units. The type of

Figure 1. Assumptions and hypotheses about organizational interdependence

Assumptions:
  I. Internal organizational diversity stimulates organizational innovation.
 II. Organizational innovation increases the need for resources.
III. As the need for resources intensifies, organizations are more likely to develop greater interdependencies with other organizations, joint programs, in order to gain resources.
 IV. Organizations attempt to maximize gains and minimize losses in attempting to obtain resources.
  V. Heightened interdependence increases problems of internal control and coordination.
 VI. Heightened interdependence increases the internal diversity of the organization.

Hypotheses:
  1. A high degree of complexity varies directly with a high number of joint programs.
  2. A high degree of program innovation varies directly with a number of joint programs.
  3. A high rate of internal communication varies directly with a high number of joint programs.
  4. A high degree of centralization varies inversely with a high number of joint programs.
  5. A high degree of formalization varies inversely with a high number of joint programs.

ORGANIZATIONAL INTERDEPENDENCE

304 interdependency with which we are concerned here is the establishment of joint, cooperative activities with other organizations. If we accept Gouldner's (1959) premise that there is a strain toward organizations maximizing their autonomy, then the establishment of an interdependency with another organization would seem to be an undesirable course of action. It is the view here that organizations are "pushed" into such interdependencies because of their need for resources—not only money, but also resources such as specialized skills, access to particular kinds of markets, and the like (cf. Levine et al., 1963).

One source of the need for additional resources results from a heightened rate of innovation, which in turn is a function of internal organizational diversity. In several ways internal diversity creates a strain towards innovation and change. The conflict between different occupations and interest groups, or even different theoretical, philosophical, or other perspectives, results in new ways of looking at organizational problems. The likely result of this is a high rate of both proposals for program innovations as well as successful implementation of them (Hage and Aiken, 1967). But organizational diversity also implies a greater knowledge and awareness of the nature of and changes in the organizational environment, particularly when organizational diversity implies not only a spectrum of occupational roles in the organization, but also involvement in professional societies in the environment by the incumbents of those occupational roles, itself a type of organizational interdependency. Together the internal conflicts and awareness of the nature of the organization's environment create strains towards organizational change.

But innovation has its price. There is a need for more resources to pay the costs of implementing such innovations —not only money, but staff, space, and time. The greater the magnitude of the change or the number of changes within some specified period of time, the greater the amounts of resource that will be needed and the less likely that the normal sources will be sufficient. Some have called organizations that successfully accomplish this task effective ones (Yuchtman and Seashore, 1967). Thus, the leaders of innovating organizations must search for other possibilities, and the creation of a joint, cooperative project with another organization becomes one solution to this problem.

This mechanism for gaining resources, i.e., the establishment of a joint program, is best viewed as a type of organizational exchange. The leaders sacrifice a small amount of autonomy for gains in staff, funds, etc. While there are strong organizational imperatives against such exchanges, since they inevitably involve some loss of autonomy, as well as necessitate greater internal coordination, the increased intensification of needs for greater resources makes such an alternative increasingly attractive. Still another factor involved here is that some objectives can only be achieved through cooperation in some joint program. The goal may be so complicated or the distribution of risk so great that organizations are impelled to enter into some type of joint venture. Of course the creation of interdependencies with other organizations also has its costs. The organization must utilize some of its own resources in order to perform whatever coordination is necessary. Hence an organization with no surplus resources available could hardly afford a joint program. Thus there must be some slack in the resource base in the organization before any innovation or cooperative venture is likely.

This is not to argue for the perfect rationality of organizational leaders. Some decisions about change or the choice of a cooperative activity may be quite irrational, and perhaps non-logical (Wilensky, 1967). Indeed much of our argument about the conditions that lead to organizational innovation, i.e., conflict among different occupations, interest groups, or perspectives, is that this is hardly the most rational way to bring about change. Perhaps it is best to view the process as a series of circumstances that propel such events.

While we feel that this line of reasoning is a valid explanation of why organizations enter into interdependent relationships with other organizations via such mechanisms as the joint program, alternative explanations have been offered and must be considered. Lefton and Rosengren (1966) have suggested that the lateral and longitudinal dimensions of organizational commitment to clients are factors, at least in health and welfare organizations. These are probably not the primary factors in other types of organizations, such as economic ones. However, our concern has been to attempt to find the most general argument possible to explain organizational interdependence. At the same time we have left unanswered the question of why organizations become diverse in the first place, and their framework may provide one possible answer. Reid (1964) has indicated that complementary resources are also an important factor in understanding organizational interdependence. Without necessarily agreeing or disagreeing with these points of view, we do believe that the first three assumptions in Figure 1 represent *one* causal chain showing why organizations become involved in more enduring interorganizational relationships.

The next theoretical problem is what kind of organization is likely to be chosen as a partner in an interdependent relationship. Here we assume that organizations attempt to maximize their gains and minimize their losses. This is our fourth premise. That is, they want to lose as little power and autonomy as possible in their exchange for other resources. This suggests that they are most likely to choose organizations with complementary resources, as Reid (1967) has suggested, or partners with different goals, as Guetzkow (1966) has indicated. This reduces some of the problem of decreased autonomy because the probability of conflict is reduced and cooperation facilitated in such symbiotic arrangements (cf. Hawley, 1951). This assumption also implies that other kinds of strategies might be used by the leaders of the organization once they have chosen the joint program as a mechanism of obtaining resources. Perhaps it is best to develop interdependent relationships with a number of organizations in order to obtain a given set of resources, thus reducing the degree of dependence on a given source. Again, we do not want to argue that organizational leaders will always choose the rational or logical alternative, but rather that they will simply *attempt* to minimize losses and maximize gains. Under circumstances of imperfect knowledge, some decisions will undoubtedly be irrational.

Our last theoretical problem is consideration of the consequences for the organization of establishing interdependent relationships as a means of gaining additional resources. Such joint activities will necessitate a set of arrangements between the participating organizations to carry out the program. This will mean commitments to the other organization, resulting in constraints on some aspects of organizational behavior. This in turn will mean an increase in problems of internal coordination, our fifth assumption. It is often difficult to work with outsiders, i.e., the partner in a joint activity. In this circumstance a number of mutual adaptations in a number of different areas will become necessary. One solution to this problem is the creation of extensive internal communication channels, such as a broad committee structure which meets frequently.

But perhaps a more interesting consequence of the joint program is that it can in turn contribute to organizational diversity. There is not only the likelihood of the addition of new staff from other organizations, but, more importantly, the creation of new communication links with other units in the organization's environment. New windows will have been opened into the organization, infusing new ideas and feeding the diversity of the organization, which means that the cycle of change, with all of its consequences, is likely to be regenerated.

In this way a never-ending cycle of diversity—innovation—need for resources —establishment of joint programs—is created. What may start as an interim solution to a problem can become a long-term organizational commitment which has a profound impact on the organization. In the long run, there is the tendency for units in an organizational set to become netted together in a web of interdependencies. (Cf. Terreberry, 1968).

With these six assumptions, a large number of testable hypotheses can be deduced. Indeed this is one of the advantages of a general theoretical framework. Not only does it provide the rationale for the hypotheses being tested, but it can suggest additional ideas for future research. Since we are mainly concerned with the factors associated with high interdependency, and more particularly the number of joint programs, all of the hypotheses in Figure 1 are stated in terms of this variable.

Organizational diversity implies many different kinds of variables. We have examined three separate indicators of it: diversity in the number of occupations or the degree of complexity; diversity in the number of power groups or the degree of centralization; and diversity in the actual work experience or the degree of formalization. If assumptions I–III are correct, then the stimulation of change, and more particularly innovation brought about by each of these kinds of diversity, should be associated with a large number of programs. But this is not the only way in which these variables can be related; and that observation only emphasizes how the internal structure of the organization affects the extent of the enduring relationships with other organizations. The problems of internal coordination and the increased diversity, assumptions V and VI, are also related. Both mechanisms of coordination—communication and programming —are undoubtedly tried, but communication is probably preferred. This increases the advantages of diversity and also helps to bring about greater decentralization and less formalization. Similarly, the greater awareness of the environment, via the infusion of staff from other organizations, feeds this cycle of cause and effect relationships. Therefore, we have hypothesized that the number of joint programs varies directly with the degree of complexity (hypothesis 1) and inversely with the degree of centralization and formalization (hypotheses 4 and 5).

Since our arguments also involve statements about the stimulation of innovation, which in turn heightens the need for resources, it is clear that we would expect the degree of innovation to co-vary with the number of joint programs. This is hypothesis 2 of Figure 1. While program change is only one kind of organizational innovation, it is probably the most important, at least from the standpoint of generating needs for additional resources, and thus it goes to the heart of the argument presented in Figure 1. Program innovation in turn has consequences for the degree of centralization and formalization in the organization, but here we are mainly concerned about the relationship between the rate of organization innovation as reflected in new programs and the number of joint programs, and not about these other mediating influences.

The degree of attempted internal coordination is measured by only one variable, namely the rate of communication, but again we feel that this is an important indication of this idea. Given the desire to minimize the loss of autonomy (assumption IV), organizational members must be particularly circumspect when dealing with staff and other kinds of resources from their organizational partners. This largely reduces the options about programming and encourages the elite to emphasize communication rates. Probably special "boundary spanning" roles (Thompson, 1962) are created; these men negotiate the transactions with other organizations and in turn keep their organizational members informed. The problems of interpenetration by other organizational members will keep the communication channels open and filled with messages as internal adjustments are made. Thus this is the rationale for the third hypothesis.

Study Design and Methodology

The data upon which this study is based were gathered in sixteen social welfare and health organizations located in a large midwestern metropolis in 1967. The study is a replication of an earlier study conducted in 1964. Ten organizations were private; six were either public or branches of public agencies. These organizations were all the larger welfare organizations that provide rehabilitation, psychiatric services, and services for the mentally retarded, as defined by the directory of the Community Chest. The organizations vary in size from twenty-four to several hundred. Interviews were conducted with 520 staff members of these sixteen organizations. Respondents within each organization were selected by the following criteria: (a) all executive directors and department heads; (b) in departments of less then ten members, one-half of the staff was selected randomly; (c) in departments of more than ten members, one-third of the staff was selected randomly. Non-supervisory administrative and maintenance personnel were not interviewed.

AGGREGATION OF DATA

This sampling procedure divides the organization into levels and departments. Job occupants in the upper levels were selected because they are most likely to be key decision-makers and to determine organizational policy, whereas job occupants on the lower levels were selected randomly. The different ratios within departments ensured that smaller departments were adequately represented. Professionals, such as psychiatrists, social workers and rehabilitation counselors, are included because they are intimately involved in the achievement of organizational goals and are likely to have organizational power. Non-professionals, such as attendants, janitors, and secretaries are excluded because they are less directly involved in the achievement of organizational objectives and have little or no power. The number of interviews varied from eleven in the smallest organization to sixty-two in one of the larger organizations.

It should be stressed that in this study the units of analysis are *organizations,* not individuals in the organizations. Information obtained from respondents was pooled to reflect properties of the sixteen organizations, and these properties were then related to one another. Aggregating individual data in this way presents methodological problems for which there are yet no satisfactory solutions. For example, if all respondents are equally weighted, undue weight is given to respondents lower in the hierarchy. Yet those higher in the chain of command, not the lower-status staff members, are the ones most likely to make the decisions which give an agency its ethos.[1]

We attempted to compensate for this by computing an organizational score from the means of social position within the agency. A social position is defined by the level or stratum in the organization and the department or type of professional activity. For example, if an agency's professional staff consists of psychiatrists and social workers, each divided into two hierarchical levels, the agency has four social positions: supervisory psychiatrists, psychiatrists, supervisory social workers, and social workers. A mean was then computed for each social position in the agency. The organizational score for a given variable was determined by computing the average of all social position means in the agency.[2]

The procedure for computing organizational scores parallels the method utilized in selecting respondents. It attempts to represent organizational life more accurately by not giving disproportionate weight to those social positions that have little power and that are little involved in the achievement of organizational goals.

Computation of means for each social position has the advantage of avoiding the potential problem created by the use of different sampling ratios. In effect, responses are standardized by organizational location—level and department—and then combined into an organizational score. Computation of means of social position also has a major theoretical advantage in that it focuses on the sociological perspective of organizational reality.

We make no assumption that the distribution of power, regulations, or rewards is random within any particular social position. Instead, each respondent is treated as if he provides a true estimate of the score for a given social position. There is likely to be some distortion due to personality differences or events unique in the history of the organization, but the computation of means for each social position hopefully eliminates or at least reduces the variation due to such factors. By obtaining measures from all levels and all departments, the total structure is portrayed and reflected in the organizational score.

THE MEASUREMENT OF ORGANIZATIONAL INTERDEPENDENCE

The degree of organizational interdependence is measured by the number of joint programs with other organizations. There are several possible measures of the nature and degree of organizational interdependence among social welfare and health organizations. Among these are:

1. The number of cases, clients or patients referred or exchanged.
2. The number of personnel lent, borrowed, or exchanged.

3. The number, sources, and amounts of financial support.
4. The number of joint programs.

The first two of these were used in an earlier study of interorganizational relationships (Levine and White, 1961). In our research we found that organizations such as rehabilitation workshops and family agencies simply did not keep records of the number of walk-ins or calls referred by other organizations. Similar problems were encountered with exchanges of personnel. Thus, we found great difficulty in using these measures of interdependence. While the nature and amounts of financial support are interesting and important aspects of interorganizational analysis, they are not included in this study.

We asked the head of each organization to list every joint program in which his organization had been involved in the past ten years, whether terminated or not. A profile of each program was obtained, including the name of participating organizations, goals of the program, number and type of clients or patients involved, and source of financial and other resources for the program. Only existing programs and those involving the commitment of resources by all participating organizations—such as personnel, finances, space—were included in our analysis.

Since a number of our sixteen organizations had participated in joint programs with each other, it was possible to check the reliability of their responses. We did not find any difficulties of recall for this period of time. In part this is probably because most of the joint programs, once started, tended to continue over time. Some organizations had maintained their organizational relationships for as many as twenty years. Then too, the fact that the joint program

is not a minor incident in the life of an organization also facilitates recall. We did discover that organizational leaders tended to think of the purchase of services as a joint program. To solve this problem we included in our interview schedule a series of follow-up questions about the amount of staff shared and the amount of funds contributed by each organization involved in the joint program.

Another problem of measurement centered on the difficulty of defining separate joint programs. For example, there was a tendency for an organization with a history of successful relationships (those that endured for more than two years) to develop a number of joint programs with the same organization. The relationships would grow in scope and depth in much the way that one would predict from Homans' (1950) hypotheses about the interaction between people. This raised the problem of whether joint programs with the same organization should be counted as separate programs. Our solution was to count the program separately if it involved different activities. Thus a research program and an education program with the same organization, two common kinds of programs, would be counted as separate joint programs. The key in making this decision was the idea of separate activities. In fact, programs were usually developed at different dates, suggesting again that our solution was a correct one. At the same time, if an organization developed the same joint program with three organizations, this was counted only once. From a practical standpoint these attempts at refinement were not so important because it is clear that the differences in number of joint programs among the sixteen organizations in our study are so great that similar ranking would occur regardless of how one counted the programs.

ORGANIZATIONAL INTERDEPENDENCE

TABLE 1. Average number of joint programs by type of organization.

Type of organizations	Number of organizations	Average number of joint programs	Range
Rehabilitation Centers	3	20.7	8–33
Special Education Department—Public Schools	1	15.0	15
Hospitals	3	8.3	6–12
Homes for Emotionally Disturbed	3	2.3	1–3
Social Casework Agencies	6	1.2	0–4
All organizations	16	7.3	0–33

The number of existing joint programs among these sixteen organizations ranged from none to 33. Rehabilitation centers had the highest average number of joint programs, although the range was quite extensive among some other kinds of organizations in our study (Table 1). The special education department and the hospitals had an intermediate range of programs. Social casework agencies and homes for the emotionally disturbed had the least number of joint programs. In every case, however, there was some variation within each organizational category.

Findings

A strict interpretation of data would allow us to discuss only the consequences of interorganizational relationships on the internal structure and performance of an organization. This is true because the period of time during which measurement of the number of joint programs, our measure of organizational interdependence, was made occurred prior to most of our measures of structure and performance. Yet the reasoning in our theoretical framework suggests that these variables are both causes and effects in an on-going process. Strictly speaking, our data reflect the consequences of increased joint programs, but we shall still make some inferences about their causes.

(1) Organizations with many joint programs are more complex organizations, that is, they are more highly professionalized and have more diversified occupational structures. By complexity we do not mean the same thing as Rushing's (1967) division of labor, a measure of the distribution of people among different occupations, but rather the diversity of activities. There are essentially two aspects of complexity as we have defined it: the degree to which there is a high number of different types of occupational activities in the organization; and the degree to which these diverse occupations are anchored in professional societies.[3] One of the most startling findings in our study is the extremely high correlation between the number of different types of occupations in an organization and the number of joint programs ($r = 0.87$).

The relationship between the occupational diversity of the organization and the number of joint programs in 1967 is very high, whether we use the number of occupations in 1959 ($r = 0.79$), the number of occupations in 1964 ($r = 0.83$), or the number of occupations in 1967 ($r = 0.87$). While time sequence is not the same as causation, this does suggest that occupational diversity is not solely a function of new programs.

Rather it suggests that organizations that have a high number of joint programs are organizations that have been occupationally diverse for a number of years.

The addition of joint programs evidently makes an organization aware of the need for still more specialties. One rehabilitation center used social workers in a joint program involving the mentally retarded with several other agencies. It then decided to add social workers to a number of its other programs. The addition of new specialties may also be necessary in order to help solve some of the problems of coordination created by the joint programs.

The dependent variable, number of joint programs, is quite dispersed with a range from 0 to 33 and a mean of 7.3. It is entirely possible that the unusually high correlations for some variables in Table 2 are simply a function of a highly skewed distribution on this variable. Therefore, we computed two non-parametric measures of correlation, Spearman's rank order correlation coefficient (rho) and Kendall's rank correlation coefficient (tau) for the relationship between number of occupations in 1967 and the number of joint programs as shown in Table 3. The relationship between these two variables remains strong even when using the non-parametric statistics.

The objection could be raised that the very strong relationship between number of occupational specialties and the number of joint programs may also be a function of the type of organization. In Table 1, it was shown that rehabilitation

TABLE 2. Relationships between the number of joint programs and organizational characteristics.

Organizational characteristics	Pearsonian product-moment correlation coefficients between each organizational characteristic and the number of joint programs
1. Degree of Complexity	
Index of Professional Training	.15
Index of Professional Activity	.60**
Number of Occupations: 1967	.87****
2. Degree of Organizational Innovation: 1959–1966	
Number of New Programs (including new programs that are joint programs)	.71***
Number of New Programs (excluding new programs that are joint programs)	.74****
3. Internal Communication	
Number of Committees	.47*
Number of Committee Meetings per Month	.83****
4. Degree of Centralization	
Index of Participation in Decision-Making	.30
Index of Hierarchy of Authority	.33
5. Degree of Formation	
Index of Job Codification	.13
Index of Rule Observation	−.06
Index of Specificity of Job	−.06

* P<.10. ** P<.05. *** P<.01. **** P<.001.

TABLE 3. Comparison of Pearsonian correlation coefficient (r), Spearman's rank order correlation coefficient (rho), and Kendall's rank correlation coefficient (tau) for the four largest correlations shown in Table 2.

Organizational characteristic	Correlation coefficient between number of joint programs and organizational characteristics		
	r	rho	tau
Number of Occupations: 1967	.87	.81	.74
Number of New Programs: 1959–1966 (including new programs that are joint programs)	.71	.84	.75
Number of New Programs: 1959–1966 (excluding new programs that are joint programs)	.74	.80	.70
Number of Committee Meetings per Month	.83	.61	.54

centers had the most joint programs, followed by the special education department, hospitals, homes for the emotionally disturbed, and finally social casework agencies. The observation that there is a positive relationship between these two variables is valid within three of the four categories of organizations shown in Table 4. That is, within the categories of rehabilitation centers, mental hospitals, and homes for the emotionally disturbed the organizations having the highest number of occupations have the most joint programs while those having the fewest occupational specialties have the smallest number of joint programs. Only among social casework agencies does the relationship not hold. It might be noted that only one social casework organization had more than one interorganizational tie.

The degree to which an organization is professionalized is also strongly related to the number of joint programs. We measured the degree of professionalism in organizations in two ways: first, the degree to which the organizational members received professional training; and second, the degree to which organizational members are currently active in professional activities, i.e., attending meetings, giving papers, or holding of-

fices. The measure of current professional activity was also quite highly related to our measure of the number of joint programs ($r = 0.60$).[4] The degree of professional training had little relationship with the number of joint programs ($r = 0.15$).[5]

(2) *Organizations with many joint programs are more innovative organizations.* The degree of organizational innovation is measured by the number of new programs that were successfully implemented in the organization during the eight-year period from 1959 to 1966. The correlation coefficient between joint programs and new programs is 0.71, as shown in Table 2. Of course, there is an element of spuriousness in this relationship, since some of the new programs are joint programs. If the correlation coefficient is recomputed, eliminating all new programs that are also joint programs, we find the same result ($r=0.74$).

As in the case of number of occupational specialties in the organization, the finding based on non-parametric measures of association between each of these two measures of organizational innovation and the number of new programs is little different from the results based on the parametric statistical measure (See Table 3).

COMPETITION, COOPERATION, AND CRISIS

	Number of occupations 1967	Number of joint programs
Rehabilitation Centers		
Rehabilitation Center A	27	33
Rehabilitation Center B	24	21
Rehabilitation Center C	13	8
Department of Special Education		
Educational Organization D	19	15
Mental Hospitals		
Mental Hospital E	18	12
Mental Hospital F	18	7
Mental Hospital G	11	6
Homes for Emotionally Disturbed		
Home H	11	3
Home I	10	3
Home J	7	1
Social Casework Agencies		
Casework Agency K	7	1
Casework Agency L	6	0
Casework Agency M	5	1
Casework Agency N	5	1
Casework Agency O	4	4
Casework Agency P	1	0

It could be that the above relationships between degree of organizational innovation and number of joint programs may simply be a function of complexity. We have argued that the degree of complexity gives rise not only to joint programs, but also to new programs. While there is no relationship between professional training and the number of new programs ($r = -0.18$), there are relatively strong relationships between this variable and professional activity ($r = 0.74$) as well as occupational diversity ($r = 0.67$). When the relationships between the number of joint programs and the number of new programs (excluding new programs that are joint programs) is controlled for each of these three indicators separately, the relationship between these two variables remains relatively strong (see Table 5). This illustrates that the number of new programs is related to the number of joint programs independently of these various indicators of complexity.

The key idea in our interpretation is that it is the rate of organizational innovation that intensifies the need for new resources. The higher this rate, the more likely organizations are to use the joint program as a mechanism for cost reduction in such activities. The fact that some new programs are joint programs only strengthens our argument that the joint program is a useful solution for the organization seeking to develop new programs.

This interplay between new programs and joint programs can be made clear with several examples from our study. One rehabilitation center with a high rate of new programs developed joint programs with several organizations that were primarily fund-raising organiza-

TABLE 5. Partial correlation coefficients between number of joint programs and organizational innovation, controlling for indicators of complexity.

Control variables	Partial correlation between number of joint programs and number of new programs 1959–1966 (excluding new programs that are joint programs), controlling for the variable indicated
Indicators of Complexity	
Index of Professional Training	.77
Index of Professional Activity	.55
Number of Occupations: 1967	.46

tions, as a solution for funding its growth. But in turn these organizations recognized new needs and asked the organization to develop still more new programs in areas for their clients. This particular agency is presently exploring the possibility of developing special toys for the mentally retarded because one of its joint programs is with an organization concerned with this type of client.

We may also re-examine the relationships between indicators of complexity and the number of joint programs. As shown in Table 6, only the relationship between the number of occupations and the number of joint programs remains strong when the number of new programs (excluding new programs that are joint programs) is controlled (partial $r = 0.75$).

(3) Organizations with many joint programs have more active internal communication channels. We measured the degree of internal communication in two ways. First, the number of committees in the organization and, second, the number of committee meetings per month. An active committee structure in an organization provides the potential for viable communication links in an organization. As shown in Table 2, there was a moderately strong relationship between the number of organizational committees and joint programs ($r = 0.47$) and a very strong relationship between the number of committee meetings per

month and the number of joint programs ($r = 0.83$).

The relationship between the number of joint programs and the number of committee meetings per month remains moderately strong when the two nonparametric measures of association are computed. (See Table 3.)

Actually the system of communication for joint programs is even more complex than this. For example, one rehabilitation agency with the largest number of joint programs had a special board with the university with which it had many joint programs and was in the process of establishing another joint board with a second university. Another rehabilitation agency created a special steering committee to suggest and supervise joint programs: the members of this committee were representatives from other organizations.

Controlling for the indicators of complexity and program change reduces the relationship between the number of committees and number of joint programs almost to zero in every case except that of professional training. Thus, the number of committees is evidently a function of these factors. On the other hand, the very strong relationship between the number of joint programs and the frequency of committee meetings is only moderately reduced when these controls are applied as shown in Table 7. This shows that the frequency of

TABLE 6. Partial correlation coefficients between number of joint programs and indicators of complexity, controlling for number of new programs (excluding new programs that are joint programs).

Indicators of complexity	Partial correlation between number of joint programs and indicators of complexity, controlling for number of new programs (excluding new programs that are joint programs)
Index of Professional Training	.32
Index of Professional Activity	.11
Number of Occupations: 1967	.75

committee meetings is not simply a function of the complexity of the organization or the degree of organizational innovation, but has an independent relationship with the number of joint programs.

(4) *Organizations with many joint programs have slightly more decentralized decision-making structures.* In our study, staff members were asked how often they participated in organizational decisions about the hiring of personnel, the promotion of personnel, the adoption of new organizational policies, and the adoption of new programs or services. The organizational score was based on the degree of participation in these four areas of decision-making.[6] As shown in Table 2, there is a weak, positive rela-

tionship between the degree of participation in agency-wide decisions and the number of joint programs ($r = 0.30$). This appears to be measuring the way resources are controlled. A second kind of decision-making concerns the control of work. We measure the degree of decision-making about work with a scale called the "hierarchy of authority."[7] This scale had a relationship with the number of joint programs in the opposite direction to our expectation ($r = 0.33$). While highly interdependent organizations have slightly more decentralization of decisions about organizational resources there is slightly less control over work in such organizations. It is difficult to account for this other than that the organizations with a high degree of pro-

TABLE 7. Partial correlation coefficients between number of joint programs and indicators of internal communication, controlling for indicators of complexity and innovation.

Control variables	Partial correlations between number of joint programs and number of committees, controlling for the variable indicated	Partial correlation between number of joint programs and frequency of committee meetings, controlling for the variable indicated
Indicators of Complexity		
Index of Professional Training	.45	.83
Index of Professional Activity	.13	.76
Number of Occupations: 1967	.11	.57
Indicator of Organizational Innovation		
Number of New Programs: 1959–1966 (excluding new programs that are joint programs)	.08	.64

TABLE 8. Partial correlation coefficients between number of joint programs and indicators of centralization of decision-making, controlling for indicators of complexity, innovation, and internal communication.

Control variables	Partial correlations between number of joint programs and participation in decision-making, controlling for the variable indicated	Partial correlations between number of joint programs and hierarchy of authority, controlling for the variable indicated
Indicators of Complexity		
Index of Professional Training	.27	.33
Index of Professional Activity	.01	.21
Number of Occupations: 1967	−.10	.31
Indicator of Organizational Innovation		
Number of New Programs: 1959–1966		
(excluding new programs that are		
joint programs)	.20	−.28
Indicators of Internal Communication		
Number of Committees	.16	.17
Number of Committee Meetings		
per Month	.43	.22

gram change during the period 1964–1966 had less control over work decisions in 1967 than in 1964. This suggests that the rate of change was so high in such organizations during this period that some more rigid mechanisms of social control were adopted in these organizations. Since the highly innovative organizations were also those with more joint programs, this helps to explain the reversal.

Partial correlations between the number of joint programs and the degree of participation in decision-making, controlling for each of the indicators of complexity, innovation, and internal communication, are shown in Table 8.

The relatively low relationship between these two variables is reduced, and in one case reversed, when these other factors are controlled by using partial correlations. Only in the case of frequency of committee meetings is the relationship strengthened. What this means is that the degree of participa-

tion in decision-making is largely a function of some of the previously discussed variables—professional activity, number of occupations, and number of committees. Thus, it has little independent relationship with the number of joint programs.

The relationship between hierarchy of authority and the number of joint programs is little affected by indicators of complexity, but somewhat more by the indicators of internal communication. (See Table 8.) On the other hand, the relationship between these two variables is reversed when the number of new programs is controlled, and the relationship is now in the expected direction, i.e., members of organizations with many joint programs having more control over individual work tasks. This finding buttresses our earlier interpretation that it was the dramatic increase of new programs that brought about less control over individual work decisions in organizations with many joint programs.

(5) There is no relationship between formalization and the number of joint programs. Rules and regulations are important organizational mechanisms that are often used to insure the predictability of performance. There are several important aspects of rules as mechanisms of social control. One is the number of regulations specifying who is to do what, when, where, and why; this we call job codification.[8] A second is the diligency with which such rules are enforced; this we call rule observance.[9] A third is the degree to which the procedures defining a job are spelled out; this we call the index of specificity of jobs.[10]

Two of these three indicators of formalization, the degree of rule observation and the degree of specificity of jobs, had very small inverse relationships with the number of joint programs (r = −0.06 in each case), but each of these is hardly different from zero. The index of job codification was directly related to the number of joint programs (r = 0.13), but it too is little different from zero, although it is in the opposite direction to our expectation.

We conclude from these findings that formalization is unrelated to the degree of organizational interdependence, suggesting that either this kind of internal diversity is not very important or that we do not have valid measures of this phenomenon. However, there is some problem of interpretation because there was also some movement of the highly innovative organizations toward greater formalization. For example, there is a negative partial correlation between the number of joint programs and each of the indicators of formalization, i.e., job codification (partial r = −0.11), rule observation (partial r = −0.37), and degree of specificity of the jobs (partial r = −0.29), when the number of new programs during the period 1959–1966 is partialled out.

CONTROLS FOR SIZE, AUSPICES, AGE, AND TECHNOLOGY

The sixteen organizations included in this study are, from one point of view, relatively homogeneous. All of them provide either psychiatric, social, or rehabilitation services of one kind or another. In comparison to economic organizations, they are indeed homogeneous. In addition, they are all located in a single metropolitan area. The reader might wonder, therefore, how far we can generalize from our study to other kinds of organizations or to organizations in other communities.

There are several ways in which some estimate of the generality can be made. One approach would be to divide the organizations into different categories, as was done in Tables 1 and 4. Here we emphasized the differences among a set of organizations that, considering the range of all organizations, are relatively homogeneous. The difficulty with this approach is that we are making comparisons among so few cases in each category.

An alternative approach is to look at some general variables that describe the conditions of all organizations. The size of the organization is one such variable. Similarly the auspices of the organization, i.e., whether private or public, is another. And the age of the organization may also be an important factor here. Perrow (1967) has recently suggested another variable, the degree of routinization of technology. Undoubtedly there are others, but these represent some of the variables that one is likely to encounter in the literature and, therefore, are a good starting place for controls.

ORGANIZATIONAL INTERDEPENDENCE

Since there were such great differences in the size of organizations in the study, a rank ordering of size is used. The correlation coefficient between size and the number of joint programs is positive and moderate ($r = 0.34$), which means that larger organizations have slightly more joint programs.

The auspices of the organization is measured by a dummy variable of private (1) versus public (0). The correlation coefficient between auspices and number of joint programs is 0.20, meaning that private organizations have slightly more joint programs.

The age of the organization was measured by constructing a trichotomous variable: (0), the organization was started in the post-Depression years (1938 to present); (1), the organization was started in the years following World War I (1918–1923); and (2), the organization was started prior to 1900. The correlation coefficient between age of the organization and the number of joint programs is -0.15, indicating that the younger organizations have slightly more joint programs.

Finally we looked at the type of technology, measured by the degree of routineness of work activities. By routineness of work we mean the degree to which organizational members have non-uniform work activities (Perrow, 1967; Woodward, 1965).[11] The correlation coefficient between routineness of work and the number of joint programs is -0.24, meaning that organizations with many joint programs have less routine technologies.

None of these four variables has strong relationships with the number of joint programs. When each of the relationships between the number of joint programs and the indicators of complexity, organizational innovation, internal communication, centralization, and formalization are controlled by each of these four variables separately, the relationships shown in Table 2 are little affected. (See Table 9.) This means that the factors of organizational size, auspices, age, and technology (as we have measured them) have little or no effect on the findings of this study.

Discussions and Conclusions

We now return to the issues raised at the outset of this paper. How are organizational structure and interdependence related? How can the study of an organization and its environment be combined? What kinds of organizations are more cooperative and integrated with other organizations?

We noted that there is a greater degree of complexity, i.e., more occupational diversity and greater professionalism of staff, in those organizations with the most joint programs. The participation in joint programs is evidently one mechanism for adding new occupational specialties to the organization at a reduced cost. By combining the resources of the focal organization with one or more others, there is the possibility of adding new occupational specializations to the organizational roster. This is especially true because joint programs are likely to be of a highly specialized nature, providing services and activities that the focal organization cannot support alone.

The involvement of staff in interorganizational relationships introduces them to new ideas, new perspectives, and new techniques for solving organizational problems. The establishment of collegial relationships with comparable staff members of other organizations provides them with a comparative framework for understanding their own

TABLE 9. Partial correlations between the number of joint programs and indicators of complexity, innovation, internal communication, centralization, and formalization, controlling separately for organization size, auspices, age, and technology.

	Partial correlation coefficient between number of joint programs and the organization characteristic indicated, controlling for			
	Size	Auspices	Age	Technology
Complexity				
Index of Professional Training	.35	.14	.16	.02
Index of Professional Activity	.56	.61	.64	.60
Number of Occupations: 1967	.88	.86	.89	.86
Innovation				
Number of New Programs: 1959–1966 (excluding new programs that are joint programs)	.73	.76	.74	.75
Internal Communication				
Number of Committees	.41	.45	.48	.48
Number of Committee Meetings per Month	.81	.82	.82	.83
Centralization				
Index of Participation in Decision-Making	.25	.27	.40	.18
Index of Hierarchy of Authority	.38	.35	.29	.33
Formalization				
Index of Job Codification	.18	.12	.07	.19
Index of Rule Observation	−.27	.00	−.10	−.02
Index of Specificity of Job	−.19	.03	−.16	.12

organizations. This is likely to affect their professional activities—attendance at meetings of professional societies—as well as reinforce professional standards of excellence. In these ways the involvement of organizations in joint programs has the effect of increasing the complexity of these social and health welfare organizations.

The heightened interdependence has other important implications for the internal structure of organizations. The partial or total commitment of organizational resources to other organizations is likely to affect various departments and the business office as well as the central programs of such an organization. Problems of coordination are likely to become particularly acute under such circumstances. The organization is forced to overcome these problems by heightening the frequency of internal communication. A more diverse committee structure and more committee meetings are mechanisms for handling such problems.

We would have expected that the heightened rates of communication would have resulted in more decentralization than appears to be the case. It is entirely possible that the problems of internal coordination may be reflected in some attempts to tighten the power structure, thus leading to less movement towards decentralization than we had expected. Also, the problems of internal coordination may be reflected in greater programming of the organization, or at least attempts in that direction, and this may be the reason why there is a small relationship between heightened inter-dependency, as we have measured it, and the degree of centralization.

Diversity in occupations (the degree of complexity) and power groups (the degree of decentralization) are related to the number of joint programs, but diversity in work, as reflected in the absence of rules, is not related to this measure of interdependence. In part this may be a consequence of the sudden increase in the rate of program innovation. But it may also be that the degree of formalization is not a good measure of diversity. It is the diversity of occupations, including their perspectives and self-interests, along with the representation of these points of view in a decentralized structure, that allows for diversity with the most critical consequences.

Our assumptions help to explain the steadily increasing frequency of organizational interdependency, especially that involving joint programs. As educa-tion levels increase, the division of labor proceeds (stimulated by research and technology), and organizations become more complex. As they do, they also become more innovative. The search for resources needed to support such innovations requires interdependent relations with other organizations. At first, these interdependencies may be established with organizations with different goals and in areas that are more tangential to the organization. Over time, however, it may be that cooperation among organizations will multiply, involving interdependencies in more critical areas, and involve organizations having more similar goals. It is scarcity of resources that forces organizations to enter into more cooperative activities with other organizations, thus creating greater integration of the organizations in a community structure. The long range consequence of this process will probably be a gradually heightened co-ordination in communities.

NOTES

1. For a discussion of some of the basic differences between individual and collective properties, see Lazarsfeld and Menzel (1960) and Coleman (1964).
2. One advantage of this procedure is that it allows for the cancellation of individual errors made by the job occupants of a particular position. It also allows for the elimination of certain idiosyncratic elements that result from the special privileges a particular occupant might have received as a consequence. An alternative procedure for computing organizational means is to weight all respondents equally. These two procedures yield strikingly similar results for the variables reported in this paper. The product-moment correlation coefficients between the scores based on these two computational procedures were as follows for the variables indicated:

Hierarchy of authority	0.93	Index of specificity of jobs	0.93
Participation in decision making	0.85	Index of routinization of technology	0.94
Job codification	0.89	Professional training	0.90
Rule observation	0.89	Professional activity	0.93

3. It should be noted that our count of occupational specialties is not based on the number of specific job titles. Instead, each respondent was asked what he did and then this was coded according to the kind of professional activity and whether it was a specialty. This procedure was used for two reasons. First, it allows for comparability across organizations. Second, it avoids the problem of task specialization where one activity might be divided into many specific and separate tasks. (See Thompson, 1964.)

4. The index of professional activity, which ranged from 0 to 3 points, was computed as
follows: (a) 1 point for belonging to a professional organization; (b) 1 point for attending at least two-thirds of the previous six meetings of any professional organization; (c) 1 point for the presentation of a paper or holding an office in any professional organization.

5. The index was scored as follows: (a) high school graduates or less education, with no professional training, received a score of 0; (b) high school graduates or less education, with some professional training, received a score of 1; (c) staff members with a college degree or some college, but an absence of other professional training, received a score of 2; (d) staff members with a college degree or some college, and the presence of some other professional training, received a score of 3; (e) the presence of training beyond a college degree, and the absence of other professional training, received a score of 4; (f) the presence of training beyond a college degree, and the presence of other professional training, received a score of 5.

6. The index of actual participation in decision making was based on the following four questions: (1) How frequently do you usually participate in the decision to hire new staff? (2) How frequently do you usually participate in the decisions on the promotion of any of the professional staff? (3) How frequently do you participate in decisions on the adoption of new policies? (4) How frequently do you participate in the decisions on the adoption of new programs? Respondents were assigned numerical scores from 1 (low participation) to 5 (high participation), depending on whether they answered "never," "sometimes," "often," or "always," respectively, to these questions. An average score on these questions was computed for each respondent, and then the data were aggregated into organizational scores as described above.

7. The empirical indicators of these concepts were derived from two scales developed by Richard Hall (1963), namely, hierarchy of authority and rules. The index of hierarchy of authority was computed by first averaging the replies of individual respondents to each of the following five statements: (1) There can be little action taken here until a supervisor approves a decision. (2) A person who wants to make his own decisions would be quickly discouraged here. (3) Even small matters have to be referred to someone higher up for a final answer. (4) I have to ask my boss before I do almost anything. (5) Any decision I make has to have my boss's approval. Responses could vary from 1 (definitely false) to 4 (definitely true). The individual scores were then combined into an organizational score as described above.

8. The index of job codification was based on responses to the following five statements: (1) A person can make his own decisions without checking with anybody else. (2) How things are done here is left up to the person doing the work. (3) People here are allowed to do almost as they please. (4) Most people here make their own rules on the job. Replies to these questions were scored from 1 (definitely true) to 4 (definitely false), and then each of the respondent's answers was averaged. Thus, a high score on this index means high job codification.

9. The index of rule observation was computed by averaging the responses to each of the following two statements: (1) The employees are constantly being checked on for rule violations. (2) People here feel as though they are constantly being watched, to see that they obey all the rules. Respondents' answers were coded from 1 (definitely false) to 4 (definitely true), and then the average score of each respondent on these items was computed. Organizational scores were computed as previously described. On this index, a high score means a high degree of rule observation.

10. The index of specificity of job was based on responses to the following six statements: (1) Whatever situation arises, we have procedures to follow in dealing with it. (2) Everyone has a specific job to do. (3) Going through the proper channels is constantly stressed. (4) The organization keeps a written record of everyone's job performance. (5) We are to follow strict operating procedures at all times. (6) Whenever we have a problem, we are supposed to go to the same person for an answer. Replies to these questions were scored from 1 (definitely false) to 4 (definitely true), and then the aver-

322 age score of each respondent on these items was computed as the other measures. A high score means a high degree of specificity of the job.

11. The index of routinization of technology was based on responses to the following five statements: (1) People here do the same job in the same way every day (reversed). (2) One thing people like around here is the variety of work. (3) Most jobs have something new happening every day. (4) There is something different to do every day. (5) Would you describe your job as being highly routine, somewhat routine, somewhat non-routine, or highly non-routine? The first four items were scored from 1 (definitely true) to 4 (definitely false). On the fifth item scores ranged from 1 (highly non-routine) to 4 (highly routine).

REFERENCES

Barth, Ernest A. T. 1963. "The causes and consequences of interagency conflict." Sociological Inquiry 33 (Winter): 51–57.

Black, Bertram J. and Harold M. Kase. 1963. "Inter-agency cooperation in rehabilitation and mental health." Social Service Review 37 (March): 26–32.

Caplow, Theodore. 1964. Principles of Organization. New York: Harcourt, Brace & World, Inc.

Clark, Burton R. 1965. "Interorganizational patterns in education." Administrative Science Quarterly 10 (September): 224–237.

Coleman, James S. 1964. "Research chronicle: The Adolescent Society." Phillip Hammond (ed.), Sociologist at Work. New York: Basic Books.

Coser, Lewis. 1956. The Functions of Social Conflict. Glencoe, Ill.: The Free Press of Glencoe.

Crozier, Michel. 1964. The Bureaucratic Phenomenon. Chicago: The University of Chicago Press.

Dahrendorf, Ralf. 1958. "Out of Utopia: toward a reorientation of sociological analysis." American Journal of Sociology 64 (September): 115–127.

Dill, William R. 1958. "Environment on an influence on managerial autonomy." Administrative Science Quarterly 2 (March): 409–443.

————. 1962. "The impact of environment on organizational development." Pp. 94–109 in Sidney Mailick and Edward H. Van Ness (eds.), Concepts and Issues in Administrative Behavior. Englewood Cliffs, N.J.: Prentice-Hall, Inc.

Elling, R. H. and S. Halbsky. 1961. "Organizational differentiation and support: a conceptual framework." Administrative Science Quarterly 6 (September): 185–209.

Emery, F. E. and E. L. Trist. 1965. "The causal texture of organizational environment." Human Relations 18 (February): 21–31.

Evan, William M. 1966. "The organization-set: toward a theory of interorganizational relations." Pp. 173–191 in James D. Thompson (ed.), Approaches to Organizational Design. Pittsburgh, Pa.: University of Pittsburgh Press.

Form, William H. and Sigmund Nosow. 1958. Community in Disaster. New York: Harper and Row.

Gouldner, Alvin. 1959. "Reciprocity and autonomy in functional theory." Pp. 241–270 in Llewellyn Gross (ed.), Symposium on Sociological Theory. New York: Harper and Row.

Guetzkow, Harold. 1950. "Interagency committee usage." Public Administration Review 10 (Summer): 190–196.

————. 1966. "Relations among organizations." Pp. 13–44 in Raymond V. Bowers (ed.), Studies on Behavior in Organizations. Athens, Ga.: University of Georgia Press.

Hage, Jerald and Michael Aiken. 1967. "Program change and organizational properties: a comparative analysis." American Journal of Sociology 72 (March): 503–519.

Hall, Richard. 1963. "The concept of bureaucracy: an empirical assessment." American Journal of Sociology 69 (July): 32–40.

Harbison, Frederick H., E. Kochling, F. H. Cassell and H. C. Ruebman. 1955. "Steel management on two continents." Management Science 2:31–39.

COMPETITION, COOPERATION, AND CRISIS

Harrison, Paul M. 1959. Authority and Power in the Free Church Tradition. Princeton, N.J.: Princeton University Press.

Hawley, Amos H. 1951. Human Ecology, New York: The Ronald Press.

Homans, George. 1950. The Human Group. New York: Harcourt, Brace and World, Inc.

Johns, Ray E. and David F. de Marche. 1951. Community Organization and Agency Responsibility. New York: Association Press.

Kornhauser, William. 1959. The Politics of Mass Society. Glencoe, Ill.: The Free Press of Glencoe.

Lawrence, Paul R. and Jay W. Lorsch. 1967. Organization and Environment. Boston: Graduate School of Business Administration, Harvard University.

Lazarsfeld, Paul and Herbert Menzel. 1960. "On the relation between individual and collective properties." Pp. 422–440 in Amitai Etzioni (ed.), Complex Organizations: A Sociological Reader. New York: The Macmillan Company.

Lefton, Mark and William Rosengren. 1966. "Organizations and clients: lateral and longitudinal dimensions." American Sociological Review 31 (December): 802–810.

Levine, Sol and Paul E. White. 1961. "Exchange as a conceptual framework for the study of interorganizational relationships." Administrative Science Quarterly 5 (March): 583–601.

———. 1963. "The community of health organizations." Pp. 321–347 in Howard E. Freeman, S. E. Levine, and Leo G. Reeder (eds.), Handbook of Medical Sociology. Englewood Cliffs, N.J.: Prentice-Hall.

Levine, Sol, Paul E. White and Benjamin D. Paul. 1963. "Community interorganizational problems in providing medical care and social services." American Journal of Public Health 53 (August): 1183–1195.

Litwak, Eugene. 1961. "Models of bureaucracy which permit conflict." American Journal of Sociology 67 (September): 177–184.

Litwak, Eugene and Lydia F. Hylton. 1962. "Interorganizational analysis: A hypothesis on coordinating agencies." Administrative Science Quarterly 6 (March): 395–426.

Miller, Walter B. 1958. "Inter-institutional conflict as a major impediment to delinquency prevention." Human Organization 17 (Fall): 20–23.

Morris, Robert and Ollie A. Randall. 1965. "Planning and organization of community services for the elderly." Social Work 10 (January): 96–102.

Perrow, Charles. 1967. "A framework for the comparative analysis of organizations." American Sociological Review 32 (April): 194–208.

Reid, William. 1964. "Interagency coordination in delinquency prevention and control." Social Service Review 38 (December 1964): 418–428.

Richardson, Stephen A. 1959. "Organizational contrasts on British and American ships." Administrative Science Quarterly 1 (September): 189–207.

Ridgeway, V. F. 1957. "Administration of manufacturer-dealer systems." Administrative Science Quarterly 1 (June): 464–483.

Rushing, William A. 1967. "The effects of industry size and division of labor on administration." Administrative Science Quarterly 12 (September): 273–295.

Selznick, Philip. 1949. TVA and the Grass Roots. Berkeley, Cal.: University of California Press.

Simpson, Richard L. and William H. Gulley. 1962. "Goals, environmental pressures, and organizational characteristics." American Sociological Review 27 (June): 344–351.

Terreberry, Shirley. 1968. "The evolution of organizational environments." Administrative Science Review 12 (March): 590–613.

Thompson, James D. 1962. "Organizations and output transactions." American Journal of Sociology 68 (November): 309–324.

———. 1966. Organizations in Action. New York: McGraw-Hill.

Thompson, James D. and William J. McEwen. 1958. "Organizational goals and environment: goal-setting as an interaction process." American Sociological Review 23 (February): 23–31.

Thompson, Victor R. 1961. Modern Organizations. New York: Alfred A. Knopf, Inc.

Tocqueville, Alexis de. 1945. Democracy in America. New York: Alfred A. Knopf, Inc.

ORGANIZATIONAL INTERDEPENDENCE

324 Warren, Roland L. 1965. "The impact of new designs of community organization." Child Welfare 44 (November): 494–500.

———. 1967. "The interorganizational field as a focus for investigation." Administrative Science Quarterly 12 (December): 396–419.

Wilensky, Harold L. 1967. Organizational Intelligence. New York: Basic Books, Inc.

Willer, David. 1967. Scientific Sociology: Theory and Method. Englewood Cliffs, New Jersey. Prentice-Hall.

Wilson, James Q. 1966. "Innovation in organization: notes toward a theory." Pp. 193–218 in Approaches to Organizational Design. Pittsburgh, Pa.: University of Pittsburgh Press.

Woodward, Joan. 1965. Industrial Organization. London: Oxford University Press.

Wrong, Dennis. 1961. "The oversocialized conception of man in modern society." American Sociological Review 26 (April): 183–193.

Yuchtman, Ephraim and Stanley E. Seashore. 1967. "A system resource approach to organizational effectiveness." American Sociological Review 32 (December): 891–903.

A BALANCE THEORY OF COORDINATION BETWEEN BUREAUCRATIC ORGANIZATIONS AND COMMUNITY PRIMARY GROUPS[1]

Eugene Litwak and Henry J. Meyer

The general problem discussed here is how bureaucratic organizations and external primary groups (such as the family and neighborhood) coordinate their behavior to achieve optimal social control. It will be argued that mechanisms exist to coordinate the two forms of organizations, and that these mechanisms of coordination can be systematically interpreted by what is called a "balance theory of coordination." It will also be argued that this "balance theory" provides a formulation that accounts for current trends more adequately than traditional sociological theories.

Traditional Theory

BUREAUCRATIC AND EXTERNAL PRIMARY GROUP COORDINATION

A number of sociologists have analyzed the characteristics of industrial bureaucratic organizations and primary groups such as the family and the

"A Balance Theory of Coordination Between Bureaucratic Organizations and Community Primary Groups," *Administrative Science Quarterly*, 11, 1 (June 1966), 31–58. Reprinted with the permission of the authors and of the publisher, *Administrative Science Quarterly*.

neighborhood so as to imply that their relationships are antithetical. Weber, in his discussion of China, for example, suggests that one reason why a modern industrial bureaucratic system did not develop was because it was contrary to the strong extended family ties of the Chinese family.[2] This is also an implication of Tonnies' remarks in so far as relations characterized as "gemeinschaft" are viewed as dominated by primary group ties, whereas "gesellschaft" relations are characteristic of the bureaucratic organization.[3] Schumpeter is very explicit on the issue and points out how the rationalistic elements of the work situation tend to undermine affective family bonds.[4] The analyses of contemporary theorists such as Parsons and his associates contradict this view only partially.[5] They accept the view that the two types of organizations are antithetical; but they point out that the family has distinctive functions that cannot be performed by any other type of organization, and that these functions are necessary for the survival of a society. They argue that the bureaucratic organization and at least one type of primary group (the nuclear family) can exist in the same society provided they are kept relatively insulated from each other.

The positions seem to suggest that bureaucratic and external primary groups, unless they are isolated, tend to conflict with each other.[6] Coordination between them is not explicitly entertained in such a conclusion.

RELATION OF TRADITIONAL THEORY TO OBSERVED TRENDS

Such theoretical formulations are surprising in view of developments that can be observed in the more advanced bureaucratic organizations in American society. If the largest and most successful of the industrial bureaucratic organizations are examined, there is evidence that they have made increased efforts in recent decades to establish closer ties with families and neighborhood groups.[7] First, management in such large bureaucracies has come to recognize that work morale and productivity are closely tied to family and local community conditions. Second, these large organizations have realized that they are increasingly exposed to public view. Decisions within these giant corporations which were previously thought to be private decisions of management have now to be reinterpreted in terms of the public welfare, so that they are now as often political as business decisions (e.g., the fixing of prices in the steel industry now clearly involves public policy).

Furthermore if diverse areas of social life are examined—such as the political, the educational, the military areas; delinquency programs; and welfare fund raising—the formal organizations exhibit concern for closer contact with external primary groups such as the family, neighborhood, or local community.[8] More to the point, this concern grows with the final stages of bureaucratization within a society, where the issues of power and control are especially crucial to the organization. Since they are subject to public scrutiny because of magnitude, industrial or political centrality, and dependence on extensive markets, such organizations become sensitive to the need for organizing and maintaining community primary-group support.

IMPLICIT ASSUMPTIONS OF TRADITIONAL THEORY

Underlying the discrepancy between the theoretical position usually presented and the observed trends are some assumptions of the traditional theory that should be made explicit. Two will be stated in exaggerated form in order to expose their implications.

The first assumption is that the primary group and the bureaucratic organization have antithetical, mutually destructive atmospheres. Bureaucracies operate on an instrumental basis, stress impersonality, specificity, the use of rules, professional expertness, and so on. Primary groups operate on a kinship or affective system of evaluation, and stress diffuse, personal, face-to-face contact, and similar relationships.

The second assumption is that the activities of the primary group are for the most part directly replaceable by those of the bureaucratic organization. Thus, if the bureaucratic organization can perform a task, there is no reason why the family should do so as well. This assumption rests, in turn, on the premise that in a mass society bureaucratic organization is the most efficient way to achieve most social goals. Consequently if the two types of organization compete, the bureaucracy will tend to supplant the primary group.[9]

Balance Theory

AN ALTERNATIVE ASSUMPTION

The assumption that the two forms of organization have antithetical atmospheres can be accepted with some reservations, although much of the research of industrial sociology has sought to show that bureaucracies can be operated in a more "human relations" atmosphere than Weber would have anticipated. Nevertheless, there are basic differences between the bureaucracy and the primary group, and such differences are partly a matter of degree and partly a matter of quality. For instance, the family operates primarily on the basis of nepotism and permanence of membership whereas industrial bureaucracy operates primarily on notions of merit and transitory membership.[10] Bureaucracy and family may both permit positive affect but differ in degree, with the family permitting deep love relations.

The assumption that bureaucracies and primary groups are alternative means for the achievement of most goals must be seriously questioned. Here it is suggested that these forms of organization are complementary and that each provides necessary means for achieving a given goal. This position does not deny that the family, for example, has unique social functions, but it does assert that both primary groups and bureaucratic organizations operate in most major task areas of life and that they bring different attributes to the achievement of a given end. From a structural point of view, instead of suggesting the isolation of primary groups and bureaucracies, the position proposed here necessitates close communication between the two forms of organization.

Some of the very characteristics that have been ascribed to the formal organization and to the primary group lend plausibility to this view. One common observation notes that the bureaucratic organization is unable to deal with nonuniform or relatively unique events.[11] This inability is usually attributed to the necessity for *a priori* rules and standardized role specifications as well as to the length of time required for the large organization to deal with an issue not previously defined. Thus, messages must move up and down long chains of communication before policy decisions can be made to meet nonuniform events. The strength of bureaucratic organizations, it is claimed, lies in the professional expertness they can provide as well as their capacity to deal with large numbers of people.

In contrast, the strength of the primary group is seen to be in speed of adaptation and flexibility in meeting nonuniform events.[12] The primary group is incapable of dealing with large numbers of people and is deficient in professional expertness.

Thus, the very virtues claimed for bureaucratic organizations are the defects of the primary groups; the virtues claimed for the primary group are the defects of bureaucratic organizations. For optimum achievement of many social goals—i.e., for social control—it would appear necessary to have both expert knowledge and flexibility, both breadth of coverage and speed of reaction.[13] In short, bureaucratic and primary groups share in the achievement of functions in all areas of life. They are not necessarily competitive, nor is there a division of labor which requires each to function independently.

A BALANCE THEORY OF COORDINATION

The dilemma that must be faced by a theory of interorganizational relations and social control is posed by two propositions:

1. The contributions of both bureaucratic organizations and primary groups are frequently necessary to achieve maximum social control in a mature industrial society.
2. The characteristics of bureaucracies and of primary groups tend to make them incompatible, if not antithetical, as forms of social organization.

A theory of coordination acknowledging both these propositions must avoid two kinds of errors. If the bureaucratic organization and external primary group are too isolated from each other, they are likely to interfere with each other and reduce the contribution of one or the other in achieving a social goal. However, if the two organizational forms are brought too close together, their antithetical atmospheres are likely to disrupt one or both organizations, again impeding the achievement of optimum social goals.

This reasoning prompts a balance theory of coordinating mechanisms that can be stated as follows: Optimum social control is most likely to occur when coordinating mechanisms develop between bureaucratic organizations and external primary groups that balance their relationships at a midpoint of social distance where they are not too intimate and not isolated from each other. This formulation requires recognition of the importance of a variety of mechanisms of coordination, ranging from those capable of bridging great social distances to those capable of increasing distance, while maintaining communication.

The idea of variable social distances bridged by varied mechanisms of coordination becomes obvious once any given large bureaucracy is examined empirically. For instance, where school systems are involved with families in which parents identify strongly with the goals of the school (e.g., middle-class families with parents in professional occupations), there is a minimum of social distance between the bureaucracy and the external primary groups. By contrast, where the schools are dealing with families who do not identify with the goals of the school (e.g., low-income migrants from the Southern Appalachian Mountains with a fundamentalist religious position), there may be a great distance between the bureaucracy and the external primary groups. Likewise industrial organizations seeking to influence the families of their employees on work conditions and worker productivity need to relate to families who identified with them as well as those families who do not. Similarly, the police seeking citizen cooperation in law enforcement must deal with persons and groups that disapprove as well as those in sympathy with the purposes of the organization.

Acknowledging variability in social distance between bureaucratic organization and external primary groups, the balance theory provides a criterion for deciding which mechanisms of coordination will provide optimum social control: mechanisms that permit communication and reduction of social distance in the case of great social distance, mechanisms that increase social distance in cases where social distance is too intimate.

MECHANISMS OF COORDINATION AND BALANCE THEORY

Theoretical consideration of issues involved in coordinating bureaucratic organizations with external primary groups is noticeably lacking in the literature on social organization.[14] Because organizations are very much concerned with maintaining communication with external primary groups, however, it is relatively easy to find many illustrations of mechanisms of coordination. From a review of some of this literature eight reasonably distinct types have been identified, although they are often found in combination and they are not completely exclusive.

For convenience, the mechanisms are viewed as approaches by which a formal organization might seek to influence external primary groups to identify with values and norms of the organization.

(1) *Detached Expert.* Professional persons (such as social workers or public health nurses) act with relative autonomy and by direct participation in external primary groups to bring group norms and values into harmony with those of the organization. They operate by becoming trusted members of the primary group the organization is seeking to influence. The use of "street gang workers" to deal with delinquent groups is an illustration.[15]

(2) *Opinion Leader.* The organization seeks to influence the members of the primary groups through "natural" leaders in neighborhoods and local communities. The Shaw-McKay area approach to delinquency control illustrates this procedure.[16] Katz and Lazarsfeld point out that those utilizing mass media may unintentionally also be using an opinion leader approach.[17] Analysis of community power suggests that in large industries management frequently uses this procedure to exercise influence.[18]

(3) *Settlement House.* A change-inducing milieu is provided through physical facilities and proximity, and through availability of professional change agents. The approach combines the traditional community center with focused educational programs. One illustration is the work at Provo described by Empey and Rabow.[19]

(4) *Voluntary Association.* A voluntary association, bringing together members of the formal organization and the primary groups, is used as a means of communication between the two, as, for example, parent-teacher associations. The same kind of associations can be seen among other types of bureaucra-

cies. The police have various recreational groups for children; churches have church-related clubs; hospitals have voluntary associations like the Gray Ladies; the army maintains close ties to veterans' associations; business organizations and unions often sponsor recreational associations. In all instances, the voluntary associations, whatever their explicit function, also serve as communication between the bureaucratic organizations and significant outside primary groups.

(5) *Common Messenger.* Messages intended to influence are communicated through an individual who is regularly a member of both the organization and the primary groups. The school child often serves as such a messenger for communication between school and family. Communication may be very explicit as in some large industrial organizations, where employees are urged to go out and sell the idea of a better business environment to their friends and families; or it may be more subtle, such as a company's attempt to influence the wives of management by indirect socialization.[20]

(6) *Mass Media.* The formal organization tries to influence primary groups through mass communication media. The characteristics of communication through such media have been thoroughly considered in many studies.[21] Examples of the use of this approach are common throughout the entire range of bureaucratic organizations, e.g., church, governmental, business, and other organizations.

(7) *Formal Authority.* Legal or well-established norms are a basis for communicating with external primary groups. The truant officer, for example, has a legal right to link school and family. The relations of certain agencies, such as the police, to the outer community are almost solely guided by legal power. Other agencies, such as the schools, utilize some legal and some voluntary forms of communication; whereas other agencies, like business and social work agencies, depend almost solely on voluntary arrangements for communicating with outside primary groups.[22]

(8) *Delegated Function.* The organization acts through another organization, which is assumed to have better access, greater expertise, more appropriate facilities, or greater legitimacy in the society. For instance, schools are frequently asked by organizations such as the fire department and safety councils to pass information to the homes through the school children.[23]

PRINCIPLES OF COMMUNICATION IN MECHANISMS OF COORDINATION

These mechanisms described, their utility and limitations for narrowing or increasing social distance can be made more explicit.

For convenience, the analysis approaches the mechanisms as communications *from* the bureaucratic organization *to* the primary group. With relatively minor modifications, however, the principles can be restated so as to characterize communication *from* the primary group *to* the formal organization. The mechanisms will here be thought of as though they are purposive, that is, intended to influence.

Principle of Initiative. Where the social distance is great, it is hypothesized that those mechanisms of coordination that permit the organization to take great initiative in contacting these groups will promote communication, otherwise selective listening may prevent the message from reaching the group for which it is intended.[24] Some of the mechanisms of coordination permit initiative by the bureaucratic organization more effectively than others. Thus, in using the detached worker approach, the bureaucratic organization sends its experts to make contact with the primary group member, in his home territory if necessary. By contrast, the voluntary association and the settlement-house approach are passive approaches requiring more initiative of the primary group. The mass-media approach, although it requires organizational initiative, leaves the decision to accept the message almost completely to the primary group members.

Principle of Intensity. To communicate across the boundaries of resistant primary groups, it is necessary to have intensive relations with primary group members in order to surmount barriers of selective interpretation and selective retention. Messages that reach a distant primary group without strong support from a trusted member are likely to be put aside or distorted.[25] The opinion leader approach, because it depends on pre-existing influence relationships represents a mechanism of considerable intensity; so does the detached worker approach. In contrast, the mass media and common messenger approaches exert the least intensity in the coordinating process.

Principle of Focused Expertise. Much communication between bureaucratic organizations and primary groups involves simple information, such as times of meetings, announcements about speakers, descriptions of new programs, and similar details. Some communications, however, involve complex kinds of messages; for example: communicating a fundamental change in the educational policy of a school to families; communicating the employ-

ment norms of a northern, urban factory to southern rural migrants; and communicating the kind of behavior that will help a returning mental patient to his family.

The principle of focused expertise implies that the more complex the information, the more necessary the close contact between a professional expert and the group to be influenced. Furthermore, since the presentation of complex information requires the communicator to take account of unique problems any given group may have in absorbing the information and to adapt the communication accordingly, immediate feedback and response are necessary. Because of such factors, an expert in close touch with the group is required.[26] The detached worker approach, the settlement-house approach, and the voluntary association approach are all procedures which put the expert in face-to-face contact with the external primary groups; whereas the opinion leader, the mass media, and the common messenger approaches permit only indirect access. It may be noted that great social distance usually implies that complex information must be transmitted and therefore suggests the need for focused expertise.

Principle of Maximum Coverage. It is hypothesized that better coordination will occur when a procedure can reach the largest number of external primary groups. This is not only a principle of economy, but also one of extensiveness. Procedures that reach more people without loss of effectiveness are preferred to those of limited scope. The detached expert approach is limited in the number of primary groups it can reach at a given level of resources because it requires almost a one-to-one relation between expert and group. One expert is restricted to one—maybe two groups. By contrast, the settlement house and the voluntary association can reach more people because a given expert can deal with many more groups in a given day. The common messenger approach has an even wider scope, and the mass media approach has the widest scope of all.

This enumeration of some of the major principles of communication governing the mechanisms of coordination is intended only to suggest differences in efficacy of communication procedures. Table 1 summarizes how these principles relate to the eight designated mechanisms of coordination. This table applies the principles as criteria to evaluate the suitability of a mechanism of coordination for any given state of imbalance. Obviously, there are many logical combinations of principles which have not been considered here or represented in Table 1.

Application of Balance Theory

BALANCE THEORY OF COORDINATION RE-EXAMINED

From the preceding presentation of mechanisms of coordination and some of the underlying communication principles involved, specific predictions can be derived from the balance theory of coordination. As illustration, the detached expert approach can be examined in terms of the principles of communication. This approach as applied to the organizations seeking to influence a primary group has the following characteristics (see Table 1):

1. It requires great initiative of the bureaucratic organization.
2. It involves intensive relations between change agent and external group.
3. It entails focused expertise, or close contact between the professional and his target group.
4. It has limited scope.

With the exception of scope, all characteristics of this mechanism are highly useful for communicating across great social distance; i.e., achieving a balance when the bureaucratic organization must deal with distant primary groups. Thus, when a school or a business seeks to communicate its goals and program to a distant family, it must take the initiative; it must use intensity of interaction to penetrate primary group boundaries, and it must make use of focused expertise to effect changes in social norms through communications of very complex messages. In northern urban communities, migrant southern white families often seem to require

TABLE 1. Theoretical dimensions of communication, hypothesized to be operative in each mechanism of coordination.

Coordinating mechanisms	Initiative	Intensity	Focused expertise	Coverage
Detached expert	highest	high	highest	lowest
Opinion leader	moderate	highest	low	moderate
Settlement house	moderate to low	high	high	moderate
Voluntary associations	lowest	moderate	moderate	high
Common messenger	moderate	low	lowest	high
Mass media	moderate to low	lowest	lowest	highest
Formal authority	high	moderate to low	high to low	high to low
Delegated function	high to low	high to low	high to low	high to low

such an approach to achieve balance between school and family for the educational motivation of the children. Unions seeking to organize in communities unfriendly to union or management seeking to sway strong labor groups have analogous problems.

This approach is less effective for coordination when primary groups are overidentified with the bureaucratic organizations. The bureaucratic organization then does not require initiative, since the primary group will take the initiative. Intensive relations are unnecessary since there are no resistant primary group boundaries to pierce and may, indeed, evoke too much affectivity. School teachers, for example, might be tempted to evaluate children on the basis of their positive or negative feelings toward the parents, and parents might evaluate their children too exclusively on the basis of their school performance. In industry, bringing the families too close may lead to nepotism and favoritism within the organization; and among the families, it may lead to undue evaluation of family members in terms of occupational success or utility. In either case, it is likely to lead to a loss in ability to achieve occupational goals. Furthermore, the detached expert approach is extremely wasteful where families already identify with the organization, since there are other procedures (mass media and voluntary association) which can communicate to such families and reach many more of them without incurring excessive intimacy.

By similar analyses, the balance theory of coordination suggests that where great social distance exists, mechanisms such as the detached worker, opinion leader, and settlement house are more effective than mass media, common messenger, formal authority, or voluntary association approaches. These statements are intended to give only an idea of the broad applications of the theory. More precise hypotheses relating given mechanisms of coordination for different family types to optimal goal achievement depend on a more detailed analysis of the primary groups involved.

BUREAUCRATIC ORGANIZATIONS AND BALANCE THEORY

Thus far, only two elements involved in balance theory have been explicitly considered in the formulation—mechanisms of coordination and external primary groups (e.g., whether they are distant or close). Little has been said about the other element of the hypothesis—the bureaucratic organization. The proposed theory of balance should be able to take account of all types of bureaucratic organizations in industrial societies.

A balance theory of coordination must be formulated to take account of two observations about bureaucratic organizations in our society: (1) that most bureaucracies must coordinate their behavior with that of outside primary groups if they are to achieve their goals successfully, and (2) that our society contains a bewildering variety of bureaucratic structures. Thus, the theory must encompass the relatively small, collegial bureaucracy of the private social work agency; the large, legalistic structure of the police force; the large industrial bureaucracy with the production and marketing goals; and the school system and the mental hospital, where requirements to conform to organizational rules may conflict with norms of professional autonomy.

Earlier in this paper it was argued that coordination with external primary groups was necessary if their contributions were to complement those of formal organizations to maximize goal achievement. It can be further argued that apparent variations in the need for such coordination by different types of bureaucracies are related to varying degrees of legitimacy which our society accords organizational efforts to influence community primary groups. Thus, welfare organizations, schools, hospitals, and churches can legitimately expose their efforts to affect the primary groups with which they are concerned. In contrast, industrial organizations and most governmental agencies do not have the legitimate privilege to influence the primary groups that concern their successful performance; therefore their coordinating efforts must operate less visibly. For example, utilization of a detached expert approach by the public relations department of an industrial concern might take the covert form of his joining social clubs and civic organizations; nevertheless, this approach does not differ structurally from the overt use of the detached expert by a school.

Litwak's conceptual scheme is used to describe the generic characteristics of bureaucracies so as to reduce the apparent great variety of such organizations to a limited number of types.[27] He points out that organizational structure and goal achievement are related, in part, to the organization's goals and to its tasks in pursuit of the goals. Where goals are relatively unambiguous, criteria for their realization, relatively determinate, and tasks relatively standardized and repetitive, the rationalistic structure of bureaucracy described by Weber appears to emerge and become efficient. In contrast, where goals are ambiguous, criteria uncertain, tasks nonuniform and likely to require interpersonal techniques, a "human relations"

form of bureaucracy is more likely to appear and to represent the more efficient structure. Finally, when organizational goals and criteria are mixed, tasks both uniform and nonuniform, techniques both impersonal and interpersonal, a third bureaucratic type that combines both rationalistic and human relations elements seems to emerge as the more efficient form. This type has been called a "professional bureaucracy," since one of its most obvious features seems to be the conflict between the organizational and professional orientations of its members.

TYPES OF BUREAUCRATIC ORGANIZATION

The types of bureaucratic organizations in terms of this presentation of a balance theory of coordination can be described in somewhat more detail.

Rationalistic Model. Characterized by impersonal social relations, detailed rules governing most actions, strict hierarchy of authority, job specialization, narrow delimitation of occupational duties and privileges, evaluation on the basis of merit (knowledge, training, success on the job). This is the model of bureaucracy described by Max Weber. This type is illustrated by government bureaucracies which follow detailed legal regulations, such as those involved in administering income tax, processing applications for licenses, and so on. It is the type most familiar in industrial bureaucracies.

Human Relations Model. Exhibits personal relations, general policies rather than detailed rules, colleague rather than hierarchical structure, broad definition of the organization's goals, and evaluation on the basis of merit. Except for evaluation (employment, pay, promotion) on the basis of merit, the human relations model exhibits char-

334 acteristics opposite to those of the
rationalistic model. This type may be
illustrated by small social work agencies, small scientific laboratories, small
graduate schools, and others.

Professional Model. Incorporates both
rationalistic and human relations elements, and found where both standardized, recurrent tasks and tasks requiring
interpersonal skills to deal with non-
standardized events are regularly required. This type of organization
develops internal arrangements (such as
parallel structures of authority, segregated departments) to reconcile contradictory administrative approaches.[28]
This is illustrated by hospitals, school
systems, and industrial organizations
with major involvements in research as
well as production.

Nonmerit Model. Unlike each of the
other forms, this is characterized by
significant intrusion of bases other than
merit for evaluation of personnel and
performance; consequently criteria
irrelevant to the achievement of organizational goals are introduced. Dependence on nepotism, personal friendship,
discrimination on the basis of race, religion, or social class, and excessive
emphasis on personal rather than organizational goals illustrate nonmerit
bases of evaluation. Although these conditions may appear, intentionally or
unintentionally, in the other types of
organizations, when they predominate
the result is distinctive enough to identify a separate organizational form. Most
typical of small organizations, some
large organizations as well, appear to
approach this model.

BUREAUCRATIC ORGANIZATIONS AND COORDINATING MECHANISMS

At the present stage of knowledge, the
relationship between bureaucratic structures and the mechanisms that link them
to the outer community can be stated in
a straightforward fashion if one makes
the following simplifying assumption:

When administrative style and mechanisms of coordination are structurally
consistent, each will operate most effectively, in achieving the given goal.
Structural consistency is defined in
terms of the dimensions of organization
already suggested: hierarchical vs. colleague relations, impersonal vs. personalized relations, specific rules vs.
policy, and so on. Each of the mechanisms may be analyzed to see which of
these attributes it demands in order to
operate. The detached worker approach
(intended to change values or deal with
distant populations, and requiring integration of the worker into the primary
group) is a mechanism that promotes
localized decision making, affective
rather than impersonal relations, internalization of policy rather than specific
rules, and diffused rather than delimited
duties. In contrast, sending messages
through mass media is an approach that
is highly consistent with centralized authority, specific rules, impersonal work
situations, delimited tasks, and so on.

The opinion leader approach requires
that the good will of the leader be obtained so as to make use of his primary
group attachment. This approach therefore demands affective rather than impersonal relations, localized autonomy
(for the opinion leader), use of internalization of policy rather than specific
rules, etc. Katz and Lazarsfeld have
pointed out that this approach is often
an unrecognized aspect of the more
rationalistic mass media approach.[29] Our
analysis would lead to the hypothesis
that it is optimally effective (e.g., the
bureaucratic organization has maximal
control) when it is used by a human relations administrative structure.

In contrast, agencies that use legal authority as their major means of communication must operate through rationalistic organizational structure. There are some counter trends among organizations using legal authority such as the juvenile court's stress on treatment; however, permitting localized organizational discretion often tends to subvert one of the basic tenets of the law—due process. As a consequence the use of formal authority as a means of communication puts very definite rationalistic restrictions on organizational structures.

The settlement house approach, as defined here, stresses attitude and value change. It therefore requires decentralized authority, affective and diffuse relations, and internalization of policies. It would seem most consistent with the human relations structure. In contrast, the voluntary association tends to deal with individuals who are already in sympathy with the organizational goals and who are often involved primarily in getting factual information or keeping informed. They could well operate, therefore, within the boundaries of a rationalistic administrative style. This would also hold for the common messenger approach.

When effective coordination requires the use of a range of coordinating mechanisms—where the organization is confronted by both distant and supporting primary groups—the professional organizational structure might be expected to be more effective. Thus, a school might develop a detached worker program for deviant families and at the same time promote a parent-teacher association for families who conform. The professional structure permits these mechanisms (with markedly different organizational demands) to operate within the same organization with minimal friction.

It is assumed that none of the mechanisms of coordination will be consistent with the nonmerit type of organization; that is, any other organizational structure combined with any mechanism of coordination is more likely to be effective than a nonmerit type, regardless of the mechanism of coordination employed. This assumption is based on the expectation that where the organization does not select or assign people in terms of task performance, it is less likely to achieve its task than the organization that does.

In summary, five significant combinations of coordinating mechanisms and administrative styles can be noted.[30]

1. Human relations administrative style with detached expert, opinion leader, and settlement house mechanisms.
2. Rationalistic administrative style with formal authority, voluntary association, mass media, and common messenger mechanisms.
3. Professional administrative style with combinations of mechanisms from both preceding items; e.g., detached worker and delegated function, opinion leader and mass media, etc.
4. Mismatched administrative style and mechanisms of coordination, e.g., rationalistic style and detached expert, human relations style and formal authority, and so on.
5. Nonmerit administrative style and any mechanism.

BUREAUCRACY, PRIMARY GROUPS, AND MECHANISMS OF COORDINATION

With these combinations, the relationships between the three independent elements of this balance theory—the primary groups, the bureaucratic organi-

TABLE 2. Hypothesized relations of primary groups, bureaucratic structure, and mechanisms of coordination in optimum balance for goal achievement.*

Bureaucratic structure	Mechanisms of coordination	Deviant primary groups	Con- forming primary groups	Mixture of deviant and groups conforming
Human relations	Opinion leader, settlement house, detached expert, delegated function	5*	3	3.5
Rationalistic	Common messenger, mass media, formal authority, voluntary association	3	5	3.5
Professional	Both human relations† and rationalistic‡ coordinating mechanisms	4	4	5
Human relations or rationalistic	Mismatched, with human relations† or rationalistic mechanism‡	2	2	2
Nonmerit	Any mechanism	1	1	1

* The larger the numbers the more likely that balance and therefore goals will be achieved. Numbers represent rankings within each column.

† Human relations coordinating mechanisms are opinion teacher, settlement house, detached expert, delegated functions.

‡ Rationalistic coordinating mechanisms are common messenger, mass media, formal authority, voluntary association.

zations, and the mechanisms of coordination—can be systematically stated and the hypothesized consequences for achieving balance and hence maximizing social control can be derived. These are presented schematically in Table 2.

Where the organization is confronted with deviant families or neighborhood groups, it must have some mechanism of coordination that permits communication over social distance (initiative, intensity, and focused expertise). The use of such mechanisms is most consistent with a human relations organizational structure. Thus, in the first column of Table 2 it is hypothesized that the first row would lead to maximum control (given the largest weight, 5). In contrast, where the organization is dealing with conforming primary groups, those mechanisms that permit wide scope and prevent too much intimacy are hypothesized to be most efficient (mass media, voluntary association, etc.). These are most

consistently located in a rationalistic administrative structure. As is indicated in the second column, it is hypothesized that mechanisms in the second row would lead to maximum control. Where the organization must simultaneously deal with deviant and conforming primary groups, it requires both sets of mechanisms and the organizational structure most consistent with contradictory dimensions is the professional model. Therefore, it is hypothesized that mechanisms in the third row will lead to maximum control.

It is assumed that where the organizational structure is mismatched with the mechanisms of coordination, it will lead to less balance than where they are matched because of the internal organizational conflict that such inconsistency implies. As mentioned earlier, the nonmerit organizational model is always hypothesized to achieve the least balance and goal achievement.

Conceptual and Research Problems

SOME CONCEPTUAL PROBLEMS

Given this type of formulation, several questions arise sufficiently often to warrant some further comments.

Definition of Distance. Up to this point the concept of social distance has been used in an intuitive commonsensical way. In its most general sense it means that a family is socially distant from a bureaucracy where their values differ or where their capacity to implement common values differs. So a family would be most socially distant which had different values from the organization and a great capacity to implement these deviant values. By contrast, a family would be less distant which had the same values as the organization, but did not have the capacity to implement them. A family with deviant values but unable to implement them would be intermediate. This kind of general formulation will have to be elaborated and improved upon as the theory develops, but this rather general definition is no real barrier to research. Thus from the viewpoint of any given bureaucracy, whether military, school, business, or others, it is much easier to classify families as being socially close or distant from the organization empirically than to provide a general definition valid in all circumstances. More modestly put, it becomes a typical problem of measurement in the social sciences.

Definition of a Midpoint. In addition, much greater attention has to be paid to the metric of social distance. What is the "precise midpoint" of balance? Again what is a difficult problem in the abstract becomes a typical social science problem in specific cases. It is not too difficult roughly to classify most of the families as being too involved, too dis-

tant, or intermediate, in relation to school, or military, or business organizations. The problem of measurement here is no different from that of differentiating between a middle class and a working class, a prejudiced and a nonprejudiced person, a religious or a nonreligious person. What is central about the formulation here is that it alerts the observer to three categories rather than two.

Psychological Theories of Balance. The term "balance" as used here differs in at least two important respects from its use in Heider's and other psychological theories of balance. First, these other workers deal with cognitions of individuals, whereas here, the behavior of organizations, not individuals, both cognitive and noncognitive, is of interest. Secondly, these other theories are based on a simple principle of direction and consistency. Thus, if the cognitions are consistently positive, interaction will take place. By contrast, at least two conditions have been pointed out as contradictory, both of which must be met if the desired interaction is to occur. The problem then is how contact is maintained despite the inconsistencies of cognitive or noncognitive aspects of the situation.

Values and Social Conflict. In the discussion about social control and values, the question might well arise as to which values the proposed theory is addressed —social, individual, or which. What is crucial in these analyses of values or social goals is not who defines them, but the extent to which they require professional expertise (which bureaucracies can provide) in dealing with uniform situations as well as the nonprofessional expertise (which the primary groups can provide) when dealing with nonuniform situations.[31] For most goals in society, both uniform and nonuniform aspects are important; therefore both bureaucracies and primary groups are necessary to maximize them. For instance, if one takes a highly personal goal, e.g., a man wants to keep the love of his wife; he could go to a professional psychiatrist; he could seek to impress her by material goods (a new car, a new house, a fur coat); or he could take her to vacation spots in far-off lands. What is characteristic of all these examples is the reliance in each case on formal organizations to provide services (e.g., cars, houses, etc.) to achieve a highly personal goal—maintaining a love relationship. It is possible to think of certain extreme situations where it would not be necessary to have both the primary group and the formal organizations, but these are not frequent. For instance, members of a classical extended family structure might consider that any help received from a bureaucracy is unnecessary. But especially in an advanced industrial society, goals that can be achieved by the primary group or the bureaucracy alone are very uncommon.[32]

The theory formulated does not discuss potential conflicts. If the primary group has goals that are contradictory to those of the formal organizations, or if two groups in general have contradictory goals, which one is desirable? The theory gives no answer to such problems. However, it does throw some light on who might win in such a conflict. Presumably those people who have a formal organization in a balanced relationship with their primary groups are more likely to win a conflict with any other people who are missing either the formal organizations, the primary groups, or the balanced relationship between the two (all other factors held constant). This particular kind of a formulation provides an organizational basis for analyzing conflict.

SOME RESEARCH DIRECTIONS

To point out that there is some ideal point of social distance, as well as various linking mechanisms which increase and decrease these social distances, is still to leave many questions. This section suggests some of the initial questions and some possible research directions.

In much of the presentation, it has been assumed that the initiative for linkages comes from the formal organization. Both in principle and in fact, this is not true. There are many obvious instances where formal organizations have been the target of local primary groups, as for example the Civil Rights movements in the South. Since linkages can be initiated from either the primary group or the formal organization, the question arises—are they symmetrical? Can they be initiated from the formal organization in the same manner as the primary group? It would seem that they are not symmetrical and that this is, in part, a function of the structural characteristics of the bureaucratic organization and the primary group. It is hypothesized that the bureaucratic organization in general has more manpower and financial resources than any primary group; therefore, it can initiate community contact with almost any mechanism of coordination. By contrast, the primary group can only start with those mechanisms that require minimal financial and professional resources. For instance, the bureaucratic organizations can initiate their linkages to the community with the detached worker and the settlement house approaches, whereas the primary group might have to start with a voluntary association. The differences in group structure and the consequent asymmetry in sequencing coordinating mechanisms is an important research problem which might well be explored.

Because of their size and need for large-scale cooperation in order to exist, the bureaucratic organizations are generally more visible than the primary groups and therefore less likely to tolerate extreme forms of deviance. They can, therefore, generally be reached by much less intensive form of coordinating mechanism (e.g., the mass media) than the primary groups. Or put as a research question—are bureaucracies more susceptible to formal linkages than primary groups? It should also be noted that bureaucracies differ in the degree of their vulnerability to the public. A political machine a week before an election is more vulnerable than a week after, while wholesalers may be less vulnerable to public pressure than retailers. The entire dimension of organizational vulnerability becomes important for understanding how coordinating mechanisms affect the bureaucracy.

It is also quite clear that some bureaucracies have more of a normative base for linking to the community than others. Thus youth delinquency agencies have stronger social support than business organizations for reaching into the community. What is interesting is that business organizations have people performing many of the same functions that the social work agencies perform, but they must do so with low visibility. The differences between the public relations man in an industrial concern and the community organizer in a Community Chest program would be most interesting for highlighting the consequence of an organization needing to use their coordinating mechanisms in a latent rather than in a manifest way. More generally, the consequence of normative support for linkages becomes an interesting research question.

If an organization is not selfconscious about its coordinating mechanisms, then certain mechanisms will always be operative, such as the common messenger and the opinion leaders. What characterizes these coordinating mechanisms is their informality. When one considers that leadership in the organization is generally class related and living conditions outside the organization are generally class related, then as a consequence of these informal mechanisms, different parts of the organization become linked to different parts of the community. This, in turn, can lead to considerable tension within the organization. This is, in part, the problem to which Selznick addresses himself.[33] More generally, the research question becomes: When do linkages lead to internal organizational cohesion and when to disruption? These are a few of the research issues which might profitably be pursued if one holds to the view that a bureaucracy should be neither isolated from primary groups nor brought too closely in contact with them.

Summary and Conclusion

A brief review of the major points presented may be useful. First, current sociological theory generally neglects the problem of coordination between bureaucratic organizations and community primary groups because it has overemphasized their incompatibilities and underemphasized their complementary contributions to the contemporary social order. The unique function of each rather than their joint functioning has been emphasized. Second, conclusions from a theory that sees continuous tension or extreme insulation of bureaucratic from primary forms of organization do not seem to correspond to observable trends in American society. Third, it is hypothesized that social control and goal achievement in modern society are accomplished through the joint contributions of both types of social forms and that optimal control and achievement will obtain when these forms are in balance. Fourth, it is argued that balance between these two types of organizations is a function of coordinating mechanisms, the most obvious of which are described and analyzed in terms of underlying principles of communication. Fifth, some of the relevant research directions are indicated.

Our presentation of this theory and associated hypotheses is not meant to be exhaustive. Indeed, elaborations will be necessary in order to specify the data necessary to examine the theory empirically. The statement is merely a first attempt to study a neglected but important problem in the understanding of contemporary society. The approach proposed seems plausible, but it is research now in progress that must determine its utility and suggest modifications in the balance theory of coordinating mechanisms between bureaucratic and primary forms of social organization.

NOTES

1. To John Leggett and Cheryl Mickelson we express thanks for helpful comments. This paper is one part of a research project being supported by the Office of Education, Project #1796.
2. T. Parsons, *The Structure of Social Action* (Glencoe, Ill.: The Free Press, 1949), pp. 542–552. Max Weber, *The Theory of Social and Economic Organization*, A. M. Henderson and T. Parsons (trans.) (New York: Oxford University, 1947), pp. 354–358.
3. F. Tonnies, *Fundamental Concepts of Sociology* (New York: American Book, 1940), pp. 18–28.
4. J. A. Schumpeter, *Capitalism, Socialism, and Democracy* (2nd ed.; New York: Harper, 1947), p. 157.
5. T. Parsons, "The Social Structure of the Family," in Ruth N. Anshen (ed.), *The Family: Its Function and Destiny* (rev. ed.; New York: Harper, 1959), pp. 260–263; George A. Theodorson, Acceptance of Industrialization and its Attendant Consequences for the Social Patterns of Non-Western Societies, *American Sociological Review*, 18 (October 1953), 480–481.
6. There are significant exceptions to this statement. James D. Thompson, Organizations and Output Transactions, *American Journal of Sociology*, 68 (November 1962), 309–324, has pointed to the need to consider boundary-spanning relations of large organizations systematically, and he has developed a general framework for doing this. For an article that covers some of the same issues from a different perspective, see Charles Kadushin, Social Distance Between Client and Professional, *American Journal of Sociology*, 57 (March 1962), 517–531. An approach to community linkages of organizations through role analysis is represented by Robert C. Hanson, The System Linkage Hypothesis and Role Consensus Patterns in Hospital-Community Relations, *American Sociological Review*, 27 (June 1962), 304–313. The more general concept of system linkage is found in Charles P. Loomis, *Social Systems: Their Persistence and Change* (Princeton, N.J.: D. Van Nostrand, 1960), pp. 32–34.
7. Irving A. Fowler, Local Industrial Structures, Economic Power, and Community Welfare, *Social Problems*, 6 (Summer 1958), 41–51; R. J. Pellegrin, and C. H. Coats, Absentee-owned Corporations and Community Power Structure, *American Journal of Sociology*, 61 (March 1956), 413–419; William H. Whyte, Jr., *The Organization Man* (New York: Simon and Schuster, 1956), pp. 295–296; Eugene Litwak, Voluntary Associations and Neighborhood Cohesion, *American Sociological Review*, 26 (April 1961), 258–262.

COMPETITION, COOPERATION, AND CRISIS

8. The revival of local organizing efforts of political parties—"volunteers," neighborhood units, clubs, etc.—expresses what an early study of political behavior documented—that to understand how people vote it is necessary to take account of their family and friends. See Paul F. Lazarsfeld, Bernard Berelson, and Helen Gaudet, *The People's Choice* (New York: Duell, Sloan, and Pearce, 1944), pp. 153 ff. S. Martin Lipset, Martin Trow, and James Coleman, *Union Democracy* (Glencoe: The Free Press, 1956), pp. 67–83, suggest more generally that governmental systems when under stress will seek to organize and control primary type organizations, and they point to the Nazis' development of block clubs during World War II as illustration. In delinquency control efforts, there is growing recognition that delinquents cannot be treated as isolated individuals, but must be reached through their significant primary groups, such as gangs. In Detroit, a special, new position has been created—the school-community agent—to facilitate this linkage in low-income areas where educational efforts have had limited success.

   For a case study of how hospital and local community volunteers coordinate their behavior to maximize goal achievement, see Otto Von Mehring, "The Social Self-Renewal of the Mental Patient and the Volunteer Movement," in Milton Greenblatt, Daniel J. Levinson, and Richard Williams (eds.), *The Patient and the Mental Hospital* (Glencoe, Ill.: The Free Press, 1957), pp. 585–593. Close dependence of fighting morale on family stability has long been recognized and was pointed out by Edward Shils and Morris Janowitz as one of the few appeals that made the German soldier susceptible to surrender. See their article, Cohesion and Disintegration in the Wehrmacht in World War II, *Public Opinion Quarterly*, 12 (1948), 280–315.

9. H. H. Gerth and C. Wright Mills (trans. and eds.), *From Max Weber: Essays in Sociology* (New York: Oxford University, 1946), pp. 196–244. Perhaps the clearest statement of this point with reference to the family is made by William F. Ogburn, "The Changing Functions of the Family," in Robert F. Winch and Robert McGinnis (eds.), *Selected Readings in Marriage and the Family* (New York: Henry Holt, 1953), pp. 74–76.

10. For a discussion of reasons why the atmospheres may not be as antithetical as formerly, see E. Litwak, The Use of Extended Family Groups in the Achievement of Social Goals: Some Policy Implications, *Social Problems*, 7 (Winter 1959–1960), 184–185.

11. P. Blau, *Bureaucracy in Modern Society* (New York: Random House, 1956), pp. 58, 62; Julian Franklin, "Bureaucracy and Freedom" in *Man in Contemporary Society, Vol. I*, (Contemporary Civilization Staff; New York: Columbia University, 1955), pp. 941–942; Eugene Litwak, Models of Bureaucracy Which Permit Conflict, *American Journal of Sociology*, 67 (September 1961), 178–179.

12. Elihu Katz and Paul F. Lazarsfeld, *Personal Influence* (Glencoe, Ill.: The Free Press, 1955), pp. 1–100.

13. It is assumed that both uniform and nonuniform events will be important for modern society. Nonuniformity is assumed because as a result of scientific and technological progress new areas of ignorance and uncertainty are exposed even though areas formerly considered uncertain are reduced to uniform predictions. In addition, a society committed to rapid technological change is subject to many unanticipated social consequences that must be dealt with as regular features of urban life. Finally, in a complex society with highly specialized roles and intricate socialization procedures, it cannot be expected that all persons will be perfectly socialized. In the welter of interactions there are always areas of uncertainty.

14. With exceptions as noted in note 5.

15. For a description of such a program see P. L. Crawford, D. I. Malamud, and J. R. Dumpson, *Working with Teenage Gangs* (New York: Welfare Council, 1950). In some school systems a school-community agent enters family and neighborhood groups in an effort to increase educational motivation of the child by strengthening family life. The chaplain will sometimes act as a detached worker to the families of service men who are accessible or the public relations officer might perform this function with

342 key community leaders around the army base. Regardless of the present social norms on the use of detached experts, in principle any bureaucratic organization can make use of the detached expert. Thus, in Russia where the norms of political behavior are different from ours, the "agitator" as described by Inkeles, tends to operate as a detached worker connecting the bureaucratic mass media with the local primary groups. See Alex Inkeles, *Public Opinion in Soviet Russia* (Cambridge, Mass.: Harvard University, 1951), pp. 67–83.

16. S. Kobrin, "The Chicago Area Project: A Twenty-Five Year Assessment," *Annals of the American Academy of Political and Social Sciences* (1959), pp. 19–37. In industry the opinion leader approach is illustrated by management's encouragement of executives to join key groups in the community and to develop through them a "better business atmosphere." School systems will select opinion leaders in local neighborhoods to help in campaigns for school funds.

17. Katz and Lazarsfeld, *op. cit.,* pp. 1–100.

18. Floyd Hunter, *Community Power Structure* (Chapel Hill: University of North Carolina, 1953), pp. 60–114, 171–207.

19. L. T. Empey and J. Rabow, The Provo Experiment in Delinquency Rehabilitation, *American Sociological Review,* 26 (October 1961), 679–695. Because of its high visibility this approach is not as readily used by organizations such as industries, where there is no clear social mandate for change. Yet prototypes that come close to this approach and are often historically related to paternalistic policies are seen in the company town, and currently the development of community centers and recreation centers by some large companies for the exclusive use of their employees. Executive conferences and seminars at business schools of universities represent another example. The army (especially overseas) may assume the same paternalistic position providing not only facilities but the context of social relations for dependents as well as officers and men.

20. William H. Whyte, Jr., "The Wife Problem," in Winch and McGinnis, *op. cit.,* pp. 278–285.

21. Katz and Lazarsfeld, *op. cit.;* Carl I. Hovland, "Effects of the Mass Media of Communication," in Gardner Lindsey (ed.), *Handbook of Social Psychology* (Cambridge, Mass.: Addison Wesley, 1950), vol. 2, pp. 1062–1103; Eugene Litwak, "Some Policy Implications in Communications Theory with Emphasis on Group Factors," in the *Proceedings,* of Seventh Annual Program Meeting of the Council on Social Work Education, *Education for Social Work* (New York: Council on Social Work Education, 1959), pp. 96–109; Herbert I. Abelson, *Persuasion: How Opinions and Attitudes Are Changed* (New York: Springer, 1959).

22. Some agencies that have depended almost entirely on legal authority in the past have moved toward other means (e.g., the trend toward "treatment" of offenders by courts), while others might seek more legal authority to achieve their goals (e.g., raising the legal age at which children must stay in school). Cf. F. James Davis, et al., *Society and the Law* (New York: The Free Press, 1962), pp. 88–90.

23. Other examples: Schools refer children to outside medical services; large business concerns might seek to affect public opinion where they have no social mandate by delegating the communication function to other organizations such as schools, civic groups, or churches. The delegated function approach assumes certain interorganizational relationships and recognizes that once the function has been delegated, the agency undertaking the communication will have recourse to the other mechanisms of coordination.

24. Herbert H. Hyman and Paul Sheatsley, Some Reasons Why Information Campaigns Fail, *Public Opinion Quarterly,* 11 (Fall 1947), 412–423.

25. Hyman and Sheatsley, *loc. cit.;* Katz and Lazarsfeld, *op. cit.,* pp. 48–66; Litwak, "Some Policy Implications in Communications Theory with Emphasis on Group Factors," *op. cit.,* pp. 97–101.

26. See P. F. Lazarsfeld, P. F. Berelson, and H. Gaudet, "The People's Choice" in William Peterson (ed.), *American Social Patterns* (New York: Doubleday, 1956), pp. 164–169.

COMPETITION, COOPERATION, AND CRISIS

27. Litwak, "Models of Bureaucracy Which Permit Conflict," *op. cit.* For an alternative   343
   formulation see James D. Thompson and Arthur Tuden, "Strategies, Structures, and
   Processes of Organizational Decision," in James D. Thompson, *et al.* (eds.), *Compara-*
   tive Studies in Administration (Pittsburgh: University of Pittsburgh, (1959), pp. 195–
   216. For a general discussion of organizational typologies see Peter M. Blau and W.
   Richard Scott, *Formal Organizations* (San Francisco: Chandler, 1962), pp. 40–58.
28. For a discussion of strains and adaptive mechanisms involving professionals in
   bureaucracies, see Blau and Scott, *op. cit.,* pp. 60–74; David Solomon, "Professional
   Persons in Bureaucratic Organizations," *Symposium on Preventive and Social Psy-*
   chiatry (Washington: Walter Reed Army Institute of Research, 1957), pp. 253–256;
   William Kornhauser, *Scientists in Industry: Conflict and Accommodation* (Berkeley
   and Los Angeles: University of California, 1962), ch. vii.
29. Katz and Lazarsfeld, *op. cit.*
30. The five combinations noted here do not exhaust either the theoretical or the empirical combinations. Only combinations which can easily be illustrated are cited.
31. For an elaborated discussion of uniform and nonuniform events and the differential
   effectiveness of bureaucratic and primary groups for dealing with them see Eugene
   Litwak "Extended Kin Relations in an Industrial Democratic Society" in E. Shanas
   and G. F. Streib (eds.), *Social Structure and the Family Generational Relations* (New
   Jersey: Prentice-Hall, 1965), pp. 294–302.
32. E. Litwak, *Ibid.,* pp. 302–303.
33. P. Selznick, *TVA and the Grass Roots: A Study in the Sociology of Formal Organiza-*
   tion (Berkeley and Los Angeles: University of California, 1949), *in passim.*

SOME CONSEQUENCES OF CRISIS WHICH LIMIT THE VIABILITY OF ORGANIZATIONS[1]

Charles F. Hermann

The initial interest in examining crises resulted from the observation of recurrent crises in contemporary international relations. It became apparent, however, that in its reaction to external crises a foreign office or other agency (i.e., an international organization) operating in the international arena shared certain characteristics with the generic class of formal or complex organizations.[2] In a crisis an organization may initiate far-reaching consequences both for its environment and for the organization itself. The internal effects of a crisis on an organization are diverse and, on occasion, contradictory. Richard C. Snyder[3] has outlined two polar effects that an external crisis can bring about in an

"Some Consequences of Crisis Which Limit the Viability of Organizations," *Adminis-*
trative Science Quarterly, 8, 1 (June 1963), 61–82. Reprinted with the permission of the
author and of the publisher, *Administrative Science Quarterly.*

organization: The crisis may be associated with the closer integration of the organization, the appropriate innovations for meeting the crisis, and the clarification of relevant values, or at the other extreme, it can lead to behavior which is destructive to the organization and seriously limits its viability.

A thorough exploration of organizational crises should account for the mechanisms in both polar types. The present inquiry, however, is confined to a fragment of the total response patterns, considering only a small, manageable number of variables associated with processes which are dysfunctional to the organization's goals and the satisfactions of its personnel.

To explore how certain responses may hinder an organization's viability, the paper will offer a series of interrelated propositions, or a model. As a demonstration that the propositions occur in the "real" world, some empirical evidence from organization literature will be offered. Both the political and non-political case studies, as well as the occasional experimental findings cited, should be considered as illustrative materials rather than as conclusive evidence. Treatment of the propositions to ensure the comparability of the relevant aspects of each case and the exclusion of plausible alternative hypotheses must await more systematic research. This paper attempts to serve as a guide for such an endeavor. A brief discussion of the definition of crisis will be followed by propositions and illustrative data and by possible operational indices of the variables involved.

The Concept of Crisis

Studying crisis phenomena provides an opportunity to examine an instrument of both organization and societal change,

highlights some of the essential features of organizational and decisional processes, and differentiates them from less vital factors under the extreme conditions associated with a crisis. Crises seem to appear frequently enough to permit systematic study and are of such a nature that they not only *permit* but also *warrant* investigation. As noted, crises are devices of change—change that may be associated with extreme behavior. Referring to the inordinate nature of crises in international politics, Charles McClelland has suggested that they "are perceived vividly as the avenues that are most likely to lead into extensive or general nuclear war."[4]

In spite of the potential value of studying crises, little distinction has been made between the concept of crisis and a number of seemingly related terms (e.g., tension, stress, anxiety, disaster, and panic). Crisis has been separated from some of these other concepts by the concept of stimulus and response.[5] In this conceptualization a crisis is conceived as a stimulus to which certain kinds of behavior—like anxiety or panic —are possible responses. Some of the distinctions appear to be, in part, the usage of different disciplines. Psychologists are inclined to employ concepts such as anxiety, threat, or stress,[6] sociologists and political scientists use such terms as panic and crisis.[7] An interdisciplinary group has focused on the concept of disaster.[8] Recently some efforts have been made to describe crisis in terms of an occasion for decision.[9]

No attempt is made here to link the term with all possible related terms, but a working definition of crisis will be formulated along three dimensions. An organizational crisis (1) threatens high-priority values of the organization, (2) presents a restricted amount of time in which a response can be made, and (3) is unexpected or unanticipated by the organization. Both the involvement of major organizational values and short decision time have been indicated as aspects of crisis in several definitions of the concept.[10] Fewer definitions have incorporated the element of surprise or the unanticipated quality of a crisis situation. The notion of programmed versus unprogrammed activity may be a component of the lack-of-anticipation dimension, but as a foreign policy planner has observed, it is not possible to have a program for every contingency, since "the number of theoretically possible crises in the years ahead is virtually infinite."[11] The lack of a programmed response, however, does not necessarily imply that the contingency has not been at least recognized. As used here, "unanticipated" implies not only the lack of a program, but lack of prior recognition of the possibility of the event occurring. An assertion of the importance of this dimension is made by Richard LaPiere who states that only when phenomena are unpredictable can they be defined as crises.[12]

It is possible that the three dimensions can be varied to yield different types of crises. In surveying the literature on the apparently related concept of disaster, Guetzkow[13] has concluded that the variables frequently are identical with those used in general psychology and sociology. The distinctive quality is that the values assumed by variables in disaster research often fall outside the limits of variable intensity incurred in other studies. Lanzetta's study of stress variation in experimental groups[14] may be indicative of the kind of exploration that could be done with the dimensions of a crisis. For the exploratory purposes of this paper, however, no effort will be made to compare the extent to which each dimension is present in the various materials used in supporting the propositions.

The relationship between the proposed working definition of crisis and seven other variables will be outlined in the following pages. An over-all view of the linkages among these variables is diagramed in Figure 1. The propositions suggested by the lines on the diagram can be broken into three subareas: (1) direct consequences of crisis stimuli, (2) stress on authority units and its transfer, and (3) organizational response to transfer.

Consequences of Crisis Stimuli

In the present model four variables are represented as being directly dependent upon the occurrence of a crisis stimulus.[15] They are represented in four propositions, which are stated and illustrated in the discussion which follows.

PROPOSITION 1.

As precrisis organizational integration decreases, a crisis will increase the tendency of members of an organization (both individuals and suborganizational units) to exercise withdrawal behavior. The withdrawal variable in this proposition is the terminal dependent variable considered in this model, but the major portion of the system suggests a series of intervening mechanisms. In effect, the first proposition is a short-circuiting of the model. As employed here, "withdrawal behavior" refers to more than the physical activity of "leaving the field." Operational measures of withdrawal might include the reduction in rates of production, increased absenteeism and employee turnover, increased subunit failure to meet deadlines, and various attitude measures of dissatisfaction. It is

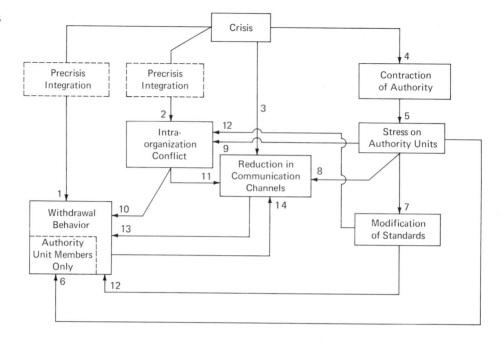

Figure 1. Summary Diagram of Relationships Between Crisis and Selected Organization Variables (the Numbers Correspond to Numbered Propositions in Text).

hypothesized that the short cut represented by Proposition 1 is more likely to occur if organizational integration is low prior to the crisis. Integration (represented by the broken-line box in Figure 1) is used here as the sum of all forces operating to keep units in the organization performing their tasks for the attainment of organization goals.[16] There is a close relationship between integration and withdrawal behavior, which might be defined as the negative aspect of integration. Thus, high precrisis organizational integration could be characterized as having low tendencies toward withdrawal behavior.

A. W. Gouldner found evidence of the withdrawal mechanism operating in a plant where a crisis occurred in the form of technological innovations and where the integration between employees and management had been previously strained.[17] A Senate investigation dis-covered a crisis in the United States Patent Office resulting in part from increases in the complexity of search procedures and from a large backlog of applications. The subcommittee report on the situation observed that "the turnover of trained personnel becomes more acute each month."[18] Indications of similar behavior are reported in a small-group study in which the group leaders withdrew under extreme stress[19] and in a proposition based on a survey of disaster studies.[20] Despite the tendency of the illustrations to suggest a direct linkage between crisis and withdrawal, it is possible that this is a spurious effect of a more complex relationship which the research efforts did not uncover.

PROPOSITION 2.

As precrisis organizational integration decreases, a crisis will tend to intensify any conflicts existing prior to the crisis. As in Proposition 1, it seems important to identify one intervening variable—the level of precrisis organizational integration. Following the nationalization of British hospitals, top administrators gained increased authority over doctors. This change in their authority relationship led to conflict.[21] Summarizing his survey, N. J. Demerath states "predisaster dissatisfactions . . . are heightened or triggered in the disaster situation."[22] In a small-group experiment, groups participated in a game in which time restrictions were imposed.[23] A crisis was induced in one-half the groups by unannounced changes in the scoring rules midway through the game, thus making successful solution of the problem (high scores) unattainable. Under such circumstances, group conflict increased. One demonstration of this change was the difference between the control and crisis groups on verbal antagonism (significant at .0002 level). Another investigator, using sociometric measurements, found that the stability of group affective linkages decreased under stress, and also found other indicators of group conflict.[24]

PROPOSITION 3.

With the introduction of a crisis, the total number of communication channels used for the collection and distribution of information will be reduced. This proposition suggests the relationship of communication channels to crisis. The aspect of communication used in this proposition deals with the network that connects the information transmitter and receiver. Essentially, a communication channel is a routinized means of exchanging information, ranging from a frequent pattern of face-to-face contacts to the employment of some mechanized transmission system (e.g., written orders, telephone, commercial mass media).

In the study of communication networks in military organizations it has been discovered that in combat there is a tendency for communication "to decrease and break down."[25] This phenomenon appeared to occur at a number of different levels from organization to individual. A psychologist working in another governmental department found that there was a reduction in the number of people consulted in a problem-solving task when time pressures increased.[26] Based on data from a series of interviews, a chi-square test indicated that this relationship (time pressure and reduction in consultation) was significant at the .02 level. If the number of personnel consulted can be taken as an index of the communication channels involved, then this might be cited as partial support for Proposition 3. If public information about the U-2 aircraft brought down inside the Soviet Union in 1960 was accurate, the United States government was confronted with a crisis in which some evidence of closure of communication channels appeared. A selected group drawn from the National Security Council is reported to have met with the President, and a decision reached that the prearranged story should be invoked with all statements issued by the Department of State. A critical delay in relating this decision to the White House press secretary, however, resulted in an announcement that bulletins would be released by the State Department and the National Aeronautics and Space Administration (NASA). Communication channels between the White House and NASA, and between NASA and the State Department are also reported to have been defective.[27]

Before exploring the next proposition, the reduction in communication channels in an organizational crisis must be reconciled with apparently contradictory reports of information overload in a crisis.[28] The proposition in this paper involves the number of communication *channels* employed, resulting in a decrease in the total distribution and collection of information in the organization. But in those channels that remain, the information load (quantity of binary units) may well reach overload proportions.

PROPOSITION 4.

In response to a crisis stimulus, there is a tendency toward contraction of authority in the organization. In terms of the remainder of the model the most important direct dependent variable of a crisis stimulus may be the contraction of authority. Authority is conceived as legitimate power, or the power of individuals and groups, the acceptance of which is recognized as obligatory by the rest of the organization. The power of an individual or larger organizational unit, A, is stated as the ability of A to get some other unit or individual, B, to act when instructed to do so by A. "Contraction," is intended here to represent one of several alternatives: (1) the shifting of authority activities to higher levels in a hierarchical structure. (2) a reduction in the number of persons or units participating in the exercise of authority without reference to a hierarchy, and (3) an increase in the number of occasions for the exercise of authority, although the actual number of authority units remains constant.

Contraction of authority is illustrated in the hypothesis formulated by Snyder and Paige based on their study of the decisions of the United States to take military action in Korea: "When crucial choices are forced on an organization from the environment, the decisional subsystem will be characterized by smaller decisional units.[29]

In the analysis of what might be described as a crisis-oriented organization, Janowitz found that as a military situation takes on aspects of a crisis "the more feasible it becomes for officer personnel to claim that new problems are outside their jurisdiction and require directives from higher authorities.[30] Considering only the dimension of high-priority values, Dean Pruitt has revealed that the increase in danger of a problem to United States objectives correlated with both an increase in the coordination required for the problem and in the level of approval (rank of signer) required.[31] These correlations are statistically significant at less than the .05 level. In the United States Patent Office several factors are creating a contraction of authority. As previously noted, there has been some turnover among the personnel with the authority to decide patent applications. At the same time, the number of applications filed and the slowdown resulting from the increasing "complexity of disclosures and the growing burden of search load"[32] has produced a large backlog of applications. Two types of contraction of authority are operating: a reduction in the number of persons in positions of authority and, simultaneously, an increase in the number of occasions for authority decisions.

Stress on Authority Units and Its Transfer

Richard Meier has suggested that "much of the stress is transmitted to component groups and individuals" and "to its clients in the milieu" by the executive leadership of an organization when it is placed under acute stress.[33] The increase in the stress on authority units and the attempts to transfer some of this stress to other parts of the organization are the subject of several propositions which are illustrated in the discussion which follows.

PROPOSITION 5.

As contraction of authority increases, the stress upon existing authority units increases. The increase in stress on authority units as a result of the contraction of authority is the mechanism in the system which brings about attempts to transmit the stress to other units in the organization. The proposition suggested here is that when authority is contracted, the stress felt by authority units is intensified beyond that induced in other organizational units. Richard Meier's comment that a crisis occurs when stress "reaches a peak at the executive level"[34] is relevant here.

The association of crisis with such terms as stress has been noted. One author has observed that "high stress . . . is almost universally characteristic of international crisis situations."[35] In the present context stress will be differentiated as a characteristic of the organization's response to a crisis. Although it frequently may involve affective components of the organization's personnel, a wide range of possible indicators of stress can be listed. It might be identified by overtime work, an increase in the number of errors made in routine tasks, greater tendencies toward problem-solving rigidity, reduction in the time spent on long-range projects, and increased scores on such psychometric instruments as the Manifest Anxiety Scale[36] as compared with scores in less stressful periods.

Several examples of this proposition can be cited. In a case study of a wildcat strike, decisions made by top management are reported to have displayed evidence of problem-solving rigidity.[37] Thus, as management-employee relations deteriorated and the problem was sent to higher authorities for resolution (contraction of authority), there were signs of stress on authority units; that is, some failure by management to explore possible alternative courses of action. The U-2 incident involved an effort to contract authority with respect to the agency responsible for releasing statements on the missing aircraft. Some indicators of subsequent stress have already been noted in terms of the communication-clearance problem and others are mentioned by David Wise and T. B. Ross.[38] Although it falls outside the range of formal organizations, an interesting analogy can be drawn from the activities of an anthropologist who became involved in Polynesian society. The small island society was experiencing a combination of natural disasters and difficulties in its governmental operation. When the existence of the people was threatened, the anthropologist catapulted to a position of authority after the natural leadership had contracted. He recalls:

> The immediate situation and succession of crises had been so overwhelming that I had not even thought of the obvious long-term solution, migration, as a practical possibility. It was not until several days after the crisis . . . that it really occurred to me.[39]

In this incident, stress is evident in the loss of attention to long-range solutions and to some extent in problem-solving rigidity.

PROPOSITION 6.

As authority unit stress increases, the tendency of authority units to withdraw from organizational tasks increases. If the occurrence of a crisis can lead directly to withdrawal behavior, it seems reasonable that further stress beyond that of the initial crisis stimulus will also lead to withdrawal. This proposition, however, is confined to the withdrawal patterns of members of authority units. On the basis of observation in communications-oriented institutions, one investigator suggests that when leaders believe that a crisis has become intolerable, they may permit "a takeover, bankruptcy or mass resignation."[40] A number of examples of stress can be found in the appropriate authority units of major European foreign offices in the crisis preceding the outbreak of World War I. There were also signs of withdrawal behavior as evidenced by a report from one source that German Chancellor Bethmann-Hollweg offered his resignation to the Kaiser a few days prior to the outbreak of the war.[41] A recent attempt to simulate critical aspects of the outbreak of World War I also resulted in a resignation attempt by one of the principal participants.[42] Summarizing findings on groups under stress, drawn from small-group research, E. P. Torrance states that when stress reaches a certain intensity "the leader feels so threatened that he either takes away all power from others or abdicates his own power role."[43]

PROPOSITION 7.

Under increasing stress, an authority unit is more likely to institute modifications in organization standards. Organization standards represent criteria (usually determined by management or their representatives, e.g., efficiency experts) for the measurement of performance and production rates within the organization. As used here, organization standards may involve the objectives or goals (as defined by the organization's authority units) for which the organization exists. This variable is the only one in the present miniature system which can readily be identified as a major crisis-solving device. It is included here because of some negative effects that may be associated with its use.

In his discussion of the American Red Cross, D. L. Sills notes that the crisis of declining membership after the end of World War I "was surmounted by adopting a new program—the preservation and improvement of public health."[44] Thus, new standards were introduced. When faced with the post-war business slump and increased competition, the management of one company made technological changes to increase production rates.[45] Richard Meier reports on the modification of standards made in a major library, whose administrators were faced with increasing stress.[46] Certain standards of performance were relaxed or countermanded, e.g., the time required to fill a request for a book from the stacks, or the speed with which overdue notices were dispatched. Several political scientists, using a content analysis of diplomatic documents, have uncovered an apparent change in requirements (or standards) for war held by Germany and Austria-Hungary.[47] There is evidence that, prior to the crisis in the summer of 1914, those governments strongly wished to avoid war until their military capabilities placed them in a more favorable position with respect to their potential enemies. As the stress upon the official decision makers increased—reflected in the increased amount of affect in their statements—the objective of avoiding immediate hostilities was abandoned. Some consequences of modifications in organization standards will be deferred to a later proposition.

PROPOSITION 8.

The increase in stress on authority units will reduce the number of communication channels used for the distribution and collection of information. Another dependent variable of stress on authority units is the reduction in the number of communication channels used by the unit. If the assumption is made that any search activity frequently involves the use of communication channels, then the proposition by March and Simon, with its accompanying evidence, becomes pertinent: "Search becomes less fruitful as stress and time pressure are pushed to the limit."[48] Persons responsible for proposing a solution to a problem also tend to consult others less frequently when time pressures became great, as noted by Dean Pruitt.[49] A recent volume on the opening campaigns of World War I indicates that in the first month of the war, General Joseph Joffre and the French General Staff, under the stress of the German attack, are reported to have adhered rigidly to a designated offensive strategy.[50] In that action they neglected certain field commanders (as well as part of the civilian government) as channels of communication—channels which were attempting to warn of needed defensive moves to prevent a German envelopment. A comment based on the study of disaster materials also might be linked to Proposition 8: "One way a feedback control system can react more rapidly is to cut down the signal range. Both individuals and community systems revert, in sudden disaster, to a restricted set of referents."[51] Like the disaster materials, the small-group studies are not directly applicable to an organizational model; but, if the findings are recognized as only suggestive, then the probability that a communication breakdown between a leader and members of his group increases under severe stress is worth consideration.[52]

PROPOSITION 9.

Increased stress on authority units will increase the probability of conflicts between the authority units and other units in the organization. This proposition, concerned with efforts to transfer stress in a crisis, relates stress in authority units to intraorganization conflict. For the present exploratory purposes, reference will be made only to two manifestations of conflict—factionalism and role conflicts. Factionalism results when a course of action is favored by one or more members of a unit more or less consistently and opposed by one or more other groups within the unit. Operational measures might be recorded by means of action preferences of various subunits as registered in interviews or questionnaires. Role conflict is the conflict between two or more patterns of behavior expected from a single position in an organization. One means of determining role conflicts is by use of the S technique in factor analysis.[53]

Both role conflicts and factionalism were reported in the wildcat strike study. Union leaders found themselves caught between their role of representing all union grievances and their identification with management and its problems. As a result "union leadership at the Oscar Center plant was divided into two, not completely stable cliques."[54] Another study indicates that a government laboratory experienced a redefinition of goals in order to obtain financial support (the stress situation). "A number of factional splits appeared, the most striking of which was that between the 'old guard' and the new leaders supporting the development."[55]

R. H. McCleery presents a case study

of an attempt by prison management to change their institution's policy from a custodial to a treatment orientation.[56] Although the stress upon the authority unit or management in this case is not clearly documented, it seems to be present along with the given disorders and difficulties which followed the policy change and eventually led to an investigation by the state legislature. What is clearly presented is the role conflicts that confronted both the staff and prisoners. A final example of stress on authority units creating intraorganization conflict is drawn from international relations. The Japanese cabinet faced a severe stress situation in deciding on the response to the Potsdam Declaration —the Allied request for unconditional surrender. The subsequent conflict was such that the cabinet agreement was reportedly violated by one of the factions.[57]

Contradicting the evidence cited are the small-group experiments of J. T. Lanzetta: "It was found that as stress increased there was a decrease in behaviors associated with internal friction in the group; a decrease in number of disagreements, arguments, aggression, deflations and other negative social-emotional behaviors."[58] A possible explanation for this contrary evidence can be drawn from Torrance's work on leadership and stress.[59] He reports one kind of behavior under mild stress and another under more intense stress. Thus, assuming a curvilinear relationship, leadership may delegate authority under mild stress but centralize it under acute stress or establish strong communication links under moderate stress which break down as stress increases. If this explanation is correct, it is important for the accuracy of the present proposition to establish that the added stress to authority units under crisis is beyond the ap-

parent threshold for acute stress.

Alternatively, the contradiction may stem from a difference between small groups, which are not embedded in organizations, and organizations. The conflicts in organizations might be accounted for by an intervening variable, such as precrisis factionalism between organizational units or the extent of independence of units within the organization. Neither of these intervening variables would be applicable to an isolated face-to-face group. But, in an organizational context, stress on authority units might produce intraorganizational conflict, depending on whether the larger organization splintered—as a result of factionalism or suborganization independence—into sections with strong in-group and out-group perceptions. A possible illustration of this alternative is displayed in the study of prison officials discussed at the beginning of Proposition 10.

Organizational Response to Transfer of Stress

In this final section some propositions will be advanced to suggest how an organization's response to attempts by an authority unit to transfer consequences of its stress can weaken organizational viability.

PROPOSITION 10.

As intraorganization conflict increases, there is a greater tendency for organization members to withdraw from organization tasks and activities. This proposition suggests that conflict leads to an increasing tendency toward withdrawal. In a study of prison officials, conflict led to the general atomization of the prison staff. There was a general "decline of the old informal groups among the staff" and the treatment-oriented guards, in particular, "responded to this new minority position by becoming more cohesive and remaining apart from the other officials."[60] With reference to similar behavior in the military establishment, Morris Janowitz concludes: "A small, homogeneous, isolated professional group is less likely to be subjected to role conflicts,"[61] which indicates that one reason for withdrawal is to escape role conflicts. In the wildcat strike case study the top union leadership escaped their role conflict by abdicating their authority, and the union members attempted a withdrawal in the form of a strike.[62] Attention might be directed to several nonorganizational examples. One interesting parallel to this proposition is Alexander Mintz's theory of nonadaptive group behavior.[63] Using an experimental group, he demonstrated that when the reward for co-operative behavior became uncertain in a threatening situation, competitive behavior occurred, each person attempting to withdraw and act independently of the group. In a Polynesian society, conflict over scarce resources resulted in a similar withdrawal pattern: "Tikopia society, as a result of the crisis, was atomizing into smaller and smaller kin groups."[64]

PROPOSITION 11.

As intraorganization conflict increases, the number of communication channels used for the collection and distribution of information in the organization decreases. Two of the examples cited above can also be applied to illustrate briefly the possible operation of this proposition, relating conflict to a reduction in the number of communication channels. Studying the developments leading to the strike, A. W. Gouldner observed a breakdown in the informal channels of upward communication: "The tensions that had developed after the first succession, and the impersonal demotion of the old supervisors after the second succession, had destroyed the workers' desires to be friendly with their supervisors."[65] A second illustration is offered by Grusky,[66] who found a reduction in communication between prison management factions, particularly between the supervisor and the treatment-oriented guards.

PROPOSITION 12.

Modification of organization standards *may* tend to increase intraorganization conflict and withdrawal behavior. This proposition cautiously links modifications in organization standards with two dependent variables—intraorganization conflict and withdrawal behavior. Withdrawal mechanisms are apparent in an examination of modifications introduced in a library's standards: "Morale . . . drops precipitately when standards are compromised. Absenteeism, sickness rate, and labor turnover (all of them partial indicators of the state of morale) may be expected to show sizeable increases."[67] In Gouldner's case study there is evidence that both withdrawal and eventually conflict followed modification of production standards. Regarding withdrawal, the author observes that workers "tended to remove themselves either from emotional participation or even physical participation in the plant."[68] The ultimate expression of conflict in that study was the wildcat strike, but, even before it occurred, indicators appeared in the reorganization of primary groups and the denial of legitimate authority to management. If modifications of standards lead to dissatisfaction, then a psychological explanation can be offered. "Aggression, withdrawal, and regression are certainly observable reactions to dissatisfaction that lead to frustration."[69]

Despite the evidence in support of the proposition, however, contrary findings were also discovered. When a study of changes in prison standards was quantified, short-run effects were found that tended to support the present proposition. Long-run effects, on the other hand, ran counter to it.[70] Also the change in Red Cross goals, cited earlier, was held to have provided a solution to the crisis.[71] These contradict the hypothesis offered in the proposed model. Will changes in standards contribute to crisis solutions or increased withdrawal and conflict tendencies? From the evidence given, modifications in organization standards may lead to withdrawal and conflict immediately after they are introduced, or when they are accompanied by certain side effects, or perhaps, when they are of a certain substantive nature. This suggests that the illustrative material reported in this paper is not sufficient to indicate the conditions for differentiating between alternative outcomes. Although there is evidence to warrant inclusion of the proposition in the model, the conditions for its operation remain open and uncertain for the present.

PROPOSITION 13.

A reduction in the number of communication channels connecting a unit to the remainder of the organization, increases the unit's withdrawal behavior. This proposition and a complementary feedback proposition—withdrawal reduces information—constitute the final propositions of the system.

A study of a military organization reveals that when communication channels are weakened in combat, field units feel that higher authority is not only "remote and distant" but "acting capriciously and arbitrarily."[72] Rejection of legitimate authority might well be interpreted as an indication of withdrawal behavior. In a similar type of finding, industrial workers were reported to have increasingly hostile attitudes toward authority as they failed to receive information in response to their grievances.[73]

PROPOSITION 14.

Withdrawal behavior by a unit of an organization reduces the number of communication channels connecting it with the remainder of the organization. The final proposition reverses the relationship between the variables incorporated in the preceding proposition. Common sense suggests that when a unit elects to withdraw from an organizational environment the probability of a reduction in communication channels linking that unit with the organization is increased. It has been noted, for example, that when the employees in the wildcat strike study began to withdraw from their supervisors, there was a reduction in upward communication.[74] An interesting incident from the early days of World War I is also pertinent. The commander of the French Fifth Army in the Battle of Charleroi became concerned about his exposed right flank and ordered the withdrawal of his forces from the engagement, thus terminating the French hopes of bringing the war to a quick conclusion. It is reported that the commander took the action without communicating to his military superiors, because he anticipated their disapproval.[75] Indirect evidence is found for the proposition in a study of small-group communication. When there were good feelings and satisfaction among the group participants (nonwithdrawal behavior), then communication between them was facilitated.[76]

The final proposition suggests the possible role of feedback in the model. If the feedback to authority units, which are responsible for selecting and initiating a response to meet a crisis, are weakened by withdrawal behavior, conflict, or some other behavior, then greater difficulty may be experienced in resolving a crisis. It is interesting to observe that the military organization—which must be constantly prepared to deal with crises—has elaborate procedures for maintaining feedback to authority units: "The informal and unofficial channels of communication are so important that they become institutionalized in the oral 'briefing.' "[77] What can happen if feedback systems fail is demonstrated in the study of prison management. "The lack of direct communication channels from the inmates to the guards to the supervisor . . . resulted in a lack of immediate knowledge by the chief policy maker of the impact of his decisions."[78]

By definition crises are situations unanticipated by the organization. In an unfamiliar situation some degree of trial and error is present in seeking a response. When, for lack of feedback, an authority unit fails to discover that an error has been made, the organization's viability may be seriously challenged. The model presented here indicates how an organization may be critically affected by changes brought about by a crisis, which may increase the possibility of error and block feedback.

NOTES

1. The author wishes to acknowledge his appreciation to the members of the International Relations Program at Northwestern University for their comments on an earlier draft of this paper, particularly the senior members: Professors Richard Snyder, Harold Guetzkow, James Robinson, Chadwick Alger, and Lee Anderson. Professor James W. Gladden of the University of Kentucky also gave the author the benefit of his insights.
2. The term "crisis" is not uncommon in organization literature. At least six selections in a recent reader used crisis. See Amitai Etzioni, *Complex Organizations* (New York, 1961), pp. 154, 182, 192, 203, 359, 399. There is, however, a dearth of material using crisis as a theoretical variable in the study of organizations.
3. "The Korean Decision (1950) and the Analysis of Crisis Decision-Making," paper presented at the Conference on Decision-Making in Crises, Stanford University, January 12–13, 1962.
4. Decisional Opportunity and Political Controversy: The Quemoy Case, *Journal of Conflict Resolution*, 6 (1962), 211. For an author who defines political and economic crises as extreme turning points, see Kenneth E. Boulding, *Conflict and Defense* (New York, 1962), pp. 250–251.
5. For example, see P. B. Foreman, Panic Theory, *Sociology and Social Research*, 37 (1953), 300; and R. T. LaPiere, *Collective Behavior* (New York, 1938), pp. 437 ff.
6. See R. S. Lazarus, J. Deese, and S. F. Osler, The Effects of Psychological Stress upon Skilled Performance, *Psychological Bulletin*, 49 (1952), 293–317; F. E. Horvath, "Psychological Stress: A Review of Definitions and Experimental Research" in L. von Bertalanffy and A. Rapoport, eds., *General Systems Yearbook* (Society for General Systems Research; IV, Ann Arbor, 1959), pp. 203–230; and also J. T. Lanzetta, G. R. Wendt, P. Langham, and D. Haefner, The Effects of an Anxiety-Reducing Medication on Group Behavior under Threat, *Journal of Abnormal and Social Psychology*, 52 (1956), 103–108.
7. Sociological examples might include Foreman, *op. cit.*; R. I. Kutak, Sociology of Crises: The Louisville Flood of 1937, *Social Forces*, 17 (1938), 66–72; E. L. Quarantelli, The Nature and Conditions of Panic, *American Journal of Sociology*, 60 (1954), 267–

275. The long-standing use of crisis by political scientists is reflected in E. H. Carr, *The Twenty Years' Crisis, 1919–1939* (New York, 1939); and in the recent interaction approach found in C. A. McClelland, The Acute International Crisis, *World Politics*, 14 (1961), 182–204.

8. See Instituut voor Sociaal Onderzoek van het Nederlandse Volk, *Studies in Holland Flood Disaster 1953*, I–IV (Washington, D.C., 1955); and G. W. Baker and D. W. Chapman, eds., *Man and Society in Disaster* (New York, 1962).

9. H. B. Williams, Some Functions of Communication in Crisis Behavior, *Human Organization*, 16 (1957), 15–19; T. W. Milburn, "Design for the Study of Deterrence," unpublished paper, Program of Graduate Training and Research in International Relations, Northwestern University (Summer, 1961); J. A. Robinson, "The Concept of Crisis in Decision-Making," in National Institute of Social and Behavioral Science, *Series Studies in Social and Economic Sciences* (Symposia Studies Series No. 11; Washington, D.C., 1962); and Snyder, *op. cit.*

10. High-priority values are mentioned by Lasswell, "Style in the Language of Politics," in H. D. Lasswell, N. Leites, *et al.*, *Language of Politics* (New York, 1949), p. 23; and Williams, *op. cit.*, p. 15. A. R. Ferguson refers to an "action which will be costly" to a group, but confines crisis to a situation in which the group can act to reduce its net losses. See his *Tactics in a Local Crisis* (Memorandum RM-3034-ISA, Rand Corporation; Santa Monica, Calif., September, 1962), p. 4. Limitation on time available for response is suggested by R. L. Hamblin, Group Integration during a Crisis, *Human Relations*, 11 (1958), 67. Both dimensions are cited by Milburn, *op. cit.*, p. 5; Robinson, *op. cit.*, p. 6; and Snyder, *op. cit.*, pp. 6, 11.

11. G. A. Morgan, Planning in Foreign Affairs: The State of the Art, *Foreign Affairs*, 39 (1961), 278. For a detailed consideration of the distinction between programmed and unprogrammed, see H. A. Simon, "The Role of Expectations in an Adaptive or Behavioristic Model," in M. J. Bowman, ed., *Expectations, Uncertainty and Business Behavior* (New York, 1958), pp. 49–58.

12. *Op. cit.*, pp. 438–439; on this dimension see also, Kutak, *op. cit.*, p. 66.

13. H. Guetzkow, "Joining Field and Laboratory Work in Disaster Research," in Baker and Chapman, *op. cit.*, p. 339.

14. J. T. Lanzetta, Group Behavior under Stress, *Human Relations*, 8 (1955), 32–33.

15. The use of "crisis stimulus" in this paper does not refer to a means of distinguishing crisis from possibly related terms. "Crisis stimulus" and "crisis response" or reaction will be used to separate aspects of the same concept.

16. "Organizational integration" may be somewhat comparable to what Peter M. Blau and W. Richard Scott have called "group solidarity"—a concept broader than the notion of cohesion. See their *Formal Organizations* (San Francisco, 1962), pp. 108–109. Their term was avoided in this presentation to emphasize the applicability of the term used to an entire organization and not only to small groups.

17. *Wildcat Strike* (Yellow Springs, Ohio, 1954), p. 82.

18. Report to United States Senate Committee on the Judiciary by its Subcommittee on Patents, Trademarks, and Copyrights, *Patents, Trademarks, and Copyrights* (87th Congress, 1st sess. as extended, pursuant to Senate Resolution 55 [Washington, D.C., May 9, 1962]), p. 2.

19. E. P. Torrance, "A Theory of Leadership and Interpersonal Behavior under Stress," in L. Petrullo and B. M. Bass, eds., *Leadership and Interpersonal Behavior* (New York, 1961), p. 108.

20. N. J. Demerath, Some General Propositions: An Interpretative Summary, *Human Organization*, 16 (1957), p. 29.

21. See C. Sofer, Reactions to Administrative Change, *Human Relations*, 8 (1955), 313. Whether this nationalization constitutes a crisis in accordance with the proposed working definition is open to question. High-priority values were involved and the time for response was comparatively short, but was it unanticipated? It might be argued that the details for executing the new regulations were unanticipated by the hospitals, therefore consistent with the definition.

COMPETITION, COOPERATION, AND CRISIS

22. *Op. cit.*, p. 29.

23. Hamblin, *op. cit.*, p. 72.

24. Torrance, *op. cit.*, p. 107.

25. M. Janowitz, *Sociology and the Military Establishment* (New York, 1959), p. 76.

26. D. G. Pruitt, "Problem Solving in the Department of State" (unpublished MS, Northwestern University, Evanston, Ill., 1961), p. 60.

27. See D. Wise and T. B. Ross, *The U-2 Affair* (New York, 1962), pp. 78–87; and W. H. Blanchard, National Myth, National Character, and National Policy: A Psychological Study of the U-2 Incident, *Journal of Conflict Resolution,* 6 (1962), 143–148. Attention should be directed to the fact that a programmed response had been prepared for the contingency that a U-2 might be lost in the USSR. Some debate occurred, however, on whether the "cover story" should be used. The other dimensions of the crisis definition appear to have been present.

28. For references to communication overload in a crisis, see Williams, *op. cit.*, p. 17; and R. L. Meier, *Social Change in Communications-oriented Institutions* (Mental Health Research Institute, University of Michigan, Report No. 10; Ann Arbor, 1961).

29. R. C. Snyder and G. D. Paige, The United States Decision to Resist Aggression in Korea: The Application of an Analytical Scheme, *Administrative Science Quarterly,* 3 (1958), 362. Also reprinted in R. C. Snyder, H. W. Bruck, and B. Sapin, eds., *Foreign Policy Decision-Making* (New York, 1962), 206–249.

30. *Op. cit.*, p. 88.

31. *Op cit.*, pp. 43, 124.

32. Report to United States Senate Committee on the Judiciary, *op. cit.*, p. 2.

33. *Op. cit.*, pp. i–ii.

34. *Ibid.*

35. R. C. North, Decision-Making in Crisis: An Introduction, *Journal of Conflict Resolution,* 6 (1962), 197.

36. J. A. Taylor, A Personality Scale of Manifest Anxiety, *Journal of Abnormal and Social Psychology,* 48 (1953), 285–290.

37. Gouldner, *op. cit.*, p. 85.

38. *Op. cit.*, see particularly chs. vi, vii, viii.

39. Spillius, Natural Disaster and Political Crisis in a Polynesian Society, *Human Relations,* 10 (1957), 18.

40. Meier, *op. cit.*, p. 43.

41. L. Albertini, *The Origins of the War of 1914* (New York, 1953), II, 437.

42. C. F. and M. G. Hermann, *The Potential Use of Historical Data for Validation Studies of the Inter-Nation Simulation: The Outbreak of World War I as an Illustration* (Report under Contract N123 (60530) 25875 A to United States Naval Ordnance Test Station, China Lake, Calif., 1962).

43. *Op. cit.*, p. 108. R. L. Hamblin also has completed some laboratory experiments in this area, revealing a change in leadership imposed by group members when a solution is not found; see his Leadership and Crises, *Sociometry,* 21 (1958), 322–335.

44. "The Succession of Goals," in Etzioni, ed., *op. cit.*, p. 154.

45. Gouldner, *op. cit.*, p. 67 ff.

46. *Op. cit.*, p. 41.

47. D. A. Zinnes, R. C. North, and H. E. Koch, Jr., "Capability, Threat and the Outbreak of War," in J. N. Rosenau, ed., *International Politics and Foreign Policy* (New York, 1961), pp. 469–482.

48. J. G. March and H. A. Simon, *Organizations* (New York, 1958), p. 116.

49. *Op. cit.*, p. 60.

50. B. W. Tuchman, *The Guns of August* (New York, 1962), pp. 209–211.

51. Williams, *op. cit.*, p. 19.

52. Torrance, *op. cit.*, p. 113.

53. This device is advanced by R. B. Cattell, who defines role for purposes of factor analysis as "a pattern of responses to different occasions which is modal among individual patterns; i.e., it is a cluster or factor among people in responses to social

occasions." See his Three Basic Factor-Analytic Research Designs—Their Interrelations and Derivations, *Psychological Bulletin,* 49 (1952), 499–520.

54. Gouldner, *op. cit.,* pp. 95, 102.
55. P. Brown and C. Shepherd, "Factionalism and Organizational Changes in a Research Laboratory," in R. T. Livingston and S. H. Nilberg, eds., *Human Relations in Industrial Research Management* (New York, 1957), p. 268.
56. "Policy Change in Prison Management," in Etzioni, ed., *op. cit.,* pp. 376–400.
57. See K. Kawai, Mokusatsu: Japan's Response to the Potsdam Declaration, *Pacific Historical Review,* 19 (1950), 409–414; and R. C. Batchelder, *The Irreversible Decision 1939–1950* (Boston, 1962), pp. 91–97.
58. *Op. cit.,* p. 46.
59. *Op. cit.,* pp. 108, 113.
60. O. Grusky, Role Conflict in Organization: A Study of Prison Camp Officials, *Administrative Science Quarterly,* 3 (1959), 465.
61. *Op. cit.,* p. 89.
62. Gouldner, *op. cit.*
63. Non-adaptive Group Behavior, *Journal of Abnormal and Social Psychology,* 46 (1951), 150–159.
64. Spillius, *op. cit.,* p. 16.
65. *Op. cit.,* p. 83.
66. *Op. cit.,* p. 466.
67. Meier, *op. cit.,* p. 41.
68. *Op. cit.,* p. 77, also see pp. 79, 83.
69. March and Simon, *op. cit.,* p. 50.
70. A. H. Barton and B. Anderson, "Change in an Organizational System: Formalization of a Qualitative Study," in Etzioni, ed., *op. cit.,* 400–418.
71. Sills, *op. cit.,* p. 154.
72. Janowitz, *op. cit.,* p. 77.
73. Gouldner, *op. cit.,* p. 93.
74. *Ibid.,* p. 74.
75. Tuchman, *op. cit.,* p. 253.
76. C. Shepherd and I. R. Weschler, The Relation between Three Inter-Personal Variables and Communication Effectiveness: A Pilot Study, *Sociometry,* 18 (1955), 108.
77. Janowitz, *op. cit.,* p. 85.
78. Grusky, *op. cit.,* p. 465.

COMPETITION, COOPERATION, AND CRISIS

Adler, Lee. 1966. "Symbiotic Marketing," *Harvard Business Review,* 44 (November–December), 59–71.

Argyris, Chris. 1960. "Organizational Effectiveness Under Stress," *Harvard Business Review,* 38 (May–June), 137–146.

Bliss, Perry. 1960. "Schumpeter, The 'Big' Disturbance and Retailing," *Social Forces,* 39 (October), 72–76.

Boulding, Kenneth E. 1962. *Conflict and Defense.* New York: Harper & Row.

Colvard, Richard. 1961. "Foundations and Professions: The Organizational Defense of Autonomy," *Administrative Science Quarterly,* 6 (September), 167–184.

Cyert, R. M. and J. G. March. 1955. "Organizational Structure and Pricing Behavior in an Oligopolistic Market," *American Economic Review,* 45 (March), 129–136.

Dimock, Marshall E. 1952. "Expanding Jurisdictions: A Case Study in Bureaucratic Conflict." In *Reader in Bureaucracy,* R. K. Merton, *et al.,* eds. Glencoe, Ill.: Free Press.

Friesema, H. Paul. 1970. "Interjurisdictional Agreements in Metropolitan Areas," *Administrative Science Quarterly,* 15 (June), 242–252.

Gusfield, Joseph R. 1957. "The Problem of Generations in an Organizational Structure," *Social Forces,* 35 (May), 323–330.

Kaufman, Felix. 1966. "Data Systems that Cross Company Boundaries," *Harvard Business Review,* 44 (January–February), 141–155.

Phillips, Almarin. 1960. "A Theory of Interfirm Organization," *Quarterly Journal of Economics,* 74 (November), 602–613.

Pruden, Henry O. 1969. "Interorganizational Conflict, Linkage, and Exchange: A Study of Industrial Salesmen," *Academy of Management Journal,* 12 (September), 339–350.

Rose, Arnold M. 1955. "Voluntary Associations Under Conditions of Competition and Conflict," *Social Forces,* 34 (December), 159–163.

Siegel, Bernard J. 1970. "Defensive Structuring and Environmental Stress," *American Journal of Sociology,* 76 (July), 11–32.

Smigel, Erwin O. 1960. "The Impact of Recruitment on the Organization of the Large Law Firm," *American Sociological Review,* 25 (February), 56–66.

Steele, H. Ellsworth. 1964. "Oligopoly in the American Rubber Industry," *Business Topics,* 12 (Spring), 47–56.

Wallace, S. Rains, Jr. 1952. "Cooperative Research," *Personnel Psychology,* 5 (Spring), 51–57.

Wren, Daniel A. 1967. "Interface and Interorganizational Coordination," *Academy of Management Journal,* 10 (March), 69–81.

CHAPTER SEVEN

Legitimation, Social Responsibility, and Regulation

Legitimation is the process whereby an organization justifies to a peer or superordinate system its right to exist, that is, to continue to import, transform, and export energy, material, or information. W. H. Ferry (1962, p. 66) defines responsibility as "the capability to distinguish right from wrong, and also accountability, both legal and moral, for actions taken and actions not taken." According to Terreberry (see chapter 2), "Legitimacy is mediated by the exchange of other resources. Thus the willingness of Firm A to contribute capital to X and of Agency B to refer personnel to X and Firm C to buy X's products testifies to the legitimacy of X."

James Thompson (1967, p. 11) views the legitimation process as occurring at the organization's institutional level. He, of course, refers to purposive justification as do Thompson and McEwen in Chapter 8. However, what occurs in and around the technical or managerial levels may also be functional or dysfunctional for the organization's legitimacy, at both the manifest and the latent levels.

Why the current concern about legitimacy and social responsibility? Selznick (1952, p. 242) provides the answer:

> The rule is: those who wield power must establish their right to do so. This is not a pious wish, or a peculiarly democratic canon, but a general political necessity. Every ruling group that presumes to gather prerogatives for itself, or to inflict deprivations on others, must identify itself with a principle acceptable to the community as justification for the exercise of power. Such doctrinal tenets are known as principles of legitimacy.

Many theorists indicate that, for reasons explored in the articles to follow, corporations are facing a crisis of legitimacy. One might speculate whether Hermann's crisis model (Chapter 6) or a variation thereof could be used to explore dysfunctional responses to this crisis.

In the first paper, Cheit reviews the history of the "Free Enterprise Campaign" and the new "Gospel of Social Responsibility." He views the latter as a reaction to the changing political and social environment of business in which the public wields power via public opinion. He examines the argument that businessmen "are trying to sell changes that have occurred *inside* the world of business," that is, that the Gospel of Social Responsibility "is designed to justify the power of managers over an ownerless system," or, "managers must say they are responsible, because they are *not*." He objects to views such as these on six counts, and considers social responsibility not a device to attempt to gain legitimacy, but as a response to demands of the firm's organization-set. He assumes that the Gospel of Social Responsibility is selling corporate autonomy, and that this in turn calls for the study of autonomy.

Kariel's paper suggests that corporations may be able to prevent further erosion of legitimacy by keeping the political machinery in good repair and by keeping society open-ended, private, pluralistic, and uncongealed. This involves acting in behalf of means rather than ends, and acting in terms of procedures rather than substance.

The hand of regulatory agencies is quite visible in our society. The fiscal and monetary policies of the federal government affect the firm's input-transformation-output activities. Specific legislation and the acts of regulatory agencies (local, state, and national) also serve to restrain the organization's internal and boundary behaviors.

Clee demonstrates the manner in which a firm is caught up in a web of regulatory agency relationships. He details eleven specific decision areas that are influenced by federal or state agencies, or by congressional legislation. Mr. Ellis' memo to the Operating Committee reflects an open-system thought pattern.

In the final paper, Holton presents a taxonomy of business-government relationships that examines categories of government policy related to the growth rate of the economy, market performance, programs related to social goals, and corrections for external diseconomies. Within each category the policy effects on business attitudes and behavior are discussed. Holton's discussion of business influence on the governmental process demonstrates how an organization's boundary spanner (the firm's representative in Washington) is related to the firm's inputs, be they information, regulations, or contracts. Finally, Holton makes interesting distinctions between the big and small businessman's attitudes toward government.

While all of the articles in this chapter are concerned with the inputs of pressure for legitimacy and regulation of economic organizations, every organization has to deal also with the question of "socially-responsible" transformation processes and outputs. In addition to governmental regulatory agencies, professional and quasiprofessional regulatory agencies also serve as checks on the behaviors of nonbusiness organizations. If the perception of an organization's outputs or conversion processes is one of "social irresponsibility," this will affect not only legitimacy and regulatory inputs, but possibly other energic inputs as well. On the other hand, governmental and other regulatory agencies must also obtain and maintain legitimacy, and this process will affect when, how, and what they regulate.

REFERENCES

Ferry, W. H. 1962. "Forms of Irresponsibility," *Annuals of the American Academy of Political and Social Science,* 343 (September), 65–74.

Selznick, P. 1952. *The Organizational Weapon.* New York: McGraw-Hill.

Thompson, James. 1967. *Organizations In Action.* New York: McGraw-Hill.

WHY MANAGERS CULTIVATE SOCIAL RESPONSIBILITY

Earl F. Cheit

For the second time in twenty years, American businessmen are engaged in a campaign to justify their autonomy, to fortify their image, and to promote new understanding of their place in society. In the late 1940's, they were preaching Free Enterprise; today, it is the Gospel of Social Responsibility. While the historical basis for the former is easy to understand, the reasons why corporate managers today are portraying themselves as responsible have been variously explained and, I think, often misinterpreted.

I am now convinced that, in general, the significance of this new posture of corporate managers has been underestimated and that:

1. It has not arisen from the much discussed attenuation of corporate ownership control.
2. It is best understood as a response to the changing social and political environment of business. The change is slow, its magnitude difficult to assess, but its direction is clearly toward an increasing assignment of responsibility to the corporation for the uses of its influence, both inside and outside the plant gates. And so American businessmen, long accustomed to creating their own environment, are adapting to a new circumstance: the increasing necessity to be responsive to the environment in which they find themselves.

There is no single "business view" of this change. Some businessmen are resisting it, and many others can easily restrain their enthusiasm. A few, such as J. Irwin Hiller, Board Chairman of Cummins Engine Company, have developed a cost/benefit rationale for the new concern of business with its environment. But, whatever their personal assessment of the increasing demand for business accountability, most corporate executives are responding to their changing environment by adapting their ideology to their interest.

Business, and the men who pursue it, have almost always enjoyed a secure and honorable place in American life. But never were they more admired than in the good years of the 1920's—a time, Frederick Lewis Allen observed, when one could pay one's clergyman high praise by telling him he had delivered his sermon in a business-like manner. The protests of the depression era and the policies of the New Deal heretically challenged the wisdom of canonizing business and its ideals, but American business was vindicated by its dramatic record of wartime production and rapid peacetime economic recovery.

So it is often said that American business was put on trial during the 1930's and won its acquittal during the 1940's.

If businessmen found satisfaction with the verdict, they apparently felt the need, typical of successful defendants, to repair the damage by setting the record straight and, in the process, to win some additional satisfaction. In retrospect, it is clear from their response that American businessmen saw it as their task to fill an ideological gap between business and society. They launched a massive campaign to sell Free Enterprise which became the subject of William H. Whyte, Jr.'s entertaining and somewhat impatient, *Is Anybody Listening?* (1952), a study which revealed that the American phenomenon of selling had taken a new and interesting turn. According to Whyte, during the late 1940's and early 1950's, ". . . businessmen appeared . . . gripped with a single idea . . . . We must *sell* Free Enterprise."[1]

An Intensive Campaign

Many, if not most, of the country's largest business corporations actively, almost frenetically, promoted a great campaign of inspirational speeches, car cards, outdoor posters, radio "listener impressions," inplant conferences, and institutional advertisements, supported by visual aids ranging from General Motors' full-length Hollywood movie on the profit system to the Free Enterprise Comic Books of Procter and Gamble and Republic Steel.

Unlike earlier efforts such as those of the American Liberty League, this campaign, according to Whyte, was one of the greatest and most intensive sales jobs in history, with expenditures for advertising and public relations running at least $100,000,000 a year, not counting the time and energy of many of America's top business executives and their assistants. In short, at the beginning of the 1950's, the campaign to sell Free Enterprise had become a substantial industry in itself.

The series of operations which made up this campaign presented a special message based on the premise that American business had been "out-sold" by collectivism. The public was told that if it did not recognize that the good things of life—the American dream— were the result of the Free Enterprise system, it would soon be victimized by the nightmare of state socialism.

The packaging and distribution of this product may have been an exciting endeavor. Certainly the speeches of the campaign reflected a high degree of excitement. At the same time, the campaign itself must have been puzzling, for although it enjoyed the support of the greatest sales apparatus in history, it seemed to fall on deaf ears. Mr. Whyte observed:

> Never before has the businessman had so much paraphernalia with which to communicate to those about him, and never before has he spent so much time using it. And more and more, as he looks about him, he is coming to wonder . . . is anybody really listening?[2]

If the samples of rhetoric collected by Mr. Whyte are typical—"The challenge I am placing before you tonight is to pioneer in reselling the virtues of our American way of life to our own American people"—it is easy to appreciate why the audience was inattentive.

Its graceless prose aside, there are more revealing reasons why the sell-America copy of the great Free Enterprise campaign failed to command attention. Masquerading as a nonpartisan effort, its actual aims—reducing high marginal rates of income taxation and reversing a labor policy favorable to union organization—were frankly political. And they came too late. Americans had not lost faith in their system; rather, they had found enough faith to try to improve it.

The New Deal

The coming to power in 1952 of a conservative government hastened the same realization among businessmen.[3] Faced with the realities of working with New Deal legislation and the obvious public support for it, a responsible government could find no way to divest itself of its economic inheritance. The abortive attempt to abandon the President's Council of Economic Advisors and thereby to tamper with the obligations of the Employment Act is a case in point.

Today the Free Enterprise sales campaign seems over. To a surprising degree, American businessmen and writers about business have followed Mr. Whyte's advice to stop interpreting our co-operative society as individualistic; to stop concealing our quest for security in phrases like competition and incentive system; to stop trying to resurrect pre-New Deal capitalism and to make legitimate our adoption of the present economic order. In short, not to sell old ideology as the solution for new, practical problems, and not to talk more but rather to listen to the real concerns Americans and others have about American business today.

Many American businessmen have apparently taken this difficult prescription seriously. Never before have corporate officials so openly acknowledged the responsibilities of business to society, and never before have they spent so much time discussing them.

The new gospel of business stresses responsibility to shareholders, to customers, to the industry, to the nation, to everyone. Its tone is restrained. Where the Free Enterprise campaign was aggressive and loud, the Gospel of Social Responsibility is self-conscious and subdued.

At the same time that the sell has become softer, however, a good deal of energy and money is now being channeled into more outright political efforts, devoted to specific issues, often supporting the proliferating fringe groups of the ultra-right.[4] Advertisements such as those of the power and light companies which equate the police state with public power, or those of Timken Roller Bearing which created the "quotation" from Lenin "we shall force the United States to *spend* itself to destruction," are examples.[5] Yet these persistent flashes of economic revivalism make the Gospel of Social Responsibility all the more conspicuous by comparison.

Roots of Responsibility

Of course, the profession of responsibility is not new. Its roots can be traced back to the Progressive era. In the late 1930's, Wendell Willkie, writes historian William Leuchtenburg, ". . . helped educate the businessman to a new sense of social responsibility."[6] By 1948, the Annual Harvard Business School Alumni Association conference was devoted to the same task. With "Business Responsibility" as his theme, the president of the Association introduced that meeting by observing, "Every day we hear more of the need for business and the men who manage business to live up to their responsibilities."

During the past few years, the meeting of middle-ranked corporate managers which did not stress the responsibility of the modern manager would have been very hard to find. In January 1963, at the annual seminar of the National Industrial Conference Board, company presidents "looked at their jobs." As in previous sessions of this series, it was an off-the-record seminar; however, I am sure I will reveal no confidences when I report that the six corporation presidents were, to a man, self-consciously responsible. According to audience members I checked with, the same theme was presented the year before.

To test my impression that this was a recent but rather general change, I consulted the American Management Association and learned that its leaders had become so interested in the subject that the Association had commissioned a study and published a revealing document entitled *Management Creeds and Philosophies*.[7]

Some 700 companies were queried for documents which each firm regarded as "a managerial creed or statement of basic objectives." One hundred and three firms responded, and a detailed follow-up was made with fifty-one companies. Three-fourths of these creeds had been formulated in the previous two to five years, about eighty per cent of them since the peak of the Free Enterprise campaign. Significantly, the creeds were developed because executives thought it desirable to ask such qustions as: "What are we doing in business?" "What are our responsibilities as managers?"

It was in response to four full days of discussion of these and other questions, the AMA reports, that the Canadian Marconi Company developed a formal statement of its primary responsibilities, which is representative of the views repeatedly expressed by American corporate executives:

PRIMARY RESPONSIBILITIES
OF
Canadian Marconi Company

1

TO THE SHAREHOLDERS,
for successful results.

2

TO OUR CUSTOMERS,
for price, quality, and service.

3

TO OUR EMPLOYEES,
for fair dealing and continuing opportunity.

4

TO OUR INDUSTRY AS A WHOLE,
for constructive and ethical action.

5

TO CANADA,
for economic and social advancement.

There is every reason to believe that if the AMA were doing another study of creeds today, it would find even greater concern with social responsibility. Corporate executives seem increasingly possessed by the idea that they must define and formulate their responsibilities to their publics, both inside and outside the firm. Almost every session of the 1964 NICB Seminar had some overtone of "Social Responsibility" and this year the Conference Board's panel of top executives chose to discuss: "Company 'Social Responsibility'—Too Much Or Not Enough?"

IBM Board Chairman, Thomas J. Watson, Jr., in his *A Business and Its Beliefs* (1963),[8] records his firm on the roster of the responsible and by prescription advises those who have not yet done so to join it. Even the most casual sampling of recent literature, professional journals, and business advertising produces countless other examples. This goes well beyond the concept of the stewardship of wealth, as Howard Bowen notes in his treatise on the subject. "Only within the past few years," he writes,[9]

. . . have large numbers of business leaders publicly acknowledged and actively preached the doctrine that they are servants of society and that management merely in the interests (narrowly defined) of stockholders is not the sole end of their duties. Indeed, discussion of the "social responsibilities of business" has become not only acceptable in leading business circles, but even fashionable.

LEGITIMATION, SOCIAL RESPONSIBILITY, AND REGULATION

Business documents professing responsibilities, he reported, run into the hundreds, perhaps thousands.

A Fashionable Discussion

In fact, by the mid-1950's, professions of responsibility had become so common that Peter Drucker[10] chided American businessmen, "you might wonder, if you were a conscientious newspaper reader, when the managers of American business had any time for business." A study of newspapers for a single month led Mr. Drucker to report that America's well-known businessmen felt responsible for (among other things) support of the community chest, employment of the handicapped, research in the social sciences, symphony orchestras, religious tolerance, the United Nations, economic education of the American people, liberal foreign trade policy, intellectual refugees from China, freedom of the press, conservation of forests, and maintenance of private colleges.

This new posture is anything but disagreeable and seems clearly an improvement over the old "public be damned" attitude. But this new attitude, which Wilbert Moore aptly calls "The public be cultivated,"[11] poses problems of its own, not the least of which is the need for a deeper understanding, if not a definition, of what it is that is being offered and why.

When a corporate executive says his firm is socially responsible, as Mr. B. C. Shaul of Tidewater Oil Company recently told the San Francisco Bay Area Pollution Control Board, he is saying that he realizes his decisions may have consequences outside his firm, and that he will try to make these private decisions so that the consequences accord with generally accepted values (in this case, the desire to keep the arsenic used in a hydrogen-generating plant from turning leaves ashen).

Performance Test

There is a close parallel here between the "business responsibility" approach to the social and political environment and the once fashionable "human relations" approach to the work environment. Both imply that before making a decision, the other fellow's feelings and interests should be taken into account.

As with human relations, some students have attempted to enumerate the interests served by the socially responsible business firm.[12] These lists typically include (though not in any particular order) such laudable objectives as economic stability, a high level of employment, technical and economic progress, improved living standards, personal freedom, and more recently, community development and improvement, and, as Mr. Drucker's inventory shows, many others.

But what happens when the critical questions often asked of human relations policies are put to any specific business action or decision; questions such as, "Is it done only where it pays? What are the other fellow's interests and are they truly being served? Who decides what the other fellow's interests are?" Not many of the firms which profess social responsibility are confronted with the rigid performance test faced by Mr. Shaul's plant. Even when they are, most acts, like the six million or so dollars spent on smog control by this Tidewater refinery, can be fully justified in terms of long-term profit maximizing. Moreover, even when exceptional instances can be cited, there is no real test of business responsibility since, for the most part and regrettably, the definitions of the public interest generally come from businessmen themselves.[13] For this reason alone some scholars argue that the Gospel of Social Responsibility is more rhetoric than reality. But it is the subject of other charges as well.

In the view of the law, for example, there is little evidence that management has been freed from its legal obligation to maximize profits for the benefit of the stockholders. A recent analysis by Mr. Wilber G. Katz[14] shows that corporate gifts, a frequently cited example of corporate action in the broad social interest, do not require new legal justification or doctrine. Like other expenditures that hope to achieve community or customer good will, they come well within the traditional doctrine of managerial duty.

Legal Responsibility

With respect to output and prices, again the legal responsibility of management has not changed. The same is true with respect to plant location or relocation. Katz concludes that with the possible (and in his view not highly significant) exception of some gifts the legal view of managerial responsibility is still that expressed in the famous decision in which the Dodge Brothers won additional dividends from Henry Ford. The court concluded.[15]

> . . . a business corporation is organized and carried on primarily for the profit of the stockholders. The powers of directors are to be employed for that end. The discretion of directors is to be exercised in the choice of means to attain that end and does not extend to a change in the end itself, to the reduction of profits or to the nondistribution of profits among stockholders in order to devote them to other purposes.

In actual practice, most large American corporations make decisions and expenditures of funds which might, by some agreed-upon standards, be counted as acts of social responsibility—scholarship programs, research awards, and aid-to-education grants by companies like DuPont are often-cited examples; less publicized are the attempts by firms like Thompson Ramo Wooldridge at leadership in race relations or by Alcoa in rebuilding of decaying urban centers. A recent innovation is the program of Equitable Assurance and others to hire and train school dropouts.

The nation's top money award for creative writing, the $5,000 Roos/Atkins Literary award, was established when, according to the board chairman of this northern California clothing firm, "it became quite clear to me that business has a responsibility to the culture of the community in which it operates." A collection of Thomas Williams's short stories won the first award in October 1963, the same month that American Export and Isbrandtsen Lines presented New York's Metropolitan Opera with a gift of $135,000 to underwrite the cost of producing *Aida*.

It is often pointed out, however, that when profit maximizing is looked at in somewhat longer-run terms, even acts such as these can usually be seen to fit the traditional doctrine of what it is that business managers are supposed to do. Thus writers like Herrymon Maurer, who have most vigorously defended the greater social role of the modern large corporation, have at the same time provided more evidence that profit-maximizing is truly its goal.[16] Admittedly, it has now become a longer-run goal, but this makes good sense and coincides with any organization's long-run major interest: survival.

Those most critical of the Gospel of Social Responsibility point out that none of our studies of human and social relations has produced decisive and reliable norms to replace the competitive pricing process and profit-maximizing for the benefit of shareholders. No other norm has been found that would allocate and utilize resources as efficiently, nor is there another norm that would be enforceable.

Moreover, if social obligations require concerted action by several companies, there is an implication that antitrust powers, already weak, might be further weakened. And this fear is fed by proposals that the voting rights of shareholders, meaningless as they are, be taken away.

Finally, and most persuasively, these critics assert that for the powerful corporation to extend its sphere of influence into social affairs with approval under the guise of social responsibility could be disastrous both for the corporation and society at large. The most extreme statement of this view comes from Professor Milton Friedman, who contends that the doctrine of management social responsibility is "fundamentally subversive . . . Few trends could so thoroughly undermine the very foundations of our free society as the acceptance by corporate officials of a social responsibility other than to make as much money for their stockholders as possible."[17]

Since it can be demonstrated that the Gospel of Social Responsibility is not in competition with but is helped by the profit motive, the awkward possibility that businessmen might undermine free society by claiming they are responsible to it seems remote. Mere mention of this possibility would dismay those managers for whom the profession of responsibility is little more than a public relations program to fend off critical attacks. Most businessmen would probably agree with a recent speech[18] by Pierre S. Du Pont, in which he asserts that a method better than the "mass communications techniques" used in the past is needed to sell Free Enterprise, and that its key point should be performance.

The broad character, the all-pervasiveness, and the timing of this new campaign, however, warrant the claim that something more than profits and public relations is involved. But what?

A Bid for Approval?

In recent years many scholars have provided one possible answer in their renewed concern about the social implications of giant corporations and the separation of their control from their ownership. They assert that "social responsibility" is the managers' attempt to seek legitimacy, to gain sovereign approval of an awkward, if bountiful, de facto status that is a natural by-product of big corporations with dispersed stock ownership. Basing their work on a hypothesis that emerged from the celebrated study, The Modern Corporation and Private Property, by Adolph A. Berle, Jr., and Gardiner C. Means,[19] these scholars have questioned whether the corporation has outgrown the controls designed to keep its managers behaving in the public interest and, even more fundamentally, whether separation from its property base strips managerial power of its legitimacy.

In his more recent writing, Mr. Berle contends that the managers of large corporations are restrained by a public consensus which has required the development of a "corporate conscience" which speaks the language of social responsibility. Mr. Berle and his followers contend that although managers are in the embarrassing position of having (in his happy phrase) power without property, they say they are responsible because the force of public consensus makes them so.

Inadequate Descriptions

On the other hand, to Mr. Berle's critics,[20] this is a vague, unconvincing "philosophy" which does not succeed in explaining away this embarrassing situation. Bernard Nossiter's recent attack[21] on the concept of "corporate conscience" contends for example that it fails in its mission to fill the gap between the lost world of competition where business decisions were constrained and the present one in which managers are increasingly able to act free of restraint.

The public is coming increasingly to realize that classical economic and legal descriptions of our system are inadequate. A business executive who uses these antiquated descriptions in the face of what we now know of corporate size and control is forced, as Eric Goldman has said in another connection, "to act as if his ideological slip was showing." Thus managers must *say* they are responsible because they are *not*.

The ingredient common to these opposing views of business responsibility is an ideological embarrassment which makes the profession of business responsibility necessary in the first place. As in the great Free Enterprise campaign, it appears that businessmen are trying to fill an ideological gap between business and society. They are not, however, trying to reweave a weakened moral fibre, or to temper new, reckless thought with older, more secure truths about business; rather the argument is that they are trying to sell changes that have occurred *inside* the world of business. In the following discussion, I shall examine this argument and, at length, disagree with it.

Although no one knows exactly how many business enterprises there are in the United States, IRS estimates[22] for the accounting year 1960–61 indicated 11,165,875 business enterprises in the nation: four-fifths, sole proprietorships; 9 per cent, partnerships; the remaining 10 per cent, corporations. According to Dun and Bradstreet, about 15,000 new corporate charters are granted each month. Since the number of failures is slightly lower, the number of corporations is increasing—IRS estimates show a 6 per cent increase from accounting year 1959–60 to 1960–61. These one million corporations employ about one-half of the labor force and generate more than one-half of the national income.

Mr. Berle has repeatedly observed that the actual assets owned by about 150 corporations equal about half the assets owned by all of American manufacturing industry. In its annual examination of the 500 largest industrial corporations (ranked by sales) *Fortune* confirms this general picture. These corporations now account for more than one-half of all United States manufacturing and mining company sales and more than 70 per cent of profits.

Moreover, as Mr. Berle has pointed out, ". . . in terms of power, without regard to asset position, not only do 500 corporations control two-thirds of the nonfarm economy but within each of that 500 a still smaller group has the ultimate decision-making power."[23] Thus, our search for the causes of ideological embarrassment leads directly to a relatively small number of corporations.

Myths Obscure Facts

THE CONTROL OF POWER— CORPORATE MYTHS

The real facts about this corporate power, we are told by a growing managerial literature,[24] have been dangerously obscured by a series of widely accepted myths. We are assured that, given the broad, general incorporation acts, the corporation creates itself. It is not an active grant of power from the state and furthermore is put to no close or meaningful scrutiny or control by the state. And we are told further that the shareholder in the large corporation is not an owner in any meaningful sense of the concept of ownership. The fact that he can sell, receive or not receive a dividend, or vote on those issues presented to him by management can hardly be construed as ownership. Nor does the shareholder have control, another mythical status popularly accorded to him.

We delude ourselves, it is contended, when we automatically regard management as protector of the shareholders or representative of the shareholder's (or somebody else's) will. How is that will determined? Or indeed, does it exist?

We must not suppose that significant, independent checks on managerial power come from consumer sovereignty, product market competition, or the scrutiny of the capital market. These checks, to a considerable extent, have been rendered malleable, if not impotent, by advertising, administered prices, and internal financing.

These myth writings seek to show that textbook descriptions of the controls on corporate power today are more appropriate to the classic period of the corporation, which was already a business fossil in 1932 when Berle and Means published their study. They describe the corporation up to 1835 as:[25]

> . . . a group of owners, necessarily delegating certain powers of management, protected in their property rights by a series of fixed rules under which the management had a relatively limited play. The management of the corporation indeed was thought of as a set of agents running a business for a set of owners; and while they could and did have wider powers than most agents, they were strictly accountable and were in a position to be governed in all matters of general policy by their owners. They occupied, in fact, a position analogous to that of captain and officers of a ship at sea; in navigation their authority might be supreme; but the direction of the voyage, the alteration of the vessel, the character of the cargo, and the distribution of the profits and losses were settled ahead of time and altered only by the persons having the underlying property interest.

Still relatively free of mutations or other evolutionary change, this concept of the corporation corresponds closely to its original form. When Sir Edward Coke expounded the law of corporations as it developed in the fifteenth and sixteenth centuries, it was clear that the members of the corporation ran its internal relations; and that a vote of the majority of members determined the corporate will.[26]

MUTINY OF THE MANAGERS

It is now widely held (in no small measure because of the original revelations and persuasiveness of Mr. Berle and Mr. Means) that there has been a mutiny of sorts, that the captain and officers of the ship have dispossessed the owners by extending their authority far beyond mere matters of navigation. It is they, and not the persons having the underlying property interest, who are directing the voyage, altering the vessel, determining the character of the cargo, and distributing the profits and losses. Even if the dispossession was unwitting, the agents now have control; yet the very law which allowed control of the nation's business shift to managers denies them legitimate legal status for the exercise of that power.

It is a long and complicated journey from Coke's *Institutes* and *Reports* to the modern business corporation, yet its direction has been rather consistently (and necessarily) toward redistributing the power to act to a smaller and smaller group of members: the managers. It is they who dictate the rate of investment, allocate research and development expenditures from retained earnings, decide what products will be introduced, determine, through advertising, what demand will be stimulated, and because of the size of the firms they manage, shape communities and often the lives of their employees. It is no accident that the researches that led Mr. Whyte to *Is Anybody Listening?* took him next to *The Organization Man.*[27] Indeed, "Within its internal world and in its far-reaching relations with its external world, it is not clear," observes George Leland Bach, "that the modern business corporation has much less pervasive influence than, say, the medieval church in its society."[28]

CRISIS OF LEGITIMACY

The power of the medieval church was legitimate because it emanated from a coherent body of accepted social thought, but, as we have been told, the modern corporation cannot make a similar claim today. And so it is held that the managers of the modern corporation face a crisis of legitimacy. When pressing issues of public interest arise, Harlan Cleveland[29] writes, there is no "agreed-upon *procedure* for facing them . . . the ultimate source of legitimation is the managers' own perpetuating powers, the survival of their own purposes and functions as the managers define them." As this becomes understood, he continues, the likelihood of further restriction on corporate freedom increases. In defense of their freedom, managers are seeking to blur the distinction between "public" and "private" interests, in part by "a drumfire of public relations, the primary purpose of which is to justify the manager's present and future actions in terms of some concept of the public interest . . ."

Professor Edward Mason contends that if modern managerial writing cannot supply a substitute for the undermined precepts of classical economics, the cost will be reduction of institutional stability and opportunities for economic growth, for these depend heavily on an ideology acceptable to leaders of thought in the community. "It cannot be too strongly emphasized," he writes, "that the growth of nineteenth century capitalism depended largely on the general acceptance of a reasoned justification of the system on moral as well as on political and economic grounds."[30] Managerial literature has successfully attacked these justifications, but offers in their place only vague generalizations about managerial conscience and the "transcendental margin."

Internal Problem

NEED FOR ACCOUNTABILITY

This same brace of problems—government intervention and reduced rate of economic growth—is cited by a second group of writers who view the corporate problem primarily as an internal one: the adverse effects on the behavior of managers of increasing attenuation of ownership.

Ernest Dale, in his recent *The Great Organizers,*[31] attempts to list some of these problems and also to measure their effect on performance. He starts from the premise that since manager and shareholder interests are not the same, the self-perpetuating managers will think first of their own positions should a conflict arise. Their exalted role tends to remove them from the consequences of their own acts; it inhibits free discussion and enforces conformity in the organization; it is likely to produce expenditures on staff and salaries which are too high. Dale cites the interesting example of a firm which was losing money and was afraid it would lose its key employees because of poor morale. Its executives decided to reward themselves and the key employees with a reduced option price on shares. It did not occur to them that the bad financial position was their responsibility and that the company might be better off if they resigned.[32]

He concludes that this conflict between the personal goals of the unchecked manager and the goals of the organization can only lead to poorer performance, that the organization will not release the same initiative as if it were proprietor-controlled (or at least partially so). Mr. Dale has little faith in the restraining influence of such "inherent checks" as the professionalism of management or its professed social responsibilities.[33]

Mr. Nossiter's plaint is not that managers will lack initiative, but rather that they may have too much. Since, in many industries, the restraining effects of competition are diminished, a few key executives make decisions which may or may not be in the public interest. Thus ". . . some business theoreticians have invented a new doctrine, the concept of the Corporate Conscience, to assure us that all is well."[34]

In sum, one view holds that since the growth of corporations has created a crisis of legitimacy, we must find an explanation (apologetic) for the new status of corporations that will lead the public to accept them today as it did in the last century. A second view is concerned, not with the behavior of the public, but with the behavior of managers. Here the concern is to find ways in which managers can be made to behave as if they were owners, and to be as responsible as if they were competitive. Offered as a solution to these problems, the Gospel of Social Responsibility or the concept of the "corporate conscience" has few supporters.

Since organizations ranging from the Roman Curia to contemporary worker-managed undertakings in Yugoslavia[35] have been accused of succumbing to the Iron Law of Oligarchy, there is no reason to assume that the large business corporation would be immune. The debate around the Berle thesis is now over a third of a century old. Its still unanswered questions remain fascinating and useful. In the context of this debate, the social responsibility of business has been shown to be a vague and even potentially dangerous concept; the new doctrine has merely restated existing market and profit norms in longer-run terms, but is certainly not a substitute for them.

The desire to justify power is a natural impulse, and its chronicles represent much of the political history of nations. The facts of corporate ownership and behavior, however, hardly warrant the

WHY MANAGERS CULTIVATE SOCIAL RESPONSIBILITY

assumption that the Gospel of Social Responsibility is designed to justify the power of managers over an ownerless system. I contend that these facts warrant rather different conclusions.

Owners Retain Control

It is far from clear that attenuation of ownership control is as complete as is generally assumed. The most recent attempt to bring up to date the famous Temporary National Economic Committee reports published in 1940 is Don Villarejo's detailed analysis of stockholdings by directors in the nation's 250 largest industrial firms.[36] His study concludes that, in a minimum of 141 corporations out of 232, concentrated ownership on the Board of Directors was sufficient to secure potential working control in the corporation in question. In the case of the other 91 corporations, the evidence available did not indicate highly concentrated holdings by directors or other large stockholders, but the data were inconclusive and centers of control may well exist.[37]

Villarejo generally uses a yardstick of 5 per cent as the amount of stock ownership required to control a corporation where the stock is widely dispersed, though the necessary figure clearly will vary in individual cases. Of course, definitions of "control" differ from student to student as do the criteria used to separate owner-controlled from management-controlled enterprises.[38] But the Villarejo estimates seem conservative at every point since in a highly uncertain field he relies only upon data which are known with certainty.

Additional Evidence

Another recent investigation of this point has been made by Gabriel Kolko who calculated the voting stock, based on proxy statements for 1957, of directors in the top 100 corporations. He includes stock managed by professional representatives sitting on boards—either for personal trusts or holding companies—and directors' beneficial interests in partnerships, trusts, and estates, including the known holdings of their direct families. Kolko concludes that the minimum percentage of voting stock owned or represented by the directors was, on the average, 9.9 per cent of the corporation's shares.

> That figure would probably be increased by several percentage points if it were possible to include the stock ownership in several closely owned giants that do not issue proxy statements. In only 23 of these 100 companies are directors listed as owning more than 10 per cent of the voting stock; in 36, they are listed as owning less than 1 per cent. As in 1937, the vast majority of stock owned by directors is held by no more than 300 men.[39]

These figures are undoubtedly lower than they would be if full information were available, because of the splitting of blocks of stock among family members for tax purposes and the placing of stocks in professionally managed trusts and investment companies where identities can be obscured. For example, when TNEC and current stock ownership figures for the same corporations are compared in board after board, the same family names appear but with very much less stock ownership visible in the current figures.

Another weakness of the attenuation of ownership control position is the fact that directors are increasingly synonymous with management.

> In 1937–39, 36 per cent of the directors of the top industrials were also key officers in their respective companies. By 1957, that figure was 50 per cent. This meant, taking into account interlocking

directorates, that the majority of the 1,477 directors of the 100 top companies were active officers in some of these companies. In 47 of the top 100, officer-directors held absolute majorities.[40]

It is also significant that as a group, the wealthiest 1 per cent of adults has increased its concentration of stock ownership over the last thirty years. Robert J. Lampman, in *Changes in the Share of Wealth Held by Top Wealth Holders, 1922–1956* (Occasional Paper 71, National Bureau of Economic Research, Inc., New York, 1960, p. 26), gives the percentage of corporate stock held by the wealthiest one per cent of adults for selected years in the following table. (Note that Lampman warns that these figures are very rough and should be used with caution.)

Year	1922	1929	1939	1945	1949	1953
Amt.	61.5	65.6	69.0	61.7	64.9	76.0

A recent *New York Times* article ("Multi Millionaire Stockholders Still Rule Big Business") reviews a new University of Pennsylvania study which adds further evidence in support of this conclusion.[41] Persons with incomes over $100,000 a year, it reports, own more than 19.5 per cent of all the stock in the country. It would be surprising if the people who hold these substantial ownership rights in corporations did not wield great influence over them.

Villarejo concedes that the issue of management control can only be settled finally "if lists of say, the largest 150 shareholders in each corporation of interest became available to the public." He also willingly concedes that there are some cases in which management appears to enjoy a dominant position, but his impressive array of facts leads him to conclude that "a relatively small group of persons, the propertied rich" (whom he names) "both own and, sub-

stantially, control the giant enterprises of the nation."

Public Acceptance

Whether or not private ownership confers legitimacy to the extent just suggested, it is clear that managers already enjoy the legitimacy conferred by public acceptance. The ironic fact is that at the very time that the great Free Enterprise campaign was at its peak, Americans were beginning to lay to rest their traditional economic fears about large-scale enterprise. More important still, many were actively endorsing the very big businesses which, out of fear, were supporting the Free Enterprise campaign. Today bigness is widely, if not unanimously, accepted as an economic necessity, even a social good.[42]

One measure of this acceptance is the quiet, almost knowing, reception and early assignment to oblivion accorded the writings of Mr. T. K. Quinn, a man whose credentials and writing skill would have won him a secure place in the journals of economics just a few years earlier. As senior vice-president of the General Electric Corporation, he had access to a view of the large business corporation available only to the top man and his heir-apparent. His views about the dangers of big business organizations led Mr. Quinn out of G.E. and to the writing, in 1953, of *Giant Business: Threat to Democracy* and in 1956, *Giant Corporations: Challenge to Freedom*[43]— both now all but forgotten. In 1956 when William H. Whyte, Jr., poked fun at the managers of organizations, we were ready to laugh at them but not to fear them.

A further measure of this acceptance of managerial capitalism is the apparent lack of impression made by the current writings which bemoan it. In fact, this lack of response is sometimes posed as the major issue in the problem itself. David Bazelon complains bitterly at the conclusion of his "Facts and Fictions of U.S. Capitalism" that when the fictions and power concentrations of our system are pointed out, people are unwilling to confront these facts, or even if they do, they respond, "So what? The System works!" Certainly there is no discernible move toward implementing the reforms that have been proposed.[44] Nor, indeed, is there much evidence outside of managerial literature of a serious intellectual involvement with the problem posed.

But what of the views of the shareholders, whose involvement is more than an intellectual one? Do they accept increasing managerial independence?

If there is serious shareholder dissatisfaction with this situation, it cannot be very widespread. Twice during the past decade, the American Society of Corporate Secretaries has queried its member firms (which include most United States blue chip companies) on matters of shareowner attendance and representation at meetings. The findings[45] show a uniform increase in both, with a marked increase in shareowner representation. In 1958 nearly two-thirds of the companies responding to the questionnaire show between 81 and 90 per cent representation at annual meetings.

Shareholders are more anxious than ever for financial reporting, and the company that overlooks its owners runs the risk of feeling their influence in annoying ways.[46] A discussion with Mr. Lewis D. Gilbert, a man whose professional life has been devoted wholly to advancing the cause of shareholder interests, confirms this view. In the 1962 annual report[47] of his activities, Mr. Gilbert,

who is no friend of managers, stresses the progress made by shareholders in advancing their interests. His list of needed reforms is long, but no less impressive is his case that shareholder influence is increasing. Thus the group most directly concerned with managers, the shareholders, not only is not in revolt, but behaves as if shareholder democracy still has meaning. In short, they too accept the managers.

Behavior of Managers

Prominent among the reasons for this acceptance is that managers behave like owners. Where performance is concerned, it is control, not ownership, that is important. And there is no generally convincing evidence that managers act differently as managers than they would as owners. There is much evidence, on the other hand, that they share the profit interests of stockholders and conduct themselves accordingly.

Their share of the stock of the corporation for which they work may be an insignificant percentage of that stock, but it is nevertheless exceedingly significant for their own personal fortunes. Kolko points out that in early 1957, 25 General Motors officers owned an average of 11,500 shares each. Even together, they certainly could not have obtained control of GM through their stockholdings. But each of these men had a personal stake of roughly one-half million dollars in the company— plus the tantalizing prospect of the corporation's continued growth.

Top management, in fact, is committed more strongly than ever to the corporation's profit position as a result of the growth of stock option plans, because without profits the options are largely worthless. By 1957 option plans had been instituted by 77 per cent of the manufacturing corporations listed on the New York or American stock exchanges. Of the largest 100 industrials, only 13 did not have option plans in 1959. Of the 87 with option plans, the 83 for which public data were available had granted key officers options on an average of 1.9 per cent of their outstanding voting stock by 1959. And the percentage of outstanding stock reserved for executive options is suggestive. By 1960, for example, Inland Steel had assigned the equivalent of 11 per cent of its outstanding voting stock for options; Ford, 6.7 per cent.

Furthermore, top corporation executives are extraordinarily well-paid men —the median income of 1,674 top executives of the 834 largest corporations in 1957 was $73,583—and they have been buying stock. In fact, the managerial class is the largest single group in the stockholding population, and a far greater proportion of this class (44.8 per cent) owns stock than any other. Thus their personal fortunes are bound not only to the money-making success of their own companies, but also to that of the larger corporate structure in which they have invested.

The Measure of Success

Managers are part of the culture which counts gain the main measure of success. If there were nothing else, the tradition of seeking gain alone would remain a strong influence on their behavior. But in addition to the stock option plans and other perquisites clearly linked to profitable return, an even more important factor is that the corporation's internal operating rules are established on a profit-return basis. Profitability becomes the test of investment decisions, the operating rule for corporate divisions. If survival is the first test of the corporation, maximum return is its test of efficient operation. It is the test by which managers survive in the face of competition from their peers and subordinates; it is the way company divisions gain favors from corporate level executive committees. The profit level provides strength in wage negotiations and leverage in seeking favors from a local community.

Thus, even in the absence of an immediate ownership interest, managers have remained remarkably true to the interests of others. When one considers a company like A.T.&T. (with 245 million shares and 2.3 million shareholders), ownership is so widely diffused that it becomes meaningless to talk about it in the customary sense. Indeed, one wonders that companies like this have enjoyed the financial success they have, not that they have not done better.

When looked at objectively, the salaries and perquisites of some managers seem inordinately high, higher than would be necessary to attract needed talent by market considerations alone. Wilbert Moore observes that this seems a polite way for managers to have their hands in the till. While this is probably true, it too is part of the managerial culture and not primarily a function of the attenuation of ownership. Managers' salaries in large family-controlled firms (such as Ford and du Pont) are also very high.

By their professions of social responsibility, managers reflect characteristics long associated with ownership. If the stewardship of wealth was formerly a concern for the rich owners of big corporations, the expression of social responsibility by managers today seems not a rejection of ownership values but an affirmation of them.

The motives and values of the men who make the top decisions in large firms have long been the subject of study. Since it is obvious that many decisions cannot be explained by a simple profit-maximizing assumption, and clear that there is some freedom of action away from this norm, many attempts have been made to construct models to predict the behavior of managers. Typically these emphasize longer-run profit goals or a satisfactory combination of several objectives. A very recent model is that of Robin Marris, who contends that managers act primarily out of concern for the growth rate of their firms, subject to concern for their job security.[48]

None of these studies contends that managers reject the values of ownership or the goal of profitmaximizing. Some suggest, in fact, that the freedom of the managers enables them more ably to maximize long-run profits. It is clear that managers have not made the bid for power predicted by James Burnham nor have they abandoned the system under a socialist onslaught as foreseen by Schumpeter. This test has never come. Instead managers have assumed the entrepreneurial position primarily as a technical role.

In their study of the process of industrialism,[49] Kerr, Harbison, Dunlop and Myers contend that this is a world-wide phenomenon:

> . . . despite the fact that the ranks of professional management are destined to expand in all industrializing societies, the managerial class has neither the capacity nor the will to become the dominant ruling group. The managers are characteristically the agents of stockholders, of state bureaucracies, or in some cases of workers' councils. Since they are preoccupied with the internal affairs of enterprise, which become ever more complex, the members of the managerial class are prone to become conformists rather than leaders in the larger affairs of society.

Public Demands Grow

Although the big corporation and its managers enjoy public acceptance, more and more demands are being made of them. The resident American managers of European firms are working today in a political and social environment which, they report to their home offices, is simply a more advanced stage of changes they see occurring in the United States. Direct United States investment abroad, while small in relative terms, is large enough to attract considerable blame for the balance of payments deficit and, in several industries, successful enough to cause governments to seek methods of curbing it. It is also large enough to have an impact on managerial thinking. For in Europe, although much enterprise remains securely private and profitable, the public, represented by the political process, is gaining increasing influence in the direction of the corporation.

The forms vary from worker representation on boards of directors, to so-called partnership-in-planning arrangements between the state and various economic interests. Although the Scandinavian countries have pioneered in the latter arrangement, France, because of the size, diversity, and private character of its industry, attracts most current attention with its Plan. By no means is the attention unfavorable, even from American businessmen, for, as *Business Week* has pointed out,[50] voluntary planning in France shows that economic freedom and planning can mix.

In broadest terms, the Plan's objective is to bring economic power under political control, a point clearly understood by American executives operating in France. "At home we think about autonomy," one told me. "Over here we look for influence."

In specific terms, the French government, after consultation with economic interest groups, sets a desired growth rate. Policy directives and eventually their technical execution are then carried on through tripartite planning commissions which translate general goals into specific targets for each sector. No direct authority is applied to firms, but fiscal and monetary policy are used to provide incentives to private industry, which has been made aware of the general framework of growth and assured of its place therein.

The French Plan

Intrigued by their success with the first four stages of this experiment, the French express enthusiasm for the fifth, and for defining more fully the responsibilities of the private corporation. A new book by Francois Bloch-Laine,[51] which seeks to do just that, has become required reading in the business community. While some of Mr. Bloch-Laine's specific programs for assuring corporate accountability might arouse little enthusiasm in the United States,[52] he notes that Americans have already made considerable progress toward his main objective: "social integration of the corporation."

Americans have accepted the big corporation, and they expect much of it. The large corporation has come to play an important role in American society, and has come to bear responsibility for many areas of the quality and tone of American life. As Abram Chayes writes:

The neglect of basic research, the dilution of the college degree, the organization man, the dullness and superficiality of the mass media, the level of political morality—all these off-spring, wanted or unwanted, find their way in the end to the doorstep of the modern corporation.[53]

It is often pointed out in the writings about managerial capitalism that the position of the managers is getting closer and closer to that of the public administrators; that their function is increasingly that of reconciling and mediating among the many conflicting interests which lay claim to the corporation and its fruits.

Problems of All Managers

No one understands this better than the managers who are caught between these interests. Shortly after World War II, when large-scale industrial unionism emerged faster than the attitudes accommodating it, a new type of manager emerged—the personnel manager or industrial relations director—who, as he worked with the realities of union power and grievances, found himself spending most of his time convincing top management of the essential merits of the union position. Since this job had to be performed at the same time that the great Free Enterprise campaign was gaining momentum, its difficulties cannot be overestimated. It was not by choice that many of these managers changed careers and are today public servants or members of college and university faculties.

In recent years the problem of the industrial relations manager is becoming the problem of all managers. Because of its importance to the realization of national objectives, the corporation is becoming an instrument of national policy. This is especially true in Britain where, during the period of nationalization, the problem was to ap-

382 point managers who would be efficient but at the same time serve the goals of nationalization. In lesser degree it is also true in the United States, where we have begun to look to the corporation to maintain price stability in the face of wage demands, to restrain inflationary pressures by behaving as if it faced competitive markets, to help sustain domestic expansion, and assist with the balance-of-payments problem. At the request of President Kennedy, C. W. Greenewalt, Board Chairman of Du Pont, is seeking $12,700,000 from United States business to finance Radio Free Europe. U.S. Steel concedes that its decision to open higher-paying jobs to Negroes in its Fairfield, Alabama, plant was made because of federal government pressure and the leverage of government contracts.

Given these pressures, it is not surprising that willingly or otherwise managers are developing a sense of social awareness and that they act (or at least speak) in response to it. Managers of large corporations cannot help but respond to the demand for social responsibility—the same demand which helped to create a tradition of responsibility in medicine and which has led many firms, as we have seen, to develop their own oaths and creeds in the tradition of Hippocrates.

Their motives undoubtedly include profit and job security, but basic to all of these is their desire to maintain their autonomy. In a recent full-page ad, the Celanese Corporation announces that it "proudly cherishes its freedom to innovate, and considers that corporate self-discipline, like personal self-discipline, is the chief condition of retaining that freedom."

If this lesson was slowly learned, it was not for lack of evidence.

An accommodation with the American labor movement, a somewhat more realistic view of the world position of capitalism, the discovery that within "socialized" nations such as Britain and Sweden much private enterprise goes on, that in others the official definition of socialism is one which members of the NAM would not find too unpalatable —all these have helped American businessmen to the realization that their immediate existence was not being threatened. Many of them have come to understand that the way to long-run assurance of getting what they want most —autonomy—is not the old ideology but a new one, an attempt to show that business serves the public interest. General Motors' public relations program is certainly geared to this point. The Free Enterprise campaign presented the corporation as the business on the corner of main street. But no more. GM public relations vice-president, Anthony De Lorenzo states: "We don't try to make ourselves look small, but to look good."[54]

When the discussion of the Gospel of Social Responsibility is limited to assertions that it is self-serving or inadequate to prop up an antiquated ideology, however, its importance is underestimated. It has produced not only the most agreeable posture struck by American business to date, but, as we saw earlier, it has produced socially useful results as well. The businessman's new sense of awareness, of being responsible to society in general, has, among other things, produced the Committee for Economic Development, has put students through college, helped their professors gain increased income, and through the Business Committee for Tax Reduction (led by the presidents of Ford Motor Company and the Pennsylvania Railroad) helped the United States get a badly needed tax cut.

Corporate Autonomy

The importance of corporate autonomy should be recognized, its limits defined, and the discussion of its terms not limited to ideology. "One may hazard a guess," George Lichtheim wrote recently, "that in a good many, if not all, backward countries . . . to the despairing question 'How can we sell capitalism to the masses?' the obvious answer would appear to be: 'By calling it socialism!' "[55] And in our country? By calling it social responsibility? Mr. Lichtheim continues:

> Such stratagems need not be conscious; they are indeed more likely to be successful if the exponents of the official creed are in good faith. But for obvious reasons they can work only in backward countries and with fairly unsophisticated electorates (if indeed there is any intention of consulting the electorate at all). Where democracy and literacy have already had a trial run, most people are likely to see through such conscious or unconscious maneuvers . . . .

Perhaps this explains the failure of the great Free Enterprise campaign, but if I am correct in assuming that the Gospel of Social Responsibility is selling corporate autonomy, then by Mr. Lichtheim's test it is worthy of our attention.

In law and in practice, we have recognized that if managers are to do their job they must be given the necessary independence. TWA managers are currently engaged in a lawsuit, the major aim of which is to keep the corporation's largest stockholder from interfering in their affairs. John K. Galbraith, when he was Ambassador to India, urged developing nations to resist the temptation to interfere with corporate autonomy, noting that the corporation's goals will be best served if it has independence.[56] As the experiences with co-determina-tion in Germany and nationalization in Great Britain and even the Soviet Union have demonstrated, corporate autonomy is a condition to which ideology must adjust, not the other way around.

Corporate autonomy should be viewed pragmatically. In their daily affairs, large corporations confront and create a wide range of complex issues the solution of which requires managerial freedom. When this freedom has been abused, as, for example, in labor and financial matters in the past, we have enacted codes and created agencies to administer them.

This approach, combined with a viable democracy, can best advance such national goals as balanced economic growth, more equitable income distribution, employment opportunities, and freedom.

In each of these areas, however, it cannot be said that business does not live up to its social responsibilities, unless we are prepared to define these responsibilities.[57]

Burden on Government

In the literature on managerialism the conflict between the recognized need for autonomous private organizations and the growing concern about the uses of their power is typically resolved by concluding, "If corporations ought to be doing things they are not now doing . . . then it is up to government to tell them so."[58] While this correctly places the burden on government, it leaves unanswered the more difficult questions of how socially responsible business behavior is to be defined, and the role of private organizations in defining that interest. The fields of agriculture, international trade, labor, and conservation, among others, are replete with evidence that the same diffusion of power which has induced social awareness makes more difficult the development of policies which reflect the public interest. A crisis such as the thalidomide scandal may momentarily disperse public apathy and provoke a prompt definition of business responsibility by Congress, but more often, conflicting interests paralyze legislative action. For this reason the use of presidential power is often prescribed. While President Kennedy won support in April 1962 when he defined for U.S. Steel its social responsibilities, clearly presidential power cannot often be used in this way. An appeal to President Kennedy by many health groups to appoint a commission to determine "the social responsibilities" of business and government led two years later to the surgeon general's report on health and smoking. Whether and how these social responsibilities of government and business are to be defined is still unknown.

In an essay on "Conglomerate Bigness as a Source of Power," Corwin Edwards concludes[59] that as the large corporation comes to typify the organization of the business community,

> its general direction would be toward an authoritarian system of business, within which the significant checks and balances would be, not those of the market, but whatever safeguards might be built into the structure of the corporation or into the relationships between the corporations and the state.

In the decade since Professor Edwards' article appeared, most discussion about the dangers of corporate power stresses either the need for citizens to become alert to the dangers of power, or the need for some as yet unspecified institutional forms of assuring that power is made responsive. In the end it may be the process of the discussion itself, and the factors that stimulate it, which produce the most lasting effects.

During the past year businessmen from various parts of the nation were invited by the Religion and Labor Council of America to participate in a conference on "Channeling Corporate Power in the Public Interest," where they may have been reminded that seventy years ago the Standard Oil Company aroused fear in Henry Demarest Lloyd because the men who ran it lacked the "restraints of culture, experience, pride, inherited caution of class or rank." But today the growing discussion does not emphasize fear so much as the challenge of defining a mission for the corporation. Should its power be confined to that of a limited-purpose organization for the production and distribution of goods and services? Or should business play a larger role in our achievement of widely desired national goals? And if so, how can we create an environment in which business self-interest coincides with doing the right thing?

Response to Change

The Gospel of Social Responsibility is important as a conservative response to a changing environment. In his classic volume, *The Organizational Revolution,* Professor Kenneth Boulding observes that change can be orderly and peaceful only when the leadership group can absorb the challengers. Thus he notes[60] that

> the aristocratic class, especially in England, responded to the challenge of the rising business class by marrying its heiresses. The business class is likewise responding to the challenge of the rising labor and farm group, not perhaps quite in the traditional manner of the earlier aristocracy, but by developing a work-

ing relationship of industrial government through collective bargaining and by submitting to the economic encroachments of the social-democratic state.

Pressures on Corporations

I have already noted some of the current pressures and expectations faced by the corporation. Even if businessmen were not listening to their critics in recent years, it would have been hard to avoid still others. President Kennedy's confrontation of U.S. Steel is the most spectacular instance, but there are many more. For several years now there have been antitrust proposals to split up corporations which have "unreasonable" market powers; during the last steel strike legislation was proposed to require firms in basic industries to give public notice of price increases and afford the public a chance for a hearing before an agency without power to decide prices, only to manage the hearings. The impact of the growing literature of managerialism, the significance of the attempt to define wage guide-posts, and the dozens of other ways in which political authority influences corporate decisions are increasingly felt by businessmen who frequently ask, "What does it all mean?" Mr. Harold Brayman, Director of Public Relations for Du Pont and an elder statesman in corporate public relations, provided an answer at the last annual meeting of the Public Relations Society of America. Advances in education and communications have made public opinion a new dominant power. It is not a hostile government that business must reckon with, he warned. It is the new authority wielded by the public.

In my view, the Gospel of Social Responsibility is best understood as part of this process of absorbing the impact of this changing environment. In this essay I have contended that rules internal to the corporation are important in determining the behavior of managers and that insofar as corporate goals have become enlarged through the managers' increased sense of social awareness, this is due to influences outside the firm.

The magnitude of these changes should not be overestimated, however. Neither Admiral Rickover's revelations of faulty work on atomic submarines, nor the NASA criticisms of defects in the work of missile contractors brought serious new pressures on the private corporation. And when the Russians launched the first satellite into space, it was the educational system, not the business system, which was criticized. Barring another depression, or external economic threat, there is no imminent likelihood that American business will again be put on trial as it was in the 1930's.

Nevertheless, the environment has changed, and business with it. Once closed in behind locked gates, the industrial plant of today is coming more and more to resemble the college campus, and its officers behave more like college deans than business moguls. As Stewart Holbrook notes, businessmen during *The Age of the Moguls*[61] could get away with behavior that today would produce 100-year jail terms. The influences producing this changing environment manifest themselves in many ways beyond those discussed in this essay. An example is the debate now in process between some insurance carriers and their policy holders. The carriers are trying to find ways of eliminating "business risk" losses—losses due to poor management, rather than to accident or negligence. Why? Because the responsibility of manufacturers and sellers for the risks of injury due to de-

386 fective products is expanding and, in the view of underwriters, is being carried forward by a "social and economic philosophy" of responsibility which is approaching "the concept of absolute liability regardless of privity or negligence."[62]

Cumulative Effects

The recent action of a grand jury which accused an advertising agency of fraud in its campaign to sell a weight-reducing drug suggests still another form the changed environment may take: Will advertising agencies be held responsible for the goods they promote?

While these environmental changes have proceeded slowly, their cumulative effects have resulted in something approaching a textbook example of the behavior organizations need for survival. When the environment changes and the organization no longer fits, its listening devices report the change. If the organization is to survive over a long period, it must make the necessary alterations in its behavior. These changes, in turn, influence the environment and set in motion a continuing chain of adjustments until a satisfactory fit is achieved.

"We, as managers of business and industry," Pierre S. Du Pont told his audience of manufacturers, ". . . . have got to take a good look at what we do and how we do it in order to make sure that we deserve popular support. And if the facts do not fit our words, I am afraid we must change the facts to bring them into conformity."

Organizations, as Professor Boulding points out, not only adapt to the changing environment, they also defend themselves against change. As we have seen, in recent years along with the new campaign of business responsibility, businessmen have renewed their interest in political activity as they did during the Free Enterprise campaign. The same companies sometimes participate in both. Summer of 1963 saw the formation of a new political group: the Business-Industry Political Action Committee. Its creation set a national precedent, marking the first time that finance and industry leaders have openly joined political forces. Their announced purpose: to help finance candidates "who support the principles of constitutional government."

Every business gathering reflecting a forward look and a willingness to adapt to change can probably be matched by another which sounds all too familiar as it girds itself to resist change. There are sharp variations in business attitudes by region and by industry, as well as differences between spokesmen for the smaller firm and the large corporation. An interesting confirmation that the latter tend to be more concerned with social responsibility comes from a study of annual reports which found that companies with large assets and with considerable contact with household consumers, the general public, and regulatory commissions are more likely to give attention in their annual reports to "objectives outside of or superior to the profit motive."[63]

It is still too early to tell to what extent this defensive action can offset the changing environment, but there is ample reason to suspect that, barring a depression or some other source of momentum, the defensive efforts will succeed in delaying change. One can safely predict that if a movement to codify autonomy and extend the definitions of corporate responsibility gains momentum, the old ideology will be revived at crucial times. We have two recent examples. In the fall of 1963, an irreconcilable conflict emerged from President Kennedy's Business Committee for Tax Reduction. Pulled forward by the economic need for tax reduction but held back by their views about budgetary deficits, several businessmen urged that a tax cut be conditioned on reduced government spending. When this view failed to gain support of the Committee, they resigned from it.

A few days earlier, after impassioned debate, the British Trades Union Congress enthusiastically endorsed the idea that its leaders join government and employers in planning the national economy. At the same time, it rejected wage restraint as part of planning. A reporter observed that the workers seemed to realize they were facing both ways, but debate alone would not resolve the clash between "head and heart: an eagerness for a growing role in the conference rooms of Government and industry, and a refusal to let go of the slogan-filled past."[64]

In 1955, Professor Galbraith in his book, *Economics and the Art of Controversy,* spoofed the absurd situation in which labor and management, and other economic interest groups, responded to each other's demands in ideological terms, as if survival were constantly at stake. He showed that this behavior has an economic base: people made a living doing it. What was needed in most instances was not new economic policies, he concluded, but new clichés.

A recent analysis of comparative European and American growth rates leads Everett M. Kassalow to conclude that the price of old ideology is greater than fresh language. He argues that private enterprise is the dynamic in both systems, but that a pragmatic attitude by European business has permitted innovations which stimulate growth that are impossible in this country because too many American businessmen still have entrenched views about the role of government.[65]

We should welcome the Gospel of Social Responsibility on both Mr. Galbraith's and Mr. Kassalow's grounds: it has replaced the Free Enterprise campaign with a new cliché and, depending on our response, may provide the basis for more flexible use of private enterprise in our mixed economy.

NOTES

This article appears in the volume, *The Business Establishment* along with essays by Robert Heilbroner, Richard Hofstadter, Paul Samuelson, Henry Nash Smith, and John William Ward. Edited by Earl F. Cheit, the book was published by John Wiley and Sons in September 1964. I wish to acknowledge the valuable assistance of Mrs. Laurent Frantz, my Research Assistant in the Institute of Industrial Relations.

1. William H. Whyte, Jr., and the Editors of *Fortune, Is Anybody Listening?* (New York: Simon and Schuster, 1952), pp. 4–6.
2. *Ibid.,* p. 1.
3. In his recent book, *The Economy, Liberty and the State* (New York: Twentieth Century Fund, 1959), Calvin Hoover has a brilliant chapter devoted to "The Conservative Acquiescence in the Changed American Economic System."
4. The National Association of Manufacturers, which Whyte calls the "bellwether of the free enterprise campaign," could claim three of its former presidents among the members of the first governing council of the John Birch Society in 1959. It is not always possible to separate the old Free Enterprise campaign and the present efforts of the radical right. One of the leading supporters of the Schwartz Christian Anti-

Communism Crusade has been Joe Crail of the Coast Federal Savings and Loan Association in Los Angeles, the third largest savings and loan group in the country. Crail set up a Free Enterprise Bureau in 1961, has spent over $250,000 annually to promote his views, and has mailed two million pieces of propaganda to depositors, borrowers, and business concerns. Crail claims that 5,000 companies have inquired about the Bureau and no less that 2,000 firms have established similar bureaus.

Harding College in Arkansas Whyte calls a "sort of ideological center for the job of 'reeducating Americans in the American way of life.' " Its "National Education Program" made the movie "Communism on the Map" (produced by Birch member Glenn Green) and widely used by radical right groups, but so inaccurate and vulnerable to criticism that even Fred Schwartz of the Anti-Communism Crusade repudiated it. The National Education Program lists on its letterhead executives from Monsanto Chemical, Swift, Mississippi Power Company, U.S. Steel, Lone Star Cement, Olin Mathieson Chemicals, American Iron and Steel Institute, and General Electric. One General Electric vice-president wrote, "It is a pleasure to endorse without reservation this organization . . . ." While many of these firms were old mainstays of the Free Enterprise campaign, some of them also were simultaneously sounding the Gospel of Social Responsibility. For more facts on business support of the radical right, see Alan F. Westin, "Anti-Communism in the Corporations," *Commentary*, December 1963, pp. 479–487, and Fred J. Cook, "The Ultras," *Nation*, June 30, 1962.

5. See the instructive and delightful article by David Spitz, "The Timken Edition of Lenin," *Harpers*, March 1961, pp. 56–57.
6. *Franklin D. Roosevelt and the New Deal 1932–1940* (New York: Harper and Row, 1961), p. 322.
7. Stewart Thompson, *Management Creeds and Philosophies, Top Management Guides in Our Changing Economy* (New York: American Management Association, 1958, Research Study No. 32).
8. (New York: McGraw Hill, 1963).
9. *Social Responsibilities of the Businessman* (New York: Harper, 1953), p. 44.
10. "The Responsibilities of Management," *Harpers*, November 1954, pp. 67–72.
11. *Conduct of the Corporation* (New York: Random House, 1962), p. 282.
12. See Bowen, *op. cit.*, chap. 2; Harlan Cleveland and Harold D. Lasswell, *Ethics and Bigness* (New York: Harper and Brothers, 1962), pp. xxiii–xlvi, and Peter L. Bernstein, "Can Business Grasp the Future?" *Nation*, January 13, 1964, pp. 49–51.
13. Henry G. Manne, "Corporate Responsibility, Business Motivation and Reality," *Annals of the American Academy*, Vol. CCCXLIII (September 1962), 55–64.
14. "Responsibility and the Modern Corporation," *Journal of Law and Economy*, Vol. III (October 1960), 75–85; I have drawn upon Katz' work in this section.
15. *Ibid.*, 82.
16. *Great Enterprise* (New York: Macmillan, 1955).
17. *Capitalism and Freedom* (Chicago: University of Chicago Press, 1962), p. 133. For a more elegant statement of this viewpoint, see Ben W. Lewis, "Economics by Admonition," *American Economic Review Supplement*, Vol. XLIX (May 1959), 384–398.
18. "The Hard Way Is the Only Way," a speech presented before the Annual Meeting of the Manufacturers Association of Connecticut, Inc., September 12, 1963.
19. (New York: Macmillan, 1932).
20. See, for example, Philip Green, "A. A. Berle—New Myths for Old," *New Republic*, June 22, 1963; Manne, *op. cit.*; and Robert L. Heilbroner's review of Berle's *The American Economic Republic* in the *New York Review of Books*, Vol. I, No. 2 (n.d.).
21. "The Troubled Conscience of American Business," *Harper's*, September 1963, pp. 37–43.
22. U. S. Internal Revenue Service, *Statistics on Income 1960–61: U. S. Business Tax Returns* (Washington, D.C.: Internal Revenue Service Publication No. 453 [November, 1962], preliminary report).
23. *Economic Power and the Free Society* (New York: Fund for the Republic, 1957), p. 14.
24. See, for example, David Bazelon, "The Facts and Fictions of U. S. Capitalism," *Reporter*, September 17, 1959, pp. 43–48; Dow Votaw, "The Mythology of Corpora-

Reagan, *The Managed Economy* (New York: Oxford University Press, 1963).

25. Berle and Means, *op. cit.*, p. 135.
26. In his two-volume treatise, *Corporations*, written in 1897, John P. Davis concluded: ". . . the corporation could act only through its organization; consequently, if an integral part of it should be wanting, the activity of the corporation was suspended until the wanting part should be supplied; thus during the vacancy of the headship, if one were a part of the corporation constitution, the corporation could perform no act until it had first elected a head. Nor might the head, in most matters, act without a body" (New York: Capricorn Giant, 1961, Vol. II), p. 213.

He cites Coke's authority: "A sole body politic that hath the absolute right in them, as an abbot, bishop, and the like, may make a discontinuance; but a corporation aggregate of many, as dean and chapter, warden and chaplains, master and fellows, mayor and commonalty, etc., cannot make any discontinuance; for if they join, the grant is good; and if the dean, warden, master, or mayor makes it alone, where the body is aggregate of many, it is void and worketh a disseisin . . . ."

27. (New York: Simon and Schuster, 1956).
28. Melvin Anshen and G. L. Bach, eds., *Management and Corporations 1985* (New York: McGraw-Hill Book Co., 1960), p. 3.
29. Cleveland and Lasswell, *op. cit.*, pp. xxviii, xxxi.
30. Edward S. Mason, "The Apologetics of 'Managerialism'," *The Journal of Business*, Vol. XXXI (January 1958), 6. For a somewhat different view, see H. J. Habakkuk, *American and British Technology in the 19th Century* (Cambridge: Cambridge University Press, 1962).
31. (New York: McGraw-Hill, 1960), chap. 6.
32. Another example comes from the recent revelation that the costly decision by General Dynamics to build ". . . the 990 was signed, sealed, and delivered without board approval." See Richard Austin Smith, *Corporations in Crises* (New York: Doubleday, 1963), p. 83.
33. In the place of the partial proprietors who are passing from the scene, he advocates professional directors, who will be put on boards by the large financial institutions (who now tend not to vote at all). These men would devote full time to directorial duties, assure an atmosphere of free discussion on boards, and serve as an independent review on an otherwise unchecked management.
34. Nossiter, *op. cit.*, p. 37.
35. See "Pope Paul Calls for Reform of the Curia," *New York Herald Tribune* (Int. Ed.), September 23, 1963; and *Workers' Management in Yugoslavia* (Geneva: International Labour Office, 1962), p. 277. In the latter case it is called "following the directorial line."
36. Don Villarejo, "Stock Ownership and the Control of Corporations," *New University Thought*, Vol. II (Autumn 1961 and Winter 1962), 33–77 and 47–65. The list of the 250 largest firms, as ranked by total assets, was taken from *Fortune*, July 1960. Usable data could be obtained for 232 of the corporations studied.
37. The data gathered were from SEC reports, which require a complete current listing of securities owned by the officer or director of each corporation. The major shortcoming of this type of data is that there is no guarantee of finding either the largest holding in a given corporation or the control block of stock. Officers and directors need not report holdings of relatives. Where the controlling group is indirectly represented on the board, there is no available information on the over-all holding of the group. Trust holdings of banks in a corporation need not be reported even if a director of the bank is a director of the corporation in question.
38. The TNEC Monograph No. 29, p. 99, defines control as "the power of determining the broad policies guiding a corporation and not . . . the actual influence on the day-to-day affairs of an enterprise." Berle and Means use the definition also adopted by R. A. Gordon, "Possession of the power to select or change management" (see reference 44). Berle argues (in *Power without Property*, p. 74) that "management control"

WHY MANAGERS CULTIVATE SOCIAL RESPONSIBILITY

is the "locus of power over and the norm of control of the bulk of American industry now." Management control is defined to mean that "no large concentrated stockholding exists which maintains a close working relationship with the management or is capable of challenging it" (p. 73).

39. Gabriel Kolko, *Wealth and Power in America* (New York: Frederick A. Praeger, 1962), pp. 61–63.

40. *Ibid.*, p. 60.

41. *New York Times*, September 13, 1963, pp. 35, 42. The study is entitled "Characteristics of Stock Ownership" by Jean Crockett and Irwin Friend. Preliminary draft (mimeographed), table 1.5, p. 1.24–25. Part of a large-scale study of stock ownership and trading financed by the Ford Foundation and directed by Professor Friend.

42. See, for example, David Lilienthal, *Big Business, A New Era* (New York: Harper, 1953), serialized in *Collier's* in 1952 and later reprinted as a Pocket Book; John Kenneth Galbraith, *American Capitalism* (Boston: Houghton Mifflin, 1952); and Leonard Sayles, *Individualism and Big Business* (New York: McGraw-Hill, 1963).

43. Both published by Exposition Press, New York.

44. For example, those of R. A. Gordon in *Business Leadership in the Large Corporation* (Berkeley: University of California Press, 1961), pp. 347–351, or those of Ernest Dale mentioned in reference 33.

45. American Society of Corporate Secretaries, Inc., *Shareowner Communications and Related Subjects* (March 1960), pp. 3–4.

46. See Oscar M. Beveridge, *Financial Public Relations* (New York: McGraw-Hill Book Company, 1963).

47. *Twenty-Third Annual Report of Stockholder Activities at Corporation Meetings 1962*, Lewis D. and John J. Gilbert, 1165 Park Avenue, New York.

48. See Robin Marris, "A Model of the 'Managerial' Enterprise," *Quarterly Journal of Economics*, Vol. LXXVII (May 1963), 185–209.

49. "Industrialism and Industrial Man," *International Labour Review*, Vol. LXXXII (September 1960), 10. Also their other work cited therein.

50. April 7, 1962, pp. 80–92.

51. *Pour Uné Reforme De L'Enterprise* (Paris: Éditions du Sevil, 1963).

52. Particularly his proposed system of economic courts which, among other functions, would resolve conflicts about corporate leadership and attest to the accuracy of its accounting.

53. Edward S. Mason, *The Corporation in Modern Society*, pp. 26–27.

54. Quoted in Irwin Ross, *The Image Merchants* (London: Weidenfeld and Nicolson, 1960), p. 166.

55. See his "Post-Bourgeois Europe," *Commentary*, January 1963, p. 2.

56. *Economic Development in Perspective* (Cambridge, Mass.: Harvard University Press, 1962), chap. 5.

57. For a parallel argument on the social responsibility of science, see Bernard Barber, *Science and the Social Order* (Glencoe: The Free Press, 1952), pp. 225–232, esp. p. 229.

58. Andrew Hacker, "Business Role in Social Reform," *New York Times*, Western Edition, November 22, 1963.

59. *Business Concentration and Price Policy* (Princeton, N.J.: Princeton University Press, 1955), p. 351.

60. (New York: Harper & Brothers, 1953), pp. 132–133.

61. (Garden City, New York: Doubleday, 1953), p. x.

62. See R. J. Wendorff, "The 'Business Risk' Problems of Products Liability Insurance," *Wisconsin Bar Bulletin*, October 1962, pp. 29–50.

63. "The Ethical Content of Annual Reports," *Journal of Business*, Vol. XXXVI, October 1963, p. 387.

64. *New York Times* (Int. Ed.), September 5, 1963, p. 1.

65. Everett M. Kassalow, "U.S. Ideology vs. European Pragmatism," *Challenge*, Vol. XI (July 1963), 22–25.

LEGITIMATION, SOCIAL RESPONSIBILITY, AND REGULATION

THE CORPORATION AND THE PUBLIC INTEREST

Henry S. Kariel

If corporate managers still believe themselves free to consider whether or not to permit "the public interest" to affect their decisions, they operate under cover of a most agreeable myth: the public interest will be attended to not by them individually but by the unforced, barely visible, always benign operations of "the economic system." As they are self-seeking, the system will be altruistic. The Myth of the Unseen Hand is an understandably durable one. Though treated with secure irony in Economics 1 courses, it remains the common theoretical foundation of both our economic and our political conduct.

Its unadorned, classic formulation was supplied in the eighteenth century. Immanuel Kant defended a state in which even "a people of devils" would work for the common good—"provided they have intelligence," he added. David Hume defended a republican form of government because, in it, even "bad men" would find it in their private interest to act for the public good. James Madison defended the fragmentation of power ordained by the Constitution on the ground that "men are not angels." The specifically economic accent was fashioned by Adam Smith's engaging formula: the rational pursuit of self-interest on the part of individuals—and, by implication, on the part of groups which are genuinely theirs—will ineluc-

tably ensure the emergence of a just economic order. This formulation continues to surround our self-seeking economic action with an atmosphere of public respectability. It is our great apology for selfishness.

Yet, when we voice it today, we do so with increasing diffidence. We look about to see that no congressman at home and no socialist abroad will overhear us. After we claim that the policy decisions in the interest of our corporation, our labor union, or our professional association are really good for the country, we feel vaguely impelled to retract our statement.

Why has Adam Smith's defense lost force? Why do we apologetically grope for a new basis of legitimacy?

The facts, as we know but will not acknowledge, have corrupted our case for the pursuit of private interests. After all, the modern corporation is a large-scale, multiple-purpose organization. It no longer belongs to a group of individuals who have banded together to pursue a single, shared purpose. If it can be said to belong to anyone at all, it is today the property of various groups whose interests conflict.

Corporate Expansiveness

A growing scholarly literature has amply shown how extensively the states

"The Corporation and the Public Interest," *The Annals of the American Academy of Political and Social Science,* 343 (September 1962), 40–47. Reprinted with the permission of the author and of the publisher, The American Academy of Political and Social Science.

392 circumscribed the business corporation prior to the Civil War. As a condition for granting corporate charters, the states acted as if to make sure that the facts would continue to accommodate the economic science of the eighteenth century. In effect, they insisted that the new artificial creature remain publicly accountable. To this end, they sought to make it likely that it would really belong to individual persons who saw eye to eye on the corporation's goal and that the corporation itself would remain a single-purpose organization. A good number of the states consequently kept the corporation small in scale, confined it to only one type of business, and limited the amount of land it could own. To give meaning to these restrictions, they authorized court-appointed visitors to scrutinize its operations, and they made the corporate charter subject to review after a specified number of years.

Today, these restraints have been thrown off. Modern technology has widened the span of the corporation's control beyond all eighteenth-century presentiments. It needs no stressing that giant-size corporations in fact determine the level and the distribution of national income, that they direct the allocation of resources, that they decide the extent and the rate of technological and economic development. They fix the level and the conditions of employment, the structure of wage rates, and the terms, tempo, and season of production not only for themselves but also for their smaller neighbors who obligingly use their bargaining agreements as models. They decide which labor markets and skills to use and which to reject. And they control the quality of goods and services as well as the quantities and standards of consumption. As they engage in their myriad operations, they embrace—generally with unfeigned tenderness—equity owners, employees, suppliers, distributors, and, despite incredibly humble protestations to the contrary, the mass of consumers.

These facts alone testify to the nature of the new role that has had to be assumed by corporate decisions makers. Top management no longer advances the common cause of a homogeneous group but has clearly emerged in the position where it has to resolve conflicts of interests, and this even when those interests themselves cannot meaningfully participate in the decision-making process. This new managerial role has precipitated the crisis in legitimacy and the quest for a new apologetics.

But, thanks to an additional development, the legitimacy of corporate power is in still greater doubt. Since corporations control an actual surfeit of material and financial resources, they have acquired the means to promote not only economic policies but social ones as well. Innocently obedient to the dictates of mass production, they have been able to retain earnings which have made it possible for them to engage in activities hard to place on balance sheets. Corporate managers have been led to assume the roles of industrial statesmen, quite naturally emerging as stewards of the public interest. They have begun to act as if duly commissioned to form a more perfect union, to promote the general welfare, and, ultimately, to secure the blessing of liberty to ourselves and our posterity. Their conscience, if not their sense of prudence, has summoned them to invade, occupy, and govern the realm of human ends—that is, to define and supply cultural, spiritual, private goods.

Impending Controls

Clearly, the modern corporation no longer represents the limited and shared interest of its owners. It no longer belongs to a homogeneous group of individuals who have banded together to pursue their own well-defined objective. To ask it to make decisions in reference to its interest is, therefore, to give it most ambiguous advice. Which of its alternative decisions—whether in the field of pricing, research, relocation, advertising, styling, or investment—is truly in its interest? Is it not true that the adoption of any corporate policy necessarily discriminates against some group embraced by the corporation? Since adversely affected groups have no institutionalized channels for monitoring and controlling corporate policy, and since ownership has ceased to bestow title to power, what enables corporate legislators to claim legitimacy for their laws? In the face of these questions, it is no wonder that industrial leaders have become uneasy and defensive, going as far as to employ specialists to write elevated institutional commercials, compose well-publicized speeches, and summarize academic articles on the ethics of business enterprise. They have begun to sense that their pursuit of a whole range of objectives and their massive power to implement their decisions have transformed their private affairs into public ones.

It is this transformation which has made it apparent that large-scale corporations are subject, in principle, to public control. Exercising the power to make public law, they are subject to those checks and balances which we are by tradition committed to impose on all public agencies—even those it still pleases us to call "private" so that we can imply "Keep Out!" Public government, we know, has every warrant to use whatever power is at its disposal to force merely nominally private concerns to act in the public interest.

Assuming the power to govern conflicting interests and aiming less at short-term profit and more at long-range welfare, business corporations are doubly exposed to public regulation. They invite us to judge their public policies not by economic criteria but by political ones. They make the test of the validity of their decisions what has been the test of all public policy, at least since the eighteenth century: its acceptability in the political arena, not in the market place. As the effectiveness of their pricing and advertising techniques subvert the classical check on their operations, as they become free to act as public benefactors, corporations make economic criteria increasingly irrelevant. The checks on their activities gradually cease to be calculable economic ones. And, as economic criteria —which always assume given ends— erode, the channels are open for the application of public standards upheld through public agencies.

If this analysis is sound, it is understandable why corporate managers are concerned with the effect of their decisions on the public interest. At whatever dollars-and-cents loss, they must consider and accept public values, lest they provoke the state to assert itself vis-à-vis the economy. Their failure to do so exposes their enterprises to state regulation.

The New Critique

It is true, of course, that those who have pressed for state regulation have gained no across-the-board victories, that socialism has indeed been merely creeping. Yet the case for more thorough-going state action has been made with increasing cogency during the last two decades. Given the recent sensitivity of corporate managers to public concerns and given our relative prosperity, this would seem paradoxical. But, in fact, it is the very solicitude of corporations and our very affluence which have given an edge to critical voices.

As we are moving toward material abundance, so it is being maintained, technological efficiency should not be the sole criterion for determining what is economical. There are nontechnological, noneconomic values in life, and the centralized, large-scale corporation does not take due account of them. Thus, instead of making assembly-line work more various and exciting, it prefers to maintain dull routines in the interest of wages and profits. Failing to make social calculations, industry adheres to a narrow standard of efficiency and economy. It fails to jettison some of the economies of large-scale production. It is insensitive to alternative ways of imposing an industrial discipline and rearranging the work process. It is unprepared to pay for experiments which are unprofitable except in human terms. All this, so it has become plausible to argue, is intolerable when profits and wages show a clear excess over need, an excess which enables well-incorporated workers, managers, and stockholders to "consume" leisure.

Since corporations are institutionally incapable of making policy in reference to standards other than those of efficiency and economy, so the criticism runs, the state will have to act. It may either supervise them so that social values will be introduced or else it may break them into fragments so that the classical competitive market will automatically take care of social values.

However soft the rhetoric, the first of these criticisms is directed toward the socializing or nationalizing of economic enterprise. It is certainly too easy to dismiss the argument for socialization summarily by calling it politically unrealistic. But perhaps it suffices to say that the liberal-democratic conditions for socialization—namely, a public government consistently responsible in its operations and immune to capture by the very groups it is empowered to regulate—are simply not present today. Without such government, let it be said bluntly, socialization would surely be a disaster for liberty.

What of the alternative of shattering the corporation so that workers and consumers become free to bid for the jobs and goods they value? Such a program, although it would feed the antitechnological nostalgia manifest in our national fondness for hobbies, barbecue pits, and Grandma Moses primitives, would give us an economy we are unprepared to accept voluntarily. In practice, we will not deprive ourselves of the mass-produced article, though we may want it to be tastier, more quiet, or less perishable. And, although the statistics leave room for doubt, it would seem that to sacrifice the giant corporation is to surrender the efficiencies of large-scale research, purchasing, production, and distribution. If, then, both socialization and fragmentation are undesirable—that is, if the large-scale business corporation is to be maintained as a viable entity—corporate managers themselves will have to consider nontechnological and noneconomic factors as they make their decisions. At a price that has not yet been discussed, they will have to consider the public interest.

Procedures as Norm

To affirm this is to lead up to one of the central questions of contemporary political theory: Precisely what is the public interest? To be sure, political philosophers have asked, "What is the just state?" since the days of classical antiquity. But the conditions under which we speculate about the goals of public action today have changed dramatically, so that only a newly formulated response can strike us as pertinent. The steady extension of the right to participate in politics, the virtually unlimited application of machine power to merely human industry, and the concurrent organizational revolution of the modern age have all created conditions which beg not so much for a novel answer as for the use of an idiom so compellingly relevant that it will drive us to gear our institutions to our ideals.

Of the major themes of political philosophy, the one which has traditionally been associated with the ideal of liberal-democratic constitutionalism is the belief that all claims to power are suspect. Every race, caste, class, or elite which presumes to know what is just must be considered to be fallible. It is not that power tends to corrupt—a dubious generalization in any case—but, rather, that man's knowledge of the public interest is always merely human. From this perspective of skepticism, it follows that to establish a just regime we must simultaneously grant and withhold authority to govern. On the one hand, we must empower our legislators to preserve the integrity of the political order against insurgents who presume to know the public interest and are prepared to impose it. Where the integrity of the state is concerned, we must limit the power of our rulers, as Hamilton noted in *Federalist Number 23*, only by the exigency which calls for its exercise—a formula prescribing few limits indeed. And, on the other hand, we must subject our rulers to a system of checks, lest they obey their private sense of justice and seek to do more than preserve the political order. Here we must require that those who, in fact, exercise the power to govern in the public realm do not themselves presume to establish justice, welfare, or happiness. However estimable their private notions, they must be kept from impregnating the state with them.

In this political tradition, the state is not itself an engine for the creation of virtue. It merely makes it possible for individuals—and the associations which truly belong to them—to pursue ultimate goods. It provides the conditions for the pursuit of happiness in private life. Its function is not to make us virtuous, to define our tastes, or to orient our preferences, but rather to keep us from becoming overbearing in public. It is thus concerned with preserving enough public order to enable us to carry on our own affairs. Its perpetual task, so we should continuously remind ourselves, is the preservation of politics—and the preservation of nothing else.

This must imply that, in constitutional democracies, the public interest has no substantive content whatever. It is exclusively procedural in character. Its sole objective is to facilitate public debate of issues so as to provide all interests significantly affected by public enactments with the opportunity to participate in their formulation. The only authentic public concern is to keep the ends of life open and uncongealed, to provide the conditions for, but not the substance of, our various private lives.

This conception of the public interest demands acceptance of a limited state. But, at the same time, it fully encourages state support of whatever makes men self-reliant and public-spirited, whether this be physical health, decent housing, nondiscriminatory employment, respectable education, or meaningful recreation. These matters require public sponsor-

THE CORPORATION AND THE PUBLIC INTEREST

ship not because such sponsorship is just—about this we can never be certain —but merely because it is in the public interest to nurture those habits of mind and conduct which make us genuinely civil.

Policy Alternatives

If, then, we believe it to be desirable to do no more than to keep the political machinery in good repair, what should we expect of corporate managers as they proceed to make policy in reference to the public interest? It should be evident that they will have to contribute financial resources at their disposal to the maintenance of the procedures of an operating constitutional democracy. At bottom, this requires that they themselves initiate and underwrite policies which support whatever may be conducive to making the right to vote meaningful. This imperative entails much that remains undiscussed. Corporate managers will have to ask themselves a whole set of questions, asking these not as citizens but as legislators. What kind of associations are essential to give force to our conflicting political views? What kind of education makes us charitable in our public life? What kind of political campaigns are necessary to give us a maximum of choice? What degree of economic and social equality must be achieved to undercut our alienation from conventional politics? What kind of technological disciplines and organizational blueprints are essential for cultivating our sense of self-esteem and civility? The effect of answering these questions is to outline practical programs whose direct financial support by the corporation is in the public interest. To follow them up is to keep ours an open-ended society in which no public

law is ever beyond amendment. It is to act in behalf of means, not ends.

To do so is certainly no easier for corporate managers than for elected public officials. In the face of a politics which is intentionally interminable, we readily lose patience and determine to do what may seem so obviously right— whether it be the fluoridation of water or the support of General Walker. The danger is precisely that we do not merely attend to procedures but move into the realm of substance, attempting to set the tone, texture, and flavor of public life, standardizing leisure, patterning freedom, and thereby hoping to give individuals fulfillment and purpose. Thus we are ever tempted to attach strings to our aid, to give grants to research institutes, municipal agencies, or educational centers with an explicit or implicit concern for the outcome of supported ventures. The danger is that we foster more than the public interest demands, that we remain unsatisfied when we merely extend the range of private judgment and private conduct. In short, public action in the public interest prescribes vigorous action but within a delimited sphere.

The Need for Restraints

Should these recommendations for more clearly defensible corporate projects have force, this will be because they happen to appeal to that corporate elite which today exercises immense power over our work and leisure. To say this is at once to concede a major imbalance in our governmental system—for we certainly do not traditionally seek to appeal to those whom we have entrusted with the instrument of government. It should not sit well with Americans to make recommendations which may be graciously accepted or dismissed as gratuitous. We should care not whether our lawmakers operate with a clear conscience but whether they must listen to us. We consider their attentiveness to be the price of their office. We know that those who govern us are more likely to restrain themselves when institutions impose restraints, not when we trust their good will. Thus we still hold with Jefferson that a just government "is founded in jealousy and not in confidence; it is jealousy and not confidence which prescribes limited constitutions to bind down those whom we are obliged to trust with power . . . ." And we agree with Hamilton that:

> . . . in contriving any system of government and fixing the several checks and controls of the constitution, every man ought to be supposed a knave; and to have no other end, in all his actions, but private interests. By this interest we must govern him; and, by means of it, make him co-operate to public good, notwithstanding his insatiable avarice and ambition.

Traditionally and rightly, we have distrusted the custodians of the public interest, even those who have been most generous in the exercise of their trusteeship. Rather than worry about a lack of moral zeal, we have been made anxious by that excess which enthusiastic men of good will feel impelled to translate into public projects. Thus we have been concerned with perfecting devices for compelling our rulers to repress their crusading spirit. It is this concern, in the final analysis, which has made us separate church from state, private morality from public politics. We have consequently deemed it of prime importance to maintain institutional checks on all who have the power to act in the public interest.

If we similarly desire to restrain corporate policy makers, we will have to develop the institutions to make the restraints effective. In practice—that is, in the light of our present-day acquiescence in the uncontrolled exercise of corporate power—this may mean that corporations themselves must reconsider their organizational charts, thereby at least postponing their nemesis. They may have to experiment with arrangements which separate officers making policy in behalf of the corporation from those making policy in behalf of the public. To encourage friction between those two branches of corporate government, to prevent their collusion, what may be required is a deliberate effort to establish offices whose guiding spirits will not be corporation men. Its members will have to be devoted not to polishing the corporate image by sound public relations but to fostering the conditions for public life in America. To preserve the independence of such branches of public affairs, they may have to be protected against their necessarily profit-minded co-ordinate branches. It is by no means clear how such protection may be assured. Conceivably, as has been suggested, one member of the board of directors may be committed to public affairs, and the new public-affairs branch may be held accountable to him alone. More radically, the corporation may divest itself entirely of its public concerns, to do what the Ford family attempted in establishing an independent Ford Foundation.

The Voice of Prudence

None of these steps will satisfy those who fear, not without reason, the emergence of a new corporatism operating under cover of democratic professions and pseudodemocratic practices. They will not satisfy those who insist that publicly responsible officers must directly participate in the affairs of the large-scale business corporation especially when the distinction between its self-regarding and its socially oriented policy becomes a fiction. Direct public control of public enterprises is, after all, a time-tested American principle. To recall this is to recognize that self-initiated innovation in corporate organization is dictated by prudence. Principle reinforced by tradition demands more. To disregard the principle is to provoke the kind of general public regulation for which our political institutions are scarcely prepared—at least so far.

Advice such as this does not, unfortunately, solve the altogether practical problem of the extent to which corporate managers should now allocate the men and money at their disposal to public purposes. However, this question is not one which can be settled theoretically, in the abstract. To answer it requires political talent, the ability to weigh unstable competing demands—including barely audible ones—and to perceive the probable consequences of their satisfaction. Such skill and insight come from experience, not from following the abstract formulas of philosophers, moralists, or even political scientists. They come from experience gained not in corporate life but in political life.

Political life, however, is infinitely tougher. It knows many more losers than winners. It is more full of disappointments and defeats. Should corporate managers become fully aware of the agony of politics, they may yet persuade themselves to withdraw from the public arena altogether and do their utmost to maximize economic profits. They may yet encourage legislation which frankly taxes their noneconomic ventures and frees them to devote themselves fully to the clearcut economic interest of stockholders. They would thereby provide the wealth which makes political life—and its inevitable defeats—possible to bear. Directly enriching the private sphere of our activities, they would provide the precondition for the politics of democratic regimes. Such private enterprise should be enough to fill their days.

THE APPOINTMENT BOOK
OF J. EDWARD ELLIS

Gilbert H. Clee

"Sorry, Miss Allison, but this has to be in Washington tomorrow morning."

Miss Allison turned toward the door with an impatience that had been mounting during the 30 minutes of distracted dictation. If Mr. Ellis had been

Gilbert H. Clee, "The Appointment Book of J. Edward Ellis," *Harvard Business Review*, 40, 6 (November–December 1962), 79–92. © 1962 by the President and Fellows of Harvard College; all rights reserved.

his usual to-the-point self, it wouldn't have taken him 10 minutes. Now she was going to be more than an hour late for her date.

She mustered a cheery, "They'll be there. Good night, Mr. Ellis."

He dialed home. "I'll be late for dinner .... I know I promised .... I have something to clean up here .... No, I'm not tired. I don't know why I sound tired if I'm not tired .... No, nothing is bothering me .... As a matter of fact, things look pretty good. Better than I expected. See you soon ...."

J. Edward Ellis, President of Universal Equipment Company, swiveled slowly around in his chair toward the window and let his eyes wander over the city skyline. How many presidents in those other offices were telling the same white lies to their solicitous wives? Something *was* bothering him, but he couldn't tell her what it was—because he didn't know himself. He had come in early that morning, refreshed by a weekend of sailing, ready to tackle the week's decisions. There were the usual problems, but they seemed routine. As a matter of fact, sales and net profits for the quarter *were* in fine shape, much better than the previous year. The backlog was in fine shape, too, and the next quarter was going to show a per-share-earnings increase. But he felt as if he had spent the day jabbing energetically at a feather pillow.

He turned back to his desk, groping for something specific to pin his feeling on. Probably because it was perched in the middle of his tidy desk, his appointment book caught his eye. There had not been as many meetings that day as usual—and certainly no really tough ones. Yet a half-formed feeling told him that his mood had something to do with that appointment book, and the neatly written notes from which he had just

finished dictating.

They guided his mind back over the events of the day ....

8:30—Operating Committee— Space Instruments Merger

This was all set, *he thought.* Everyone agrees it's a good deal, despite some obvious antitrust implications .... But that article I read last week ... warning that Justice was getting tougher about companies buying up control of important customers. In one case Justice had used a new merger as a basis for reexamining some acquisitions that went back ten years or more. What have we done to make sure that Justice understands that we need Space Instruments to broaden our capabilities? Have we done all that we could to see that they understand the competitive trends in our industry? Do they know what we have to cope with if we are going to survive, much less grow? *He read what he had written in his appointment book.*

To Rodgers - any chance Justice will question last three acquisitions if they don't like S. I. merger? Are risks serious enough to give up S. I. deal? Can he get across to Justice why merger makes so much sense?

APPOINTMENT BOOK OF J. EDWARD ELLIS

Groves's figures show that we ought to get a lot more for these pumps. The market will take the increase, too. Maybe the FTC will look cross-eyed at a price rise, however—especially if the others raise prices too. We're damned if we raise, and damned if we lower. FTC is already asking questions about our price reduction on limit switches. If this keeps up, we may end up in the same position as GE did, with an across-the-board action against us. That would be just great! We can't afford to take any chances now because of the debenture issue. Bad publicity wouldn't do us any good on the Street. It would help if Rogers can find out in Washington which way we ought to move.

Rodgers - FTC advisory opinion on fuel pump price hike?

9:30—Peterson—Six-Month Projections

Pete expects business to continue to increase. If it does, we may need more working capital than we planned on. But Pete says that he really can't estimate how much we should borrow until he knows more about how Washington is going to interpret the new depreciation schedules. Are we going to modify our own equipment expenditure schedule? How many of our customers will modify theirs? If we change or they change, it will influence our need for cash because of the effect on our own cash flow. Also, it'd have a lot to do with earnings over

the long term, and might affect dividend policy, too. Pete says any figures he produces will probably have to be changed, because so much depends on what is going on in Washington.

Put depreciation on agenda next board meeting. Write Rodgers: how soon can have better idea of what interpretation will be?

Three jobs in a row for the Washington office! Am I overloading Rogers? Maybe this is more than one man can handle. On the other hand, we aren't selling much to the government—and we don't want any more government business than we have now.

10:00—Jones—Ohio Plant

That Ohio plant expansion sure looks like a good investment. And Jones said he'd go ahead and hire an architect if it weren't for one small animal in the ointment. What about the new Trade Bill? As a matter of fact, with the possibility of lower tariffs on both sides, it may be that we ought to forget the Ohio project and build in West Germany. Jones thinks we should take that up with our people in Hamburg. But what about Kennedy's proposal to tax overseas investment?

Rodgers: latest info re tariff and overseas investment tax

There's more to this one than meets the eye. When we made those improvements at the Ohio plant last year, 40 jobs could have been washed out. Jones only suggested keeping the men on because we could use them when we expanded the plant. They were all old employees, and there was a lot of unemployment around Columbus. Now if the expansion is going to be held up, or maybe even cancelled because of this tariff and tax situation, we'll have that problem back in our lap again. Maybe Jones had better let the 40 go, but that won't be easy. The community will raise Cain about that, sure as shooting. We'll try to find some way of helping them find work—and public relations had better do what it can to get the community to understand.

10:30—Fox—West Virginia

Fox tells me he's ready to make a final offer to the union in the Huntington plant. It's a fair offer, too, but the leadership down there is in no mood to talk sense. Actually, we can stand a strike right now a lot better than the union can, and they know it. But suppose the Secretary of Labor sends one of his people down to get into the act? There's no doubt about it; any intervention by the Labor Department will weaken our bargaining position. It's a little late to do anything about it, but it's worth a try.

Rodgers - make sure somebody in Labor understands our competitive costs problems before this thing comes to head.

Lewis says if we revise our salary schedules, he can pick up a few key marketing people and some engineering graduates at the end of the school year. He thinks stock options have been pretty useful in the compensation program, especially in competition with some of the big companies. It's true, we've snared some pretty good talent that way.

But Lewis is worried by a lot of talk in Washington about eliminating the tax break on stock options as part of the new tax bill. Could they make that stick? Could they make it retroactive?

Ask Rodgers re tax treatment stock options

Should I get Rogers into the Ohio situation too? Maybe the Area Redevelopment Program applies to the 40 men we may have to let go. How would we go about it? I'd better tell Lewis to check in Columbus and also contact Rogers about the retraining situation.

Maybe I ought to ask Rogers if he wants to pick up some free-lance help for a few weeks to get all these chores done.

11:15—Thompson— Road-Building Sales

Thompson's last sales report was unusually interesting and needed discussion. A shift from asphalt to more concrete in the highway program and the possible switch to a new method of laying and maintaining concrete could be important. If Thompson's information is right, the change would cut our sales to

APPOINTMENT BOOK OF J. EDWARD ELLIS

asphalt equipment manufacturers and users. But it sure would put us in a position to go to town with our concrete equipment customers. It might even double our sales the first year! Maybe $8 or $9 million in five years. Thompson says the Corps of Engineers is spearheading a concrete test program for the federal highway group, but that all final decisions will be made by state highway departments. He thinks that unless someone gets behind the program, it could rapidly get nowhere. However, any company that does get into it now could grab a good piece of business—and maybe keep it.

It will be interesting to see Thompson's detailed projections of the sales and profit potential over the next five years, and know who could coordinate a 50-state campaign and tie it in with Washington. How does he think Universal might go about getting a state-by-state program organized?

Rodgers - re Corps Engineers and fed. highway group - info on concrete shift?

11:30—Product Planning Committee—Q3 Switch

This is a tough one. Should we tighten our schedule on developing the miniaturized Q3 switch? The Q2 is still selling well. Sales this quarter are a bit ahead of target, and our share of the market has jumped to 38%. Forecasts for next year indicate a 12% increase in volume, with prices firm. Sales to the Air Force are down to less than 4% of the total, well within the company policy of keep-ing direct sales to the military as low as reasonably possible.

Now Dynatronics is coming out in the spring with their new model, the one that meets the specifications for the new Starfire jet fighter. They really got the jump on us this time. Starting to work with Wright Field a year ago on developing those specifications, long before we even knew about the changeover, was darn good business. They've wanted to get into switches for years, and this was their chance.

Next meeting of P.P.C.-did we know about this changeover soon as we could have? Why didn't we do something about it? Was P.P.C. aware of competitive implications? What other product plans ought to be updated in view possible defense changeover?

We'd better send somebody out to Dayton pronto and see whether we can get a strong bid in. Whether we get in on this contract or not, we ought to accelerate our program and get the Q3 on the market as soon as we can.

If Dynatronics gets the contract, it will put them in this business—with new equipment and enough volume to manufacture at low cost. They can match our price or undercut us, and they'll have the know-how to broaden their line of miniaturized switches, too. Now we've got another full-scale competitor in our industrial switch markets, courtesy of the Department of Defense.

12:30—Lunch—Homeland Hospital—Executive Board Meeting

Thought we just had to make a yes-or-no decision on going ahead with plans to build the new hospital annex. Sounded like a simple question of raising the $6 million until Dr. MacLennon presented that report on the status of the Hill-Burton program in our state. Imagine, not a single hospital in the county even applying for funds, though the state and federal authorities put our county high on the priority list! Naturally, they gave the money to other counties. Still, if we could meet the requirements, we could get a $9-million hospital for our $6 million. If we don't go ahead with the $9-million project—including a diagnostic laboratory and a research center—MacLennon says that the Westward Hospital undoubtedly will attract some of our younger staff doctors away. And, just to make sure we didn't miss the point, he underscored the fact that the Hill-Burton people told him a very important criterion in evaluating an aid application is the support of local industry.

MacLennon also brought up Kerr-Mills and Medicare. Whether we like it or not, he says, some additional medical care for the aged will be provided, sooner or later. He's worried over how these bills will affect the caseload at the hospital. How will they affect the community? And how will they affect Universal? That's what worries me. The increased contribution he expects would be substantial, of course, but that's not the point. Will the hospital be able to serve all the needs of our employees? If not, what additional company medical facilities will we need? And what effect will the government programs have on our company health insurance policy?

Obviously, we've got to know a lot more about all three of these bills. We asked MacLennon to make a more extensive analysis of the various government hospital programs and the opportunities available. Just what strings are attached to each of them?

2:30—Scott—R & D

This is a sticky one. Defense wants more detailed monthly reports of performance on the new telecommunications project. But why should we get involved in more paper work, much less institute a new control system—PERT they call it—just so they can have more detailed status reports by the first of every month? After all, we've never missed a delivery date in our entire history, have we?

Scott's figures on government-sponsored R & D are significant, though. Next year, over 20% of our own R & D will be government supported. That's less than the industry average, and we want it that way. But it is important to us as well as to the national defense. It's probably better to keep in the good graces of the Pentagon and look into the cost of developing, equipping, and operating a PERT system. Actually, if this new control system or any other gimmick can keep Defense suppliers on their toes, it is probably all to the good. Another job for Rogers . . . .

Rodgers - tell Defense OK on PERT

Maybe I ought to write a personal note complimenting the Under Secretary for the job he's doing in controlling performance on defense contracts. That's not a bad idea, but it can wait until tomorrow.

2:45—Smith and Davis—Convertible Debenture

We never even got around to discussing the date of the debenture issue. All Davis wanted to talk about was the state of the money market, the effect of the Federal Reserve and the Treasury on short-term interest rates, and so on. And he thinks that this, plus the state of the stock market, makes it necessary to raise the interest rate on the convertibles. *Now* he tells us that we might have saved $185,000 if we had gone to the market last March!

Why hadn't Davis anticipated the hike in interest rates? Isn't it his job to assess the money market trends? What's so new about Treasury and Fed influencing interest rates? All he could say was that as deficits and debt increase, the impact of the actions of the Treasury and federal government increases. And now the government has to take into account the international pressures on our gold flow which make it desirable to keep our short-term interest rates competitive with the interest rates abroad. Meanwhile, the increase in the rates on savings here has caused money to flow into the banks so that they're loaded with cash and looking for good-risk borrowers. That certainly needs a lot closer scrutiny.

3:15—Finance Committee—Second Half 1962 and 1963

This meeting was really valuable. Without a doubt, Brown's analysis of projected trends in the economy from now until the end of 1963 was convincing.

Finance Committee—prepare analysis and projection of comparative cost of getting money from banks, rather than going convertible route at this time

What were those two critical points Brown made? I've got a copy of his presentation in my briefcase somewhere. Oh, yes, here it is . . . .

(1) In view of fundamental trends in the economy—and especially the failure of corporate return on investment to achieve higher levels—I question whether the rate of business investment is going to increase as rapidly as some of the government and industry spokesmen were predicting early in 1962. This means that we're probably going to have to scratch harder for business in all of our product lines. And don't think that our competitors won't be scratching hard, too. The resulting competition is going to keep prices from rising enough to absorb increasing costs, especially the cost of scratching for more business.

(2) My analysis of government spending confirmed my feeling that both military and nonmilitary budgets would most likely increase in the foreseeable future. The military expenditures—and the related space and foreign aid items—will go up, I think, because there is nothing in the international picture that would support any reduction in our defense or foreign aid posture. Increasing efficiency—especially in procurement—will save money, but the best we can count on is that this will slow down the rate of increase.

Brown has really put his finger on some of the problems we've got to face.

His analysis of nonmilitary government spending is equally sound. There's bound to be enormous pressure-group influence to support deficit spending as a way of maintaining economic growth and full employment. But what is really interesting is his analysis of some of the ways in which companies like Universal might be affected. Let me see, where did he discuss that? Here it is . . . .

(3) Projections of increased government spending from a level of 99.7 in 1962 to 127.4 in 1964 and 172.8 in 1970 are, I am sure, generally familiar. Spending on space alone by NASA and the military, running between $3 and $4 billion this year, will increase steadily, and probably top $10 billion by 1970. I would like to point out that while most of us tend to think of these expenditures in terms of missile hardware, a great deal of the money goes to other aspects of space, as far afield from hardware as new textiles, new food concentrates, and special medical and scientific instrumentation.

The same applies to the more than 60% of all expenditures for research and development (public and private) now being made by the Department of Defense, AEC, NASA, and other federal agencies. Although we tend to think of this research as specifically related to supersonic fighters or space platforms, there is increasing evidence that these projects have ramifications that touch much closer to home. Just consider, for example, the implications of government research for new trends in metallurgy which, in turn, will affect raw materials, the processing, and even the marketing of our company's products.

Any product we make might be affected, quickly and drastically. We know the effect miniaturization has had on many of our commercial products. We have to be prepared to accept further and constant changes resulting from government-sponsored R & D.

(4) Since purchases by federal, state, and local government reached about $100 billion in 1960—or, in other words, some 20% of our gross national product—no matter how little we sell the government, directly, our customers, and our customers' customers, are inevitably going to be involved more and more with the federal government.

The direction their businesses take, therefore, will be affected by governmental programs, both military and nonmilitary. And what they are going to need, and expect, from us will also be affected.

As a specific example, let me cite the utility industry, a major customer for many of our products. As a direct result of government research and procurement, it is reasonable to assume that by 1975 a major part of the nation's new electrical utility capacity may well be powered by nuclear fusion. Already several of our clients have built atomic generating plants on a private enterprise basis. Meanwhile, the government is moving ahead to develop practical small plants, one of which is already at work at one of our Arctic bases. These plants could substantially change the kind of equipment our customers are going to need. As time goes on, they will want fewer of our present products, and more and more of an entirely new range of products and lines. Certainly, this kind of impact will affect almost every product and every market we serve.

Capital invested in over 2,500 government-owned commercial and industrial facilities within the Department of Defense alone exceeds $15 billion. Again, no matter how little we participate directly, our customers and their customers are going to be involved. In addition, the government is operating —or controlling—uncounted assets in gas and oil, forests and power, and ports and highways. As an example of how we can expect to be affected, just consider what will happen to us as a result of the new developments in highway construction and maintenance. What we have to keep asking ourselves continually is just how state and local expenditures for urban renewal, transportation, education, and medical services will affect our business.

All this growth in government activity, according to Brown, would also intensify the impact of government monetary and fiscal policies on levels of purchasing power, the distribution of that purchasing power, and, consequently, on specific economic factors such as interest rates and the availability of capital. Brown's conclusion—and no one seemed prepared to argue with him —was that one way or another, one of the fastest growing sectors of the economy was the business of government. This in turn would influence the rate of growth of the economy as well as the direction that growth is going to take. No industry, no company, Brown had concluded, could escape its increasing impact.

That had been J. Edward Ellis's day, and in its events he recognized the seeds of his own discontent. Everything he had done that day, or not done, everything that was neatly catalogued in his appointment book, had involved him in a way of doing things that was totally at odds with his own deep-rooted system of values. He had always felt that managing a business effectively meant having enough knowledge of the factors affecting his decisions, and sufficient control over at least the critical factors, so that he could validly accept the responsibility for the consequences of his actions. If what he did proved to be wrong, then he was prepared to accept the responsibility. By the same token, when things went right, he expected the credit and the profit. This was his value system. He applied it not only to himself but to those around him. It was the only way he knew how to measure his subordinates' contribution and reward them accordingly.

Government Influence

This way of doing business had, he realized, been progressively eroded by increasing governmental participation in the economy. For that very reason, he had always tried to run the company in a way that had kept it clear—as clear as possible—of entangling alliances with Washington. Despite this, all that day he, and those he relied on, had been repeatedly in a position of having the validity of decisions depend on what might happen in Washington. As a result, the kind of responsibility he could take for these decisions was qualified in an important way by what the government might do. And this applied to everyone in the company.

The logic of events (right or wrong, avoidable or unavoidable) had made the government the greatest single influence, and very frequently the dominant influence, in many aspects of his business— its growth, its policies, its prices and wages, and its profits. He, or his people, could make the best possible decision, and then some unilateral action in Washington could make right wrong, or, for that matter, wrong right. Under these conditions, how could he discharge his responsibility for making decisions in the interest of his stockholders, his customers, his employees, or those who would succeed him in running the business?

It was this fundamental conflict between values and circumstances, between responsibility and reality, which had been, for some time, lurking just below the level of his consciousness. Now the simple sum of one day's events had brought this conflict out into the open.

Perhaps what had brought it into focus was the awareness that this whole problem of government and business was reaching much more deeply into his company's affairs than he had realized. There was almost no area of decision making, including some areas that superficially seemed to be still in the "private sector," in which the government was not directly—or indirectly—involved. He thought back over past events, and it wasn't hard to trace just how this had happened.

First, the government had taken on some specific "policing" duties—regulating monopolies and then, more broadly, curbing monopolistic restraint of trade. Next, after the revision of the banking system, the government got involved in regulating the financial institutions. In the 1930's, though, a major change took place when the government's involvement became both greater and more affirmative. Certain areas of the economy that had formerly been the private preserve of free enterprise, and subject only to "policing," had been taken over by the government. During those depression years, and during and after World War II, one responsibility after another had been added to the areas of active government participation. Every time a new responsibility was assumed by the government, often to enable the nation to meet a temporary crisis, it was rarely relinquished. Thus, responsibilities had been piled one on top of the other.

Ellis could almost recall the words used by President Eisenhower as he traced the impact of military expenditures by the United States after World War II:

> "We have been compelled to create a permanent armaments industry of vast proportions. Added to this, three-and-a-half-million men and women are directly engaged in the defense establishment. We annually spend on military security alone more than the net income of all U.S. corporations.

"This conjunction of an immense military establishment and a large arms industry is new in the American experience. The total influence—economic, political, even spiritual—is felt in every city, every statehouse, every office of the Federal Government. We recognize the imperative need for this development. Yet we must not fail to comprehend its grave implications. Our toil, resources and livelihood are all involved; so is the very structure of our society."

Now these words took on added significance to Ellis. He realized that they applied to other areas of government activity—federal, state, and local—at home and abroad.

He could now see this same trend being foreshadowed in the technical area. It was obvious to him that the direction of a great deal of technological development was largely a function of government spending. For example, what industries became growth industries was often determined by decisions made in Washington. And where the government decided to spend its money might determine which sections of the country were to grow and prosper.

Effect on Company

Within this framework, how well many companies did was also going to be more and more a matter of how effectively they related to the government—and this included even some details of company operations that Ellis had not thought of before today.

For example, who his company hired had always been the company's own affair. But now Ellis remembered having wondered on his way to luncheon whether Fox was really the right man for his job as director of labor relations. He was an old-timer, with a lot of know-how in working with the union people, and especially with the shop stewards.

But Fox was hardly up to dealing with the new Labor Department group. The thought had crossed his mind that maybe it would be better to have somebody in the job who was more knowledgeable about Washington—someone who could handle the "public interest" discussions at a more sophisticated level. Possibly somebody with a Washington background.

He remembered stopping in the middle of the thought. There he was considering shelving a loyal and experienced employee, just because he could not deal effectively with somebody in Washington. These were the facts of life. Ellis remembered being angry with himself for even entertaining the idea of shelving Fox. Fox was going to stay right where he was!

But the point was still valid. One of the skills an executive needs is the ability to work with that special species —the government official. He recalled that he had been thinking for some time that Groves was probably not as sharp on this whole pricing question as he should be. He knew Groves was friendly with a few of his contemporaries in the industry and probably knew many of them socially. However, with the trend in Washington, what was once an asset had now become almost a liability. He jotted down another note, this time to warn all of his people again about business conversations with competitors. He thought, with some irritation, this was how far Washington's involvement had gone, how deeply it had affected his company, its policies, and its people.

Getting Help

It was discomforting to Ellis to keep thinking so negatively. Then there was the other side of the coin. Not everything the government does is *necessarily* bad for the company, he reminded himself. As a matter of fact, as he thought back over the history of the company, he could identify a number of specific occasions when one government policy or another had been pretty good for the company.

There was, for example, that RFC loan that had helped them to get back on their feet in 1931. And he hadn't liked NRA —it was as unconstitutional as a law could be—but he had to admit that it had stopped some of the ruinous competition that could have bankrupted the company. Then, too, the "arsenal-of-democracy" buildup had helped him get into some new product lines he just couldn't have found the funds to develop if it hadn't been for the government contracts. Several of these new fields would have gone by default to the industry giants if he hadn't been able to get in on some of the contracts during World War II.

There was also that well-equipped new plant that he had been able to buy after the war at much less than it would have cost to build. And when the government's R & D effort really began to move ahead, the company had done pretty well with its efforts in electronic controls. He then realized that his company never could have put together its systems engineering team if it hadn't been for those Polaris submarine subcontracts. And it was that know-how which, having spilled over into the Industrial Controls Division, actually turned in over 30% of the company's profits in the past year, he thought. Not one cent of the stockholders' equity had gone into that division.

And when government spending had shifted to space and missiles and moved westward so that 45% of the military budget was spent on the West Coast, the company's Palo Alto operation was sitting there ready to subcontract. As much as he was frustrated by the government's involvement in his business, Ellis had to admit that a fair amount of the company's growth and a substantial chunk of its profits had come directly or indirectly from government—federal, state, or local.

Moreover, "big government" probably would get bigger. Certainly, there was nothing that he could see to point in any other direction. The rapidly changing world environment and our national acceptance of leadership in the Free World probably would require increased government spending. Also our national safety would continue to require vast expenditures for defense and for the development of highly complex military weapons systems and space vehicles. Leadership of the Free World would demand a careful husbanding of our economic strengths. This, in turn, would require fiscal stability, steady economic growth, and a sound dollar in international trade. But many people, probably a majority, he thought, were in favor of trying to reconcile these requirements with a continuing high level of foreign aid.

Ellis had to admit that on balance the reality of world conditions perhaps justified a greater interest in economic affairs by the government than was required prior to World War II. But what did this mean for what was left of private enterprise? And, specifically, what did it mean for his company? No matter how big or powerful the government might become, it could not achieve great national objectives without a strong and thriving private enterprise—that is, unless our whole political, social, and economic system were scrapped.

This no one can argue with, he had thought. Economic growth in the United States is based on the success of private enterprise. When new plants and equipment go up, the American economy rises. When they go down, the American economy goes down. The flexibility, creativity, and power of the private segment of our economy have been proved time and time again. During World War II, we produced the means for winning the war—and then we turned around and rebuilt the broken economies of both friend and foe after it. And too many people forgot that it was our private enterprise economy that helped rebuild some economies that had strongly socialistic underpinnings.

This same power and vitality, he thought, is a potent factor in the Cold War and it will be in the East-West economic struggle still to come. Moreover, although the government will probably have to direct the development of such major national efforts as weapons systems and space technology, it will only succeed in its objectives by mobilizing large segments of private enterprise to create and produce the systems and hardware and to develop the technical capability that further progress will require.

The same held true, Ellis realized, for the economic development of the less advanced nations. Money and technical aid supplied by the U.S. government haven't done—and couldn't do—the job. Only the joint efforts of government, by helping to create an environment conducive to investment, and of private enterprise, with its ability to get the job done, will accomplish the common purpose. Alone, neither government nor private enterprise can be fully effective.

410　This reminded him of the chart which Brown had displayed that afternoon, showing how the movement of U.S. industry abroad was accelerating. U.S. private investment overseas then exceeded $32 billion, or roughly three times that of a decade before. Brown's point had been well taken. Private investment, and the consequent participation of U.S. enterprise in foreign economies, can have either a substantial negative or positive effect on our political and economic relationships abroad. It can also affect our long-term balance of payments, employment, and economic position at home. Brown's conclusion had been that as American industry's investment and impact increased, it no longer would consist of a group of individual companies that merely "do business" abroad. American industry would become an instrument of national purpose, whether it wanted to or not.

Brown's remarks recalled to Ellis a speech that he had read by Rawleigh Warner, Jr., executive vice president of Mobil International Oil Company. He had been impressed then by some of Warner's comments, and he had put a copy of the speech aside for future reference. "There is an increasing need for a fuller realization by our own government," it read, "that United States companies operating abroad, in all lines of commerce, are in the front line of action in the economic war with Russia . . . . We are not asking anyone to hold us by the hand and make life easy. We are simply asking for something that in the long run, we believe, is in the interests of every American and everyone else in the free world."

There was no question about it—the support given to business by our government and the controls which the government imposes or does not impose on business will be a critical factor in our economic drive abroad. But, on the other hand, private business policy and business operations will have a major effect on our international relationships in the Free World.

What bothered him most, Ellis supposed, was the fact that his company was not really organized to deal with all these factors. As a matter of fact, his man in Mexico City probably knew more about what the Mexican government was doing, how its programs were likely to move into the future, and what its requirements were likely to be, than anyone in the company knew about the U.S. government—much less the governments of fifty states and hundreds of localities around the country.

Need to Understand

As he thought over the frustrations of the day, he realized that his dilemma might in part be of his own making. Because the whole idea of big government was so foreign to him, Ellis had been quite willing to play ostrich, burying his corporate head in some kind of philosophical sand, as if hoping vaguely that the government might go away and leave him alone. But the government wasn't going to go away, and he was going to have to do something about organizing his company to live effectively and profitably within the framework of a bigger—if not a better—government. He had to do this not only for his company, but to help preserve the Free World and the independence of the individual.

The whole problem, he realized, was hardly simple. He knew that this country had evolved a political-economic mix that appeared, at least to him, to have no philosophic base or logical rationale. In his own lifetime, the United States had moved rapidly away from a high degree of free enterprise. But what had it moved to? It was not true, he knew, that (as some of his friends seemed to believe, judging by the way they extolled the past and lamented about the future) the United States had moved from Adam Smith to socialism or any other known "ism." What existed now seemed to Ellis politically and economically to be an undefined and indefinite agglomerate. But the fact that this country was operating in a nameless philosophic limbo that eluded definition was hardly a source of satisfaction.

He had to admit that the system (or lack of system) worked—but did it work well enough? Would it improve? Would the growing network of casually created, interlocking relationships result in achieving our national objectives fast enough to ensure survival? Was there a recognizable pattern emerging that would permit the nation to mobilize its resources to gain its national goals, yet do so in a manner that would salvage the greatest possible degree of free enterprise and individual self-determination? These were the questions that nagged Ellis.

He felt sure that this search for a highly effective political-economic structure could be "muddled through" in a world of peace, isolation, or unchallenged power. But the race run by the United States against the Communist world for military superiority, economic strength, and the support of the uncommitted nations would require more than a structure that just "works." In fact, it would require the most highly effective structure it could achieve—and as soon as possible.

Need for Positive Rationale

Ellis was enough of a realist to know that a rationale for a more effective joint

effort between government and private enterprise would not spring full-blown from philosophic discourse or academic study. He felt that it would have to evolve, painstakingly, and bit by bit, from continuous research, out of the ferment of discussion and effective communications, and be fused in the crucible of experience.

While there were many things coming out of Harvard that he did not agree with, Ellis had clipped a quote from a speech by Harvard's president, Nathan M. Pusey, which he thought dealt rather forthrightly with the problem as it related to federal aid to education. He removed it from his desk drawer and read:

"We at Harvard do not want the Federal Government to take over financial responsibility for us. Far from it! Rather we are working as hard as we can to maintain our financial independence as the basic requirement for maintaining any independence at all . . . . And we shall go on doing this. But we shall also continue our new association with Government wherever learning and research can strengthen national policy.

"We stand ready now, as in times of emergency in the past, to work with the Federal Government in the nation's interest. We hope, as we proceed, to be able with the Government to discover and establish fully acceptable methods of collaboration in carrying out this new, large, urgently important, shared obligation. But we move into the relationship, on guard and wary, filled with suspicion, ready to be helpful where we can, but at the same time eager to concede nothing to our more powerful partner. We fear that at some future time our new associate may begin to make demands upon us inconsistent with the true character of an independent university. When that time comes perhaps we should anticipate, when those repeated times come—we wish to be able, and we firmly intend, to say no."

The questions inherent in this effort, Ellis knew, had been explored and debated since the United States was founded. He also realized that they never had been nor could be resolved definitively, for relationships among groups are always in a state of flux. They result from reactions to an ever-changing and undisciplined environment. They are products of the backgrounds, cultures, objectives, and strengths and weaknesses of the leadership of these groups. And they are created by compromise with political feasibility.

Yet it was neither practical nor praiseworthy, Ellis felt, to sit back and let someone else generate the ideas and establish the rules as to the relative position of government and private enterprise. If he and others like him in business simply allowed a vacuum to exist, economic power would move further toward the government—by default.

Personally, he knew he was not a crusader; but, at least for the company, his course of action was clear.

J. Edward Ellis addressed the microphone of his dictating machine with more conviction than he had voiced in many months.

To: Operating Committee
From: J. Edward Ellis

During our next few meetings I propose that we systematically examine the relationships of our company with the government.

For whatever help it may be to you, I want you to know that I am convinced the government is going to wield a substantial, and probably an increasing, impact on our company during the next few years. I realize that many of us wish this were not so. But this wish has no realistic relationship to the facts of life in our country or to the trends in international affairs. Many of these facts or trends we may personally deplore. One way or another, I urge you to take whatever personal action you consider appropriate by participating in civic and political affairs. However, as far as the company is concerned we must recognize and deal with things as they exist. We have two areas of basic responsibility:

> To manage our company in the best interests of stockholders, employees, and customers.
> To manage our business so that it supports existing national policies, and at the same time exerts whatever influence it can on future policies, in ways that we consider consistent with the ideals of a free enterprise system.

In the interests of both these objectives, we must organize to make our company as strong as possible. This means taking advantage of *appropriate opportunities* to work with the government, for example, by entering into contracts for our products and our services, and by participating in research and development activities. At the same time, however, we must also organize ourselves in the most effective manner possible, to bring to the attention of the proper government officials how government actions or policies affect us, favorably or adversely.

I think that we ought to proceed on the assumption that if we ever do anything that is contrary to the national interest, we will be prepared to accept with good graces the controls that may be imposed on us. On the other hand, I feel that we should do everything we can to call the attention of government people to policies and actions that in our judgment are not in the national interest.

At the next meeting of the committee, we will begin our discussion of this whole subject. In my opinion, this may well be one of the most important discussions that we have held in a number of years. Our objective is to establish during the next year the following program.

Proposal for Consideration

We must develop an inventory of relationships between the government and our company. Our relationships can be categorized as:

(1) *Direct relationships*—Included in this group are supply contracts, research and development contracts, or systems management arrangements where the government and the company are dealing directly with each other to accomplish a common objective. In addition to listing these direct relationships and the importance of them in dollars and cents to the company, I would analyze the contractual provisions to measure the effect of such contracts on business policy, prices, wages, working conditions, and so forth.

(2) *Indirect relationships*—By this term I mean relationships such as taxes, regulatory provisions, and antitrust rulings that have a measurable or semi-measurable impact on company operations.

(3) *Subtle relationships*—These are more difficult to define, but at least the major ones can be determined. Illustrations of subtle relationships are government policies that may affect interest rates, export and import regulations or tariffs, and government aids to special interest groups—i.e., the aged—that may create a favorable or unfavorable environment for the corporation's present activities, or open up new profit opportunities.

An inventory of this nature will identify the total relationships that exist between the corporation and the government and provide the information we need to make some judgment about relative importance. It should show the relationships that each organizational unit in the company has with government departments or agencies. It should demonstrate the nature and magnitude of government action and policy on our direction, growth, and profitability.

Proposal for Improvement

Based on this information, we are going to be looking for specific answers to four questions:

(1) *How can our company best organize to deal with the government in all areas of critical concern?*

One of the problems we will face stems mainly from the fact that we are a diversified and decentralized company dealing with an equally far-flung and segmented government. As I grope for a word to describe the way we have been trying to deal with this difficult situation, the only one that comes to my mind is "anarchy." But the times and circumstances require a more disciplined approach.

Therefore, I want to arrive at answers to such questions as: What kind of Washington organization should we have? And what should this organization's responsibility be in relation to the responsibilities of each division and each sales office of the company? For example, in defense contracts, when and where does direct selling begin and who is responsible for what? We also need to think through the question of how we can best develop an appropriate relationship between our technical and research groups and their opposite numbers in the government, again in relation to the responsibilities of our Washington group and our various sales operations.

Another critical problem that must be solved is the responsibility of our headquarters management for coordinating the government involvements of our various divisions and our separate staff functions. For example, who has what responsibility in relation to the FTC? Who is going to coordinate any action we might want to take on tariff matters, so that we don't meet ourselves coming around the corner? Who has the responsibility for deciding what action we take through the trade association, and which actions do we want to take directly?

(2) *What should we add to our present management information and control system?*

The inventory of our relationships with government should point out areas of critical concern to us; areas where government policy or action can have or does have a major effect on our prices, wages, profits, or corporate strategy. We must determine what information we need in these specific areas in order to anticipate government action or, at least, to adapt quickly to changes in government policy. For example, since developments in metallurgy are vital to us, we should know what trends or developments are contemplated as a result of government action that are likely to change metallurgical technology. Similarly, we should know the developments in the foreign aid program that may create a demand for our products abroad. We should have up-to-date information on the thinking of the government relative to tariffs as a prerequisite to our facilities planning. And, finally,

we should be aware of other critical areas, and other important steps we need to take to bring our information flow in line with our needs.

(3) *What actions and policies do we want the government to undertake in order to make us a more effective and more profitable part of the United States economic structure?*

We cannot criticize every program of the government, nor do we want to. But we should be in a position to present facts to appropriate government departments or Congressional committees that point out the impact of pending legislation or administrative rulings on our willingness to make new investments, our profits, or our level of employment. Also, we should be in a position to support those federal actions that would be beneficial to us as well as to the economy as a whole.

For example, concerning taxation of overseas investment, who should be responsible for the development and documentation of a company point of view? And who should coordinate our approach to the government?

(4) *What policies should we as a company adopt to support the federal government in the achievement of national objectives?*

With the particular product line and managerial strengths we have, what additional participation should we seek, if any, in government research programs designed to strengthen the country's military and scientific capability? Who should be responsible for integrating our relations with the Corps of Engineers and with 50 state and innumerable urban highway departments? What participation would it be appropriate for us to have in programs of economic development for the less developed nations? Perhaps we should not participate, but we owe it to ourselves and to the country at least to explore the possibilities of taking part in these programs.

To the extent that these analyses are possible, we can begin to develop a body of facts and policies that may result in improvements in both the operations of government and our business and their relationships with each other.

When J. Edward Ellis placed the microphone on its cradle, he noticed that it was almost 7:30 P.M. He dialed. "I was a little longer than I thought I'd be," he said apologetically. "Yes, I know. I ought to sound better—I *feel* better .... I have the feeling that I have accomplished something important . . . ."

BUSINESS AND GOVERNMENT

Richard H. Holton

Government regulations of business are pictured, perhaps not inaccurately, as being so pervasive that most major decisions in the large firm must be reviewed for consistency with federal law and administrative regulations before they are carried out. Corporate plans for advertising campaigns, for mergers and acquisitions, for changes in employment practices, for new stock issues, for changes in the manner of computing and reporting earnings, for pricing to different groups of customers—all can raise questions that the management must put to its legal staff.[1]

Although businessmen are inclined to date the great intrusion of government into business from the days of Franklin D. Roosevelt's tenure in the White House, the role of government in business life was by no means insignificant before then. Before 1890 government intervention in the form of protective tariffs and subsidies was clearly intended to promote business. Although much of the legislation since the Sherman Antitrust Act of 1890 has had a different emphasis, business spokesmen often overlook the many ways in which, even now, government promotes and assists business. The government's monetary and fiscal policies are designed to keep employment and incomes (and therefore profits) at high levels; depletion allowances, subsidized construction programs, the mail subsidy, and other policies are also of positive assistance to business.

Restrictions on business behavior are designed to improve the functioning of the system; thus, the loss of some freedom of action for some parties ideally represents not a net loss of freedom, but rather a gain for the system as a whole.[2]

Debates on business-government relations will long be with us, but in recent years the antagonism seems to have been diminishing. Indeed, on some is-

Reprinted by permission from *Daedalus,* Journal of the American Academy of Arts and Sciences, Boston, Massachusetts, Volume 98, Number 1.

sues, especially the problems of the cities, business and government are working more closely together than ever before. The extent of the *rapprochement* should not be overstated, however, since much of the business community lies outside the world of the more enlightened corporations.

Evolution of Business-Government Relations

Until the late-nineteenth century, legislation was designed, on the whole, to encourage business and commerce. After the War of 1812 it was clear that the new nation could not rely on the Old World as a source of manufactured goods, and protective tariffs were enacted to promote the growth of American industry. Government also subsidized business directly, especially the transportation industry. The canal system was developed during the 1830's and 1840's in part through government subsidy. In the 1860's and 1870's massive land grants promoted railroad development, and some 130 million acres were given away by the federal government—establishing a railroad empire twice the size of New York, New Jersey, and Pennsylvania combined. This action perhaps set a record (in one sense or another) for government support and encouragement of business in the United States.

Government regulation of business in its present pattern probably dates from the passage of the Interstate Commerce Commission Act of 1887 and the Sherman Act of 1890, which were responses to changes that had taken place in the twenty-five years following the Civil War. Not only was there rapid industrial development in the eastern part of the country and in the Midwest, but the agricultural West grew markedly in economic and political strength. The farmers and ranchers of the Midwest and West became increasingly suspicious of the railroads and the financial interests of the East. Discriminatory freight rates infuriated the farmers, yet were directly attributable to ruinous competition among the railroads. The Interstate Commerce Act of 1887 attempted to solve these problems by setting up the Interstate Commerce Commission to regulate freight rates and other aspects of competition in the transportation field.

At the same time, collusive agreements to soften competition and predatory tactics to drive rivals out of business led to the Sherman Act of 1890. It was becoming increasingly apparent that competitive behavior had to be policed in some degree. The Food and Drug Act of 1906, the Clayton Act of 1914, and the Federal Trade Commission Act of the same year were all designed to set up "rules of the game" for competition. World War I brought an end to this first major wave of regulatory legislation.

The business prosperity of the 1920's, marked by relative calm in business-government relations, was smashed by the stock market crash and the ensuing Depression. New federal agencies—the Securities and Exchange Commission, the Federal Communications Commission, the Civil Aeronautics Board, and the National Labor Relations Board, to cite a few—imposed new requirements on American business. The public, at least as represented by the President and the Congress, viewed the Depression as evidence that all does not necessarily go well in an economy following the 1920's version of a *laissez-faire* policy. From the passage of the I.C.C. Act until World War II, much legislation supportive of business was enacted; the recitation of regulatory bills above should not cause one to overlook, for example, the Hawley-Smoot Tariff of 1930 or the depletion allowance provisions in the federal income tax.

World War II again brought a cessation of significant new restrictive legislation, and the 1950's witnessed for the most part only relatively minor modifications of regulatory statutes already on the books. The Celler-Kefauver Act of 1950 amended the Clayton Act and significantly increased the power of the federal government to prevent mergers considered contrary to the public interest. In the 1950's and 1960's, government regulation of business was modified by court decisions and administrative interpretations, with little new legislation.

A Taxonomy of Business-Government Relationships

The current status of business-government relations can be clarified by considering four categories of government policy. One consists of measures to maximize the rate of growth of the economy and, thereby, reach and maintain full employment. A second is directed at the performance of markets— the market for goods and services, for capital, and for labor. A third set of programs is designed to redirect resources toward agreed-upon social goals, such as improved housing and education. Finally, certain government programs are directed toward correcting for "external diseconomies," such as environmental pollution. Since segments of the business community have complained about the rationale of these policies and the implementation of them, each group of policies warrants brief examination.

Government and Economic Growth

The first half of the 1960's has been especially notable because of the implementation of a set of neo-Keynesian policies designed to promote economic growth and employment. Illustrative are the investment tax credit of 1962, aimed at increasing aggregate demand by stimulating the demand for new capital equipment, and the 1964 tax cut, passed to offset a budgetary deficit. It is a sobering thought that the effective translation of Keynesian economics from the printed page into action required more than two decades, although the landmark Employment Act of 1946 at least recognized the role of government in the employment problem. After eighty years of steady expansion, the number of former doubters who have been persuaded of the virtues of the so-called "New Economics" is now impressive. The federal government has recently encountered difficulty with the "fine tuning" of the economy through fiscal and monetary policy. Its efforts to design and carry out a combination of policies to reduce unemployment, especially in the ghettos, but to avoid at the same time an uncomfortably high rate of inflation have been frustrated, in part, by pressures generated by the war in Vietnam. These problems do not, however, signify failure of the so-called New Economics; indeed, they would not have been encountered had the New Economics not been successful.

The business community's low acceptance of modern theories of taxation and

418 expenditure stems from a deep suspicion of government spending in general and is reinforced by its concern about a growing national debt. Yet society as a whole, as reflected in the Congress of the United States, has now made the judgment that policies designed to facilitate continuing economic growth and low unemployment are definitely in the public interest. An expanding economy can more easily adjust to problems of technological change and shifts in demand than can an economy that is limping along with 6 or 7 percent of its work force unemployed. Such structural difficulties as regional unemployment or discrimination in hiring can be corrected more readily if the system as a whole is dynamic rather than static. In an atmosphere of economic expansion, risk-taking by new entrepreneurs as well as by established firms is more attractive, and technological change is accelerated. Social problems requiring new government expenditures can be more comfortably financed in a context of growth. Furthermore, the business community itself is a prime beneficiary of high employment policies, since profits suffer more in a recession than do the other shares of the national income. And partly because a growing number of businessmen are aware of this phenomenon, the resistance to monetary and fiscal policies designed to maintain a high rate of economic growth will surely continue to diminish over time.

Government and the Performance of Markets

The many regulatory laws that have been enacted since the I.C.C. Act and the Sherman Act have been a sore spot with most businessmen over the years, yet the business community does, on the whole, agree that it would be a mistake to abandon such government regulation. Business executives may have suggestions for modifying either a law's language or interpretation, but few would call for its repeal. Businessmen do, however, complain about overzealous bureaucrats who allegedly have an inadequate understanding of the real world of commerce and therefore fail to realize the full consequences of their actions. In private, if not in public, discussions, it is agreed that regulatory legislation has helped to keep the competitive environment in the United States considerably livelier and healthier than it would otherwise have been. Contrasts with the cartelized industries in Europe underscore this point.

The individual firm may well find it difficult to live with the regulatory legislation as it is enforced. The legislation is usually rather vague, and its interpretation is left to the regulatory agencies and to the courts. Interpretations can and do shift as new faces appear on the regulatory commissions and on the courts of law. The absence of clear, reasonable, and consistent guidelines in the antitrust area, for example, is a continuing problem for the individual firm, although the complexity and diversity of individual situations preclude significant departures from the case-by-case approach.

Economists evaluate the state of competition in the market by looking at the conduct and performance of market structure. By the crudest measure, competition appears to be eroding in the manufacturing sector of the economy; the percentage of manufacturing assets held by the two hundred largest manufacturing companies in the country rose from 46.7 percent to 55.4 percent between 1950 and 1965.[3] Yet examination of the conduct and performance of the individual industries suggests to many that these markets are, in a sense, highly "competitive." Although economic concentration is high in them, they exhibit the innovation and efficiency that one would expect from firms trying to best one another in the market. Anti-competitive behavior is difficult to ferret out and to prove except in instances of blatant collusion, such as the electrical equipment conspiracy of the 1960's.

Over the last few years the market for consumer goods and services has received unusual attention. The position of Special Assistant for Consumer Affairs has been established in the Office of the President; "truth-in-packaging" and "truth-in-lending" legislation has been passed; automobile safety has been the subject of more regulation; and product warranties are being reviewed. At first glance, it seems paradoxical that the consumer's problems in the market place should draw such comment precisely when the average consumer is better off than ever before, judging by disposable income per capita. Furthermore, the body of consumer legislation on the books before the new wave of concern was perhaps as comprehensive and as effective as that to be found anywhere in the industrial world. Perhaps the issue surfaced at this particular time only because its apparent political appeal was accidentally discovered; or perhaps the concern of an increasingly sophisticated public about advertising and merchandising practices finally grew to some critical mass.

The technology of consumer goods is increasingly complex. More and more features of goods and services cannot be judged intelligently by the typical consumer. The rate of technological change may be increasing, and sellers' marketing tactics are becoming more imaginative and (at least in part) confusing.

The so-called "professional consumers" argue that the average consumer has too little information at his disposal to make an intelligent decision. The defendants of the *status quo* reply that ample information is available, but that few consumers use it. Both sides may miss the important point—namely, that the consumer faces an increasing need for an *efficient* information system. The simplest models of competitive markets assume that buyers and sellers have perfect information about the options open to them. Since information is not costless, any improvement in the efficiency of the informational process should make competition more effective. Given the multitude of decisions that must be made in, say, the supermarket, proliferation in package sizes makes it extremely time-consuming for the consumer to compute values in terms of price per ounce or per pound. Although there are obviously other important components of an item's "value," price per ounce or pound is presumably a major one for the consumer. If we believe what we say about the desirability of the competitive process, we should not oppose measures designed to make that process more efficient. In practice, of course, the problem is not so simple, since the proposed "truth-in-packaging" measures may increase manufacturing costs or inhibit development of better packaging.

Business commonly responds to the demand for more regulation in consumer markets by contending that competition and the legislation already in effect amply protect the consumer. A retailer or manufacturer who does not satisfy his customers will lose them. This argument assumes, however, that the buying public learns rather quickly which sellers do the better job, yet in many cases the learning process is slow and

The consumer may learn to judge his suppliers fairly rapidly if the item is bought quite frequently, if the quality and performance characteristics of the item are either apparent at the point of purchase or immediately after the item is used, and if the rate of technological change is slow, relative to the frequency of purchase. Certain items bought weekly in the supermarket might well meet all three of these conditions, but many goods and services do not. For example, automobile tires are difficult for the individual consumer to evaluate because they are bought so seldom and are subject to relatively rapid technological change. And how quickly does one learn whether Company A or Company B offers the best casualty insurance coverage for a given premium? One rarely files a claim, and the differing circumstances of each claim make it difficult for the consumer to judge whether or not some competing company would provide better service on that claim. Hearsay evidence and advertising provide additional information, but both sources are imperfect. Competition is reduced to rivalry among selling and merchandising techniques, with little relation to qualitative differences in product. When the learning process is slow and imperfect, a brand may prosper not because it is the "best buy," but rather because it is "best merchandised."

Differences in the frequency of purchase, the susceptibility to objective measurement of quality and performance, and the rate of technological change lead to important differences in the nature of the competitive discipline imposed on sellers in the markets for consumer goods and services. In some markets the consumer can assess the value of a good or service, while in many others he must rely largely on information provided by the seller. The model of the competitive economy assumes that all consumer markets are of the first sort; in markets of the second type, consumer satisfaction might not be maximized simply because the consumer is not fully aware of the alternatives. It is interesting to note how often opponents of further government rule-making for consumer products cite the markets for high-frequency items, usually those encountered in supermarkets, as evidence of the proper functioning of consumer markets.

The federal government's regulation of the market for goods and services may well be shifting away from *intermediate* markets (markets in which goods are bought by firms) toward consumer markets. Given the rapidly growing varieties of goods and services available, the imaginative new marketing techniques, and the increasing technical complexity of consumer goods, consumers will have less time and less relative ability to judge the quality of their purchase options. This situation would seem to call for more rule-making by federal agencies in the area of consumer goods and services. If the analysis above is correct, the recent legislation regarding packaging, disclosure of financing charges on consumer purchases, and tire standards is but a harbinger of things to come. The present concern about the welfare of the nation's poor people serves to reinforce the pressures for consumer legislation since poor people are, for a variety of reasons, least able to evaluate properly the purchasing options they face.

Further regulating activity may also be expected in the capital market, where innovations were especially notable during the 1930's. The Securities Act of 1933, the Securities Exchange Act of 1934, and related legislation were clearly a reaction to the speculative excesses of the 1920's. The resulting improvements in the quality and quantity of information available about individual companies, coupled with such safeguards as penalties for manipulation of stock by insiders, have been largely responsible for the marked difference in the role of the equity capital market in the United States and other industrialized countries. Although corporate financial officers can criticize the burden of detailed corporate reporting to the S.E.C., there can be little doubt that federal regulation of capital markets has been essentially salutary.

The complexity of the modern corporation in the United States and certain institutional features of our capital markets are raising new questions, however, about the efficiency of the country's capital allocation mechanism. The informational requirements imposed by the S.E.C. help investors make better investment decisions. The quantity of information on all publicly traded equities is so great that the individual investor needs a screening device to select essential information for his consideration; the community of brokerage firms, investment advisory services, and ancillary institutions provides this service. But the growing importance of corporate and conglomerate firms has made this screening more difficult in recent years.

The conglomerate is in some ways comparable to a mutual fund that is not required to report on its portfolio, since it need not report its financial results by division. Consequently, the prospective investor does not know whether the corporation's total performance reflects some mix of good and bad records among the divisions or whether all components of the firm have performed in a comparable manner. Two conglomerates conceivably might file identical reports with the S.E.C., yet one might be far

more dependent on the profits from one or two divisions than the other. Were this information known, it could make one corporation more or less attractive to the investor than the other. If this is the case, the capital market does not work so well as it should, and the growing concern about the components of the conglomerate may well lead to further regulation.

This question is related to a second—namely, the role of the corporation in making investment decisions on behalf of its stockholders. Corporations are major capital-generating machines. They retain and invest roughly half of their after-tax earnings. One can ask whether society would utilize this reinvested capital in any different pattern if all corporate earnings were paid out to stockholders who would then have the option of buying new issues of equity stock offered by firms in need of additional capital. Under such circumstances, the steel industry, for example, would be forced to go to the equity market to raise capital for any expansion not financed by the cash flow from depreciation charges. It is difficult to imagine that stockholders would not reinvest their earnings differently than the corporations are presently doing on their behalf. It may well be, however, that investment decisions under the present system are better informed and hence more productive for society as a whole than they would be with a 100 percent pay-out rule.[4]

Regulation of the labor market seems to have been singularly stable in recent years. The basic labor legislation of the 1930's, as modified by the Taft-Hartley Act of 1947 and the Landrum-Griffin Act of 1959, seems quite durable. The National Industrial Relations Board faces a continuing stream of cases, it is true, and further refinement of acceptable practices can be expected. But no major legislative changes in business-government relations affecting the negotiating process seem imminent.

Instead, attention will continue to be focused primarily on the wage-determination process as it affects prices and the price level. Under conditions of high-level employment, employers bargaining on an industry-wide basis are able to pass wage increases onto buyers through increases in prices more easily than when the level of aggregate demand is low. The Kennedy Administration's attempt to institute voluntary wage-price guidelines was relatively unsuccessful. The guidelines policy was weak largely because it lacked sanctions and favorable public sentiment. The individual parties in bargaining situations have considered the cost of compliance with the guidelines too high. This has been more true of those situations involving local contracts than of the major industry-wide contracts. Unless mandatory wage and price controls are instituted, the country might not be able to lower unemployment to 3 percent without generating an uncomfortably high rate of inflation.

The nation's effort to find jobs for the hard-core unemployed promises to lead to modifications of business-government relations in the unskilled and untrained labor market. Federal minimum wage legislation and minimum wages under existing labor contracts discourage employers from using workers whose productivity is so low that the applicable minimum wage is not recovered. Pressure appears to be mounting for tax incentives or direct subsidies to employers hiring the hard-core unemployed. This may well be the next major innovation in business-government relations in the labor market if an adequate control and enforcement mechanism can be devised.

Redirection of Resources Government and the

Business-government relations extend well beyond the regulatory legislation designed to improve market performance; much (if not more) business-government contact stems from government policy designed to alter the pattern of the nation's resource use. The government accomplishes some redirection of resources by purchasing goods and services that would not otherwise be produced, such as military weapons systems. It also redirects resources without becoming a buyer—for example, by levying tariffs.

Business objections to redirection of resource use are milder than the feelings about the regulation of market behavior. The steel industry does not seem to object to tariffs on steel as a form of government intervention. Many business leaders may speak out for free trade, but few cite specific tariffs or quotas as an unwarranted government intervention for fear of alienating suppliers, customers, or others in the business community. The Federal Reserve Board of Governors and the Treasury influence the level and structure of interest rates, thus serving not only to redirect resources toward or away from housing and investment goods, but also to control the level of aggregate demand and hence the price level. Objections to high interest rates, even from the housing industry, seem to be couched in relatively understanding terms. Business-government relations in the defense sector of the economy are such that President Eisenhower warned the public about the military-industrial complex as he was leaving office.

The federal government's influence on the resources engaged in research and development in the nation is especially clear. About two thirds of the R & D expenditures in the country are federally financed.[5] Government dollars are underwriting the defense and space R & D work. The R & D budget of the Atomic Energy Commission assures that the country is spending far more to develop nuclear power than to improve coal utilization. The government-financed R & D work in universities and in nonprofit organizations is drawing talent away from other areas. The growing concern about present social problems is causing a modest alteration in the predominant pattern of the last decade, but as yet the redirection of funds is not significant. As R & D efforts lead to new products and processes, the development of business is furthered along the lines of those products and processes. Thus, government decisions about R & D financing can definitely influence the pattern of industrial growth.

Government can also shift the pattern of resource use by means of tax incentives or subsidies. In terms of funding, this method of control lies between the tariff, which requires little expenditure, and R & D programs in space exploration and defense, which necessitate great outlays. The maritime subsidies, the subsidization of the feeder airlines, and the oil depletion allowance are illustrative. Here, too, business objections to government intervention in the market place are mild despite the increased public expenditures or loss of revenues that the programs entail.

Governmental programs redirecting resource use are not subject to the intense and continuing criticism that business brings to bear on efforts to regulate market performance. Perhaps because certain industries clearly benefit from government intervention to direct resource allocation, the individual businessman hesitates to object publicly to such programs. He is more likely to restrict his criticisms of government policy to those areas in which business can present a more united front.

Government and External Diseconomies

Some costs of production are not borne by the firm, but shifted to the public at large. In the economist's terms, these costs are generally known as external diseconomies. For example, a paper mill may deposit untreated waste into a stream because that is the easiest and cheapest means of disposal. The costs arising from the pollution of the stream —the value of the lost recreational benefits and the increased cost of purifying the water downstream for drinking purposes—are costs or diseconomies that the general community must bear. Programs designed to correct for these diseconomies might be viewed as redirecting resource use, but certain diseconomies are becoming so important that they warrant special attention.

Air and water pollution are of growing concern, and new programs and controls are being designed and introduced, especially at the state and local government level. Expenditures to improve urban transportation can be considered an attempt to offset at least some of the diseconomies of urban agglomeration, diseconomies that arise because firms have found it desirable to operate in the central city.

Business Influence on the Governmental Process

Prior to the turn of the century, the influence of the corporate community on the legislative process in Washington was scandalous. A number of senators and congressmen were known to be "in the pocket" of one corporate group or another. The Senate of 1889 was called the "millionaires club," and the railroads in particular could count on reliable spokesmen. The Tillman Act of 1907 and subsequent legislation have attempted to outlaw corporate financial contributions to campaign funds. Corporate funds can, nevertheless, be used for certain types of campaign activity, and corporate officers are often expected to make contributions to pooled campaign funds. Thus the corporate community, if not the individual corporation, can make its financial importance felt in particular campaigns.[6]

The growing complexity of the federal government has forced the corporation to shift some of its attention from the election process to the day-to-day operations of legislative committees and executive agencies. A firm's representative in Washington—whether he be a full-time employee or an attorney retained to keep his ear to the ground as well as to represent the firm in actual legal proceedings—is expected to maintain continuing contact with key individuals in the government bureaucracy and in Congress. These relations are not limited to Cabinet officers and chairmen of selected congressional committees. The staff director of a legislative committee or a career civil servant several echelons down in an executive agency might be more important in the lobbyist's network of information and influence.

Within the executive branch, the Department of Commerce would appear to be the most logical spokesman for the business community, paralleling the importance and influence the Departments of Labor and Agriculture have for their constituencies. But for a variety of reasons it is not. Its major bureaus perform service functions that have little to do with the policy matters of greatest interest to the business community. The corporate executive may be most concerned about the award of public contracts or about actions taken by the Internal Revenue Service, the Antitrust Division of the Department of Justice, the Federal Trade Commission, the S.E.C., the N.L.R.B., and the other regulatory agencies. The Department of Commerce cannot bring much influence to bear on these agencies since most of its twenty-seven thousand employees are in such agencies as the Weather Bureau, the National Bureau of Standards, the Bureau of the Census, the Patent Office, the Bureau of International Commerce, and the Economic Development Administration. The Business and Defense Services Administration, which consists largely of industry specialists, is a spokesman on certain industry problems, but never has enough money or expertise to be particularly effective. Furthermore, on numerous issues the business community is so divided that the Department of Commerce finds it difficult to take a strong stand.

There is evidence that the trade association is playing a relatively less important role in Washington than it played a generation ago. On some issues the association finds disagreement among its own members; it is often short of funds, which limits the talent it can bring onto its staff; and the key men in government are likely to shun association executives with an obvious ax to grind. At the same time the major corporations have adopted a "do-it-yourself" approach to representation in Washington. The increase in government contracting alone now justifies a corporation's having a Washington office with a full-time representative. Direct access has reduced the corporation's reliance on the trade association.

The Washington representative may play two roles—that of the marketing specialist skilled in arranging sales to government agencies and that of the lobbyist. The two roles often overlap: The cocktail party and reception staged by the Washington office when the company president is in town will include as guests not only selected congressmen and senators, but representatives from customer agencies as well.

The Washington lobbyist is a popular target for contempt and criticism, but his power to influence legislation has probably been exaggerated. The communications media have converted Washington into a goldfish bowl, and the congressman or presidential appointee who is a lackey for one interest group or another must be prepared at any moment to be exposed by a zealous columnist. Thus, the threat of adverse publicity disciplines the recipient of the lobbyist's influence.

The lobbyist who survives in Washington performs a useful function in the governmental process. Given the chronic shortage of staff to generate the information and analysis needed to deal with any particular policy issue, the government official often welcomes the lobbyist's contribution. The lobbyist is disciplined in the exercise of this informational power by the knowledge that his opponents in the particular struggle will also be offering information and testimony to defend their views. If he presents a weak or misleading case to a congressman, the congressman may well refuse to see him again. Since contacts with the right people are the representative's stock in trade, he dares not alienate the people through whom his influence on public policy becomes operative. He is forced, therefore, to become a more useful part of the government process than he might otherwise be.

Although the business lobbyist's influence in Washington is limited by the fear of adverse publicity or the possibility of losing valuable contacts, this influence is clearly substantial. Furthermore, over the last decade or so the corporate community has become conscious of the importance of public relations as a means of generating public support for business, thus laying the foundation for more effective lobbying The new emphasis on business cooperation with government in the solution of social problems may well serve to reinforce this support. Although the net impact of this public relations effort may be impossible to assess, the public acceptance of, if not explicit enthusiasm for, the large corporation would seem to suggest that the effort has been successful. It has surely helped to establish a more sympathetic environment for business in Washington.[7]

Big Business, Small Business, and the Smaller Governments

Discussions of business-government relations generally cover only the relationships between the giant corporation and the federal government. The business community is typically pictured as "Fortune's 500" largest firms. Little study has been accorded the relationship between small business and government or between business, large or small, and state and local governments.

The rhetoric of today's corporate chiefs about the social responsibilities of business and the importance of closer cooperation between business and government is heartening, but this is probably not the voice of business as a whole. Of the 3,293,000 non-agricultural enterprises in the country in 1963, about 3,114,000, or 95 percent, had fewer than

426　twenty employees. Not quite 40 percent had no employees at all.[8] The owner-managers of these small firms have been growing further apart from the corporate executive in recent years, and the business-government *rapprochement* one perceives is limited to the large corporate sector of the business community.

The top operating official of the large corporation may now be more sympathetic with the federal government first because of his necessary interest in the health of the economy. He watches the forecasts of the Gross National Product with considerably more care and interest than does the local retailer, insurance broker, or real-estate agent, who believes his firm's performance depends primarily on his own prowess rather than on the G.N.P. By contrast, the corporation with operations across the country is more closely tied to the national indices. The corporate leader is also especially concerned about what is now commonly called the "corporate image"; it is important for the corporation, as represented by its top management, to demonstrate concern about the problems of the country and (publicly, at least) to take a constructive attitude toward their solution. The small businessman may want to be known as a good citizen of the community; but, being less visible, he is not under the same pressure as the chief executive of a large firm.

The top echelons of the modern corporation are filled with men who have come to know Washington, while Washington is still a dirty word to the small businessman. Flattered by an invitation to a White House breakfast with other corporate leaders, the executive finds himself impressed by the President's problems. When presenting testimony for his firm before a congressional committee, he may be exposed to some reasoned rebuttals, but he may also find himself shifting his position or at least appreciating the need for compromise. If he himself has not served on a special committee set up by the President, a Cabinet officer, or the head of one of the regulatory agencies, he knows people who have. Moving in this milieu, he can scarcely avoid developing sympathy for the nature and magnitude of the problems in drafting public policy. He may even take a tour of duty in Washington himself and emerge with a higher regard for the efficiency and dedication of the career civil servant.

The suburban automobile dealer, the owner of the local lumber yard, or the local attorney is denied this depth of contact with Washington. To him government appears as the source of a steady demand for reports to be filled out and taxes to be paid. Since he signs these reports himself (he may even complete them without assistance), he is much more aware of them than is the corporate executive whose staff performs this function. The local businessman's impression of the efficiency of the civil service is colored by his contact with state and local government offices, where efficiency of management is probably below that of the federal government offices. Thus, his image of waste in government may vary substantially from that of the corporate official.

The small businessman's attitude toward government may be reinforced by his resentment over government salaries. The corporate president with a salary several times that of the top government officials is at least spared the bitterness of the small businessman who sees himself living no better than some civil servants who, in his view, enjoy a good income without the worries of entrepreneurship.

Finally, the small businessman may

have less time to participate in government. He must be his own specialist in everything, and he is often too busy to do well the various functions he should perform in his business, to say nothing of taking time for outside activities. An exception must be made here for the small businessman whose business or professional position is strengthened by public exposure. Thus, the insurance agent or the real-estate broker may reason that the publicity associated with running for election helps this vocation, and that political life multiplies his contacts.

If these observations are not overly wide of the mark—they all deserve more qualification than has been entered here—certain conclusions may follow. First, business-government relations may be improving if one considers only the top executives of the *"Fortune* 500" and the leaders of the federal government. The countless small businessmen in the country, less exposed to Washington than the corporate leaders, may still be as unsympathetic to the programs of the federal government as ever.

This difference in attitude toward government becomes clear if one compares the tone of the articles and editorials in *Nation's Business,* the monthly magazine of the U.S. Chamber of Commerce, and the speeches on business-government relations given by the top executives of the major corporations or the articles in *Business Week* and *Fortune.* As a rule, the latter are much more likely to recognize the grounds for cooperation and to make constructive and realistic suggestions. *Nation's Business,* by contrast, caters to the views of the owners of small and medium-sized businesses (who account for most of the Chamber of Commerce membership) and still employs the anti-New Deal rhetoric of the Roosevelt era. Thus, the *rapprochement*

between business and government may not reach far into the ranks of business.

A second conclusion may be warranted. The major corporation is not so deeply involved at the level of state and local government as at the federal level. There are exceptions, of course: The large public utility, regulated by the state, is interested in state legislation affecting utility rates; the major insurance company watches the state legislature's debates about insurance rates; the nationally known manufacturer planning a new plant deals with local officials about zoning regulations; and in some states a handful of corporations are so dominant that they, perforce, play an influential role in the state capital. But the large corporation is primarily concerned with the policies of the federal government. Its influence at the state and local level is typically less significant. Although the top executive in the company may exhort the troops to become involved in politics, the rising young executive in the company is not likely to wield much power at the state and local level. He is struggling up the corporate ladder and has limited time for politics. More important, he is transferred so often that he cannot build a solid political base from which to be effective. Thus, business influence on state and local governments may be primarily the influence of the owners of the medium-sized and small firms, while the business influence on the federal government may be much more heavily weighted toward the views of the major corporations.

If this line of reasoning is defensible, it suggests that the state and local governments are not so likely as the federal government to obtain the help of business in the development of new and imaginative programs for solving particular social problems. To the extent that business influences public policy—and other influences, of course, may often dominate—the state and local government will opt for minimizing taxes and expenditures and avoiding new programs. Competition among states and local jurisdictions in offering a good "business climate" for new industry reinforces this tendency. Thus business interests most influential at the state and local level, those most concerned about keeping government activity to a minimum, may by their inaction force policy designs to surface in Washington rather than in the state capital or in city hall.

NOTES

1. For documentation of the common business view of the role of government in the business environment, see Francis X. Sutton, Seymour E. Harris, Carl Kaysen, and James Tobin, *The American Business Creed* (Cambridge, 1956), especially Ch. 9. Different capitalist ideologies are discussed in R. Joseph Monsen, *Modern American Capitalism, Ideologies and Issues* (Boston, 1963).
2. See Paul A. Samuelson, "Personal Freedoms and Economic Freedoms in the Mixed Economy," in Earl F. Cheit (ed.), *The Business Establishment* (New York, 1964), pp. 193–227.
3. Statement of Dr. Willard F. Mueller, Director, Bureau of Economics, Federal Trade Commission, before the Select Committee on Small Business, U.S. Senate, March, 15, 1967, p. 50.
4. A mild version of an undistributed profits tax was actually enacted in 1936. For a discussion of the nature of the debate, see Arthur M. Schlesinger, Jr., *The Politics of Upheaval*, Vol. 3 of *The Age of Roosevelt* (Boston, 1960), pp. 505–509.
5. Richard R. Nelson, Merton J. Peck, and Edward D. Kalachek, *Technology, Economic Growth and Public Policy* (Brookings, 1967), p. 46.
6. For a review of the status of this question, see Edwin M. Epstein, *Corporations, Contributions, and Political Campaigning: Federal Regulation in Perspective* (Berkeley, 1968). The author argues that corporations should be permitted to spend corporate funds for election purposes if such expenditures are subject to proper reporting and publicity requirements.
7. See V. O. Key, Jr., *Politics, Parties, and Pressure Groups* (fifth edition; New York, 1967), pp. 93–96; and Harold Brayman, *Corporate Management in a World of Politics* (New York, 1967), especially Ch. 5.
8. Bureau of the Census, *1963 Enterprise Statistics*, Part I, Table 8.

Adams, Walter. 1968. "The Military-Industrial Complex and The New Industrial State." *Papers and Proceedings of the Eightieth Annual Meeting of the American Economic Association*, 58 (May), 652–665.

Barber, Bernard. 1963. "Is American Business Becoming Professionalized? Analysis of a Social Ideology." In *Sociological Theory, Values, and Sociocultural Change*, E. A. Tiryakian, ed., New York: Free Press.

Brooks, Robert C., Jr. 1964. "A Neglected Approach to Ethical Business Behavior," *The Journal of Business*, 37 (April), 192–194.

Crozier, Michel. 1969. "A New Rationale for American Business," *Daedalus*, 98 (Winter), 147–158.

Eells, Richard. 1959. "Social Responsibility: Can Business Survive the Challenge?" *Business Horizons*, 2 (Winter), 33–41.

Frederick, Williams C. 1959. "The Growing Concern over Business Responsibility," *California Management Review*, 1 (Summer), 54–61.

Galambos, Louis P. 1964. "The Cotton-Textile Institute and the Government: A Case Study in Interacting Value Systems," *Business History Review*, 38, 186–213.

Gluck, Samuel E. 1962. "'Philosophies of Management' in Philosophical Perspective," *The Annals Of The American Academy Of Political And Social Science*, 343 (September), 10–19.

Goldman, Marshall I. 1960. "Product Differentiation and Advertising: Some Lessons from Soviet Experience," *The Journal of Political Economy*, 68 (August), 346–357.

Grether, E. T. 1965. "An Emerging Apologetic of Managerialism?: Theory in Marketing, 1964," *Journal of Marketing Research*, 2 (May), 190–195.

Hacker, Andrew. 1963. "Do Corporations Have a Social Duty?" *The New York Times Magazine* (November 17), 21, 116, 118.

Heilbroner, Robert L. 1968. "Rhetoric and Reality In The Struggle Between Business and the State," *Social Research*, 35 (Autumn), 401–425.

Howton, F. William. 1963. "The Moral Crisis Of Corporations," *Social Research*, 30 (Summer), 253–260.

Katz, Wilber G. 1960. "Responsibility And The Modern Corporation," *The Journal of Law and Economics*, 3 (October), 75–85.

Lewis, Ben W. 1959. "Open Season On Bigness," *Harvard Business Review*, 37 (May–June), 106–113.

Lewis, Ben W. 1959. "Power Blocs And The Operation Of Economic Forces: Economics By Admonition," *Papers and Proceedings of the 71st Annual Meeting of the American Economic Association*, 49 (May), 384–398.

Leys, Wayne A. 1968. "Ethics in American Business and Government: The Confused Issues." *The Annals of the American Academy of Political And Social Science*, 75 (October), 772–774.

Marx, Fritz M. 1967. "Intersections Between Management Thinking And Political Thinking," *Management International Review*, 7, 117–124.

McGuire, Joseph W. 1966. "The *Finalité* of Business," *California Management Review*, 8 (Summer), 89–94.

Moore, Wilbert. 1962. *The Conduct of the Corporation*. New York: Random House.

Phillips, Charles F., Jr. 1963. "What Is Wrong with Profit Maximization?" *Business Horizons*, 6 (Winter), 73–80.

Reagan, Michael D. 1960. "The Seven Fallacies of Business in Politics," *Harvard Business Review*, 38 (March–April), 60–68.

Sabatino, Richard A. 1966. "The Responsible Corporation," *The American Journal of Economics and Sociology*, 25 (July), 255–266.

Schlusberg, Malcolm D. 1969. "Corporate Legitimacy and Social Responsibility: The Role

430   of Law," *California Management Review,* 12 (Fall), 65–76.

Sethi, S. Prakash, and Dow Votaw. 1969. "Do We Need a New Corporate Response to a Changing Social Environment? Part II," *California Management Review,* 12 (Fall), 17–31.

Silk, Leonard S. 1969. "Business Power, Today and Tomorrow," *Daedalus,* 98 (Winter), 174–189.

Sofer, Cyril. 1955. "Reactions to Administrative Change," *Human Relations,* 8 (August), 291–316.

Staats, Elmer B. 1969. "Industry-Government Relationships," *California Management Review,* 12 (Fall), 83–90.

Taylor, John F. A. 1965. "Is the Corporation Above the Law?" *Harvard Business Review,* 43 (March–April), 119–130.

Turner, Robert C. 1958. "The Apologetics Of 'Managerialism,' " Comment, *The Journal of Business,* 31 (July), 243–248.

Van Cise, J. 1966. "Regulation By Business or Government," *Harvard Business Review,* 44 (March–April), 53–63.

Votaw, Dow. 1961. "The Politics of a Changing Corporate Society," *California Management Review,* 3 (Spring), 105–118.

Votaw, Dow, and S. Prakash Sethi. 1969. "Do We Need a New Corporate Response to a Changing Social Environment? Part I," *California Management Review,* 12 (Fall), 3–16.

Weaver, David B. 1962. "The Corporation and the Shareholder," *The Annals of the American Academy of Political and Social Science,* 343 (September), 84–94.

Decisions,
Goals, and
Effectiveness

In the first paper, McWhinney correlates the type of role of the decision maker and the appropriate decision modality with each of the ideal types of environment proposed by Emery and Trist (see Chapter 2).

A table may serve to explicate his model:

Complexity of environment	Role of the decision maker	Appropriate decision modality
Placid, randomized	Used at all levels within the organization	Certainty
Placid, clustered	Technician: delegation and control of decisions; proper placement of decision makers	Risk
Disturbed, reactive	Manager: competing, bargaining, and coordinating	Uncertainty
Turbulent field	Directional leadership	Definition and selection of domain; appreciative decisions

Thompson and McEwen view goal-setting as a dynamic and recurring (goal reappraisal) aspect of organizational activity that involves determining the relationship of the organization to the larger society.[1] They delineate four forms of interaction with the environment that the organization can employ in order to garner support: competition, bargaining, co-optation, and coalition. Because the organization must interact with its environment, elements in that environment (outsiders) can enter into or constrain the organization's decision process. Thompson and McEwen conceptualize this decision process in terms of five sequential activities. Because the potential power of any environmental element increases the earlier it can enter into the sequence of decision-making activities, selection of one of the four forms of organization-environment interaction is a strategic decision for an administrator.

Perrow's paper examines the relationship of tasks (independent variables) to the determination of operative goals (dependent variables) via the intervening variable of group domination. According to Perrow, every organization must accomplish tasks that require interaction with its external environment, including capital and human inputs, legitimation, and coordination of the organization's relations with other organizations and with clients or consumers. Each task area provides a *partial* basis for domination of the organization by a group competent to solve the problems that the task presents. This dominant group, because of its power and orientation, shapes or limits the types of operative goals that the organization is likely to pursue. In Perrow's voluntary general hospital example, the need for capital inputs and community acceptance (independent variables) led to a trustee domination (intervening variable). The resultant operative goals (dependent variables) reflected the power and orientations of the trustees. Perrow indicates that his scheme applies to voluntary service organizations as well as business organizations.[2]

In the last paper, Yuchtman and Seashore attempt to develop a different conceptual framework to describe and assess organizational effectiveness. They examine two traditional approaches, the "goal approach" and the "functional approach." They conclude that "both contain serious methodological and theoretical shortcomings." They define the effectiveness of an organization "in terms of its bargaining position, as reflected in the ability of the organization, in either absolute or relative terms, to exploit its environment in the acquisition of scarce and valued resources." This definition focuses attention on behavior. Goals are means to enhance the bargaining position of the organization while members' personal goals depend upon the bargaining position of the organization. The authors propose that "the highest level of organizational effectiveness is reached when the organization maximizes its bargaining position and optimizes its resource procurement."

NOTES

1. David Sills reports examples of organizations that, because their goals had either been achieved or had become irrelevant, began working to-

ward "new or sharply modified goals." Among these are the American Legion, the Birth Control Federation, the Y.M.C.A., and the American National Red Cross. Two organizations, the Woman's Christian Temperance Union, and Townsend Organization ". . . failed to adjust themselves to a changed environment." See *The Volunteers.* 1958. New York: The Free Press, pp. 253–268.

2. Moore provides some support for Perrow's ideal-typical sequence for profit-making organizations. See: Moore, David G. 1959. "Managerial Strategies." In *Industrial Man,* W. Lloyd Warner and Norman H. Martin, eds., New York: Harper. See also: Chandler, Alfred D., Jr., 1966. *Strategy and Structure.* Garden City, New York: Doubleday (Anchor Books).

ORGANIZATIONAL FORM, DECISION MODALITIES AND THE ENVIRONMENT[1]

William H. McWhinney

One of the functions which formal organizations perform is to buffer the individual member from the impact of the chaotic interrelation of everything to everything. Ideally, organizations free the member effectively to deal with just so much of the environment as his intellect and psyche permit. The organization, through compartmentalization of tasks and responsibilities, circumscribes for each member the domain of environmental factors with which he must be concerned and permits a match to be established between the *complexity of the environment*, the *type of role* and the *modalities of decision-making* which are appropriate in the functions performed by the members. This paper presents a view of the organization as such a structure. It draws on a number of broad conceptualizations in the work of Emery and Trist (1963), Talcott Parsons (1960) and Frank Knight (1921), to develop a scheme through which to select the most appropriate decision modality according to the environment and the role of the decision-maker. The exposition begins with the description of the environment, then develops the role-decision modality relationship as a response to the occurrence of given degrees of complexity in the environment and to the needs of the members and to the elements of the organization. The pairing of environments with decision modalities indicates the need to recognize another modality, which I call *domain selection,* beyond Knight's three modalities. The resultant picture of the behavior and role relation of the members differs considerably from the depiction of a bureaucracy in the Weberian tradition or from the behavioral theory model represented by the work of Cyert and March (1963).

Causal Texture of the Organizational Environment

The causal texture of the environment is relevant to this view of the organization in two ways; as related to the total environment in which the organization is embedded, and as related to those portions of the environment which the sub-units and individual members experience as occupants of organizational space. For an elementary organization consisting of one man this dichotomy is not applicable. When, however, a second man enters an organization in which division of labor has occurred he need not confront the total environment. He is buffered from some certain parts; the worker is to some extent isolated from the market by the finished goods inventory; the financial planner is protected

"Organizational Form, Decision Modalities and the Environment," *Human Relations,* 21, 3 (August 1968), 269–281. Reprinted with the permission of the author and of the publisher, *Human Relations.*

436 from the vagaries of daily operations by the liquidity of the organization and the availability of loans; the production engineer is secured against variability in the characteristics of raw material by tolerance specifications. The texture of the environment for the member is "degraded" by such buffering into one appropriate to the task and to the persons carrying it out. The total organization, however, must recognize the complexity of the environment in which it operates and develop its strategy accordingly; only by moving the locus of its operation can it mitigate or enrich the impact.

Emery and Trist (1963) have performed an important service in classifying these environments (especially in recognizing the need to identify the range). They employ a continuum in the causal texture which differs in the degree of uncertainty and in the degree of interdependence exhibited between the parts or regions of the environment. Four ideal types are defined by Emery and Trist:

> The first three of these types have already, and indeed repeatedly been described in a large variety of terms and with the emphasis on an equally bewildering variety of special aspects . . . The fourth type, however, is new, at least to us, and is the one that for some time we have been endeavouring to identify . . . Together, the four types may be said to form a series in which the degree of causal texturing is increased, in a new and significant way, as each step is taken.

I. PLACID, RANDOMIZED ENVIRONMENTS

In the simplest type, goals and noxiants are relatively unchanging in themselves and randomly distributed. A critical property from the organization's viewpoint is that there is no difference between tactics and strategy, and organizations can exist adaptively as single, and indeed quite small, units.

The environment represented by extremely low organizational density has the strange double aspect of placing the member of one of the organizations which do exist in a position totally *dependent* on his environment—for the inhabitant of an organized area has no ability to predict what his environment will do—and totally *independent* of it for there is nothing to know about it so concern with it is useless. In the extreme there is both the total dependence of the slave naked before his master and the total disaffection of the powerless and disfranchised "citizen."

II. PLACID, CLUSTERED ENVIRONMENTS

The next type is also static, but goals and noxiants are not randomly distributed; they hang together in certain ways. Now the need arises for strategy as distinct from tactics. Under these conditions organizations grow in size, becoming multiple and tending towards centralized control and coordination.

In such environments it is possible to identify sources (causes) of events; one can make (probabilistically) useful statements about future occurrences and can select "best" actions. Most of our physical science knowledge assumes and/or bears on such environments. The process of study is typified by the near independence of the observer from the observed.

III. DISTURBED REACTIVE ENVIRONMENTS

The third type is dynamic rather than static. It consists of a clustered environment in which there is more than one system of the same kind, i.e., the objects of one organization are the same as, or relevant to, others like it. Such competitors seek to improve their own chances by hindering each other, each knowing the others are playing the same game. Between strategy and tactics there emerges an intermediate type of organizational response—what military theorists refer to as operations. Control becomes more decentralized to allow these to be conducted. On the other hand, stability may require a certain coming-to-terms between competitors.

In such environments an interactional relationship exists between the observer and his environment such that one cannot make statements about the world independent of the knowledge of the position and intents of other individuals and organizations which populate such dense environments.

IV. TURBULENT FIELDS

The fourth type is dynamic in a second respect, the dynamic properties arising not simply from the interaction of identifiable component systems but from the field itself (the "ground"). The turbulence results from the complexity and multiple character of the causal interconnections. Individual organizations, however large, cannot adapt successfully simply through their direct interactions. An examination is made of the enhanced importance of values, regarded as a basic response to persisting areas of relevant uncertainty, as providing a control mechanism, when commonly held by all members in a field.

The interactions in a turbulent field are of such a nature and magnitude that the natural buffering is eliminated. One cannot stand off (in one's own organization) and be uninvolved, for such a negative action affects others. Daniel Bell (1967) labels this condition as a "loss of

insulating space." Perhaps our most immediate awareness of a turbulent environment is in the microcosm of a deep personal relationship, particularly when one or both members are growing and changing in their self-awareness.

The degree of buffering provided by the *medium* in which the individual and the organization interact provides another means by which to classify these environments. The density of the medium is the degree to which it absorbs, delays, smooths, filters, diffuses the various forms of energetic emanations arising in the relevant universe. As Bell's phrase indicates, the turbulent environment is one in which the medium is too thin to provide insulation between the elements of society. The reactive, clustered and random placid environments display increasingly dense media. We can develop our organizational theory more richly in terms of variable media rather than with specific reference to the distribution of organizations. Doing so supports the concept that the environment is not simply given but is manipulatable through the development of media which can provide environment appropriate to the needs of the organization and its members.

Modalities of Decision-Making

In each environment there is a modality of decision-making which fully uses the available information but doesn't require further assumptions. These will be called the *appropriate* modalities. Knight (1921) established a simple and much used trichotomy of *certainty, risk,* and *uncertainty* to label the decision types he found in economics problems. This scheme needs to be expanded to handle the full range of problems existing in the organizational setting. A fourth class of problems, at least, must be added; in keeping with Knight's terminology I call these *domain problems*. These are the problems, often associated with the leadership function, which deal with the question of *what* aspects of the environment are to be of *concern*, of what phenomena should be *noticed* and of what variables should be introduced into the criterion function for the organization's performance. The deepest problem of leadership is that of selecting the domains of concern, just as the significant question of scientific research is the choice of the domain of phenomena to be investigated and the domain of criterion of evaluation.[2] This problem of domain selection has received little attention from administrative theorists. There has been considerable concern with the problem in political spheres, though these seem more to be attempts to avoid the problem than explore it. See for example, Braybrooke and Lindblom (1963) and Quade (1964). Two major studies of decision-making which discuss the problem in a relevant terminology are Selznick's *Leadership in Administration* (1957) and a recent British work, Sir Geoffrey Vickers' *The Art of Judgment* (1965). Material from these studies is introduced below. The organizational use of these modalities is coupled with the environmental conditions in the following paragraphs.

USES OF CERTAINTY

Certainty, natural or established by fiat, is pervasive in human affairs. It is the only modality appropriate in the Emery-Trist random placid environment. In such an environment contingency and relativity of events and values do not exist with sufficient strength to be accorded any notice. In the extreme scarcity of organization in the environment

learning is not possible so one behavior is apparently as good as any other. Under such primitive circumstances "certainty" is the cheapest stance. In the simplest environments, and in the more complex, certainty introduced by fiat provides for *maintenance* of the social fabric. A child's socialization and formal education provide a basis of things he knows to be true, for examples, "2+2=4" and "the spoon is always placed to the right side of the place." Areas of certainty are also required for maintenance of intra- and interpersonal structure; the child requires boundaries (constraints) on his behavior to permit him to grow to the mature person who can cope with uncertainty.

Certainty continues to be a useful stance in highly buffered enclaves of a causally complex environment. In the environment of our physical universe (as seen by a modern man) such buffering acts through physical and temporal seclusion. The inhabitant of a remote mountain village is isolated from (scientific) knowledge and world turmoil. The earth is similarly uninvolved in cosmological events by distance (and thus, time). Rarely, if ever, need we take any other than a certainty stance to the universe though just as a new technology or holocaust could intrude upon the village, so a cosmological event could intrude over vast distance in unforetellable ways.

Isolation from uncertainty and risk can also be achieved within complex interactive organizational environments by many forms of buffering. Typically the buffers in the organizational setting operate on information, though they may also be realized directly via physical and temporal seclusion as well. If such buffering is made reasonably complete, the members of the secluded unit can come to view their unit as the universe. Thus the buffering reproduces a relation to the complex environment that resembles a unit's relation to a simpler environment. As the isolation moves to such an extreme it is likely to lead to parochial behavior, restrictive norm setting and finally pathological rigidity. Buffering so used is protective though dysfunctional; the isolation achieved through buffering can also be used to simplify the decision environment in ways which are systematically chosen to be efficient, and in the case of temporary withdrawal provide the "retreat" one may require to regain strength for dealing with more complex environments.

The scientific stance holds that the portions of our world held to be certain are simply events with which we should associate very small variances. Unassailable as is the modern position, certainty is reintroduced into almost every aspect of organizational life, even by the scientifically minded, as an administrative convenience. Almost all money transactions and accounts are in the form of logical (or arithmetical) statements rather than in probabilistic form. Next year's tax receipts, orders for goods, specifications of plant and equipment, inventories are commonly treated as certainties and only occasionally is it useful to admit that propositions concerning such items stand for a near zero variance statement. From the viewpoint of the management process the most significant use of certainty is in the *uncertainty absorption*[3] provided by the stipulation of the future for the purpose of planning. Such absorption allows the separate development of detailed response plans by various subdivisions of an organization. The translation of an estimate of market demand into a specific "next year's gross sales" or of a welfare demand into so many unemployed and so many fatherless families makes it possible for each of the involved departments to construct plans which are mutually coordinated. Without such fiats, the subdivisions would require an unending round of plan readjustment to get some semblance of a coordinated plan.

Certainty may also appear as an explicit surrogate for a probabilistic proposition where one can use a certainty equivalent such as a mean value to replace full information about a distribution with little or no degradation in the quality of the resultant decisions.[4] Also, we can see the development of planning devices, such as critical path methods, as attempts to make dependable the uncertainty absorption occurring in scheduled commitments, i.e., to make more likely the truth of a logical proposition such as, "Project '66 will be completed by the end of December, 1966."

Certainty has a role in the turbulent environment as a device for providing stability in the criteria by which the organization or society operates. The adoption of an ideology (a system of beliefs) buffers the organization from directionlessness, permits planning, and develops commitment, but as such buffering may be a dysfunctional response in the sub-group, so certainty at the ideological level may restrict creativity, produce narrow dogma and obsessional mechanisms, and foster messianic crusades and genocides.

More than any of the other modalities of decision-making, certainty appears to be usable at all levels of causal texturing of the environment and at all levels within the organizational fabric. Its usage cannot be assigned as primary to any level or role in the decision structure.

THE SUPERVISION OF RISK

Risk (and the knowledge of the probability of future occurrences) becomes an economically meaningful modality for decision-making in the second type of environment—in the environment in which the density of organized clusters provides the investigator with the possibility of making much better than random predictions about the behavior of his environment. Risk-taking, making decisions based on data samples and subjective expectations, is the province of the expert who studies the distributions and formulates appropriate decision paradigms. The ability to predict opens the possibility of delegation and control. If we have some idea of the future behavior of a system we can instruct another on how to handle a range of contingent events and on when he should return "control" to ourselves. Also, since (a portion of) our predictions can be judged as to their accuracy, we can meaningfully locate decision-makers with greater and lesser skills in various domains. In a given domain we can recognize one decision-maker to have better procedures for selecting the appropriate procedure than some other decision-maker. We can assume, and test for, competence in a way that could not be done in the random placid environment. In this better ordered environment it is meaningful to assign one decision-maker to supervise (i.e., instruct and evaluate) another who has been judged in advance to be less competent.

Much of what Parsons (1960) calls *technical management* I would include in the risk supervision modality. Parsons includes in the technical stratum all forms of research, but the more innovative and basic the research, the more it extends beyond risk supervision into the modality of domain selection. I associate supervision of risk with bureaucratic administration. Response to risk can be as fully "formalized and recorded in writing" as can response via certainty fiat. In both theoretic frameworks supervision is basically viewed as classification of events and responding by calling out the proper rules from the "book." The techniques of identification in risk supervision may be more sophisticated than those Weber considered, but the basic activity is the same, and thus propositions concerning bureaucratic operations would usually apply to risk supervision. For example, reduction of operations to supervision of risk is increasingly important as the size of the organization grows and its needs for centralization increase.

MANAGEMENT OF UNCERTAINTY

If the organization operated within an unchanging set of domains (and these domains remained themselves relatively unchanged) eventually all propositions about nature would reduce to risk statements. We would learn the distribution of possible consequences of our acts. But there will always be "new" domains of which so little is known that we cannot make useful probability judgments on future occurrences. This novelty is one source of uncertainty. A second source arises in the mutual interdependence of decision-makers; in the disturbed reactive environment the facts of one's environment are significantly modified by the decisions others make. Even though we may have intimate knowledge of the "nature" of the domains in which we are mutually involved, the effects of the interacting organizations on the environment may still not be anticipated. Predictions are dependent on the knowledge of the current and future acts of these *other organizations* which operate in the relevant domains. Given technical delays in communication or intended withholding or falsification, the organization must treat the world as uncertain (not just risky).

The responses of the decision-maker in such an environment are *competition* and *coordination*—precisely those which Parsons has assigned to the managerial function. Parsons indicates the major concern of the manager (of uncertainty) is with the acquisition of the required goods and resources and disposal of the organization's products; both involve predictions of tastes, market prices and quantities and of developing technologies. To some degree market and technology are subject to risk evaluations, and to that degree these are technical tasks. As Georg Simmel (1955) pointed out, any combat that endures will develop certain conventions, restraints and civilities. The American Civil War and the desert campaigns of World War II were characterized by fraternization and "fair play." When such rudimentary super-organization evolves it provides a stability that allows calculation to identify the better alternatives. The longer the game goes on the more difficult it becomes to hide totally one's proclivities for particular patterns of response and the greater the usefulness of the opponents' "intelligence."

If the opponents concede to the necessity of continuing interchange the tendency is to continue toward a merger (or to centralization of decision-making if merger is not permitted). With recognition of the formulation of a super-organization the gaming behavior takes on a coordinative aspect. Resource allocation and internal pricing are initiated to further the common goal. These activities constitute the second role of the manager. Ideally gaming and cooperation are incompatible behavior patterns but it is common for a manager to engage in an unstable game of cooperation and bargaining. Rather a negotiation begun

under one guise may shift to another as additional facts and values are exposed, as is well illustrated in the labor negotiations which might start in explicit conflict but find solution in cooperative problem-solving and in legislative committees where the inverse sequence is not uncommon. A prominent example of the managerial dilemma appears in the electrical equipment industry conspiracy of the late 1950's. The environment in which this bizarre anti-trust case occurred must have appeared to fit perfectly Emery and Trist's description of a disturbed reactive environment and the various managers' responses illustrate the variety of skills needed to *operate* in the multi-organizational market under organizational conditions which required them to come-to-terms amongst their competitors to attain stability. As Emery and Trist hypothecated, the management functions in the reactive, oligopolistic environment of the electric industry were highly decentralized. General Electric during the 1950's was organized as a collection of separate profit center sub-companies joined only at the directorate level. The need to be able to make rapid and local "moves" in order to retain command of the situation was recognized in developing this organizational form.

The skills of inter-organizational bargaining and of coordination may be supported by an understanding of the technological information the risky decision-maker uses, but the handling of the reactive environment requires quite different skills. The training for one style may in fact be dysfunctional for another.[5] The essential orientation of the manager is to the others with whom he deals; "what will he do in response to what I do?" The manager must take the other's view without losing sight of his own—a consideration which is irrelevant to one in the role of the technical decision-maker. Parsons highlights this difference in expressing the doubt that it is appropriate for a manager of uncertainty to "supervise" a risk evaluator, holding that these are separate, mutually dependent activities, not representable even by interpenetrating ranges in a simple hierarchy. An administrative paradox results from this view. Parsons places the technical and managerial in separate sub-systems which react to each other in competing and coordinating ways. The skills required for operation in this relationship are, by definition, assigned to the managerial sub-system and are not appropriate to the technical. This leads to the unsurprising conclusion that the technician is at a disadvantage. Of course the technician is not necessarily devoid of nor unable to learn the characteristic skill of the manager, but as soon as he becomes proficient he tends to be recruited for the ranks of management.

DIRECTION AMONG DOMAINS

Domain problems, while as pervasive as the other three modalities, have been neglected in the administrative literature.[6] Beyond Selznick's few comments there is so little discussion of this modality in print, that it is necessary to take a few paragraphs to discuss it prior to looking at it in the organizational setting.

Domain problems arise in grand and in intimate affairs: a young Negro suddenly offered a chance to attend a major university; a personality crisis in a middle-aged man who comes to recognize his life as meaningless; research chemist with a chemical displaying wholly unexpected properties; the city council facing the concept of overall transportation redesign; a citizens' committee coming to grips with euthanasia; evaluation of an artistically creative design for a sewage plant; a war crimes tribunal trying to define personal guilt for genocidal acts; and the redirection of the Polio society on its achieving its grandest goal are examples of the conscientious search for valuations of domains which are new to the organization's executives.

The elements of a domain problem are not so easily isolated and studied as well-defined problems, say, in revenue forecasting or price determination of a new soap on the American market. In the terminology of Vickers (1965) solving a domain problem is an *act of appreciation,* and in turn, "An appreciative system [is] a net, of which the weft and warp are reality concepts and value concepts. Reality concepts classify experiences in ways which may be variously valued. Value concepts classify types of relations which may appear in various configurations of experience."

Both valuing and awareness of reality begin in an act of noticing. Once awareness has been accorded to some phenomenon of the environment, the involved object or event has been valued; it has, perhaps at a trivial level, *competed* for attention and at least momentarily has been accepted. The development of elemental awareness into a domain of concern is one of joint development of the evaluation of facts provided by a search and of the reality testing of the value concepts in the context of other prior valuations. Vickers indicates the confounding in the processes of domain selection that carries over into risk evaluation and bargained decision:

The value judgments of men and societies cannot be *proved* correct or incorrect; they can only be *approved* as right or condemned as wrong by the exercise of another value judgment .... By what criterion can conservatives or reformers prove that resources now devoted to this should be reallocated to that; or that the total resources available for public spending by the authority should be increased or reduced and the residue in the private sector change correspondingly? There are abundant arguments which our further "appreciations" may distinguish as legitimate or illegitimate (a judgment of value) and as likely to be more or less cogent (a judgment of reality); but there are no "external," "objective" criteria (in the narrow sense which we have come to attach to the term) to which appeal can directly be made. In the endless political debate on such matters, which include most of the most vital valuations of our time, each disputant can only expose to the others those aspects of the proposal which he thinks most likely to bring the others' appreciative settings into line with his own. If no change results, he can accuse his unconvinced opponent of inhumanity or irresponsibility, of being out of date or deviant, even of being unable or unwilling to "face facts"; but not of placing an "illogical" value on the facts faced.

. . . Reality judgments are more susceptible of "proof"; yet if we examine the reality judgment of the commissioners, how few, in fact, are probable, even after the event. Some are estimates of probability. In the event, the improbable may happen; but the estimate is not thereby proved faulty. Some are of facts essentially unobservable and never cleary demonstratable, such as the state of people's opinions; and of these a special and extensive class are facts which are changed by every reported observation—as public opinion is changed by every published report, purporting to describe its state. The word "judgment" is appropriately used even of reality judgment; for the more complex the subject matter, the more the relevant facts are matters of judgment.

Moreover the relevant facts are necessarily only a selection of all that might have been noticed. They are selected for their "relevance"—to what? To the value judgment which makes them interesting and significant. Their selection no less than their validity is a matter of judgment. (Vickers 1965; pp. 71–72).

Acts of appreciation appear to be quite similar to *adaptive* acts; the Negro simply may adapt to a higher goal state; the Polio society may simply have adapted to a related goal on achievement of the primary goal. The difference lies in the degree of domain of selection. Problem-solving, no matter how ingenious, is simply adaptive if it does not cause the individual or organization to consider domains he (it) has yet to evaluate. The appreciate act involves forming a novel value for the goal object or domain. The novelty may only be for the appreciator; each man's existential crisis does not discover new appreciations for mankind. And even if the appreciation is novel it is not necessarily momentous; a fine pun may have appreciative aspects. But the most significant characteristic is that appreciation is not a decision-making approach to the established goal; it is the elemental social act of attaching value and as such it is also the elemental act of *leadership*.[7]

An appreciative decision differs in another fundamental way from an adaptive response. It is not clear that there is any meaning to optimality in a domain problem. Let us see why. The domain problem does not begin with a set of initial states, a set of possible transformations and a criterion function. For optimality to be a meaningful concept, at least initial conditions should be known and the goal states should be ordered. For the domain problem each of the problem elements is incompletely formulated at the start. The perception of reality and the criterion function emerge out of the process of selection. The developing search locates new dimensions or elements of reality and assigns values to them.[8]

The importance of domain problems in the organization is to a great degree a function of the causal richness of the environment. Noticing can occur in any environment though probably that which is noticed in the placid random environment is "unappreciable." In the clustered environment, noticing will provide "economic" advantage if the awareness is properly evaluated (in risk terms), but there is little drive to notice in a placid environment. Innovation may be a means to improvement but in such an environment failure to innovate does not bring swift sanctions. Tribes of man have existed for millennia without significant acts of appreciation or innovation. But with the appearance of competing organizations in a disturbed environment appreciation takes on a critical role and particularly those appreciations of the other (reactive) persons in one's environs. But in distinction to appreciation of the novel in the simpler environment appreciation of the other can be confined to a given domain of the competitive-coordinative behavior repertoire. The anti-trust laws of the USA define such a domain of reactiveness between competitors. Manners and social convention may define the domain of intercourse on cooperative behavior between members of an organization (or society). The encompassing *status quo* is a buffer which allows one to interact without new acts of appreciation.

When the density of environment increases to produce turbulent fields the *status quo* fails as a buffer. The domains of intercourse are no longer well-bounded and new appreciation becomes a central modality for society at large. But for every person to be involved in appreciation is a defining condition of anarchy.[9] Where society as a whole provides stability in the simple environment, in the turbulent field the organization takes the role of providing the individual protection against the need for continued reappreciation. This may be an unattractive role from the liberal reforming view, but it is a necessary role to the conservative. By assigning the vast majority of appreciative decisions to a limited element of the organization—and equivalently, of the larger society—the members may continue to operate as though they were in simpler reactive and clustered environments. The organization and society which exist in the causally richest textural state must reconstruct for its members the full range of environments so that the members can operate within the tolerable modalities without interference from excessive turbulence. By absorbing uncertainty regarding value questions within the *institutional* levels the manager and politician are freed to limit their concerns to deciding how to *operate* in the prescribed domains and the technician can limit his concern to optimizing in environments rendered stable by fiat.

But conversely, all domain problems are not confined to a high executive level. Leadership (in the institutional sense) is a pervasive even if rare phenomenon. The creative evaluation, the aroused conscience, the entrepreneurial innovation can emerge anywhere in the organization but their acceptability is limited, depending on the separability of the domain on which the new appreciation bears. If action based on the new appreciation stays within a natural unit of the organization it can be accepted or rejected on local grounds, but if it bears on a variety of units, its acceptance can undermine the ability of the organization to provide the shelter necessary in a turbulent environment. Therefore, new appreciations are not to be judged solely on their own merits, but also on the possible loss in organizational structure that may occur through accepting the new domain. The rejection may simply result in disaffection of the proposer, but there are numerous instances in which the circumstances provided the occasion for great drama as in the confrontation of Galileo and the Pope and of General Billy Mitchell and the military establishment.[10] It is also a source of schism which has resulted in the formation of new enterprises, new nations and new faiths.

If the characterization of the domain defining process is reasonably accurate it is even more different from managers' decision-making under uncertainty than it is from the planful processes of the technical decision-maker and from the simplest certainty processes used at the most fully buffered enclaves in the body of the organization. In fact, *certainty*, in the form of specific policy, goals and constraints, is introduced by fiat into the organization more by the directorate than by any other level except possibly that imposed by supervision in mass clerical and production units. From this view it does seem reasonable to attach to the directorate the major planning staffs. With such placement the technical staff can serve to explore and test the feasibility of new appreciations of the leadership without increasing the domains of relevant uncertainty for the "operating managers." The sharpness of the difference between the manager's role and that of the institutional leadership supports Parsons' conjecture that there will be a second administrative articulation between the institutional level and the managerial. Between the two, the interrelationship of manager or supervisor as interpreted at lower levels is inappropriate. Recognition of this articulation also throws light on the behavior of the actors in the electrical conspiracy case. From this model one would predict that a chief executive could be as uninvolved with the "operations" of his chief sales man-

agers as the man involved claimed. And it possibly would have been an appropriate disinvolvement if the world were simply a *reactive* one which, as Emery and Trist point out, requires decentralization to facilitate the bargaining and coordinating actions necessary to maintain stability and growth. However, the environment of the post-industrial society is better viewed as *turbulent*, rendering that decentralization ineffective in attaining the goals either of the individual companies or of the society in which they operated. At a most abstract level we might assign the cause of that fiasco to a misidentification of the environment in which the electrical manufacturers and their customers operated.

The importance of recognizing the tripart nature of an organization is a relatively new phenomenon. In Weber's and Fayol's world the slow change in technology may have made it possible for the director to be technician and manager. He could supervise and manage. The articulation of roles could be hidden within a single man's province or at most within that of the top echelon of executives of the organization. But, increasingly, the disturbance in the environment renders even the competitively alert organization non-viable and raises a question as to the need for the emergence of new societal institutions. Extrapolating from the gaming behavior of the manager and the appreciations of the leadership one is led to the hypothesis that the mere presence of organizations in a clustered placid environment may be a sufficient condition for the appearance of disturbed and turbulent environments. The delays, the intended and unintended distortion of information, and the fluctuation of boundaries caused by new domain selections produces the disturbance. If these are aspects of a self-perpetuating disturbing force the environment would move through the turbulent state into eventual system breakdown—explosively into anarchy or possibly into a more appropriate combination of institutions which would bound the turbulence.[11]

A Speculation

This paper has taken as its prime reference the formal organization, and to a limited degree, the individual as a psychological complex. Three functions and four modalities of decision-making have been discussed in relation to the environment of the organization (individual) and the environments which the organization can create within itself both for its own explicit efficiency of operation and to facilitate the functioning of its membership. The juxtaposition of environmental types and decision modalities provides the basis for integrating into a general framework the appreciative decision, here identified as the domain selection problem. It also provides support for Parsons' conjecture as to the variation in the form of authority relationships existing between the organizational members who perform the different functions, technical, managerial and directional.

With somewhat less confidence we can speculate that this analysis of organizational structure and behavior is appropriate to the total turbulent society characteristic of much of the contemporary world. These three functions and the four modalities of decision employed in the organization may not only be replicated in the sub-units of the formal organization, but I hypothesize that we can identify in the overall society elements fulfilling the same basic functions; governments provide the institutional direction and, hopefully, significant appreciations; business provides the allocative, market component and the university-research foundation provides the technical. At first impression this parallelism may seem wholly without merit, and so it may be in the Industrial Society. But in the Post-Industrial Society which we have entered, the industrial technology is replaced by science and a science-derived productive capacity to which non-scientific labor is increasingly ancillary. And just as technicians may have a role as staff to the directorate, so do scientists come to be counsels to top governmental leaders, yet are still likely to continue their subordination to the managing politician and manipulator of the market-place. There is already evidence of the emergence of this encompassing arrangement in what Michael Harrington (1967) labels the socio-industrial complex in which the scientist is sometimes advisor to the government and sometimes the productive technician in the entrepreneur organization. If there is a reasonable parallel in the organizational and social roles, then it seems appropriate that we consider the parallel functional (and dysfunctional) buffering of the citizen from the turbulence and disturbed environments in the design of the political state.

NOTES

1. The author wishes to express his indebtedness to Eric L. Trist and Samuel H. Nerlove for their helpful comments.
2. Peter Vaill, Graduate School of Business Administration, UCLA, has pointed to the similarity of concern of the leader and the scientist in his epigram, "Management Is Research."

3. Uncertainty here simply means *doubt* including risk as well as uncertainty.
4. See Holt *et al.* (1960) regarding the use of certainty equivalents.
5. See Haire (1968).
6. Katz and Kahn (1966), though organizing their discussion on a different basis, also face many of the same issues as are handled here.
7. For this reason alone administrative studies cannot appropriately be seen as a subdiscipline of economics or praxeology. I find this to be one of the central messages in Selznick's *Leadership in Administration*.
8. The technique of systems analysis has also come to the position, e.g., "It cannot be emphasized too strongly that a (if not the) distinguishing characteristic of systems analysis is that the objectives are either not known or are subject to change" (Wildavsky, 1966). However, it is not clear whether the analysts are merely recognizing their limitations or whether they would admit that search can be an act of appreciation.
9. See Santayana (1951, p. 236).
10. Ruth Leeds presents several more examples in her insightful "The Absorption of Protest" (Cooper *et al.* 1964).
11. See McWhinney (1968) for further discussion of the related dynamics and of the transturbulent environment.

REFERENCES

Bell, Daniel (1967). Toward the Year 2000: Work in Progress. *Daedalus,* **96.**
Braybrooke, David and Lindblom, Charles E. (1963). *A Strategy for Decision.* Glencoe, Ill.: Free Press.
Cooper, W. W., Leavitt, H. J. and Shelly, M. W., Jr. (Ed) (1964). *New Perspectives in Organizational Research.* New York: Wiley & Son.
Cyert, R. M. and March, J. G. (1963). *A Behavioral Theory of the Firm.* Englewood Cliffs, N.J.: Prentice-Hall, Inc.
Emery, F. E. and Trist, Eric L. (1963). The Causal Texture of Organizational Environments. *Hum. Relat.* **18,** 20–6.
Haire, Mason (1968). An Integrated Approach to Personnel Management. *Indust. Relat.* **17.**
Harrington, M. (1967). The Socio-Industrial Complex. *Harpers* (November).
Holt, C. C., Modigliani, F., Muth, J. F. and Simon, H. A. (1960). *Planning Production, Inventories and Work Force.* Englewood Cliffs, N.J.: Prentice-Hall.
Katz, Daniel and Kahn, R. L. (1966). *The Social Psychology of Organizations.* New York: Wiley.
Knight, F. H. (1921). *Risk, Uncertainty and Profit.* Boston: Houghton Mifflin Co.
McWhinney, Wm. H. (1968). Dualities in Organization Theory. (Mimeographed) Graduate School of Business, UCLA.
Parsons, Talcott (1960). *Structure and Process in Modern Societies.* Glencoe, Ill.: The Free Press.
Quade, E. J. (Ed.) (1964). *Analysis for Military Decisions.* Chicago: Rand McNally.
Santayana, George (1951). *Dominations and Powers,* New York: Scribners.
Selznick, P. (1957). *Leadership in Administration.* Evanston, Ill.: Row Peterson & Co.
Simmel, Georg (1955). *Conflict.* Trans. K. H. Wolff. Glencoe, Ill.: The Free Press.
Vickers, Geoffrey (1965). *The Art of Judgment.* New York: Basic Books.
Wildavsky, A. (1964). *The Politics of the Budgetary Process.* Boston: Little, Brown.
Wildavsky, A. (1966). The Political Economy of Efficiency: Cost-Benefit Analysis, Systems Analysis and Program Budgeting. *Public Admin. Rev.* December, 292–310.

ORGANIZATIONAL GOALS AND ENVIRONMENT
Goal-Setting as an Interaction Process

James D. Thompson and William J. McEwen

In the analysis of complex organizations the definition of organizational goals is commonly utilized as a standard for appraising organizational performance. In many such analyses the goals of the organization are often viewed as a constant. Thus a wide variety of data, such as official documents, work activity records, organizational output, or statements by organizational spokesmen, may provide the basis for the definition of goals. Once this definition has been accomplished, interest in goals as a dynamic aspect of organizational activity frequently ends.

It is possible, however, to view the setting of goals (i.e., major organizational purposes) not as a static element but as a necessary and recurring problem facing any organization, whether it is governmental, military, business, educational, medical, religious, or other type.

This perspective appears appropriate in developing the two major lines of the present analysis. The first of these is to emphasize the interdependence of complex organizations within the larger society and the consequences this has for organizational goal-setting. The second is to emphasize the similarities of goal-setting processes in organizations with manifestly different goals. The present analysis is offered to supplement recent studies of organizational operations.[1]

It is postulated that goal-setting behavior is purposive but not necessarily rational; we assume that goals may be determined by accident, i.e., by blundering of members of the organization and, contrariwise, that the most calculated and careful determination of goals may be negated by developments outside the control of organization members. The goal-setting problem as discussed here is essentially determining a relationship of the organization to the larger society, which in turn becomes a question of what the society (or elements within it) wants done or can be persuaded to support.

Goals as Dynamic Variables

Because the setting of goals is essentially a problem of defining desired relationships between an organization and its environment, change in either requires review and perhaps alteration of goals. Even where the most abstract statement of goals remains constant, application requires redefinition or interpretation as changes occur in the organization, the environment, or both.

The corporation, for example, faces changing markets and develops staff specialists with responsibility for con-

"Organizational Goals and Environment: Goal-Setting as an Interaction Process," *American Sociological Review*, 23, 1 (February 1958), 23–31. Reprinted with the permission of the authors and of the publisher, The American Sociological Association.

tinuous study and projection of market changes and product appeal. The governmental agency, its legislative mandate notwithstanding, has need to reformulate or reinterpret its goals as other agencies are created and dissolved, as the population changes, or as non-governmental organizations appear to do the same job or to compete. The school and the university may have unchanging abstract goals but the clientele, the needs of pupils or students, and the techniques of teaching change and bring with them redefinition and reinterpretation of those objectives. The hospital has been faced with problems requiring an expansion of goals to include consideration of preventive medicine, public health practices, and the degree to which the hospital should extend its activities out into the community. The mental hospital and the prison are changing their objectives from primary emphasis on custody to a stress on therapy. Even the church alters its pragmatic objectives as changes in the society call for new forms of social ethics, and as government and organized philanthropy take over some of the activities formerly left to organized religion.[2]

Reappraisal of goals thus appears to be a recurrent problem for large organization, albeit a more constant problem in an unstable environment than in a stable one. Reappraisal of goals likewise appears to be more difficult as the "product" of the enterprise becomes less tangible and more difficult to measure objectively. The manufacturing firm has a relatively ready index of the acceptability of its product in sales figures; while poor sales may indicate inferior quality rather than public distaste for the commodity itself, sales totals frequently are supplemented by trade association statistics indicating the firm's "share of the market." Thus within a

matter of weeks, a manufacturing firm may be able to reappraise its decision to enter the "widget" market and may therefore begin deciding how it can get out of that market with the least cost.

The governmental enterprise may have similar indicators of the acceptability of its goals if it is involved in producing an item such as electricity, but where its activity is oriented to a less tangible purpose such as maintaining favorable relations with foreign nations, the indices of effective operation are likely to be less precise and the vagaries more numerous. The degree to which a government satisfies its clientele may be reflected periodically in elections, but despite the claims of party officials, it seldom is clear just what the mandate of the people is with reference to any particular governmental enterprise. In addition, the public is not always steadfast in its mandate.

The university perhaps has even greater difficulties in evaluating its environmental situation through response to its output. Its range of "products" is enormous, extending from astronomers to zoologists. The test of a competent specialist is not always standardized and may be changing, and the university's success in turning out "educated" people is judged by many and often conflicting standards. The university's product is in process for four or more years and when it is placed on the "market" it can be only imperfectly judged. Vocational placement statistics may give some indication of the university's success in its objectives, but initial placement is no guarantee of performance at a later date. Furthermore, performance in an occupation is only one of several abilities that the university is supposed to produce in its students. Finally, any particular department of the university may find that its reputation lags far

450 behind its performance. A "good" department may work for years before its reputation becomes "good" and a downhill department may coast for several years before the fact is realized by the professional world.

In sum, the goals of an organization, which determine the kinds of goods or services it produces and offers to the environment, often are subject to peculiar difficulties of reappraisal. Where the purpose calls for an easily identified, readily measured product, reappraisal and readjustment of goals may be accomplished rapidly. But as goals call for increasingly intangible, difficult-to-measure products, society finds it more difficult to determine and reflect its acceptability of that product, and the signals that indicate unacceptable goals are less effective and perhaps longer in coming.

Environmental Controls over Goals

A continuing situation of necessary interaction between an organization and its environment introduces an element of environmental control into the organization. While the motives of personnel, including goal-setting officers, may be profits, prestige, votes, or the salvation of souls, their efforts must produce something useful or acceptable to at least a part of the organizational environment to win continued support.[3]

In the simpler society social control over productive activities may be exercised rather informally and directly through such means as gossip and ridicule. As a society becomes more complex and its productive activities more deliberately organized, social controls are increasingly exercised through such formal devices as contracts, legal codes, and governmental regulations. The stability of expectations provided by these devices is arrived at through interaction, and often through the exercise of power in interaction.

It is possible to conceive of a continuum of organizational power in environmental relations, ranging from the organization that dominates its environmental relations to one completely dominated by its environment. Few organizations approach either extreme. Certain gigantic industrial enterprises, such as the *Zaibatsu* in Japan or the old Standard Oil Trust in America, have approached the dominance-over-environment position at one time, but this position eventually brought about "countervailing powers."[4] Perhaps the nearest approximation to the completely powerless organization is the commuter transit system, which may be unable to cover its costs but nevertheless is regarded as a necessary utility and cannot get permission to quit business. Most complex organizations, falling somewhere between the extremes of the power continuum, must adopt strategies for coming to terms with their environments. This is not to imply that such strategies are necessarily chosen by rational or deliberate processes. An organization can survive so long as it adjusts to its situation; whether the process of adjustment is awkward or nimble becomes important in determining the organization's degree of prosperity.

However arrived at, strategies for dealing with the organizational environment may be broadly classified as either *competitive* or *co-operative*. Both appear to be important in a complex society—of the "free enterprise" type or other.[5] Both provide a measure of environmental control over organizations by providing for "outsiders" to enter into or limit organizational decision process.

The decision process may be viewed as a series of activities, conscious or not, culminating in a choice among alternatives. For purposes of this paper we view the decision-making process as consisting of the following activities:

1. Recognizing an occasion for decision, i.e., a need or an opportunity.
2. Analysis of the existing situation.
3. Identification of alternative courses of action.
4. Assessment of the probable consequences of each alternative.
5. Choice from among alternatives.[6]

The following discussion suggests that the potential power of an outsider increases the earlier he enters into the decision process,[7] and that competition and three sub-types of co-operative strategy—bargaining, co-optation, and coalition—differ in this respect. It is therefore possible to order these forms of interaction in terms of the degree to which they provide for environmental control over organizational goal-setting decisions.

COMPETITION

The term competition implies an element of rivalry. For present purposes competition refers to that form of rivalry between two or more organizations which is mediated by a third party. In the case of the manufacturing firm the third party may be the customer, the supplier, the potential or present member of the labor force, or others. In the case of the governmental bureau, the third party through whom competition takes place may be the legislative committee, the budget bureau, or the chief executive, as well as potential clientele and potential members of the bureau.

The complexity of competition in a heterogeneous society is much greater than customary usage (with economic overtones) often suggests. Society judges the enterprise not only by the finished product but also in terms of the desirability of applying resources to that purpose. Even the organization that enjoys a product monopoly must compete for society's support. From the society it must obtain resources—personnel, finances, and materials—as well as customers or clientele. In the business sphere of a "free enterprise" economy this competition for resources and customers usually takes place in the market, but in times of crisis the society may exercise more direct controls, such as rationing or the establishment of priorities during a war. The monopoly competes with enterprises having different purposes or goals but using similar raw materials; it competes with many other enterprises, for human skills and loyalties, and it competes with many other activities for support in the money markets.

The university, customarily a non-profit organization, competes as eagerly as any business firm, although perhaps more subtly.[8] Virtually every university seeks, if not more students, better-qualified students. Publicly supported universities compete at annual budget sessions with other governmental enterprises for shares in tax revenues. Endowed universities must compete for gifts and bequests, not only with other universities but also with museums, charities, zoos, and similar non-profit enterprises. The American university is only one of many organizations competing for foundation support, and it competes with other universities and with other types of organizations for faculty.

The public school system, perhaps one of our most pervasive forms of near-monopoly, not only competes with other governmental units for funds and with

452 different types of organizations for teachers, but current programs espoused by professional educators often compete in a very real way with a public conception of the nature of education, e.g., as the three R's, devoid of "frills."

The hospital may compete with the midwife, the faith-healer, the "quack" and the patent-medicine manufacturer, as well as with neighboring hospitals, despite the fact that general hospitals do not "advertise" and are not usually recognized as competitive.

Competition is thus a complicated network of relationships. It includes scrambling for resources as well as for customers or clients, and in a complex society it includes rivalry for potential members and their loyalties. In each case a third party makes a choice among alternatives, two or more organizations attempt to influence that choice through some type of "appeal" or offering, and choice by the third party is a "vote" of support for one of the competing organizations and a denial of support to the others involved.

Competition, then, is one process whereby the organization's choice of goals is partially controlled by the environment. It tends to prevent unilateral or arbitrary choice of organizational goals, or to correct such a choice if one is made. Competition for society's support is an important means of eliminating not only inefficient organizations but also those that seek to provide goods or services the environment is not willing to accept.

BARGAINING

The term bargaining, as used here, refers to the negotiation of an agreement for the exchange of goods or services between two or more organizations. Even where fairly stable and dependable expectations have been built up with important elements of the organizational environment—with suppliers, distributors, legislators, workers and so on—the organization cannot assume that these relationships will continue. Periodic review of these relationships must be accomplished, and an important means for this is bargaining, whereby each organization, through negotiation, arrives at a decision about future behavior satisfactory to the others involved.

The need for periodic adjustment of relationships is demonstrated most dramatically in collective bargaining between labor and industrial management, in which the bases for continued support by organization members are reviewed.[9] But bargaining occurs in other important, if less dramatic, areas of organizational endeavor. The business firm must bargain with its agents or distributors, and while this may appear at times to be one-sided and hence not much of a bargain, still even a long-standing agency agreement may be severed by competitive offers unless the agent's level of satisfaction is maintained through periodic review.[10] Where suppliers are required to install new equipment to handle the peculiar demands of an organization, bargaining between the two is not unusual.

The university likewise must bargain.[11] It may compete for free or unrestricted funds, but often it must compromise that ideal by bargaining away the name of a building or of a library collection, or by the conferring of an honorary degree. Graduate students and faculty members may be given financial or other concessions through bargaining, in order to prevent their loss to other institutions.

The governmental organization may also find bargaining expedient.[12] The police department, for example, may overlook certain violations of statutes in order to gain the support of minor violators who have channels of information not otherwise open to department members. Concessions to those who "turn state's evidence" are not unusual. Similarly a department of state may forego or postpone recognition of a foreign power in order to gain support for other aspects of its policy, and a governmental agency may relinquish certain activities in order to gain budget bureau approval of more important goals.

While bargaining may focus on resources rather than explicitly on goals, the fact remains that it is improbable that a goal can be effective unless it is at least partially implemented. To the extent that bargaining sets limits on the amount of resources available or the ways they may be employed, it effectively sets limits on choice of goals. Hence bargaining, like competition, results in environmental control over organizational goals and reduces the probability of arbitrary, unilateral goal-setting.

Unlike competition, however, bargaining involves direct interaction with other organizations in the environment, rather than with a third party. Bargaining appears, therefore, to invade the actual decision process. To the extent that the second party's support is necessary he is in a position to exercise a veto over final choice of alternative goals, and hence takes part in the decision.

CO-OPTATION

Co-optation has been defined as the process of absorbing new elements into the leadership or policy-determining structure of an organization as a means of averting threats to its stability or existence.[13] Co-optation makes still fur-

ther inroads on the process of deciding goals; not only must the final choice be acceptable to the co-opted party or organization, but to the extent that co-optation is effective it places the representative of an "outsider" in a position to determine the occasion for a goal decision, to participate in analyzing the existing situation, to suggest alternatives, and to take part in the deliberation of consequences.

The term co-optation has only recently been given currency in this country, but the phenomenon it describes is neither new nor unimportant. The acceptance on a corporation's board of directors of representatives of banks or other financial institutions is a time-honored custom among firms that have large financial obligations or that may in the future want access to financial resources. The state university may find it expedient (if not mandatory) to place legislators on its board of trustees, and the endowed college may find that whereas the honorary degree brings forth a token gift, membership on the board may result in a more substantial bequest. The local medical society often plays a decisive role in hospital goal-setting, since the support of professional medical practitioners is urgently necessary for the hospital.

From the standpoint of society, however, co-optation is more than an expediency. By giving a potential supporter a position of power and often of responsibility in the organization, the organization gains his awareness and understanding of the problems it faces. A business advisory council may be an effective educational device for a government, and a White House conference on education may mobilize "grass roots" support in a thousand localities, both by focussing attention on the problem area and by giving key people a sense of participation in goal deliberation.

ORGANIZATIONAL GOALS AND ENVIRONMENT

Moreover, by providing overlapping memberships, co-optation is an important social device for increasing the likelihood that organizations related to one another in complicated ways will in fact find compatible goals. By thus reducing the possibilities of antithetical actions by two or more organizations, co-optation aids in the integration of the heterogeneous parts of a complex society. By the same token, co-optation further limits the opportunity for one organization to choose its goals arbitrarily or unilaterally.

COALITION

As used here, the term coalition refers to a combination of two or more organizations for a common purpose. Coalition appears to be the ultimate or extreme form of environmental conditioning of organizational goals.[14] A coalition may be unstable, but to the extent that it is operative, two or more organizations act as one with respect to certain goals. Coalition is a means widely used when two or more enterprises wish to pursue a goal calling for more support, especially for more resources, than any one of them is able to marshall unaided. American business firms frequently resort to coalition for purposes of research or product promotion and for the construction of such gigantic facilities as dams or atomic reactors.[15]

Coalition is not uncommon among educational organizations. Universities have established joint operations in such areas as nuclear research, archaeological research, and even social science research. Many smaller colleges have banded together for fund-raising purposes. The consolidation of public school districts is another form of coalition (if not merger), and the fact that it does represent a sharing or "invasion" of goal-setting power is reflected in some of the bitter resistance to consolidation in tradition-oriented localities.

Coalition requires a commitment for joint decision of future activities and thus places limits on unilateral or arbitrary decisions. Furthermore, inability of an organization to find partners in a coalition venture automatically prevents pursuit of that objective, and is therefore also a form of social control. If the collective judgment is that a proposal is unworkable, a possible disaster may be escaped and unproductive allocation of resources avoided.

Development of Environmental Support

Environmental control is not a one-way process limited to consequences for the organization of action in its environment. Those subject to control are also part of the larger society and hence are also agents of social control. The enterprise that competes is not only influenced in its goal-setting by what the competitor and the third party may do, but also exerts influence over both. Bargaining likewise is a form of mutual, two-way influence; co-optation affects the co-opted as well as the co-opting party; and coalition clearly sets limits on both parties.

Goals appear to grow out of interaction, both within the organization and between the organization and its environment. While every enterprise must find sufficient support for its goals, it may wield initiative in this. The difference between effective and ineffective organizations may well lie in the initiative exercised by those in the organization who are responsible for goal-setting.

The ability of an administrator to win support for an objective may be as vital as his ability to foresee the utility of a new idea. And his role as a "seller" of ideas may be as important to society as to his organization, for as society becomes increasingly specialized and heterogeneous, the importance of new objectives may be more readily seen by specialized segments than by the general society. It was not public clamor that originated revisions in public school curricula and training methods; the impetus came largely from professional specialists in or on the periphery of education.[16] The shift in focus from custody to therapy in mental hospitals derives largely from the urgings of professionals, and the same can be said of our prisons.[17] In both cases the public anger, aroused by crusaders and muck-rakers, might have been soothed by more humane methods of custody. Current attempts to revitalize the liberal arts curricula of our colleges, universities, and technical institutes have developed more in response to the activities of professional specialists than from public urging.[18] Commercial aviation, likewise, was "sold" the hard way, with support being based on subsidy for a considerable period before the importance of such transportation was apparent to the larger public.[19]

In each of these examples the goal-setters saw their ideas become widely accepted only after strenuous efforts to win support through education of important elements of the environment. Present currents in some medical quarters to shift emphasis from treatment of the sick to maintenance of health through preventive medicine and public health programs likewise have to be "sold" to a society schooled in an older concept.[20]

The activities involved in winning support for organizational goals thus are not confined to communication within the organization, however important this is. The need to justify organization goals, to explain the social functions of the organization, is seen daily in all types of "public relations" activities, ranging from luncheon club speeches to house organs. It is part of an educational requirement in a complicated society where devious interdependence hides many of the functions of organized, specialized activities.

Goal-Setting and Strategy

We have suggested that it is improbable that an organization can continue indefinitely if its goals are formulated arbitrarily, without cognizance of its relations to the environment. One of the requirements for survival appears to be ability to learn about the environment accurately enough and quickly enough to permit organizational adjustments in time to avoid extinction. In a more positive vein, it becomes important for an organization to judge the amount and sources of support that can be mobilized for a goal, and to arrive at a strategy for their mobilization.

Competition, bargaining, co-optation, and coalition constitute procedures for gaining support from the organizational environment; the selection of one or more of these is a strategic problem. It is here that the element of rationality appears to become exceedingly important, for in the order treated above, these relational processes represent increasingly "costly" methods of gaining support in terms of decision-making power. The organization that adopts a strategy of competition when co-optation is called for may lose all opportunity to realize its goals, or may finally turn to co-optation or coalition at a higher "cost" than would have been necessary

456 originally. On the other hand, an organization may lose part of its integrity, and therefore some of its potentiality, if it unnecessarily shares power in exchange for support. Hence the establishment *in the appropriate form* of interaction with the many relevant parts of its environment can be a major organizational consideration in a complex society.

This means, in effect, that the organization must be able to estimate the position of other relevant organizations and their willingness to enter into or alter relationships. Often, too, these matters must be determined or estimated without revealing one's own weaknesses, or even one's ultimate strength. It is necessary or advantageous, in other words, to have the consent or acquiescence of the other party, if a new relationship is to be established or an existing relationship altered. For this purpose organizational administrators often engage in what might be termed a *sounding out process.*[21]

The sounding out process can be illustrated by the problem of the boss with amorous designs on his secretary in an organization that taboos such relations. He must find some means of determining her willingness to alter the relationship, but he must do so without risking rebuff, for a showdown might come at the cost of his dignity or his office reputation, at the cost of losing her secretarial services, or in the extreme case at the cost of losing his own position. The "sophisticated" procedure is to create an ambiguous situation in which the secretary is forced to respond in one of two ways: (1) to ignore or tactfully counter, thereby clearly channeling the relationship back into an already existing pattern, or (2) to respond in a similarly ambiguous vein (if not in a positive one) indicating a receptiveness to further advances. It is important in the sounding out process

that the situation be ambiguous for two reasons: (1) the secretary must not be able to "pin down" the boss with evidence if she rejects the idea, and (2) the situation must be far enough removed from normal to be noticeable to the secretary. The ambiguity of sounding out has the further advantage to the participants that neither party alone is clearly responsible for initiating the change.

The situation described above illustrates a process that seems to explain many organizational as well as personal inter-action situations. In moving from one relationship to another between two or more organizations it is often necessary to leave a well defined situation and proceed through a period of deliberate ambiguity, to arrive at a new clear-cut relationship. In interaction over goal-setting problems, sounding out sometime is done through a form of double-talk, wherein the parties refer to "hypothetical" enterprises and "hypothetical" situations, or in "diplomatic" language, which often serves the same purpose. In other cases, and perhaps more frequently, sounding out is done through the good offices of a third party. This occurs, apparently, where there has been no relationship in the past, or at the stage of negotiations where the parties have indicated intentions but are not willing to state their positions frankly. Here it becomes useful at times to find a discrete go-between who can be trusted with full information and who will seek an arrangement suitable to both parties.

Conclusion

In the complex modern society desired goals often require complex organizations. At the same time the desirability of goals and the appropriate division of labor among large organizations is less self-evident than in simpler, more homogeneous society. Purpose becomes a question to be decided rather than an obvious matter.

To the extent that behavior of organization members is oriented to questions of goals or purposes, a science of organization must attempt to understand and explain that behavior. We have suggested one classification scheme, based on decision-making, as potentially useful in analyzing organizational-environmental interaction with respect to goal-setting and we have attempted to illustrate some aspects of its utility. It is hoped that the suggested scheme encompasses questions of rationality or irrationality without presuming either.

Argument by example, however, is at best only a starting point for scientific understanding and for the collection of evidence. Two factors make organizational goal-setting in a complex society a "big" research topic: the multiplicity of large organizations of diverse type and the necessity of studying them in diachronic perspective. We hope that our discussion will encourage critical thinking and the sharing of observations about the subject.

NOTES

1. Among recent materials that treat organizational goal-setting are Kenneth E. Boulding, *The Organizational Revolution*, New York: Harper and Brothers, 1953; Robert A. Dahl and Charles E. Lindblom, *Politics, Economics, and Welfare*, New York: Harper and Brothers, 1953; and John K. Galbraith, *American Capitalism: The Concept of Countervailing Power*, Boston: Houghton Mifflin, 1952.
2. For pertinent studies of various organizational types see Burton R. Clark, *Adult Education in Transition*, Berkeley and Los Angeles: University of California Press, 1956; Temple Burling, Edith M. Lentz, and Robert N. Wilson, *The Give and Take in Hospitals*, New York: G. P. Putnam's Sons, 1956, especially pp. 3–10; Lloyd E. Ohlin, *Sociology and the Field of Corrections*, New York: Russell Sage Foundation, 1956, pp. 13–18; Liston Pope, *Millhands and Preachers*, New Haven: Yale University Press, 1942; Charles Y. Glock and Benjamin B. Ringer, "Church Policy and the Attitudes of Ministers and Parishioners on Social Issues," *American Sociological Review*, 21 (April, 1956), pp. 148–156. For a similar analysis in the field of philanthropy, see J. R. Seeley, B. H. Junker, R. W. Jones, Jr., and others, *Community Chest: A Case Study in Philanthropy*, Toronto: University of Toronto Press, 1957, especially Chapters 2 and 5.
3. This statement would seem to exclude antisocial organizations such as crime syndicates. A detailed analysis of such organizations would be useful for many purposes; meanwhile it would appear necessary for them to acquire a clientele, suppliers, and others, in spite of the fact that their methods at times may be somewhat unique.
4. For the *Zaibatsu* case see Japan Council, *The Control of Industry in Japan*, Tokyo: Institute of Political and Economic Research, 1953; and Edwin O. Reischauer, *The United States and Japan*, Cambridge: Harvard University Press, 1954, pp. 87–97.
5. For evidence on Russia see David Granick, *Management of the Industrial Firm in the U.S.S.R.*, New York: Columbia University Press, 1954; and Joseph S. Berliner, "Informal Organization of the Soviet Firm," *Quarterly Journal of Economics*, 66 (August, 1952), pp. 353–365.
6. This particular breakdown is taken from Edward H. Litchfield, "Notes on a General Theory of Administration," *Administrative Science Quarterly*, 1 (June, 1956), p. 3–29. We are also indebted to Robert Tannenbaum and Fred Massarik who, by breaking the decision-making process into three steps, show that subordinates can take part in the "manager's decision" even when the manager makes the final choice. See "Participation by Subordinates in the Managerial Decision-Making Process," *Canadian Journal of Economics and Political Science*, 16 (August, 1949), pp. 410–418.

458   7. Robert K. Merton makes a similar point regarding the role of the intellectual in public bureaucracy. See his *Social Theory and Social Structure,* Glencoe: The Free Press, 1949, Chapter VI.

8. See Logan Wilson, *The Academic Man,* New York: Oxford University Press, 1942, especially Chapter IX. Also see Warren G. Bennis, "The Effect on Academic Goods of Their Market," *American Journal of Sociology,* 62 (July, 1956), pp. 28–33.

9. For an account of this on a daily basis see Melville Dalton, "Unofficial Union-Management Relations," *American Sociological Review,* 15 (October, 1950), pp. 611–619.

10. See Valentine F. Ridgway, "Administration of Manufacturer-Dealer Systems," *Administrative Science Quarterly,* 1 (March, 1957), pp. 464–483.

11. Wilson, *op. cit.,* Chapters VII and VIII.

12. For an interesting study of governmental bargaining see William J. Gore, "Administrative Decision-Making in Federal Field Offices," *Public Administration Review,* 16 (Autumn, 1956), pp. 281–291.

13. Philip Selznick, *TVA and the Grass Roots,* Berkeley and Los Angeles: University of California Press, 1949.

14. Coalition may involve joint action toward only limited aspects of the goals of each member. It may involve the complete commitment of each member for a specific period of time or indefinitely. In either case the ultimate power to withdraw is retained by the members. We thus distinguish coalition from merger, in which two or more organizations are fused permanently. In merger one or all of the original parts may lose their identity. Goal-setting in such a situation, of course, is no longer subject to inter-organizational constraints among the components.

15. See "The Joint Venture Is an Effective Approach to Major Engineering Projects," *New York Times,* July 14, 1957, Section 3, p. 1 F.

16. See Robert S. and Helen Merrell Lynd, *Middletown in Transition,* New York: Harcourt Brace, 1937, Chapter VI.

17. Milton Greenblatt, Richard H. York, and Esther Lucille Brown, *From Custodial to Therapeutic Patient Care in Mental Hospitals,* New York: Russell Sage Foundation, 1955, Chapter 1, and Ohlin, *loc. cit.*

18. For one example, see the Report of the Harvard Committee, *General Education in a Free Society,* Cambridge: Harvard University Press, 1945.

19. America's civil air transport industry began in 1926 and eight years later carried 500,000 passengers. Yet it was testified in 1934 that half of the $120 million invested in airlines had been lost in spite of subsidies. See Jerome C. Hunsaker, *Aeronautics at the Mid-Century,* New Haven: Yale University Press, 1952, pp. 37–38. The case of Billy Mitchell was, of course, the landmark in the selling of military aviation.

20. Ray E. Trussell, *Hunterdon Medical Center,* Cambridge: Harvard University Press (for the Commonwealth Fund), 1956, Chapter 3.

21. This section on the sounding out process is a modified version of a paper by James D. Thompson, William J. McEwen, and Frederick L. Bates, "Sounding Out as a Relating Process," read at the annual meeting of the Eastern Sociological Society, April, 1957.

THE ANALYSIS OF GOALS
IN COMPLEX ORGANIZATIONS*

Charles Perrow

Social scientists have produced a rich body of knowledge about many aspects of large-scale organizations, yet there are comparatively few studies of the goals of these organizations. For a full understanding of organizations and the behavior of their personnel, analysis of organizational goals would seem to be critical. Two things have impeded such analysis. Studies of morale, turnover, informal organization, communication, supervisory practices, etc., have been guided by an over-rationalistic point of view wherein goals are taken for granted, and the most effective ordering of resources and personnel is seen as the only problematical issue. Fostering this view is the lack of an adequate distinction between types of goals. Without such clarification it is difficult to determine what the goals are and what would be acceptable evidence for the existence of a particular goal and for a change in goals.

It will be argued here, first, that the type of goals most relevant to understanding organizational behavior are not the official goals, but those that are embedded in major operating policies and the daily decisions of the personnel. Second, these goals will be shaped by the particular problems or tasks an organization must emphasize, since these tasks determine the characteristics of those who will dominate the organization. In illustrating the latter argument, we will not be concerned with the specific goals of organizations, but only with the range within which goals are likely to vary. Though general hospitals will be used as the main illustration, three types of organizations will be discussed: voluntary service organizations, non-voluntary service organizations and profit-making organizations.

The Overrationalistic View

Most studies of the internal operation of complex organizations, if they mention goals at all, have taken official statements of goals at face value. This may be justified if only a limited problem is being investigated, but even then it contributes to the view that goals are not problematical. In this view, goals have no effect upon activities other than in the grossest terms; or it can be taken for granted that the only problem is to adjust means to given and stable ends. This reflects a distinctive "model" of organizational behavior, which Gouldner has characterized as the rational model.[1]

"The Analysis of Goals in Complex Organizations," *American Sociological Review*, 6, 26 (December 1961), 854–866. Reprinted with the permission of the author and of the publisher, The American Sociological Association.

* Some of this material was presented in a paper titled, "A Reassessment of Authority and Goals in Voluntary General Hospitals," at the Fifty-fifth Annual Meeting of the American Sociological Association (1960). I should like to thank the following for their perceptive criticism: Morris Janowitz, Eliot Freidson, and Hanan Selvin.

460 Its proponents see the managerial elite as using rational and logical means to pursue clear and discrete ends set forth in official statements of goals, while the worker is seen as governed by nonrationalistic, traditionalistic orientations. If goals are unambiguous and achievement evaluated by cost-accounting procedures, the only turmoil of organizational life lies below the surface with workers or, at best, with middle management maneuvering for status and power. Actually, however, nonrational orientations exist at all levels, including the elite who are responsible for setting goals[2] and assessing the degree to which they are achieved.

One reason for treating goals as static fixtures of organizational life is that goals have not been given adequate conceptualization, though the elements of this are in easy reach. If making a profit or serving customers is to be taken as a sufficient statement of goals, then all means to this end might appear to be based on rational decisions because the analyst is not alerted to the countless policy decisions involved. If goals are given a more elaborate conceptualization, we are forced to see many more things as problematic.

Official and Operative Goals

Two major categories of goals will be discussed here, official and "operative" goals.[3] Official goals are the general purposes of the organization as put forth in the charter, annual reports, public statements by key executives and other authoritative pronouncements. For example, the goal of an employment agency may be to place job seekers in contact with firms seeking workers. The official goal of a hospital may be to promote the health of the community through curing the ill, and sometimes through preventing illness, teaching, and conducting research. Similar organizations may emphasize different publicly acceptable goals. A business corporation, for example, may state that its goal is to make a profit or adequate return on investment, or provide a customer service, or produce goods.

This level of analysis is inadequate in itself for a full understanding of organizational behavior. Official goals are purposely vague and general and do not indicate two major factors which influence organizational behavior: the host of decisions that must be made among alternative ways of achieving official goals and the priority of multiple goals, and the many unofficial goals pursued by groups within the organization. The concept of "operative goals"[4] will be used to cover these aspects. Operative goals designate the ends sought through the actual operating policies of the organization; they tell us what the organization actually is trying to do, regardless of what the official goals say are the aims.

Where operative goals provide the specific content of official goals they reflect choices among competing values. They may be justified on the basis of an official goal, even though they may subvert another official goal. In one sense they are means to official goals, but since the latter are vague or of high abstraction, the "means" become ends in themselves when the organization is the object of analysis. For example, where profit-making is the announced goal, operative goals will specify whether quality or quantity is to be emphasized, whether profits are to be short run and risky or long run and stable, and will indicate the relative priority of diverse and somewhat conflicting ends of customer service, employee morale, competitive pricing, diversification, or liquidity.

Decisions on all these factors influence the nature of the organization, and distinguish it from another with an identical official goal. An employment agency must decide whom to serve, what characteristics they favor among clients, and whether a high turnover of clients or a long run relationship is desired. In the voluntary general hospital, where the official goals are patient care, teaching, and research, the relative priority of these must be decided, as well as which group in the community is to be given priority in service, and are these services to emphasize, say, technical excellence or warmth and "hand-holding."

Unofficial operative goals, on the other hand, are tied more directly to group interests and while they may support, be irrelevant to, or subvert official goals, they bear no necessary connection with them. An interest in a major supplier may dictate the policies of a corporation executive. The prestige that attaches to utilizing elaborate high speed computers may dictate the reorganization of inventory and accounting departments. Racial prejudice may influence the selection procedures of an employment agency. The personal ambition of a hospital administrator may lead to community alliances and activities which bind the organization without enhancing its goal achievement. On the other hand, while the use of interns and residents as "cheap labor" may subvert the official goal of medical education, it may substantially further the official goal of providing a high quality of patient care.

The discernment of operative goals is, of course, difficult and subject to error. The researcher may have to determine from analysis of a series of apparently minor decisions regarding the lack of competitive bidding and quality control that an unofficial goal of a group of key executives is to maximize their individual investments in a major supplier. This unofficial goal may affect profits, quality, market position, and morale of key skill groups. The executive of a correctional institution may argue that the goal of the organization is treatment, and only the lack of resources creates an apparent emphasis upon custody or deprivation. The researcher may find, however, that decisions in many areas establish the priority of custody or punishment as a goal. For example, few efforts may be made to obtain more treatment personnel; those hired are misused and mistrusted; and clients are viewed as responding only to deprivations. The president of a junior college may deny the function of the institution is to deal with the latent terminal student, but careful analysis such as Clark has made of operating policies, personnel practices, recruitment procedures, organizational alliances and personal characteristics of elites will demonstrate this to be the operative goal.[5]

The Task—Authority—Goal Sequence

While operative goals will only be established through intensive analysis of decisions, personnel practices, alliance and elite characteristics in each organization, it is possible to indicate the range within which they will vary and the occasion for general shifts in goals. We will argue that if we know something about the major tasks of an organization and the characteristics of its controlling elite, we can predict its goals in general terms. The theory presented and illustrated in the rest of this paper is a first approximation and very general, but it may guide and stimulate research on this problem.

Every organization must accomplish four tasks: (1) secure inputs in the form

462 of capital sufficient to establish itself, operate, and expand as the need arises; (2) secure acceptance in the form of basic legitimation of activity; (3) marshal the necessary skills; and (4) coordinate the activities of its members, and the relations of the organization with other organizations and with clients or consumers. All four are not likely to be equally important at any point in time. Each of these task areas provides a presumptive basis for control or domination by the group equipped to meet the problems involved. (The use of the terms control or dominance signifies a more pervasive, thorough and all-embracing phenomenon than authority or power.) The operative goals will be shaped by the dominant group, reflecting the imperatives of the particular task area that is most critical, their own background characteristics (distinctive perspectives based upon their training, career lines, and areas of competence) and the unofficial uses to which they put the organization for their own ends.

The relative emphasis upon one or another of the four tasks will vary with the nature of the work the organization does and the technology appropriate to it,[6] and with the stage of development within the organization.[7] An organization engaged in manufacturing in an industry where skills are routinized and the market position secure, may emphasize coordination, giving control to the experienced administrator. An extractive industry, with a low skill level in its basic tasks and a simple product, will probably emphasize the importance of capital tied up in land, specialized and expensive machinery, and transportation facilities. The chairman of the board of directors or a group within the board will probably dominate such an organization. An organization engaged in research and development, or the pro-

duction of goods or services which cannot be carried out in a routinized fashion, will probably be most concerned with skills. Thus engineers or other relevant professionals will dominate. It is also possible that all three groups—trustees, representatives of critical skills, and administrators—may share power equally. This "multiple leadership" will be discussed in detail later. Of course, trustees are likely to dominate in the early history of any organization, particularly those requiring elaborate capital and facilities, or unusual legitimization. But once these requisites are secured, the nature of the tasks will determine whether trustees or others dominate. The transfer of authority, especially from trustees to another group, may be protracted, constituting a lag in adaptation.

Where major task areas do not change over time, the utility of the scheme presented here is limited to suggesting possible relations between task areas, authority structure, and operative goals. The more interesting problems, which we deal with in our illustrations below, involve organizations which experience changes in major task areas over time. If the technology or type of work changes, or if new requirements for capital or legitimization arise, control will shift from one group to another. One sequence is believed to be typical.

Voluntary General Hospitals

We will discuss four types of hospitals, those dominated by trustees, by the medical staff (an organized group of those doctors who bring in private patients plus the few doctors who receive salaries or commissions from the hospital), by the administration, and by some form of multiple leadership. There has been a general development among hospitals from trustee domination, based on capital and legitimization, to domination by the medical staff, based upon the increasing importance of their technical skills, and, at present, a tendency towards administrative dominance based on internal and external coordination. (The administrator may or may not be a doctor himself.) Not all hospitals go through these stages, or go through them in this sequence. Each type of authority structure shapes, or sets limits to, the type of operative goals that are likely to prevail, though there will be much variation within each type.[8]

TRUSTEE DOMINATION

Voluntary general hospitals depend upon community funds for an important part of their capital and operating budget. Lacking precise indicators of efficiency or goal achievement, yet using donated funds, they must involve community representatives—trustees— in their authority structure. Trustees legitimate the non-profit status of the organization, assure that funds are not misused, and see that community needs are being met. Officially, they are the ultimate authority in voluntary hospitals. They do not necessarily exercise the legal powers they have, but where they do, there is no question that they are in control.

The functional basis for this control is primarily financial. They have access to those who make donations, are expected to contribute heavily themselves, and control the machinery and sanctions for fund raising drives. Financial control allows them to withhold resources from recalcitrant groups in the organization, medical or non-medical. They also, of course, control all appointments and promotions, medical and non-medical.

Where these extensive powers are exercised, operative goals are likely to reflect the role of trustees as community representatives and contributors to community health. Because of their responsibility to the sponsoring community, trustees may favor conservative financial policies, opposing large financial outlays for equipment, research, and education so necessary for high medical standards.[9] High standards also require more delegation of authority to the medical staff than trustee domination can easily allow.[10] As representatives drawn from distinctive social groups in the community, they may be oriented towards service for a religious, ethnic, economic, or age group in the community. Such an orientation may conflict with selection procedures favored by the medical staff or administration. Trustees may also promote policies which demonstrate a contribution to community welfare on the part of an elite group, perhaps seeking to maintain a position of prominence and power within the community. The hospital may be used as a vehicle for furthering a social philosophy of philanthropy and good works; social class values regarding personal worth, economic independence and responsibility; the assimilation of a minority group;[11] or even to further resistance to government control and socialized medicine.

Such orientations will shape operative goals in many respects, affecting standards and techniques of care, priority of services, access to care, relations with other organizations, and directions and rate of development. The administrator in such a hospital—usually called a "superintendent" under the circumstances—will have little power, prestige or responsibility. For example, trustees have been known to question the brand of grape juice the dietitian orders, or insist that they approve the color of paint the administrator selects for a room.[12] Physicians may disapprove of patient selection criteria, chafe under financial restrictions which limit the resources they have to work with, and resent active control over appointments and promotions in the medical staff.

MEDICAL DOMINATION

Trustee domination was probably most common in the late nineteenth and twentieth century. Medical technology made extraordinary advances in the twentieth century, and doctors possessed the skills capable of utilizing the advances. They demanded new resources and were potentially in a position to control their allocation and use. Increasingly, major decisions had to be based upon a technical competence trustees did not possess. Trustees had a continuing basis for control because of the costs of new equipment and personnel, but in many hospitals the skill factor became decisive. Some trustees felt that the technology required increased control by doctors; others lost a struggle for power with the medical staff; in some cases trustees were forced to bring in and give power to an outstanding doctor in order to increase the reputation of the hospital.[13] Under such conditions trustees are likely to find that their legal power becomes nominal and they can only intervene in crisis situations; even financial requirements come to be set by conditions outside their control.[14] They continue to provide the mantle of community representation and non-profit status, and become "staff" members whose major task is to secure funds.

It is sometimes hard to see why all hospitals are not controlled by the medical staff, in view of the increasing complexity and specialization of the doctors' skills, their common professional background, the power of organized medicine, and the prestige accorded the doctor in society. Furthermore, they are organized for dominance, despite their nominal status as "guests" in the house.[15] The medical staff constitutes a "shadow" organization in hospitals, providing a ready potential for control. It is organized on bureaucratic principles with admission requirements, rewards and sanctions, and a committee structure which often duplicates the key committees of the board of directors and administrative staff. Nor are doctors in an advisory position as are "staff" groups in other organizations. Doctors perform both staff and line functions, and their presumptive right to control rests on both. Doctors also have a basic economic interest in the hospital, since it is essential to most private medical practice and career advancement. They seek extensive facilities, low hospital charges, a high quality of coordinated services, and elaborate time and energy-conserving conveniences.

Thus there is sufficient means for control by doctors, elaborated far beyond the mere provision of essential skills, and sufficient interest in control. Where doctors fully exercise their potential power the administrator functions as a superintendent, or as his coprofessionals are wont to put it, as a "housekeeper." The importance of administrative skills is likely to be minimized, the administrative viewpoint on operative goals neglected, and the quality of personnel may suffer. A former nurse often serves as superintendent in this type of hospital. Policy matters are defined as medical in nature by the doctors,[16] and neither trustees nor administrators, by definition, are qualified to have an equal voice in policy formation.

The operative goals of such a hospital are likely to be defined in strictly medical terms and the organization may achieve high technical standards of care, promote exemplary research, and provide sound training. However, there is a danger that resources will be used primarily for private (paying) patients with little attention to other community needs such as caring for the medically indigent (unless they happen to be good teaching cases), developing preventive medicine, or pioneering new organizational forms of care. Furthermore, high technical standards increasingly require efficient coordination of services and doctors may be unwilling to delegate authority to qualified administrators.

Various unofficial goals may be achieved at the expense of medical ones, or, in some cases, in conjunction with them. There are many cases of personal aggrandizement on the part of departmental chiefs and the chief of staff. The informal referral and consultation system in conjunction with promotions, bed quotas, and "privileges" to operate or treat certain types of cases, affords many occasions for the misuse of power. Interns and residents are particularly vulnerable to exploitation at the expense of teaching goals. Furthermore, as a professional, the doctor has undergone intensive socialization in his training and is called upon to exercise extraordinary judgment and skill with drastic consequences for good or ill. Thus he demands unusual deference and obedience and is invested with "charismatic" authority.[17] He may extend this authority to the entrepreneurial aspects of his role, with the result that his "service" orientation, so taken for granted in much of the literature, sometimes means service to the doctor at the expense of personnel, other patients, or even his own patient.[18]

ADMINISTRATIVE DOMINANCE

Administrative dominance is based first on the need for coordinating the increasingly complex, non-routinizable functions hospitals have undertaken. There is an increasing number of personnel that the doctor can no longer direct. The mounting concern of trustees, doctors themselves, patients and prepayment groups with more efficient and economical operation also gives the administrator more power. A second, related basis for control stems from the fact that health services in general have become increasingly interdependent and specialized. The hospital must cooperate more with other hospitals and community agencies. It must also take on more services itself, and in doing so its contacts with other agencies and professional groups outside the hospital multiply. The administrator is equipped to handle these matters because of his specialized training, often received in a professional school of hospital administration, accumulated experience and available time. These services impinge upon the doctor at many points, providing a further basis for administrative control over doctors, and they lead to commitments in which trustees find they have to acquiesce.

The administrator is also in a position to control matters which affect the doctor's demands for status, deference, and time-saving conveniences. By maintaining close supervision over employees or promoting their own independent basis for competence, and by supporting them in conflicts with doctors, the administrator can, to some degree, overcome the high functional authority that doctors command. In addition, by carefully controlling communication between trustees and key medical staff officials, he can prevent an alliance of these two groups against him.

If administrative dominance is based primarily on the complexity of basic hospital activities, rather than the organization's medical-social role in the community, the operative orientation may be toward financial solvency, careful budget controls, efficiency, and minimal development of services. For example, preventive medicine, research, and training may be minimized; a cautious approach may prevail towards new forms of care such as intensive therapy units or home care programs. Such orientations could be especially true of hospitals dominated by administrators whose background and training were as bookkeepers, comptrollers, business managers, purchasing agents, and the like. This is probably the most common form of administrative dominance.

However, increasing professionalization of hospital administrators has, on the one hand, equipped them to handle narrower administrative matters easily, and, on the other hand, alerted them to the broader medical-social role of hospitals involving organizational and financial innovations in the forms of care. Even medical standards can come under administrative control. For example, the informal system among doctors of sponsorship, referral, and consultation serves to protect informal work norms, shield members from criticism and exclude non-cooperative members. The administrator is in a position to insist that medical policing be performed by a salaried doctor who stands outside the informal system.

There is, of course, a possibility of less "progressive" consequences. Interference with medical practices in the name of either high standards or treating the "whole" person may be misguided or have latent consequences which impair therapy. Publicity-seeking innovations may be at the expense of more humdrum but crucial services such as the out-patient department, or may alienate doctors or other personnel, or may deflect administrative efforts from essential but unglamorous administrative tasks.[19] Using the organization for career advancement, they may seek to expand and publicize their hospital regardless of community needs and ability to pay. Like trustees they may favor a distinctive and medically irrelevant community relations policy, perhaps with a view towards moving upward in the community power structure. Regardless of these dangers, the number of administration dominated hospitals oriented towards broad medical-social goals will probably grow.

MULTIPLE LEADERSHIP

So far we have been considering situations where one group clearly dominates. It is possible, however, for power to be shared by two or three groups to the extent that no one is able to control all or most of the actions of the others. This we call multiple leadership: a division of labor regarding the determination of goals and the power to achieve them.[20] This is not the same as fractionated power where several groups have small amounts of power in an unstable situation. With multiple leadership, there are two or three stable, known centers of power. Nor is it the same as decentralized power, where specialized units of the organization have considerable autonomy. In the latter case, units are free to operate as they choose only up to a point, when it becomes quite clear that there is a centralized authority. In multiple leadership there is no single ultimate power.

Multiple leadership is most likely to appear in organizations where there are multiple goals which lack precise criteria of achievement and admit of considerable tolerance with regard to achievement. Multiple goals focus interests, and achievement tolerance provides the necessary leeway for accommodation of interests and vitiation of responsibility. Many service organizations fit these criteria, but so might large, public relations-conscious business or industrial organizations where a variety of goals can be elevated to such importance that power must be shared by the representatives of each.

In one hospital where this was studied[21] it was found that multiple leadership insured that crucial group interests could be met and protected, and encouraged a high level of creative (though selective) involvement by trustees, doctors, and the administration. However, the problems of goal setting, assessment of achievement, and assignment of responsibility seemed abnormally high. While the three groups pursued separate and conflicting operative goals in some cases, and were in agreement on still other goals, in areas where interests conflicted the goal conflicts were submerged in the interests of harmony. In the absence of a single authority, repetitive conflicts threatened to erode morale and waste energies. A showdown and clear solution of a conflict, furthermore, might signal defeat for one party, forcing them to abandon their interests. Thus a premium was placed on the ability of some elites to smooth over conflicts and exercise interpersonal skills. Intentions were sometimes masked and ends achieved through covert manipulation. Assessment of achievement in some areas was prevented either by the submergence of conflict or the preoccupation with segmental interests. Opportunism was encouraged: events in the environment or within the hospital were exploited without attention to the interests of the other

groups or the long range development of the hospital. This left the organization open to vagrant pressures and to the operation of unintended consequences. Indeed, with conflict submerged and groups pursuing independent goals, long range planning was difficult.

This summary statement exaggerates the impact of multiple leadership in this hospital and neglects the areas of convergence on goals. Actually, the hospital prospered and led its region in progressive innovations and responsible medical-social policies despite some subversion of the official goals of patient care, teaching, research, and preventive medicine. The organization could tolerate considerable ambiguity of goals and achievements as long as standards remained high in most areas, occupancy was sufficient to operate with a minimum deficit, and a favorable public image was maintained. It remains to be seen if the costs and consequences are similar for other organizations where multiple leadership exists.

Application to Other Organizations[22]

VOLUNTARY SERVICE ORGANIZATIONS

Other voluntary service organizations, such as private universities, social service agencies, privately sponsored correctional institutions for juveniles, and fund raising agencies resemble hospitals in many respects. They have trustees representing the community, may have professionals playing prominent roles, and with increasing size and complexity of operation, require skilled coordination of activities. Initially at least, trustees are likely to provide a character defining function which emphasizes community goals and goals filtered through their own social position. Examples are religious schools, or those emphasizing one field of knowledge or training; agencies caring for specialized groups such as ethnic or religious minorities, unwed mothers, and dependent and neglected children; and groups raising money for special causes. Funds of skill and knowledge accumulate around these activities, and the activities increasingly grow in complexity, requiring still more skill on the part of those performing the tasks. As the professional staff expands and professional identification grows, they may challenge the narrower orientations of trustees on the basis of their own special competence and professional ideology and seek to broaden the scope of services and the clientele. They may be supported in this by changing values in the community. Coordination of activities usually rests with professionals promoted from the staff during this second character defining phase, and these administrators retain, for a while at least, their professional identity. Trustees gradually lose the competence to interfere.

However, professionals have interests of their own which shape the organization. They may develop an identity and ethic which cuts them off from the needs of the community and favors specialized, narrow and—to critics—self-serving goals. Current criticisms of the emphasis upon research and over-specialization in graduate training at the expense of the basic task of educating undergraduates is a case in point in the universities.[23] There is also criticism of the tendency of professionals in correctional institutions to focus upon case work techniques applicable to middle-class "neurotic" delinquents at the expense of techniques for resocializing the so-called "socialized" delinquent from culturally deprived areas.[24] The latter account for most of the delinquents, but professional identity and techniques favor methods applicable to the former. Something similar may be found in social agencies. Social workers, especially the "elite" doing therapy in psychiatric and child guidance clinics and private family agencies, may become preoccupied with securing recognition, equitable financial remuneration, and status that would approach that of psychiatrists. Their attitudes may become more conservative; the social order more readily accepted and the deviant adapted to it; "worthy" clients and "interesting cases" receive priority.

It is possible that with increasing complexity and growth in many of these voluntary service organizations, administrators will lose their professional identity or be recruited from outside the organization on the basis of organizational skills. In either case they will be in a position to alter the direction fostered by selective professional interests. Of course, the problem of coordinating both internal and external activities need not generate leadership seeking broadly social rather than narrowly professional goals, any more than it necessarily does in the hospital. Administrative dominance may stunt professional services and neglect social policy in the interest of economy, efficiency, or conservative policies.

NON-VOLUNTARY SERVICE ORGANIZATIONS

A different picture is presented by non-voluntary service organizations— those sponsored by governmental agencies such as county or military hospitals, city or county welfare agencies, juvenile and adult correctional agencies.[25] Authority for goal setting, regulation, and provision of capital and operating expenses does not rest with voluntary trustees, but with governmental officials appointed to commissions. In contrast to volunteers on the board of a private service organization, commissioners are not likely to be highly identified with the organization, nor do they derive much social status from it. The organizations themselves often are tolerated only as holding operations or as "necessary evils." Commission dominance is sporadic and brief, associated with public clamor or political expediency. On the other hand, the large size of these organizations and the complex procedures for reporting to the parent body gives considerable importance to the administrative function from the outset, which is enhanced by the tenuous relationship with the commissioners. Consistent with this and reinforcing it is the low level of professionalization found in many of these agencies. The key skills are often non-professional custodial skills or their equivalent in the case of public welfare agencies (and schools). Administrators are often at the mercy of the custodial staff if, indeed, they have not themselves risen to their administrative position because of their ability to maintain order and custody.

Nevertheless, professional influence is mounting in these organizations, and professional groups outside of them have exercised considerable influence.[26] Professionals may assume control of the organization, or administrators may be brought in whose commitment is to the positive purposes of the organization, such as rehabilitation of the clients, rather than the negative custodial functions. This appears to have happened in the case of a few federal penal institutions, a few state juvenile correctional institutions, and several Veterans Administration mental hospitals. Even where this happens, one must be alert to the influence of unofficial goals. The or-

ganizations are particularly vulnerable to exploitation by the political career interests of administrators or to irresponsible fads or cure-alls of marginal professionals. In summary, the sequence of tasks, power structure, and goals may be different in non-voluntary service organizations. The importance of administrative skills with system maintenance as the overriding operative goal does not encourage a shift in power structure; but where new technologies are introduced we are alerted to such shifts along with changes in goals.

PROFIT-MAKING ORGANIZATIONS

Our analysis may appear less applicable to profit-making organizations for two reasons. First, it could be argued, they are not characterized by multiple goals, but relate all operations to profit-making. Second, skill groups are not likely to dominate these organizations; owners control the smaller firms, and professional executives the larger ones. Thus power structure and possibly goals may merely be a function of size. We will discuss each of these points in turn.

If profit-making is an overriding goal of an organization, many operative decisions must still be made which will shape its character. Even where technology remains constant, organizations will vary with regard to personnel practices, customer services, growth, liquidity, an emphasis upon quality or quantity, or long or short run gains. An adequate understanding of the organization will require attention to alternatives in these and other areas.

Furthermore, it has often been asserted that the importance of profits, *per se*, has declined with the increased power of professional management, especially in large organizations. The argument runs that since management does not have a personal stake in profits, they consider them less important than stability, growth, solvency, and liquidity.[27] The impressionistic evidence of those who assert this is not supported by a study of James Dent.[28] When asked, "What are the aims of top management in your company?" the response of executives of 145 business firms showed no greater mention of "to make profits, money or a living" among large than small firms, nor among those with professional managers than owner-managers. Because goals stated in this form may not reflect actual policies and because of other limitations, one is somewhat reluctant to take this as a fair test of the hypothesis.

Even though his sample was not representative, and the question asked does not get at what we have called operative goals, his study provides good evidence of variations of stated goals in profit-making organizations. Responses coded under the category "to make money, profits, or a living" were mentioned as the first aim by 36 percent of the executives; "to provide a good product; public service" by 21 percent, and "to grow" was third with 12 percent. When the first three aims spontaneously mentioned were added together, profits led; employee welfare tied with "good products or public service" for second place. Dent found that the variables most associated with goals were size of company and "proportion of employees who are white-collar, professional or supervisory."[29] While goals no doubt are influenced by size, this accounted for only some of the variance. Holding size constant, one might discover the effect of major task areas. The association of goals with the "proportion of employees who are white-collar . . ." supports this argument.

R. A. Gordon and others have asserted that in large corporations it is the executive group, rather than stockholders or the board of trustees, that generally dominates.[30] A study of the role of trustees, frankly in favor of their exercising leadership and control, actually shows through its many case studies that trustees exercise leadership mainly in times of crisis.[31] The generalization of Gordon, almost a commonplace today, appears to be sound; he asserts that the common pattern of evolution is for active leadership by owners in the early years of the firm, then it is passed on to new generations of the families concerned, and gradually responsibility for decision-making passes to professional executives who frequently have been trained by the original leaders.[32] Goals likewise shift from rapid development and a concern with profits to more conservative policies emphasizing coordination, stability and security of employment.[33]

But does this mean that for large, old, and stable firms that operative goals are substantially similar, reflecting professional administration? Does it also mean that for profit-making organizations in general there are only two alternative sources of domination, trustees (including owners) and professional administrators? Our theoretical scheme suggests that neither may be true, but the evidence is scanty. Certainly within the organizations dominated by professional managers there is ample opportunity for a variety of operational goals less general than, say, stability and security of employment. Even these are likely to vary and to shape the nature of the firm. (We exclude, of course, the failure to achieve these broad goals because of poor management or environmental factors over which the organization has no control; we are dealing with operating policies which may not be achieved.) Gordon notes that the "historical background" of a company (he does not elaborate this phrase) and especially the training received by its leading executives may be a powerful factor in shaping management decisions. "It is the 'Rockefeller tradition' rather than the present Rockefeller holdings which actively conditions the management decisions in the Standard Oil companies. This tradition is largely responsible for present methods of management organization and internal control, use of the committee system and the domination of boards of directors by [company executives]."[34] Historical factors will certainly shape decisions, but the nature of technology in the oil industry and the trustees' awareness of the prime importance of coordination may have been decisive in that historical experience.

Domination by skill groups is possible in two ways. On the one hand, a department—for example, sales, engineering, research and development, or finance—may, because of the technology and stage of growth, effectively exercise a veto on the executive's decisions and substantially shape decisions in other departments. Second, lines of promotion may be such that top executives are drawn from one powerful department, and retain their identification with the parochial goals of that department. Gordon asserts that chief executives with a legal background are conservative in making price changes and find "order in the industry" more appealing than aggressive price competition.[35] It is possible that engineers, sales executives, and financial executives all have distinctive views on what the operating policies should be.

Thus, goals may vary widely in profit-making organizations, and power may rest not only with trustees or professional administrators, but with skill groups or administrators influenced by their skill background. Of course, one task area may so dominate a firm that

there will be no shifts in power, and operative goals will remain fairly stable within the limits of the changing values of society. But where basic tasks shift, either because of growth or changing technology, the scheme presented here at least alerts us to potential goal changes and their consequences. An ideal-typical sequence would be as follows: trustee domination in initial stages of financing, setting direction for development and recruitment of technical or professional skills; then dominance by the skill group during product or service development and research, only to have subsequent control pass to coordination of fairly routinized activities. As the market and technology change, this cycle could be repeated. During the course of this sequence, operative goals may shift from quantity production and short-run profits as emphasized by trustees, to the engineer's preoccupation with quality at the expense of quantity or styling, with this succeeded by a priority upon styling and unessential innovations demanded by the sales force, and finally with an emphasis upon the long-run market position, conservative attitude towards innovation, and considerable investment in employee-centered policies and programs by management. It is important to note that the formal authority structure may not vary during this sequence, but recruitment into managerial positions and the actual power of management, trustees or skill groups would shift with each new problem focus. Multiple leadership is also possible, as noted in an earlier section.

There are many critical variables influencing the selection of key problem areas and thus the characteristics of the controlling elite and operative goals. They will be applicable to the analysis of any complex organization, whether business, governmental, or voluntary. Among

ANALYSIS OF GOALS IN COMPLEX ORGANIZATIONS

those that should be considered are capital needs and legitimization, the amount of routinization possible, adaptability of technology to market shifts and consumer behavior, possible or required professionalization, and the nature of the work force. Our analysis of profit-making organizations suggests that we should be alert to the possibility of a natural history of changes in task areas, authority, and goals which parallels that of hospitals and other voluntary service organizations. Non-voluntary service organizations may systematically deviate from this sequence because of the source of capital (government) which influences the commitments of appointive trustees (commissioners), and the character of the administrative tasks. The scheme presented here, when used in conjunction with the concept of operative goals, may provide a tool for analyzing the dynamics of goal setting and goal changing in all complex organizations.

NOTES

1. Alvin Gouldner, "Organizational Analysis," in Robert Merton, Leonard Broom and Leonard S. Cottrell, Jr., editors, *Sociology Today*, New York: Basic Books, 1959, p. 407.
2. A strong argument for considering changes in goals is made by James D. Thompson and William J. McEwen, "Organizational Goals and Environment: Goal-Setting as an Interaction Process," *American Sociological Review*, 23 (February, 1958), pp. 23–31.
3. A third may be distinguished: social system goals, which refers to those contributions an organization makes to the functioning of a social system in which it is nested. In Parsons' terminology, organizations may serve adaptive, gratificatory, integrative, or pattern-maintenance functions. See Talcott Parsons, "Sociological Approach to the Theory of Organizations," *Administrative Science Quarterly*, 1 (June–September, 1956), pp. 63–86, 225–240. This alone, however, will tell us little about individual organizations, although Scott, in a suggestive article applying this scheme to prisons and mental hospitals, implies that organizations serving integrative functions for society will place particular importance upon integrative functions within the organization. See Frances G. Scott, "Action Theory and Research in Social Organization," *American Journal of Sociology*, 64 (January, 1959), pp. 386–395. Parsons asserts that each of the four functions mentioned above also must be performed within organizations if they are to survive. It is possible to see a parallel between these four functions and the four tasks discussed below, but his are, it is felt, too general and ambiguous to provide tools for analysis.
4. The concept of "operational goals" or "subgoals" put forth by March and Simon bears a resemblance to this but does not include certain complexities which we will discuss, nor is it defined systematically. See J. G. March and H. A. Simon, *Organizations*, New York: Wiley, 1958, pp. 156–157.
5. Burton Clark, *The Open Door College*, New York: McGraw-Hill, 1960.
6. For an illuminating discussion of organizations which emphasizes technological differences, see James D. Thompson and Frederick L. Bates, "Technology, Organizations, and Administration," *Administrative Science Quarterly*, 2 (December, 1957), pp. 325–343.
7. Many other factors are also important, such as the legal framework, official and unofficial regulatory bodies, state of the industry, etc. These will not be considered here. In general, their influences are felt through the task areas, and thus are reflected here.
8. The following discussion is based upon the author's study of one hospital which, in fact, passed through these stages; upon examination of published and unpublished studies of hospitals; and upon numerous conversations with administrators, doctors, and trustees in the United States. Sophisticated practitioners in the hospital field recognize and describe these types in their own fashion. See Charles Perrow, "Au-

thority, Goals and Prestige in a General Hospital," unpublished Ph.D. dissertation, University of California, Berkeley, 1960, for fuller documentation and discussion.

9. Exceptions to conservative financial policies appear to occur most frequently in crisis situations where accreditation is threatened or sound business principles are violated by run down facilities, or inefficient management. See Temple Burling, Edith M. Lentz, and Robert N. Wilson, *The Give and Take in Hospitals*, New York: G. P. Putnam, 1956, Chapters 4, 5, 6.

10. Burling *et al.*, (*ibid.*, p. 43), note that active trustees find delegation difficult.

11. Perrow, *op. cit.*, chapter 5.

12. Edith Lentz, "Changing Concepts of Hospital Administration," *Industrial and Labor Relations Research*, 3 (Summer, 1957), p. 2. Perrow, *op. cit.*, p. 86.

13 Berthram Bernhein, *The Story of Johns Hopkins*, New York: McGraw-Hill, 1948, pp. 142–148.

14. For a detailed analysis of such a shift of power, see Perrow, *op. cit.*, pp. 43–50.

15. There is a small group of doctors on the medical staff, who may or may not bring in private patients, who receive money from the hospital, either through salary or commissions—pathologists, anesthetists, roentgenologists, paid directors of the out-patient department, etc. These are members of the organization in a direct sense.

16. Oswald Hall, "Some Problems in the Provision of Medical Services," *Canadian Journal of Economics*, 20 (November, 1954), p. 461.

17. Albert F. Wessen, "The Social Structure of a Modern Hospital," unpublished Ph.D. dissertation, Yale University, 1951, p. 43.

18. Wessen notes that the doctor "sees ministering to the needs of doctors as a major function of the hospitals." (*Ibid.*, p. 328.)

19. Charles Perrow, "Organizational Prestige: Some Functions and Dysfunctions," *American Journal of Sociology*, 66 (January, 1961), pp. 335–341.

20. As in small group analysis, there is an increasing though belated tendency to recognize the possibility that there may be more than one leader in an organization. For a recent discussion of the problem in connection with army groups, see Hanan Selvin, *The Effects of Leadership*, Glencoe, Ill.: The Free Press, 1960, Chapters 1, 7. Amitai Etzioni goes even further in discussing "professional organizations." For a provocative discussion of goals and authority structure, see his "Authority Structure and Organizational Effectiveness," *Administrative Science Quarterly*, 4 (June, 1959), pp. 43–67.

21. Perrow, Authority, Goals and Prestige . . . , *op. cit.*, chapters 4, 10.

22. The dogmatic tone of this concluding section is, unfortunately, the consequence of an attempt to be brief.

23. Earl J. McGrath, *The Graduate School and the Doctrine of Liberal Education*, New York: Bureau of Publication, Teachers College, Columbia University, 1960.

24. Robert Vinter and Morris Janowitz, "Effective Institutions for Juvenile Delinquents: A Research Statement," *Social Service Review*, 33 (June, 1957), pp. 118–122; Donald Cressey, "Changing Criminals: The Application of the Theory of Differential Association," *American Journal of Sociology*, 56 (September, 1955), p. 116; Lloyd Ohlin and W. C. Lawrence, "Social Interaction Among Clients as a Treatment Problem," *Social Work*, 4 (April, 1959), pp. 3–14.

25. Public schools are excluded here because of the elective status of school boards; however, with some revisions, the following analysis would be applicable.

26. Thompson and McEwen note that the "importance of new objectives may be more readily seen by specialized segments (professionals) than by the general society" and argue that public clamor for change has not been the initiating force. *Op. cit.*, p. 29.

27. Robert A. Gordon was perhaps the first to deal at length with this proposition, and many have subsequently argued along the same lines. See Robert A. Gordon, *Business Leadership in the Large Corporation*, Washington, D.C.: Brookings Institution, 1945, pp. 308–312, 322, 327–329, 336, 340. For similar assertions see C. E. Griffin, *Enterprise in a Free Society*, Chicago: Irwin, 1949, pp. 96–104; H. Maurer, *Great*

Enterprise, New York: Macmillan Co., 1955, pp. 77–78; and F. X. Sutton, et al., The American Business Creed, Cambridge: Harvard University Press, 1956, pp. 57–58. For a contrary view see G. Katona, Psychological Analysis of Economic Behavior, New York: McGraw-Hill, 1951, p. 197.

28. James K. Dent, "Organizational Correlates of the Goals of Business Managements," Journal of Personnel Psychology, 12 (Autumn, 1959), pp. 375–376.

29. Ibid., pp. 378, 380, 383. Data on types of business, unfortunately, are not presented, except as reflected in the variable "proportion of employers who are white collar . . ."

30. Gordon, op. cit., pp. 114, 131–132, 145–146, 180, 347.

31. M. T. Copeland and A. Towl, The Board of Directors and Business Management, Boston: Harvard University, 1947. For a similar conclusion and excellent discussion of these matters see R. H. Dahl, "Business and Politics," American Political Science Review, 53 (March, 1959), p. 6. The argument for increasing managerial control was, of course, also put forth by Burnham in 1941, but he was only faintly interested in the effects upon organizations, his thesis being that managers would supplant capitalists in the national and world power elite. See The Managerial Revolution, New York: John Day, 1941.

32. Gordon, op. cit., p. 180.

33. Ibid., pp. 327, 339. See his illustrations from General Motors and U.S. Rubber Company in chapter 7.

34. Ibid., p. 188.

35. Ibid., p. 264.

A SYSTEM RESOURCE APPROACH TO ORGANIZATIONAL EFFECTIVENESS*

Ephraim Yuchtman and Stanley E. Seashore

We are badly in need of an improved conceptual framework for the description and assessment of organizational effectiveness. Nearly all studies of formal organizations make some reference to effectiveness; the growing field of comparative organizational study depends in part upon having some conceptual scheme that allows comparability among organizations with respect to effectiveness and that guides the empirical steps of operationalization and quantification.

Aside from these needs of social scientists, consideration should also be given to the esthetic and applied requirements of organization managers. They experi-

"A System Resource Approach to Organizational Effectiveness," American Sociological Review, 32, 6 (December 1967), 891–903. Reprinted with the permission of the authors and of the publisher, The American Sociological Association.

* The preparation of this paper was financially supported by the National Science Foundation under Grant GS–70. Since the preparation of this paper, the first author has taken up his new post at the University of Tel-Aviv.

DECISIONS, GOALS, AND EFFECTIVENESS

ence high emotional involvement, pleasurable or otherwise, in the assessment of the relative success of their organizations; they are, of course, intensively and professionally engaged, informally, in the formulation and testing of hypotheses concerning the nature of decisions and actions that alter organizational effectiveness. They need a workable conception of "effectiveness" to sustain their egos and their work.

The social scientist designing or interpreting an organizational study is presently in a quandary. Most of the research concerned with the problem has been devoted to the study of the *conditions* under which organizations are more or less effective. The classic paradigm consists of some measurement of effectiveness—productivity or profit, for example —as the dependent variable, and of various sociological and social-psychological measures as the independent variables. The independent variables are usually treated in a relatively sophisticated manner; little attention, however, has been given to the concept of effectiveness itself. The latter remains conceptually a vague construct; in consequence there is available a large amount of empirical data with little understanding of these data. As stated recently by Katz and Kahn:

> There is no lack of material on criteria of organizational success. The literature is studded with references to efficiency, productivity, absence, turnover, and profitability—all of these offered implicitly or explicitly, separately or in combination, as definitions of organizational effectiveness. Most of what has been written on the meaning of these criteria and on their interrelatedness, however, is judgmental and open to question. What is worse, it is filled with advice that seems sagacious but is tautological and contradictory.[1]

Similar conclusions, on the same or on different grounds, have been reached by other students of organizations.[2] While emphasizing different aspects of the problem, all agree that results from studies of organizational effectiveness show numerous inconsistencies, and are difficult to evaluate and interpret, let alone compare. The inconsistencies arise, often, from discrepant conceptions of "organizational effectiveness." In the present paper an attempt is made, first, to show some of the limitations inherent in traditional approaches to organizational effectiveness and, second, to provide an improved conceptual framework for dealing with that problem.

Traditional Approaches to Organizational Effectiveness

In spite of the variety of terms, concepts and operational definitions that have been employed with regard to organizational effectiveness, it is hardly difficult to arrive at the generalization that this concept has been traditionally defined in terms of goal attainment. More specifically, most investigators tend implicitly or explicitly to make the following two assumptions: (1) that complex organizations have an ultimate goal ("mission," "function") toward which they are striving and (2) that the ultimate goal can be identified empirically and progress toward it measured. In fact, the orientation to a specific goal is taken by many as the defining characteristic of complex organizations. A few organizational theorists[3] avoid making these assumptions, but they represent the exception rather than the rule.

Beyond these two common assumptions, however, one may discern different treatments of the matter, especially with regard to the rationale and operations for identifying the goals of organizations. It is useful to distinguish between two major doctrines in this respect. The first may be called the "prescribed goal approach." It is characterized by a focus on the formal charter of the organization, or on some category of its personnel (usually its top management) as the most valid source of information concerning organizational goals. The second may be referred to as the "derived goal approach." In it the investigator derives the ultimate goal of the organization from his (functional) theory, thus arriving at goals which may be independent of the intentions and awareness of the members. The prescribed and derived doctrines will be referred to as the *goal approach* and the *functional approach,* respectively.

The Goal Approach to Organizational Effectiveness

The goal approach, which itself has taken many forms, is the most widely used by students of organizations. Some have adopted it only as part of a broader perspective on organizations.[4] Others have employed it as a major tool in their study of organizations.[5] The goal approach has been attacked recently on various grounds. Katz and Kahn, while noting that ". . . the primary mission of an organization as perceived by its leaders furnishes a highly informative set of clues," go on to point out that:

> Nevertheless, the stated purpose of an organization as given by its by-laws or in the reports of its leaders can be misleading. Such statements of objectives may idealize, rationalize, distort, omit, or even conceal some essential aspects of the functioning of the organization.[6]

The goal approach is often adopted by researchers because it seems to safeguard them against their own subjective biases. But Etzioni attacks precisely this assumption:

> The (goal) model is considered an objective and reliable analytical tool be-

cause it omits the values of the explorer and applies the values of the subject under study as the criteria of judgment. We suggest, however, that this model has some methodological shortcomings, and it is not as objective as it seems to be.[7]

Furthermore, argues Etzioni, the assessment of organizational effectiveness in terms of goal attainment should be rejected on theoretical considerations as well:

> Goals, as norms, as sets of meanings depicting target states, are cultural entities. Organizations, as systems of coordinated activities of more than one actor, are social systems.[8]

We understand this statement as rejecting the application of the goal approach in the study of organizational effectiveness for two reasons: first, goals as ideal states do not offer the possibility of realistic assessment; second, goals as cultural entities arise outside of the organization as a social system and cannot arbitrarily be attributed as properties of the organization itself. A similar criticism is offered by Starbuck, who calls attention to a hazard in the inferring of organizational goals from the behavior of organizational members:

> To distinguish goal from effect is all but impossible. The relation between goals and results is polluted by environmental effects, and people learn to pursue realistic goals. If growth is difficult, the organization will tend to pursue goals which are not growth oriented; if growth is easy, the organization will learn to pursue goals which are growth oriented. What one observes are the learned goals. Do these goals produce growth, or does growth produce these goals?[9]

It should be noted that the authors cited above tend to treat the problem as a methodological one even though, as we will show, theoretical differences and uncertainties are present as well. In order to escape some of these methodological shortcomings, several investigators have attempted to rely upon inferential or impressionistic methods of goal identification. Haberstroh, for example, makes the distinction between the formal objectives and the "common purpose" of the organization, the latter serving as the "unifying factor in human organizations."[10] But how, one may wonder, can that factor be empirically identified? Haberstroh maintains that it can be discovered through a systematic inquiry into the communication processes of the organization and by knowledge of the interests of its leadership, especially those in key positions. An empirical investigation conducted in accordance with that advice resulted in a list of operational (task) goals that, according to the investigator's own acknowledgment, do not adequately represent his notion of the "common purpose" of the organization. The latter remains therefore a rather vague concept and, it may be added, not surprisingly so. If one assumes that Haberstroh's "common purpose" stands for those objectives that are shared by the organization's members, he is reminded by several students of organizations[11] that such objectives are generally highly ambiguous, if not controversial, and therefore difficult to identify and measure.

The same kind of criticism can be applied to those who rely on the organization's charter, whether formal or informal, as containing the main identifying features of the organization, including its goals. Such an approach is represented by Bakke; he refers to the organization's charter, in the broad sense of the term, as expressing ". . . the image of the organization's unique wholeness." Such an image is created by ". . . selecting, highlighting, and combining those elements which represent the *unique* whole character of the organization and to which

uniqueness and wholeness all features of the organization and its operations tend to be oriented."[12] The reader is left puzzled about how to discover the goals of the organization even after knowing that they are contained somewhere in the "image of the organization's unique wholeness."

The difficulty of identifying the ultimate goal of an organization is illustrated by some of the research on mental hospitals and other "total" institutions, as discussed by Vinter and Janowitz and, particularly, by Perrow and Etzioni.[13] Many of these institutions have been judged to be ineffective since they fail to achieve their presumed therapeutic goals. Vinter and Janowitz demonstrate, however, that the goal of therapy is held only by a limited segment of the public, and that the institutions themselves are oriented mainly to custody, not therapy.

Etzioni elaborates upon this issue as follows:

> When the relative power of the various elements in the environment are carefully examined, it becomes clear that, in general, the sub-publics (e.g., professionals, universities, well-educated people, some health institutions) which support therapeutic goals are less powerful than those which support the custodial or segregating activities of these organizations. Under such conditions, most mental hospitals and prisons must be more or less custodial.[14]

This observation, like Starbuck's argument quoted above, amounts to saying that organizational goals are essentially nothing more than courses of action imposed on the organization by various forces in its environment, rather than preferred end-states toward which the organization is "striving." Such a perspective on the nature of organizational goals seems to undermine the rationale behind the use of goals as a yardstick for assessing organizational effective-

478 ness. How, we may ask, can a given social unit be regarded as "effective" if it cannot even determine its goals for itself, i.e., if the reference is wholly to the needs of entities other than itself? It would seem that the capacity of an organization to attain its own goals is a consideration of higher priority than that of success in attainment of imposed goals. An adequate conceptualization of organizational effectiveness cannot therefore be formulated unless factors of organization-environment relationships are incorporated into its framework.

Finally, it is not only in its external environment that the organization is faced with a variety of forces exerting influence on its behavior. The organization itself is composed of a large variety of individuals and groups, each having its own conceptions about any claims on the organization. The managers of an organization do not wholly agree among themselves about the organizational goals; in addition it is not certain that these goals, even if agreed upon, would prevail. This complicated reality is highlighted by the analysis of Cyert and March. They warn against the confusion in understanding organizational behavior whenever any one individual or group, such as the top management, is selected to represent the organization as a whole:

> The confusion arises because ultimately it makes only slightly more sense to say that the goal of the business organization is to maximize profit than it does to say that its goal is to maximize the salary of Sam Smith, Assistant to the Janitor.[15]

These considerations, taken together, seem to cast a serious doubt on the fruitfulness of the goal approach to organizational effectiveness. This is not to suggest that the concept of organizational goals should be rejected in toto. For certain analytical purposes it is useful to abstract some goal as an organizational property. In the study of persons in organizational settings, the concept of goal is useful and perhaps essential.[16] In the study of organizational effectiveness, however, the goal approach has appeared as a hindrance rather than as a help.

The Functional Approach to Organizational Effectiveness

The functional approach to organizational effectiveness can be characterized as "normative" in the sense that the investigator reports what the goals of an organization are, or should be, as dictated by the logical consistency of his theory about the relationship among parts of larger social systems. From this point of view, the functional, or derived goal, approach has an important advantage over the prescribed goal doctrine since it appears to solve the problem of identifying the ultimate goals of complex organizations: Given the postulates and premises of the functional model about the nature of organizations and their interconnectedness with the total social structure one can derive from it the specific goals of an organization, or of a class of organizations. This is evident mainly in the work of Parsons, one of the outspoken advocates of functional analysis, in his suggestions for a theory of organizations.[17] The Parsonian scheme also illustrates, however, a major weakness inherent in the functional approach. This weakness can be usefully discussed in terms of "frames of reference."

Organizations, or other social units, can be evaluated and compared from the perspectives of different groups or individuals. We may judge the effectiveness of an organization in relation to its own welfare, or we may assess how successful the organization is in contributing to the well-being of some other entities.

While the selection of a given frame of reference is a question of one's values and interests, the distinction among them must be clearly made and consistently adhered to. Vital as this requirement appears to be, one encounters various treatments of effectiveness that implicitly or explicitly refer to different frames of reference interchangeably, as if effectiveness from the point of view of the organization itself is identical with, or corresponds to, effectiveness viewed from the vantage point of some other entity, such as a member, or owner, or the community, or the total society.

The point of departure for Parsons' analysis of complex organizations is the "cultural-institutional" level of analysis. Accordingly, "The main point of reference for analyzing the structure of any social system is its value pattern. This defines the basic orientation of the system (in the present case, the organization) to the situation in which it operates; hence, it guides the activities of participant individuals."[18] The impact of the value pattern, furthermore, is felt through institutional processes which ". . . spell out these values in the more concrete functional contexts of goal-attainment itself, adaptation to the situation, and integration of the system."[19] These functional prerequisites, including the value pattern, are universally present in every social system. Their specific manifestations and their relative importance, however, vary according to the defining characteristic of the system and its place in the superordinate system. In the case of complex organizations, their defining characteristic is the primacy of orientation to the attainment of a specific goal. This goal, like all other organizational phenomena, must be legitimated by the value pattern of the organization. The nature of this legitimation is a crucial element in Parsons' analysis; the following quotation shows its relevance for the present discussion as well:

> Since it has been assumed that an organization is defined by the primacy of a type of a goal, the focus of its value-system must be the legitimation of this goal in terms of the functional significance of its attainment for the superordinate system, and secondly, the legitimation of the primacy of this goal over other possible interests and values of the organization and its members.[20]

In terms of our analysis, this states explicitly that the focal frame of reference for the assessment of organizational effectiveness is not the organization itself but rather the superordinate system. Not only must the ultimate goal of the organization be functionally significant in general for that system but, in the case of a conflict of interests between it and the organization, the conflict is always resolved in favor of the superordinate system—since the value pattern of the organization legitimates only those goals that serve that system. In other words, the *raison d'être* of complex organizations according to this analysis, is mainly to benefit the society to which they belong, and that society is, therefore, the appropriate frame of reference for the evaluation of organizational effectiveness. In order to avoid misunderstanding in this respect the following illustration is provided by Parsons:

> For the business firm, money return is a primary measure and symbol of success and is thus part of the goal structure of the organization. But it cannot be the primary organizational goal because profit-making is not by itself a function on behalf of the society as a system.[21]

Now there is no argument that the organization, as a system, must produce some important output for the total system in order to receive in return some vital input. However, taking the organization itself as the frame of reference, its

A SYSTEM RESOURCE APPROACH

480   contribution to the larger system must be regarded as an unavoidable and costly requirement rather than as a sign of success. While for Parsons the crucial question is "How well is the organization doing for the superordinate system?" from the organizational point of view the question must be "How well is the organization doing for itself?"

It was suggested earlier that a major weakness of the goal approach has been its failure to treat the issue of organizational autonomy in relation to organizational effectiveness. This seems to be the Achilles heel of the functional approach as well. In Parsons' conception of organizations, and of social systems in general there exists the tendency to overemphasize the interdependence among the parts of a system and thus, as argued by Gouldner, fail ". . . to explore systematically the significance of variations in the degree of interdependence," ignoring the possibility that ". . . some parts may vary in their dependence upon one another, and that their interdependence is not necessarily symmetrical."[22]

Gouldner's proposition of "functional autonomy" may be examined on several different levels. For example, one may regard the organization itself as the total system, looking for variations in the degree of autonomy among its own parts; this has been the focus of Gouldner's analysis. But the same line of analysis can be attempted at a different level, where society is taken as the total system. Here the investigator may be exploring variations in the degree of autonomy of various parts and sub-systems, an instance of which are complex organizations. Such an analysis underlies the typology offered by Thompson and Mc-Ewen, in which the relations between organizations and their environments are conceived in terms of the relative autonomy, or dominance, of the organization vis-à-vis its environment.[23]

The proposition of functional autonomy implies that organizations are capable of gearing their activities into relatively independent courses of action, rather than orienting themselves necessarily toward the needs of society as the superordinate system. Under such assumptions it is difficult to accept as a working model of organizations the proposition that the ultimate goal of organizations must always be of functional significance for the larger system.

Comparing the goal and the functional approaches, it can be concluded that both contain serious methodological and theoretical shortcomings. The goal approach, while theoretically adhering to an organizational frame of reference, has failed to provide a rationale for the empirical identification of goals as an organizational property. The functional approach, on the other hand, has no difficulty in identifying the ultimate goal of the organization, since the latter is implied by the internal logic of the model, but the functional model does not take the organization as the frame of reference. Furthermore, neither of the two approaches gives adequate consideration to the conceptual problem of the relations between the organization and its environment.

A System Resource Approach to Organizational Effectiveness

The present need, to which we address our attention, is for a conception of organizational effectiveness that: (1) takes the organization itself as the focal frame of reference, rather than some external entity or some particular set of people; (2) explicitly treats the relations between the organization and its environment as a central ingredient in the definition of effectiveness; (3) provides a theoretically general framework capable of encompassing different kinds of complex organizations; (4) provides some latitude for uniqueness, variability and change, with respect to the specific operations for assessing effectiveness applicable to any one organization, while at the same time maintaining the unity of the underlying framework for comparative evaluation; (5) provides some guide to the identification of performance and action variables relevant to organizational effectiveness and to the choice of variables for empirical use.

A promising theoretical solution to the foregoing problems can be derived from the open system model as it is applied to formal social organizations. This model emphasizes the distinctiveness of the organization as an identifiable social structure or entity, and it emphasizes the interdependency processes that relate the organization to its environment. The first theme supports the idea of treating formal organizations not as phenomena incidental to individual behavior or societal functioning but as entities appropriate for analysis at their own level. The second theme points to the nature of interrelatedness between the organization and its environment as the key source of information concerning organizational effectiveness. In fact, most existing definitions of organizational effectiveness have been formulated, implicitly or explicitly, in terms of a *relation* between the organization and its environment, since the attainment of a goal or the fulfillment of a social function imply always some change in the state of the organization vis-à-vis its environment. The crucial task, then, is the conceptualization of that relation. The system model, with its view of the nature of the interaction processes between the organization and its environment, provides a useful basis for such a conceptualization.

According to that model, especially as applied to the study of organization by Katz and Kahn,[24] the interdependence between the organization and its environment takes the form of input-output transactions of various kinds relating to various things; furthermore, much of the stuff that is the object of these transactions falls into the category of *scarce and valued resources*. We shall have more to say about "resources" below. For the moment it will suffice to indicate that the value of such resources is to be derived from their utility as (more or less) generalized means for organizational activity rather than from their attachment to some specific goal. This value may or may not correspond to the personal values of the members of the organization, including their conception of its goals. It should be noted also that scarce and valued resources are, for the most part, the focus of competition between organizations. This competition, which may occur under different social settings and which may take different forms, is a continuous process underlying the emergence of a universal hierarchical differentiation among social organizations. Such a hierarchy is an excellent yardstick against which to assess organizational effectiveness. It reflects what may be referred to as the "bargaining position" of the organization in relation to resources and in relation to competing social entities that share all or part of the organization's environment.[25]

We propose, accordingly, to define the effectiveness of an organization in terms of its bargaining position, as reflected in the ability of the organization, in either absolute or relative terms, to exploit its environment in the acquisition of scarce and valued resources.

The concept of "bargaining position" implies the exclusion of any specific goal (or function) as the ultimate criterion of organizational effectiveness. Instead it points to the more general capability of the organization as a resource-getting system. Specific "goals" however can be incorporated in this conceptualization in two ways: (1) as a specification of the means or strategies employed by members toward enhancing the bargaining position of the organization; and (2) as a specification of the personal goals of certain members or classes of members within the organizational system. The better the bargaining position of an organization, the more capable it is of attaining its varied and often transient goals, and the more capable it is of allowing the attainment of the personal goals of members. Processes of "goal formation" and "goal displacement" in organizations are thus seen not as defining ultimate criteria of effectiveness, but as strategies adopted by members for enhancing the bargaining position of their organizations.

The emphasis upon the resource-getting capability of the organization is not intended to obscure other vital aspects of organizational performance. The input of resources is only one of three major cyclic phases in the system model of organizational behavior, the other two being the throughput and the output. From this viewpoint the mobilization of resources is a necessary but not a sufficient condition for organizational effectiveness. Our definition, however, points not to the availability of scarce and valued resources as such, but rather to the bargaining position with regard to the acquisition of such resources as the criterion of organizational effectiveness. Such a position at a given point of time is, so far as the organization's own behavior is concerned, a function of all the three phases of organizational behavior —the importation of resources, their use (including allocation and processing),

and their exportation in some output form that aids further input.

By focusing on the ability of the organization to exploit its environment in the acquisition of resources we are directed by the basic yet often neglected fact that it is only in the arena of competition over scarce and valued resources that the performance of both like and unlike organizations can be assessed and evaluated comparatively. To put it somewhat differently, any change in the relation between the organization and its environment is affected by and results in a better or worse bargaining position vis-à-vis that environment or parts thereof.

It should be noticed that the proposed definition of effectiveness does not imply any specific goal toward which an organization is striving, nor does it impute some societal function as a property of the organization itself. Our definition focuses attention on *behavior*, conceived as continuous and never-ending processes of exchange and competition over scarce and valued resources.[26] We shall now discuss some of the concepts central to our definition of organization effectiveness.

Competition and Exchange

Our emphasis upon the competitive aspects of interorganizational relations implies that an assessment of organizational effectiveness is possible only where some form of competition takes place. This raises the question of how general or limited is the scope of applicability of our definition, since interorganization transactions take forms other than competition. An old and useful distinction in this respect has recently been formulated by Blau:

A basic distinction can be made between two major types of processes that characterize the transactions of organized collectivities—as well as those of individuals, for that matter—competitive processes reflecting endeavors to maximize scarce resources and exchange processes reflecting some form of interdependence. Competition occurs only among like social units that have the same objectives and not among unlike units . . . Competition promotes hierarchical differentiation between more or less successful organizations, and exchange promotes horizontal differentiation between specialized organizations of diverse sort.[27]

Blau's assessment that ". . . competition promotes hierarchical differentiation between more or less *successful* organizations" is, of course, in line with our definition of organizational effectiveness; furthermore, there is no question about the mainly competitive character of relations among "like" social units.

However, Blau's contention that competition occurs *only* among like organizations is an oversimplification. Indeed, it is difficult to point to any interrelated organizations that are not in competition with respect to some kinds of resources, and it is easy to point to organizations that are dominantly competitive, yet have some complementarity and interdependence in their relations. A university and a business firm, for example, may be involved in an exchange of knowhow and money, and still compete with respect to such resources as manpower and prestige. The type of pure complementarity of exchange is very limited indeed. We suggest, accordingly, that exchange and competition are the extremes of a continuum along which interorganizational transactions can be described. The proposed definition of effectiveness allows then for the comparative evaluation of any two or more organizations that have some elements of rivalry in their relations. Such a comparative evaluation becomes more meaningful—in the sense of encompassing the crucial dimensions

of organizational behavior—as the variety and number of competitive elements in these relations increases. The clearest and most meaningful comparison obtains when the evaluated organizations compete directly for the same resources. This condition implies that the compared organizations are engaged in like activities and share to a large degree the same temporal and physical life space. In such cases the comparison is facilitated by the fact that the competition refers to the same kinds of resources and that the assessment variables—both of input and output—are measured in like units. Comparisons are also possible, however, in the case of organizations that do not compete directly, but that compete in environments that are judged to be similar in some relevant respects.

As the characteristic transactions between organizations come closer to the exchange pole of the continuum the problem of comparison becomes more complex: first, the elements of competition may be very few in number and peripheral in importance, thus making the comparison trivial; second, the more unlike the organizations, the more difficult it is to measure their performance units on common scales. In any case, the identification of the competitive dimensions in interorganizational transactions is the key problem in the assessment of organizational effectiveness. Some clarification and possible ways of solution for this problem can be achieved through an examination of the concept of "resources."

Resources

A key element in this definition is the term "resources." Broadly defined, "resources" are (more or less) generalized means, or facilities, that are potentially controllable by social organizations and that are potentially usable—however indirectly—in relationships between the organization and its environment. This definition, it should be noted, does not attribute directionality as an inherent quality of a resource, nor does it limit the concept of resources to physical or economic objects or states even though a physical base must lie behind any named resource. A similar approach to "resources" is taken, for example, by Gamson. He argues that the "reputation" of individuals or groups as "influentials" in their community political affairs is itself a resource rather than simply ". . . the manifestation of the possession of large amounts of resources. . . ."[28]

One important kind of resource that is universally required by organizations, that is scarce and valued, and that is the focus for sharp competition, is energy in the form of human activity. The effectiveness of many organizations cannot be realistically assessed without some accounting for the organization's bargaining position with respect to the engagement of people in the service of the organization. One thinks, of course, of competition in the industrial or managerial labor market, but the idea is equally applicable to the competition, say, between the local church and the local political party, for the evening time of persons who are potentially active in both organizations.

Since human activity is such a crucial class of organizational resource, we elaborate on the meaning that is intended and one of the implications. We view members of an organization as an integral part of the organization with respect to their organizational role-defining and role-carrying activities, but as part of the environment of the organization with respect to their abilities, motives, other memberships, and other characteristics that are potentially useful but not utilized by the organization in role performance. An "effective" organization competes successfully for a relatively large share of the member's personality, engaging more of the personality in organizationally relevant ways, thus acquiring additional resources from its environment.

A number of other distinctions may usefully be made with respect to the resources that are involved in the effectiveness of organizations:

1. *Liquidity*. Some resources are relatively "liquid" in the traditional economic sense of that term and are readily exchangeable by an organization for resources of other kinds. Money and credit are highly liquid, being exchangeable for many other (but not all) kinds of resources. By contrast, the resource represented by high morale (among members) is relatively low in liquidity; under some conditions, it is not directly exchangeable at full value in transactions with other organizations but must be internally transformed, e.g., into products or services, before exchange. Some organizations are characterized by having a large proportion of their resources in relatively non-liquid forms.

2. *Stability*. Some resources are transient in the sense that they must be acquired and utilized continuously by an organization, while other resources have the property of being stored or accumulated without significant depreciation. An organization that acquires a rapidly depreciating resource and fails to utilize this resource within an acceptable period will suffer loss of part of the value. The current high turnover among technical staff in some industrial firms is an example of loss of effectiveness through failure to utilize transient resources. By contrast, money is a highly stable resource that can be stored indefinitely at small loss and can be accumulated against future exchange requirements.

Political influence is a resource of notorious instability.

3. *Relevance.* In principle, all resources are relevant to all organizations to the extent that they are capable of transformation and exchange. The degree of relevance, however, is of considerable interest, since identification of resources of high relevance offers a guide to a useful classification of organizations and serves to direct priority in comparative analyses to those kinds of resources that most clearly reflect the relative bargaining power of organizations. Degree of relevance also has a bearing upon the analysis of symbiotic relationships among organizations (high rates of exchange with relatively little bargaining and high mutual benefit) and upon the analysis of monopolistic forces (dominance of a given resource "market" and consequent enhancement of bargaining power). The degree of relevance of a given resource can be estimated on an *a priori* basis from a knowledge of the typical outputs of an organization and a knowledge of its characteristic throughput activities. Critical resources might be discerned from an analysis of changes in the pattern of internal organizational activity, for such changes can be interpreted to be a response to an enhanced requirement or a threatened deficit with respect to a given type of resource. Organizations are frequently observed to mobilize activities in a way that enhances their power to acquire certain resources. A judgment of future organizational effectiveness might accordingly be improved by information concerning the organization's ease of adaptation to shifts among classes of resources in their degree of relevance.

4. *Universality.* Some resources are of universal relevance in the sense that all organizations must be capable of acquiring such resources. The universally required classes include: (1) personnel; (2) physical facilities for the organization's activities; (3) a technology for these activities; and (4) some relatively liquid resource, such as money, that can be exchanged for other resources. The amount required of each class may in some cases be very modest, but all organizations must have, and must be able to replenish, resources of these kinds. The non-universal resources are, in general, those for which competition is limited, either because of irrelevance to many organizations or because the particular resource is ordinarily obtained amply through symbiotic exchange.

5. *Substitution.* Organizations with similar typical outputs competing in a common environment do not necessarily share the same roster of relevant and critical resources. One reason for this is that the internal processes of organizational life may be adapted to exploit certain readily available resources rather than to acquire alternative scarce resources in hard competition. An example of this is seen in the case of a small, ill-equipped guerrilla army facing a force of superior size and equipment. While exploiting rather different resources, they may compete equally for the acquisition of territorial and political control.

A crucial problem in this context is the determination of the relevant and critical resources to be used as a basis for absolute or comparative assessment of organizational effectiveness. In stable, freely competitive environments with respect to relatively liquid resources, this determination may be rather easy to make, but under other conditions the determination may be problematic indeed. The difficulties arise primarily in cases in which the competing organizations have differential access to relatively rich or relatively poor environments, where symbiotic exchange relationship may develop, where the resources are not universal, and where the possibilities of substitution are great. In such situations, the analytic approach must employ not a static conception of the relationships between an organization and its environment but rather, a conception that emphasizes adaptation and change in the organizational patterns of resource-getting.

Optimization vs. Maximization

In their recent analysis of complex organizations, Katz and Kahn proposed defining organizational effectiveness as "the maximization of return to the organization by all means."[29] This definition shares with the one we propose an emphasis on resource procurement as the sign of organizational success; it differs, however, in invoking the notion of maximization, a concept we have avoided. The position taken here is that maximization of return, even if possible, is destructive from the viewpoint of the organization. To understand this statement it should be remembered that the bargaining position of the organization is equated here with the ability to exploit the organization's environment—not with the maximum use of this ability. An organization that fully actualizes its exploitative potential may risk its own survival, since the exploited environment may become so depleted as to be unable to produce further resources. Furthermore, an organization that ruthlessly exploits its environment is more likely to incite a strong organized opposition that may weaken or even destroy the organization's bargaining position. Thus, the short-run gains associated with over-exploitation are likely to be outweighted by greater long-run losses. Also, the resource itself may lose value if over-exploited; for example, an effective voluntary community organization may enjoy extraordinary bargaining power in the engagement of prestigeful people, but this power may not safely be used to the maximum, because excessive recruitment risks the diminishing of the value of membership when membership ceases to be exclusive.

These considerations lead to the proposition that the highest level of organizational effectiveness is reached when the organization maximizes its bargaining position and optimizes its resource procurement. "Optimum" is the point beyond which the organization endangers itself, because of a depletion of its resource-producing environment or the devaluation of the resource, or because of the stimulation of countervailing forces within that environment. As stated by Thompson and McEwen:

> It is possible to conceive of a continuum of organizational power in environmental relations, ranging from the organization that dominates its environmental relations to one completely dominated by its environment. Few organizations approach either extreme. Certain gigantic enterprises, such as the Zaibatsu in Japan or the old Standard Oil Trust in America, have approached the dominance-over-environment position at one time; most complex organizations, falling somewhere between the extremes of the power continuum, must adopt strategies for coming to terms with their environment.[30]

We may add, however, that the need "for coming to terms with their environments" applies to organizations that approximate the dominance-over-environment extreme as well. A powerful enterprise like General Motors must exercise its potential power with much restraint in order to avoid the crystallization of an opposition which may weaken its bargaining power considerably, through legislation or some other means.

It is of course very difficult, if possible

at all, to determine in absolute terms the organization's maximum bargaining position and the optimal point of resource procurement that is associated with that position. Since most organizations, however, fall short of maximizing their bargaining position, the optimization problem, though theoretically important, is only of limited empirical relevance. In practice, organizational effectiveness must be assessed in relative terms, by comparing organizations with one another. The above discussion on the nature of "resources" provides at best a general outline for carrying out such a task. A more detailed discussion and a preliminary effort to apply empirically the conceptual scheme presented here is reported elsewhere.[31] Briefly, the following steps seem necessary for a meaningful comparative assessment of organizational effectiveness: (1) to provide an inclusive taxonomy of resources; (2) to identify the different types of resources that are mutually relevant for the organizations under study; and (3) to determine the relative positions of the compared organizations on the basis of information concerning the amount and kinds of resources that are available for the organization and its efficiency in using these resources to get further resources.

Some Implications

We end this discussion with a few speculations about the impacts that might arise from a general acceptance and use of the conception of organizational effectiveness that we have proposed. These may affect theorists, empirical researchers and managers in various ways:

1. The rejection of the concept of an ultimate goal, and the replacement of this singular concept with one emphasizing an open-ended multidimensional set of criteria, will encourage a broadening of the scope of search for relevant criterion variables. Past studies have tended to focus too narrowly upon variables derived from traditional accounting practice or from functional social theory, or on narrowly partisan "goals" attributed to organizations. A conception of organizational effectiveness based upon organizational characteristics and upon resource-acquisition in the most general sense will encourage the treatment as criteria of many variables previously regarded as by-products or incidental phenomena in organizational functioning.

2. Past comparative studies of organizations have, in general, been of two kinds: (1) Comparison of organizations differing markedly in their characteristics, e.g., prisons and factories, so that issues of relative effectiveness were deemed irrelevant and uninteresting as well as impractical; and (2) comparisons among organizations of a similar type, so that they could be compared on like variables and measurement units. The conception we offer provides the possibility of making accessible for study the large middle range of comparisons involving organizations that have only limited similarities such that they compete with respect to some but not all of their relevant and crucial resources.

3. Case studies of single organizations will be aided by the provision of a conceptual basis for treating a more inclusive and more realistic range of variables that bear on the effectiveness of the organization.

4. The meaning of some familiar variables will need to be reassessed and in some cases changed. For example, distributed profit, a favorite variable for the comparative assessment of business organizations, will be more widely recognized as a cost of organizational activity and not as an unequivocal sign of success or goal achievement. Some

managers have already adopted this view. Similarly, growth in size, usually interpreted as a sign of organizational achievement, can now be better seen as a variable whose meaning is tied closely to environmental factors and to the position of the organization with respect to certain other variables; the conception we have presented highlights the idea that growth in size is not in itself an un- mitigated good, even though it may mean greater effectiveness under some conditions. In a similar fashion, it will be seen as necessary that the judgment of the meaning of each criterion variable rests not upon an absolute value judgment or a universal conceptual meaning, but rather upon the joint consideration of an extensive integrated set of organizational performance and activity variables.

NOTES

1. Daniel Katz and Robert L. Kahn, *The Social Psychology of Organizations,* New York: Wiley, 1966, p. 149.
2. Basil S. Georgopoulos and Arnold S. Tannenbaum, "A Study of Organizational Effectiveness," *American Sociological Review,* 22 (October, 1957), pp. 534–540; Mason Haire, "Biological Models and Empirical Histories of the Growth of Organizations," in Mason Haire, ed., *Modern Organization Theory,* New York: Wiley, 1959, pp. 272–306; Amitai W. Etzioni, "Two Approaches to Organizational Analysis: A Critique and a Suggestion," *Administrative Science Quarterly,* 5 (September, 1960), pp. 257–278; Robert M. Guion, "Criterion Measurement and Personnel Judgments," *Personnel Psychology,* 14 (Summer, 1961), pp. 141–149; Charles Perrow, "Organizational Goals," in *International Encyclopedia of Social Sciences,* 1964 edition, pp. 854–866; Stanley E. Seashore, "Criteria of Organizational Effectiveness," *Michigan Business Review,* XVII (July, 1965), pp. 26–30.
3. James G. March and Herbert A. Simon, *Organizations,* New York: Wiley, 1958; Etzioni, *op. cit.;* Perrow, *op. cit.;* Seashore, *op. cit.;* Katz and Kahn, *op. cit.*
4. Chester I. Barnard, *The Functions of the Executive,* Cambridge: Harvard University Press, 1938; Peter F. Drucker, *The Practice of Management,* New York: Harper, 1954.
5. Robert Michels, *Political Parties,* Glencoe, Ill.: The Free Press, 1949; William J. Baumol, *Business Behavior, Value and Growth,* New York: Macmillan, 1959; James K. Dent, "Organizational Correlates of the Goals of Business Management," *Personnel Psychology,* 12 (Autumn, 1959), pp. 365–393; Carl M. White, "Multiple Goals in the Theory of the Firm," in Kenneth E. Boulding and W. Allen Spivey, editors, *Linear Programming and the Theory of the Firm,* New York: Macmillan, 1960, pp. 181–201; Bertram M. Gross, "What Are Your Organization's Objectives? A General-System Approach to Planning," *Human Relations,* 18 (August, 1965), pp. 195–216.
6. Katz and Kahn, *op cit.,* p. 15.
7. Etzioni, *op. cit.,* p. 258.
8. Etzioni, *op. cit.,* p. 258.
9. William H. Starbuck, "Organizational Growth and Development," in James G. March, ed., *Handbook of Organizations,* Chicago: Rand McNally, 1965, p. 465.
10. Chadwick J. Haberstroh, "Organization Design and Systems Analysis," in James G. March, ed., *Handbook of Organizations,* Chicago: Rand McNally, 1965, pp. 1171–1211.
11. Abraham D. H. Kaplan, Joel B. Dirlam, and Robert F. Lanzillotti, *Pricing in Big Business,* Washington: Brookings Institution, 1958; Richard M. Cyert and James G. March, "A Behavioral Theory of Organizational Objectives," in Mason Haire, ed., *Modern Organization Theory,* New York: Wiley, 1959, pp. 76–90.
12. E. Wight Bakke, "Concept of the Social Organization," in Mason Haire, ed., *Modern Organization Theory,* New York: Wiley, 1959, pp. 16–75.
13. Robert Vinter and Morris Janowitz, "Effective Institutions for Juvenile Delinquents: A Research Statement," *Social Service Review,* 33 (June, 1959), pp. 118–130; Charles Perrow, "The Analysis of Goals in Complex Organizations," *American Sociological*

14. Etzioni, op. cit., p. 264.

15. Cyert and March, op. cit., p. 80.

16. Alvin F. Zander and Herman M. Medow, "Individual and Group Levels of Aspiration," Human Relations, 16 (Winter, 1963), pp. 89–105; Alvin F. Zander and Herman M. Medow, "Strength of Group and Desire for Attainable Group Aspirations," Journal of Personality, 33 (January, 1965), pp. 122-139.

17. Talcott Parsons, "Suggestions for a Sociological Approach to a Theory of Organizations—I," Administrative Science Quarterly, 1 (June, 1956), pp. 63–85; Talcott Parsons, Structure and Processes in Modern Societies. New York: The Free Press, 1960, pp. 16–96.

18. Parsons, op. cit., 1956, p. 67.

19. Parsons, op. cit., 1956, p. 67.

20. Parsons, op. cit., 1956, p. 68.

21. Parsons, op. cit., 1956, p. 68.

22. Alvin W. Gouldner, "Organizational Dynamics," in Robert K. Merton et al., eds., Sociology Today, New York: Basic Books, 1959, p. 419.

23. James D. Thompson and William J. McEwen, "Organizational Goals and Environment: Goal-Setting as an Interaction Process," American Sociological Review, 23 (February, 1958), pp. 23–31.

24. Katz and Kahn, op. cit.

25. The differential amounts of success of organizations with regard to their bargaining positions implies the possibility of exploitation of one organization by another, a possibility which may endanger the stability of social order. The asymmetry in inter-organizational transactions and its consequences for the problem of social order underlie the sociological interest in exchange processes and their normative regulation. As pointed out recently by Blau:

    Without social norms prohibiting force and fraud, the trust required for social exchange could not serve as a self-regulating mechanism within the limits of these norms. Moreover, superior power and resources, which often are the results of competitive advantages gained in exchange transactions, make it possible to exploit others. (Exchange and Power in Social Life, New York: Wiley, 1964, p. 255.)

    Blau's discussion is concerned mainly with the more limited case of exchange between individuals as social actors. Nevertheless, it points to the potential asymmetry involved in exchange processes in general and the consequences of such asymmetry, namely, the emergence of a hierarchical differentiation among the interacting units with regard to their exploitative ability. For the purposes of the present discussion it is important to note that such an advantageous bargaining position, which may be dysfunctional for the system as a whole, is from the organization's point of view a sign of its success.

26. One reader of an early draft of this paper, Dr. Martin Patchen, inquired about the sources of directive energy in goal-less organizations. The answer is that persons who are members of the organizations, and acting both within their role prescriptions and in idiosyncratic deviations from role prescriptions, import personal values and goals which may modify the system in a directed way.

27. Peter Blau, Exchange and Power in Social Life, New York: Wiley, 1964, p. 255.

28. William A. Gamson, "Reputation and Resources in Community Politics," American Journal of Sociology, 72 (September, 1966), pp. 121–131.

29. Katz and Kahn, op. cit., p. 170.

30. Thompson and McEwen, op. cit., p. 25.

31. Stanley E. Seashore and Ephraim Yuchtman, "The Elements of Organizational Performance." A paper prepared for a symposium on "People, Groups and Organizations: An Effective Integration of Knowledge," Rutgers University, November, 1966. (This paper will appear in Administrative Science Quarterly, 1967.); Ephraim Yuchtman, A Study of Organizational Effectiveness, unpublished Ph.D. dissertation, the University of Michigan, 1966.

A SYSTEM RESOURCE APPROACH

ADDITIONAL READINGS

Clark, Burton R. 1956. "Organizational Adaptation and Precarious Values: A Case Study," *American Sociological Review,* 21 (June), 327–336.

Frederickson, H. George. 1967. "Human Resources in Public Organization," *International Review of Administrative Sciences,* 33, 336–344.

Grusky, Oscar. 1959. "Role Conflict in Organization: A Study of Prison Officials," *Administrative Science Quarterly,* 3 (March), 452–472.

Lynton, Rolf P. 1969. "Linking an Innovative Subsystem into the System," *Administrative Science Quarterly,* 14 (September), 398–416.

McNulty, James E. 1962. "Organizational Change in Growing Enterprises," *Administrative Science Quarterly,* 7 (June), 1–21.

Simon, Herbert A. 1964. "On the Concept of Organizational Goal," *Administrative Science Quarterly,* 9 (June), 1–22.

Simpson, Richard L., and William H. Gulley. 1962. "Goals, Environmental Pressures, and Organizational Characteristics," *American Sociological Review,* 27 (June), 344–351.

CHAPTER NINE

General
Studies

The papers in this final chapter are "general" in that either they introduce dimensions of the external environment previously unexplored, or they discuss the effects of some combination of environmental factors on the organization. The reader should apply concepts, models, and theories from previous chapters while perusing these general studies.

Ditz's studies of three business organizations lead him to the generalization that "different functions require different structures." This insight and his practical-level suggestions are highly consonant with the empirically based "contingency theory" of Lawrence and Lorsch (1967). According to this theory, there is no one best way to organize or manage. The decision to use either "classical" or "human-relations" organization theory depends on external environmental conditions. Neither theory is a panacea. Following Lawrence and Lorsch, it appears that an organization characterized by an informal structure and widely shared influence (that is, one characterized by a "human-relations" orientation) is in a good position to cope with uncertain, unstable, and heterogeneous environmental elements. On the other hand, organizations or their subsystems transacting with certain, stable, and homogeneous environmental elements can cope most advantageously by using a "tighter" organizational structure, in terms of formalization of structure and concentration of influence nearer the top of the structure (that is, an organization characterized by a more "classical" orientation).

Ditz views the internal organizational system as determinate, or closed, by means of status ascription, bureaucratic controls and organization men. The external system is conceptualized as indeterminate, or open, because of status achievement, charismatic relationships, and marginal men. In terms of James Thompson's output-structure typology (Chapter 4), the members of the external system would probably be slotted in cell IV.

In a seminal paper, Thompson identifies three sources of conflict in organizations, two of which are clearly exogenous. He delineates the type of conflict associated with each source and discusses the organization's sequential defense mechanisms for each type. He advances a series of propositions about vulnerability to and control over conflict in three types of organizations and situations. Administrators who hope to understand and deal with conflict effectively will find Thompson's organizational rather than interpersonal approach to conflict instructive and will find it valuable to reflect upon the propositions he advances and the defense mechanisms he describes.

In a scenario of the twenty-first century, Shonfield attempts to determine whether the social authority of the large corporation will be expanded. He examines some probable trends in the relationships between the large corporation and significant others in its organization-set, namely, consumers, shareholders, organized labor, and government. Each relationship is viewed as providing constraints on as well as opportunities for the expansion of corporate authority. The reader may find it interesting to isolate those predictions that pertain to the firms' continuing search for more certainty in their relationships with environmental elements.

Two papers in the additional reading section are noteworthy. In a classic article, Dill reports the effect of different task environments on the autonomy of top-management groups in two Norwegian business firms. The task environment, comprised of four elements, is defined as "stimuli that the organization might respond to," in terms of their relevancy for goal-setting and goal attainment. Dill found that the key men in the clothing manufacturing firm had less autonomy "both with respect to their direct superiors and with respect to one another" than did those in the sales-engineering-contracting firm.

A comparison of the task environments of the two firms indicated that the differences in autonomous executive behaviors appeared to be associated with six differences in external task environments and seven internal constraints. James Thompson (1967, pp. 72–73) has built a model relating the impact of the task environment on the structure of boundary-spanning units that uses two of Dill's descriptions of the task environment, homogeneity-heterogeneity and stable-shifting. Lawrence and Lorsch's (1967) comparative case study of firms in three different industries, and the derivation of a contingency theory therefrom, provides more recent support of Dill's data, finding

that instability, uncertainty, and heterogeneity are associated with a
"looser" organization structure.

In a case study of professional architectural-engineering firms,
Brown relates the effects of a shifting task environment on the perspective of personnel, the addition of new roles, and the firms'
strategies and domains. One might speculate whether the architectural-engineering firms' environments are moving into the turbulent-
field stage (see papers by Emery and Trist, and by Terreberry in
Chapter 2, and by McWhinney in Chapter 8).

REFERENCES

Lawrence, Paul, and Jay Lorsch. 1967. *Organization and Environment.*
   Boston: Division of Research, Graduate School of Business Administra-
   tion, Harvard University (Ch. 7 and 8).
Thompson, James. 1967. *Organizations in Action.* New York: McGraw-
   Hill.

THE INTERNAL-EXTERNAL DICHOTOMY IN BUSINESS ORGANIZATIONS

Gerhard W. Ditz

Sociologists may contribute to the understanding of business organizations by applying relevant sociological concepts and generalizations, derived and validated from sociological research at large, in the analyses of specific business problems. This paper is based on a re-examination of certain data collated originally in a series of discrete studies for three business organizations. These companies are leaders in their respective industries of life insurance, communications services, and advertising directories. The original studies covered such topics as effectiveness and morale of sales and marketing organizations, compensation systems, and supervisory and personnel practices compared in sales and nonsales (engineers, office workers) groups.

External Versus Internal

For purposes of this study, "external" operations were defined as those activities in which the employee's primary task requires directly relating himself to people outside his company. All other business operations or functions—plant, office, engineering, and accounting—are referred to as "internal." In these three companies, sales constituted by far the most important external operation. Other external operations such as marketing, advertising, public relations, and cus-tomers' services are therefore generally ignored here.

This conceptual distinction between internal and external operations reflects in some degree current administrative practices and verbal usages. Organization charts, job descriptions, compensation systems, office locations, and hiring practices often reveal this distinction. Where other indicators are absent, the employees concerned may acknowledge this dichotomous structure when describing their work situation.

Separate but Equal

The degree of structural differentiation between external and internal operations depends on the comparative status of the two functions in the corporate image. If management views the two as equally important, the differentiation tends to be larger. Alternatively, when one group of functions is clearly subordinate to the other, the differentiation is minimized.

Comparing the three companies in this study, it may be said that the co-equal status of internal and external operations was most clearly acknowledged in the insurance company, and the structural differentiation was stronger there than in the other two companies. Insurance company sales were handled by organizationally separate agency depart-

"The Internal-External Dichotomy in Business Organizations," *Industrial Management Review*, 6, 1 (Fall 1964), 51–57. Reprinted with the permission of the author and of the publisher, the *Industrial Management Review*.

496 ments, each having its own management hierarchy. The agency managements were connected with the internal (home office) organizations only at the next-to-the-highest corporate level. The agency departments had their own supporting staff groups, maintained distinct recruitment, training, and compensation systems, and at most levels occupied separate office locations. In addition, there were attribute variances between external and internal personnel, both on expected variables such as age and sex and on less obvious characteristics such as religious, ethnic, and national background; for example, minority groups were much more heavily represented among sales personnel. Significantly different earnings and turnover distributions were associated with the structural differentiation. Further, though transfers between different home office departments (that is, within the internal organization) and transfers between different agencies (that is, within the external organization) were quite frequent, such transfers were infrequent between home offices and agencies. This held true at all levels and geographical locations.

The communications services company exemplified weak structural differentiation, with the external function subordinate to the internal. The company's quasi-public utility status inhibited vigorous marketing. The sales groups were attached at a fairly low level to the management hierarchy of the internal system. Marketing and related staff functions operated parallel to sales. The latter came under the same personnel controls as the internal departments. Thus sales people were recruited largely from the same pool as were plant and office workers. Essentially the same compensation system prevailed, and the same career opportunities were open to

all. Crossing of personnel between sales and non-sales was as frequent as between any other departments. Differences in background and performance between external and internal personnel, as noted in the insurance company, were absent here.

The directory publisher, too, exemplified minimal structural differentiation, but here the external function was superordinate. Publication of the directory depended directly upon successful sale of advertising space. Management consisted of persons moving up from successful selling experience. All external and internal operations reported to them. Personnel systems and practices were not differentiated. Whatever their starting job, the more ambitious gravitated toward sales. Those who had made the grade in selling, but no longer could or wanted to pursue it, found a niche in the internal operations. The customary contrast between insiders' salaries and salesmen's commissions was partly erased through flexible salary ranges and individualized bonuses, and the results pointed up again the dominance of the external system. Differences in backgrounds between external and internal personnel were small. The characteristics identified with external personnel in the insurance company (e.g., high minority group representation, high turnover, and high income variability) predominated throughout the directory publishing company. (In the communications services company the characteristics of the internal personnel were dominant in the sales division.)

Examining the Proposition Against Changes over Time

These cases support the proposition that where external and internal functions have equal recognition their structural differentiation will be maximized; and to the extent that there is inequality, the stronger function will impose its structure on the weaker one.

Such a proposition can be strengthened if it can be shown to hold true through changes in the organization or operating goals of a company. Such changes did indeed occur in two of the companies studied. The communications service company undertook changes to focus more sharply on marketing, as indicated by increases in its market research, advertising budget, and product diversification efforts; this was accompanied by an increase in structural differentiation, in accordance with the proposition. The sales management line was extended and strengthened, and some marketing functions were subordinated to it. Changes were introduced into sales recruiting, training, and compensation, making these distinct from the overall corporate systems. The directory company moved to isolate and strengthen some of the internal functions against the overpowering status of sales. Internal departments and staff positions, at one time subordinate to sales, now reported directly to higher management. Outsiders were brought in for some jobs in internal functions, and it was understood that theirs would be career positions, rather than niches for super-annuated or tired sales personnel.

How Valid Are These Propositions?

Apart from the obvious limitation that our propositions are empirically validated by only three cases, what is their theoretical and practical significance? The proposition that a business will keep external and internal functions administratively apart to the extent it recognizes their co-equal status expresses the abstract generalization that different functions require different structures. At a more practical level, it suggests that an increase in structural differentiation will improve the performance of both functions and particularly will improve the performance of the subordinate activities.

In support of these propositions is the common observation that the organization of the typical sales force differs significantly from that of the typical office; these differences are meaningfully inter-related. For example, office supervision tends to be more direct, sales supervision more indirect. Associated with this are typical differences in compensation methods based on salaries in contrast to commissions. Inter-related with these are differences in turnover, work attendance, and earning fluctuations. Less obviously connected are differences in recruiting, selection, and training policies, in work incentives and motivation, and in the types of persons attracted to these varying work situations. Indeed, these many and meaningfully inter-related variances suggest that we are dealing here with different patterns or social systems which can be characterized by conventional sociological attributes.

Status Ascription and Achievement[1]

Like all organizations, business firms develop and maintain status systems. These are collections of rights and duties associated with different positions. They express themselves in the reciprocal behavior of the individuals occupying these positions. Sociologists distinguish between two types of status; that which is ascribed to the individual without distinct reference to his special ability and that which can be achieved only through individual ability as expressed in competitive performance.

Our external-internal division constitutes a reference line for this status typology. Ascribed status is more commonly found internally, whereas status achievement is characteristic for the external system. In internal operations, management assigns the rights and duties associated with a particular position; included here are span of control, range of supervision, level and mode of compensation, title, size of office, and other tangible and symbolic status attributes. Status is not ascribed arbitrarily. Management stands and falls by its ability to match positions and individuals. The goodness of fit must be recognized eventually by associates and subordinates alike. In the long run management must back the natural winner, but in the short run the appointee's prestige will reflect the status of those who have appointed him. For a while, at any rate, he will receive the prestige of his new position, regardless of his actual performance.

Ascribing status ahead of individual performance increases the probability that all required roles will be enacted and that gaps in the institutionalized behavior patterns will be minimized. But as assignments precede the demonstration of the individual's suitability, performance tends to be adequate, not exceptional. Status ascription promotes average collective performance rather than above-average individual performance; it makes for stable, uniform, and continuous organizational behavior. Such attributes are desirable in internal systems, relatively isolated from their external environment. External operations lack this isolation, which is, indeed, one reason why status has to be achieved here. External encounters take place in the ever-changing market, the moving frontier of business. Though influencing customers and public are traditional business objectives, as long as the customer is sovereign management cannot ascribe rights and duties to the reciprocal behavior of salesman and customer. Thus the status situation of salesman and others dealing with the public differs radically from that of internal employees. Management may give the salesman a larger territory, better accounts, more and different lines of goods, superior compensation, a better sounding title, a larger office. All these however, are only pseudo-attributes of status. They do not make the customer buy. Nor will the salesman's associates acknowledge these status symbols, unless they are backed up by personal accomplishments. Management status cannot be deflected here; all management can do is acknowledge ex-post-facto the individual achievement.

A status system based on achievement does not assure that all roles will be enacted. It tends instead to enhance variations in performance as between individuals. This means that in the typical sales organization, at any particular time, some salesmen will not sell at all and others will do exceptionally well, partly because of variations in individual talent and partly because of outside factors. There is less stability and continuity in the performance of external groups compared to internal ones, but there is a higher probability of exceptional individual performance.

Bureaucracy Versus Charisma

The concepts of bureaucracy and charisma, originating in the historical sociology of Max Weber, match in some significant respects the dichotomy developed here.[2] Bureaucratic controls in Weber's sense are eminently suitable for such internal operations as the organization of an office. They promote efficiency through clearly defined work roles and through a formal hierarchy of authority. Impersonal procedures govern the minutiae of individual and collective behavior. The results are orderly, stable work relations, predictable actions, calculable results. These usually compensate for typical bureaucratic drawbacks such as red tape, ritualism, and over-routinization.[3]

By contrast, bureaucratic controls are inappropriate for external operations such as selling, advertising, and promotion. Marketing targets and promotional strategies are too impermanent to be usefully controlled by formal rules. External roles are less definable and results less calculable; customer relations are too personal to be effectively subjected to impersonal supervisory authority. Formal procedures cannot identify and mobilize the highly individualized abilities which produce results. These depend on charismatic relationships, with emphasis on the novel, unique, and creative.[4] Natural leadership here takes the place of formal authority. Charismatic abilities are not acquired or learned; they appear in the form of unpredicted accomplishments. Notwithstanding claims to the contrary, the secret of success in a particular advertising or selling campaign is identified only after the event, if at all. Such success usually defies imitation or replication by other individuals and in other situations. It cannot be formalized or routinized.

On the external side managerial methods are bound to be less scientific in external groups than in internal ones. Personnel actions in external groups are typically confined to eliminating obvious failures and thus improving the group average. The charismatic or extraordinary talent can best be discovered or attracted by providing a favorable organizational environment.

Organization Man Versus Marginal Man

Our typology can further be refined against the frame of reference of two other conceptual models which, independently from one another, codify personality types and social processes. In *The Organization Man*, William H. Whyte, Jr., depicts the inordinate influence of the contemporary business organization on its employees, whose total personality becomes integrated into the organizational image.[5] The ensuing over-adjustment and over-conformity spills into the nonbusiness sphere, becoming a way of life which threatens traditional values of initiative and individuality.

Whyte's characterization is pertinent for the attitudes of our internal personnel. But it fits members of external groups so poorly that the latter in this context appear as antiorganization men. Whyte thus supports indirectly the validity of our polarization. His characterization applied to both internal and external systems, on the assumption that there is only one organization, would show that the internalist is most integrated into the organizational image and the externalist is least so. The salesman tends to be a nonconformist in regard to his company's rules and customs. He is unstable in his work habits, unpredictable in his results, uncertain and ambivalent in his loyalties. These traits are consistent with our proposition that the salesman does not belong to the company's internal system. He cannot meaningfully conform to rules which do not

500 effectively apply to the market. The salesman must divide his loyalties between employer and customer, choosing between demands on his behavior which originate in both these domains.

This profile puts the externalist into another and quite different model described by Everett V. Stonequist in *The Marginal Man*.[6] This construct describes the racial or cultural hybrid and other socially dislocated individuals "who through migration, education, marriage, or some other influence leave one social group or culture without making a satisfactory adjustment to another, find themselves on the margin of each but a member of neither."[7] Though original model and applications did not explicitly encompass occupationally engendered marginality, they describe behavior patterns which are frequently encountered in external groups.[8] The externalist, too, lives in two societies—in intimate association with the world about him but never so identified with it that he is unable of critical detachment.[9] Notwithstanding his appearance of personal warmth, the salesman, like the marginal man, operates with cool calculation, for only thus is he able to cope with the cross-pressures to which he is inevitably exposed.[10] These manifestations of marginal behavior do not result exclusively from an individual's efforts to adapt to his occupation; sales positions attract persons whose backgrounds stimulate such traits. Earlier cited observations showing that socially ambitious members of underprivileged groups are statistically overrepresented in sales, are appropriate to this point. It is the marginal person's social frustration which encourages uninhibited occupational climbing and makes sales jobs attractive to him. Business can profit from these private frustrations and compulsive strivings if the compensatory aggressiveness is turned outwards rather than allowed to produce internal friction. Marginal man and external job therefore constitute a natural match. Moreover, frequent role-switching, needed in direct selling, is endemic to the marginal personality. So is another important trait of the salesman: the ability to combine overt empathy with covert emotional detachment. Just as the organization man constitutes an ideal typical model for our internal system, the marginal man provides the ideal for the external system.

Formal Organization and Informal Groupings[11]

In all organizations there are spontaneous clusters of congenial associates, friendship and gossip groups, cliques, and grapevines. Their structure may reflect spatial, occupational, or status proximity. Small in size and developing through face-to-face encounters, these groups constitute foci around which powerful sentiments are mobilized. Feelings of togetherness, the team spirit, and the illusion that the big corporation is only one large family are generated here.

Relative to the large, formal organization, these informal groupings have rightly been viewed as primary. They can as easily impede as support the formal organization.[12] To cite examples from the author's own studies, informal groups favorably propagandized management policy, helped newcomers to get adjusted, and enhanced the objectives of work contests by organizing unscheduled overtime; but cliques also undermined a new incentive plan, mobilized discontent to unseat an unpopular supervisor, and demoralized trainees by spreading false rumors.

Informal groupings arise in both internal and external operations. Where the two structures are insufficiently differentiated, the informal groups tend to orient themselves in opposition to the formal objectives because the latter are felt to discriminate against the weaker system. The informal groups then act as a protection or evasion device for the disaffected personnel and as a rallying point for the opposition to centralized management. If these informal activities are effective they may modify the formal organization towards structural differentiation. However, informal groups also may be the mechanism through which the formal organization develops its cohesiveness. To promote cohesion, management brings together employees from across departments and levels to meet face-to-face in informal gatherings such as parties, outings, and athletic activities.

External operations in general require less organizational cohesion than do internal operations. Management should not over-stimulate informal groupings in its external system. Salesmen perform better with less group integration, and they require less group support than employees in plant or office. Salesmen's need for sociability is normally satisfied through the relationship with the customer. The salesman must not become so attached to the familiarity and social warmth of his office that he shuns the cold canvass of strange prospects. Closeness to his fellow-salesmen must not pre-empt his capacity to get close to his customers.

Conclusion and Applications

The internal-external polarity results from variances in social systems rather than business objectives. The internal system is determinate in so far as its members can be expected to act out prescribed roles. Though adherence to these is never perfect, the more complete is this adherence the more efficient is the operation. The internal system can be viewed as closed to the extent that internal activities and behavior can be controlled and predicted. This reiterates earlier discussions of "ascribed status," "bureaucracy" and "organization man."

The external system is indeterminate or open. Actions of customers, prospects, and public can only be influenced, not prescribed. The effectiveness of company prescriptions is problematic even for its own external employees.

Roles constitute interactions based on reciprocal expectations. Within the internal system the company can effectively prescribe how employee X should act towards employee Y, because it can at the same time prescribe how Y is to react to X. But to prescribe effectively for salesmen requires predicting the prospects' reactions, and the prospects' independence renders such predictions hazardous indeed. Our proposition as to the structural differentiation of external operations is based upon the sovereignty of the customer.

In the absence of adequate differentiation, the stronger function imposes its structure on the weaker one; our communications services company imposed its internal structure on an already weak marketing operation and the directory publisher structured its internal departments according to the needs of its sales force. The ensuing incongruities were due to the fact that administrative controls and supervisory techniques appropriate to one system do not fit the other.

External roles (as different from internal) cannot be reliably defined in an organization chart alone. External behavior is less amenable to planning be-

502 cause it has to adjust to forces outside of management's purview; occupational success and the employee's contribution to the company are more dependent on abilities developed before the employee joined the company. Salesmen typically operate within plural and competing loyalties. They switch roles easily and always remain emotionally detached. These traits are not acquired in the company's training course; they are inherent in marginal personalities. Recruiting and selection skills are thus of great importance in the external group, whereas training and direct supervision are relatively more important internally. These differences are further accentuated by the fact that when non-conformist, anti-organization personalities are recruited into the external departments they enter minimally organized groups. The desirable charismatic qualities can only be demonstrated through unpredictable accomplishments, and these alone produce status here. These qualities, however, are associated with marginal backgrounds or personalities prone to social maladjustment. The recruiting manager's problem is to decide how much maladjustment and how many marginal personalities his organization can safely tolerate.

Beyond recruitment, management's external task is largely to successfully deploy the newly found talent and to determine the boundaries within which members of the external group can operate autonomously. Apart from this, the supervisory role should preferably be confined to supportive counselling and problem-solving, with the manager acting as the resource man; there is little place for systematic rules and routinized procedures.

The validity of our typology does not require the two systems to be mutually exclusive. Internal operations can also become too bureaucratized, their personnel starved of competitive stimuli and unable to adjust to change. On the other hand, the marginal or non-conformist disposition of the externalist may go too far and disrupt the minimally cohesive external organization. Some status ascriptions occur externally, too, and the internal system has to allow for some individual status achievements. Finally, structural differentiation does not mean that there cannot and should not be a sphere of common policy and administration embracing the two systems. The need is for distributions of the cited variables which are distinctly different for the external and internal groups, each constituting a consistent and meaningful pattern justifying the notion of polarized systems.

NOTES

1. Sociological concepts and definitions used here are standard to many contemporary texts; for example, see [1].
2. See [2], pp. 196–216, 245–252; and [3], pp. 363–373, 386–392.
3. For these disadvantages of bureaucracy, see [4], pp. 195–206.
4. "Charisma," meaning "special grace" in its Scriptural origin, was used by Weber in various typological contexts, including as the polar opposite to "bureaucracy;" see [2], pp. 245–252.
5. See [5], pp. 1–13, *passim*.
6. See [6].
7. *Ibid.*, pp. 2–3.
8. The special relevance of the "marginal man" to the modern marketplace was already recognized by Professor Robert E. Park of the University of Chicago, who guided Stonequist's study; see *ibid.*, p. xiv.

9. *Ibid.*, pp. 2–9, *passim.*
10. *Ibid.*, pp. 2–9, 201–222.
11. This basic dichotomy is discussed in practically every sociology primer; see, for example, [7], pp. 218 ff.
12. See [8].

REFERENCES

Linton, Ralph, "Status and Role," a chapter in Wilson and Kolb, *Sociological Analysis*, New York, Harcourt, Brace and Company, 1949, pp. 211–233.

Gerth, Hans H., and Mills, C. Wright, *From Max Weber*, New York, Oxford University Press, 1958.

Weber, Max, *The Theory of Social and Economic Organization*, translated and edited by T. Parsons and A. M. Henderson, Glencoe, Illinois, The Free Press, 1947.

Merton, Robert K., *Social Theory and Structure*, Glencoe, Illinois, The Free Press, 1957.

Whyte, William H., Jr., *The Organization Man*, New York, Simon and Schuster, Inc., 1956.

Stonequist, Everett V., *The Marginal Man*, New York, Russell and Russell, Inc., 1961.

MacIver, R. M., and Page, Charles M., *Society*, New York, Rinehart and Company, Inc., 1949.

Roethlisberger, F. J., and Dickson, William J., *Management and the Worker*, Cambridge, Massachusetts, Harvard University Press, 1947.

ORGANIZATIONAL MANAGEMENT OF CONFLICT[1]

James D. Thompson

Conflict in organizations is usually considered by students of organizations and by administrators in our culture as something to be avoided or eliminated. This reflects a popular preoccupation with morale, human relations, and co-operation, and the general value that peace is good and conflict bad. As a result the literature of organization and administration has focused on the settlement of specific instances of conflict, for which human-relations, morale-building techniques may be appropriate.[2]

But there are important questions to be raised about organization-wide management of conflict, as distinct from the local settlement of conflict. The purpose of this paper is to add to our understanding of (1) the sources of conflict within organizations, (2) the vulnerabilities of different organizations to conflict, and (3) the devices employed by organizations to control conflict.

Attention will not be confined to de-

"Organizational Management of Conflict," *Administrative Science Quarterly*, 4, 4 (March 1960), 389–409. Reprinted with the permission of the author and of the publisher, *Administrative Science Quarterly*.

504 vices deliberately employed by administrators to control conflict, but will include patterns that may have been developed for very different purposes. In specific cases they may even have evolved without formal, conscious consideration; they may have been borrowed, unwittingly, from other organizations. Whether organizations employ control mechanisms out of habit, tradition, or design is not an important question here. If planned processes are to be understood, they must first be seen as part of the larger context.

Conflict is identified here simply as *that behavior by organization members which is expended in opposition to other members.*

Sources and Forms of Organizational Conflict

TECHNOLOGY AND
ADMINISTRATIVE ALLOCATION

It has long been known that specialization of activity and responsibility in complex organizations is accompanied by questions about the division of rewards and of resources for achieving rewards.

Some standards for equating inducements and contributions arise in every organization to handle problems associated with division of labor and resources, but official standards do not always prevent feelings of relative deprivation,[3] which may, in turn, lead to conflict. Soldiers, for example, may feel that the "top kick" runs the army but that the "shavetail" gets the privileges. Foremen may feel that they keep the company going, although the boss participates in a stock bonus plan. Professors may believe that *they* are the university but that fund-raising officers get the high salaries.

The more complex the division of labor, the more difficult the formulation and application of standards for equating inducements and contributions. Even when organization members accept abstract standards as fair and legitimate, they may complain about their interpretation and application in specific instances. When organization members compare themselves to other members, to the extent that they believe they contribute more in proportion to their awards, to that degree will they have feelings of deprivation.

A particular technology may set minimum requirements, not only for differentiation but also for communication or interaction between those performing differentiated activities. While differentiation per se may not lead to conflict, interaction of members of different categories makes comparisons likely and may lead to conflict. But while differentiation and interaction are intrinsic to modern technologies, organizations usually have alternatives in assigning specific activities and responsibilities to specific members, and also in dividing inducements. These matters are largely subject to administrative discretion, to be settled by habit, precedent, or deliberate decision. We may therefore refer to conflict based on feelings of relative deprivation as *conflict generated by administrative allocations.*

That alternatives are available within the framework of a given technology is easily illustrated. In industrial circles, the relative merits of functional versus product division for the same kind of work are often debated. In governmental circles, similar debates occur over areal and functional divisions.

Chester I. Barnard has pointed out that specialization may be based on (a) the place where work is done; (b) the time at which work is done; (c) the persons with whom work is done; (d) the things upon which work is done; and (e) the method or process by which work is done.⁴ But it must be emphasized that the choice of one criterion for specialization does not necessarily exclude the others; it simply specifies which has priority. The manufacturing firm which organizes along product-division lines, for example, often finds that the geography of its market requires sales staffs and warehousing and delivery systems which cut across and blur product lines. Whatever the form of organization, the differences in the aggregate of activities is probably far less significant than the differences of grouping and hence of interaction required of members.⁵

The systems by which inducements are allocated are also subject to administrative discretion within rather wide limits established by organizational technologies. Hierarchical differentiation is an indispensable feature of organizations containing two or more primary groups, but the number of categories and their pervasiveness are not fixed. The number of ranks in the military organization, for example, has not been constant through even modern history. The military organization also affords a good example of categorization which in the official ideology is all pervasive: officer and enlisted distinctions are to be maintained in every type of relationship.

In addition to hierarchical differentiation, most organizations also categorize their members in other ways to facilitate the distribution of rewards and penalties. The American military system classifies its members as regular, reservist, or National Guard; the Air Force distinguishes rated (qualified to fly) from nonrated (or ground duty only) personnel. Rewards or penalties are distributed partly on the basis of the member's category.

While categorizations of these types seem indispensable for modern complex organizations, their number and nature are not necessarily fixed; administrators have choices in these matters.

In summary we are saying that technologies require differentiation and interaction, but that organizations have some control over (1) the number of categories and (2) the patterns of interaction among members of different categories. *Hence within limits administrative allocations determine the relative deprivations experienced by organization members, and thereby control potential conflict inherent in modern technologies.*

LABOR FORCE AND LATENT ROLES

In the complex cultures in which formal organizations exist, there is a wide variety of distinctions between categories of persons. Many of these social and cultural distinctions are irrelevant to the official roles and technologies of a particular organization, but they may "spill over" into it. Each individual recruited into an organization brings to it not only the particular skills, beliefs, dispositions, and the like that are appropriate but also talents, beliefs, or attitudes that are irrelevant to the technology. Individuals may distinguish among themselves on a great many criteria, separating old from young, Yankees from rebels, Republicans from Democrats, friendly drinkers from abstainers. Racial and ethnic origins, family lineage, socioeconomic class, and religious beliefs are frequently applied.

In the "ideal type" conception of formal organization or bureaucracy the roles associated with such distinctions are usually irrelevant to the purposes and technology of the organization, and thus *remain latent* whenever members are acting on behalf of the organization.[6] We know, however, that empirically these nonorganizational roles of members can become active in organizational contexts. Nepotism, patronage, and favoritism are some examples.

The vulnerability of an organization to conflict based on latent roles depends largely on the composition of that portion of society from which the organization recruits.[7] The more heterogeneous the labor force, the greater the likelihood that members will possess differentiated latent roles as well as skills. The occupational needs of the organization thus place both imperatives and limitations on the types of individuals who can be considered potential members. To the extent that occupational qualifications are associated with particular latent roles, the organization seeking those qualifications must also accept the related latent roles. But the organization retains some discretion in the matter. *To the extent that recruitment and selection procedures limit diversity or maintain it within manageable patterns, the organization can manage the potential conflict in latent role diversity.*[8]

COMPETING PRESSURES AND ORGANIZATIONAL POSTURE

Organizations and their environments are interdependent, and actions by elements of the environment can create dilemmas for the organization. Whether dilemmas are handled by "minimax" methods, hunch, or other means, dissension often occurs among members who feel handicapped in their spheres of operation, and conflict between winning and losing factions may result. Debate over dilemma decisions may be as heated among those lacking power to make such choices as among the decision makers, and the debates may continue long after a commitment is made.

"The environment," of course is a residual term, and it seems useful to restrict our consideration to *task environments*.[9] We are not referring, therefore, to the total community or society, but to those parts of it that are not indifferent to the organization. The more heterogeneous the task environment, the more likely is the organization to be caught up in conflicting demands, expectations, or pressures. The extent of differentiation in the task environment may be beyond the control of the organization (although it may have some choice even here), but to the extent that the organization can choose between various *postures* relative to the task environment, it can manage conflict stemming from competing pressures.

The concept of "organizational posture" requires elaboration. We are referring to the *relationship* between an organization and its task environment, not to characteristics of either the organization or the environment per se. Since it is the relationship which is at issue, the organization does not have full discretion over its posture, but it can, by changing its structure, affect the relationship. Hence the management of organizational posture seems to have elements of gamesmanship, and game theory might be appropriately applied to its analysis.

One important aspect of organization posture is the degree of distinctiveness or eliteness possessed by the organization in relation to the task environment. The organization with a prestigefully unique, unusual, esoteric, or important competence is likely to enjoy appreciation, respect, or awe of the task environment, and thereby have members' identification and loyalty reinforced through interaction with the environment.[10]

Another important aspect of posture is the nature of exposure to the environment.[11] Under some conditions, at least, constant exposure of members tends to erode their identification with the organization. Apparently this is especially true when organization members are regularly in interaction with the same elements of the task environment, and less true when members interact with clients or customers on a one-visit basis.

The proportion of members exposed may vary from organization to organization and also make a difference in the kinds and numbers of problems faced. Where many members are exposed and their loyalties pull in different directions, the problems of maintaining membership identification undoubtedly are different from where conflicting demands and interests are focused on a few central offices and are resolved before being translated into programs for the organization at large.

Thus by varying the distinctiveness of the organization, the proportion of members exposed, and the frequency and regularity of their exposure, the organization gains a measure of control over conflict stemming from potential reactions to competing pressures.

Dynamics of Conflict Management

We have hypothesized so far that organizations face three types of potential conflict, that each rests on a different set of conditions, and that for each there is an appropriate defense:

In this section we will attempt to make the analysis somewhat more concrete and specific, and suggest that: (1) there are rather wide variations in the vulnerabilities of different organizations to the three sources of conflict, and (2) the defensive tactics may be interrelated. For this purpose a series of propositions will be advanced about vulnerability and control in three types of organizations and situations. The examples will not exhaust the possible combinations of technologies, labor forces, and task environment, but were chosen because they are sufficiently distinct to illustrate the possibilities. When available, supporting studies will be cited.[12]

THE IDEOLOGICAL ORGANIZATION

Many organizations have as their primary purpose the perpetuation or propagation of certain belief systems. This is particularly true of such voluntary associations as churches, "movement" organizations like the Women's Christian Temperance Union or the United Nations Association, and splinter political parties. But other organizations may on occasion adopt primarily ideological objectives, as, for example, the resistance army, the college committed to a great books program, or the established political party in a period of crisis. Welfare organizations and governmental agencies with a pioneering or reform mission may also operate as ideological organizations.

For the ideological organization a

Type of conflict	Source of conflict	Defense device
Administrative allocation	Technology	Organizational structure
Latent roles	Labor force	Recruitment and selection
Competing pressures	Task environment	Organizational posture

508   common belief in the objective or identification with it is essential and this requirement presents serious problems of conflict management to such organizations.

PROPOSITION 1: For the ideological organization, administrative allocation poses a threat, since it creates a basis for distinctions which may destroy or override the homogeneity of beliefs.

Defense 1A: If this organization can remain small and informal, it may escape the necessity for official allocation. Dynes concludes that "sectarian groups with their organizational simplicity and congregational similarity produce a type of loyalty, satisfaction, and religious intensity that complex religious organizations do not reproduce."[13] Tsouderos, in a study of growing voluntary associations, notes that increasing size brings both increasing heterogeneity of membership and formalization of administrative activities, which tend to alienate portions of the membership and lead to secession en masse.[14]

Defense 1B: If this organization cannot avoid the necessity for allocation of undesirable assignments, it may rely on volunteers on the basis of duty or the opportunity to demonstrate conviction, worthiness, or sincerity.

Defense 1C: If volunteers are not available, this organization may solve its allocation problems by reducing technical, economic, or efficiency norms. Personnel may be assigned to types of tasks consistent with their general social status, irrespective of demonstrated ability. In our society, for example, men would not be subordinated to women, older people to younger, veteran members to newcomers. Soemardjan noted that during the Indonesian revolution, when ideological solidarity of the population was essential, bureaucratic positions left vacant by the Japanese were filled not simply in terms of capability but also in terms of "acceptability."[15]

Defense 1D: If the organization cannot avoid noticeable allocation, it may rely on membership consensus for the allocation of rewarding or prestigeful responsibilities. Thus, if forced to employ a formal authority system, this organization may base it on member control or "democracy," thus taking the sting out of authoritative decisions and directives.

PROPOSITION 2: For the ideological organization, a heterogeneous labor force calls for special defenses to prevent the emergence of latent role conflict.

Defense 2A: This organization can exercise care in preadmission screening, with emphasis less on technical abilities than on latent-role factors such as "character." Sponsorship by members in good standing is a device frequently employed. Minnis, studying women's organizations in a heterogeneous city, found that at least 90 percent of the organizations in her sample were racially exclusive, 76 percent were religiously exclusive, and that within large religious divisions, further differentiation of clubs occurred according to race, ethnic origin, and social prestige. Division according to religion was found to take place *even when the type of association and the services rendered to the community were not of a religious nature.*[16] Soemardjan notes that in the emergent Indonesian army during revolution, military units were formed out of pre-existing groups; members of one unit were formerly fellow members of the same village, members of another unit had been members of the same religious organization, those in still another had been fellow students in the same school.[17]

Defense 2B: If initial recruitment cannot prevent heterogeneity of recruits, then training, testing, and the elimination of "misfits" may solve the problem of latent role differences. Complete or near-complete isolation of recruits from the environment while they are being indoctrinated, initiated, or "hazed" is not unusual. The isolation is frequently coupled with stern discipline, which indoctrinates recruits to the importance of giving priority to organizational norms and needs, and therefore of suppressing antagonistic latent-role attitudes.

Defense 2C: If this organization emphasizes the distinctiveness of its ideology, it may ensure the psychological insulation of members and thereby prevent the activation of latent roles. Thus ritualistic ceremonies, awards for meritorious service, and reaffirmations of faith are employed frequently, for they serve as reminders of the distinctiveness of the organization.

Defense 2D: If distinctiveness does not override latent role differences, the ideological organization may segregate its members and thereby confine interaction within groups of compatible backgrounds. Protestant denominations in small Southern communities thus maintain white and Negro congregations. Gusfield's study of the WCTU reveals that this organization, presumably founded on common convictions, contains two conflicting elements, grouped largely by age. He reports that conflict between the age groups is partially prevented by prevention of contact. Iota Sigma units, of younger people, meet in evenings, while the regular WCTU meets in the afternoons.[18]

PROPOSITION 3: The ideological organization is in a sense a combat organization,[19] and thus oriented to possible conflict with the task environment. Yet it must take special steps to ensure that its members do not subvert organizational objectives in their struggles with outsiders.

Defense 3A: If distinctiveness has been achieved (Defense 2C), it serves as a defense against the pressures of the task environment. But if the organization cannot gain sufficient distinctiveness, it may overcome the effects of competing stimuli by restricting exposure to a few members of tested and reinforced loyalty.

Defense 3B: If the organization cannot limit exposure to the few it may guard against competing stimuli by limiting the frequency of member exposure, or distributing exposure so that all members are exposed to all elements of the environment. Thus it may rotate members from one post to another, to give all members an opportunity to serve without developing sympathy for or identification with any one portion of the environment. Or it may practice periodic rotation of exposed members for reindoctrination, including periodic retreats, conventions, or training programs, which exhort rather than instruct. Blau observes in a federal law enforcement agency that agents' duties require that they remain detached, conciliatory, and constantly alert in complex investigations and negotiations, even in the face of aggressive respondents. Their needs to restore composure and depleted energies were met through relaxing contacts with friendly colleagues. In a governmental employment agency, Blau also notes that employment interviewers who engaged more often in private discussions with coworkers generally treated clients more objectively.[20]

THE GIANT ENTERPRISE

The phrase "giant enterprise" is used here to refer to those organizations which have nonideological purposes,

510 highly subdivided technologies, and which do not confine their activity to a local community. Our largest industrial firms fit this category, as do federal and state governments, and the military services. America's larger universities probably tend to fall here, although they often contain overtones of ideological orientation.

PROPOSITION 4: Required technological specialization makes differentiation of members unavoidable, the number of possible categories of distinction quite large, and hence the potential for feelings of relative deprivation enormous.

Defense 4A: This organization may become distinctive, in fact or by myth, so that the net advantages of membership are felt to outweigh the disadvantages, compared with other members' rewards. The institutional advertising of the Marine Corps or the Bell Telephone System may be as important in maintaining membership as in recruiting.

Defense 4B: The myth of homogeneity and equality being impossible, the giant enterprise may take pains to show that administrative allocation of responsibilities, resources, and rewards is done strictly on the basis of technical, economic, or efficiency considerations. Gouldner, reporting on a wildcat strike in a gypsum plant, notes that the agreement which ended the strike did so by way of delimiting spheres of competence and authority, centralizing the hierarchical system, extending the sway of formal rules, and reinforcing the propriety of impersonal attitudes within the plant.[21]

Defense 4C: When empirical criteria for allocation are lacking, the organization may seek legitimacy for its administrative allocations by calling on outside authorities, such as consultants, thus transferring the responsibility for unpopular decisions.

Defense 4D: This organization may reduce interaction of different specialized members or groups by organizing them into technologically homogeneous units. Thus accountants frequently are grouped with other accountants, sociologists with other sociologists.

Defense 4E: This organization, moreover, may de-emphasize comparisons, by underprivileged members, of other members. It may emphasize instead the situations of similarly classified persons in other organizations. The complexity of the giant enterprise and, usually, of its environment, affords a large number of possible *reference groups.*[22] Therefore sociologists may be discouraged by the university from comparing their inducements and contributions with those of accountants in the same university and may be urged instead to remember how many sociologists elsewhere are in worse positions. To the extent that the organization has a role in influencing the *saliency* of certain possible reference groups over others, it may control conflict in some measure.

PROPOSITION 5: For the giant enterprise it is the lack of active latent (or unofficial) roles, rather than their activation, which constitutes a threat to harmony. Repeated official emphasis on technical, economic, and efficiency norms tends to reinforce differentiation and to minimize communication or interaction, and the inadequacy of communication between interdependent parts becomes a source of conflict in the organization.

Defense 5A: The giant enterprise may group members drawn from a heterogeneous labor force in ways which will foster the activation of homogeneous latent roles. Shils and Janowitz, studying cohesion and disintegration of Wehrmacht units in World War II, note that cohesion as evidenced by low rates of desertion and surrender was highest in those units composed exclusively of Germans, and was less in groups of heterogeneous ethnic composition in which Austrians, Czechs, and Poles were intermixed with each other.[23]

Defense 5B: The giant enterprise may promote the activation of latent roles by masking latent role differences which would set members apart. By reducing those factors which would discourage interaction and solidarity, it may thus permit the identification by members of common bonds.[24] Dornbusch notes that the military organization requires "uniform" apparel as a means of masking latent role differences. In the military academy, uniforms are issued on the first day and discussions of wealth and family background are taboo. Dornbusch concludes that "there are few clues left which will reveal social status in the outside world."[25]

Defense 5C: The giant enterprise may promote the activation of latent roles that crisscross official distinctions. As has frequently been noted, overlapping roles and values in heterogeneous groups may reduce cleavage on any one issue and may also serve to facilitate the resolution of conflict. Thus bowling teams, office parties, coffee breaks, football pools, and other "mixers" may activate latent roles, help members discover that other members are "human," and help them "find something in common." Blau notes that the Christmas party "enhanced the solidarity of the members of the entire agency in several ways." It permitted the official to experience a feeling of "belonging." By providing interactions between members of different departments and between different hierarchical positions, it strengthened the relations between officials who had little opportunity for informal contacts during office hours. Drinking lowered the barriers against convivial inter-

action created by differences in official status. Dancing forced officials to cross status lines, since most women occupied clerical positions and most men professional ones.[26]

Defense 5D: As a final defense against those latent roles which are not easily controlled, giant organizations frequently develop training programs to ensure the *local* settlement of conflict based on latent role differences.

PROPOSITION 6: The strains and stresses generated by technological differentiation make the giant enterprise particularly vulnerable to conflict generated by actions of the task environment, since the giant enterprise usually faces a heterogeneous task environment.

Defense 6A: This organization may try to homogenize its task environment by standardizing its treatment of environmental elements, so that clients get uniform client-treatment, suppliers get standardized receptions, and so on. Differential treatment of elements of the task environment may be perceived as discriminatory treatment, and elements that feel relatively deprived can direct hostility toward the organization. Rules and procedures may therefore be sought to ensure that each exposed member of the organization reacts in identical fashion to similar situations.

Defense 6B: If the task environment cannot be homogenized, this organization may establish semiautonomous branches, each dealing with one class of environmental element. This not only tends to reduce the potential threat of competing stimuli, but may also have the added advantage of reducing vulnerability to administrative allocations. To the extent that branches are autonomous, interaction between heterogeneous branches is reduced, and hence feelings of relative deprivation are less

512　likely to develop. The advantages of wholly-owned subsidiaries may not be confined to the legal and income-tax aspects. Chandler's survey of large American firms reveals trends toward decentralized autonomous management units, with centralized firms prominent only if their activities were restricted to one line of products.[27] In Dill's study of Norwegian firms, the firm with the more heterogeneous task environment revealed considerably more decentralization and autonomy of departments. Where the nature of outside demands precluded complete autonomy, conflict was likely. Moreover, in the more centralized firm, new policies or relationships with the environment suggested by one group were more likely to interfere with the plans or commitments of others.[28]

Defense 6C: If the giant enterprise in a heterogeneous task environment is unable to avoid conflict either by altering its internal structure or by changing its posture, it may resort to widening its boundaries, thus encompassing what formerly were elements of the task environment. This may be achieved through co-optation or through merger. This seems to be the most difficult defense, for it involves inevitably (a) change of environment, (b) change of structure, and (c) change of posture.[29]

THE LOCAL ENTERPRISE

By this we mean organizations employing highly elaborated, differentiated technologies, but differing from the giant enterprise not only in size but also in their markets or clienteles, which tend to be restricted to the same geographic territory that supplies the labor force and other resources. The community hospital and community college usually fall into this category, which also includes the local government or social work agency. Often business firms in service industries would fit here, to the extent that they employ elaborate technologies.

Because of space limitations, we will deal only with the local enterprise in a relatively homogeneous community. One of the significant characteristics of this situation is that relationships among members of the community, whether members also of the organization or of its task environment, are highly intertwined. When the community hospital asks elements of the task environment for monetary contributions, it often is asking individuals who have been patients, or who sell materials to the hospital, or who have been involved in disputes with the hospital over tax exemptions. Members of the community college staff may interact with neighbors who pay taxes to support the college or have children attending it.

We suggest that despite the technological similarities of local and giant enterprises, the local enterprise has conflict vulnerabilities and defenses that tend to be parallel to those of ideological organizations. Yet the local enterprise differs from the ideological organization, too, for it cannot be as selective in recruitment and has greater interdependence with the task environment than does the combat-oriented ideological organization.

PROPOSITION 7: The local enterprise in a relatively homogeneous community unavoidably has a disruptive role, for it must allocate responsibilities and rewards differentially among members drawn from that homogeneous community.

Defense 7A: This organization often will relax technical, economic, or efficiency norms, and attempt to train recruits to acceptable levels of performance of technical tasks, thereby ensuring that latent-role traditions will be stronger than the divisive forces. Garceau, in his study of libraries, found that in old, stable, homogeneous communities, library boards tended to favor local librarians, and it was a great advantage to be a native, if not of the town, county, or state, at least of the section. This was particularly true of the South, he reported, where the necessity of recruiting trained personnel from the North presented a serious problem in library and community relations.[30] Gouldner found the personnel selection criteria in the gypsum plant tended to exclude "city" people and to favor local community people, especially farmers, people adhering to traditional values and respected by their community. He also found an "indulgency" pattern whereby supervisors tempered the performance of their managerial roles by taking into account obligations that would be relevant for relationships among friends and neighbors.[31] Kennedy, reviewing research on industrial grievance negotiation, noted that despite the usefulness of formal systems and procedures, a great many disputes were settled through a highly informal process in most plants and shops. Settlements were negotiated in face-to-face contact between people who ordinarily knew each other well. Informality, in this context, meant among other things a minimum of preoccupation with legalism or with consistent interpretation of agreements. This informality, he concluded, was "amenable to many 'bootleg' and extra-legal tactics and pressures."[32]

Defense 7B: The local enterprise in a homogeneous environment may take pains to disclaim distinctiveness, emphasizing that its members are "your neighbors." If forced to import specialists for its technology, this organization encourages them to become part of the community by establishing homes there and taking part in community events.

Defense 7C: If the organization cannot blend into its environment, it may reduce the competing effects of stimuli by reducing the exposure of its members, focusing exposure on its most presentable members and hiding the more atypical ones.

PROPOSITION 8: If the homogeneous community is suddenly divided, the local enterprise is particularly vulnerable to latent role conflict. Because of the many linkages among members of the local community, a community issue is not easily confined to a few channels. Elements of the task environment may press the enterprise to take a stand, and latent roles may be activated in organizational contexts.

Defense 8A: This organization may attempt to foresee events in the environment, which threaten harmony with that environment, and may attempt to find early solutions—even when such action is beyond the scope of the organization's "real" purpose. Coleman observed that the charge "subversive" against school teachers will divide some communities into opposing camps; other communities will unite to protect the teachers, while still others will unite against teachers. In an issue over children's books, he found that the early, unified response of prestigeful people drew to their side the whole community, and Coleman concludes that if there had been any split in opinion among the really prominent men in town, the concern over their children's books expressed by ordinary citizens in the beginning of the dispute would undoubtedly have grown into a conflict of sizable proportions.[33] It would seem that astute leaders would take an early and active part in securing such "unified response of prestigeful people."

Defense 8B: If the organization is not able to prevent environmental controversies, it may attempt to remain aloof from them. If it has achieved indistinction (see Defense 7B) it is probably more able to avoid being drawn into the issue. Coleman observes strong pressures for an organization to remain neutral when the community in which it operates develops controversies. If organization members hold opposing sentiments, he reports, their disharmony forces the organization itself to remain neutral. Moreover, the organization must maintain a public position in the community which might be endangered by taking sides in a partisan battle.[34] In studying the church, Glock and Ringer observe not only that the membership is divided in its attitudes toward labor, but also that the church exists in a broader community in which this divergency of viewpoint is also reflected, and that the church's equivocal official position on these matters seems to represent an attempt to conciliate both sides.[35]

PROPOSITION 9: The local enterprise in a homogeneous community often faces a dilemma, stemming from competing pressures to optimize technological considerations on the one hand and to acquiesce to the local climate on the other. These stresses are likely to divide the more highly skilled or professional members from the less skilled members, and imported specialists may form the nucleus of those critical of the efforts of the local community.

This generalization may not hold for those instances where the local community is composed of highly skilled, professional families. The public school system in a suburban community composed of highly educated professional families seems to support rather then challenge school objectives, although conflict may occur over means.

Defense 9A: The only defense for this situation seems to be the appointment of one or more administrators who are able to maintain the commitments of organization members in spite of compromises. To the extent that this is the main mechanism, it suggests that the local enterprise in a homogeneous community may be uniquely dependent on the personality characteristics and social interaction skills of its administrators.

Conclusion

It is hoped that this essay will stimulate further analysis of conflict viewed as an organizational phenomenon rather than only as an interpersonal phenomenon. This approach seems to hold promise of bringing into closer relation what is known about organizational structure, labor force, and task environment as parts of a dynamic system. While it seems plausible that each of those elements produces a different type of potential conflict, it should be noted that there is no one-to-one correlation between the type of conflict and a possible defense against it. A given defensive mechanism, in other words, may provide defenses against more than one source of conflict.

Illustrative of the kinds of hypotheses which this approach can generate are the following:

A. Racial integration may be more easily introduced into the giant enterprise (for example, the military system) than into the Southern church, whose ideology places all men equal before God, because homogeneity is a necessary defense for the voluntary church but not for the giant enterprise.

B. The ideological organization is limited in its choice of technologies to those which call only for the kinds of skills possessed by those espousing the ideology. If necessary skills cannot be found among ideologically acceptable members of the labor force, then the voluntary organization's homogeneity is shattered; it must look for new defenses and it may have to be converted into another kind of organization.

With respect to administrative processes, this analysis suggests a reason why the present ethos of administration in the United States militates against the deliberate introduction of conflict as a means of advancing toward organization goals. The forces leading toward conflict are only in part subject to control by the organization. These forces also appear to be interrelated, so that once started, conflict may continue in chainlike fashion. Lacking adequate understanding of conflict, administrators may tend to guard against it even when they believe there are advantages to be gained from controlled conflict.

On the other hand administrators worry and complain about conflict engendered by their administrative reallocations, and they plead for techniques for "overcoming resistance to change." The preceding analysis suggests some reasons why change may lead to conflict. Organization patterns developed solely on technological grounds may so alter patterns of interaction that feelings of relative deprivation are increased, latent roles activated, and the organizational posture changed. Or an administrative device borrowed from another organization, having different vulnerabilities may destroy basic defenses. "Scientific management" techniques, for example, might reinforce basic defenses in the giant enterprise, but destroy the defenses of a local enterprise.

NOTES

1. For helpful comments on earlier versions of this paper I am indebted to my colleagues, Robert W. Avery, Richard O. Carlson, Peter B. Hammond, Robert W. Hawkes, and Arthur Tuden.
2. The positive functions of conflict have received occasional attention in sociological theory, especially by Lewis Coser, The Functions of Social Conflict (Glencoe, Ill., 1956). For an unusual study of industrial conflict and a theory of group tensions, see Alvin W. Gouldner, Wildcat Strike (Yellow Springs, O., 1954).
3. This concept is taken from S. A. Stouffer et al., The American Soldier (Princeton, 1949), I. For a more formal analysis of the concept and its utility, see Robert K. Merton and Paul Lazarsfeld, eds., Continuities in Social Research (Glencoe, Ill., 1950).
4. Chester I. Barnard, The Functions of the Executive (Cambridge, Mass., 1938), pp. 128–129.
5. Despite the fact that these are age-old questions of concern to many organizations on a recurring basis, there have been few objective, empirical investigations of the impact of various organizational forms on organizational behavior.
6. For a penetrating analysis of latent roles and their impact on organizations, see Alvin W. Gouldner, Cosmopolitans and Locals: Toward an Analysis of Latent Social Roles —I and II, Administrative Science Quarterly, 2 (1957–1958), 281–306 and 444–480.
7. Diversity of latent roles does not necessarily result in organizational conflict, because such roles may remain latent. The problem, from the standpoint of the organization, is that it is difficult to foresee or prevent the triggering that activates such roles. If latent role differences create a potential for conflict, and if the organization lacks control over that potential, the safest procedure is to eliminate the potential.
8. In reviewing knowledge of voluntary associations, C. Wayne Gordon and Nicholas Babchuk use the concept "degree of accessibility," or the exclusiveness of membership criteria. See their A Typology of Voluntary Associations, American Sociological Review, 24 (1959), 22–29.

516   9. The concept of task environment, defined somewhat differently, is taken from William R. Dill, Environment as an Influence on Managerial Autonomy, *Administrative Science Quarterly*, 2 (1958), 409–443. There have been few attempts to describe and differentiate environments *from the point of view of an organization.* Economic characterizations of markets (competitive, monopolistically competitive, oligopolistic, etc.) might serve to describe environments for economic organizations just as characteristics of international relationships might serve as a basis for describing the environments of nation states. For a recent suggestive work in the latter category, see Morton Kaplan, *System and Process in International Politics* (New York, 1957). James Coleman, focusing on controversies in communities, suggests four variations in the social organization of the community: *(a)* variation in member identification with the community, *(b)* density of organizations and associations in the community, *(c)* distribution of participation among citizens, and *(d)* interlocking of organizational memberships. See Coleman, *Community Conflict* (Glencoe, Ill., 1957). Frank A. Pinner, studying high schools in relation to the value structure of the environing community, writes in terms of "degrees of 'looseness' and 'tightness' of a community structure." See Robert K. Merton, *Social Theory and Social Structure* (rev. ed.; Glencoe, Ill., 1957), p. 404, note 13a.

10. Gordon and Babchuk, *op. cit.,* refer to "status conferring capacity," or the ability of an organization to bestow prestige or to be associated with prestige, which accrues to its members. They suggest that this is associated with the degree of accessibility referred to earlier.

11. In a study of sect development, Bryan Wilson finds two principal types of mechanisms by which sects govern their own and members' relationships to the external world: isolation and insulation. See his An Analysis of Sect Development, *American Sociological Review*, 24 (1959), 3–14. It seems probable that distinctiveness is one means of insulation.

12. There is little direct evidence available in reports of research, since the variables and relationships involved here have seldom been examined explicitly. There are a number of descriptive reports about various kinds of organizations facing different conditions. Our citations frequently will rely on the authors' inferences, *which would not necessarily* be concurred in by those cited.

13. Russell R. Dynes, The Consequences of Sectarianism for Social Participation, *Social Forces*, 35 (1957), 334.

14. John E. Tsouderos, Organizational Change in Terms of a Series of Selected Variables, *American Sociological Review*, 20 (1955), 208–209.

15. Selo Soemardjan, Bureaucratic Organization in a Time of Revolution, *Administrative Science Quarterly*, 2 (1957), 186.

16. Mhyra S. Minnis, Cleavage in Women's Organizations: A Reflection of the Social Structure of a City, *American Sociological Review*, 18 (1953), 48–49.

17. *Op. cit.,* p. 191.

18. Joseph R. Gusfield, The Problem of Generations in an Organizational Structure, *Social Forces*, 35 (1957), 329.

19. This concept is taken from Philip Selznick, *The Organizational Weapon* (New York, 1952).

20. Peter M. Blau, *The Dynamics of Bureaucracy* (Chicago, 1955), pp. 83, 137.

21. Gouldner, *Wildcat Strike*, p. 119.

22. For an extended discussion of this concept see Robert K. Merton and Alice S. Kitt, "Contributions to the Theory of Reference Group Behavior," in Merton and Lazarsfeld, *op. cit.,* pp. 40–105.

23. Edward A. Shils and Morris Janowitz, Cohesion and Disintegration in the Wehrmacht in World War II, *Public Opinion Quarterly*, 12 (1948), 285.

24. Robert W. Avery, in personal communication, has observed that in giant enterprises there seem to be unwritten rules against discussing subjects about which there may be ideological controversy. During the coffee break or in the car pool, the World Series or the Rose Bowl game may be debated loudly, but in our society religion and

25. Sanford M. Dornbusch, The Military Academy as an Assimilating Institution, *Social Forces,* 33 (1955), 317.

26. Blau, *op. cit.,* p. 132.

27. Alfred D. Chandler, Jr., Management Decentralization: An Historical Analysis, *The Business History Review,* 30 (1956), 111–179.

28. Dill, *op. cit.,* pp. 438–439.

29. For elaboration of the idea that co-optation and coalition (and ultimately merger) are successively costly or "desperate" defenses against environmental realities, see James D. Thompson and William J. McEwen, Organizational Goals and Environment, *American Sociological Review,* 33 (1958), 23–31.

30. Oliver Garceau, *The Library in the Political Process* (New York, 1949), p. 113.

31. Alvin W. Gouldner, *Patterns of Industrial Bureaucracy* (Glencoe, 1954), pp. 53–55, 65. The reader will note that Gouldner's study of the gypsum plant as reported in *Wildcat Strike* was cited in the section on the giant enterprise. My understanding of his findings is that in the early period, the plant revealed a highly developed indulgency pattern, recruitment from a relatively homogeneous local community, and management which was relatively free from central office pressures. Later the firm reversed these features, thus converting the plant into something of a giant enterprise. It was during this period of conversion that the wildcat strike occurred, and the "solution" was to move the plant still further in the direction of the giant enterprise, as noted in Defense 4B.

32. Van D. Kennedy, "Grievance Negotiation," in Arthur Kornhauser, Robert Dubin, and Arthur M. Ross, eds., *Industrial Conflict* (New York, 1954), pp. 290–291.

33. Coleman, *op. cit.,* pp. 4, 20.

34. *Ibid.,* p. 12.

35. Charles Y. Glock and B. B. Ringer, Church Policy and the Attitudes of Ministers and Parishioners on Social Issues, *American Sociological Review,* 31 (1956), 153.

BUSINESS IN THE TWENTY-FIRST CENTURY

Andrew Shonfield

Any attempt to speculate systematically about the long-term future of business enterprise forces one to take a view about the evolution of the whole institutional apparatus of modern society. The corporation occupies a commanding position in that portion of the system which is most obviously destined to grow. And it can hardly grow in importance without jostling other established centers of power. How will they respond to being jostled? The answer will very

Reprinted by permission from *Daedalus,* Journal of the American Academy of Arts and Sciences, Boston, Massachusetts, Volume 98, Number 1 (Winter 1969).

518　largely influence the relations between the corporation and the groups on which it most intimately depends—the consumers of its products, the labor that produces them, the shareholders that own its property, and the government that intermittently interferes with the way in which the business is run.

A simplifying device is to think of these relations in the framework of the crucial confrontation between the corporation and the state—rivals in certain areas of activity, close collaborators in others. I use the term "state" here as a convenient shorthand for public authority in its most general sense—that is, to include both the courts and the smaller agencies of collective power which are subject in the last resort to the central government, but operate from day to day with a considerable measure of independence. One has the impression nowadays that the dialogue between the corporation and the state consists largely of a simple assertion by the former: "Anything you can do, I can do better." And the claim is widely conceded by the public, indeed by many of the servants of the state itself. This is a remarkable reversal of roles compared with two or three decades ago. The reversal is so complete that it is worth reminding ourselves of how the relative authority and efficiency of these two rivals used to be regarded in the 1930's and 1940's. The failure of business enterprise as an instrument of social progress was celebrated at length in America during the New Deal and later on in Europe in a spate of postwar legislation transferring vast quantities of industrial and commercial property from private to public ownership.

The disenchantment with private enterprise was more complete in Europe than it was in the United States. The popular antipathy toward it had a systematic ideological content of a politically respectable kind in European social democracy. There has never been any anti-capitalist movement comparable to this either in political power or popular respectability in the United States. So the European reversal of opinion is especially noteworthy. It seems likely that one reason why the corporation has been rehabilitated so rapidly in the face of the established prejudice against it is the general disappointment with the performance of the postwar state as the manager of economic enterprise.

Yet this, too, is strange on the face of it. State intervention in the economy since the Great Depression almost certainly represents the biggest single achievement of a nonmilitary character in the history of modern government. The advance of social welfare and the maintenance of an orderly and stable economic structure during a period of exceptionally rapid growth have demonstrated the capacity of the state in new fields of economic and social management. Why, then, is there so little popular sentiment, even among the socialists in Western Europe, in favor of any general extension of the role of the state as entrepreneur displacing the conventional business corporation? The answer is largely that the state, through the changes it has wrought in the economic environment during the last quarter of a century, has provided the corporation with a splendid opportunity to demonstrate its flexibility and responsiveness as an instrument for meeting people's changing wants. The agencies of the state have seemed, by contrast, to be ponderous and insensitive.

The following are some of the specific elements in the rehabilitation of large-scale business enterprise. First, it has managed to establish rather better personal relations with the consumers of its goods and services than has the state. It is true that the typical products of the two are different, and the public does not have much opportunity for comparing like with like. Still, the overwhelming impression emerges that the average consumer in an advanced Western country does not believe that he would secure better service for his personal needs if more of the things which he buys today were produced and sold by the state. The second point is related to this: It is that the large corporation, which had a bad reputation, sometimes bordering on the sinister, for pursuing a variety of restrictive policies during the period between the wars, has come to be seen as an exceptionally powerful instrument of innovation. It is not that it is more fecund than its rivals in generating important new ideas; its strength lies in its proved ability to convert ideas, especially in the field of technology, very rapidly into useful products. The contrary reputation, reflected in the writings of critics like J. K. Galbraith—that the chief talent of contemporary business is in the creation of frivolous desires whose satisfaction makes no significant difference to the sum of human happiness—has so far not dented the image of the corporation as a beneficent innovator.

The social position of the large corporation has also been improved by its well-publicized attachment to the techniques of scientific management. This is the opposite of the nepotism that was widely believed, on quite plausible grounds, to be an inherent feature of organizations in which the ultimate power was held by the owners of share capital. While the corporation management liberated itself from the tutelage of the owners of the business, it also set about establishing a closer and more amicable relationship with the organized labor in its employ. In a growing number of instances, the active participation of trade unions has been sought in the process of innovation. And the new kind of wage bargain recognized certain prior claims of the wage-earners on the extra income that the innovating corporation expected to obtain. Thus, the brute fact of ownership, which had for so long dominated the political debate, lost some of its portentous quality.

Instead, the issue has come to be seen to be about the form of organization of large-scale enterprise—the powers of the management, the rights of the employees, the relationship between the management and the owners, whether the latter are private shareholders, a government, or some mixture of public and private interests. The final element in the structure of respectability which the large corporation has successfully established for itself in the postwar world is its position in several countries as the active and willing partner of the state in the conduct of major national policies. Outside the Anglo-Saxon world, big business commonly held a position in the past which was recognized as being analogous to that of a quasi-public authority. But that did not mean that it was particularly amenable to the public interest as the government of the day defined it. The strengthening of governmental power, together with the taming of some of the primitive ideological urges of an earlier generation of big business, have provided the basis for the practice of economic planning in contemporary capitalist society. The dependence of the planners on bargains made with a comparatively small number of major enterprises in key sectors of industry has come to be increasingly recognized—on both sides. The small group of major firms in an industry, sometimes fewer than half a dozen, are

520 also aware that their business operations may be profoundly affected, for good or ill, by the interventions of government in a steadily growing range of economic and social activities.

The Expansive Giants

Thus, while the large business corporation has a secure status as a powerful and reliable social instrument, its position still depends on acting in the role of junior partner to the state in the pursuit of certain public purposes. The next stage in this exploration is to ask whether there are any identifiable forces that would tend to enlarge the social authority of the corporation vis-à-vis the conventional agencies of the state. To do this, I propose to examine some probable trends in the future relationship between the large corporation and the other bodies with which it is, and will remain, in close day-to-day contact: the consumers of its products, its shareholders, organized labor, government in the forms of executive power and of judicial power.

The method is to discover what constraints and what opportunities for expansion of corporate authority each of these relations seems likely to provide. For this exercise a number of assumptions have to be made about the basic economic climate during the remainder of this century. My own can be briefly stated. They are based on an extrapolation of trends which have become increasingly marked in the past two decades. I assume that production will continue to grow, and that although there may be variations from year to year, the average pace at which it grows will not be less in the Western developed world than it has been so far during the 1960's. It might well be slightly faster. I also assume that there is no economic slump in this period and no large-scale war involving the present industrial world.

In these circumstances, the very big business corporation is likely to grow faster than the average business. The experience of recent years suggests that it may grow a great deal faster than its competitors, both in terms of the assets that it owns and of the labor it employs. Allowing for the fact that the giant corporations tend to be more highly capitalized than the average, it is remarkable how much additional manpower they have managed to absorb during the 1960's. The *Fortune* Directory shows that General Motors, the world's largest employer with a current payroll of three quarters of a million workers, added 25 per cent more employees to its books between 1960 and 1966.[1] Ford more than doubled the number of its employees during the same period, and General Electric registered a rise of 40 per cent. These are the three largest manufacturing companies in the United States, measured in terms of numbers employed. Exceptionally among the giant corporate employers, U.S. Steel showed a decline during this period; but this was due to the special circumstance, also exceptional among big business enterprises, that its prosperity was dependent on the fortunes of a single industry which was growing very slowly.

It is not simply by the extrapolation of past trends that one is led to the conclusion that the very big will probably get a great deal bigger. R. Marris (in *The Theory of Managerial Capitalism*) has convincingly argued that the drive of professional business management in contemporary capitalist society is directed—once the minimum condition of "financial security" has been achieved—toward the maximum expansion of the gross assets which the particular corporate managers control. The growth of these assets is, on the evidence which Marris provides, a more compelling objective than obtaining the highest possible rate of return per unit of capital employed. The two motives are, of course, entirely compatible with each other in the long run; what is important to establish is that actual behavior in the short- and medium-range is more readily explained in terms of the pursuit of the maximum rate of growth of the individual company. Marris makes a further point which is relevant to the future balance of power between states and corporations. The managerial motive of expanding one's area of authority is, of course, not lacking among the servants of the state; but "the most fundamental difference between business firms and government departments," he says, "lies in the former's capacity for autonomous growth."

It is worth adding to this that changes in the technology of management, above all the use of computers of increasing sophistication as a tool of decision-making, have removed many of the traditional constraints on the size of organizations which can be efficiently run by a single board of management. A more subtle point is that modern techniques of social and political analysis, tracing the precise routes by which power and influence are exercised within organizations, provide the opportunity for the more efficient design of their structure. In particular, the hierarchical relationships, which are an essential feature of the corporate type of organization, can be modulated to serve the different purposes of the various types of decision and action in which the corporation has to engage. A less authoritarian structure, offering scope for considerable initiative on the periph-

ery while maintaining even stricter control over essential matters at the center, is likely to be better equipped for the process of expansion by osmosis between the giant and the small firm.

Whether the outcome will be quite so dramatic by the end of the century as the situation foreshadowed by Professor H. V. Perlmutter — a world industrial landscape dominated by some two hundred "monster" enterprises responsible for the greater part of output—is more doubtful. At any rate, it is necessary to envisage some countervailing social and political forces to the unlimited growth of the giant corporation. It might take the form of a popular political movement with a power base among the smaller firms—among which there will be some with ten to twenty thousand people on their payrolls—appealing to a widespread anxiety about preserving alternative and more decentralized sources of economic power in society. Tax concessions or subsidies will surely be employed to help to secure the independence and prosperity of enterprises separate and different from the giants.

This separateness will be the more readily maintained in practice because the odds are that the giants themselves will not develop an appetite for takeovers and mergers that is either unlimited in volume or unselective in content. Two considerations will serve to illustrate the spontaneous restrictions on appetite that are likely to assert themselves. First is the minimum critical size that firms will have to reach before they become worthwhile takeover prospects for giant corporations, which are envisaged here as organizations with a million or more employees. There will be a natural anxiety about spreading the inevitably scarce resource of skilled managerial manpower too thin. The resources of management are used particularly heavily in the process of integrating relatively small enterprises, taken over by the giant, into the purposes and the way of life of the expanding corporation. The second consideration is simply that certain kinds of industrial mergers—for example, vertical integration of some manufacturing process to include a variegated retail outlet—are sometimes judged to be positively inconvenient. The big corporation may feel that it retains more freedom for maneuver in the process of profitable expansion if it avoids tying itself indissolubly to particular partners, either in the conduct of its sales strategy or in its buying of materials for processing. There is too little evidence so far about the long-term prospect for companies based on an indiscriminate policy of conglomerate mergers. It is too soon to argue on the basis of facts available that in modern business the crucial resource of good management can be generalized at short notice to any product or process in which the expanding giant corporation identifies the prospect of profitable operation. There is at least a suspicion, which remains to be disproved, that the management know-how of successful companies is more specific than that.

Corporate Customers

The contemporary business corporation, as Bernard Cazes has observed,[2] seems to be increasingly concerned to achieve a wider or longer-lasting contractual relationship with its customers than the traditional relationship represented by a series of isolated selling transactions. It tries to get the customer to commit himself to the firm, either as the purchaser of a whole range of products instead of a single item or as a regular buyer of a particular product or service over an extended period of time. The inducement offered to the customer is frequently some form of discount on the price, in return for providing his supplier with an assured outlet. Cazes connects this trend with the desire of the modern automated enterprise to plan its production on the basis of secure outlets. There is, I believe, a further motive connected with the evolution of a society oriented increasingly toward the provision of services that is likely to reinforce the trend toward commerce in the form of a commitment over time rather than an individual transaction.

Services that are repeatedly performed for customers tend to involve the enterprise performing them in an initial investment, sometimes of a substantial kind, for each one of its clients. It is of the essence of the kind of service that people in the urban societies of the second half of the twentieth century will increasingly require that they must be first of all reliable and, secondly, fast. Individual transport in cities is perhaps the most obvious case in point. It is hardly likely that the vast and crowded conurbations, which will contain the majority of the population of the industrial world by the end of the century, will be able to accommodate individually owned cars in town centers. People, who will be on the average more than twice as rich as they are today, will be willing to pay a great deal in order to be assured of 100 per cent reliability and promptness of their transport service.

The issue goes a great deal deeper than consumer preferences. The population in the twenty-first century will contain a greatly increased proportion of very old people in the age bracket eighty to one hundred years plus. These people will be much more vulnerable to the failure of services, such as the delivery of food at stated times or the repair and maintenance of household equipment, than the rest of the population. The guarantee of the prompt delivery of services in the crowded urban conditions of the year 2000 will present acute problems of organization, and it becomes apparent that there will have to be a new set of relationships between the service corporation and its customer, giving the latter more security and the former more power to ensure that services promised are delivered on time to those who depend on them.

The problem of the very old and vulnerable is a particular instance of a more general proposition about the service relationship between the corporation and its customers. It is, for example, barely conceivable that societies in which the majority live in high apartment blocks will tolerate an attempt by the elevator operators to stage a lightning strike. Moreover, corporations which have entered into guarantees to provide precisely timed services will have to be supported by whatever means public authority can command in their efforts to meet their obligations. It seems likely indeed that their employees, going about the provision of certain services, will be endowed with official public service status; they will need to have the right, in the last resort, to exercise police powers to cope with obstacles that impede them in fulfilling their tasks.

The process envisaged here would put the service corporation in its relations with the consumer on a footing analogous to that of an enterprise fulfilling a government military contract in time of war. Failure to fulfill commitments undertaken might lay the enterprise open to the penalities of the criminal law. The contract for certain kinds of services, like the contracts undertaken to supply a nation with equipment essential for its defense, will tend to acquire a special sanctity because people's lives will hang on its performance. By an extension, it is plausible to speculate that popular sentiment about inflicting severe discomfort on the helpless old will develop an intensity similar to that felt about cruelty to children. Corporations will be subject to exigent standards. But concomitantly their status as a social instrument will be enhanced. They will be recognized as performing certain services that are not different in essence from the public law functions of the police or other bodies clothed with the authority of the state. At the same time, the committed customers of the service corporation, with their long-standing contracts and their guaranteed price discounts, will have some of the benefits that go with membership in a consumer's cooperative. This sense of consumer participation is something the corporation may well wish to foster.

All this is based on certain assumptions about consumer preferences and about the future of the economic system. It is assumed that the conventional bias will be against the accumulation of more and better consumer durable goods and in favor of an uncluttered style of living—an offset to the crowded environment of the future—based on the reliable provision of services by outside specialist organizations. People living in city apartments will have shed any illusions about their ability to fend for themselves and will recognize unashamedly their necessary and constant dependence on what others do for them. Secondly, the consumer of the future will not have readily at his disposal the traditional remedy against the supplier of a poor or unattractive product—the transfer of his very next purchase to a competing supplier. It is in the nature of the case that the number of possible suppliers of certain kinds of services, involving the special priority attached to performance and the tight guarantees for the customer indicated above, will be limited. Only a small number of franchises will be granted, and consumers in some areas may find that no alternative supplier is anxious to compete for their custom.

Moreover, the cult of guaranteed service, in which the competitive struggle between firms will be considerably muted, will not be confined to corporations selling directly to individual consumers. It is to be expected that an increasing number of services vitally important to the inhabitants of packed and lively urban communities—such services as noise reduction, weather control, or getting rid of air pollution—will have to be arranged on a collective basis. Once a corporation has undertaken a contract of this sort, it will be difficult for a community to change quickly to a new supplier if it is dissatisfied with the results. Again, the corporation will be treated as having some of the attributes of a public law body.

It is worth noting that there is no reason why these personal and collective services should not be provided by publicly owned corporations. Public transport, electricity, and gas are commonly provided in this way in Europe. But there is no widely held conviction in Europe, emerging out of this experience, that public ownership provides a better guarantee of performance in these fields of economic activity than private ownership. In any case it is not the ownership issue which is regarded as being important, but rather whether the enterprise is conducted on the lines of a conventional business corporation. It is essentially because corporate enterprise is obsessed by the desire for growth that it organizes itself in a demonstrative fashion to please consumers and to cajole them into buying more.

Corporate Shareholders

As indicated earlier, the business corporation has acquired its enhanced status as a social instrument partly by liberating itself from an exclusive concern with the interests of its owners. In future the bond between management and shareholders is likely to be loosened still further. Managements, however, have hitherto found it convenient to be formally subject to the orders of private property owners. This enables them to speak to governmental agencies, when they make awkward demands on them, as the representatives of people whose personal property they hold in trust on the understanding that it will be employed in ways that yield a solid profit.

The trouble is that the traditional mythology of ownership has increasingly come to lack verisimilitude in a situation where the management is overwhelmingly concerned with the long-term destiny of a great corporation in society, while many of the shareholders whom it purports to serve are solely interested in the short-term impact made by the corporation on the stock market between the moment when they buy shares and the moment when they sell them. Few people would accept the argument that the managers of a company ought to concern themselves exclusively with maximizing the gains of this changing group of temporary holders of the company's shares. The whole notion of ownership in relation to corporate enterprise will have to be re-thought and put on a fresh basis if it is to be treated in the future as a persuasive element in guiding management policy. The prospect is that there will be increasing numbers of consumers and of employees with a long-term interest in the policies of the giant corporation, to which many of its legal masters will be indifferent.

A solution to this problem which has been suggested by Bloch-Lainé is that shareholders should be divided into two categories, the long-term and the short-term holders, and that voting rights should be wielded only by the former.[3] The suggestion is interesting because it points to the possibility of a new general system of legal rights based on time as a measure of the degree of commitment, whether of shareholder, consumer, or worker. It is not fanciful to foresee a fresh set of definitions centered on the duration of commitment replacing the simplicities, already somewhat archaic, of laws resting on the doctrine of absolute property.

With the different interest groups crowding in on company boards and asserting their rights to a say in management decisions, it may come to be something of a problem to reassert the claims of the owners. Their right to demand policies which will assure them of at least the conventional rate of return on their capital, plus a measure of capital appreciation, will no doubt be conceded. But beyond that, they may well have to struggle to be heard above the din of competing claims. In addition to the long-term committed consumer groups and the long-service worker groups, the state itself may be expected to wish to assert its right to influence the management decisions of giant corporations and to do so at an early stage in boardroom discussions. To achieve this purpose it will not need to go through the motions of becoming an actual shareholder, in the style of the "mixed companies" which are a familiar feature today of France and other West European countries. If the techniques of se-

lective intervention by the state in the industrial policies pursued by large corporations become, as seems likely, an established part of economic planning, then, as one British journalist has put it recently, the government will take on a position "almost akin to that of a large shareholder, even when it does not actually own any equity."[4]

It is possible, however, that a revival of the rights of mere ownership may be brought about by the institutional investors. Certainly the insurance companies and pension funds will be especially well placed, as time goes on, to assert their claim to influence the decisions of corporate management, as long-term professional investors representing a mass interest in achieving the highest possible level of profits.

Organized Labor

The corporation, with its considerable investment in each new recruit to its work force, will have an increasing interest in the immobility of labor. It is possible that the Japanese convention of lifelong engagement will come to be nearer the norm of labor relations in Western industrial countries than the traditional idea of a labor market from which a business draws its fluctuating manpower requirements from time to time. If it is going to be usual for a worker to be retrained for new jobs two or three times in the course of a working lifetime as old jobs become obsolescent, then the great corporation, which will itself be in the constant travail of adapting itself to new technology, could well provide the natural context for the re-education of people in new skills. The sheer size of the giant corporation should greatly facilitate the process of job-changing. Indeed, this facility may

526 come to be one of the particular attractions of employment in this type of enterprise. The corporation for its part will have to apply substantial resources to the business of education. The degree of efficiency in retraining redundant workers, cutting the idle time between the cessation of an old job and the performance of a new one, will plainly have a significant effect on its own costs.

The performance of this kind of function is also likely to affect profoundly the personal feelings of a corporation's employees. No doubt the general sense of insecurity caused by rapid technological change will be mitigated by generous welfare payments from public funds, in the form of redundancy grants and finance for retraining. But it will, nevertheless, be felt to be a considerable advantage to be able to move securely into one's next job under a familiar management and in the shelter of the corporation in which one started one's career. How far will the new kind of corporate loyalty affect traditional trade-union attitudes? Paternalistic companies have sometimes, though less frequently in the recent past, set out to rival the worker's loyalty to his trade union. The question is whether the special function of the trade union in an advanced welfare state enjoying full employment—namely, the representation of sectional or particular plant interests —will be so important in the future.

But whether it is or not, there will certainly be a continuing need for the professional representation of organized labor in the policy-making bodies of the giant corporation. The form that this will take will no doubt vary from one country and one legal system to another. But in one way or another the outcome seems likely to involve something analogous to the present system of worker representatives on the Super-

visory Boards of German companies. Trade-union power and influence may well come to be concentrated at this point in particular. Just as a corporation nowadays appoints outside directors from banks, insurance companies, and other businesses, so the "worker-directors" of the future may have the recognized function of reflecting the wider interests of labor in a given industry, including the interests of those employed in competing corporations or in smaller enterprises.

Relations with Governments

Having mobilized the mass loyalties of the consumers of its products and of its employees, the giant corporation may appear in certain situations as a formidable rival to governments. How formidable will depend in large part on the size of the government concerned. A giant corporation in the United States will obviously be differently placed in a power struggle with the federal government than in a contest with the government of a country like Denmark or Ireland. It is to be observed that an international corporation with a work force one million strong would be supporting a dependent family population equal to the present size of these nations. The value of the physical assets controlled by such a corporation will be greater than those belonging to a small nation—if only because national assets, unlike those belonging to a corporation, are to a large extent an accidental agglomeration, including barren mountains and heaths and awkward towns developed for forgotten purposes. The corporation's command of scarce and specialized skills is also much greater. It can, after all, pick and choose among a world population of talented specialists to man its top posts. The corporation, in short, will be in a position to bully some governments. And the latter will be vulnerable to pressure because they will be loath to forgo the benefits of high technology at low cost which local enterprises controlled by international corporations will be able to offer.

On the other hand, the giant corporations will be the target of powerful popular suspicion. Governments are bad enough, but at least they can occasionally be teased into articulate honesty by parliaments; corporations are harder to crack open. It is inevitable that there will be demands for much closer public surveillance of their activities than anything to which they have been subjected hitherto. With the progressive accretion of corporate power, the pressures for new forms of public accountability will grow. The corporation's claim to a large measure of privacy, in order to be able to conduct its competitive activities without being spied upon by its business rivals, will seem less and less tenable. The public service function of the great corporate enterprise, in effective occupation of a large chunk of the economic terrain, will be seen as the ultimate justification for the special privileges, and obligations, enjoyed by it in its relations with consumers and with the planning organizations of the government. In its early days the great corporation assumed some of the attributes of a robber baron—the moat and the thick fortress wall surrounding its activities, the right to sally forth without warning to destroy its rivals and to disappear again behind its postern gate without being stopped and questioned. By contrast, the symbol of the giant enterprise of the future, as of the bank of the mid-twentieth century, will be the glass wall. The change in banking architecture from the old model of a fortress to that of a public show behind well-protected but transparent windows illustrates the progression.

Some of the demands for accountability may be met by the devices outlined earlier. Consumer representatives in the boards of management may be expected to exercise a watching brief on prices and to impose a curb on the temptations arising from established quasi-monopolistic positions in certain industries and trades. The traditional threat of the dynamic new business challenging the sitting occupants to do combat with it will grow less credible as great corporate enterprises become firmly embedded in positions of trust at a number of key points in the late-twentieth-century economy. Indeed, it may quite likely come to seem wrong to allow them to be challenged by an upstart entrepreneur not carrying any comparable burden of public responsibility. Traveling light and therefore maneuvering fast in a competitive situation will be regarded as less of a virtue than it was thought to be in the small-business phase of early capitalism. That will not prevent the mythology of this earlier phase, which gave the great corporation so much more room for maneuver—so long as it could keep up the charade of being just another small man grown somewhat taller than the rest—from being the subject of nostalgic devotion by some corporate managers. And they will no doubt try to use the myth in their struggle against the tutelage of interest groups with special rights, like the consumers of their products or the workers in their plants.

Meanwhile, the state, in those places where states are strong enough to insist on their rights as guardians of the public interest, may be expected to press for a great deal more information. It will not be enough for a corporation to be able to show that it makes a reasonable average profit on its operations and does not charge excessive prices. It will also be held accountable for the efficiency with which it uses the factors of production at its disposal—land, capital, and natural resources—in particular lines of production. Since the scope for offsetting losses in one branch of production against gains in another will be enormously increased, it will be difficult to establish whether a particular management is, for example, making effective use of the additional manpower which is absorbed into some new enterprise or not. If, as seems probable, labor, especially skilled labor, continues to be in short supply in advanced societies by the end of the century, then organizations which are especially well placed to acquire this scarce resource in the market may well be called upon to show, by objective measurement of the performance of labor in their different enterprises, that the marginal product of labor is higher there than it would be if it were employed for some alternative purpose. In other words, the "opportunity cost" of the marginal labor supply of an enterprise would be measured against the value of its product.

The principle behind these techniques of measurement—which may seem impossibly complicated today, but which are likely to be developed rapidly in response to planning needs during the coming decades—is that the employment of a social resource like labor requires a social justification. Similar criteria will be applied to the use of capital. It could, for instance, happen that a giant corporation, which was able to obtain investment funds cheaply and was also economical in its use of labor, employed the capital in its business in a relatively wasteful manner. Finally, and most obviously, corporate enterprise has hitherto been able to use up natural resources, like land, water, and clean air, with little or no regard for the social costs of its operations. The bias of latter-day capitalism toward what Albert Hirschman has described so shrewdly under the heading of the "internalization of external diseconomies"[5] is likely to go a great deal further rather fast. And the intrusion of social costs and benefits into commercial calculations of profit and loss will make for large changes in the kind of enterprise which is deemed to be successful because it yields the highest net rate of return.

My expectation is that the large corporation will adapt itself to this change, but will do so with a struggle. Wherever it has the opportunity to escape from the trammels on entrepreneurial initiative imposed by social costings, organized consumer pressures, and workers' representation in management, it will. Its political power will not be negligible. It may be able to play one or more of the forces with which it has to contend against another. For example, a body of consumers might be mobilized in a dispute with the state about some costly government proposal concerned with the preservation of the environment for the benefit of people a generation ahead. Or circumstances might arise in which it was convenient for a corporation to enter into an alliance with the planning department of the government in order to press some unpopular decision on organized labor. I assume that corporations, in spite of the pluralistic character of their boards of directors, will not lose their distinctive persona. Indeed, it is to be expected that the giant corporation of the future will be even more anxious to give expression to its own individual style, doctrines, and traditions. Differences in the corporate culture of particular giants will no doubt become the subject of erudite works by learned scholars; and as these fine points are established, managers will stoutly proclaim their mission of defending the individual ethos of the organization entrusted to their leadership.

Nevertheless, there will be occasions when the giants will find it convenient to band together. They will all hanker for an environment away from centers of powerful government, such as the United States, in which they can flex their muscles without being constantly asked what they are doing. The natural escape route will be via the further internationalization of the enterprise. It is no secret that some U. S. companies which currently invest abroad are partly influenced by the escape motive. It may come to be argued in time that a country so powerful and nationalistic as the United States, with so large a domestic market, does not provide an appropriate headquarters for a truly international company. The export of capital may then be followed, as it has been already in the case of some big British companies, by the emigration of the corporation itself to a more congenial environment in a foreign land. Governments will be invited to compete for its favors.

At that stage of the power struggle between corporations and governments, the small states in Europe and elsewhere may, in turn, find a compelling motive for banding together, as the only means of imposing a due regard for the public interest on the footloose giant.

NOTES

1. See July 1961 and June 1967 issues.
2. Bernard Cazes, *Futuribles,* Vol. 5, No. 4 (Paris, 1968).
3. Francois Bloch-Lainé, Pour une reforme de l'enterprise (Paris, 1963).
4. Christopher Tugendhat, *Financial Times* (January 31, 1968).
5. Albert O. Hirschman, *The Strategy of Economic Development* (New Haven, 1959).

ADDITIONAL READINGS

Becker, S. W., and G. Gordon. 1966. "An Entrepreneurial Theory of Formal Organizations. Part I: Patterns of Formal Organizations," *Administrative Science Quarterly,* 11 (December), 315–344.

Becker, Selwyn W., and Thomas L. Whisler. 1967. "The Innovative Organization: A Selective View of Current Theory and Research," *Journal of Business,* 40 (October), 462–469.

Bennis, Warren G. 1966. *Changing Organizations.* New York: McGraw-Hill.

Brown, Warren B. 1969. "The Impact of a Dynamic Task Environment: A Study of Architectural-Engineering Firms," *Academy of Management Journal,* 12 (June), 169–177.

Burns, Tom. 1961. "Micropolitics: Mechanisms of Institutional Change," *Administrative Science Quarterly,* 6 (December), 257–281.

Davis, Keith, and Robert L. Blomstrom. 1966. *Business and Its Environment.* New York: McGraw-Hill.

Dill, William R. 1958. "Environment as an Influence on Managerial Autonomy," *Administrative Science Quarterly,* 2 (March), 409–443.

Drucker, Peter F., ed. 1969. *Preparing Tomorrow's Business Leaders Today.* Englewood Cliffs, N.J.: Prentice-Hall (Part 1, "The Changing Environment").

Easton, David. 1965. *A Systems Analysis of Political Life.* New York: Wiley.

Evan, William M., and Ezra G. Levin. 1966. "Status-Set and Role-Set Conflicts of the Stockbroker: A Problem in the Sociology of Law," *Social Forces,* 45 (September), 73–83.

Faunce, William A. 1968. *Problems of an Industrial Society.* New York: McGraw-Hill.

Guetzkow, Harold. 1966. "Relations Among Organizations." In *Studies on Behavior in Organizations,* Raymond V. Bowers, ed. Athens: University of Georgia Press.

Hawkes, Robert W. 1961. "The Role of the Psychiatric Administrator," *Administrative Science Quarterly,* 6 (June), 89–106.

Hegland, Tore Jacob, and Borre Nylehn. 1968. "Adjustment of Work Organizations to Critical Environmental Factors," *Acta Sociologica,* 11 (Fasc 1–2), 31–54.

Johnson, Harold L. 1960. "A Behavioral Approach to the Business Enterprise," *The Southern Economic Journal,* 27 (July), 1–10.

Kriesberg, Louis. 1955. "Occupational Controls Among Steel Distributors," *The American Journal of Sociology,* 61 (November), 203–212.

Lawrence, Paul R., and Jay W. Lorsch. 1967. "Differentiation and Integration in Complex Organizations." *Administrative Science Quarterly,* 12 (June), 1–47.

Lawrence, Paul R., and Jay W. Lorsch. 1967. *Organization and Environment.* Boston: Division of Research, Graduate School of Business Administration, Harvard University.

LeCompte, Kilburn. 1962. "Organizational Structures in Transition." In *Organization Theory in Industrial Practice,* Mason Haire, ed. New York: Wiley.

Lorsch, Jay W. 1965. *Product Innovation and Organization.* New York: Macmillan.

Lorsch, Jay W., and Paul R. Lawrence, eds. 1970. *Studies in Organization Design.* Homewood, Ill.: Irwin.

McGuire, Joseph W. 1963. *Business and Society.* New York: McGraw-Hill.

Meade, J. E. 1968. "Is 'The New Industrial State' Inevitable?" *The Economic Journal,* 78 (June), 372–392.

Moore, Wilbert E. 1962. *The Conduct of the Corporation.* New York: Random House. (Chapters 1, 13, 16–21).

Parsons, Talcott. 1956. "Suggestions for a Sociological Approach to the Theory of Organizations—I," *Administrative Science Quarterly,* 1 (June), 63–85.

Parsons, Talcott. 1957. "The Mental Hospital as a Type of Organization." In *The Patient and the Mental Hospital,* Milton Greenblatt, Daniel J. Levinson, and Richard H. Williams, eds. Glencoe, Ill.: Free Press.

GENERAL STUDIES

Parsons, Talcott. 1958. "Some Ingredients of a General Theory of Formal Organization." 531
In *Administrative Theory in Education*, Andrew W. Halpin, ed. Chicago: The Midwest
Administration Center, University of Chicago.

Parsons, Talcott. 1959. "General Theory in Sociology." In *Sociology Today*, Robert K.
Merton, Leonard Broom, and Leonard S. Cottrell, Jr., eds. New York: Basic Books.

Randell, G. A. 1966. "A Systems Approach to Industrial Behavior," *Occupational Psychology*, 40 (July), 115–127.

Reiss, A. J., Jr., and D. J. Bordua. 1967. "Environment and Organization: A Perspective
on the Police." In *The Police: Six Sociological Essays*, D. J. Bordua, ed. New York:
Wiley.

Thompson, James D. 1964. "Decision Making, the Firm, and the Market." In *New Perspectives in Organization Research*, W. W. Cooper et al., eds. New York: Wiley.

Thorelli, Hans B. 1967. "Organizational Theory: An Ecological View," *Papers and Proceedings of the 27th Annual Meeting of the Academy of Management* (December),
66–84.

Triandis, Harry C. 1966. "Notes on the Design of Organizations." In *Approaches to
Organizational Design*, James D. Thompson et al., eds. Pittsburgh, Pa.: University of
Pittsburgh Press.

Wilson, A. T. M. 1961. "The Manager and His World," *Industrial Management Review*,
3 (Fall), 1–26.